Lecture Notes in Computer Science 16508

The series Lecture Notes in Computer Science (LNCS), including its subseries Lecture Notes in Artificial Intelligence (LNAI) and Lecture Notes in Bioinformatics (LNBI), has established itself as a medium for the publication of new developments in computer science and information technology research, teaching, and education.

LNCS enjoys close cooperation with the computer science R & D community, the series counts many renowned academics among its volume editors and paper authors, and collaborates with prestigious societies. Its mission is to serve this international community by providing an invaluable service, mainly focused on the publication of conference and workshop proceedings and postproceedings. LNCS commenced publication in 1973.

Ping Li · Lizhuang Ma · Liang Wan · Bin Sheng ·
Jinman Kim · Daniel Thalmann ·
Nadia Magnenat-Thalmann
Editors

Advances in Computer Graphics

42nd Computer Graphics International Conference, CGI 2025
Hong Kong, China, July 14–18, 2025
Proceedings, Part II

Springer

Editors
Ping Li
The Hong Kong Polytechnic University
Hong Kong, China

Lizhuang Ma
Shanghai Jiao Tong University
Shanghai, China

Liang Wan
Tianjin University
Tianjin, China

Bin Sheng
Shanghai Jiao Tong University
Shanghai, China

Jinman Kim
The University of Sydney
Sydney, NSW, Australia

Daniel Thalmann
EPFL
Lausanne, Switzerland

Nadia Magnenat-Thalmann
University of Geneva
Geneva, Switzerland

ISSN 0302-9743 ISSN 1611-3349 (electronic)
Lecture Notes in Computer Science
ISBN 978-3-032-22263-3 ISBN 978-3-032-22264-0 (eBook)
https://doi.org/10.1007/978-3-032-22264-0

This Springer imprint is published by the registered company Springer Nature Switzerland AG
The registered company address is: Gewerbestrasse 11, 6330 Cham, Switzerland

Preface

Computer Graphics International (CGI) is one of the oldest annual international conferences on Computer Graphics in the world. Through a half century of influence, we are dedicated to making CGI a top conference on graphics and media. Researchers are invited to share their experiences and novel achievements in various fields of Computer Graphics, Media, and Virtual Reality. Previous recent CGI conferences have been held in Sydney, Australia (2014), Strasbourg, France (2015), Heraklion, Greece (2016), Yokohama, Japan (2017), Bintan, Indonesia (2018), and Calgary, Canada (2019). CGI was virtual between 2020 and 2022 due to the COVID pandemic, and was held in Shanghai, China (2023), and Geneva, Switzerland (2024). This year, CGI 2025 was organized by Hong Kong Polytechnic University, and supported by the Computer Graphics Society (CGS). The conference was held during July 14 to 18, 2025.

These CGI 2025 LNCS proceedings are composed of 124 papers from a total of 402 submissions, which include 59 papers that were reviewed highly and recommended to be published in The Visual Computer journal track. To ensure the high quality of the CGI 2025 LNCS proceedings, each paper was reviewed by at least two experts in the field (all reviews were double blind) and the authors of accepted papers were asked to revise their paper according to the review comments prior to publication.

The CGI 2025 conference also organized the ENGAGE (Empowering Novel Geometric Algebra for Graphics & Engineering) 2025 Workshop, focused specifically on important aspects of geometric algebra, including graphics, motion, AI, quantum science, geography and power systems. The workshop has been part of CGI conferences since 2016, and has been featured as a separate volume in LNCS this year.

We would like to express our sincere gratitude to all the PC members and external reviewers who provided timely high-quality reviews. We would also like to thank all the authors for contributing to the conference by submitting their wonderful works.

July 2025

Ping Li
Lizhuang Ma
Liang Wan
Bin Sheng
Jinman Kim
Daniel Thalmann
Nadia Magnenat-Thalmann

Organization

Honorary Conference Chairs

Enhua Wu	Chinese Academy of Sciences/University of Macau, China
Yiannis Aloimonos	University of Maryland, College Park, USA
Jian Jun Zhang	Bournemouth University, UK

Conference Chairs

Nadia Magnenat-Thalmann	University of Geneva, Switzerland
Ping Li	Hong Kong Polytechnic University, China
Bin Sheng	Shanghai Jiao Tong University, China
Jinman Kim	University of Sydney, Australia

Program Chairs

Liang Wan	Tianjin University, China
Lizhuang Ma	Shanghai Jiao Tong University, China
Daniel Thalmann	EPFL, Switzerland

International Steering Committee

Nadia Magnenat-Thalmann	University of Geneva, Switzerland
Jinman Kim	University of Sydney, Australia
Daniel Thalmann	EPFL, Switzerland
Marina Gavrilova	University of Calgary, Canada
Ping Li	Hong Kong Polytechnic University, China
Jian Jun Zhang	Bournemouth University, UK

Paper Awards Committee

Nadia Magnenat-Thalmann	University of Geneva, Switzerland
Ping Li	Hong Kong Polytechnic University, China

Jinman Kim	University of Sydney, Australia
Yang Wen	Shenzhen University, China
Daniel Thalmann	EPFL, Switzerland

Organization Chairs

Mingsong Lyu	Hong Kong Polytechnic University, China
Lei Zhu	Hong Kong University of Science and Technology (Guangzhou), China

Workshop Chairs

Eckhard Hitzer	International Christian University, Japan
Yang Wen	Shenzhen University, China
Younhyun Jung	Gachon University, South Korea

Web Chairs

Rui Zhang	University of Hong Kong, China
Hui Ye	Hong Kong Baptist University, China

Program Committee

Kamron Abdulkhaev	HSE University, Russia
Marco Agus	Hamad Bin Khalifa University, Qatar
Euijoon Ahn	James Cook University, Australia
Selim Balcisoy	Sabanci University, Turkey
Werner Benger	AHM Software GmbH, Austria
Lei Bi	University of Sydney, Australia
Stéphane Breuils	Université Savoie Mont Blanc, France
Yiyu Cai	Nanyang Technological University, Singapore
Juan Cao	Xiamen University, China
Mingwei Cao	Hefei University of Technology, China
Yan-Pei Cao	Tsinghua University, China
Tolga Capin	TED University, Turkey
Jian Chang	Bournemouth University, UK
Deng Chen	Wuhan Institute of Technology, China

Falai Chen	University of Science and Technology of China, China
Haoyu Chen	Hong Kong University of Science and Technology (Guangzhou), China
Jie Chen	Hong Kong Baptist University, China
Nenglun Chen	Nanjing University of Information Science and Technology, China
Qiang Chen	Jiangxi University of Finance and Economics, China
Renjie Chen	University of Science and Technology of China, China
Siming Chen	Fraunhofer IGD, Germany
Xuejin Chen	University of Science and Technology of China, China
Yadang Chen	Nanjing University of Information Science and Technology, China
Yi-Chao Chen	Shanghai Jiao Tong University, China
Zhonggui Chen	Xiamen University, China
Zhanglin Cheng	SIAT, Chinese Academy of Sciences, China
Ming-Te Chi	National Chengchi University, Taiwan
Hui-Chun Chu	Soochow University, Taiwan
Etienne Corman	CNRS, France
Remi Cozot	University of the Littoral Opal Coast, France
Hui Cui	La Trobe University, Australia
Yuchao Dai	Northwestern Polytechnical University, China
Jan De Beenhouwer	University of Antwerp, Belgium
Amal Dev Parakkat	Institut Polytechnique de Paris, France
Yoshinori Dobashi	Hokkaido University, Japan
Xiao Dong	Beijing Normal–Hong Kong Baptist University, China
Yue Dong	Tsinghua University, China
Zhiyang Dou	Massachusetts Institute of Technology, USA
Zhengjun Du	Qinghai University, China
Parris Egbert	Brigham Young University, USA
Martin Eisemann	TU Braunschweig, Germany
Hui Fang	Loughborough University, UK
Xiaonan Fang	Macau University of Science and Technology, China
Yu Fang	NVIDIA, USA
Jieqing Feng	Zhejiang University, China
Gang Fu	Hong Kong Polytechnic University, China
Qiang Fu	Beijing University of Posts and Telecommunications, China

Xiao-Ming Fu	University of Science and Technology of China, China
Ioannis Fudos	University of Ioannina, Greece
Issei Fujishiro	Keio University, Japan
Eric Galin	LIRIS, University Lyon 1, France
Lin Gao	Institute of Computing Technology, Chinese Academy of Sciences, China
Marina Gavrilova	University of Calgary, Canada
Laurent Grisoni	University of Lille, France
Frank Yunqing Guan	Singapore Institute of Technology, Singapore
Jianwei Guo	Institute of Automation, Chinese Academy of Sciences, China
Jie Guo	Nanjing University, China
Yulan Guo	Sun Yat-sen University, China
Shashi Kant Gupta	Eudoxia Research University, USA
Hugo Hadfield	University of Cambridge, UK
Osama Halabi	Qatar University, Qatar
Peter Hall	University of Bath, UK
Mahmoud Hassaballah	South Valley University, Egypt
Xiaowei He	Institute of Software, Chinese Academy of Sciences, China
Dietmar Hildenbrand	TU Darmstadt, Germany
Eckhard Hitzer	International Christian University, Japan
Fei Hou	Institute of Software, Chinese Academy of Sciences, China
Xinrong Hu	Wuhan Textile University, China
Haibin Huang	Megvii Technology, USA
Jin Huang	Wuhan Textile University, China
Shi-Sheng Huang	Beijing Normal University, China
Xiangru Huang	Westlake University, China
Xingchang Huang	Max Planck Institute for Informatics, Germany
Kei Iwasaki	Saitama University, Japan
Alberto Jaspe-Villanueva	King Abdullah University of Science and Technology, Saudi Arabia
Jinyuan Jia	Hong Kong University of Science and Technology (Guangzhou), China
Xiaogang Jin	Zhejiang University, China
Younhyun Jung	Gachon University, South Korea
Ramakrishna Kakarala	Omnivision Technologies, USA
Prem Kalra	Indian Institute of Technology Delhi, Indian
Manos Kamarianakis	University of Crete, Greece
Aouaidjia Kamel	Henan University, China
Dawar Khan	University of Haripur, Pakistan

Xumeng Wang	Nankai University, China
Yunhai Wang	Renmin University of China, China
Chun-Wang Wei	Kaohsiung Medical University, Taiwan
Laixiang Wen	Jilin Animation Institute, China
Yang Wen	Shenzhen University, China
Di Weng	Zhejiang University, China
Franz-Erich Wolter	Leibniz University Hannover, Germany
Tak-Lam Wong	Douglas College, Canada
Tien-Tsin Wong	Monash University, Australia
Huisi Wu	Shenzhen University, China
Jun Wu	Delft University of Technology, The Netherlands
Qiangqiang Wu	City University of Hong Kong, China
Burkhard Wuensche	University of Auckland, New Zealand
Shihong Xia	Institute of Computing Technology, Chinese Academy of Sciences, China
Chunxia Xiao	Wuhan University, China
Haoran Xie	Japan Advanced Institute of Science and Technology, Japan
Ke Xie	Shenzhen University, China
Shiqing Xin	Shandong University, China
Guanyu Xing	Sichuan University, China
Zhaohu Xing	Hong Kong University of Science and Technology (Guangzhou), China
Feng Xu	Tsinghua University, China
Gang Xu	Hangzhou Dianzi University, China
Kai Xu	National University of Defense Technology, China
Kun Xu	Tsinghua University, China
Pengfei Xu	Shenzhen University, China
Sen-Zhe Xu	University of Science and Technology Beijing, China
Weiwei Xu	Zhejiang University, China
Bo Yang	Hong Kong Polytechnic University, China
Meng Yang	Beijing Forestry University, China
Wenhan Yang	Pengcheng Laboratory, China
Xiaosong Yang	Bournemouth University, UK
Yijun Yang	Hong Kong University of Science and Technology (Guangzhou), China
Yin Yang	University of Utah, USA
Yongliang Yang	University of Bath, UK
Junfeng Yao	Xiamen University, China
Tatsuya Yatagawa	Hitotsubashi University, Japan

Ran Yi	Shanghai Jiao Tong University, China
Renjiao Yi	National University of Defense Technology, China
Deng Yu	Shandong University, China
Zhaoyuan Yu	Nanjing Normal University, China
Xin Yuan	Westlake University, China
Fanglue Zhang	Victoria University of Wellington, New Zealand
Jian Zhang	Bournemouth University, UK
Lei Zhang	Beijing Institute of Technology, China
Meng Zhang	Nanjing University of Science and Technology, China
Qi Zhang	City University of Hong Kong, China
Songhai Zhang	Tsinghua University, China
Wen Zhang	Wuhan University, China
Xiaoyan Zhang	Shenzhen University, China
Yun Zhang	Communication University of Zhejiang, China
Jennifer Zhao	Victoria University of Wellington, New Zealand
Jianmin Zheng	Nanyang Technological University, Singapore
Zichun Zhong	Wayne State University, USA
Wen Zhou	Anhui Normal University, China
Yang Zhou	Shenzhen University, China
Yu Zhou	Shenzhen University, China
Yuanfeng Zhou	Shandong University, China
Chenyang Zhu	Simon Fraser University, Canada
Jianlin Zhu	South-Central Minzu University, China
Lei Zhu	Hong Kong University of Science and Technology (Guangzhou), China

Contents

Detection and Recognition

Image Analysis and Processing

Reconstruction

Rendering and Animation

Detection and Recognition

Cross-Layer Feature Aggregation Object Detection Networks for Modality-enhanced UAV Images

Xiangqian Liu[1], Guangwei Zhang[2](✉), and Bing Zhou[1]

[1] The College of Computer Science and Artificial Intelligence, Zhengzhou University, Zhengzhou 450000, Henan, China
liuxiangqian@gs.zzu.edu.cn

[2] The School of Computer Sciences, Beijing University of Posts and Telecommunications, Beijing 100876, China
gwzhang@bupt.edu.cn

Abstract. Unmanned aerial vehicle (UAV) object detection has become a major challenge in remote sensing. UAV imagery often encompasses various perspectives and altitudes, leading to significant scale variations, occlusions, and dense small objects. To address these challenges, we propose a cross-layer feature aggregation object detection network for modality-enhanced UAV images, named CLFAMENet. First, the wavelet pooling modal enhancement (WPME) module is constructed to effectively utilize high-frequency and low-frequency information through wavelet domain learning, fusing these features to produce a modality-enhanced feature map. Second, the efficient spatial edge information aggregation (ESEIA) module combines edge information extracted by SobelConv with spatial information extracted by convolution, thereby generating feature representations encompassing rich edge and spatial information. Finally, the proposed cross-layer feature aggregation (CLFA) module introduces a bidirectional fusion mechanism between high-resolution and low-resolution features, enhancing the interaction between shallow and deep features. Experimental results on the VisDrone and the UAVDT datasets show that CLFAMENet effectively improves the accuracy and robustness of object detection, outperforming existing methods.

Keywords: Modality-enhanced · Wavelet domain · Edge information · Cross-Layer feature · Unmanned aerial vehicle (UAV) image

1 Introduction

Unmanned aerial vehicles (UAVs) offer advantages such as low cost and high maneuverability, making them highly valuable in fields like intelligent transportation and remote sensing [1]. When combined with object detection technology, UAVs can autonomously identify and locate targets. The primary difficulties in

P. Li et al. (Eds.): CGI 2025, LNCS 16508, pp. 3–15, 2026.
https://doi.org/10.1007/978-3-032-22264-0_1

UAV object detection is the dominance of small objects, which often suffer from low resolution, weak feature representation, and poor contrast [2]. Additionally, the wide coverage and diverse environments captured in UAV imagery introduce background interference, increasing the risk of false detections.

Currently, deep learning-based object detection methods are generally classified into two main categories: two-stage methods and one-stage methods. The two-stage method, also known as region proposal-based algorithms, follows a two-step process for object detection. First, it generates candidate regions (or proposals) that are likely to contain the objects. Then, these candidate regions are classified and refined through further processing. Representative algorithms in the two-stage category include Faster R-CNN [3], R-FCN [4], and SPP-Net [5], among others. On the other hand, one-stage methods treat object detection as a direct regression problem. These methods simplify the process by directly outputting the location and category of the target object from a single deep learning network, making them more efficient. Representative algorithms in the one-stage category include YOLO [6], SSD [7], and RetinaNet [8]. One-stage methods are particularly noted for their real-time performance and streamlined processes. However, they can be less effective when dealing with small objects in complex backgrounds, where their detection accuracy tends to decrease compared to two-stage methods. Although existing methods have achieved some results in the field of UAV target detection, they still face three major limitations: (1) feature degradation due to repeated downsampling in CNNs, (2) insufficient edge awareness caused by blurred small object boundaries, and (3) inefficient cross-scale fusion of high- and low-resolution features.

To address these issues, this paper proposes a cross-layer feature aggregation object detection network designed explicitly for modality-enhanced UAV imagery, named CLFAMENet. The main contributions of this paper are summarized as follows.

- We propose a wavelet pooling modal enhancement (WPME) module to address the challenge of detecting small and low-contrast objects. By leveraging wavelet domain decomposition, this module captures both high-frequency and low-frequency. Additionally, edge information extracted via SobelConv is fused to further enhance fine-grained object features.
- To enrich local texture and spatial semantics, we introduce an efficient spatial edge information aggregation (ESEIA) module. It combines two complementary branches: a SobelConv-based edge extractor and a standard convolutional spatial feature extractor. This design allows the network to aggregate both structural and spatial cues effectively at the early stage.
- We design a cross-layer feature aggregation (CLFA) module to bridge semantic gaps across feature hierarchies. By incorporating a bidirectional fusion strategy between high-resolution (detailed) and low-resolution (semantic) features, it enhances the networkâĂŹs capacity for multi-scale object detection.

2 Related Work

In recent years, researchers have conducted extensive research on drone object detection. Kisantal proposed an oversampling technique for small object images by repeatedly copying and pasting small objects to augment the dataset, which significantly improved instance segmentation and object detection performance for small objects [9]. Chen et al. employed an adaptive resampling enhancement strategy, logically replicating objects multiple times within the image to further enhance detection results [10]. Bosquet combined generative adversarial networks with image inpainting to increase the proportion of small objects in the dataset, leading to a significant improvement in model detection performance [11].

In addition, researchers have widely used multi-scale feature extraction to improve the performance of small target detection in drone images. Lin et al. introduced feature pyramid networks (FPN), which construct feature pyramids with high-level semantic information at various scales, enabling more accurate object detection [12]. Zhang et al. addressed the complex background interference for small objects by introducing adaptive feature fusion and densely connected pyramid structures [13]. Jiang et al. used convolution kernels of different scales to extract multi-scale information and combined the fine-grained details in the shallow feature map with the deep semantic information to achieve efficient multi-scale feature fusion [14]. Xi et al. proposed a fine-grained object focusing network, FiFoNet, for object detection in UAV imagery [15]. This network effectively selects multi-scale feature combinations for targets while blocking background interference.

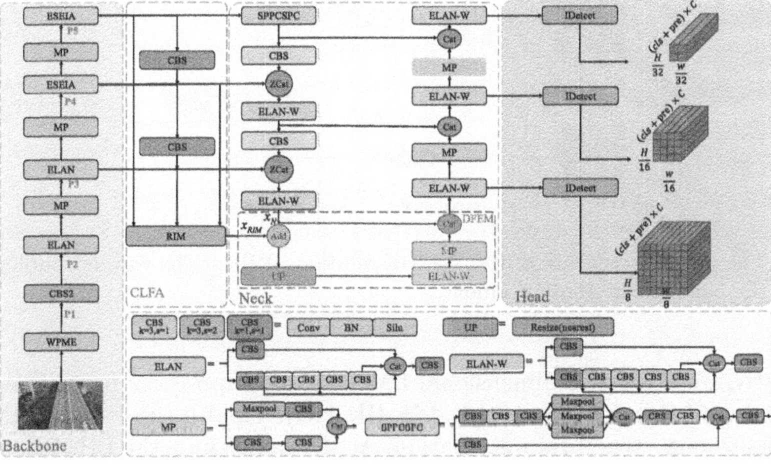

Fig. 1. The overall structure of the proposed CLFAMENet. The backbone is responsible for feature extraction. The neck performs feature fusion and enhancement. The head uses these features for object localization and classification.

3 Method

This paper proposes a small object detection network for UAV images called CLFAMENet, as shown in Fig. 1. It comprises three key modules: the WPME module, the ESEIA module, and the CLFA module. The WPME module uses wavelet domain learning to extract essential feature information while reducing noise impact. The ESEIA module generates feature representations rich in edge and spatial information to optimize the efficient layer aggregation network (ELAN). The CLFA module introduces a bidirectional fusion mechanism between high-resolution and low-resolution features, thereby improving the detection capability for targets of various scales. Spatial pyramid pooling concurrent spatial pyramid convolution (SPPCSPC) is an original component from YOLOv7.

3.1 WPME Module

To ensure the complete preservation of small object information, we employed the discrete wavelet transform (DWT) for feature extraction, utilizing both low- and high-frequency components to represent the target. The architecture of the WPME module is shown in Fig. 2. Among them, wavelet pooling layer (WPL) captures multi-scale information by decomposing features into different frequency components.

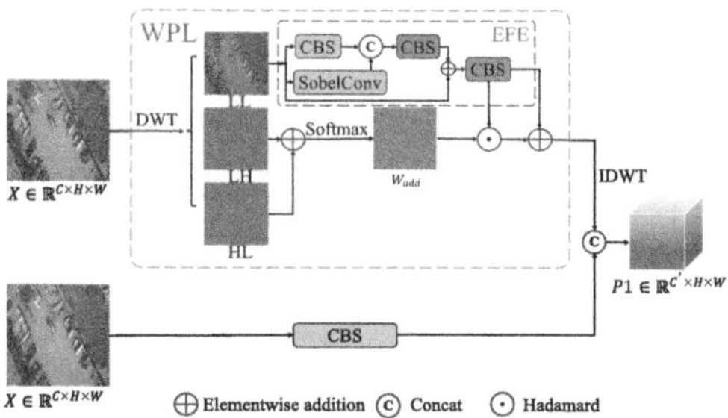

Fig. 2. The overall structure of the WPME module. WPL is the wavelet pooling layer. EFE is the edge feature enhancement.

Firstly, we use a two-dimensional DWT to decompose the input image $X \in \mathbb{R}^{C\times H\times W}$ into four sub-bands (LL, LH, HL, HH). The LL sub-band contains the target's primary structural information. At the same time, the LH, HL, and HH sub-bands represent detailed information in the horizontal, vertical, and diagonal directions, respectively. This can be expressed as:

$$\{\text{LL}, \text{LH}, \text{HL}, \text{HH}\} = \text{2D DWT}\ (X) \tag{1}$$

where the HH subband containing a lot of noise is discarded.

Secondly, LH and HL are added elementwise and apply softmax normalization to highlight essential features and suppress noise, resulting in a weighted feature map. The formula for this process is as follows:

$$W_{\text{add}} = Softmax(\text{LH} + \text{HL}) \tag{2}$$

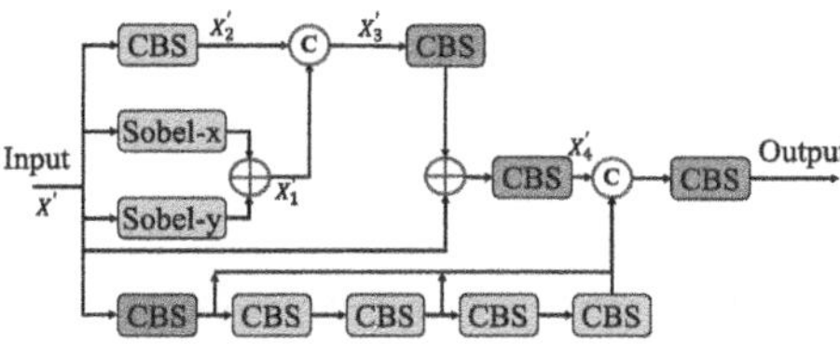

Fig. 3. Overall structure of the ESEIA module. Sobel-x and Sobel-y are the two directional components of the Sobel operator in image processing.

Then, the proposed edge feature enhancement (EFE) module enhances the low-frequency information from the LL subband by combining Sobel convolution with a standard convolution layer. Sobel convolution is an edge detection operation that effectively captures edge information in images. Specifically, the weighted high-frequency feature map is fused with the edge-enhanced LL subband feature map through the Hadamard product. This can be expressed as:

$$\text{F}_{\text{me}} = (1 + W_{\text{add}}) \odot \text{EFE}(LL) \tag{3}$$

Finally, the enhanced feature map is reconstructed back to the original space through inverse discrete wavelet transform (IDWT) and combined with the convolved original image features to obtain the initial feature P1.

$$\text{P1} = \text{2D IDWT}(\text{F}_{\text{me}}, \text{LH}_0, \text{HL}_0, \text{HH}_0) + Conv(X) \tag{4}$$

where LH_0, HL_0, and HH_0 are the zeroed-out versions of the HH, HL, and LH components.

3.2 ESEIA Module

As shown in Fig. 3, the ESEIA module aims to enhance feature representation in UAV imagery by combining edge and spatial information. The ESEIA module consists of two branches. The first branch extracts edge information from the input X' using Sobel convolution. Sobel convolution applies Sobel filters in the x and y directions.

Then, applying the Sobel filters via 3D convolutions, we obtain the edge information for both directions as:

$$X_1' = \text{Conv 3D}_x(X') + \text{Conv 3D}_y(X') \tag{5}$$

Next, the input feature map is passed through a 3×3 convolution branch to capture contextual information to obtain X_2'. Then X_1' and X_2' are concatenated along the channel to obtain X_3'. Finally, X_3' performs a 1×1 convolution operation and is added to the input X' to preserve the initial information and enhance the representation. In the second branch, X' passes through a 1×1 convolution module to change the number of channels. Then X' passes through four 3×3 convolution modules for feature extraction. As shown in Fig. 3, the four features are superimposed together to obtain the final feature result.

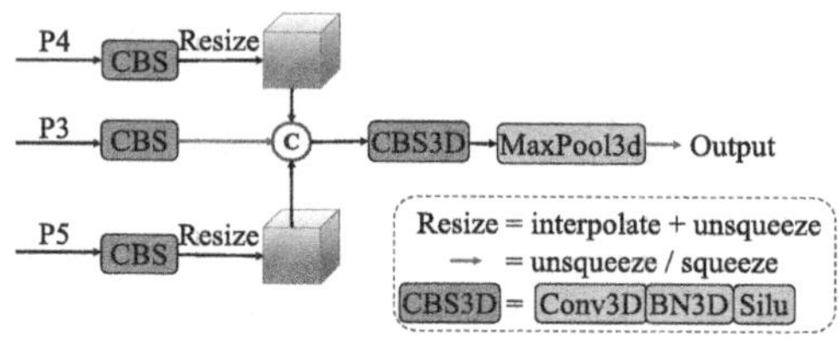

Fig. 4. Overall structure of the RIM module.

3.3 CLFA Module

The structure of the CLFA module is shown in the yellow area of Fig. 1. This module introduces a bidirectional fusion mechanism between high-resolution and low-resolution features, making the information transfer between features more sufficient, thereby improving the detection ability of multi-scale objects.

First, high-resolution and low-resolution features are extracted from different layers of the network. Then, a bidirectional fusion mechanism is used for feature interaction in Zcat. High-resolution features convey detailed information, while low-resolution features provide global contextual information. Specifically, the Zcat module takes three inputs: low-resolution features l, mid-resolution features m, and high-resolution features s. The low-resolution features l, which contain more semantic information, are adjusted to the same size as the mid-resolution features through upsampling.

$$l' = \text{Interp}(l, \text{size} = m \cdot \text{shape}[2:], \text{mode} = \text{nearest}) \tag{6}$$

The high-resolution features s can capture more texture details and are resized to the target size using max pooling and average pooling operations.

$$s' = \text{MaxPool}(s, \text{size} = m \cdot \text{shape}[2:]) + \text{AvgPool}(s, \text{size} = m \cdot \text{shape}[2:]) \tag{7}$$

Then, these feature maps are concatenated along the channel dimension to obtain a richer feature representation. The detailed process is as follows:

$$Fused = Cat(l', m, s', dim = 1) \tag{8}$$

Notably, we propose the resolution integration module (RIM) feature layer to optimize the network structure. The network structure of RIM is shown in Fig. 4. This module enhances feature representation and detection performance by fusing feature maps P3, P4, and P5 of different resolutions. Specifically, 1×1 convolutions are first used to make the number of channels in P3, P4, and P5 consistent, ensuring channel dimension consistency across different resolution feature maps. Next, upsampling operations adjust the resolution of P4 and P5 to match P3. Then, P3, P4, and P5 are expanded to the third dimension and fused using 3D convolutions, allowing deep feature fusion. 3D convolution facilitates information interaction in both spatial and channel dimensions, better combining multi-scale features. Finally, 3D pooling further compresses the feature maps and removes the third dimension, generating the final fused feature.

In addition, the deep feature enhancement module (DFEM) was added to the neck to improve the detection performance of small objects, as shown in Fig. 1. This module first adds x_{RIM} to the input from the previous layer x_N, followed by upsampling, feature extraction, and pooling operations. Finally, the generated feature map is fused with x_N, optimizing the detection of small objects.

3.4 Loss Function

To optimize the detection performance of CLFAMENet, we employ a multi-component loss function that integrates classification loss, regression loss, and IoU-based loss. The overall loss function is defined as follows:

$$L = \lambda_1 L_{\text{cls}} + \lambda_2 L_{\text{reg}} + \lambda_3 L_{\text{IoU}} \tag{9}$$

where L_{cls} represents the classification loss, implemented using Binary Cross Entropy (BCE) loss. L_{reg} denotes the regression loss, use BCE to calculate the difference between the object confidence and the IoU value of the predicted box. L_{IoU} is an IoU-based loss function, implemented using Complete IoU (CIoU).

4 Experimental Results

4.1 Implementation Details and Evaluation Metrics

Our proposed method is an improvement based on the YOLOv7 framework. The experiments were conducted using an NVIDIA GeForce RTX 4070 Ti Super GPU. We used SGD as the optimizer, with an initial learning rate of 0.01, and a momentum of 0.937. The batch size was set to 8 during the experiments, and the number of epochs was set to 300. In the data preprocessing stage, we resized the original image to a fixed size of 640×640. We used mAP, mAP_{50}, and mAP_{75} as quantitative evaluation metrics for the comparative experiments. In addition, we also evaluated the number of model parameters and FPS.

4.2 Datasets

The VisDrone 2019 dataset [16] is a pivotal resource in the field of UAV vision, featuring images of small and densely packed objects across various complex scenes. Specifically, 6,471 images are designated for model training, 548 for validation, and 1,610 for the final evaluation. The UAVDT dataset [17] is a video dataset of drone flight missions in real scenarios, primarily used for UAV object detection and tracking tasks. The targets in the dataset include three main categories: car, truck, and bus. In this paper, 24,206 images are selected for model training, and 16,170 images are used for validation.

4.3 Comparisons With State-of-the-Art Algorithms

Table 1. Comparison with state-of-the-art detectors on the VisDrone 2019 dataset.

Method	mAP	mAP_{50}	mAP_{75}	AP_S	AP_M	AP_L	$Params(M)$	FPS
RetinaNet [8]	19.4	35.9	18.3	14.3	29.5	33.6	53.0	28
Cascade R-CNN [18]	23.2	39.7	23.4	16.5	36.8	39.4	54.9	26
YOLOv7 [19]	28.1	49.0	27.8	18.9	39.4	54.9	36.9	43
YOLOv7-u6 [19]	28.7	46.2	29.2	18.3	40.2	45.8	41.5	39
EdgeYOLO [20]	26.4	44.8	26.2	16.3	38.7	53.1	40.5	34
YOLOv8 [21],	24.6	38.3	23.0	13.0	33.9	41.9	10.6	65
YOLOv9m [22]	27.1	44.3	27.7	15.7	37.6	46.2	20.1	58
YOLOv10m [23]	26.2	42.8	27.3	15.3	37.3	45.4	15.7	60
YOLO11m [24]	27.7	45.1	28.3	16.5	38.4	46.6	20.0	58
RT-DETR-L [25]	26.9	45.0	27.5	18.8	39.2	52.1	32.0	53
CGMNet [26]	29.3	50.9	29.4	20.2	40.6	47.4	43.6	31
CLFAMENet	**31.2**	**53.4**	**31.1**	**22.1**	**42.5**	**51.2**	39.2	48

Results on the VisDrone 2019 Dataset. To further demonstrate the superiority of the proposed method, we compared the performance of CLFAMENet with state-of-the-art models, as shown in Table 1. The experimental results indicate that the proposed CLFAMENet achieves optimal performance in detection accuracy (mAP, mAP_{50}, mAP_{75}) and multi-scale object detection (AP_S, AP_M, AP_L), with an mAP of 31.2%, significantly outperforming other methods (e.g., 29.3% for CGMNet and 28.7% for YOLOv7-u6). Additionally, CLFAMENet exhibits particularly outstanding performance in small object detection (APs of 22.1%) and medium object detection (APm of 42.5%), demonstrating its stronger adaptability in handling multi-scale objects in drone scenarios. Furthermore, we incorporated several advanced YOLO-based methods in our comparison, including YOLOv9m, YOLOv10m, and YOLO11m, to ensure fairness and modern

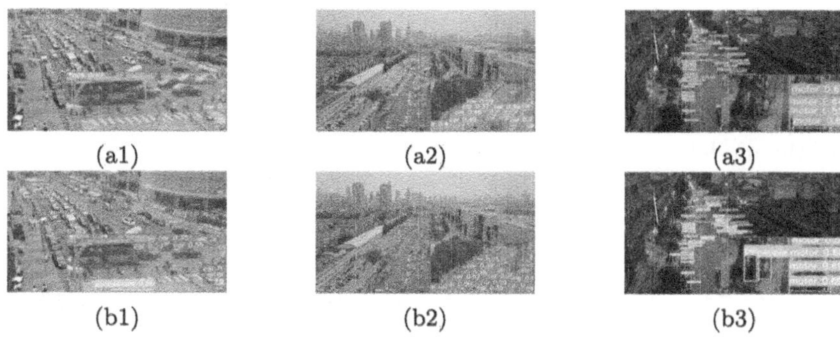

Fig. 5. Visualization results on the VisDrone 2019 dataset. The first to second rows,respectively, present the visualized results of YOLOv7 and CLFAMENet.

relevance. The proposed method achieves an excellent balance between accuracy and speed.

As shown in Fig. 5, we performed a visual analysis comparison between YOLOv7 and our proposed method. Our method obviously significantly reduces the missed detection of small aggregated objects. Furthermore, our method performs better in handling occluded objects.

Table 2. Comparison with state-of-the-art detectors on the UAVDT dataset.

Method	mAP	mAP_{50}	mAP_{75}	car	truck	bus
YOLOv7 [19]	26.8	45.0	29.4	78.4	12.6	44.0
YOLOv7-u6 [19]	27.9	46.0	24.3	78.9	11.6	47.5
YOLOv8 [21]	23.3	38.0	24.5	72.8	8.9	32.3
CGMDet [26]	29.1	48.0	**32.6**	81.3	16.0	47.4
CLFAMENet	**30.6**	**49.3**	32.5	**81.6**	**18.0**	**48.3**

Results on the UAVDT Dataset. We also conducted a performance comparison analysis on the UAVDT dataset. As shown in Table 2, CLFAMENet performed well, surpassing all existing methods and achieving the highest mAP (30.6%) and mAP_{50} (49.3%). In terms of category-specific performance measured by mAP_{50}, CLFAMENet achieves the best results for car (81.6%), truck (18.0%), and bus (48.3%). Although CGMDet slightly outperforms CLFAMENet in mAP_{75} (32.6% vs. 32.5%), our method consistently delivers better accuracy across all other metrics, demonstrating its effectiveness in multi-scale object detection on UAV imagery.

The detection results of the proposed method on the UAVDT dataset are shown in Fig. 6. It can be seen from Fig. 6 (a1, b1) that the proposed method can significantly improve the accuracy of the model in dark scenes. It can be seen from Fig. 6 (a2, b2) that the proposed method can effectively identify occluded objects and demonstrate robustness. It can be seen from Fig. 6 (a3, b3) that the proposed method improves the accuracy while reducing the missed detection rate of the model.

Fig. 6. Visualization results on the UAVDT dataset. The first to second rows, respectively, present the visualized results of YOLOv7 and CLFAMENet.

4.4 Ablation Study

As shown in Table 3, we conducted multiple ablation experiments on the VisDrone2019 dataset to verify the effectiveness of our proposed framework. The baseline methods achieved 28.1%, 49.0%, and 27.8% on mAP, mAP_{50}, and mAP_{75}, respectively.

Table 3. The result of the ablation experiments.

CLFA	ESEIA	WPME	mAP	mAP_{50}	mAP_{75}
			28.1	49.0	27.8
✓			30.9	52.8	30.8
	✓		28.2	49.1	28.2
		✓	28.4	49.7	28.7
✓	✓		30.9	53.1	30.5
	✓	✓	28.3	49.6	28.5
✓	✓	✓	31.2	53.4	31.1

Introducing CLFA improved mAP by 2.8%, mAP_{50} by 3.8%, and mAP_{75} by 3.0%, owing to its bidirectional fusion of shallow high-resolution and deep low-resolution features. ESEIA improves mAP_{50} and mAP_{75} by 0.1% and 0.4%

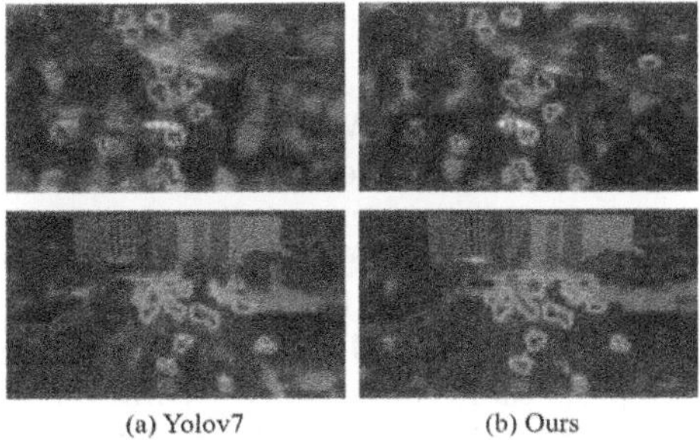

Fig. 7. The heatmap results on the VisDrone 2019 dataset.

respectively by enhancing spatial and edge information. Although ESEIA is effective for boundary refinement, its overall effect is not as good as CLFA. WPME increased mAP to 28.4%, mAP_{50} to 49.7%, and mAP_{75} to 28.7%, showing that wavelet-based frequency decomposition improves robustness to scale and occlusion. The combination of CLFA and ESEIA obtains mAP of 30.9%, indicating that edge-aware spatial features facilitate multi-scale fusion. In contrast, the combination of ESEIA and WPME only slightly improves over the baseline (mAP 28.3%). The integration of all three modules in CLFAMENet achieved the highest performance, with mAP improving to 31.2%, mAP_{50} to 53.4%, and mAP_{75} to 31.1%. The synergistic effect of multi-scale feature fusion (CLFA), spatial-edge feature enhancement (ESEIA), and wavelet-based feature enrichment (WPME) contributes to optimal detection performance.

We also visualized the effectiveness of the proposed method using heatmaps, as shown in Fig. 7. By examining the heatmap results, it is evident that the proposed method better attends to relevant regions, particularly for small and challenging objects, thus validating its robustness and accuracy.

5 Conclusion

In this paper, we propose CLFAMENet for small object detection in UAV imagery. Combining the image and spatial domain characteristics, we propose WPME to enhance the model's feature extraction capabilities. Additionally, we propose the ESEIA module, which aids in accurately delineating object boundaries and enhancing detection under challenging environmental conditions. Finally, the proposed CLFA module promotes enhanced feature aggregation by leveraging high-resolution and low resolution contexts, thereby improving detection accuracy at various object scales. Experimental results validate the effectiveness of our proposed methods in detecting small and densely packed objects in UAV imagery.

References

1. Luo, Z., Wang, Y., Chen, L., Yang, W.: Frequency spectrum features modeling for real-time tiny object detection in remote sensing image. IEEE Geosci. Remote Sens. Lett. (2024)
2. Hao, C., Zhang, H., Song, W., Liu, F., Wu, E.: Slicing-aided learning for small object detection. IEEE Sign. Process. Lett. (2024)
3. Ren, S., He, K., Girshick, R., Sun, J.: Faster r-CNN: towards real-time object detection with region proposal networks. Adv. Neural Inf. Process. Syst. **28** (2015)
4. Dai, J., Li, Y., He, K., Sun, J.: R-FCN: object detection via region-based fully convolutional networks. Adv. Neural. Inf. Process. Syst. **29** (2016)
5. He, K., Zhang, X., Ren, S., Sun, J.: Spatial pyramid pooling in deep convolutional networks for visual recognition. IEEE Trans. Patt. Anal. Mach. Intell. **37**(9), 1904–1916 (2015)
6. Redmon, J., Divvala, S., Girshick, R., Farhadi, A.: You only look once: unified, real-time object detection. In: Proceedings of the IEEE Conference on Computer Vision and Pattern Recognition, pp. 779–788 (2016)
7. Liu, W., et al.: SSD: single shot multibox detector. In: Leibe, B., Matas, J., Sebe, N., Welling, M. (eds.) ECCV 2016. LNCS, vol. 9905, pp. 21–37. Springer, Cham (2016). https://doi.org/10.1007/978-3-319-46448-0_2
8. Lin, T.-Y., Goyal, P., Girshick, R., He, K., Dollár, P.: Focal loss for dense object detection. In: Proceedings of the IEEE International Conference on Computer Vision, pp. 2980–2988 (2017)
9. Kisantal, M.: Augmentation for small object detection arXiv preprint arXiv:1902.07296 (2019)
10. Chen, C., et al.: RRNET: a hybrid detector for object detection in drone-captured images. In: Proceedings of the IEEE/CVF International Conference on Computer Vision Workshops (2019)
11. Bosquet, B., Cores, D., Seidenari, L., Brea, V.M., Mucientes, M., Del Bimbo, A.: Bimbo: a full data augmentation pipeline for small object detection based on generative adversarial networks. Patt. Recogn. **133**, 108998 (2023)
12. Lin, T.-Y., Dollár, P., Girshick, R., He, K., Hariharan, B., Belongie, S.: Feature pyramid networks for object detection. In: Proceedings of the IEEE Conference on Computer Vision and Pattern Recognition, pp. 2117–2125 (2017)
13. Zhang, R., Shao, Z., Huang, X., Wang, J., Wang, Y., Li, D.: Adaptive dense pyramid network for object detection in UAV imagery. Neurocomputing **489**, 377–389 (2022)
14. Jiang, L., et al.: Mffsodnet: multi-scale feature fusion small object detection network for UAV aerial images. IEEE Trans. Instr. Measur. (2024)
15. Xi, Y., Jia, W., Miao, Q., Liu, X., Fan, X., Li, H.: Fifonet: fine-grained target focusing network for object detection in UAV images. Remote Sens. **14**(16), 3919 (2022)
16. Zhu, P., et al.: Detection and tracking meet drones challenge. IEEE Trans. Patt. Anal. Mach. Intell. **44**(11), 7380–7399 (2021)
17. Du, D., et al.: The unmanned aerial vehicle benchmark: Object detection and tracking. In: Proceedings of the European Conference on Computer Vision (ECCV), pp. 370–386 (2018)
18. Cai, Z., Vasconcelos, N.: Cascade r-CNN: delving into high quality object detection. In: Proceedings of the IEEE Conference on Computer Vision and Pattern Recognition, pp. 6154–6162 (2018)

19. Wang, C.-Y., Bochkovskiy, A., Mark Liao, H.: Yolov7: trainable bag-of-freebies sets new state-of-the-art for real-time object detectors. In: Proceedings of the IEEE/CVF Conference on Computer Vision and Pattern Recognition, pp. 7464–7475 (2023)
20. Liu, S., Zha, J., Sun, J., Li, Z., Wang, G.: Edgeyolo: an edge-real-time object detector. In: 2023 42nd Chinese Control Conference (CCC), pp. 7507–7512. IEEE (2023)
21. Jocher, G., Chaurasia, A., J. Q.: Yolov8 by ultralytics. In: https://github.com/ultralytics/ultralytics (2023)
22. Wang, C.-Y., Yeh, I., Mark Liao, H.Y.: Yolov9: learning what you want to learn using programmable gradient information. In: European Conference on Computer Vision, pp. 1–21. Springer (2024)
23. Wang, A., Chen, H., Liu, L., Chen, K., Lin, Z., Han, J., et al.: Yolov10: real-time end-to-end object detection. Adv. Neural. Inf. Process. Syst. **37**, 107984–108011 (2024)
24. Khanam, R., Hussain, M.: Yolov11: an overview of the key architectural enhancements arXiv preprint arXiv:2410.17725 (2024)
25. Zhao, Y., et al.: DETRS beat YOLOs on real-time object detection. In: Proceedings of the IEEE/CVF Conference on Computer Vision and Pattern Recognition, pp. 16965–16974 (2024)
26. Zhou, L., et al.: A multi-scale object detector based on coordinate and global information aggregation for UAV aerial images. Remote Sens. **15**(14), 3468 (2023)

AGRC-ViMamba: A Robust Neural Network Architecture for Enhanced Small Target Detection Against Information Loss

Yang Liu[1,2], Yatu Ji[1](✉), Lei Shi[1], Qing-Dao-Er-Ji Ren[1], Bao Shi[1], Nier Wu[1], Xufei Zhuang[1], and Haiteng Xu[1]

[1] Inner Mongolia University of Technology, Hohhot 010051, China
{20221100134,mljyt}@imut.edu.cn
[2] Inner Mongolia Vocational College of Chemical Engineering, Hohhot 010080, China

Abstract. A key challenge faced by deep neural networks is the gradual loss of input data features during the layer-by-layer feature extraction process, which becomes particularly serious in the task of small object detection. Although the existing theories attribute this performance degradation to the phenomenon of information bottleneck, we propose AGRC-ViMamba, which is a new framework aimed at reducing information attenuation and improving the recognition accuracy of small targets. Our method integrates two key components: (1) Multi-level attention gated reversible column (ML-AGRC), which serves as a reversible auxiliary branch to maintain a reliable gradient flow; (2) The improved feature extractor SPD-Conv-SS2D module based on the VSS architecture. The backbone network adopts this enhanced VSS module and the auxiliary branches inspired by YOLOv9, effectively retaining fine-grained target features during forward propagation while minimizing parameter overhead to the greatest extent. A large number of experiments have proved the effectiveness of this model. Compared with the state-of-the-art (SOTA) method, without reducing the recall rate, the accuracy of this model on the VisDrone and AI-TOD datasets has increased by 1.5% and 2.3% respectively. The ablation study further verified the contributions of the ML-AGRC and SPD-Conv-SS2D modules to the model performance. The source code is available at https://github.com/wizardly1985/AGRC-ViMamba.

Keywords: Small Object Detection · Vision Mamba · Attention Gated Reversible Column

1 Introduction

Small object recognition remains a key challenge in computer vision. This paper conducts research on the Layer-wise Information Attenuation (LIA) problem that is widespread in deep neural networks. This phenomenon refers to the irreversible loss of detailed information caused by convolution downsampling and

P. Li et al. (Eds.): CGI 2025, LNCS 16508, pp. 16–28, 2026.
https://doi.org/10.1007/978-3-032-22264-0_2

nonlinear activation during the layer-by-layer transmission of feature maps. In small target recognition, it is manifested as the loss of gradient information of key texture or shape features and the degradation of spatial resolution. To solve this core bottleneck, this paper innovatively proposes the Multi-Level Attention Gated Reversible Column(ML-AGRC) architecture. Its original design intention is to construct a bidirectional feature propagation path through reversible residual connections, and achieve cross-level coupling of shallow detail features and deep semantic features in combination with the dynamic gating mechanism. Thus breaking through the information capacity limitation of the traditional one-way feature pyramid. The SS2D [1] module of visual Mamba is further introduced. Its advantage lies in the spatial dependency modeling ability based on the state space model, which can effectively capture the long-range context association of small targets. Based on the above methods, we propose a new AGRC-ViMamba framework.

The main contributions of this paper are as follows: (1)This study advocates a new neural network structure. The idea is to use reverse columns to replace the common Neck part, synchronously achieving the purpose of multi-scale feature fusion and alleviating the loss of gradient information. (2) We innovatively developed the SPD-Conv-SS2D module. By modifying the visual state space (VSS) structure in the ViM model [1], the feature representation ability of the network for microscale targets was significantly enhanced. This module optimizes the spatial-spectral feature fusion mechanism, enabling the network to effectively capture the multi-scale complex features of the target, thereby playing a key role in the detection of tiny targets in complex backgrounds. (3)We have specially designed a multi-level attention-gated reversible column subnetwork. By optimizing the gradient propagation path, it provides reliable gradient flow support for the backbone network. This structural improvement effectively resolves the information bottleneck effect in deep neural networks and ensures the accurate modeling of the correlation between the detection target and the input features during the training process through the dynamic feature calibration mechanism. This technological breakthrough has significant theoretical value for enhancing the robustness and accuracy of detecting tiny targets.

2 Related Work

Figure 1. illustrates three exemplary neural network architectures, each possessing distinctive innovations and playing specific roles in addressing the information bottleneck problem. The following subsections elaborate on these methods.: (a)Path Aggregation Network (PAN) [2] enhances semantic information in lower layers by propagating high-level features via upsampling, while its bottom-up path supplements missing details in higher layers through downsampling of high-resolution low-level features. This bidirectional architecture facilitates integrated flow of semantic and detailed information, enabling features at all levels to maintain strong semantics and high spatial resolution. (b) Reversible Columns(RevCol) [3] achieves feature decoupling through reversible transformations, enabling natural separation of low-level and high-level semantic features

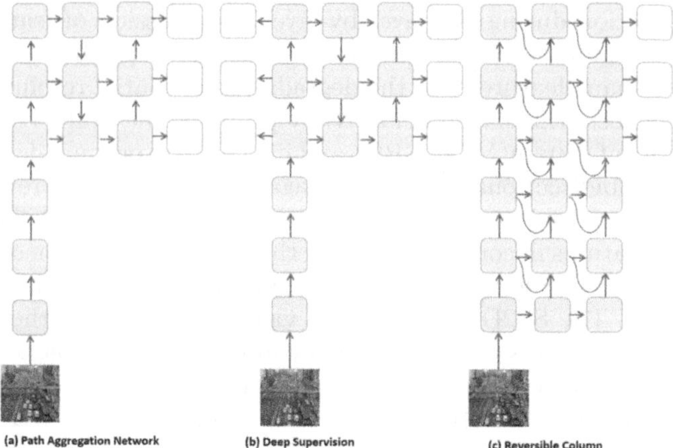

Fig. 1. related network architectures and methods.(a)Path Aggregation Network.(b)Deep Supervision.(c)Reversible Column.

across layers while ensuring lossless information propagation. This framework reconstructs activations during backpropagation to prevent information loss, with its bidirectional flow design optimizing training efficiency. The approach is applicable to diverse vision tasks including object detection. (c) Deep Supervision introduces auxiliary supervisory signals at intermediate network layers, enforcing discriminative feature learning in shallow networks through multi-level loss constraints to suppress feature degradation in deeper layers. This multi-dimensional framework transcends single-method limitations, achieving optimal efficiency-fidelity balance for fine-grained detection in complex scenarios.

3 Method and Principle

3.1 Architecture Overview

The architecture design of AGRC-ViMamba (see Fig. 2) adopts a dual-branch structure comprising two object detection branches and a Reversible Column branch. Both the Main Branch and Auxiliary Branch employ similar frameworks: they first conduct feature learning through IB-DSConv with an inverted bottleneck structure (see Fig. 4(b)), then perform feature extraction using multi-level SPD-Conv-SS2D modules, and finally predict object categories and bounding boxes via detection heads. A critical distinction lies in their detection heads: the Main Branch utilizes a single detection head (see Fig. 4(c)), while the Auxiliary Branch incorporates five detection heads to implement deep supervision. Additionally, the Reversible Column branch leverages multi-scale attention gating mechanisms to achieve cross-scale feature fusion while preserving gradient fidelity throughout the network.

$$\mathcal{L} = \lambda_{\text{cls}}\mathcal{L}_{\text{cls}} + \lambda_{\text{box}}\mathcal{L}_{\text{box}} + \lambda_{\text{obj}}\mathcal{L}_{\text{obj}} \tag{1}$$

The Eq. (1) is the loss function of the model.$\mathcal{L}_{cls}$ serves as a fundamental component of the loss function designed to quantify the model's precision in predicting target category probabilities during object detection tasks. $\mathcal{L}_{box}$ serves as the core loss function component that drives the model to precisely localize target bounding boxes by mathematically modeling spatial discrepancies between predicted and ground-truth boxes, thereby guiding the network to optimize positional parameters. $\mathcal{L}_{obj}$ serves as a core loss component designed to evaluate whether predicted bounding boxes contain valid targets. It optimizes the model's ability to distinguish between background and foreground by mathematically modeling prediction errors in object presence probability. λ_{obj} andλ_{cls} and λ_{box} dynamically adjusted loss weighting coefficients.

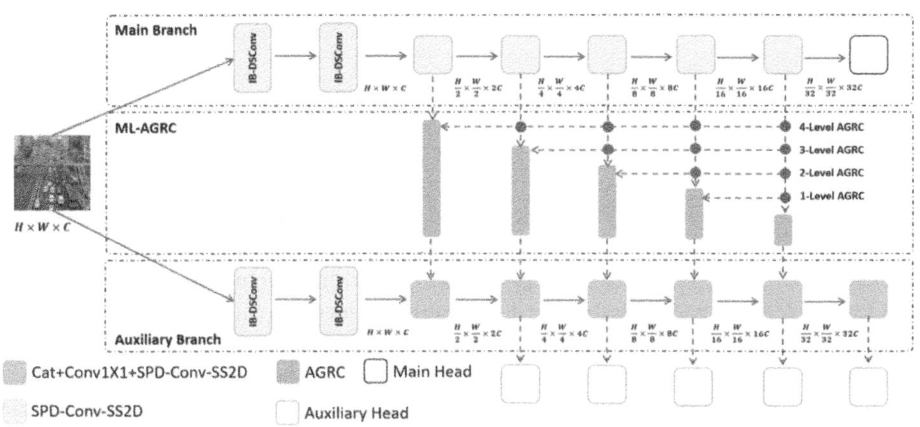

Fig. 2. Architecture of AGRC-ViMamba.

3.2 SPD-Conv-SS2D Module

This study proposes an SPD-Conv-SS2D module based on an improved VSS architecture (see Fig. 3.) specifically optimized for microscopic object recognition, which adopts a dual-path design: the first path performs spatial reorganization and channel expansion through SPD-Conv [4], while the second path implements a global dynamic selective scanning mechanism via the SS2D module, with an additional residual connection integrated to prevent feature degradation in deep networks.

The SPD-Conv introduced in this study, serving as a versatile architectural component, is centered around the Spatial-to-Depth Paradigm (SDP). It enhances feature learning efficiency, preserves critical spatial details, and achieves multi-scale feature retention. The basic mechanism of this module involves dimensional transformation of visual data through spatial compression and channel expansion, and its computational topology entails dimensional restructuring

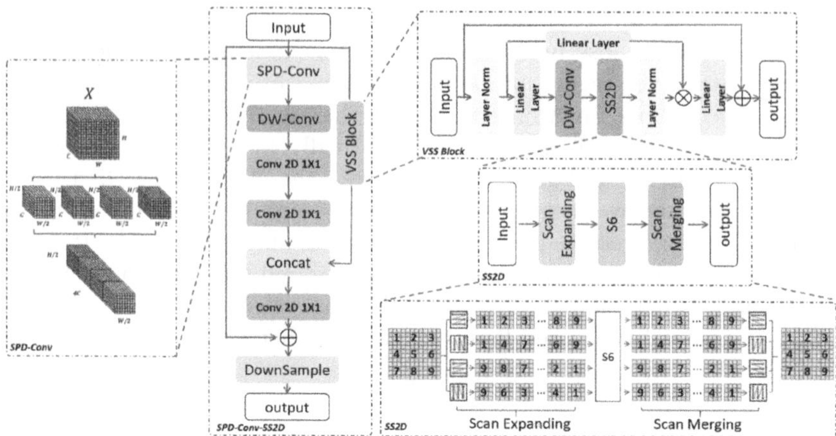

Fig. 3. SPD-Conv-SS2D module.

via spatial redistribution and channel concatenation. For an input feature tensor X with dimensions $H \times W \times C$, the spatial plane is first partitioned into hierarchical sub-regions according to the Eq. (2). Spatial reorganization is accomplished through pixel-interleaved partitioning and hierarchical aggregation along the channel axis. Each partitioned segment undergoes dimensional restructuring, reducing the spatial resolution to $H/2 \times W/2$ while proportionally expanding the channel capacity to $4 \times C$. Subsequently, dimensional stacking is achieved through channel - directional integration via Eq. (3). This geometric transformation enables the convolutional network to capture enhanced cross-channel correlations, alleviates the information degradation issue of traditional downsampling, preserves high-resolution spatial relationships during the downsampling phase to retain multi-scale visual cues, and realizes enhanced multi-scale feature retention in hierarchical abstraction through the two-stage process of controlled spatial reduction and expanded channel encoding. In particular, it can preserve discriminative features crucial for microscopic pattern recognition.

$$f_i = \mathrm{X}\left[0 : \mathrm{W} : \mathrm{i}, 0 : H : \mathrm{i}, :\right], i = 0, ..., 4 \tag{2}$$

$$output = stack(f_0, f_1, f_2, f_3) \tag{3}$$

The secondary processing pathway incorporates a Vision State Space block(VSS Block).The core of the VSS block is SS2D, which consists of three key operations: Scan Expanding, Selective Scan Spatial State Sequence (S6) block processing, and Scan Merging.As shown on the right side of Fig. 3, the Scan Expanding operation unfolds the input 2D feature map into one-dimensional sequences along four distinct directions: 1) top-left to bottom-right, 2) bottom-left to top-right, 3) bottom-right to top-left, and 4) top-right to bottom-left. This bidirectional scanning mechanism ensures that each element in the feature map aggregates information from all spatial positions along different paths, thereby establishing a global receptive field. The output of scan expansion consists of image patch sequences generated along these four directions, which are then fed as inputs into four separate S6 blocks for processing.The Scan Merging operation in Fig. 3 is responsible for reshaping and fusing the four sequences processed by the S6 blocks, ultimately reconstructing them into a 2D feature map output.The four one-dimensional sequences from scan expansion are independently processed by the S6 blocks for feature extraction. The core of the S6 block lies in its selective scan spatial state sequence model. This model enables each element in the sequence to selectively interact with information scanned before it, effectively reducing the computational complexity from quadratic (as in traditional methods like self-attention) to linear. This step ensures thorough scanning of information across all directions, thus capturing features from different dimensions.

The VSS Block essentially serves as a State Space Model (SSM) for the visual domain, typically described using time-invariant systems. The SS2D module models image processing tasks as a discretized Linear Time-Invariant (LTI) system operating on image patch sequences. Specifically, this modeling involves discretizing the continuous state transition equation, as detailed in Eq. (4).The final output y_t represents the prediction for the $t-th$ image patch of the output image y. Using Eq. (5), we can reconstruct the complete image.

$$\begin{aligned} h'(t) &= Ah(t) + Bu(t) \Rightarrow h_t = \overline{A}h_{t-1} + \overline{B}x_t, \\ y(t) &= Ch(t) + Du(t) \Rightarrow y_t = \overline{C}h_t + \overline{D}x_t \end{aligned} \tag{4}$$

$$y = [y_1, y_2, ..., y_n] \tag{5}$$

where $u(t) \in \mathbb{R}$ is the map of the input signal, $y(t) \in \mathbb{R}$ is the output response, $h(t)$ is the hidden state, and $h'(t)$ represents the derivative of $h(t)$. $A \in \mathbb{R}^{N\times N}, B \in \mathbb{R}^{N\times 1}, C \in \mathbb{R}^{1\times N}, D \in \mathbb{R}^1$ are the weighting parameters, all learned by the neural network (see Eq. (6)). Subsequently, a matrix Δ is learned through two Linear() layers. This is followed by the discretization of A, B, C, and D via Eq. (7), yielding their discretized versions($\overline{A}$,$\overline{B}$,$\overline{C}$ and $\overline{D}$). Ultimately, the discretized state transition equation is obtained, corresponding to the right-hand side of the $\Rightarrow$ operator in Eq. (4).

$$\begin{aligned} A &= Embedding(expand(x)) \quad , D = Embedding(expand(x)) \\ B &= Linear(x) \quad , C = Linear(x) \end{aligned} \tag{6}$$

where x indicates the input image,x_t denotes the image patch sequence .$expanding()$ indicates the operation of serializing image blocks by using different scanning methods. $Embedding()$ means converting the image block to an embedding vector.

$$\begin{aligned} \Delta &= Linear(Linear(x)) \\ \overline{A} &= \exp(\Delta A), \overline{B} = \Delta B, \overline{C} = \Delta C, \overline{D} = \Delta D \end{aligned} \tag{7}$$

3.3 Multi-Level Attention Gated Reversible Column(ML-AGRC)

The ML-AGRC is an auxiliary reversible branch that integrates the Path Aggregation Network, Reversible Column, and attention gating mechanism. It can not only generate reliable gradients but also achieve the fusion of deep multi-scale features.The schematic of ML-AGRC is illustrated in Fig. 4(a).

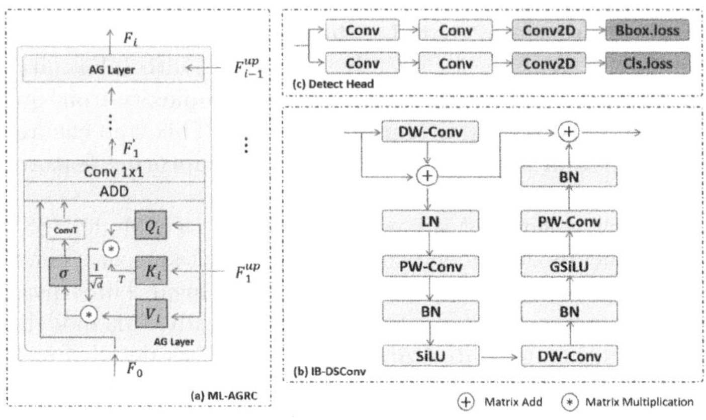

Fig. 4. Three important modules in AGRC-ViMamba. (a) Multi-Level Attention Gated Reversible Column (ML-AGRC). (b) Inverted Bottleneck Depthwise Separable Convolution (IB-DSConv). (c) Detect Head.

$$
\begin{aligned}
F_i' &= \text{AGLayer}\left(F_{i-1}', F_i^{up}\right) \\
&= \text{Conv}_{1\times 1}\left(W_\tau \cdot \sigma\left(\text{softmax}\left(\frac{Q_i K_i^T}{\sqrt{d}}\right) V_i\right) + \text{ConvT}(F_{i-1}')\right), \quad i \geq 1
\end{aligned} \tag{8}
$$

$$
F_0' = F_0, V_i = W_V F_i^{up}, K_i = W_K F_i^{up}, Q_i = W_Q F_i^{up} \tag{9}
$$

$$
F_i = AGRC(F_0', F_1^{up}, ..., F_{i-1}^{up}) = \{ \begin{matrix} AGLayer(F_0', F_1^{up}), i = 1 \\ AGLayer(F_{i-1}', F_i^{up}), i \geq 2 \end{matrix} \tag{10}
$$

where W_V and W_K and W_Q and W_τ represents four learnable matrixs,σ represents the sigmoid() function, represents the feature dimension. d indicates the feature map of the Multi-Level AGRC output of the previous level.F_i^{up} denotes the output of the i-th layer feature extractor, F_i represents the output after i applications of AGLayer(), and F_i' indicates the output of the i-th application of AGLayer().

4 Experiments

4.1 Experimental Details and Visualization

This study conducted experiments using two small object detection datasets, including the VisDrone [5] and AI-TOD [6] datasets. The experiment was conducted on the RTX 4090 GPU using the PyTorch framework for 400 epoches training, and the training data was uniformly divided into 640 × 640 pixel images. Figure 5. shows the visualization of the detection results on the above two datasets.

Fig. 5. Visualization of prediction results on VisDrone and AI-TOD dataset.

4.2 Comparison Results

Table 1. Result of comparison experiments on the VisDrone and AI-TOD dataset.

Model	Param.	FLOPs	Precision(%)	Recall(%)	mAP_{50}(%)	FPS
YOLOv9-c [7]	25.3M	102.1G	41.3/61.3	49.7/63.4	41.3/42.5	160
YOLOv10x [8]	29.3M	160.4G	53.1/70.1	**50.8/66.7**	40.8/43.6	110
YOLOv11x [9]	56.9M	194.9G	53.1/72.0	50.2/65.4	41.6/44.8	112
Drone-YOLO-L [10]	20.5M	102.4G	45.3/63.2	50.0/66.2	38.3/41.6	138
Mamba YOLO-L [11]	57.6M	156.2G	51.6/61.8	36.5/50.3	43.9/44.9	148
RemoteDet-Mamba [12]	71.3M	115.8G	49.5/68.2	49.6/53.3	42.1/43.8	150
SOAR [13]	17.1M	145.7G	55.6/71.8	36.5/50.3	42.5/43.6	148
AGRC-ViMamba	28.9M	174.0G	**57.1/74.1**	48.6/66.3	**45.5/45.3**	150

In the comparative experiments, we selected four typical object detection models and three small object detection models based on Mamba. As shown in Table 1, we compared their performance differences on two experimental datasets. The results show that AGRC-ViMamba outperformed the suboptimal model in Precision by 1.5% and 2.3%, respectively, while achieving improvements of 1.6% and 0.4% in $mAP50$(mean Average Precision at IoU = 0.50). However, it did not reach the optimal performance in Recall, falling short of the best model by 2.6% and 0.4%. Considering the characteristics of the datasets, the VisDrone dataset contains a large number of occluded objects and images under complex lighting conditions, which degrade the features of the detected objects. As a result, the model failed to effectively identify these objects but also did not misclassify them as other types. In contrast, the AI-TOD dataset primarily involves variations in object size, without complex lighting or object occlusion, leading to a smaller decline in Recall.In summary, AGRC-ViMamba exhibits a cautious tendency in object detection: if the features of the detected objects are compromised, it prefers to miss detection rather than produce false detections. In terms of the Frames Per Second (FPS) metric, there is not much difference between AGRC-ViMamba and the lightweight YOLOv9-c. AGRC-ViMamba reaches 150 FPS, a decrease of only 10 FPS, and it is at a moderate level. This is an acceptable result.

4.3 Compare the Precision and Recall Rates of Different Types of Detection Objects in the VisDrone Dataset

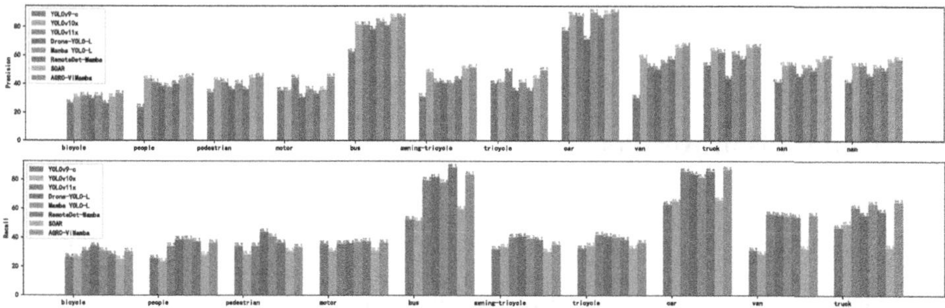

Fig. 6. Comparison of precision and recall of different object.

Figure 6. presents a comprehensive comparison of target recognition performance using bar charts. The upper panel of the figure shows the accuracy rates for ten different target categories, while the lower panel displays the corresponding recall rates. An in-depth analysis of the precision bar charts reveals that the AGRC-ViMamba model outperforms all competing models in every target category. It is worth noting that the bar chart of AGRC-ViMamba is completely higher than that of other models, clearly demonstrating its superior accuracy.The AGRC-ViMamba model exhibits significant advantages in recognizing fine-grained feature categories such as motor, pedestrians, vans, tricycles, and awning tricycles. These categories are characterized by rich and complex features, making accurate identification challenging. Compared with the second-highest-performing model, AGRC-ViMamba achieves improvements of 0.8%, 1.3%, 1.2%, 2.0%, and 0.8% respectively. Even for occlusion-prone categories like people and bicycles, the model still achieves accuracy improvements of 0.2% and 0.6%. For coarse-grained feature categories with abundant training samples and distinct features—including cars, trucks, and buses—AGRC-ViMamba maintains a competitive edge, outperforming the second-best model by 0.1%, 0.5%, and 0.1% respectively.When examining recall rates, although AGRC-ViMamba does not lead in most categories, it excels in detecting targets with dominant coarse-grained features (e.g., cars, vans, and trucks). In these categories, AGRC-ViMamba outperforms the second-best model by 1.1%, 0.1%, and 0.4% respectively.Experimental results indicate that the AGRC-ViMamba model tends to improve detection precision while avoiding false positives, particularly when object features are degraded, where this tendency becomes more pronounced.

4.4 Ablation Study

Table 2. The results of the comparison of different levels of ML-AGRC.

1-Level	2-Level	3-Level	4-Level	Precision(%)	Recall(%)	mAP_{50}(%)
✓	✓	✗	✗	16.2	14.5	14.4
✗	✓	✓	✗	18.3	17.3	16.6
✓	✗	✓	✗	30.1	21.3	18.2
✗	✗	✓	✓	42.1	37.1	30.1
✗	✓	✗	✓	39.8	34.6	26.4
✓	✗	✗	✓	35.1	28.3	21.3
✓	✓	✓	✗	43.2	38.1	31.4
✓	✓	✗	✓	45.4	39.2	33.9
✓	✗	✓	✓	48.1	40.2	37.2
✗	✓	✓	✓	50.1	43.6	40.5
✓	✓	✓	✓	**57.1**	**48.6**	**45.5**

To verify the influence of ML-AGRC on the model, the ablation experiments here are conducted from two aspects. The network structures at different reversible depths are shown in the Fig. 2. The first aspect of the ablation experiment is the impact of the lack of AGRC at different levels on the model performance. From the Table 2, we can see that the absence of AGRC at different levels will cause the decrease of Precision, Recall and mAP_{50}. Meanwhile, the lack of AGRC at a deeper level leads to a greater performance degradation. For example, the absence of 1-Level AGRC shown in the light green area of Table 2 resulted in a 7% decrease in Precision, and the absence of 4-Level AGRC resulted in a 13.9% decrease in Precision. The analysis of other data also conforms to the same rule.

The second aspect of the ablation experiment is to verify the influence on the model performance when different numbers of ML-AGRC deletions are present. By comparing the data in Table 2, we can find that the more ML-AGRC is missing, the more obvious the decline in model performance is. For example, by comparing the light green region and the light blue region in Table 2, we find that the Precision of the missing one ML-AGRC model decreases by at least 7%, but the Precision of the missing two ML-AGRC model decreases by at least 15%.We observe that other data also conform to the same rule.

Comparison of Different Information Extraction Backbone Networks. The ablation experiment as shown in Table 3 is to verify the effectiveness of SPD-Conv-SS2D in improving the model performance. In the table, ✓ indicates the use of all ML-AGRC, and ✗ indicates that feature fusion is achieved through simple skip connections between corresponding levels without using ML-AGRC. The ablation experiment compared the feature information extraction capabilities of four commonly used feature extractors and the SPD-Conv-SS2D module, as well as their influences on Pecision, Recall, and mAP_{50}.It can be seen from the light green area in the table that in the case of using ML-AGRC, the SPD-Conv-SS2D module has an improving effect on the evaluation indicators of the model. For example, Pecision has increased by at least 7.6% (57.1%–49.5%). In addition, it can be found in the light blue area of the table that the SPD-Conv-SS2D module also has an improving effect on the evaluation indicators of the model without using ML-AGRC. For example, Pecision has increased by at least 1.8% (32.3%–30.5%).The above experimental results can illustrate that the SPD-Conv-SS2D module is useful for improving the performance of the model.

Table 3. The results of the comparison of different BackBones.

Model	BackBone	ML-AGRC	Precision(%)	Recall(%)	mAP_{50}
AGRC-ViMamba	ResNet-50	✗	18.3	10.8	10.1
AGRC-ViMamba	ResNet-50	✓	32.5	39.3	31.9
AGRC-ViMamba	ResNet-101	✗	20.3	17.9	19.3
AGRC-ViMamba	ResNet-101	✓	35.3	38.1	33.3
AGRC-ViMamba	VGG-16	✗	21.5	20.6	26.1
AGRC-ViMamba	VGG-16	✓	49.5	33.9	39.5
AGRC-ViMamba	EfficientNet	✗	30.5	30.0	28.1
AGRC-ViMamba	EfficientNet	✓	40.1	39.3	35.8
AGRC-ViMamba	SPD-Conv-SS2D	✗	36.3	31.8	29.1
AGRC-ViMamba	SPD-Conv-SS2D	✓	**57.1**	**48.6**	**45.5**

5 Conclusion

In this study, to alleviate the LIA problem in small target recognition, we propose the AGRC-ViMamba model based on SPD-Conv-SS2D and ML-AGRC. This model innovatively abandons the traditional neck structure in favor of feature fusion through an attention-gated reversible branch auxiliary mechanism. Experiments on small target datasets VisDrone and AI-TOD demonstrate that AGRC-ViMamba achieves high target recognition accuracy while maintaining a modest parameter count. Furthermore, ablation studies validate the effectiveness of the SPD-Conv-SS2D module and confirm that the ML-AGRC structure significantly enhances small target recognition capability. This work not only provides a novel network architecture for efficient small target recognition but may also offer valuable insights for other dense prediction tasks.

Acknowledgments. This study is supported by Inner Mongolia Natural Science Foundation (2024MS06009), National Natural Science Foundation of China (62206138), Research program of science and technology at Universities of Inner Mongolia Autonomous Region (NJZZ23081), Science Research Foundation of Inner Mongolia University of Technology (BS2021079).

Disclosure of Interests. The authors declare no conflicts of interest.

References

1. Zhu, L., Liao, B., Zhang, Q., Wang, X., Liu, W., Wang, X.: Vision mamba: efficient visual representation learning with bidirectional state space model. In: Proceedings of the 41st International Conference on Machine Learning, pp. 62429–62442, PMLR, Kigali (2024)
2. Liu, S., Qi, L., Qin, H., Shi, J., Jia, J.: Path aggregation network for instance segmentation. In: Proceedings of the IEEE/CVF Conference on Computer Vision and Pattern Recognition (CVPR 2018), pp. 8759–8768, IEEE Computer Society, Salt Lake City (2018)
3. Cai, Y., et al.: Reversible column networks. In: International Conference on Learning Representations (ICLR 2023), pp. 1–12, OpenReview, Kigali (2023)
4. Sunkara, R., Luo, T.: No more strided convolutions or pooling: a new CNN building block for low - resolution images and small objects. In: Proceedings of the European Conference on Machine Learning and Knowledge Discovery in Databases (ECML PKDD 2022), Springer, France (2022)
5. Zhu, P., et al.: Detection and tracking meet drones challenge. IEEE Trans. Patt. Anal. Mach. Intell. **44**(11), 7380–7399 (2021)
6. Xu, C., Wang, J., Yang, W., Yu, H., Yu, L., Xia, G.: AI TOD: the tiny object detection in aerial images dataset. IEEE Trans. Geosci. Remote Sens. **60**, 1–14(2022)
7. Wang, C., Yeh, I., Liao, H.: YOLOv9: learning what you want to learn using programmable gradient information, arXiv preprint arXiv:2402.13616 (2024)
8. Wang, A., et al.: YOLOv10: real-time end-to-end object detection. arXiv preprint arXiv:2405.14458 (2024)
9. Jocher, G., Qiu, J.: Ultralytics YOLO11. https://github.com/ultralytics/ultralytics. Accessed 17 June 2025

10. Zhang, Z.: Drone-yolo: an efficient neural network method for target detection in drone images. Drones **7**(8), 526–537 (2023)
11. Wang, Z., Li, C., Xu, H., Zhu, X., Li, H.: Mamba YOLO: a simple baseline for object detection with state space model. In: Proceedings of the AAAI Conference on Artificial Intelligence(AAAI 2024), pp. 450–465. AAAI Press, Vancouver (2024)
12. Ren, K., Wu, X., Xu, L., Wang, L.: RemoteDet-mamba:a hybrid mamba-CNN network for multi-modal object detection in remote sensing images. arXiv preprint arXiv:2410.13532 (2024)
13. Verma, T., Singh, J., Bhartari, Y., Jarwal, R., Singh, S., Singh, S.: SOAR: advancements in small body object detection for aerial imagery using state space models and programmable gradients, arXiv preprint arXiv:2405.01699 (2024)

Small Object Detection Algorithm with Selective Fusion of Small Scale Features

Ming Xin, Bo Wang, Xin Wang, Kaiting Gong, Yang Zhang, and Ge Zhang(✉)

School of Computer and Information Engineering, Henan University, Kaifeng 475001, China
1534736261@qq.com

Abstract. Current object detection technologies have become relatively mature, yet significant challenges remain in the detection of small objects, such as frequent false positives and missed detections. To address the issues associated with small objects, including small scale, high noise levels, and variable shapes, several improvements have been proposed. Firstly, since small objects are prone to be missed due to their size, an additional shallow feature map was introduced to facilitate subsequent feature fusion, enhancing the ability to capture small objects. Secondly, a novel feature aggregation module, Deformable Selective Aggregation (DSA), was designed to reduce noise and focus the model more effectively on the fine features of small objects. Lastly, Focaler-IoU combined with MPDIoU was utilized as the loss function, improving the accuracy of small object bounding box localization. Experimental results demonstrate that the improved model significantly enhances performance metrics such as mAP 50 and mAP 50–95 on the VisDrone2019-DET, CARPK, and WiderPerson datasets, reflecting excellent generalization and robustness.

Keywords: Small Object Detection · Shallow Feature Map · Selective Fusion · IoU

1 Introduction

Small object detection is a critical task across multiple domains, with wide-ranging applications in disaster prevention, infrastructure inspection and maintenance, search and rescue, and crop management. With the widespread deployment of unmanned aerial vehicles (UAVs) in these fields, the demand for accurate and efficient small object detection has significantly increased. Effectively detecting small objects from the complex and vast aerial images captured by UAVs presents not only theoretical challenges but also holds substantial practical value [1, 2].

UAVs offer a unique perspective for capturing large-scale scenes but also introduce challenges such as varying altitudes, complex backgrounds, and rapid motion, which further complicate small object detection. Traditional object detection models are primarily designed for larger, ground-based targets and often struggle to maintain high accuracy when applied to UAV imagery, as small objects are represented by limited pixels and are more susceptible to noise [3, 4]. In recent years, advances in deep learning and neural

P. Li et al. (Eds.): CGI 2025, LNCS 16508, pp. 29–40, 2026.
https://doi.org/10.1007/978-3-032-22264-0_3

network architectures have offered promising solutions to these challenges. However, small object detection in UAV imagery remains a major challenge. As illustrated in Fig. 1, UAV-based object detection faces a range of challenges across different scenarios and complex conditions. For instance, UAV images often contain complex natural backgrounds, such as buildings, trees, and other structures, which may share visual characteristics with the targets, leading to noise and false detections. Additionally, the scale of objects in UAV imagery can vary significantly due to changes in distance, altitude, and environmental factors, resulting in both large and small objects appearing within the same frame. Furthermore, small objects often have irregular shapes and are prone to occlusion, complicating the detection task.

Fig. 1. Some representative images from the VisDrone2019-DET [5] and WiderPerson [6] dataset. Such as (a)small objects, (b)object occlusion and denseness, (c)dim lighting, and so on.

In summary, this paper aims to address the challenges of small object detection in UAV-captured imagery by proposing a novel method specifically designed for this task. Given the common issues of missed and false detections when detecting small objects from a UAV perspective, we present the following improvements:

- An additional Small Detection Head (SDH) was introduced, along with the design of a Deformable Selective Aggregation (DSA) module, which reduces noise and enhances the model's sensitivity to small objects, enabling more precise capture of fine details.
- The Focaler-IoU combined with MPD-IoU, termed F-MPDIoU, is employed for calculating the regression loss of bounding boxes, thereby enhancing the accuracy of small target bounding box localization.

2 Related Work

Multi-scale feature fusion has been extensively explored to improve small object detection. SAFA [7] adaptively selects processing scales per sample, while MFDS-DETR [8] fuses hierarchical features via deformable self-attention to extract fine-grained details. Contextual enhancement modules [9] and radar-vision fusion strategies [10] have also been proposed to boost performance in complex environments. However, most methods treat input features uniformly, leading to accumulated noise and high false positives, especially for similar objects. To address this, we introduce a DSA module that selectively aggregates informative features, suppresses redundancy, and enhances small object representation.

Bounding box regression losses have evolved from IoU to GIoU, DIoU, and CIoU, progressively improving convergence and localization by modeling spatial and geometric constraints [11]. For small object scenarios, Focaler-IoU [12] reweights samples based on regression difficulty, while MPDIoU [13] leverages minimum point distance to handle aspect-ratio-aligned but size-discrepant boxes. We adopt F-MPDIoU, a hybrid of Focaler-IoU and MPDIoU, to balance multi-scale adaptability with improved localization accuracy, particularly for small targets.

3 Method

In conclusion, using the RT-DETR [14] model as a baseline, we propose a new small object detection model as shown in Fig. 2. The network architecture is redesigned by introducing the fourth-stage backbone features into the fusion process, generating a high-resolution 160 × 160 shallow feature map that enhances small object detection accuracy. A DSA module is further developed to facilitate feature fusion across scales. Finally, F-MPDIoU is adopted as the loss function to preserve multi-scale detection capability while improving bounding box localization precision for small objects.

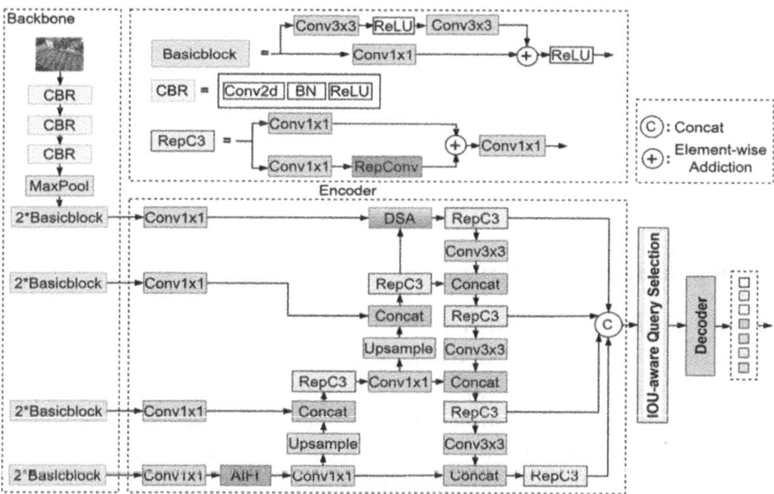

Fig. 2. The overall structure of our model.

3.1 Small Detection Head

Detecting smaller objects requires preserving high-resolution feature maps, as small objects tend to have weaker and less distinct features. High-resolution feature maps preserve crucial details often lost during downsampling, improving the network's capacity to identify small objects. Currently, most popular detection models, such as YOLOv8, YOLOv5, and RT-DETR, are not specifically optimized for detecting small objects. In UAV-captured images, many targets are smaller than the minimum detection size of the original detection heads and are often located in occluded or edge areas. Therefore, it is essential to optimize the detection heads to improve the network's ability to detect these small and distant objects effectively. As shown in Fig. 3, we add a 160 × 160 shallow feature map at an earlier stage of the network to preserve higher-resolution spatial information. This layer is designed to retain fine-grained details typically lost during deep downsampling, enabling the model to better capture subtle features of small objects.

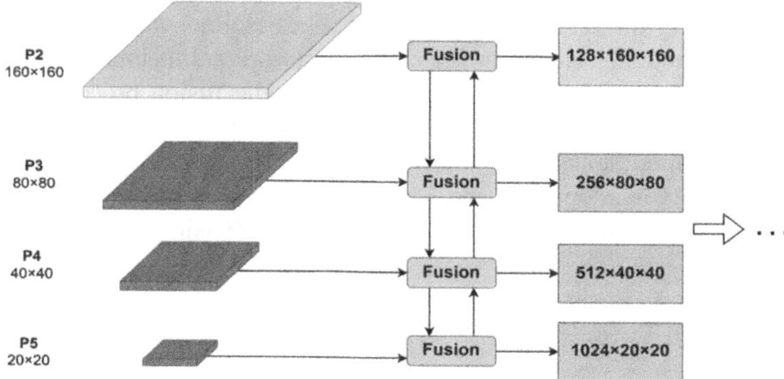

Fig. 3. Overview of Enhanced Small Object Detection Head (Simplified Feature Fusion and Subsequent Processing).

3.2 Deformable Selective Aggregation

While shallow features contain less semantic information, they are rich in detail, with clear boundaries and minimal distortion; deep features, on the other hand, carry more extensive semantic information [15]. Literature suggests that directly fusing shallow and deep features may lead to information redundancy and inconsistency [16], which inspired our approach to feature fusion. Additionally, due to the characteristics of small objects, shallow feature maps often contain substantial noise, which can significantly hinder the extraction of detailed features. Therefore, a carefully designed fusion mechanism is required. To facilitate the fusion between shallow and deep feature maps while reducing noise, we developed the Selective Aggregation (SA) module. Furthermore, to address issues related to the irregular shapes and occlusion of small objects, we incorporated deformable convolution operations to better capture their spatial features. In summary, we propose the DSA module, as illustrated in Fig. 4.

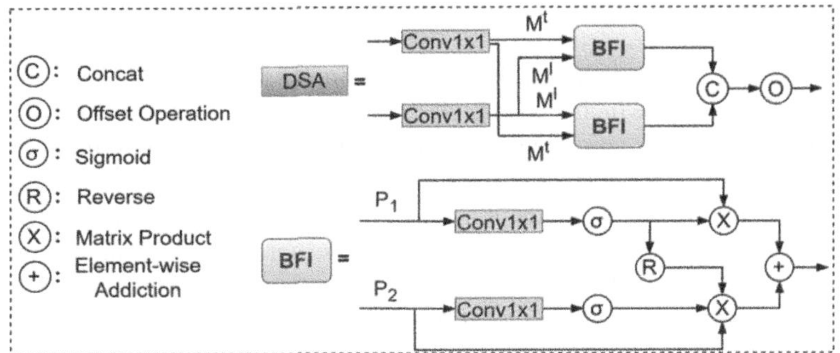

Fig. 4. The overall structure of DSA.

To effectively combine spatial boundary details from low-level features with high-level semantic information, we designed a Bidirectional Feature Interaction (BFI) module. Before feature fusion, this module selectively extracts information from both feature maps and applies weighted updates. The function of the BFI module, denoted as *BFI*(,), is as follows:

$$P_1' = T_\partial(P_1),\ \ P_2' = T_\partial(P_2) \tag{1}$$

$$BFI(P_1, P_2) = P_1' * P_1 + R(P_1') * P_2' * P_2 \tag{2}$$

where P_1 and P_2 are the input feature maps, and the function T_∂ () is a combination of a linear mapping layer with a 1×1 convolution kernel and a Sigmoid activation function. After undergoing dimensionality reduction and activation, the resulting feature maps are P_1' and P_2'. The operator $*$ denotes matrix multiplication, while the function *R*() is primarily used for the reverse operation, defined as (1- P_1').

The SA module is illustrated as follows:

$$Out = Conv\Big(Concat\Big(BFI\big(M^t, M^l\big), BFI\big(M^l, M^t\big)\Big)\Big) \tag{3}$$

The DSA module builds upon the SA module by incorporating deformable convolution operations. The overall process is described as follows:

$$offset = Conv3 \times 3\Big(Concat\Big(BFI\big(M^t, M^l\big), BFI\big(M^l, M^t\big)\Big)\Big) \tag{4}$$

$$Out = Dcn3 \times 3\Big(Concat\Big(BFI\big(M^t, M^l\big), BFI\big(M^l, M^t\big)\Big), offset\Big) \tag{5}$$

where the offset refers to the calculation of the displacement, while Conv3 × 3 denotes a 3 × 3 convolution operation with batch normalization and ReLU activation. Concat(,) represents the concatenation operation along the channel dimension. M^t, M^l correspond to the input high-level and low-level feature maps, where $M^t \in \mathbb{R}^{H \times W \times C}$, $M^l \in \mathbb{R}^{\frac{H}{2} \times \frac{W}{2} \times C}$. To enable element-wise operations between them, we upsample the lower-resolution feature map to match the spatial size of the higher-resolution one using bilinear interpolation. Dcn3 × 3 indicates the deformable convolution operation. Finally, Out represents the output of the DSA module.

3.3 F-MPDIoU

In small object detection datasets, the issue of sample imbalance is particularly pronounced. Small objects, which are difficult to precisely locate, are typically considered hard samples, while larger objects are treated as relatively easy samples. In such datasets, if the bounding box regression continues to focus on larger objects (easy samples), it may fail to effectively improve detection performance. Conversely, Focaler-IoU can prioritize the bounding box regression of small objects (hard samples), improving overall detection accuracy, particularly for small targets. In these datasets, existing bounding box regression loss functions often face difficulties in optimization when predicted boxes and ground truths have the same aspect ratio yet exhibit substantial differences in scale, such as width and height. To address this issue, MPD-IoU exploits the spatial properties of horizontal rectangles and introduces a new similarity metric for bounding boxes based on the minimum point distance. This metric incorporates all key factors considered by existing loss functions, including overlapping or non-overlapping areas, center point distance, and differences in width and height, while simplifying the computation process, leading to better optimization for small object detection. Therefore, we combined the advantages of these two IoU approaches and proposed Focaler-MPD-IoU for our loss function computation.

To enable the model to focus on different regression samples across various detection tasks, Focaler-IoU utilizes a linear interval mapping approach to reformulate the IoU loss, improving the efficiency of bounding box regression. The formula is presented below:

$$IoU^{Focaler} = \begin{cases} 0, & IoU < d \\ \frac{IoU-d}{u-d}, & d \leq IoU \leq u \\ 1, & IoU > u \end{cases} \tag{6}$$

where $IoU^{Focaler}$ represents the restructured IoU value, while IoU denotes the original IoU value. The parameters d and u are adjustable values. By adjusting the parameters d and u, IoU Focaler can focus on samples with different levels of difficulty according to requirements.

The MPDIoU loss function aims to maximize the DIoU value between two bounding boxes, guiding the model to better learn their positions and shapes. In small object detection tasks, MPDIoU outperforms traditional G/IoU loss functions when handling complex scenarios, effectively enhancing detection performance, particularly in accurately localizing small objects. The formula is as follows:

$$d_1^2 = \left(x_1^g - x_1^p\right)^2 + \left(y_1^g - y_1^p\right)^2 \tag{7}$$

$$d_2^2 = \left(x_2^g - x_2^p\right)^2 + \left(y_2^g - y_2^p\right)^2 \tag{8}$$

$$MPDIoU = IoU - \frac{d_1^2}{w^2 + h^2} - \frac{d_1^2}{w^2 + h^2} \tag{9}$$

where $\left(x_1^g, y_1^g\right)$ and $\left(x_2^g, y_2^g\right)$ represent the coordinates of the top-left and bottom-right corners of the ground truth bounding box, respectively, while $\left(x_1^p, y_1^p\right)$ and $\left(x_2^p, y_2^p\right)$ represent the coordinates of the top-left and bottom-right corners of the predicted bounding box. IoU stands for the original Intersection over Union metric. The variables w and h correspond to the width and height of the image, while d_1 and d_2 indicate the distances between the top-left and bottom-right corners of the ground truth and predicted bounding boxes, respectively.

In summary, we combine Focaler-IoU and MPDIoU to formulate F-MPDIoU, which is employed as our loss function. The equation $L_{F-MPDIoU}$ is expressed as follows:

$$L_{F-MPDIoU} = 1 - IoU^{Focaler} + \frac{d_1^2}{w^2 + h^2} + \frac{d_1^2}{w^2 + h^2} \quad (10)$$

4 Experimental Results and Analysis

The experiments were conducted on a platform running Ubuntu 20.04, equipped with an Intel(R) Xeon(R) CPU E5–2680 v4 @ 2.40GHz (7 cores), an RTX 3090 GPU, and 30.0 GB of RAM. The framework was based on PyTorch 2.0.1, with computations accelerated using CUDA 11.8. The learning rate was set to 0.0001, and the AdamW optimizer was employed. Training and validation were performed under the same hyperparameters. The batch size was 8, and the input image size was 640 × 640 × 3. The datasets used in this experiment included VisDrone2019 object detection dataset, WiderPerson dataset, and CARPK [17] dataset.

4.1 Ablation Experiment

To validate the effectiveness of the proposed improvements, including SDH, DSA, and F-MPDIoU, we conducted ablation experiments. As shown in Table 1, these experiments were performed on the training set of the VisDrone2019-Det dataset, and the performance of the proposed model was evaluated on the validation set, specifically focusing on small object detection tasks.

Table 1. Ablation experiments on Visdrone2019-Det-val.

	Parameters(M)	P	R	mAP50	mAP50–95	FPS
Baseline	19.88	0.617	0.454	47.4	29.0	44.1
+SDH	18.60	0.609	0.472	48.8	30.6	43.9
+SDH + SA	18.58	0.614	0.474	49.2	30.9	46.8
+SDH + DSA	18.59	0.619	0.477	49.7	31.3	46.8
+SDH + DSA + F-MPDIoU	18.59	**0.621**	**0.480**	**49.9**	31.1	46.5

Analysis of the results indicates that the inclusion of the SDH led to improvements in Recall (R), mAP 50, and mAP 50–95 by 4.0%, 3.0%, and 5.5%, respectively. Comparing the Selective Aggregation (SA) and DSA modules, the results confirm the effectiveness of integrating the Bidirectional Feature Interaction (BFI) module and deformable convolution. With the addition of the DSA module, R, mAP 50, and mAP 50–95 improved by 5.1%, 4.9%, and 7.9%, respectively. Finally, using F-MPDIoU as the loss function further enhanced detection performance. The final model showed improvements in Precision (P), R, mAP 50, and mAP 50–95 by 0.6%, 5.7%, 5.3%, and 7.2% over the baseline, effectively validating the utility of each proposed modification. Notably, despite these enhancements, the inference speed increased from 44.1 FPS to 46.5 FPS, demonstrating that the proposed improvements do not incur additional time costs but instead contribute to both accuracy and efficiency.

4.2 Comparison Experiment

To visually demonstrate the performance of our model, we plotted a comparison between model parameters and mAP 50 performance, as shown in Fig. 5. We selected several state-of-the-art object detection models such as YOLOv5l, YOLOv6m, YOLOv8m, DTA-FSAF, and other improved versions of YOLO series models, including CNXResNet [18], which is based on PP-YOLOE. By comparing these models, we observed that our improved model achieves outstanding performance in both parameter efficiency and mAP 50 score.

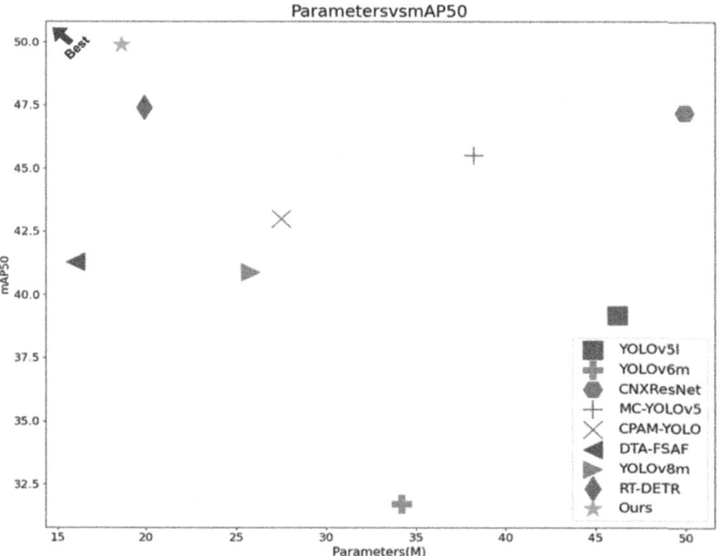

Fig. 5. Comparison of Model Parameters and mAP 50 Performance on Visdrone2019-Det-val.

To further validate the advantages of our algorithm, we compared it with other excellent models released in recent years. The models include TOOD [19], YOLOv7 [20], QueryDet [21], Final half F-T [22], CPAM-YOLO [23], DY-YOLOv5 [24], UAV-YOLOv8 [25], SF-SSD [26], Modified YOLOv5 [27], Nguyen et al. [28], FedsNet [29], UniDet [30], BSMH [31].

Table 2. Comparison with detection models in recent years on the VisDrone2019-Det.

Method	Pedestrian	People	Bicycle	Car	Van	Truck	Tricycle	Awning-tricycle	Bus	Motor	mAP50
TOOD	21.9	11.9	7.4	55.3	31.4	25.4	14.5	8.6	37.2	19.8	38.2
YOLOv7	56.9	37.6	17.3	79.9	41.9	41.6	23.2	9.9	61.9	45.8	41.6
QueryDet	56.8	37.4	17.6	80.3	41.9	41.8	24.2	10.1	62.1	44.8	41.7
Final half F-T	49.9	40.1	19.4	78.6	44.0	40.1	30.2	15.5	54.8	48.3	42.1
CPAM-YOLO	57.1	38.9	18.8	82.2	42.5	43.5	26.3	11.3	62.8	46.6	43.0
DY-YOLOv5	51.3	40.2	21.0	82.3	45.9	39.4	32.8	17.1	59.7	49.6	43.9
UAV-YOLOv8	56.8	44.9	18.8	85.8	50.8	39.0	33.3	19.7	64.3	56.2	47.0
Ours	**59.1**	**50.9**	**23.7**	**87.0**	**53.1**	40.7	**36.3**	**19.9**	**67.6**	**61.1**	**49.9**

Table 3. Comparison of detection results on the CARPK dataset.

Method	P	R	mAP50	mAP50–95
SF-SSD	/	/	90.1	/
YOLOv5m	/	/	94.6	57.8
Modified YOLOv5	/	/	57.7	/
Nguyen et al	/	/	95.8	63.1
RT-DETR	0.982	0.984	99.3	84.6
Ours	**0.987**	**0.988**	**99.4**	84.5

Table 4. Comparison of detection results on the WiderPerson dataset.

Method	P	R	mAP50	mAP50–95
FedsNet	/	/	71.3	/
UniDet	0.783	0.596	73.4	39.9
BSMH	0.804	0.602	74.2	44.5
YOLOv7	/	/	76.7	45.6
RT-DETR	0.816	0.662	77.3	48.1
Ours	0.815	**0.673**	**77.7**	**48.5**

As shown in Table 2, Our method outperforms mainstream detectors like TOOD, QueryDet, and most improved YOLO variants, achieving top precision in categories such as People and Car on the VisDrone2019-Det.

To further validate the robustness and generalization ability of our model, we conducted experiments on the CARPK and WiderPerson datasets. As shown in Tables 3 and 4, our method consistently outperformed state-of-the-art models, including YOLO variants, SSD-based models. On CARPK, our model achieved the highest precision, recall, and mAP 50 scores, while on WiderPerson, our model achieved the highest, recall, mAP 50, and mAP 50–95 scores, confirming its strong generalization across diverse detection tasks.

5 Conclusion

To address the challenges associated with small-scale targets in drone aerial imagery, such as small size, occlusion, and low lighting, which often lead to missed and false detections, we proposed three methods to mitigate these issues. First, we introduced a small object detection head to enhance the model's sensitivity to smaller targets. Next, we designed the DSA module, applying it to feature fusion operations at scales of 160×160 and 80×80. This effectively reduced noise, enabling the model to focus more on capturing information pertinent to the targets themselves. Finally, we developed F-MPDIoU as a loss function by combining Focaler-IoU and MPDIoU, improving the precision of small object bounding box localization. Experiments across multiple datasets demonstrated that our improved model can effectively detect small objects in drone-captured imagery, outperforming many current state-of-the-art detection models on various metrics.

In the future, we plan to explore further reductions in computational and parameter complexity to make the model more lightweight and suitable for deployment in more demanding aerial imagery applications.

Acknowledgments. This work was supported by Henan Provincial Science and Technology Research Project [grant number 242102210014].

Disclosure of Interests. The authors have no competing interests to declare that are relevant to the content of this article.

References

1. Li, Z., Wang, Z., He, Y.: Aerial photography dense small target detection algorithm based on adaptive collaborative attention mechanism. J. Aeronaut. **10**, 1–12 (2023)
2. Li, R., Hu, Y., Li, L., et al.: SMWE-GFPNNet: A high-precision and robust method for forest fire smoke detection. Knowl.-Based Syst. **289**, 111528 (2024)
3. Lv, Y., Tian, B., Guo, Q., Zhang, D.: A lightweight small target detection algorithm for UAV platforms. Appl. Sci. **15**(1), 12 (2025)
4. Luo, X.D.: Research progress on deep learning methods for object detection and semantic segmentation in UAV aerial images. Acta Aeronaut. Astronaut. Sin. **1–31** (2023)
5. Zhu, P., Wen, L., Du, D., et al.: Detection and tracking meet drones challenge. IEEE Trans. Pattern Anal. Mach. Intell. **44**(11), 7380–7399 (2021)
6. Zhang, S., Xie, Y., Wan, J., et al.: WiderPerson: a diverse dataset for dense pedestrian detection in the wild. IEEE Trans. Multimedia **22**(2), 380–393 (2019)
7. Huang, Z., Huang, A., Hu, X., et al.: Scale-adaptive feature aggregation for efficient space-time video super-resolution. In: Proceedings of the IEEE/CVF Winter Conference on Applications of Computer Vision, pp. 4228–4239 (2024)

8. Chen, Y., Zhang, C., Chen, B., et al.: Accurate leukocyte detection based on deformable-DETR and multi-level feature fusion for aiding diagnosis of blood diseases. Comput. Biol. Med. **170**, 107917 (2024)
9. Qin, Z.Y., Chen, D.K., Wang, H.Y.: MCA-YOLOv7: An improved UAV target detection algorithm based on YOLOv7. IEEE Access **12**, 42642–426505 (2024)
10. Li, X.H., Huo, K.X., Yan, X.F., et al.: Thunder-vision fusion vehicle detection method based on feature-weighted visual enhancement. Highway Traffic Technol. **40**(2), 182–189 (2023)
11. Zheng, Z., Wang, P., Liu, W., et al.: Distance-IoU loss: faster and better learning for bounding box regression. In: Proceedings of the AAAI Conference on Artificial Intelligence 34(7), 12993–13000 (2020)
12. Zhang, H., Zhang, S.: Focaler-IoU: More focused intersection over union loss. arXiv preprint (2024). https://arxiv.org/abs/2401.10525
13. Ma, S., Xu, Y.: Mpdiou: A loss for efficient and accurate bounding box regression. arXiv preprint (2023). https://arxiv.org/abs/2307.07662
14. Zhao, Y., Lv, W., Xu, S., et al.: DETRs beat YOLOs on real-time object detection. In: Proceedings of the IEEE/CVF Conference on Computer Vision and Pattern Recognition, pp. 16965–16974 (2024)
15. Li, X., Li, X., Zhang, L., et al.: Improving semantic segmentation via decoupled body and edge supervision. In: Computer Vision–ECCV 2020 LNCS, **12362**, pp. 435–452. Springer, Cham (2020)
16. Tang, F., Xu, Z., Huang, Q., et al.: DuAT: dual-aggregation transformer network for medical image segmentation. In: Chinese Conference on Pattern Recognition and Computer Vision (PRCV), pp. 343–356. Springer, Singapore (2023)
17. Hsieh, M.R., Lin, Y.L., Hsu, W.H.: Drone-based object counting by spatially regularized regional proposal network. In: Proceedings of the IEEE International Conference on Computer Vision, pp. 4145–4153 (2017)
18. Cai, Z., Hong, Z., Yu, W., et al.: CNXResNet: a lightweight backbone based on PP-YOLOE for drone-captured scenarios. In: 2023 8th International Conference on Signal and Image Processing (ICSIP), pp. 460–464. IEEE (2023)
19. Feng, C., Zhong, Y., Gao, Y., et al.: TOOD: task-aligned one-stage object detection. In: 2021 IEEE/CVF International Conference on Computer Vision (ICCV), pp. 3490–3499 (2021)
20. Wang, C.Y., Bochkovskiy, A., Liao, H.Y.M.: YOLOv7: trainable bag-of-freebies sets new state-of-the-art for real-time object detectors. In: Proceedings of the IEEE/CVF Conference on Computer Vision and Pattern Recognition, pp. 7464–7475 (2023)
21. Yang, C., Huang, Z., Wang, N.: QueryDet: cascaded sparse query for accelerating high-resolution small object detection. In: Proceedings of the IEEE/CVF Conference on Computer Vision and Pattern Recognition, pp. 13668–13677 (2022)
22. Pebrianto, W., Mudjirahardjo, P., Pramono, S.H.: Partial half fine-tuning for object detection with unmanned aerial vehicles. IAES Int. J. Artif. Intell. **13**(1), 399 (2024)
23. Wu, H., Zhu, Y., Cao, M.: An algorithm for detecting dense small objects in aerial photography based on coordinate position attention module. IET Image Process (2024)
24. Wei, Q., Hu, X., Hou, Q.: Dynamic-YOLOv5: An improved aerial small object detector based on YOLOv5. In: 2023 3rd International Conference on Neural Networks, Information and Communication Engineering (NNICE), pp. 679–683. IEEE (2023)
25. Wang, G., Chen, Y., An, P., et al.: UAV-YOLOv8: A small-object-detection model based on improved YOLOv8 for UAV aerial photography scenarios. Sensors. **23**, 7190 (2023)
26. Yu, J., Gao, H., Sun, J., et al.: Spatial cognition-driven deep learning for car detection in unmanned aerial vehicle imagery. IEEE Trans. Cogn. Dev. Syst. **14**(4), 1574–1583 (2021)
27. Hamzenejadi, M.H., Mohseni, H.: Real-time vehicle detection and classification in UAV imagery using improved YOLOv5. In: 2022 12th International Conference on Computer and Knowledge Engineering (ICCKE), pp. 231–236. IEEE (2022)

28. Nguyen, D.L., Vo, X.T., Priadana, A., et al.: Car detector based on YOLOv5 for parking management. In: Conference on Information Technology and its Applications, pp. 102–113. Springer, Cham (2023)
29. Peng, H., Chen, S.: FedsNet: the real-time network for pedestrian detection based on RT-DETR. J. Real-Time Image Proc. **21**(4), 1–12 (2024)
30. Zhou, X., Koltun, V., Krähenbühl, P.: Simple multi-dataset detection. In: Proceedings of the IEEE/CVF Conference on Computer Vision and Pattern Recognition, pp. 7571–7580 (2022)
31. Lu, F., Xu, Y.C., Qi, Y., et al.: BSMH: Cross-dataset object detection based on box-separated multiple-head. IET Image Process **18**(11), 3013–3027 (2024)

An Industrial Multi-machining Feature Dataset and Contrastive Learning-Based Network for Feature Recognition

Zheng Fang[1], Haochen He[1], Zhengda Lu[1], Haiyong Jiang[1], Yiqun Wang[2], and Jun Xiao[1](✉)

[1] School of Artificial Intelligence, University of Chinese Academy of Sciences, Beijing 100049, China
xiaojun@ucas.ac.cn
[2] College of Computer Science, Chongqing University, Chongqing 400044, China

Abstract. Machining feature recognition plays a crucial role in the effective integration of Computer-Aided Design (CAD), Computer-Aided Process Planning (CAPP), and Computer-Aided Manufacturing (CAM) systems. However, current machining feature datasets lack diversity and authenticity in both machining features and base models. Existing recognition methods are limited in capturing the geometric information of long-range complex intersecting features. In this paper, we first construct a novel Multi-Machining Feature model Dataset (MMFD) that includes various non-machining feature shapes as base models and complex machining features commonly encountered in real industrial manufacturing processes. We also propose CRNet, a contrastive learning-based machining feature recognition network with a Transformer encoder and Face Geometric Position Encoding (FGPE) to capture long-range contextual and spatial geometric relationship information between complex features. Our experimental results demonstrate the effectiveness and accuracy of our CRNet on MMFD compared to the state-of-the-art methods.

Keywords: Machining feature recognition · Multi-feature · Dataset · Instance segmentation · Contrastive learning

1 Introduction

Machining feature recognition aims to extract low-level geometric and topological features from CAD models and then identify the positions and types of high-level machining features. This provides essential data for Computer-Aided Process Planning (CAPP) to generate and optimize process routes and parameters. Therefore, machining feature recognition is a critical research problem in the field of intelligent automated manufacturing.

Existing machining feature datasets mainly consist of simple single-feature models [17,18,21] or synthetic multi-feature models created through Boolean

Z. Fang and H. He—These two authors contributed equally to this work.

P. Li et al. (Eds.): CGI 2025, LNCS 16508, pp. 41–53, 2026.
https://doi.org/10.1007/978-3-032-22264-0_4

operations [11–13]. However, they lack complex features commonly requiring milling tools in real machining processes, such as U-slots, T-slots, and dove tail slots. While some recent datasets [6,19] include some complex features like T-slots or fillets, they still rely on basic base models (e.g., cuboids, cylinders), lacking realistic non-machining geometries such as freeform surfaces. This results in limited diversity and authenticity, failing to reflect the complexity of real industrial machining scenarios.

Machining feature recognition methods can be broadly categorized into two main categories: rule-based [1,8,20] and learning-based [2,4,16,17,19] methods. Rule-based methods depend on expert-defined rules, but struggle with complex, intersecting features and high computational costs. In contrast, learning-based methods leverage annotated CAD datasets and deep learning to automatically learn mappings from low-level geometric features to high-level machining features, achieving better performance. However, learning-based methods still face major challenges in recognizing complex machining features. Voxel-based [9,21] and multi-view-based approaches [11–13] disrupt original geometry and topology, limiting scalability [19]. Graph-based methods [2,4,16] preserve topology but often lack instance segmentation or global geometric awareness. Point cloud-based methods [17,19] retain detailed geometry but suffer from uneven sampling and limited ability to capture long-range context. Additionally, indirect supervision strategies [16,19] reduce feature discriminability, hindering recognition of complex intersecting features.

In this work, we introduce MMFD, a novel point cloud dataset containing diverse base models and complex machining features found in real industrial scenarios. We also propose CRNet, a contrastive learning-based recognition network that captures long-range geometric context with a Transformer encoder [22] and enhances feature discrimination through a face geometric position encoding (FGPE) module. Moreover, we propose a contrastive learning loss to directly supervise the face embedding features, thereby improving the recognition and localization of intersecting complex machining features. Finally, experiments demonstrate that our method achieves the state-of-the-art performance in machining feature recognition.

2 Related Work

Machining Feature Dataset. FeatureNet [21] is a classic single-feature dataset. This dataset primarily consists of 24 types of relatively simple machining features, such as through hole and through slot. Several studies [15,17] used this dataset or constructed datasets with the same feature categories for training. Yeo et al. [18] and MFDataset [7] constructed single-feature datasets containing 16 and 32 types of machining features, respectively. However, these datasets are still single-feature and have a limited variety of complex machining feature types. Some researchers constructed multi-feature datasets by combining single-feature models from FeatureNet [21] using Boolean operations [11,13] or by using its feature categories [2,4,16]. However, these synthetic models differ from real industrial models in feature placement and construction. Datasets like ASIN [19] and Lee et al. [6] also include multiple features but are built on basic shapes such as cuboids or cylinders, limiting their ability to represent realistic non-machining geometries like freeform or curved surfaces.

Machining Feature Recognition. Rule-based approaches rely on expert-designed rules for machining feature recognition [1,8,20], but creating reliable rules is complex and time-consuming. Feature intersections and topology disruptions further increase the difficulty of rule design. Unlike explicit rule design, learning-based methods learn recognition patterns from datasets, enabling better identification of complex machining features. Multi-view-based [11–13] and voxel-based [9,21] methods suffer from loss of geometric detail and high computational cost, respectively. Graph-based methods [2,4,16] preserve topology using adjacency graphs, while point cloud-based methods [17,19] offer richer 3D geometry. However, fixed-point sampling [19] can lead to uneven data in complex features, and commonly used backbones [10] struggle to capture long-range dependencies.

3 Overview

Machining features refer to a set of specific shapes and areas to be machined that have machining semantics on a CAD model. The machining feature recognition task aims to accurately identify the semantic feature category of each face in CAD models with complex machining features and to cluster and segment the faces belonging to the same machining feature instance. Figure 1 illustrates the overall framework, which consists of the MMFD construction and the CRNet.

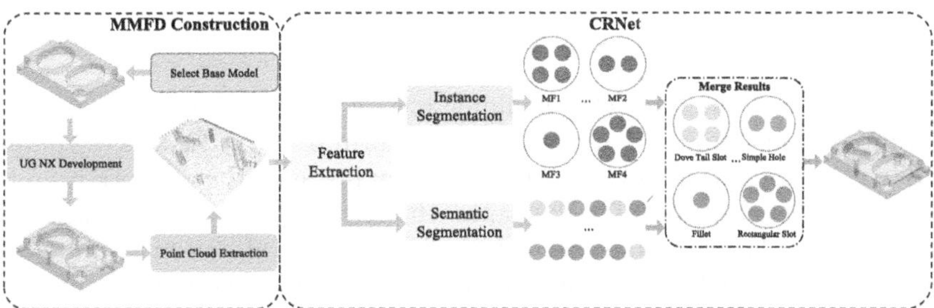

Fig. 1. The framework of the proposed method. "MF" denotes unclassified machining feature instances. Solid circles represent the faces of the CAD model, and solid circles of the same color indicate faces belonging to the same machining feature category.

Table 1. Complex machining features and non-machining feature shapes commonly found in real industrial production scenarios included in the MMFD.

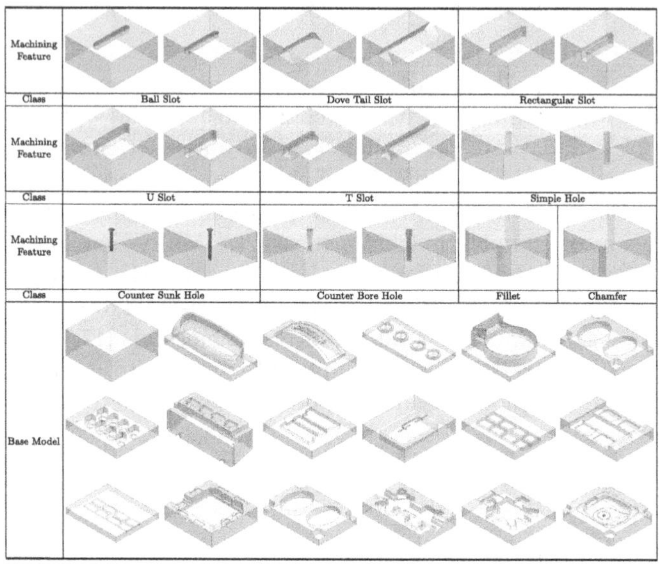

4 Dataset Construction

Data Collection. To collect the machining features and models relevant to real industrial manufacturing, we conducted comprehensive on-site investigations at some industrial factories in China, examining parts produced in actual production lines. In collaboration with experienced CAD model engineers, we identified ten common machining feature types in real manufacturing, along with their typical size and quantity ranges.

Existing datasets often rely on simple base models like cuboids or cylinders, excluding non-machining shapes such as freeform or curved surfaces commonly found in real production models. This exclusion prevents the network from learning the geometric features of such shapes, thus affecting its generalization to real machining models. To address this, we collect 17 typical non-machining feature shapes as base models, enhancing the complexity and diversity of our dataset, as illustrated in Table 1.

3D CAD Models Generation. We propose an efficient data generation algorithm using UG NX to create CAD models with multiple complex machining features, simulating realistic milling tool movements to reflect actual production processes. Specifically, we generate model samples by first selecting cuboids or common industrial models as base models, as shown in Fig. 2(a). Next, a random surface point (yellow cross) and machining direction (red lines) are chosen to simulate diverse real-world feature positions and angles. Machining feature sizes are randomly sampled within predefined ranges, and appropriate milling tools are used to add features. Fillets and chamfers are generated along random convex edges, as shown in Fig. 2(b). This process is repeated until the feature count meets the range threshold. The resulting models closely resemble actual industrial parts, as verified by experienced CAD engineers, as shown in Fig. 2(c).

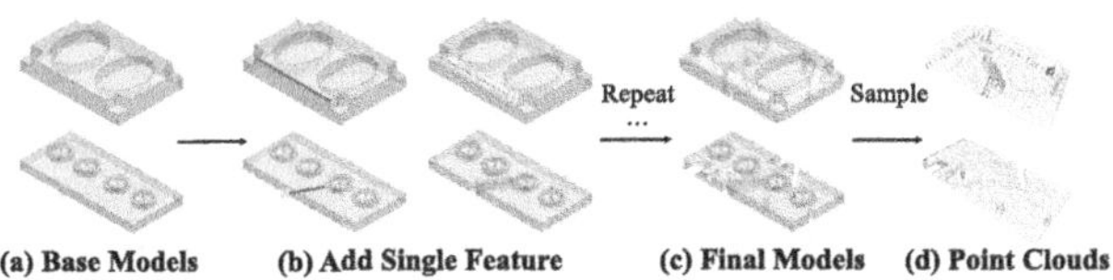

Fig. 2. The process of generating our dataset with multiple machining features.

Point Cloud Extraction. The generated CAD models cannot be directly used for neural network training, so we convert them into point clouds, which effectively preserve geometric details like positions, curvatures, and normals. Unlike ASIN [19], which samples a fixed number of points per face, our strategy ensures an even point distribution by allocating points proportionally to face areas, with a minimum of 20 points per face. This preserves geometric details across varying face sizes and yields a multi-feature point cloud dataset with machining feature category and instance labels, as shown in Fig. 2(d).

5 CRNet Architecture

The architecture of our CRNet is shown in Fig. 3, including a feature extraction module, an instance clustering segmentation module that incorporates face geometric position encoding, and a semantic segmentation module.

5.1 Feature Extraction

The feature extraction module is the initial component of the network and aims to extract representative and discriminative features from the input point cloud data for subsequent segmentation tasks. We use Point Transformer [22] as the feature extractor to capture long-range dependencies and geometric context, outperforming prior backbone networks [10] only focus on local features. It outputs point-wise features $\mathbf{P}' \in \mathbb{R}^{N\times 48}$, which are then aggregated via a face average pooling layer to produce face-level features $\mathbf{F} \in \mathbb{R}^{f\times 48}$, enhancing representation ability and reducing instance clustering cost.

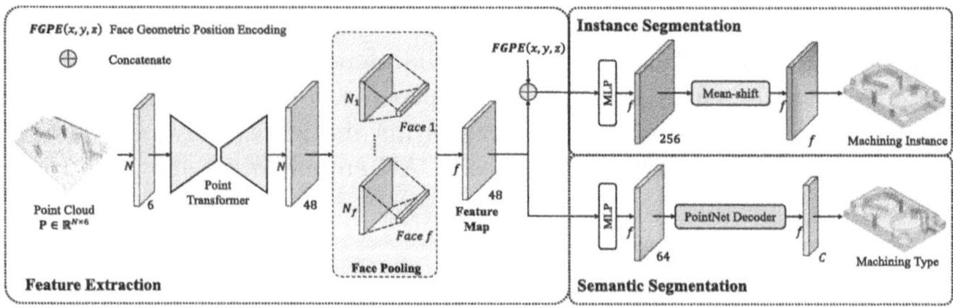

Fig. 3. The architecture of the CRNet. N represents the number of points in the point cloud data, f represents the number of faces in the CAD model, N_i represents the number of points on the ith face, $FGPE$ is the 3D coordinates of the face, and C represents the number of semantic categories for machining features.

5.2 Segmentation Based on Contrastive Learning

Face Geometric Position Encoding. In the instance segmentation module, we introduce a novel face geometric position encoding $FGPE \in \mathbb{R}^{f\times 3}$, which embeds additional geometric position information into our network. Specifically, we calculate the average coordinates of all sampled points on each face, and the coordinates of the closest point within the current face are used as the position encoding representation. And FGPE enhances the discriminability of the face features $\mathbf{F}$, which is crucial for distinguishing complex and intersecting machining features. We demonstrated the effectiveness of FGPE in ablation experiments.

Instance Contrastive Learning. After that, we employ a contrastive learning loss to directly supervise these face features enriched by FGPE, promoting feature space separation between different instances. Therefore, following the work of [5], we define the instance segmentation contrastive loss $\mathcal{L}_I$ as the sum of the intra-cluster variance term $\mathcal{L}_{var}$ and inter-cluster distance term $\mathcal{L}_{dist}$.

$$\mathcal{L}_{var} = \frac{1}{M}\sum_{m=1}^{M}\frac{1}{N_m}\sum_{i=1}^{N_m}[\|\mu_m - x_i\| - \delta_v]_+ \tag{1}$$

$$\mathcal{L}_{dist} = \frac{1}{M(M-1)}\sum_{m_A<m_B}[2\delta_d - \|\mu_{m_A} - \mu_{m_B}\|]_+ \tag{2}$$

$$\mathcal{L}_I = \mathcal{L}_{var} + \mathcal{L}_{dist} \tag{3}$$

where M is the number of instances in the ground truth, N_m is the number of faces in instance m, x_i is the 256-dimensional feature vector of the corresponding face from the instance segmentation branch, μ_m is the mean of all face features in instance m. Further, $\|\cdot\|$ represents the L2 distance, $[x]_+ = max(x, 0)$, m_A and m_B are instance indices. δ_v and δ_d denote the variance loss and distance loss margins, respectively. In this paper, $\delta_v = 0.5$, $\delta_d = 0.75$. Finally, we apply mean-shift clustering on the face features to achieve accurate and reliable instance segmentation.

Semantic Segmentation. The semantic segmentation module is designed to classify each face of a CAD model into specific machining feature categories. We use a PointNet [10] decoder to obtain the classification results for each face in this module. It enhances face-wise features with MLPs, extracts global features via max pooling, and combines local and global features to produce the final classification map through another MLP with a softmax activation function.

5.3 Network Training

We perform end-to-end training of our network using our dataset. In the following, we focus on defining a two-term loss $\mathcal{L}$ with weight to supervise the training step, which can be formulated as:

$$\mathcal{L} = \alpha \mathcal{L}_S + \beta \mathcal{L}_I \tag{4}$$

where $\mathcal{L}_S$ represents the loss function for semantic segmentation, and $\mathcal{L}_I$ represents the contrastive loss function for instance segmentation. The loss weights are denoted as α and β. Empirically, we use $\alpha = 1$ and $\beta = 10$.

Semantic segmentation loss L_S is defined by the cross-entropy loss function:

$$\mathcal{L}_S = -\sum_{i=1}^{N_c} y_i log \hat{y}_i \tag{5}$$

where N_c refers to the number of classes, y_i is the i-th element of the ground-truth vector, and $\hat{y}_i$ is i-th element of the predicted output vector.

Table 2. Comparison of machining feature categories in open source datasets. The number of features represents the range of the number of machining features contained in each CAD model.

Dataset	Ball slot	Dove tail slot	Rectangular slot	U slot	T slot	Simple hole	Counter sunk hole	Counter bore hole	Fillet	Chamfer	Number of Features
FeatureNet [21]			✓			✓			✓	✓	1
Yeo et al. [18]			✓			✓	✓	✓	✓	✓	1
MFDataset [7]		✓			✓	✓	✓	✓	✓	✓	1
MsvNet [12]			✓			✓			✓	✓	[2, 10]
MFCAD [2]			✓							✓	4
MFCAD++ [4]			✓			✓			✓	✓	7
ASIN [19]			✓		✓	✓			✓	✓	[2, 13]
Lee et al. [6]			✓			✓			✓✓	✓	[1, 4]
MFInstSeg [16]			✓			✓			✓	✓	[5, 14]
MMFD(Ours)	✓	✓	✓	✓	✓	✓	✓	✓	✓	✓	[10, 14]

Fig. 4. Visualizations of some generated models in the MMFD.

6 Experimental Results

6.1 Experimental Setup

Dataset. The proposed MMFD comprises 6400 CAD models, with 3000 models based on a cuboid as the base model and 3400 models generated based on 17 different base models. The training set consists of 5120 models, and both the validation and test sets include 640 models each, all randomly selected from the dataset. More visualizations of multi-machining feature models in the MMFD are shown in Fig. 4.

We compared the MMFD with existing open-source machining feature recognition datasets. As shown in the last column of Table 2, the MMFD contains the highest average number of machining features per model, making it more challenging for feature recognition tasks and more valuable for practical industrial applications.

Implementation Details. We implement our network using the PyTorch framework. The network is trained for 100 epochs in each experiment by Adam optimizer with $lr = 0.003$ and $batchsize = 8$. The settings for the comparative methods were adopted from their respective papers or open-source code.

Table 3. The results of the comparative experiment. Higher means better. Bold figures indicate the best results.

Method	Semantic segmentation			Instance segmentation		
	Acc	mAcc	mIoU	Acc	F1	mIoU
Cao et al. [2]	54.18	25.71	41.14	-	-	-
HCADNet [4]	64.49	84.88	50.52	-	-	-
ASIN [19]	84.60	71.24	74.47	12.89	4.78	4.00
AAGNet [16]	87.39	83.51	77.12	43.32	69.83	64.13
CRNet(Ours)	**94.98**	**90.08**	**91.04**	**67.66**	**77.25**	**72.97**

Evaluation Metrics. We adopt the Accuracy(Acc), mean Accuracy(mAcc), F1 score, and mean Intersection-over-Union(mIoU) to evaluate the performance of semantic and instance segmentation in machining feature recognition, similar to previous works [11,12,16].

6.2 Comparison Experiments

We compare the semantic and instance segmentation performance of various networks on MMFD, as shown in Table 3. First, the networks of Cao et al. [2] and Hierarchical CADNet (HCADNet) [4] lack instance segmentation functionality and exhibit inferior performance in the semantic segmentation task since they encode CAD models into attribute adjacency graphs, which underutilize the spatial geometric information of geometric primitive surfaces in CAD models. ASIN [19] and AAGNet [16] cannot effectively capture the global spatial contextual information between complex intersecting features since they construct a face link similarity matrix through the dot product and use binary cross-entropy loss for indirect supervision. In contrast, our CRNet can accurately capture point cloud long-range spatial context information. Meanwhile, we use contrastive learning loss to directly supervise high-dimensional distinguishable features with the FGPE, achieving SOTA results in both segmentation tasks.

6.3 Ablation Study

Dataset. We investigate the effects of non-machining feature shapes and sampling strategies on model performance. We train CRNet only on cuboid-based models and test it on three subsets, including the models generated from cuboids, the other test set generated from 17 basic models, and the full test set, as shown in the first three rows of Table 4. The results are the best in the test set with only cuboids and the worst in the test set composed of 17 basic models, highlighting the importance of including the 17 basic non-machining models to improve generalization. Additionally, using the fixed-point sampling strategy [19] leads to uneven point densities and lower accuracy. In contrast, our area-proportional sampling strategy better preserves geometric structure, enhancing feature recognition, as shown in Table 4.

Table 4. The results of the dataset ablation experiment. Higher means better. Bold figures indicate the best results.

Dataset	Semantic segmentation			Instance segmentation		
	Acc	mAcc	mIoU	Acc	F1	mIoU
only cuboids	89.19	88.02	81.27	68.73	74.74	70.34
only base	18.35	38.63	8.63	4.97	27.75	25.80
full test	36.87	59.57	21.35	34.86	49.78	46.68
32 points [19]	91.92	88.97	88.92	61.07	73.84	69.46
MMFD	**94.98**	**90.08**	**91.04**	**67.66**	**77.25**	**72.97**

Table 5. The results of the network components ablation experiment. Higher means better. Bold figures indicate the best results.

Components	Semantic segmentation			Instance segmentation		
	Acc	mAcc	mIoU	Acc	F1	mIoU
PointNet [10]	82.41	70.56	76.27	26.72	46.64	43.43
DGCNN [14]	87.19	85.38	83.95	40.17	62.52	58.50
Sparse Conv [3]	83.75	69.43	75.84	46.36	63.60	59.40
Without FGPE	94.01	88.59	89.67	58.55	72.17	67.87
MSE Loss	94.53	89.21	90.42	18.65	4.60	3.85
BCE Loss	93.89	88.20	89.39	50.77	59.03	52.73
Ours	**94.98**	**90.08**	**91.04**	**67.66**	**77.25**	**72.97**

Network Components. As shown in Table 5, we evaluate the impact of different network components on performance. Replacing the Point Transformer [22] with PointNet [10], DGCNN [14], or Sparse Convolution [3] leads to performance drops, confirming the superiority of self-attention in capturing long-range geometric context. Removing FGPE also significantly degrades instance segmentation, highlighting its role in enhancing face-wise feature discriminability. Following the AAGNet [16], constructing a similarity link matrix using the dot product and substituting our contrastive loss with MSE or BCE results in lower accuracy due to less effective indirect supervision. Our contrastive loss directly optimizes feature embeddings without requiring a similarity matrix, better capturing geometric relationships.

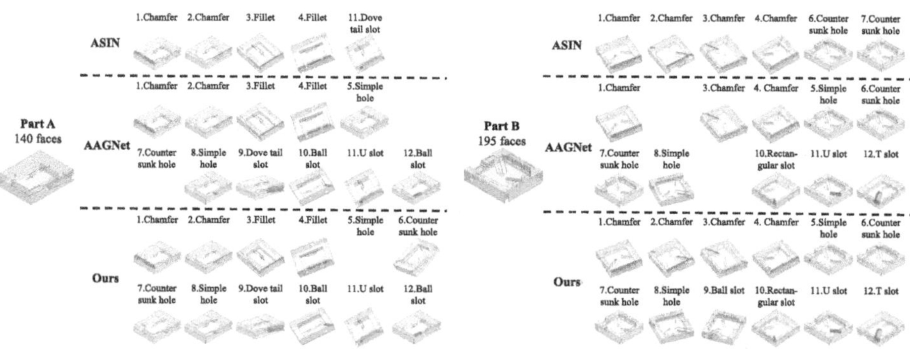

Fig. 5. The comparative case study.

6.4 Case Study

To visually assess machining feature recognition, we compare our CRNet with ASIN [19] and AAGNet [16] on two CAD models, as illustrated in Fig. 5. Cao et al. [2] and HCADNet [4] are excluded due to their lack of instance segmentation capabilities. Only correctly predicted machining feature faces are visualized. ASIN and AAGNet fail to detect all features, due to their limited ability to capture global geometric context. In contrast, CRNet accurately identifies nearly all machining features by leveraging FGPE and contrastive learning, which better preserves geometric relationships and enhances feature discrimination.

While our method is slightly less efficient computationally, it achieves significantly higher accuracy. However, it failed to detect feature 5 in Part A, likely due to its small size and subtle geometry, which may cause it to be overwhelmed by adjacent complex features during feature extraction and clustering.

6.5 Real-World CAD Dataset

To assess generalization, we invited CAD and CAM engineers to manually create 87 real-world CAD models, forming a test set distinct from MMFD, as illustrated in Fig. 6. The model trained on MMFD was directly applied to this dataset, and Table 6 show that our method maintains high accuracy and captures complex geometries effectively. This demonstrates the strong generalization of our network and the high similarity in distribution between MMFD and real industrial data. Moreover, MMFD can be further expanded using the automated generation pipeline described in Sect. 4, enhancing its scalability and applicability to broader manufacturing scenarios.

Table 6. The experimental results on the real-world CAD dataset. Higher means better. Bold figures indicate the best results.

Dataset	Semantic segmentation			Instance segmentation		
	Acc	mAcc	mIoU	Acc	F1	mIoU
Real-world	88.14	**93.70**	82.56	**71.05**	67.27	65.56
MMFD	**94.98**	90.08	**91.04**	67.66	**77.25**	**72.97**

Fig. 6. Visualizations of some real-world CAD models.

7 Conclusion

In this work, we introduce MMFD, a novel point cloud dataset with diverse machining features and complex base models reflecting real industrial scenarios.

Additionally, we propose CRNet, a contrastive learning-based network with face geometric positional encoding to enhance feature discrimination. Finally, Comprehensive experiments demonstrate that our method achieves high accuracy and generalizability of industrial machining feature recognition.

In future work, we plan to expand the scale of MMFD by collecting more real industrial base models. And we intend to enhance the efficiency of the instance segmentation module to reduce its current computational cost.

Acknowledgments. This work was partially supported by the National Natural Science Foundation of China (62476262, 62206263, 62271467, 62306297, 62306296, 62202076), the National Key R&D Program of China (2024YFC3308000), Beijing Nova Program, Beijing Natural Science Foundation (4242053, L242096), and China Postdoctoral Science Foundation (2022T150639).

References

1. Babic, B., Nesic, N., Miljkovic, Z.: A review of automated feature recognition with rule-based pattern recognition. Comput. Ind. **59**(4), 321–337 (2008)
2. Cao, W., Robinson, T., Hua, Y., Boussuge, F., Colligan, A.R., Pan, W.: Graph representation of 3D cad models for machining feature recognition with deep learning. In: International Design Engineering Technical Conferences and Computers and Information in Engineering Conference. vol. 84003, p. V11AT11A003. American Society of Mechanical Engineers (2020)
3. Choy, C., Gwak, J., Savarese, S.: 4D spatio-temporal convnets: Minkowski convolutional neural networks. In: Proceedings of the IEEE/CVF Conference on Computer Vision and Pattern Recognition, pp. 3075–3084 (2019)
4. Colligan, A.R., Robinson, T.T., Nolan, D.C., Hua, Y., Cao, W.: Hierarchical cad-net: learning from b-reps for machining feature recognition. Comput. Aided Des. **147**, 103226 (2022)
5. De Brabandere, B., Neven, D., Van Gool, L.: Semantic instance segmentation with a discriminative loss function. arXiv preprint arXiv:1708.02551 (2017)
6. Lee, H., Lee, J., Kim, H., Mun, D.: Dataset and method for deep learning-based reconstruction of 3D cad models containing machining features for mechanical parts. J. Comput. Design Eng. **9**(1), 114–127 (2022)
7. Lei, R., Wu, H., Peng, Y.: Mfpointnet: a point cloud-based neural network using selective downsampling layer for machining feature recognition. Machines **10**(12), 1165 (2022)
8. Li, H., Huang, Y., Sun, Y., Chen, L.: Hint-based generic shape feature recognition from three-dimensional b-rep models. Adv. Mech. Eng. **7**(4), 1687814015582082 (2015)
9. Ning, F., Shi, Y., Cai, M., Xu, W.: Part machining feature recognition based on a deep learning method. J. Intell. Manuf. **34**(2), 809–821 (2023)
10. Qi, C.R., Su, H., Mo, K., Guibas, L.J.: Pointnet: deep learning on point sets for 3D classification and segmentation. In: Proceedings of the IEEE Conference on Computer Vision and Pattern Recognition, pp. 652–660 (2017)
11. Shi, P., Qi, Q., Qin, Y., Scott, P.J., Jiang, X.: Intersecting machining feature localization and recognition via single shot multibox detector. IEEE Trans. Industr. Inf. **17**(5), 3292–3302 (2020)

12. Shi, P., Qi, Q., Qin, Y., Scott, P.J., Jiang, X.: A novel learning-based feature recognition method using multiple sectional view representation. J. Intell. Manuf. **31**(5), 1291–1309 (2020). https://doi.org/10.1007/s10845-020-01533-w
13. Shi, P., Qi, Q., Qin, Y., Scott, P.J., Jiang, X.: Highly interacting machining feature recognition via small sample learning. Robo. Comput.-Integrated Manuf. **73**, 102260 (2022)
14. Wang, Y., Sun, Y., Liu, Z., Sarma, S.E., Bronstein, M.M., Solomon, J.M.: Dynamic graph CNN for learning on point clouds. ACM Trans. Graphics (tog) **38**(5), 1–12 (2019)
15. Wu, H., Lei, R., Huang, P., Peng, Y.: A semi-supervised learning framework for machining feature recognition on small labeled sample. Appl. Sci. **13**(5), 3181 (2023)
16. Wu, H., Lei, R., Peng, Y., Gao, L.: Aagnet: a graph neural network towards multi-task machining feature recognition. Robo. Comput.-Integrated Manuf. **86**, 102661 (2024)
17. Yao, X., Wang, D., Yu, T., Luan, C., Fu, J.: A machining feature recognition approach based on hierarchical neural network for multi-feature point cloud models. J. Intell. Manuf. **34**(6), 2599–2610 (2023)
18. Yeo, C., Kim, B.C., Cheon, S., Lee, J., Mun, D.: Machining feature recognition based on deep neural networks to support tight integration with 3D cad systems. Sci. Rep. **11**(1), 22147 (2021)
19. Zhang, H., Zhang, S., Zhang, Y., Liang, J., Wang, Z.: Machining feature recognition based on a novel multi-task deep learning network. Robo. Comput.-Integrated Manuf. **77**, 102369 (2022)
20. Zhang, Y., Luo, X., Zhang, B., Zhang, S.: Semantic approach to the automatic recognition of machining features. Int. J. Adv. Manuf. Technol. **89**, 417–437 (2017)
21. Zhang, Z., Jaiswal, P., Rai, R.: Featurenet: machining feature recognition based on 3D convolution neural network. Comput. Aided Des. **101**, 12–22 (2018)
22. Zhao, H., Jiang, L., Jia, J., Torr, P.H., Koltun, V.: Point transformer. In: Proceedings of the IEEE/CVF International Conference on Computer Vision, pp. 16259–16268 (2021)

EX-YOLO: Improve YOLOv11 to Achieve Efficient Detection of Small Targets of Drones

WenLiang Pan(✉) and FangLin Chen

School of Computer, Electronics and Information, Guangxi University, Nanning 530004, China
ipwliang@icloud.com

Abstract. The detection of small targets in traffic scenarios still faces great challenges, where traditional algorithms struggle due to resolution and information loss issues. This paper propose EX-YOLO, an enhanced version of YOLOv11, featuring a redesigned FPN module with multi-scale feature fusion, lightweight convolution modules, and an NWD loss function. These innovations improve feature extraction for small targets while reducing computational load. Our experiments on TT100K and VisDrone datasets demonstrate EX-YOLO's superior balance between accuracy and efficiency. It achieves higher precision, recall, and mAP with lower computational cost compared to other YOLO variants, making it a promising solution for real-time drone-based small target detection.

Keywords: small-sized objects detection · feature pyramid network · context enhancement module · lightweight feature fusion module · NWD loss function

1 Introduction

When drones drive at high speed, they need to accurately identify distant traffic signs. Traditional detection algorithms are not effective due to resolution and information loss problems, and complex traffic environments have high requirements for the robustness of detection algorithms. Detection algorithms based on deep learning have become a key research topic in improving the detection ability of small targets.

Existing deep learning target detection algorithms such as R-CNN series [3, 4,10], YOLO series [1,5,12,13], SSD series [2,9], etc. have their own advantages and disadvantages. The YOLO series transforms target detection into regression problems to achieve real-time detection performance, but there are difficulties in small target detection.

The development of target detection technology stems from the rise of CNN. Early two-stage detection models, such as the R-CNN series, are highly accurate but slow. YOLO series single-stage detection is directly detected in the full map.

P. Li et al. (Eds.): CGI 2025, LNCS 16508, pp. 54–65, 2026.
https://doi.org/10.1007/978-3-032-22264-0_5

YOLOv4 adds Mish activation function, CSPDarknet backbone network [14] and SPP module, etc. to improve detection accuracy and speed; YOLOv9 introduces hybrid CNN - Transformer backbone network, etc., improve the detection performance of small targets; YOLOv11 introduces C3k2 and C2PSA modules, etc., for further optimization. However, the YOLO single-stage structure still faces challenges in the detection of small targets. Because small targets have few pixels, they are vulnerable to background interference.

In order to improve the detection performance of small targets, researchers optimize the FPN [7] structure. FPN improves multi-scale detection ability through top-down feature fusion, and PANet [8], BiFPN [11], etc. are further improved. At the same time, loss function optimization is the key. Traditional YOLO's BCE and MSE are not sensitive. Although IoU-class loss function and GWD loss [16] have been improved, they are still not sensitive to small targets. Li, Haibin and others [6] proposed E-PAN (Enhanced Path Aggregation Network), which enhances the fusion of multi-scale features through approximate sampling and residual operations between the same scale, and filters complex background information to improve detection accuracy. Zhang, Yan et al. [17] designed a lightweight and detail-sensitive DsPAN, which enhances local features and details, and reduces information loss during feature fusion.

The main contributions of this study are as follows:

1. Propose the SPPC module: improve the FPN module by introducing the context enhancement module, which improves the richness of contextual information of the feature map and enhances the detection ability of small targets.
2. Lightweight Attention Convolution DBSS Module: While improving the detection accuracy, it reduces the computing burden of the model and realizes efficient feature processing.
3. NWD loss function: In response to the recognition challenges in small target detection, the loss calculation method has been optimized and the recognition performance of small targets has been significantly improved.

2 Method

This paper proposes a series of improvement measures based on existing methods, including multi-scale fusion module SPPC module, lightweight convolution module DBSS module and more efficient loss function NWD loss function to improve detection performance while maintaining model lightweight. The model of the new method is EX-YOLO, and its process is shown in Fig. 1a.

2.1 Improved Multi-scale Fusion Module

The SPPC module integrates the multi-scale feature extraction ability of the SPPF module and the feature enhancement ability of CAM. The module structure is shown in Fig. 1b. The input feature map first compresses the number of channels through the 1×1 convolutional layer, then performs multiple pooling

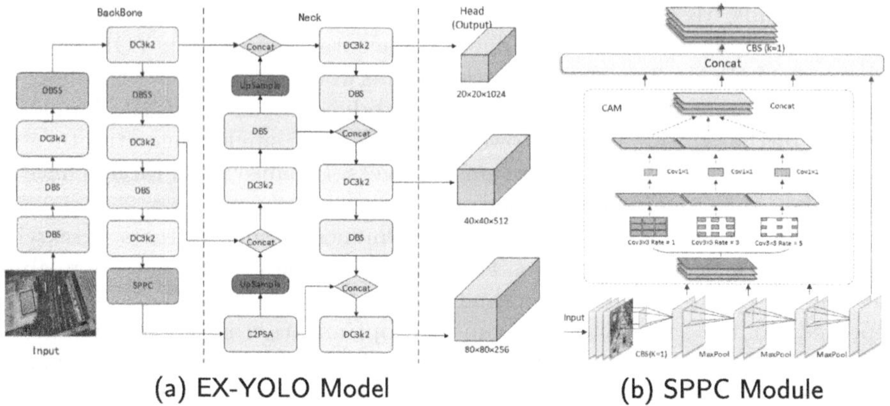

Fig. 1. The target detection model architecture of this article is shown. In Fig. 1a, it is the overall model, which is composed of three parts: BackBone, Neck and Head. BackBone contains DBS, DC3k2, DBSS, SPPC and other modules. Neck adopts C2PSA and upsampling, splicing and other operations, and Head is used for output. In Fig. 1b, it is the details of the SPPC module. After multi-branch processing such as CBS and MaxPool, with the help of CAM and Concat integration features, it realizes multi-scale feature integration and improves the target detection performance.

operations, and inserts the CAM module during the pooling process to enhance the feature expression.

The SPPC module will input the feature map x first compress the number of channels through the 1×1 convolution layer to obtain the output feature map y_0, and perform three pooling operations on y_0 to obtain the feature map y_i. Apply the CAM module to y_i respectively to enhance the feature expression.

Concat operation will be carried out on the enhanced feature map y_i'. Finally, channel fusion is carried out through the 1×1 convolutional layer, and the final feature diagram y is output:

$$y = \mathrm{Conv}(\bigoplus y_i'), \quad y_i' = \mathrm{CAM}(y_i), \quad y_i = \mathcal{P}(y_{i-1}), \quad i = 0, 1, 2, 3 \tag{1}$$

In formula 1, $\bigoplus$ represents Concat operation, and $\mathcal{P}$ represents pooling operation. The CAM module extracts features through multi-scale convolution operations and enhances feature expression through fusion.

$$\mathrm{CAM}(x) = \mathrm{Conv}(\bigoplus \mathrm{Conv}_i(x, \mathit{dilation} = j)), \quad i = 1, 2, 3, \quad j = 1, 3, 5 \tag{2}$$

In formula 2, Conv_i represent the output of different expansion rate convolutions respectively. Then the feature fusion is carried out through 1×1 convolution.

SPPC module effectively extracts multi-scale features by combining the advantages of SPPF and CAM modules. The SPPF module captures context information of different scales through pooling operations, while the CAM module further enhances the feature expression ability through multi-scale convolution and channel fusion. This design enables the model to better adapt to the feature extraction needs of small and medium-sized targets, thus improving the performance of small target detection.

2.2 Lightweight Convolutional Calculation

The method proposed in this paper focuses on enhancing the feature extraction network of YOLOv11 by introducing a lightweight weight adaptive learning convolutional unit (DSCM), aiming to reduce computational complexity and model parameters while preserving accuracy.

The DSCM is composed of three main components: depthwise convolution, pointwise convolution, and a dynamic weight adjustment module. Depthwise convolution, which applies a separate convolution operation to each input channel with the number of kernels equaling the number of input channels, significantly reduces the computational load. Its mathematical expression is:

$$O_i = \sum_{k \in K} I_i \otimes W_{k,i} \tag{3}$$

In formula 3, where O_i represents the output channel, I_i the input channel, $W_{k,i}$ the convolutional kernel for channel i, and K the kernel size.

Pointwise convolution, a 1×1 convolution operation, adjusts the output channels of depthwise convolution to the desired number. Its mathematical form is:

$$O = \sum_{i=1}^{C_{in}} I_i \otimes W_i \tag{4}$$

In formula 4, with O as the output feature map, C_{in} the input channels, and W_i the pointwise convolution weight.

To further decrease the computational burden, the dynamic weight adjustment mechanism divides the input channels into blocks, each using a shared weight parameter α to dynamically adjust the convolutional kernel weight. The final convolutional weight is generated by expanding α according to the number of blocks and channels, then multiplying it element-wise with the original weight, expressed as:

$$W_{res} = \alpha \odot W \tag{5}$$

In formula 5, where W_{res} is the adjusted weight, α the dynamic parameter, and W the original weight. This approach effectively optimizes the feature extraction process in YOLOv11 for enhanced small target detection.

Finally, SimAM [15] is introduced to enhance the ability of feature weight adjustment. Compared with the traditional attention mechanism, SimAM does not require additional parameters and convolutional pooling operations. It dynamically calculates the similarity between the activation value of the characteristic map and the channel mean, and uses energy function optimization to obtain a lightweight, efficient and integrated attention weight. By combining SimAM with lightweight convolutional units to build DBSS modules, a small target feature enhancement scheme with low computing complexity is realized, and a lightweight solution is provided to improve the fine-grained information perception ability in target detection tasks.

2.3 More Efficient Loss Function

In order to further improve the detection performance of small targets, we introduced the NWD loss function and combined it with the DIoU box loss function. The NWD loss function can more accurately evaluate the similarity between the prediction box and the real box by calculating the spatial and scale differences between the two, so as to improve the ability of the model to capture small targets.

The NWD loss function is evaluated by calculating the spatial and scale differences between the prediction box and the real box. Similarity between the two.

The specific definition is as follows:

Given the prediction box $\mathbf{p}$ and the ground truth boundary box $\mathbf{g}$, its central coordinates are $\mathbf{c}_p = (x_p, y_p)$ and $\mathbf{c}_g = (x_g, y_g)$, the width and height are (w_p, h_p) and (w_g, h_g) respectively. The NWD loss function is defined as:

$$L_{NWD} = \exp\left(-\frac{\sqrt{D_W}}{c}\right) \tag{6}$$

In the formula (6), Wasserstein distance D_W is:

$$D_W = (\Delta x)^2 + (\Delta y)^2 + \frac{(w_p - w_g)^2 + (h_p - h_g)^2}{4} + \epsilon \tag{7}$$

In the formula (7), $\Delta x = x_p - x_g$, $\Delta y = y_p - y_g$, ϵ is a very small constant to avoid division errors, c is a constant used to adjust the zoom of distance.

Take the sum of the DIoU loss function and the NWD loss function as the box loss function of YOLOv11:

$$L_{box\_loss} = \frac{L_{DIoU} + L_{NWD}}{2} \tag{8}$$

Take the average by summing the DIoU loss function and the NWD loss function, we can further enhance the detection ability of the model for small targets while maintaining the detection performance of the DIoU loss function for most targets. This combination can make full use of the advantages of the two loss functions, thus improving the overall detection performance of the model.

3 Experimental

3.1 Datasets

In drone-based small target detection research, selecting appropriate datasets is crucial for algorithm performance verification. This study employs the TT100K [19] and VisDrone [18] datasets to evaluate the enhanced YOLOv11 algorithm.

TT100K. Collected by Tsinghua University and Tencent teams via drones, focuses on traffic signs across diverse scenarios, weather, and lighting conditions, containing numerous small targets in complex environments. It also provides attributes like scene visibility, object class, and occlusion.

VisDrone. Developed by Tianjin University's AISKYEYE team, is a large-scale benchmark dataset designed for various computer vision tasks in drone image and video analysis. It comprises 288 video clips, 261,908 image frames, and 10,209 static images, covering diverse city scenes, environments, objects, and densities under various weather and lighting conditions.

(a) TT100K (b) VisDrone

Fig. 2. Figure 2a can be observed that the number of small targets in the TT100K dataset is small, the distribution is uneven, the distribution is not in the center, and there are many target categories. Figure 2a can be observed that the number of small targets in the TT100K dataset is small, the distribution is uneven, the distribution is not in the center, and there are many target categories.

Although TT100K and VisDrone are not directly drone-perspective datasets, their target types align well with those that drones need to identify in practical applications. Traffic signs are key identification objects for drones in traffic inspection and intelligent traffic fields, while people, bicycles, motorcycles, and cars are crucial detection targets in security monitoring and urban traffic management scenarios.

3.2 Analysis of Experimental Results

The system used for the experiment in this paper is Ubuntu 22, and the system hardware facilities are 64G RAM, NVIDIA GTX4090 GPU and Intel i9-13900K CPU. The software platform is cu121, Anaconda.

Comparative Studies. The algorithm validation from Table 1 was performed with the image size set to 320×320, and the confidence and IoU thresholds were established at 25% and 70%, respectively, to ensure a meticulous assessment of the model's detection capabilities under these specific parameters.

The comparative studies presented in Table 1 underscore the efficacy of EX-YOLO relative to other YOLO variants on both the TT100K and VisDrone datasets. On the TT100K benchmark, EX-YOLO achieves a precision (P) of 87.5%, a recall (R) of 83.0%, and an $mAP_{0.5}$ of 89.3%. Although YOLOv9 attains a marginally higher mAP (90.6%), EX-YOLO outperforms YOLOv11 and YOLOv10 in both precision and recall, thereby evidencing its superior detection reliability. Crucially, EX-YOLO's computational footprint–17.0 GFLOPs–is substantially lower than that of YOLOv9 (27.2 GFLOPs), YOLOv10 (25.4 GFLOPs), and YOLOv11 (21.8 GFLOPs). This reduction in FLOPs translates to a more favorable balance between accuracy and efficiency: despite the slight trade-off in mAP relative to YOLOv9, EX-YOLO maintains state-of-the-art detection capability while significantly reducing computational overhead. In other words, EX-YOLO's modest decrease in mAP (1.3% lower than YOLOv9) is more than compensated by its markedly lower GFLOPs, rendering it exceptionally well suited to resource-constrained or real-time UAV deployments.

Table 1. Comparative Studies on the TT100K dataset and VisDrone dataset

Methods	Params M	GFLOPs	TT100K				VisDrone			
			P %↑	R %↑	$mAP_{0.5}$% ↑	FPS ↑	P %↑	R %↑	$mAP_{0.5}$% ↑	FPS ↑
YOLOv11[5]	9.5	21.8	87.8	77.7	87.7	94.3	48.5	38.1	38.3	82.6
YOLOv10[12]	8.2	25.4	77.6	75.2	85.0	88.5	50.1	38.0	39.0	78.1
YOLOv9[13]	7.5	27.2	91.4	81.8	90.6	90.9	52.5	39.2	40.2	62.1
EX-YOLO	11.4	17.0	87.5	83.0	89.3	84.7	51.4	37.2	39.0	68.5

On the VisDrone dataset, EX-YOLO records a precision of 51.4%, a recall of 37.2%, and an $mAP_{0.5}$ of 39.0%, with a frame rate of 68.5 FPS. While YOLOv9 demonstrates a slightly higher mAP (40.2%), EX-YOLO nonetheless exceeds YOLOv11 and YOLOv10 in recall and offers a competitive FPS that is more than adequate for on-board processing. Specifically, EX-YOLO's recall advantage over YOLOv11/YOLOv10 supports more reliable detection of small targets, and its real-time throughput remains within acceptable bounds for aerial tracking applications. Although YOLOv11 achieves 82.6 FPS and YOLOv10 achieves 78.1 FPS, their respective recalls (38.1% and 38.0%) are marginally lower than EX-YOLO's 37.2%. Moreover, EX-YOLO's GFLOPs (17.0) are again the lowest among all compared models, underscoring its consistent computational efficiency.

Taken together, the results demonstrate that EX-YOLO attains a favorable trade-off between detection performance and resource consumption. Across both TT100K and VisDrone, EX-YOLO preserves high precision and recall while minimizing FLOPs, which is critical for lightweight drone platforms. Even in scenarios where mAP is marginally below that of the top-performing YOLOv9, EX-YOLO's efficiency gains and robust recall render it an excellent solution for real-time small-object detection in UAV contexts.

Figure 3 further illustrates EX-YOLO's resilience across varying confidence thresholds. On TT100K, EX-YOLO achieves a peak F1 score of 0.80 at a confidence threshold of 0.260 and maintains consistently strong F1 values across a broad threshold range–outperforming YOLOv11 and YOLOv10 in nearly all operating points. On VisDrone, EX-YOLO attains an F1 score of 0.42 at a threshold of 0.142, which is competitive with YOLOv9 and superior to both YOLOv11 and YOLOv10 throughout most of the curve. These F1 trends highlight EX-YOLO's ability to balance precision and recall robustly, confirming its suitability for reliable, lightweight small-object recognition on drones.

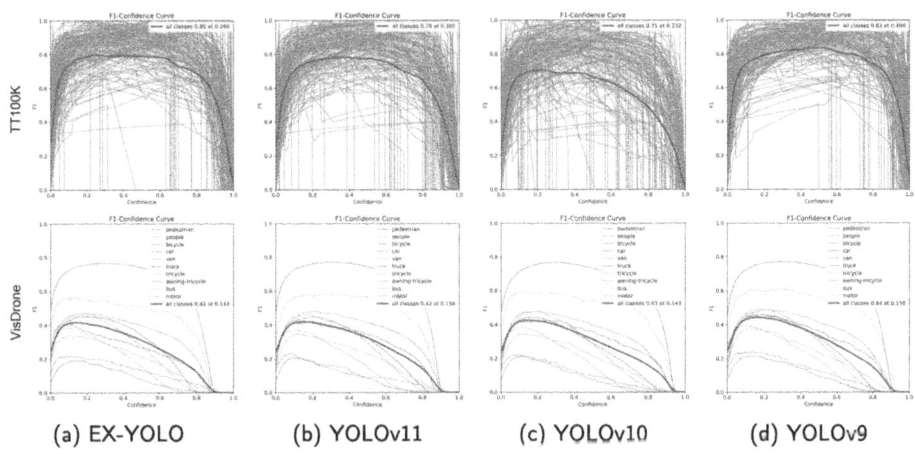

Fig. 3. F1 curve on the TT100K dataset and VisDrone dataset.

In Fig. 4, the confusion matrices reveal EX-YOLO's superior performance in minimizing both false positives (FP) and false negatives (FN). In the upper triangular regions, EX-YOLO exhibits fewer off-diagonal dark spots compared to YOLOv9, YOLOv10, and YOLOv11, indicating reduced FP predictions across most classes. For example, in the bicycle and pedestrian categories, EX-YOLO shows less dark blue coloration in non-diagonal cells, suggesting fewer misclassifications of background or other objects as these targets. The background row in EX-YOLO's matrix also has lower values for most classes, demonstrating better distinction between actual objects and background noise.

In the lower triangular areas, EX-YOLO demonstrates its advantage in reducing FN. Along the diagonal, EX-YOLO generally maintains higher intensity (darker blue) compared to other YOLO variants, signifying more accurate true positive identifications and fewer missed objects. This is particularly evident in challenging categories like tricycle and awning-tricycle, where EX-YOLO's diagonal values are more pronounced, reflecting its enhanced ability to detect smaller, potentially occluded objects.

When compared to YOLOv9, YOLOv10, and YOLOv11, EX-YOLO strikes a better balance between FP and FN reduction. YOLOv9 sometimes achieves slightly higher true positive rates for certain classes but often at the cost of increased FP predictions. YOLOv10 and YOLOv11, on the other hand, exhibit more scattered dark spots in both upper and lower triangular regions, indicating less consistent performance in managing the FP and FN trade-offs.

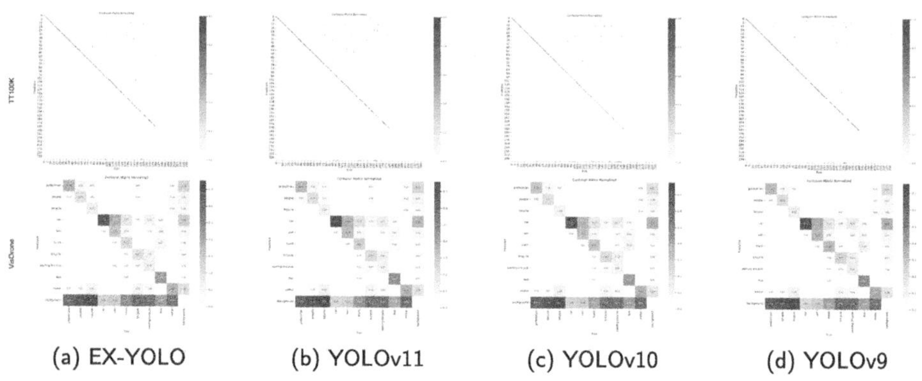

Fig. 4. Confusion matrix normalized on the TT100K dataset and VisDrone dataset.

These observations from the confusion matrices align with the previously reported metrics, further validating EX-YOLO's effectiveness as a more reliable object detection solution for drone-based applications where minimizing both FP and FN is critical for real-time decision-making.

Ablation Studies. Table 2 provides an ablation study on the TT100K and VisDrone datasets, examining the individual and combined impacts of the NWD loss function, SPPC module, and DBSS module on the EX-YOLO model's performance.

The NWD loss function, when used alone, delivers slight improvements in precision and mAP on TT100K, with a minor FPS increase. On VisDrone, it enhances precision but slightly reduces inference speed. This highlights NWD's role in improving localization accuracy for small objects through better capture of spatial correlations in bounding box regression, with minimal computational cost.

Adding the SPPC module to NWD significantly boosts performance on both datasets. On TT100K, mAP improves from 88.2% to 90.9%, while VisDrone records its highest mAP at 39.2%. These gains demonstrate SPPC's effectiveness in capturing richer spatial backgrounds and enhancing multi-scale feature integration. However, this comes with increased computational complexity, as evidenced by reduced FPS and higher GFLOPs.

Table 2. Ablation Studies On the TT100K dataset and VisDrone dataset

Methods	Params M	GFLOPs	TT100K				VisDrone			
			P %↑	R %↑	$mAP_{0.5}$% ↑	FPS ↑	P %↑	R %↑	$mAP_{0.5}$% ↑	FPS ↑
YOLOv11[5]	9.5	21.8	87.8	77.7	87.7	94.3	48.5	38.1	38.3	82.6
YOLOv10[12]	8.2	25.4	77.6	75.2	85.0	88.5	50.1	38.0	39.0	78.1
YOLOv9[13]	7.5	27.2	91.4	81.8	90.6	90.9	52.5	39.2	40.2	62.1
EX-YOLO	11.4	17.0	87.5	83.0	89.3	84.7	51.4	37.2	39.0	68.5

Introducing the DBSS module alongside NWD and SPPC optimizes the performance-efficiency balance. On TT100K, although mAP slightly decreases to 89.3%, FPS improves from 78.1 to 84.7. Similarly, VisDrone maintains a high mAP of 39.0% with an FPS increase to 68.5. DBSS mitigates the computational overhead of SPPC by promoting efficient spatial sampling and suppressing redundant activations, thus preserving key features while reducing inference cost.

(a) EX-YOLO (b) YOLOv11 (c) YOLOv10 (d) YOLOv9

Fig. 5. Detected of algorithms on TT100K dataset and VisDrone dataset.

In summary, NWD specializes in small object localization optimization, SPPC enhances multi-scale semantic representation despite increased computational demands, and DBSS restores speed with minimal performance compromise. The integration of all three components in EX-YOLO achieves an impressive balance between accuracy and efficiency, validating its design for real-world, resource-constrained detection scenarios.

3.3 Comparison of Detection Targets

In Fig. 5, the detection results of EX-YOLO, YOLOv11, YOLOv10, and YOLOv9 on the TT100K and VisDrone datasets are presented. On the TT100K dataset, the proposed EX-YOLO algorithm demonstrates better recognition of small targets, such as cars and billboards, with more accurate bounding boxes and higher confidence scores compared to other YOLO variants. For instance, EX-YOLO detected more "p5" and detected the "p29" in the middle of the picture. YOLOv11, YOLOv10 and YOLOv9 all detected the "p29" in the middle of the picture.

On the VisDrone dataset, EX-YOLO shows a more balanced performance in detecting various small targets, including cars, pedestrians, and motorcycles. It achieves confidence scores of 0.62 for pedestrians and 0.58 for motorcycles, which are competitive with other algorithms.

Overall, the visualization results indicate that EX-YOLO provides more accurate and robust small target recognition for drones across different datasets.

4 Conclusion

In this paper, we proposed EX-YOLO to enhance the detection of small targets for drones by improving YOLOv11. Our method redesigned the FPN module with multi-scale feature fusion, introduced lightweight convolution modules and NWD loss function. The comparative studies and ablation experiments demonstrate that EX-YOLO achieves a better balance between detection accuracy and computational efficiency on TT100K and VisDrone datasets. It outperforms other YOLO variants with higher precision, recall, and mAP at a lower computational cost. The inference visualization also shows its better recognition of small targets. Our work provides a promising solution for real-time small target detection in drone applications.

References

1. Bochkovskiy, A., Wang, C., Liao, H.: Yolov4: optimal speed and accuracy of object detection. arXiv (2020)
2. Fu, C., Liu, W., Ranga, A., Tyagi, A., Berg, A.: Dssd: deconvolutional single shot detector. arXiv (2017)
3. Girshick, R.: Fast R-CNN. arXiv (2015)
4. He, K., Gkioxari, G., Dollár, P., Girshick, R.: Mask r-cnn. In: Proceedings of the IEEE International Conference on Computer Vision (ICCV), pp. 2961–2969. Venice, Italy (2017)
5. Khanam, R., Hussain, M.: Yolov11: an overview of the key architectural enhancements. arXiv preprint arXiv:2410.17725 (2024)
6. Li, H., Wu, D., Zhang, W., Xiao, C.: Yolo-pl: helmet wearing detection algorithm based on improved yolov4. Digit. Signal Process. **144**, 104283 (2024)

7. Lin, T.Y., Dollar, P., Girshick, R., He, K., Hariharan, B., Belongie, S.: Feature pyramid networks for object detection. In: Proceedings of the 2017 IEEE/CVF Conference on Computer Vision and Pattern Recognition (CVPR), pp. 936–944. Honolulu, HI, USA (2017)
8. Liu, S., Qi, L., Qin, H., Shi, J., Jia, J.: Path aggregation network for instance segmentation. In: Proceedings of the IEEE Conference on Computer Vision and Pattern Recognition, pp. 8759–8768 (2018)
9. Liu, W., Anguelov, D., Erhan, D., Szegedy, C., Reed, S., Fu, C.: SSD: single shot multibox detector. In: Proceedings of the European Conference on Computer Vision (ECCV), pp. 21–37. Amsterdam, The Netherlands (2016)
10. Ren, S., He, K., Girshick, R., Sun, J.: Faster R-CNN: towards real-time object detection with region proposal networks. IEEE Trans. Pattern Anal. Mach. Intell. **39**, 1137–1149 (2015)
11. Tan, M., Pang, R., Le, Q.: Efficientdet: scalable and efficient object detection. In: Proceedings of the IEEE/CVF Conference on Computer Vision and Pattern Recognition, pp. 10781–10790 (2020)
12. Wang, A., et al.: Yolov10: real-time end-to-end object detection. arXiv preprint arXiv:2405.14458 (2024)
13. Wang, C.Y., Yeh, I.H., Mark Liao, H.Y.: Yolov9: learning what you want to learn using programmable gradient information. In: European Conference on Computer Vision, pp. 1–21. Springer (2024)
14. Wang, C., Liao, H., Wu, Y., Chen, P., Hsieh, J., Yeh, I.: Cspnet: a new backbone that can enhance learning capability of CNN. In: Proceedings of the IEEE/CVF Conference on Computer Vision and Pattern Recognition Workshops, pp. 390–391. Seattle, WA, USA (2020)
15. Yang, L., Zhang, R.Y., Li, L., Xie, X.: Simam: a simple, parameter-free attention module for convolutional neural networks. In: International Conference on Machine Learning, pp. 11863–11874. PMLR (2021)
16. Yang, X., Yan, J., Ming, Q., Wang, W., Zhang, X., Tian, Q.: Rethinking rotated object detection with gaussian Wasserstein distance loss. In: Proceedings of the 2021 International Conference on Machine Learning (ICML) (2021)
17. Zhang, Y., Zhang, H., Huang, Q., Han, Y., Zhao, M.: DSP-yolo: an anchor-free network with DSPAN for small object detection of multiscale defects. Expert Syst. Appl. **241**, 122669 (2024)
18. Zhu, P., et al.: Detection and tracking meet drones challenge. IEEE Trans. Pattern Anal. Mach. Intell. 1–1 (2021). https://doi.org/10.1109/TPAMI.2021.3119563
19. Zhu, Z., Liang, D., Zhang, S., Huang, X., Li, B., Hu, S.: Traffic-sign detection and classification in the wild. In: The IEEE Conference on Computer Vision and Pattern Recognition (CVPR) (2016)

BIDP: Brain-Inspired Dual-Process CNN-Transformer for Salient Object Detection

Wenyi Wu[1], Chen Liao[1], Qiangqiang Zhou[2](✉), Dandan Zhu[3], and Xinping Rao[2]

[1] School of Digital Industry, Jiangxi Normal University, Nanchang, China
[2] School of Software, Jiangxi Normal University, Nanchang, China
qiang@jxnu.edu.cn
[3] Institute of AI Education, East China Normal University, Shanghai, China

Abstract. While most existing salient object detection (SOD) methods achieve accurate predictions of salient regions, their performance in precisely delineating object boundaries remains suboptimal. Inspired by the brain's dual-process mechanism, we propose a novel dual-process framework: (1) a Pyramid Efficient Channel Attention U-Net (PECA-U-Net) that enhances local detail representation during initial salient feature extraction, and (2) a Residual Efficient Channel Attention Transformer (RECA-Transformer) that refines edge details through global context modeling. These modules are sequentially integrated within a feature extraction and refinement backbone architecture, enabling comprehensive boundary-aware saliency prediction. Furthermore, we design a Boundary-Aware Attention Loss (BAAL) that adaptively balances global saliency and boundary precision through a weighted combination of base and boundary losses. Extensive experiments conducted on five benchmark datasets demonstrate the effectiveness and competitiveness of our proposed model in SOD tasks. The source code is publicly available at https://github.com/1245179435/PECA-REAT.

Keywords: Salient Object Detection · Brain-Inspired · Attention Mechanisms

1 Introduction

SOD aims to imitate human vision by rapidly identifying salient regions for object localization and segmentation, and is widely used in object detection [1], segmentation, and AR/VR tasks. Most SOD methods rely on convolutional neural networks(CNNs) for multi-scale feature extraction and apply multi-level fusion [2], refinement networks, and attention mechanisms [3] to improve accuracy. However, CNNs inherently struggle with modeling global dependencies and long-range interactions, often resulting in suboptimal fine-boundary predictions. Transformer-based architectures, using query-based self-attention to capture global and hierarchical relationships, offer a promising alternative.

P. Li et al. (Eds.): CGI 2025, LNCS 16508, pp. 66–77, 2026.
https://doi.org/10.1007/978-3-032-22264-0_6

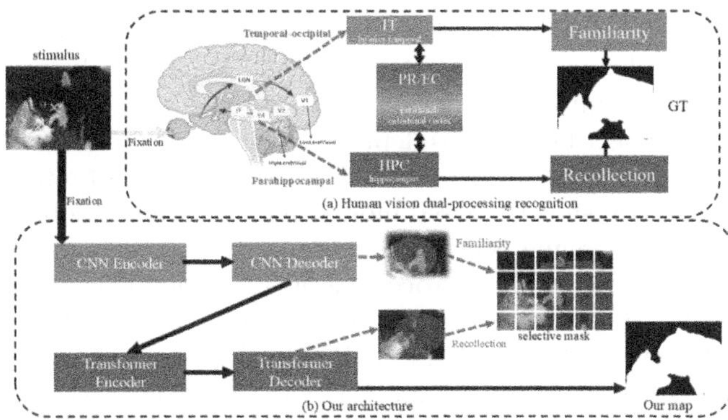

Fig. 1. An illustration comparing the human vision system and the proposed frameworks. Framework (a) is modeled after the human vision system, while our proposed framework (b) represents a dual-process approach inspired by the principles of human vision.

Empirical studies [4] demonstrate that the hierarchical operation of the human visual perception system exhibits architectural parallels with the ventral visual stream (VVS), as illustrated in Fig. 1(a). This neurobiological principle has motivated the development of hybrid CNN-Transformer architectures [5], where CNNs excel at extracting generalized shallow visual features through their inductive biases for spatial locality and translation invariance. In contrast, Transformer modules leverage self-attention mechanisms to establish global contextual relationships and generate task-adaptive high-level representations. The synergistic integration of these complementary paradigms has been empirically validated to enhance model prediction accuracy across multiple vision tasks.

Furthermore, emerging evidence from cognitive neuroscience supports the **dual-process detection theory** [6], a foundational framework for understanding human recognition and memory systems. This theory posits two distinct cognitive phases during visual saliency processing: an initial rapid **familiarity** assessment followed by a deliberate **recollection** process. When visual stimuli first reach the primary visual cortex (V1) [7], automatic feature extraction occurs at millisecond timescales, processing fundamental attributes including edge orientations, spatial frequencies, and elementary shape primitives. This subconscious processing mechanism bears functional similarities to the hierarchical feature abstraction in CNNs, where successive convolutional layers progressively aggregate local visual patterns into structured representations.

When enhanced discriminative power becomes necessary, the brain engages hippocampal-dependent recollection mechanisms through controlled memory retrieval processes [8]. This secondary stage integrates multi-modal contextual information with stored semantic knowledge to resolve perceptual ambiguities, analogous to how Transformer architectures establish global dependencies through attention-weighted feature interactions. Inspired by this theory, the conceptual framework of our method is illustrated in Fig. 1(b). Two major challenges remain unresolved in SOD. First, accurate foregroundbackground separation requires a balance between global structure and local details, which continues to pose challenges despite the adoption of multi-scale fusion techniques. Second, preserving sharp object boundaries depends on effective multi-resolution feature integration; however, CNN-based methods frequently fail to retain fine-grained details. Although Transformer-based models have enhanced global context modeling, their ability to refine object boundaries remains suboptimal.To address these issues, we propose a dual-process network inspired by the brain's visual processing. A PECA-U-Net module leverages CNNs for local feature extraction and initial saliency prediction, while a RECA-Transformer refines boundaries via long-range dependency modeling. A BAAL function further enhances edge precision by combining base loss with edge-aware attention (see Fig. 2).

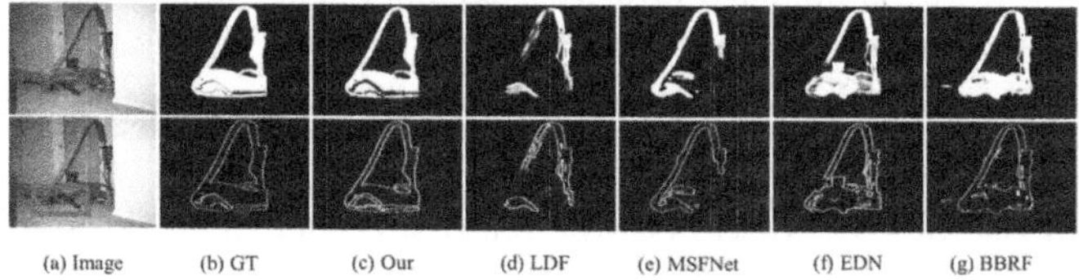

Fig. 2. Visual comparison with SOTA methods (LDF [9], MSFNet [2], EDN [10], BBRF [1]). Columns show: (a) input image with saliency details, (b) GT, (c) our results, and (d-g) competitors' outputs (each displaying both saliency map and boundary view).

This work presents the following main contributions: (1) A novel PECA-U-Net module extracts and integrates multi-scale features to generate an initial coarse saliency map. Inspired by the brain's familiarity process, the pyramidal design effectively captures local details. (2) An innovative RECA-Transformer module that augments the standard self-attention with Efficient Channel Attention (ECA) , forming a biologically-inspired recollection mechanism with multi-scale receptive fields. (3) A BAAL function is developed that fuses a base loss with an edge attention loss. The edge attention component directs refinement of boundaries, resulting in saliency maps with enhanced sharpness.

2 Related Work

2.1 Dual-Process Detection Theory

The Dual-Process Detection Theory [6] explains recognition and memory through two interrelated cognitive processes: familiarity and recollection. Inspired by this theory, some architectures adopt dual-processing mechanisms [5], and by simulating the human brain's mechanism in object detection, they have achieved promising results.

2.2 Vision Transformers

Initially used in Natural Language Processing (NLP), Transformers have been adapted for vision tasks such as image classification and semantic segmentation. The SelfReformer [3] global dependencies by tokenizing images. Recent advancements such as the enhanced Visual Saliency Transformer (VST++) [11] integrate CNNs with attention mechanisms to support multitask predictions, demonstrating strong performance in tasks like SOD.

2.3 U-Net Model

U-Net, known for its U-shaped architecture, is widely applied in semantic segmentation. Recent variants such as Attention U-Net [12] and TransUNet [13] incorporate attention modules, recurrent units, and residual links to boost feature focus, training stability, and accuracy in complex segmentation tasks.

3 Proposed Method

3.1 Network Architecture

The proposed framework comprises two principal components—a PECA-U-Net module and a RECA-Transformer module—whose combined operation yields excellent predictive performance for SOD.

3.2 Pyramid Efficient Channel Attention U-Net Module

The PECA-U-Net module encompasses the following components. **Encoder Part**: A pre-trained VGG16 functions as the primary network, employing its learned convolutional and pooling layers to extract image features progressively. The feature maps at each convolution stage gradually decrease in size, forming a pyramid structure (from the original size to 1/2 (Stage 1), 1/4 (Stage 2), 1/8 (Stage 3), 1/16 (Stage 4), and 1/32 (Stage 5)). After each convolution stage, a Spatial Attention(SA) module is incorporated. The SA module consists of convolutional layers and ECA module [14] (see Fig. 3 (i)), which enhance spatial feature representation. The formula for ECA calculation is as follows:

$$X' = X \cdot \sigma\left(\mathrm{Conv1D}_{1\times 1}\left(\mathrm{AvgPool}(X)\right)\right) \quad (1)$$

σ refers to applying the Sigmoid activation function.

The method for calculating the SA module is as follows:

$$S = \mathrm{ECA}\left(\mathrm{Conv2D}_{3\times 3}\left(\mathrm{ReLU}\left(\mathrm{Conv2D}_{1\times 1}(X)\right)\right)\right) \quad (2)$$

where $\mathbf{X} \in \mathbb{R}^{C\times H\times W}$ stands for input feature , $\mathbf{S} \in \mathbb{R}^{C\times H\times W}$ is output feature after SA module. H, W, and C denote the height, width, and number of channels of the input feature, respectively.

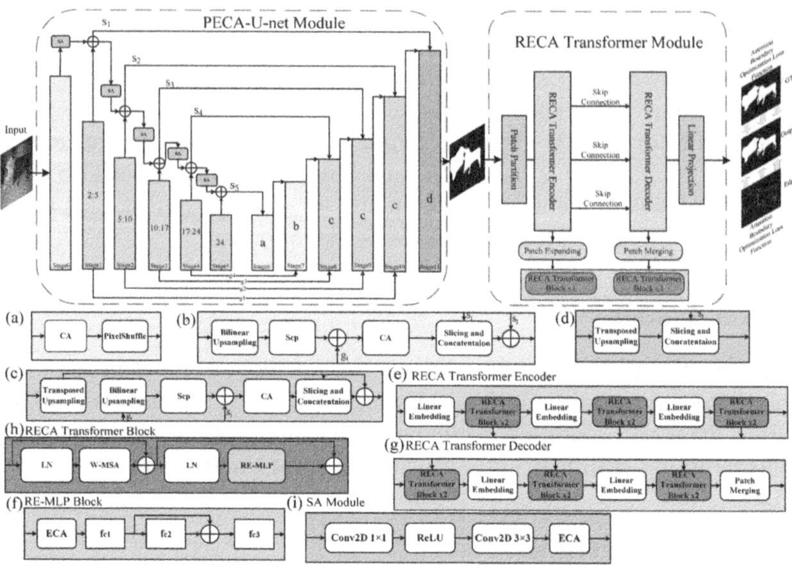

Fig. 3. The overall architecture comprises two primary modules: the PECA-U-Net and the RECA-Transformer. In the PECA-U-Net encoder, the stages of the VGG16 network are redefined to optimize feature extraction capabilities: Stage 0 represents a 1×1 convolutional layer used to adjust the input channels; Stage 1 corresponds to layers 2 to 5 of VGG16, comprising two convolutional layers followed by a pooling layer; and Stage 5 corresponds to layers 24 through the final layer of VGG16, encompassing three fully connected layers. Architectural components are denoted as (a), (b), (c), and (d) for various segments of the PECA-U-Net decoder, while (e), (f), (g), and (h) refer to the RECA-Transformer encoder, the RE-MLP Block, a secondary RECA-Transformer encoder, and the RECA-Transformer block, respectively.

Decoder Part: At Stage 6 (see Fig. 3 (a)), given the absence of corresponding high-level features, we first process the output features from the encoder. Subsequently, the features from Stage 5 (which serve as input to Stage 6) are enhanced through an Coordinate Attention(CA) module [15]. The underlying principle of the CA module is to improve the representational capacity of feature maps by harmonizing spatial and channel attention mechanisms.

Specifically, the working principle of the CA module can be described as follows: First, average pooling operations are independently applied along the horizontal and vertical directions of the input feature maps to generate spatial context descriptors for both orientations. This operation compresses global spatial information while preserving orientation-sensitive features, yielding two sets of 1D feature vectors. Subsequently, these orientation-specific feature representations are concatenated along the channel dimension to form enhanced feature representations that integrate bidirectional spatial information.

$$X_w^{(c,1,w)} = \frac{1}{|H|}\sum_{h \in H} X^{(c,h,w)} \quad X_h^{(c,h,1)} = \frac{1}{|W|}\sum_{w \in W} X^{(c,h,w)} \tag{3}$$

$$Y = concat(X_h, X_w, dim = 2) \tag{4}$$

Y denotes the concatenation of horizontal and vertical spatial features. X stands for input feature. where H (height), W (width), and C (channels) represent the spatial dimensions and channel depth.

The concatenated feature map (Y) is dimensionally reduced through a 1×1 convolution and batch normalization, with non-linearity added by the ReLU activation function. This can be described as:

$$Y' = \text{ReLU}\left(\text{BatchNorm2d}\left(\text{Conv2D}_{1\times 1}(Y)\right)\right) \tag{5}$$

The dimensionally reduced feature map (Y') is subsequently separated into horizontal and vertical feature maps (x_h, x_w). A 1×1 convolution and Sigmoid activation are utilized on the horizontal and vertical feature maps to generate attention weights. The attention weights are then applied to the original input features through element-wise multiplication, yielding the reinforced features.This can be described as:

$$\mathcal{F}_{\text{out}} = x \odot \sigma\big(\text{Conv2D}_{1\times 1}(x_h)\big) \odot \sigma\big(\text{Conv2D}_{1\times 1}(x_w)\big) \tag{6}$$

where the *identity* term corresponds to the original input x. $\mathcal{F}_{out}$ indicates the features after enhancement. $\odot$ stands for matrix multiplication. Finally, we upsample the feature map processed by CA using PixelShuffle.

In Stage 8 (see Fig. 3 (c)), given the presence of corresponding high-level features from Stage 3, deconvolution is first performed on the output of the previous decoder layer (Stage 7) using ConvTranspose2d. Thereafter, bilinear interpolation is employed to upsample the feature map from Stage 3, thereby enhancing resolution. These steps aid in restoring image details and resolution. Subsequently, the Spatial context pooling(Scp) module is leveraged to extract and bolster the spatial context information of the Stage 3 feature map. The detailed working principle of the Scp module is explained as follows: Initially, a 1×1 convolution operation is applied to input feature map $x \in \mathbb{R}^{C\times H\times W}$, mapping it to a single-channel feature map $Z \in \mathbb{R}^{1\times H\times W}$. A Softmax operation is then performed to calculate the weight for each position. Reshaped weights are then applied to the original feature map through element-wise multiplication, resulting in enhanced features.

The feature map processed by the Scp module is fused with S4. Afterward, the fused feature map is spatially enhanced using the CA module. The resulting feature map is combined with the Stage 7 feature map from the preceding decoder layer's ConvTranspose2d through a process of Slicing, concatenation and element-wise addition. This allows our module to fully consider high-level and low-level feature information at different scales, ensuring high resolution and high quality of the final feature map.

3.3 Residual Efficient Channel Attention Transformer Module

The Swin Transformer [16] captures multi-scale features through hierarchical processing and sliding windows, but its static MLP (two FC layers + activation) limits channel-wise adaptation. We address this by: (1) integrating ECA [14] for channel attention, enhancing feature discrimination; and (2) adding residual connections to improve gradient flow (Fig. 3 (f)). The resulting RECA Transformer Block (Fig. 3 (h)) combines these mechanisms, boosting both stability and predictive performance through:

$$\mathcal{F}_{\text{RE-MLP}} = \text{fc}_3\Big(\text{fc}_2(\text{fc}_1(\text{ECA}(\mathbf{x})) + \text{fc}_1(\text{ECA}(\mathbf{x}))\Big) \tag{7}$$

fc_1, fc_2, and fc_3 denote fully connected layers. $\mathbf{x}$ stands for input features.

The RECA Transformer Module employs an encoder-decoder architecture (see Fig. 3 (e), (g)), where the window attention mechanism is utilized during the encoding phase for multi-scale feature extraction, while the decoding phase progressively restores spatial details to refine target boundaries and feature representations. The formula for the RECA Transformer Block can be described as follows:

$$\begin{aligned} \mathbf{X}_{out} &= \text{RECA Transformer Block}(\mathbf{X}_{in}) \\ &= \mathcal{F}_{\text{RE-MLP}}\Big(\text{LN}\big(\text{W-MSA}(\text{LN}(\mathbf{X}_{in})) + \mathbf{X}_{in}\big)\Big) \\ &\quad + \text{W-MSA}(\text{LN}(\mathbf{X}_{in})) + \mathbf{X}_{in} \end{aligned} \tag{8}$$

LN indicates layer normalization, W-MSA implements windowed multi-head self-attention, and $\mathbf{X}_{in}$ denotes input feature maps.

3.4 Attention Boundary Optimization Loss Function

To address edge optimization limitations in conventional loss functions, we propose a Boundary-Aware Attention Loss combining: a base loss component and a boundary attention mechanism. The formulation is:

$$\begin{aligned} \mathcal{L}_{\text{BAAL}} &= \mathcal{L}_{\text{Base}} + \beta \cdot \mathcal{L}_{\text{Edge}} \\ &= \frac{1}{N}\sum_{i=1}^{N} \text{CrossEntropy}(p_i, t_i) + \beta \cdot \frac{1}{N}\sum_{i=1}^{N} \omega_i \cdot \text{CrossEntropy}(p_i, t_i) \\ &= \frac{1}{N}\sum_{i=1}^{N} \text{CrossEntropy}(p_i, t_i) \cdot (1 + \beta \cdot (1 + \alpha \cdot \text{Edges}_i) \end{aligned} \tag{9}$$

The edge-aware loss $\mathcal{L}_{\text{Edge}}$ is weighted $\beta \in \mathbb{R}^+$ to balance its contribution. For each pixel p_i and t_i denote the prediction and ground truth, respectively. An attention weight map ω_i prioritizes edge regions by scaling the edge map with a coefficient $\alpha \in \mathbb{R}^+$, where Edges_i is derived from the gradient of the ground truth mask.

4 Experimental Results

4.1 Implementation and Experimental Setup

The experiments were conducted using PyTorch 2.3 framework with an i9-13900K CPU and RTX 3090 GPU (24GB) configuration. We employed the SGD optimizer (initial learning rate 0.005, momentum 0.9) with a batch size of 15 and input image size of 224×224. The BALL parameters were set to $\beta = 2$ and $\alpha = 1.5$.

4.2 Evaluation Datasets and Metrics

We assessed our method using five standard benchmark datasets for SOD tasks. **ECSSD** [17]: 1000 images with complex backgrounds and diverse, well-annotated salient objects.**PASCAL-S** [18]: 850 challenging images with multi-category objects and precise annotations. **HKUIS** [19]: 4447 images featuring disconnected/overlapping objects and low contrast, making it challenging for SOD models. **DUT-OMRON** [20]: 5168 images with 12 detailed salient objects, offering feature diversity.**DUTS** [21]: The largest SOD dataset (15,572 images), split into 10,553 training (DUTS-TR) and 5,019 test (DUTS-TE) images. We evaluate our method using the following five metrics: Precision-Recall (PR) curve, $F_{\beta\text{-measure}}$, MAE, E-measure, and S-measure.

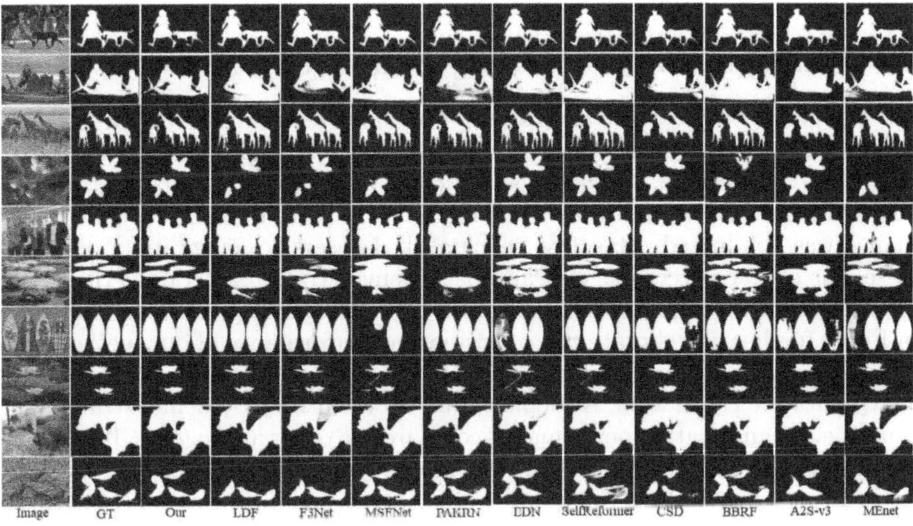

Fig. 4. Qualitative comparison of the proposed method against other methods. For the blurriness, fragmentation, and smoothness observed in some fine details, we attribute these issues to the way the Transformer's self-attention mechanism captures features.

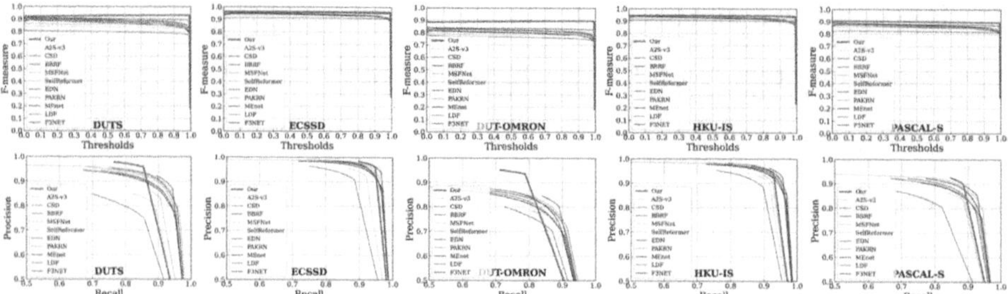

Fig. 5. Comparison of precision-recall curves (bottom row) and F-measure curves (top row) across five saliency benchmark datasets. As described above, our network achieves promising results on these five datasets.

Table 1. Quantitative evaluation of our approach versus ten other techniques across five datasets: DUTS-TE, HKU-IS, PASCAL-S, ECSSD, and DUT-OMRON. Colors Red, Green, and Blue represent the top, second, and third performance levels, respectively.

Methods	DUTS-TE				HKU-IS				PASCAL-S				ECSSD				DUT-OMRON			
	$F_\beta\uparrow$	$MAE\downarrow$	$E_\xi\uparrow$	$S_m\uparrow$	$F_\beta\uparrow$	$MAE\downarrow$	$E_\xi\uparrow$	$S_m\uparrow$	$F_\beta\uparrow$	$MAE\downarrow$	$E_\xi\uparrow$	$S_m\uparrow$	$F_\beta\uparrow$	$MAE\downarrow$	$E_\xi\uparrow$	$S_m\uparrow$	$F_\beta\uparrow$	$MAE\downarrow$	$E_\xi\uparrow$	$S_m\uparrow$
F3Net20	0.891	0.035	0.901	0.888	0.936	0.028	0.952	0.917	0.871	0.061	0.858	0.854	0.945	0.033	0.927	0.924	0.813	0.052	0.869	0.838
LDF20	0.897	0.033	0.909	0.892	0.939	0.027	0.953	0.919	0.874	0.059	0.865	0.856	0.950	0.030	0.924	0.930	0.819	0.051	0.873	0.839
MSFNet21	0.877	0.034	0.911	0.875	0.927	0.026	0.953	0.907	0.862	0.060	0.858	0.843	0.941	0.035	0.926	0.914	0.798	0.045	0.862	0.819
PAKRN21	0.906	0.032	0.916	0.900	0.942	0.027	0.954	0.923	0.873	0.065	0.857	0.851	0.952	0.032	0.923	0.927	0.834	0.049	0.885	0.853
EDN22	0.882	0.041	0.893	0.883	0.938	0.029	0.952	0.921	0.875	0.064	0.854	0.854	0.948	0.034	0.927	0.928	0.814	0.056	0.862	0.836
Selfreformer22	0.916	[illegible]	[illegible]	0.910	0.947	0.024	0.959	[illegible]	[illegible]	0.050	0.872	[illegible]	[illegible]	[illegible]	0.929	0.935	0.837	[illegible]	0.886	0.857
BBRF23	[illegible]	0.025	0.926	[illegible]	0.952	0.020	0.965	0.932	0.891	[illegible]	[illegible]	0.871	0.962	0.022	[illegible]	[illegible]	[illegible]	[illegible]	[illegible]	[illegible]
CSD23	0.843	0.046	0.891	0.843	0.915	0.037	0.944	0.890	0.846	0.071	0.855	0.824	0.926	0.044	0.921	0.894	0.790	0.061	0.859	0.812
MENet23	0.913	0.028	[illegible]	0.903	[illegible]	[illegible]	[illegible]	0.927	0.890	0.053	0.864	0.865	0.955	0.031	0.925	0.928	0.834	0.045	0.882	0.850
A2S24	0.843	0.047	0.890	0.849	0.920	0.033	0.949	0.898	0.857	0.066	0.858	0.837	0.932	0.038	0.926	0.905	0.792	0.062	0.862	0.821
Ours	0.902	0.029	0.926	0.892	0.937	[illegible]	0.953	0.927	0.896	0.041	[illegible]	0.879	0.953	0.028	0.937	0.944	0.846	0.035	0.893	0.854

4.3 Comparison with Other State-of-the-Art Methods

We compared our method against the ten most recent networks in the field: F3Net [22], LDF [9], MSFNet [2], PAKRN [23], SelfReformer [3], EDN [10], BBRF [1], MENet [24], CSD [25], and A2S-v3 [26]. Five evaluation metrics were adopted from LDF. Quantitative Evaluation: Evaluation of the model's performance was conducted using five benchmark datasets to gauge its effectiveness in salient object detection. Our approach demonstrated superior performance, as reflected in the superior metrics shown in Table 1. The precision-recall curves in Fig. 5 further corroborate the consistent outperformance of our method compared to other techniques.

Qualitative Evaluation: As depicted in Fig. 4, our method demonstrates superior object segmentation performance compared to other approaches. It can accurately delineate salient objects under various challenging conditions, including low-contrast scenes (10th row), fine-grained structures (3rd row), objects touching image boundaries (9th row), complex object boundaries (2nd row), small objects in cluttered backgrounds (4th and 8th rows), multiple salient objects (5th and 6th rows), and cluttered foregrounds and backgrounds (1st and 7th rows). The completeness and structural integrity of our predictions attest to the effectiveness of our architectural design. Overall, our method exhibits better segmentation quality and richer details than other techniques, showcasing its robust performance across diverse scenarios.

Table 2. Quantitative ablation study evaluating the contributions of each module. "Unrefine" denotes removal of the RECA-Transformer; "UnedgeLoss" replaces BAAL with cross-entropy and Dice losses; "RECA-Transformer" removes the PECA-U-Net module.

Methods	DUTS-TE				PASCAL-S				ECSSD			
	$F_\beta\uparrow$	$MAE\downarrow$	$E_\xi\uparrow$	$S_m\uparrow$	$F_\beta\uparrow$	$MAE\downarrow$	$E_\xi\uparrow$	$S_m\uparrow$	$F_\beta\uparrow$	$MAE\downarrow$	$E_\xi\uparrow$	$S_m\uparrow$
Unrefine	0.864	0.046	0.911	0.858	0.848	0.077	0.762	0.728	0.920	0.056	0.893	0.839
UnedgeLoss	0.875	0.036	0.922	0.866	0.868	0.044	0.886	0.849	0.931	0.033	0.922	0.902
RECA-Transformer	0.807	0.039	0.876	0.801	0.767	0.080	0.814	0.766	0.877	0.053	0.904	0.846
Our	**0.902**	**0.029**	**0.926**	**0.892**	**0.896**	**0.041**	**0.867**	**0.879**	**0.953**	**0.028**	**0.937**	**0.944**

5 Ablation Studies

In this section, we validate the proposed model via ablation experiments on both network architecture and loss function. The "Unrefine" variant removes the RECA-Transformer to isolate global context modeling, while "UnedgeLoss" replaces BAAL with Cross-entropy and Dice losses to assess the boundary loss. Additionally, the "RECA-Transformer" variant excludes the PECA-U-Net, isolating local feature extraction. Architecture ablation compares the full model with one using only PECA-U-Net for SOD, and loss ablations show that the boundary attention mechanism improves edge detail optimization, as evidenced by better evaluation metrics (see Table 2). Figure 6 displays ground truth and boundary maps from different settings, highlighting each module's contribution and overall efficacy. Overall, these studies confirm that the proposed architecture and loss function significantly enhance SOD performance.

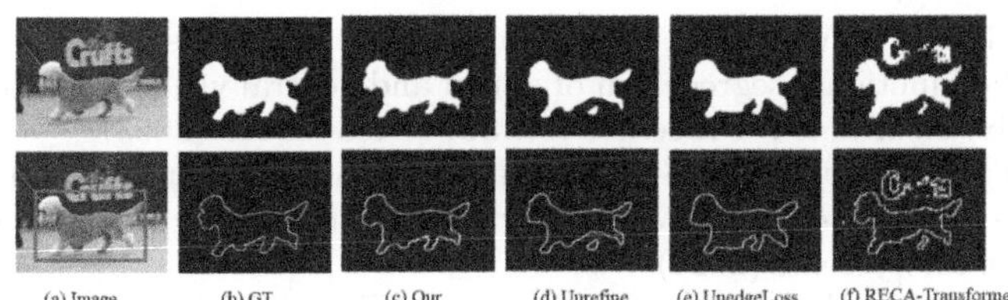

Fig. 6. (a) Original image and target object. (b) Ground truth (GT) image with its boundary map. (c) Our method with corresponding boundary map. (d) PECA-U-Net method alone with its boundary map. (e) Cross-entropy and Dice losses with its boundary map. (f) RECA-Transformer with its boundary map.

6 Conclusion

In this study, we propose a brain-inspired model that integrates PECA-U-Net, RECA-Transformer, and BAAL to enhance SOD performance. The PECA-U-Net efficiently localizes salient objects, while the RECA-Transformer refines boundaries using long-range dependencies. Our BAAL function emphasizes boundary errors during training. Experimental results on five benchmark datasets show that our model achieves superior performance on most datasets and remains highly competitive on the others, as evaluated by standard metrics.

Acknowledgments. This work was supported in part by the National Natural Science Foundation of China (Grant Nos. 62262030 and 62377011) and in part by the Natural Science Foundation of Jiangxi Province (Grant Nos. 20232BAB202021 and 20242BAB20047).

Disclosure of Interests. The authors declare no conflict of interest.

References

1. Ma, M., Xia, C., Xie, C., Chen, X., Li, J.: Boosting broader receptive fields for salient object detection. IEEE Trans. Image Process. **32**, 1026–1038 (2023)
2. Zhang, M., Liu, T., Piao, Y., Yao, S., Lu, S.: Auto-MSFNet: search multi-scale fusion network for salient object detection. In: Proceedings of the 29th ACM International Conference on Multimedia, pp. 667–676 (2021)
3. Y.K., Y., Lin, W.: SelfReformer: self-refined network with transformer for salient object detection (2022). arXiv:2205.11283 arXiv preprint
4. Siamak, K., Sorooshyari, H., Sheng, H., Vincent Poor: object recognition at higher regions of the ventral visual stream via dynamic inference. Front. Comput. Neurosci. **14**, 46 (2020)
5. Zhang, M., Bu, T., Hu, L.: A dynamic dual-processing object detection framework inspired by the brain's recognition mechanism. In: Proceedings of the IEEE/CVF International Conference on Computer Vision, pp. 6264–6274 (2023)
6. Yonelinas, A.P., Aly, M., Wang, W., Koen, J.D.: Recollection and familiarity: examining controversial assumptions and new directions. Hippocampus **20**(11), 1178–1194 (2010)
7. Choi, M., Han, K., Wang, X., Zhang, Y., Liu, Z.: A dual-stream neural network explains the functional segregation of dorsal and ventral visual pathways in human brains. Adv. Neural. Inf. Process. Syst. **36**, 50408–50428 (2023)
8. Ibrayev, T., Mukherjee, A.: Sai Aparna Aketi, and Kaushik Roy. Towards two-stream foveation-based active vision learning, IEEE Transactions on Cognitive and Developmental Systems (2024)
9. Wei, J., Wang, S., Wu, Z., Su, C., Huang, Q., Tian, Q.: Label decoupling framework for salient object detection. In: Proceedings of the IEEE/CVF Conference on Computer Vision and Pattern Recognition, pp. 13025–13034 (2020)
10. Yu-Huan, W., Liu, Y., Zhang, L., Cheng, M.-M., Ren, B.: EDN: salient object detection via extremely-downsampled network. IEEE Trans. Image Process. **31**, 3125–3136 (2022)
11. Liu, N., Luo, Z., Zhang, N., Han, J.: VST++: efficient and stronger visual saliency transformer. IEEE Trans. Pattern Anal. Mach. Intell. **46**(11), 7300–7316(2024)

12. Oktay, O., et al.: Attention U-Net: learning where to look for the pancreas. arXiv preprint arXiv:1804.03999 (2018)
13. Chen, J., et al.: TransUNet: transformers make strong encoders for medical image segmentation. arXiv preprint arXiv:2102.04306 (2021)
14. Hu, J., Shen, L., Sun, G.: Squeeze-and-excitation networks. In: Proceedings of the IEEE Conference on Computer Vision and Pattern Recognition, pp. 7132–7141 (2018)
15. Hou, Q., Zhou, D., Feng, J.: Coordinate attention for efficient mobile network design. In: Proceedings of the IEEE/CVF Conference on Computer Vision and Pattern Recognition, pp. 13713–13722 (2021)
16. Liu, Z., et al.: Swin Transformer: hierarchical vision transformer using shifted windows. In: Proceedings of the IEEE/CVF International Conference on Computer Vision, pp. 10012–10022 (2021)
17. Yan, Q., Xu, L., Shi, J., Jia, J.: Hierarchical saliency detection. In: Proceedings of the IEEE Conference on Computer Vision and Pattern Recognition, pp. 1155–1162 (2013)
18. Li, Y., Hou, X., Koch, C., Rehg, J.M., Yuille, A.L.: The secrets of salient object segmentation. In: Proceedings of the IEEE Conference on Computer Vision and Pattern Recognition, pp. 280–287 (2014)
19. Li, G., Yu, Y.: Visual saliency based on multiscale deep features. In: Proceedings of the IEEE Conference on Computer Vision and Pattern Recognition, pp. 5455–5463 (2015)
20. Yang, C., Zhang, L., Lu, H., Ruan, X., Yang, M.: Saliency detection via graph-based manifold ranking. In: Proceedings of the IEEE Conference on Computer Vision and Pattern Recognition, pp. 3166–3173 (2013)
21. Wang, L., et al.: Learning to detect salient objects with image-level supervision. In: Proceedings of the IEEE Conference on Computer Vision and Pattern Recognition, pp. 136–145 (2017)
22. Wei, J., Wang, S., Huang, Q.: F^3net: fusion, feedback and focus for salient object detection. Proc. AAAI Conf. Artif. Intell. **34**, 12321–12328 (2020)
23. Binwei, X., Liang, H., Liang, R., Chen, P.: Locate globally, segment locally: a progressive architecture with knowledge review network for salient object detection. Proc. AAAI Conf. Artif. Intell. **35**, 3004–3012 (2021)
24. Wang, Y., Wang, R., Fan, X., Wang, T., He, X.: Pixels, regions, and objects: multiple enhancement for salient object detection. In: Proceedings of the IEEE/CVF Conference on Computer Vision and Pattern Recognition, pp. 10031–10040 (2023)
25. Zhou, H., Qiao, B., Yang, L., Lai, J., Xie, X.: Texture-guided saliency distilling for unsupervised salient object detection. In: Proceedings of the IEEE/CVF Conference on Computer Vision and Pattern Recognition, pp. 7257–7267 (2023)
26. Yuan, Y., Liu, W., Gao, P., Dai, Q., Qin, J.: Unified unsupervised salient object detection via knowledge transfer (2024). arXiv:2404.14759 arXiv preprint

SDOD: Towards Reliable Object Detection Under Diverse Rainy Conditions with Deraining and Mutual Learning

Zhiyong Wei[1], Hongda Qin[1], and Ningjiang Chen[1,2](✉)

[1] School of Electrical Engineering, Guangxi University, Nanning 530004, China
[2] Graduate School, Guangxi University, Nanning 530004, China
chnj@gxu.edu.cn

Abstract. Object detection has achieved impressive performance under normal weather conditions. However, under rainy weather, raindrops and rainstreaks can significantly reduce image quality, leading to severe performance degradation of detectors. To address this issue, we propose an unsupervised domain adaptation (UDA) training framework, called Self-training with Deraining for Object Detection (SDOD), which leverages unlabeled rainy images to transfer knowledge from labeled normal images to improve the performance of detectors under rainy weather conditions. The proposed SDOD consists of a learnable lightweight deraining module and a cross-weather self-training architecture. Specifically, we introduce a deraining module as a weak augmentation to restore the rainy image, which is then input to the teacher model, thereby strengthening its ability to explore object features in the rain. Next, we employ mutual learning between the teacher model (taking images from rainy weather) and the student model (taking images from both normal and rainy weather), which iteratively optimizes the performance of both the detectors and the deraining module. Moreover, we designed a rainy object estimation strategy to produce more reliable pseudo-labels for rainy images. Extensive experiments conducted on rainy benchmarks demonstrate the superiority of our SDOD compared with existing UDA methods, showing detection performance improvements in rainy weather conditions.

Keywords: Computational imaging · Object detector · Rainy weather · Domain adaptation

1 Introduction

Over the past several years, object detectors [7,11] have had significant advancements through the development of convolutional neural networks (CNNs), which have been widely applied in fields such as autonomous driving, drone navigation, and smart robotics. Current detectors are designed under normal weather conditions as data collection is more feasible. However, the real world often encounters

P. Li et al. (Eds.): CGI 2025, LNCS 16508, pp. 78–91, 2026.
https://doi.org/10.1007/978-3-032-22264-0_7

adverse weather such as snow, fog, and rain. Among these, rainy conditions are particularly common, which significantly degrades the quality of images captured by visual sensors due to falling raindrops and streaks disrupting light transmission.

A natural approach to address this issue is to design a dedicated object detection architecture for rainy weather, incorporating specialized modules to process rain features and constructing large-scale rainy datasets [9,10]. However, such modifications to the model reduce the efficiency of deployment applications, and annotating rainy images is both time-consuming and labor-intensive. Another widely adopted method is to combine the draining with detection [3,15,26], which involves adding a rain removal module as the preprocessing step to eliminate raindrops from images. Nonetheless, standalone deraining operations often lead to image distortion and feature shift, resulting in limited performance improvements or even negative optimization. In contrast, recently proposed unsupervised domain adaptation (UDA) methods [1,17,20,29,30] can enhance the performance of detectors in rainy conditions using only unlabeled rainy images, allowing the model to adapt to rainy scenarios with domain gaps and achieve sustained optimization, thereby which has garnered significant attention due to its efficiency and effectiveness. Existing UDA methods for rainy conditions can be broadly categorized into adversarial learning and self-training. Adversarial learning [4,17,20,30] methods align the image-level and instance-level features from normal weather (source domain) and rainy weather (target domain) images to reduce the weather domain gap, which focuses on learning common object features across different weather conditions. However, the inherent instability of adversarial training has been shown to provide limited performance improvements for detectors and is prone to training failures. Self-training methods [1,29] introduce semi-supervised learning strategies to cross-weather scenarios, utilizing a teacher-student framework to learn domain-invariant features in the target weather domain and transferring instance knowledge from normal weather. Although existing methods have made significant progress in general scenarios, they often overlook the rain-specific characteristics inherent to rainy environments. Rainy scenes present unique challenges such as varying rainfall intensity, complex rain streak patterns, and atmospheric veiling effects. These diverse factors collectively exacerbate domain gaps and degrade object-level details, ultimately compromising the reliability of detectors in rainy conditions.

To address the aforementioned issues, we propose an end-to-end UDA training framework, named Self-training with Deraining for Object Detection (SDOD), which effectively leverages unlabeled rainy images to enhance detector performance under rainy conditions. Furthermore, it targets extracting features of objects in the rain to effectively transfer knowledge from normal weather conditions, avoiding bias induced by rain-specific characteristics. The proposed SDOD consists of a rain-specific teacher model and a cross-weather student model, as shown in Fig. 1. **First**, we employ a learnable lightweight deraining module (LDM) as the weak augmentation to process unlabeled rainy images which are input to the teacher model. The resulting clean features reduce the interference from rain-specific characteristics that improve the quality of generated pseudo-labels. **Second**, we designed a rainy object estimation (ROE) strategy to filter out unreliable samples in the pseudo-labels, thereby reducing the noisy supervision signals. **Third**, the deraining module iteratively optimizes its performance to achieve optimal deraining, while the student model continuously learns the features of the derained images, thus overcoming the limitations of performance improvement in conventional self-training methods. The SDOD addresses the problem of object detection in rainy conditions by innovatively integrating a deraining module with a self-training framework.

Extensive experiment results on multiple normal to rainy weather object detection benchmarks demonstrate the superiority of our method, improving detector performance under rainy conditions using only unlabeled rainy images and preventing premature training stagnation. Our contributions can be summarized as follows:

1) We propose a UDA self-training framework specifically tailored for rainy scenarios, which focuses on enhancing detection performance without the reliance on labeled rainy data. Compared to existing UDA methods, our approach mitigates the interference of rain-specific noise in images, enabling a more reliable transfer of knowledge from normal weather data.

2) We introduce a learnable lightweight deraining module that integrates the deraining task with weak-strong augmentation in the self-training and conduct a rainy object estimation. Through iterative joint training, we achieve interactive enhancement of both detection performance and deraining image quality, thereby mitigating the risk of premature training stagnation.

3) Extensive experiments conducted on both synthetic and real rainy benchmark datasets validate the superiority of our method compared with the existing UDA methods. The proposed SDOD can significantly improve detection performance in rainy conditions and simply integrate into any object detector as a plug-and-play framework.

2 Related Work

Fully supervised rainy weather detection involves creating rainy datasets by labeling rainy images or synthesizing rainy conditions for labeled normal images [9,10]. The annotations were inherited from the original normal images, allowing them to be directly used as training data for object detectors. The deraining in conjunction with the detection approach involves preprocessing images to remove rain before detection, with the focus on the selection and improvement of deraining networks [3,15,26].

UDA object detection is a wide method to address domain shift [1,17,20,29,30], aiming to bridge the domain gap between normal and rainy weather. A *et al.* [20] proposed a prior-based domain adversarial object detection framework, leveraging image formation principles to acquire weather-specific prior knowledge and construct new adversarial losses to mitigate the impact of rainy weather on detection performance. Zhou *et al.* [30] investigated a domain-specific adaptation setup to align features across different weather domains in required dimensions and introduced a self-adversarial disentanglement framework with additional supervision signals to enrich normal weather information for the domain generator. These methods effectively transfer knowledge from normal weather to rainy conditions by using feature alignment and disentanglement, significantly enhancing detector performance.

3 Proposed Method

Before demonstrating how our method transfers knowledge from labeled normal weather to rainy weather object detection, we first define the problem. We denote normal weather data as the normal domain $\mathcal{S} = (x_n^i, b_n^i, c_n^i)_{i=1}^{N_s}$, which contains N_s samples annotated with bounding boxes b_n and class labels c_n. Rainy weather data is defined as the rainy domain $\mathcal{T} = (x_r^i)_{i=1}^{N_t}$, which contains N_t samples without available annotations. Both normal weather and rainy weather share the same object categories. The proposed SDOD framework is illustrated in Fig. 1.

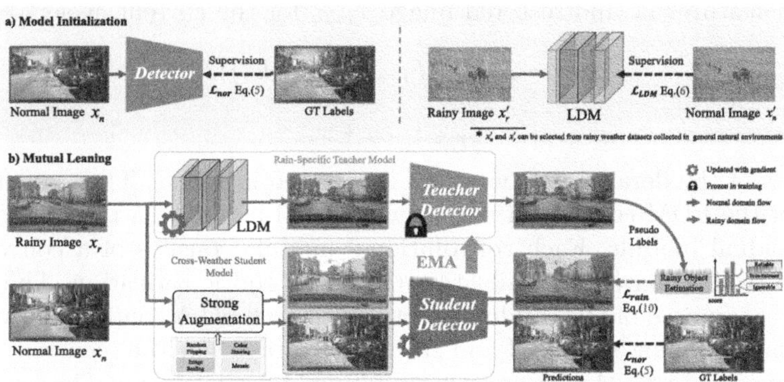

Fig. 1. The overview of our SDOD framework.

3.1 Lightweight Deraining Module

Generally, a rainy image can be conceptualized as a combination of a clean background image and a rain layer [6,14]. Existing deep learning-based deraining methods primarily utilize deep networks to map rainy images to their clean background counterparts, which has proven to be an effective approach. Given that the deraining operation serves as a data augmentation component within our training framework, we designed a learnable lightweight deraining module that balances training efficiency and deraining performance.

Different from the current complex deraining networks [3,26] based on encoder-decoder [16] or Transformers architectures [2], we utilize a simple recursive-residual module to achieve effective rain streak removal, and the recursive layers can be adjusted according to deployment scenarios to enhance application convenience, which similar to existing easy-to-use deraining networks [15].To the specific, we first input the rainy image x_r concat with the rain layer features r_{k-1} into the convolution module F_{conv1} at cycle $k-1$, resulting in the intermediate features f_k. This process can be defined by the following:

$$f_k = F_{conv1}(cat(x_r, r_{k-1})). \tag{1}$$

Subsequently, the previous state value h_{k-1} concat with the intermediate features f_k are input into the recurrent module F_{rec}. Here, we employ a classic Long Short-Term Memory (LSTM) as the recurrent module and set the current internal state v, which effectively removes the rain layer while maintaining a simpler network structure. These steps are formulated as follows:

$$h_k = F_{rec}(cat(f_k, h_{k-1}), v_{k-1}). \tag{2}$$

The current state values h_k from this stage are then input into the residual module F_{res}, and processed by the convolutional module F_{conv2}, yielding the rain layer features r_k and restored image x_{rr_k} for the current cycle:

$$r_k = F_{conv2}(F_{res}(cat(h_k, h_k)), \tag{3}$$

$$x_{rr\_k} = r_k + x_r. \tag{4}$$

Details of the deraining process are illustrated in Fig. 2. The network architecture of the LDM consists of two convolutional modules, a recurrent module, and a residual module. Each convolutional module consists of a convolutional layer, followed by batch normalization (BN) and ReLU activation. The residual module is composed of five residual blocks, with each block containing two convolutional layers, followed by BN and ReLU activation. For the recurrent module, we implement an LSTM with state gates formed by convolutional layers. All convolutional layers employ 3×3 kernels with 1×1 padding. As illustrated in Fig. 1, the LDM serves as a weak augmentation for rainy images in the SDOD framework effectively removing rain streaks. By setting multiple recursive iterations T it achieves multi-level progressive deraining.

3.2 Mutual Learning in Rainy Conditions

Model Initialization. In the self-training strategy, to enable the teacher model to generate effective pseudo-labels for rainy images during the mutual learning step, we initially train the detector using labeled normal weather data $\mathcal{S} = (x_n^i, b_n^i, c_n^i)_{i=1}^{N_s}$. This serves as the model initialization is supervised by the detection loss $\mathcal{L}_{nor}$, which can be defined as follows:

$$\mathcal{L}_{nor}(x_n, b_n, c_n) = \mathcal{L}_{reg}(x_n, b_n) + \mathcal{L}_{cls}(x_n, c_n), \tag{5}$$

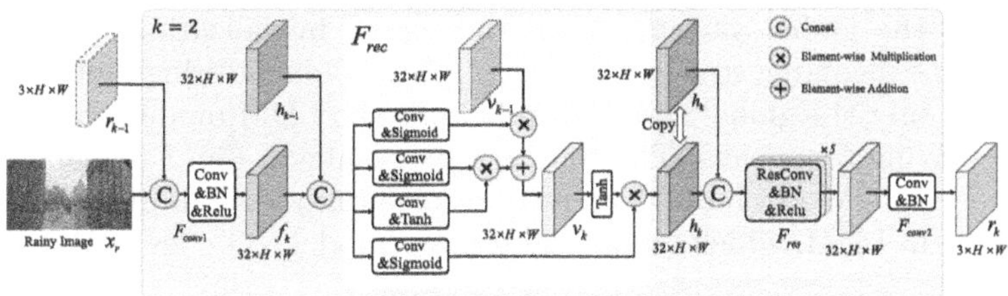

Fig. 2. One cycle of the processing structure of the LDM at $k = 2$. If the current cycle is the final one, *i.e.*, $k = T$, x_{rr} is obtained by performing an element-wise addition of r_k and x_r.

where $\mathcal{L}_{cls}$ denotes the classification loss, and $\mathcal{L}_{reg}$ represents the regression loss. The regression loss of the detector includes the Complete Intersection over Union (CIOU) [28] loss for bounding box regression, and the Distribution Focal Loss (DFL) [12] for distribution focusing.

In addition, the initialization of LDM requires paired rainy image x'_r and normal image x'_n for training. The loss function for this training can be defined as follows:

$$\mathcal{L}_{LDM} = -\sum_{k=1}^{T} \lambda_k SSIM(x'_r, x'_n), \tag{6}$$

where the $SSIM$ refers to the Structural Similarity Index Measure loss, T is the number of recursions in the LDM, and λ_k represents the corresponding weight at the recursion stage k. It is noteworthy that, due to the difficulty of obtaining paired rainy and normal images in real-world traffic scenarios, we trained our LDM using a general deraining dataset Rain100L [24]. This dataset comprises natural scene normal images x'_n with corresponding rainy counterparts x'_r, which does not include any images from the traffic scenes used in our object detection validation set. Consequently, the initialized LDM module learns only deraining features without incorporating any prior detection information.

LDM Optimization. The rain removal performance of the LDM is initially derived from the general deraining dataset. To enable the LDM to adapt to various rainy scenarios during mutual learning, we apply statistical optimization to guide the LDM in learning different rain layer information. Given the domain discrepancies across various rainfall intensities, we optimize the LDM by allowing only the global mean and variance in the batch normalization layers [18] to be updated while freezing the other LDM network layers. The update of the global mean is defined as follows:

$$\hat{\mu}_j = (1 - \rho) \cdot \hat{\mu}_{j-1} + \rho \cdot \mu_j, \tag{7}$$

where j denotes the training step, $\hat{\mu}_0$ is the global mean from the model initialization, μ is the mean of the incoming x_r batch from the rainy domain during mutual learning, and ρ represents the momentum term. The variance update follows a similar approach, as shown below:

$$\hat{\sigma}_j^2 = (1 - \rho) \cdot \hat{\sigma}_{j-1}^2 + \rho \cdot \sigma_j^2, \tag{8}$$

where $\hat{\sigma}_0^2$ is the global variance from the model initialization, and σ^2 is the variance of the incoming x_r batch from the rainy domain during mutual learning. By allowing only the global statistics to adapt, the LDM module can effectively adjust to varying rain layers. The comparative results in Fig. 3 demonstrate that the optimized LDM can more effectively restore rainy domain images compared with the origin LDM, which allows the teacher model to be less affected by rain noise.

Fig. 3. Comparison of deraining results for two rainy domain samples: (a) original rainy image. (b) LDM initialized with natural images, and (c) LDM optimized with the self-training framework. The improvement in deraining performance is visible within the red bounding boxes.

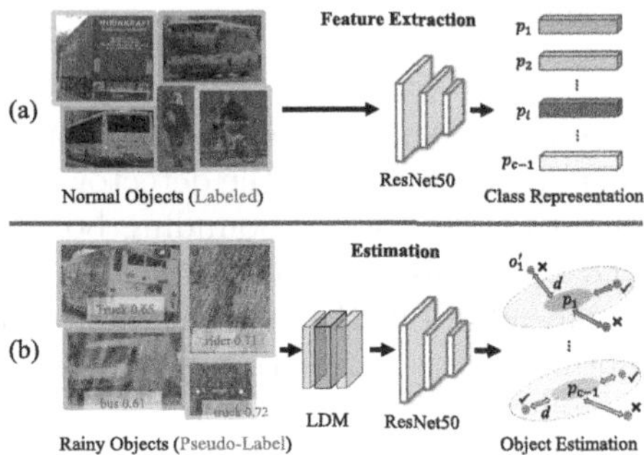

Fig. 4. (a) Perform feature extraction on labeled source domain objects to acquire their respective class representations. (b) Rainy objects from pseudo-labels may have classification errors, *e.g.*, misclassifying a bus as a truck. These class representations are then estimated, ✓ " indicates the object to be retained, while ✗ " indicates the object to be ignored.

Rainy Object Estimation and Student Optimization. In the teacher model, the LDM significantly reduces noise in the pseudo-labels by removing rain streaks from rainy images. Additionally, we apply Non-Maximum Suppression (NMS) to eliminate redundant bounding boxes and set the threshold $\{\delta_1, \delta_2\}$ of confidence score δ to categorize pseudo-labels into three groups: *reliable* ($\delta \in (\delta_2, 1.0)$), *to-be-estimated* ($\delta \in (\delta_1, \delta_2]$), and *ignorable* ($\delta \in (0.0, \delta_1]$). *Reliable* pseudo-labels are directly used as supervision signals for the student model, while *ignorable* ones are discarded. For the *to-be-estimated* pseudo-labels, an object estimation mechanism is proposed for further processing.

While the thresholded labels are generally reliable in object detection, they often suffer from classification confusion, *e.g.*, misclassifying a bus as a truck, as shown in Fig. 4 (b). Since object semantics are similar between normal and rainy domains, we apply object estimation to refine the *to-be-estimated* labels. First, we input the labeled normal domain object into an initialized ResNet50 network and extract the class representation o_i for i-th class, as shown in Fig. 4 (a). We compute the average class representation p_i based on the objects belonging to that i-th class. Next, we input the rainy domain object with the *to-be-estimated* label into ResNet50 to obtain the class representation o_i'. Finally, we compute the cosine distance d between the rainy object class representation o_i' and the corresponding average class representation p_i for estimation:

$$d = 1 - \frac{o_i' \cdot p_i}{\|o_i'\| \, \|p_i\|}. \tag{9}$$

By setting a threshold ω, the corresponding objects $d(o_i', p_i) < \omega$ in the pseudo-labels are classified as *reliable*, and the remaining objects do not utilize their classification signal. In the training process, the object estimation step only requires a forward pass, which avoids introducing extra computational costs. In this way, we can define the loss for the rainy data in the student model as follows:

$$\mathcal{L}_{rain}(x_r, b_r', c_r') = \mathcal{L}_{reg}(x_r, b_r') + \mathcal{L}_{cls}(x_r, c_r'), \tag{10}$$

where b_r' and c_r' are the bounding box and classification pseudo-labels filtered by rainy object estimation. ROE enhances pseudo-label reliability by measuring class-level semantic similarity between objects across different domains. To further reduce classification errors, we adopt threshold-based filtering strategies.

Teacher Update. During the optimization step, the performance of the student model is enhanced. We use the network parameters of the student model to iteratively update the teacher model and synchronize the improvement in the quality of pseudo-labels for rainy images. We use the Exponential Moving Average (EMA) for this operation, defined by the following:

$$\theta_j^t \leftarrow \alpha\theta_{j-1}^t + (1-\alpha)\theta_j^s, \tag{11}$$

where θ^t and θ^s represent the network weights of the teacher model and the student model, respectively, and α is the smoothing coefficient.

Full Objective. In mutual learning, the overall loss for our proposed SDOD framework can be summarized as follows:

$$\mathcal{L}_{total} = \lambda_{nor}\mathcal{L}_{nor} + \lambda_{rain}\mathcal{L}_{rain}, \tag{12}$$

where λ_{nor} and λ_{rain} are the weights used to balance the corresponding losses. We employ $\mathcal{L}_{total}$ to optimize the detector in the student model, while the teacher model is updated using the aforementioned EMA method.

4 Experiments

4.1 Datasets and Implementation Details

To validate the adaptation performance of our method under diverse rainy conditions, we designed evaluation rain scenarios that include the normal-to-single and the normal-to-compound rainy domains. For the normal-to-single rainy domain, the experiments encompass Cityscapes [5] $\rightarrow$ Rainy-Cityscapes$_1$ [8], Cityscapes $\rightarrow$ Rainy-Cityscapes$_2$ [20], Daytime-sunny [25] $\rightarrow$ Dusk-rainy, and Daytime-sunny $\rightarrow$ Night-rainy. For the normal-to-compound rainy domains, we use Daytime-sunny as the normal domain and combine Daytime-sunny and Night-rainy as the compound rainy domain.

In the experiment, we used YOLOv8-S [11] as the benchmark detector because it is a widely used real-time detector, and we followed the settings of the original version. All training and validation images were uniformly resized to 640×640. For the hyperparameter settings, we set $\lambda_k = 0.2 \times k$ in (6) , following the approach outlined in [15], and set $\omega = 0.6$ of the distance d in (9). The deraining module recursion cycles $T = 4$, and the threshold $\{\delta_1, \delta_2\}$ of pseudo labels is set to 0.2 and 0.8. we defined $\alpha = 0.9996$ in (11), $\rho = 0.1$ in (7) and (8), and $\lambda_{nor} = 1.0$ and $\lambda_{rain} = 0.1$ in (12). In the initialization step, We adopt a Stochastic Gradient Descent (SGD) optimizer during training for 100 epochs, the learning rate is set to 1×10^{-2}. The batch size is set to 16 for all experiments. In the cross-weather training step, we set the learning rate 1×10^{-4} for 20 epochs. We evaluate the adaptation performance using the mean Average Precision (mAP) metric at a IoU threshold of 0.5.

4.2 Ablation Study

We conducted a series of ablation experiments in normal to rainy scenarios, *i.e.*, Daytime- sunny $\rightarrow$ Dusk-rainy (and Daytime-sunny $\rightarrow$ Night-rainy), to validate the effectiveness of each component of our method. The detailed results are presented in Table 1. Firstly, we observed that incorporating the LDM as an image preprocessing step into the original detection pipeline (denoted as **LDM**) increased to 31.8% (19.8%) mAP, demonstrating that a deraining network trained on general rainy datasets can restore rainy images and enhance detector performance. Then employing the original teacher-student framework with the rainy object estimation (denoted as **TS + ROE**) improved the performance to 33.5% (21.6%) mAP, highlighting that naive self-training alone has limited efficacy in bridging the substantial domain gap between normal and rainy scenarios. Incorporating the LDM as an image preprocessing step in the detector trained with the teacher-student framework (denoted as **LDM + TS**) further elevated the performance to 40.6% (26.9%) mAP. Our comprehensive method, which integrates the LDM into the self-training framework with strong and weak augmentations and applies rainy object estimation (denoted as **LDM + TS + ROE**), achieved a performance of 43.3% (28.0%) mAP.

4.3 Experimental Results

Normal-to-Single Rainy Domains. The results on Cityscapes $\rightarrow$ Rainy-Cityscapes and Cityscapes $\rightarrow$ Rainy-Cityscapes are shown in Table 2 and Table 3. The comparative results on Daytime-sunny $\rightarrow$ Dusk-rainy and Night-rainy

Table 1. Ablation results of our proposed SDOD for adapting Daytime-sunny → Dusk-rainy ($S \rightarrow D$) and Daytime-sunny → Night-rainy ($S \rightarrow N$)

Method	LDM	TS	ROE	$S \rightarrow D$	$S \rightarrow N$
Baseline	-	-	-	27.5	13.7
Proposed	✓			31.8	19.8
		✓	✓	33.5	21.6
	✓	✓		40.6	26.9
	✓	✓	✓	**43.3**	**28.0**

Table 2. The results (%) on the Rainy-Cityscapes$_1$ validation set.

Method	person	rider	car	truck	bus	motor	bicycle	mAP
FRCNN [7]	23.2	55.0	35.7	2.1	51.1	10.9	27.7	29.4
SCL [6]	27.0	57.9	50.3	10.0	67.9	13.9	33.9	37.3
SAD [17]	29.3	61.0	52.7	19.2	68.2	**26.2**	34.1	41.5
YOLOv8 [21]	27.3	60.8	54.3	18.6	55.1	5.1	28.7	35.4
R-YOLO [21]	30.4	68.1	61.6	11.7	60.5	4.0	29.7	38.0
SSDA [29]	29.5	67.1	60.0	20.4	60.8	3.6	33.5	39.3
AT [13]	31.5	65.2	59.0	17.9	64.2	5.8	37.1	40.1
CMT [1]	33.2	67.9	61.4	15.2	**69.3**	6.1	37.8	41.6
SDOD (ours)	**37.3**	**68.2**	**66.8**	**25.0**	**69.3**	8.5	**37.5**	**44.6**

are shown in Table 4 and Table 5. We compared our SDOD with previously proposed UDA methods, citing the results from the original papers. Additionally, we reproduced recent UDA methods [1,13,21,29] within the benchmark detector [11] for comparison, as these methods had not been evaluated in this rainy context. This demonstrates the effectiveness of our method in enhancing detector performance for cross-domain between normal and rainy weather conditions.

Normal-to-Compound Rainy Domain. For the experiments on the normal-to-compound rainy domain, we trained on the normal and compound-rainy domain and validated on the compound-rainy domain. Table 6 shows the validation results on the compound-rainy domain, where the proposed SDOD achieved the best performance with 36.6% mAP, outperforming the recent method CMT [1] by 2.1%. This demonstrates that our method can assist the detector in generalizing in variable rainy scenarios (Fig. 5).

Table 3. The results (%) on the Rainy-Cityscapes$_2$ validation set.

Method	person	rider	car	truck	bus	train	motor	bicycle	mAP
FRCNN [7]	21.6	19.5	38.0	12.6	30.1	24.1	12.9	15.4	21.8
DAF [4]	26.9	28.1	50.6	23.2	39.3	4.7	17.1	20.2	26.3
DNN [6]	27.1	30.3	50.7	23.1	39.4	18.5	21.2	24.0	29.3
SW [17]	29.6	38.0	52.1	27.9	49.8	28.7	24.1	25.4	34.5
PDA [20]	31.3	34.8	57.8	29.3	48.6	34.4	25.4	27.3	36.1
YOLOv8 [11]	23.5	13.9	45.4	17.6	26.0	18.7	12.9	18.4	22.1
R-YOLO [21]	33.5	31.3	59.6	30.8	**55.7**	**34.5**	21.5	28.3	36.9
SSDA [29]	29.1	38.2	62.3	32.6	54.6	27.5	22.3	30.2	37.1
AT [13]	43.3	46.4	66.4	33.2	50.6	17.4	23.2	29.1	38.7
CMT [1]	43.9	46.4	66.9	37.5	52.6	24.4	22.6	29.2	40.4
SDOD (ours)	**46.2**	**50.4**	**68.5**	**38.1**	53.5	31.8	**26.1**	**33.3**	**43.5**

Table 4. The results (%) on adaptation from Daytime-sunny to Dusk-rainy.

Method	bus	bike	car	motor	person	rider	truck	mAP
FRCNN [4]	38.6	21.5	51.7	12.0	19.7	13.6	40.9	28.3
DAF [4]	43.6	27.5	52.3	16.1	28.5	21.7	44.8	33.5
SW [17]	40.0	22.8	51.4	15.4	26.3	20.3	44.2	31.5
ICCR [23]	43.8	28.5	52.4	22.7	29.2	21.9	45.6	34.9
VDD [22]	47.9	**33.2**	55.1	**26.1**	30.5	**23.8**	48.1	37.8
YOLOv8 [21]	33.5	8.4	67.6	6.5	21.8	11.1	43.7	27.5
SSDA [29]	45.3	18.6	73.7	17.2	41.0	18.8	50.5	37.9
R-YOLO [21]	43.0	16.4	74.5	21.5	41.4	22.2	51.4	38.6
AT [13]	47.7	18.2	74.3	18.3	39.1	20.5	53.7	38.8
CMT [1]	46.7	17.9	74.0	21.3	45.7	17.4	56.4	39.9
SDOD (ours)	**51.3**	21.5	**76.8**	24.9	**47.9**	22.9	**57.6**	**43.3**

Fig. 5. Qualitative results of Daytime-sunny → Dusk-rainy/Night-rainy set-up.

Table 5. The results (%) on adaptation from Daytime-sunny to Night-rainy.

Method	bus	bike	car	motor	person	rider	truck	mAP
FRCNN [7]	23.4	13.3	31.8	1.5	10.2	10.9	23.2	16.3
CT [27]	22.4	9.7	27.4	0.6	9.3	9.3	13.4	13.1
SCL [19]	20.0	9.2	33.2	0.3	11.9	10.6	26.4	15.9
DAF [4]	23.8	12.0	37.7	0.2	14.9	4.0	29.0	17.4
SW [17]	24.7	10.0	33.7	0.6	13.5	10.4	29.1	17.4
ICCR [23]	32.5	12.1	36.2	1.3	16.1	17.0	29.3	20.6
VDD [22]	34.8	**15.6**	38.6	**10.5**	18.7	**17.3**	30.6	23.7
YOLOv8 [21]	24.8	3.8	33.4	0.3	8.8	4.0	21.2	13.7
SSDA [29]	43.5	7.4	49.3	6.1	13.2	7.0	39.3	23.7
R-YOLO [21]	39.8	9.9	53.4	1.8	19.7	7.4	34.9	23.8
AT [13]	40.9	9.5	54.8	2.4	19.6	9.6	35.9	24.7
CMT [1]	40.6	10.8	55.9	5.4	21.6	8.6	**37.7**	25.8
SDOD (ours)	**41.8**	11.7	**57.9**	9.0	**24.8**	15.1	35.7	**28.0**

Table 6. The results (%) on the Compound-rainy scene.

Method	bus	bike	car	motor	person	rider	truck	mAP
FRCNN [7]	35.1	19.3	44.0	8.8	17.5	12.8	37.7	25.0
DAF [4]	35.9	18.3	44.2	10.1	22.0	17.9	39.9	26.9
CT [27]	31.3	15.4	41.7	8.4	19.1	15.3	32.3	23.4
SCL [19]	32.7	19.7	44.9	10.5	22.9	18.5	38.3	26.8
SW [17]	36.9	20.7	45.1	6.6	23.1	16.9	41.5	27.3
ICCR [23]	38.8	20.4	44.6	11.7	24.7	15.4	41.6	28.2
VDD [22]	41.8	**26.8**	48.6	**17.9**	27.0	**22.2**	44.1	32.6
YOLOv8 [21]	33.1	8.8	55.5	6.2	19.8	8.5	40.4	24.6
R-YOLO [21]	40.6	19.5	66.9	7.8	29.5	17.3	44.7	32.3
SSDA [29]	43.3	19.4	65.5	7.8	32.5	14.7	47.4	32.9
AT [13]	41.2	19.5	65.2	11.4	30.5	14.7	50.8	33.3
CMT [1]	45.4	17.2	65.8	13.4	29.5	17.5	**52.8**	34.5
SDOD (ours)	**46.8**	20.5	**67.8**	15.8	**34.5**	19.6	51.0	**36.6**

5 Conclusion

In this work, we for the first time propose an effective UDA object detection method in rainy conditions that combines deraining augmentation and self-training. We introduce a learnable deraining module that enables the teacher model in the self-training framework to generate high-quality pseudo-labels. Through mutual learning, our method iteratively enhances detection performance in rainy conditions. We conducted extensive experimental evaluations on both synthetic and real rainy datasets encompassing multiple scenarios. Moreover, SDOD permits the potential extension of LDM for other weather patterns (e.g., fog/snow) through module replacement or retraining, facilitating multi-scenario deployment without full architectural redesign.

References

1. Cao, S., Joshi, D., Gui, L.Y., Wang, Y.X.: Contrastive mean teacher for domain adaptive object detectors. In: Proceedings of the IEEE/CVF Conference on Computer Vision and Pattern Recognition, pp. 23839–23848 (2023)
2. Chen, S., Ye, T., Bai, J., Chen, E., Shi, J., Zhu, L.: Sparse sampling transformer with uncertainty-driven ranking for unified removal of raindrops and rain streaks. In: Proceedings of the IEEE/CVF International Conference on Computer Vision, pp. 13106–13117 (2023)
3. Chen, X., Li, H., Li, M., Pan, J.: Learning a sparse transformer network for effective image deraining. In: Proceedings of the IEEE/CVF Conference on Computer Vision and Pattern Recognition, pp. 5896–5905 (2023)
4. Chen, Y., Li, W., Sakaridis, C., Dai, D., Van Gool, L.: Domain adaptive faster R-CNN for object detection in the wild. In: Proceedings of the IEEE/CVF Conference on Computer Vision and Pattern Recognition, pp. 3339–3348 (2018)
5. Cordts, M., et al.: The cityscapes dataset for semantic urban scene understanding. In: Proceedings of the IEEE/CVF Conference on Computer Vision and Pattern Recognition, pp. 3213–3223 (2016)
6. Fu, X., Huang, J., Zeng, D., Huang, Y., Ding, X., Paisley, J.: Removing rain from single images via a deep detail network. In: Proceedings of the IEEE/CVF Conference on Computer Vision and Pattern Recognition, pp. 3855–3863 (2017)
7. Girshick, R.: Fast R-CNN. In: Proceedings of the IEEE International Conference on Computer Vision, pp. 1440–1448 (2015)
8. Hu, X., Fu, C.W., Zhu, L., Heng, P.A.: Depth-attentional features for single-image rain removal. In: Proceedings of the IEEE/CVF Conference on Computer Vision and Pattern Recognition (2019)
9. Huang, S.C., Hoang, Q.V., Le, T.H.: SFA-Net: a selective features absorption network for object detection in rainy weather conditions. IEEE Trans. Neural Netw. Learn. Syst. (2022)
10. Huang, S.C., Jaw, D.W., Hoang, Q.V., Le, T.H.: 3FL-Net: an efficient approach for improving performance of lightweight detectors in rainy weather conditions. IEEE Trans. Intell. Transp. Syst. **24**(4), 4293–4305 (2023)
11. Jocher, G., Chaurasia, A., Qiu, J.: Ultralytics YOLO/V8.1.0 - YOLOV8 oriented bounding boxes (2023)
12. Li, X., et al.: Generalized focal loss: learning qualified and distributed bounding boxes for dense object detection. Adv. Neural. Inf. Process. Syst. **33**, 21002–21012 (2020)
13. Li, Y.J., et al.: Cross-domain adaptive teacher for object detection. In: Proceedings of the IEEE/CVF Conference on Computer Vision and Pattern Recognition, pp. 7581–7590 (2022)
14. Qian, R., Tan, R.T., Yang, W., Su, J., Liu, J.: Attentive generative adversarial network for raindrop removal from a single image. In: Proceedings of the IEEE/CVF Conference on Computer Vision and Pattern Recognition, pp. 2482–2491 (2018)

15. Ren, D., Zuo, W., Hu, Q., Zhu, P., Meng, D.: Progressive image deraining networks: a better and simpler baseline. In: Proceedings of the IEEE/CVF Conference on Computer Vision and Pattern Recognition, pp. 3937–3946 (2019)
16. Ronneberger, O., Fischer, P., Brox, T.: U-Net: convolutional networks for biomedical image segmentation. In: Navab, N., Hornegger, J., Wells, W.M., Frangi, A.F. (eds.) MICCAI 2015. LNCS, vol. 9351, pp. 234–241. Springer, Cham (2015). https://doi.org/10.1007/978-3-319-24574-4_28
17. Saito, K., Ushiku, Y., Harada, T., Saenko, K.: Strong-weak distribution alignment for adaptive object detection. In: Proceedings of the IEEE/CVF Conference on Computer Vision and Pattern Recognition, pp. 6956–6965 (2019)
18. Schneider, S., Rusak, E., Eck, L., Bringmann, O., Brendel, W., Bethge, M.: Improving robustness against common corruptions by covariate shift adaptation. Adv. Neural. Inf. Process. Syst. **33**, 11539–11551 (2020)
19. Shen, Z., Maheshwari, H., Yao, W., Savvides, M.: SCL: towards accurate domain adaptive object detection via gradient detach based stacked complementary losses (2019). arXiv:1911.02559 arXiv preprint
20. Sindagi, V.A., Oza, P., Yasarla, R., Patel, V.M.: Prior-based domain adaptive object detection for hazy and rainy conditions. In: European Conference on Computer Vision, pp. 763–780. Springer (2020)
21. Wang, L., Qin, H., Zhou, X., Lu, X., Zhang, F.: R-YOLO: a robust object detector in adverse weather. IEEE Trans. Instrum. Meas. **72**, 1–11 (2022)
22. Wu, A., Liu, R., Han, Y., Zhu, L., Yang, Y.: Vector-decomposed disentanglement for domain-invariant object detection. In: Proceedings of the IEEE/CVF International Conference on Computer Vision, pp. 9342–9351 (2021)
23. Xu, C.D., Zhao, X.R., Jin, X., Wei, X.S.: Exploring categorical regularization for domain adaptive object detection. In: Proceedings of the IEEE/CVF Conference on Computer Vision and Pattern Recognition, pp. 11724–11733 (2020)
24. Yang, W., Tan, R.T., Feng, J., Liu, J., Guo, Z., Yan, S.: Deep joint rain detection and removal from a single image. In: Proceedings of the IEEE/CVF Conference on Computer Vision and Pattern Recognition, pp. 1357–1366 (2017)
25. Yu, F., Xian, W., Chen, Y., Liu, F., Liao, M., Madhavan, V., Darrell, T., et al.: BDD100K: a diverse driving video database with scalable annotation tooling
26. Zamir, S.W., et al.: Multi-stage progressive image restoration. In: Proceedings of the IEEE/CVF Conference on Computer Vision and Pattern Recognition, pp. 14821–14831 (2021)
27. Zhao, G., Li, G., Xu, R., Lin, L.: Collaborative training between region proposal localization and classification for domain adaptive object detection. In: European Conference on Computer Vision, pp. 86–102. Springer (2020)
28. Zheng, Z., Wang, P., Liu, W., Li, J., Ye, R., Ren, D.: Distance-IOU Loss: faster and better learning for bounding box regression. In: Proceedings of the AAAI Conference on Artificial Intelligence, vol. 34, pp. 12993–13000 (2020)
29. Zhou, H., Jiang, F., Lu, H.: SSDA-YOLO: semi-supervised domain adaptive yolo for cross-domain object detection. Comput. Vis. Image Underst. **220**, 103649 (2023)
30. Zhou, Q., Gu, Q., Pang, J., Lu, X., Ma, L.: Self-adversarial disentangling for specific domain adaptation. IEEE Trans. Pattern Anal. Mach. Intell. (2023)

An Improved Small Object Detection Method for Shuttlecock Activity Analysis

Xin Ma[1,2], Guiren Zhou[1,2], Haijun Huang[1,2], Jianwen Chen[1,2], Xiaoxu Shi[4], Yuxin Hong[1,2], Meng Sun[1,2], Xiao Zhang[1,2,3], Bo Yang[1,2], and Jianlin Zhu[1,2](✉)

[1] School of Computer Science (School of Artificial Intelligence), South-Central Minzu University, Wuhan 430074, China
Jianlin.Zhu@mail.scuec.edu.cn
[2] Hubei Provincial Engineering Research Center for Intelligent Management of Manufacturing Enterprises, South-Central Minzu University, Wuhan 430074, China
[3] School of Computer Science and Technology, University of Science and Technology of China, Hefei 230026, China
[4] College of Computer Science (College of Software, College of Artificial Intelligence), Inner Mongolia University, 235 Daxue Xi Road, Saihan District, Hohhot 010010, Inner Mongolia, China

Abstract. In the task of shuttlecock tracking and strike counting, existing methods suffer from significant limitations in detection accuracy and tracking stability due to the small size and high speed of the target. Furthermore, the lack of a dedicated shuttlecock dataset further restricts the improvement of model performance. To address these issues, this paper proposes a novel network model that integrates a small object detection branch and a convolutional attention mechanism to enhance the detection and tracking capabilities of shuttlecock targets. Specifically, a small object detection branch is added to the detection framework to strengthen high-resolution feature extraction, and a convolutional block attention module is introduced to enhance the representation of key features under complex backgrounds and scale variations. Meanwhile, a dedicated shuttlecock dataset is constructed through real-scene recording and rigorous filtering, effectively alleviating the shortage of training data. Experimental results demonstrate that the proposed method achieves significant improvements in detection precision, recall, and overall mAP metrics, with the overall mAP increasing by approximately 6% points compared to the baseline model, while maintaining high detection speed. Additionally, a Web-based client system is developed to encapsulate the model and visualize the results, further verifying the feasibility and efficiency of the proposed approach in real-world applications. This work provides new insights and technical support for small object detection and intelligent sports analysis.

Keywords: Shuttlecock tracking · Strike counting · Object detection branch · Convolutional block attention module · Small Intelligent sports analysis

P. Li et al. (Eds.): CGI 2025, LNCS 16508, pp. 92–103, 2026.
https://doi.org/10.1007/978-3-032-22264-0_8

1 Introduction

As a traditional Chinese sport, shuttlecock kicking is widely popular in universities and major competitions, playing an important role in promoting national culture and enhancing cultural identity [1]. The number of kicks is a key indicator for evaluating training performance and determining competition outcomes. However, current shuttlecock kicking instruction and competitions still heavily rely on manual counting, which often leads to inaccuracies and inefficiencies, especially in long-duration or high-intensity scenarios.

With the rapid development of technologies such as artificial intelligence, sports technology innovation has become a critical driving force in building China into a strong sporting nation [2]. Nevertheless, the development of sports technology in China is still in its early stages [3]. For example, feedback collected from the Shuttlecock Kicking Association at South-Central Minzu University through its smart coaching system shows that among 117 suggestions, the demand for intelligent counting assistance was among the most frequent [4], indicating a strong need for automation.

To address these challenges, this paper proposes an automatic detection and counting method for shuttlecock kicking. Specifically: (1) an improved detection framework is designed by adding a small-object detection branch for enhanced high-resolution feature extraction, and incorporating convolutional block attention modules to improve performance; (2) a high-quality shuttlecock kicking dataset is constructed to compensate for the lack of public datasets; and (3) a web-based interactive system is developed to visualize counting results in real time, facilitating practical deployment.

2 Related Work

Existing research on strike counting and target tracking in sports training and competition mainly falls into two categories:

IoT-based approaches deploy sensors on sports equipment or athletes to accurately perceive strike actions. For example, the Tac-Trainer system [5] and the smart shuttlecock system [6] utilize MEMS motion sensors and mobile applications to collect and visualize data, thereby improving training efficiency and teaching quality. However, such methods are limited by hardware deployment costs and application scenarios, making them less suitable for open or natural environments.

Computer vision-based methods leverage the advantages of deep learning in object detection and tracking [7], enabling automatic analysis of strike behaviors in sports videos. Popular models such as YOLO [8] and Fast R-CNN are widely used for object detection, while algorithms like DeepSORT [9] support efficient multi-object tracking. Researchers have also constructed several sports video datasets, such as Soccer-ISSIA [10] and NCAA [11], to train and evaluate vision models. However, most existing studies focus on racket-based sports like table tennis and badminton. There is a lack of targeted research on shuttlecock kicking, which involves fast motion and small-sized foot-based targets.

Therefore, there remains a pressing need for specialized methods to achieve automatic tracking and strike counting tailored to the characteristics of shuttlecock sports.

3 Shuttlecock Detection and Counting

3.1 Network Structure

To address the limitations of conventional detection networks in handling small object detection tasks, this study proposes a strategic optimization of the network architecture. Firstly, to enhance the detection capability for small-scale targets, an additional small-object detection branch is introduced. This branch operates on a high-resolution feature map with a size of 80×80, extracted from the earlier stages of the backbone network. By incorporating convolutional modules and feature enhancement mechanisms, the network captures finer-grained details, effectively compensating for the deficiencies of conventional networks in small object detection. Secondly, considering the practical challenges where targets occupy extremely small proportions of the image and undergo significant scale variations, a lightweight attention mechanism [12] is incorporated into the feature extraction process to improve the precision of feature representation. This mechanism integrates channel-wise and spatial-wise attention, enhancing important features while suppressing irrelevant information. It enables the network to dynamically adjust the focus areas of feature maps during training, thereby emphasizing crucial target features. Under complex backgrounds and rapid scale changes, this approach significantly improves the model's perception and localization capabilities. The overall optimization maintains high inference speed while further enhancing detection accuracy and stability for small objects (Fig. 1).

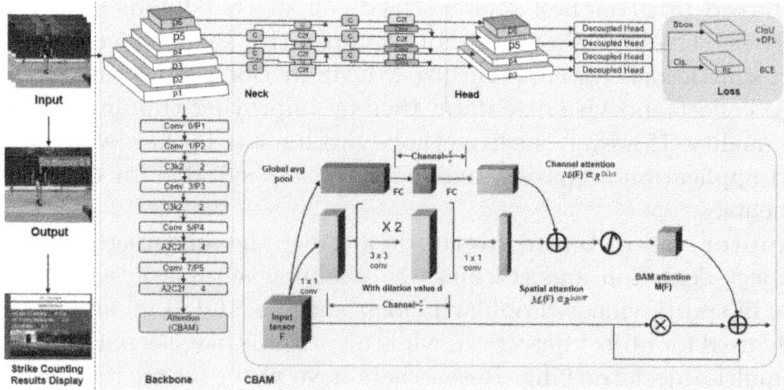

Fig. 1. Overall Architecture Diagram.

Small-Object Detection Branch Design. In the shallow layers of the network, the model can clearly distinguish object contours and capture fine-grained details, which is beneficial for detecting small-scale objects. As the network depth increases, the resolution of feature maps decreases, and the extracted features become more abstract and representative [13], but it becomes more difficult to directly recognize original image information. In standard object detection tasks, multi-scale detection is typically performed using feature maps of 80×80, 40×40, and 20×20 resolutions, which are responsible for detecting targets of various sizes such as those larger than 8×8, 16×16, and 32×32 pixels, respectively. However, when dealing with smaller or faster-moving targets, relying solely on these original-scale features often results in missed detections or localization errors. To address this, an additional detection branch is introduced in the detection head, leveraging high-resolution shallow-layer features with an 80×80 feature map for prediction. A fine-grained convolutional module is also incorporated during feature extraction to enhance the capture of information in target regions. This strategy significantly improves the recall and localization accuracy for tiny objects while maintaining the overall detection speed (Fig. 2).

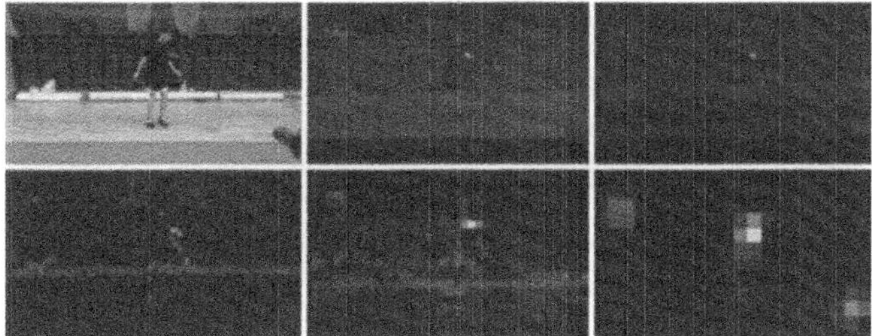

Fig. 2. Visualization of Feature Maps Across Layers.

Fine-Grained Feature Enhancement Mechanism. Due to the shuttlecock's typically small proportion in the image and its frequent dramatic scale changes, conventional detection networks often struggle to extract sufficient target features, leading to a sharp decline in detection accuracy. To address this challenge, this study incorporates a fine-grained feature enhancement mechanism that combines channel importance evaluation and spatial attention guidance. This mechanism enables the network to dynamically adjust the weights of input features, selectively focusing on critical parts of the data rather than treating all information equally. Through a two-stage process—first emphasizing key channels, then refining spatial regions—the mechanism significantly enhances feature expression for small target areas while effectively suppressing background noise. As a plug-and-play module, it can be seamlessly integrated into existing CNN architectures with minimal additional computational overhead, yet it substantially improves the model's detection and localization performance for small, fast-moving targets in complex scenarios.

3.2 Multi-component Loss Framework

To enhance detection performance, the proposed loss function considers three components: object confidence, classification accuracy, and bounding box regression. The loss is defined as:

$$\mathcal{L} = \mathcal{L}_{conf} + \mathcal{L}_{cls} + \mathcal{L}_{bbox} \tag{1}$$

where:

- $\mathcal{L}_{conf}$: confidence loss for objectness prediction,
- $\mathcal{L}_{cls}$: classification loss for category prediction,
- $\mathcal{L}_{bbox}$: bounding box regression loss.

The confidence loss considers both object and background regions:

$$\mathcal{L}_{conf} = \sum_{i \in \mathrm{obj}} (C_i - \hat{C}_i)^2 + \lambda_{noobj} \sum_{j \in \mathrm{noobj}} (0 - \hat{C}_j)^2 \tag{2}$$

Classification loss is calculated using cross-entropy:

$$\mathcal{L}_{cls} = - \sum_{i \in \mathrm{obj}} \sum_{c \in C} y_{i,c} \cdot \log(\hat{y}_{i,c}) \tag{3}$$

Bounding box regression adopts mean squared error across box coordinates:

$$\begin{aligned} \mathcal{L}_{bbox} = \sum_{i \in \mathrm{obj}} \Big[&(x_i - \hat{x}_i)^2 + (y_i - \hat{y}_i)^2 \\ &+ (w_i - \hat{w}_i)^2 + (h_i - \hat{h}_i)^2 \Big] \end{aligned} \tag{4}$$

The total loss is a weighted sum of the components:

$$\mathcal{L}_{total} = \mathcal{L}_{conf} + \lambda_{cls} \cdot \mathcal{L}_{cls} + \lambda_{bbox} \cdot \mathcal{L}_{bbox} \tag{5}$$

3.3 Shuttlecock Strike Determination

Analysis of collected shuttlecock videos shows that the shuttlecock generally moves in an approximately vertical oscillatory trajectory. The Y-axis motion data were collected, as shown in Fig. 3. In OpenCV, a larger Y-coordinate represents a lower position in the image. When the Y-coordinate transitions from increasing to decreasing, it typically indicates a strike. Based on this observation, a strike determination method is proposed: for every three consecutive detected positions, if the second Y-coordinate is greater than the first and third, a strike is recorded, incrementing the strike count. Although effective, the current method has limitations, such as difficulties distinguishing hand-held states or ground contacts, which require future refinement.

After the video analysis is completed on the web interface, the system will display the total frame count, average detection frame rate, and the number of

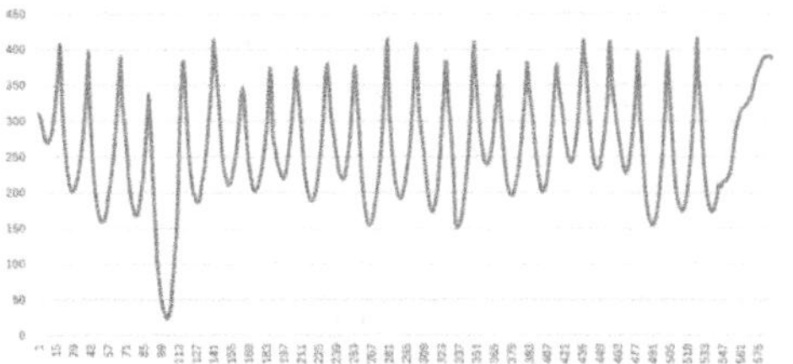

Fig. 3. Shuttlecock Y-Position Over Time.

successful hits in the left section. Below, a video showing the complete tracking path of the shuttlecock will be generated for the user to review and inspect. The right section will show all the image frames detected as hit moments. For images that are misjudged by the model, users can right-click to remove them, and the system will automatically update the total count of hits (Fig. 4).

Fig. 4. Video Analysis.

4 Experimental Results and Analysis

4.1 Dataset

Dataset Construction. Due to the lack of publicly available shuttlecock datasets, we developed a dedicated detection dataset through self-collected annotations. The construction workflow is shown in Fig. 5.

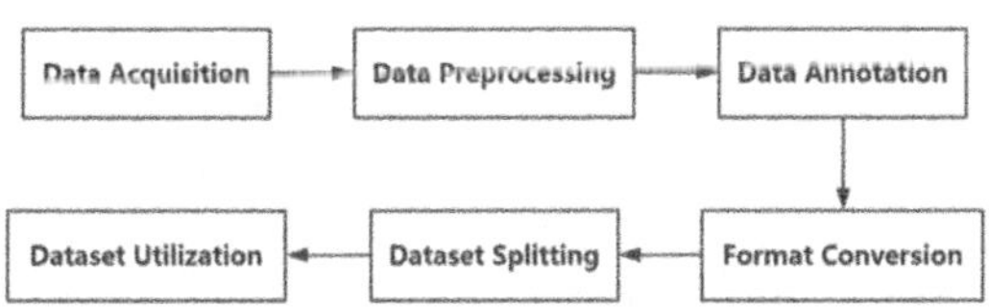

Fig. 5. Dataset Construction Workflow.

Data collection employed a 1280 × 720@30fps camera recording multi-angle shuttlecock training sessions in a university gym. Sample examples appear in Fig. 6.

Fig. 6. Examples of Captured Samples.

Frames extracted via OpenCV (Python) in JPG format underwent manual filtering: images with ¿30% occlusion were discarded. 681 valid images remained; Some samples from the dataset are shown in Fig. 7.

Fig. 7. Partial Images from the Dataset.

4.2 Experimental Environment

Experiments utilized a server with 22-core vCPU, dual NVIDIA RTX 3090 GPUs (24 GB× 2), and 120 GB RAM. The software stack comprised Ubuntu 22.04, Python 3.10.14, PyTorch 2.2.2 with CUDA 12.3/cuDNN 8.9.7. Models were trained in PyTorch and deployed via Flask-based web client for real-time visualization.

4.3 Comparison Experiments

Experimental Design and Result Demonstration. In this section, networks with different architectural modifications and the default baseline network are trained and compared. The goal is to select the model with the best performance based on evaluation metrics. The initial hyperparameters used for all networks are shown in Table 1.

Table 1. Initial parameters of the object detection network.

Parameter	Value	Description
weights	YOLOv12n	Pretrained model
lr0	0.01	Initial learning rate
weight_decay	0.0005	Weight decay rate
batch	64	Number of images per batch
workers	0	Number of data loader threads
epoch	300	Total training epochs
mosaic	1.0	Probability of Mosaic data augmentation
imgsz	640	Input image size

The total training time for all models was approximately 14 h. After training, all results were collected and saved in a designated directory.

A total of six networks were trained, including the default model. For convenience, each model is referred to by a short name. The details of their architecture depth and aliases are listed in Table 2.

Table 2. Network naming and architectural details.

Model Name	Alias	Layers	Description
v12-nc1-base	A	22	Default model
v12-nc1-cbam	B	23	Adds one attention layer
v12-nc1-cbam2	C	24	Adds two attention layers
v12-nc1-adda2c2fdet	D	23	Enhanced detection and A2C2f module
v12-nc1-cbam2a2c2f6	E	25	Lightweight attention and high-interaction channels
v12-nc1-addtinyobjdetwithdet2	F	28	Dual detection heads with enhanced feature fusion

In Network B, the CBAM convolutional attention module is added before the Conv module in the 3rd layer of the default network. In Network C, CBAM convolutional attention modules are added before the 3rd and 9th layers of the default network. In Network D, a CBAMBlock module is inserted between the P3/8 and P5/32 layers to enhance feature representation. The C3k2 module in the P2/4 layer is removed, and direct downsampling to P3/8 is applied, followed by CBAM + C3k2. This simplifies the shallow layer network structure. In Network E, a P6/64 feature layer is added to enhance small object detection capability. A preP6 branch and the A2C2f module are inserted in the Backbone to extract small object features at 80×80 resolution. In the Head, an independent small object detection path is introduced, along with a dedicated Detect head that performs small object predictions solely for the P6 branch.

The impact of the selected output layer feature map size on recognition accuracy is analyzed through comparisons of Networks A, D, and F. The impact of the number of CBAM convolutional attention modules on recognition accuracy is analyzed through comparisons of Networks B and C. The impact of the convolutional attention mechanism on model performance improvement is analyzed through comparisons of Networks D and E.

Experimental Results and Analysis. Precision and recall are two metrics that often exhibit a trade-off relationship. Ideally, both should be high, but improving one often comes at the cost of the other. As shown in Figs. 8a and 8b , model convergence occurs around the 200th epoch. Among the six networks, model F achieves the highest precision and recall.

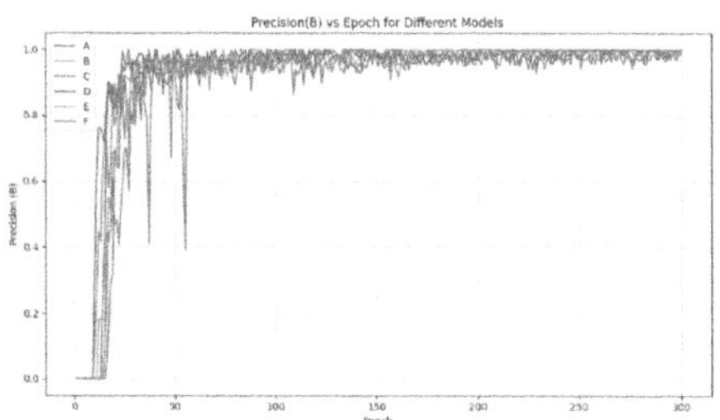

(a) Cross-Architecture Precision Analysis on Shuttlecock Dataset

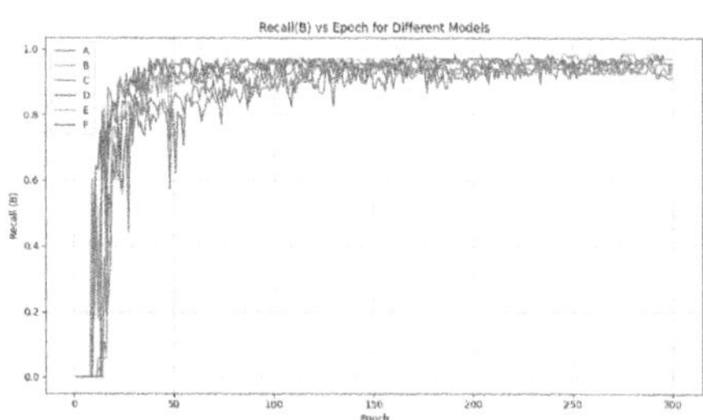

(b) Cross-Architecture Recall Analysis on Shuttlecock Dataset

Fig. 8. Comparison of Precision and Recall across architectures on the Shuttlecock dataset.

Figures 9a and 9b show the mAP@50 and mAP@5095 performance of the models during training. The mAP@50 metric calculates the mean average precision at an IoU threshold of 50%, evaluating the model's object detection capability within a certain tolerance. On the other hand, mAP@5095 considers a range of IoU thresholds from 50% to 95%, penalizing models that make imprecise predictions, providing a more comprehensive evaluation of model performance. These metrics offer a detailed measurement standard, demonstrating the model's performance in detecting objects under different levels of overlap between predicted and ground truth boxes.

By comparing models B and C, we find that adding two attention modules does not necessarily lead to better performance—model B (with one) outperforms model C. Likewise, comparing models D and E reveals that when the

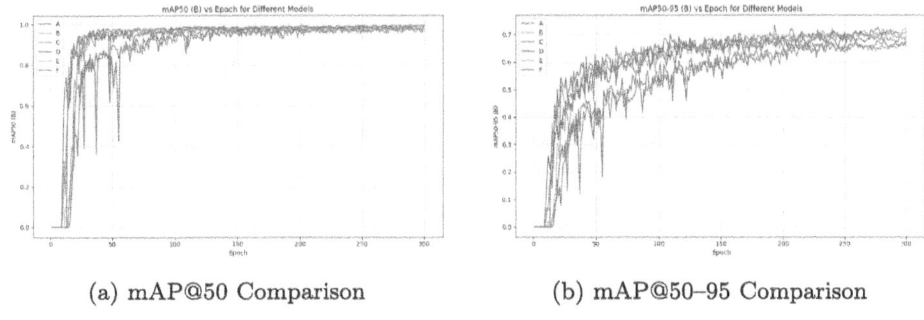

(a) mAP@50 Comparison (b) mAP@50–95 Comparison

Fig. 9. Performance comparison at different mAP thresholds.

attention blocks are appropriately placed in key fusion and upsampling layers, as in model E, the network better focuses on global cues while suppressing irrelevant background, thus enhancing detection capability.

This suggests that excessive use of attention mechanisms may not yield better results. In conclusion, model F outperforms all others across the evaluated metrics, and thus, its best checkpoint will be used in subsequent detection tasks.

To visually compare the detection performance of the six networks, a side-by-side visualization of their detection results on the same sample image is presented in Figs. 10. The figure highlights the bounding boxes and confidence scores generated by each model, providing intuitive insights into their localization precision and recall capability for small shuttlecock targets. Figure 11 illustrates the inference results of the best-performing model.

Fig. 10. Comparison of Detection Performance Across Different Models.

Fig. 11. Inference Results of the Best-Performing Model.

5 Limitation and Future Work

Although the improved network structure proposed in this paper has achieved good results in small object detection, there are still some limitations. First, despite the inclusion of a small object detection branch and feature enhancement mechanism, the model's performance still has room for improvement in extremely small object scenarios or situations with complex backgrounds. Particularly for rapidly changing shuttlecock targets, the model's positioning accuracy and recall rate may be affected in high-speed motion scenes. Secondly, although the attention mechanism has been optimized to enhance the focus on small objects, the generalization ability of this method across different datasets and scenes still needs further validation.

In response to these limitations, future work can focus on the following areas. First, training with more cross-domain data to enhance the model's generalization ability. Secondly, further optimization of the model's timeliness, especially in real-time applications, by incorporating more lightweight network structures and compression methods to improve inference speed without significantly reducing detection accuracy. Lastly, for rapidly moving small targets, more temporal information fusion methods can be explored, such as time series prediction based on video frames, to further improve the detection and localization accuracy of dynamic targets.

6 Conclusion

This paper proposes a network architecture optimization method tailored for shuttlecock target detection and constructs a dedicated dataset based on real-world recordings, addressing the scarcity of public datasets in this field. Experimental results show that the improved model achieves a mAP of 73.2%, representing an approximately 6% point improvement over the original model, while maintaining detection speed and reducing missed detections. These results validate the effectiveness of the proposed method in small object detection and offer a new perspective for detecting and tracking fast-moving, small-sized targets.

Acknowledgements. This work was supported in part by the Fundamental Research Funds for the Central Universities, South-Central Minzu University (Grant Numbers: CZQ25015, PTZ25002, XTZ24003).

References

1. Bo, H.: Research on the development path and countermeasures of shuttlecock in college physical education. Contemporary Sports Technol. **10**(15), 112–113 (2020)
2. Zipu, W., et al.: From technological development to policy innovation: theoretical logic and practical direction of sports science and technology innovation. J. Shanghai Univ. Sport **48**(04), 13–25 (2024)
3. Yuede, G., Guoqiang, P.: Measures and inspiration of world competitive sports power's technology assistance in olympic preparation. Sports Culture Guide **09**, 7–14 (2023)
4. Hong, G.: Study on the techniques of shuttlecock. J. South-Central Univ. Nationalities (Nat. Sci. Edition) **21**(3), 92–94 (2002)
5. Wang, J., Ma, J., Hu, K., et al.: Tac-trainer: a visual analytics system for IoT-based racket sports training. IEEE Trans. Visual Comput. Graph. **29**(1), 951–961 (2022)
6. Xiao, Z., Xusheng, L., Haiyao, Z., et al.: A smart shuttleball system for national physical education and training. China Comput. Commun. **35**(01), 96–100 (2023)
7. Huang, Y., Xiao, D., Liu, J., et al.: An improved pig counting algorithm based on YOLOv5 and DeepSORT model. Sensors **23**(14), 6309 (2023)
8. Girshick, R., Donahue, J., Darrell, T., et al.: Rich feature hierarchies for accurate object detection and semantic segmentation. In: Proceedings of the IEEE Conference on Computer Vision and Pattern Recognition, pp. 580-587 (2014)
9. Bewley, A., Ge, Z., Ott, L., et al.: Simple online and realtime tracking. In: 2016 IEEE International Conference on Image Processing (ICIP), pp. 3464-3468. IEEE (2016)
10. D'Orazio, T., Leo, M., Mosca, N., et al.: A semi-automatic system for ground truth generation of soccer video sequences. In: 2009 Sixth IEEE International Conference on Advanced Video and Signal Based Surveillance, pp. 559-564. IEEE (2009)
11. Ramanathan, V., Huang, J., Abu-El-Haija, S., et al.: Detecting events and key actors in multi-person videos. In: Proceedings of the IEEE Conference on Computer Vision and Pattern Recognition. pp. 3043-3053 (2016)
12. Woo, S., Park, J., Lee, J.-Y., Kweon, I.S.: CBAM: convolutional block attention module. In: Ferrari, V., Hebert, M., Sminchisescu, C., Weiss, Y. (eds.) ECCV 2018. LNCS, vol. 11211, pp. 3–19. Springer, Cham (2018). https://doi.org/10.1007/978-3-030-01234-2_1
13. Reis, D., Kupec, J., Hong, J., et al.: Real-time flying object detection with YOLOv8. arXiv preprint arXiv:2305.09972 (2023)

Enhancing Small Object Detection in Aerial Images Under Multi-weather Conditions

Zhe Yang(✉) and Haocheng Fu

School of Computer Science and Technology, Soochow University, Jiangsu, China
yangzhe@suda.edu.cn

Abstract. To address the challenges of small object detection under complex weather conditions—particularly those with blurred features caused by rain and fog—this paper proposes We-YOLO, an enhanced YOLOv10-based model. The framework integrates an Enhanced Multi-path Feature Pyramid Network (EMFPN) for improved multi-scale feature fusion, a C2f-TKSA module that combines adaptive sparse selection with channel attention to suppress weather-induced noise, and a CSP-OMni block for better scale adaptability. A Dense-Mosaic data augmentation strategy is also introduced to enhance small-object feature learning. Experimental results show that We-YOLO achieves 5.5% improvement in mAP@50 on the custom WeDrone dataset. The WeDrone dataset and code are available on GitHub: https://github.com/suda-sklcc/Wedrone.git.

Keywords: Small-object detection · Multi-weather · Data augmentation · YOLO

1 Introduction

Object detection is vital in autonomous driving and surveillance, yet small-object detection under adverse weather (e.g., rain, haze, snow) remains difficult. Image degradation and weather-induced distortions weaken feature representation. Dataset issues like annotation challenges and class imbalance further reduce robustness, making small-object detection a critical unresolved problem.

Deep learning has significantly advanced small-object detection, particularly through the YOLO [1] series, which is widely used for real-time detection. Recent improvements, such as YOLO-CCA [2] and BGF-YOLO [3], further enhance small-object detection by strengthening context fusion and utilizing attention modules and advanced feature pyramids.

Despite progress, aerial small-object detection under harsh weather still faces major challenges:

(1) Small targets lose detail and clarity, reducing detection accuracy.

(2) Real-time and accurate detection is hard to achieve due to the trade-off between speed and model complexity.

P. Li et al. (Eds.): CGI 2025, LNCS 16508, pp. 104–116, 2026.
https://doi.org/10.1007/978-3-032-22264-0_9

(3) Existing datasets lack realistic weather effects, occlusions, and very small targets ($< 20 \times 20$ pixels), limiting generalization.

2 Related Work

2.1 YOLOv10

YOLOv10 [4], introduced by Ao Wang et al. in 2024, improves upon YOLOv8 by addressing redundant predictions and enhancing both computational efficiency and detection accuracy.

The model achieves this through modifications in post-processing and network architecture, most notably by adopting an NMS-free training strategy that combines dual label assignment with consistent matching metrics. This approach eliminates redundant predictions and removes the dependency on NMS during inference, resulting in significantly improved processing speed.

2.2 Small Object Detection

Small object detection focuses on identifying targets occupying minimal image area (typically defined as objects smaller than 32×32 pixels), which presents significant challenges due to limited feature representation, susceptibility to noise interference, and frequent occlusion. Conventional detection models often underperform with small objects as their indistinct visual characteristics are easily overwhelmed by background clutter.

Current solutions primarily involve multi-scale feature enhancement approaches likeFeature Pyramid Networks (FPN) [5] to improve fine-grained feature extraction, anchor-free models such as FCOS [6] to eliminate biases from preset anchors, and data augmentation techniques including Mosaic [7] to increase small object sample diversity. Furthermore, super-resolution reconstruction networks have been employed to recover detailed features of small objects. Despite these advancements, detecting small objects remains particularly challenging in complex environments or under adverse weather conditions.

3 Our Method

To improve small pedestrian detection accuracy in multi-weather aerial imagery, this paper proposes We-YOLO, an enhanced algorithm based on YOLOv10n. Key improvements include: introducing Enhanced Multi-path Feature Pyramid Network(EMFPN) to better integrate semantic and spatial features; incorporating in the neck the Cross-Stage Top-k Sparse Attention module(C2f-TKSA) to reduce redundancy and suppress background noise; designing the CSP-Omni module to fuse multi-scale receptive fields; proposing Dense-Mosaic to enhance small-object saliency; and constructing the WeDrone dataset with diverse weather conditions to support aerial pedestrian detection tasks.

The improved We-YOLO architecture is illustrated in Fig. 1.

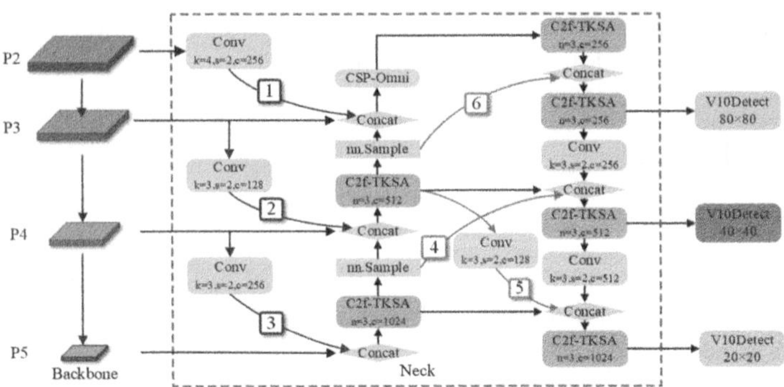

Fig. 1. We-YOLO structure.

3.1 Cross-Stage Top-k Sparse Attention Module

Small objects in detection are prone to missed detection due to low resolution and background noise, especially in weather-affected images. Traditional C2f modules improve feature flow but struggle with shallow feature usage, contextual information, and multi-scale fusion efficiency.

To address these issues, we propose the C2f-TKSA module, which combines sparse selection with channel-wise attention, improving small-object feature extraction while reducing computational overhead and enhancing contextual information efficiency.

As shown in Fig. 2, the C2f-TKSA architecture processes input images through three parallel branches (generating K, Q, V values) after Layer Normalization. Unlike traditional spatial self-attention methods, TKSA uses 1× 1 convolutions followed by 3 × 3 depth-wise convolutions to perform channel-wise attention, this reduces memory and computational complexity. An adaptive Top-k selector calculates similarity scores between query and key matrices, masking low-attention elements to generate a sparse attention matrix. This sparse representation retains only the most important attention patterns, enabling efficient information aggregation and enhancing detail processing for key regions. Mathematically, the sparse attention mechanism can be expressed as:

$$\text{Sparse}_{\text{Att}}(Q, K, V) = \text{softmax}\left(T_k\left(\frac{QK^T}{\lambda}\right)\right)V \tag{1}$$

The $T_k(\bullet)$ selection operator is formally defined as:

$$[(T_k(S))]_{ij} = \begin{cases} S_{ij} & S_{ij} \in \text{top-}k(\text{row } j) \\ 0 & \text{otherwise} \end{cases} \tag{2}$$

The above equation defines the $T_k(\bullet)$ selection operator, which selects the top k values for each row in the matrix S. Specifically, for each element S_{ij} in the matrix S, if it belongs to the top k largest values in its respective row, it is retained; otherwise, it is set to zero. Importantly, k is not a fixed value, but rather a learnable parameter that can adapt during training. This operation helps preserve only the most relevant features, which is critical for small object detection, where background noise often overwhelms small target signals. Subsequently, a scatter operation is applied to generate an initialized feature map with the same dimensions as the QK matrix. Based on the values and indices retained after the Top-k selection, only the most important information is preserved while all other entries are set to zero. This filtered representation is then passed through a softmax function to obtain a sparsified attention score matrix, effectively highlighting the most critical query-key relationships.

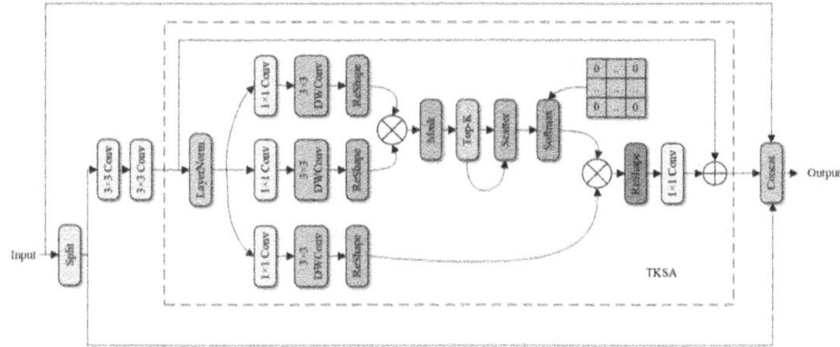

Fig. 2. C2f-TKSA module.

3.2 Enhanced Multi-Path Feature Pyramid Network

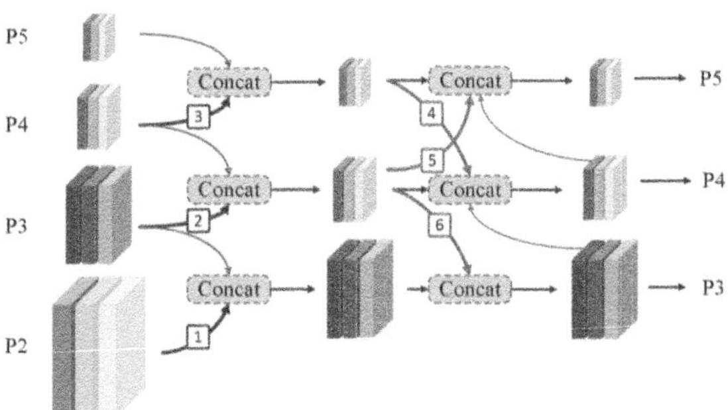

Fig. 3. EMFPN structure.

The Feature Pyramid Network (FPN) is a widely used multi-scale feature extraction architecture that enhances object detection and segmentation by fusing cross-layer features via a top-down pyramid. However, traditional FPN has two limitations: unidirectional top-down propagation may weaken small-object information, and suboptimal feature reuse can introduce redundancy and dilute key features.

To address these issues, we propose an Enhanced Multi-path Feature Pyramid Network (EMFPN). As shown in Fig. 3, EMFPN introduces a complementary fusion mechanism between shallow and deep features at the backbone-FPN junction. Shallow features, rich in fine-grained details (e.g., small-object local features), are directly reused to enhance feature representation and stabilize deep learning (Branches 1âĂŞ3).

In deeper stages, EMFPN employs bidirectional fusion (Branches 4âĂŞ6), combining bottom-up and top-down flows to optimize feature representation. At the output, multi-resolution P4-level features are concatenated with high-level maps, preserving low-level context while strengthening semantic representation. This design improves multi-scale feature learning and significantly boosts small-object detection.

3.3 Multi-receptive Field Fusion Module

In the FPN architecture, small-object detection relies on high-resolution feature maps, but large feature maps have small receptive fields and high computational costs. Although CNNs introduce large convolutional kernels to expand the receptive field, this increases computational cost, and a single convolutional kernel cannot meet the demands of multi-scale feature extraction.

To address these issues, this paper proposes a novel CSP-OMni module, as illustrated in Fig. 4. In the CSP-OMni module, the input feature map is first processed by a 1×1 convolution for channel adjustment. Then, the feature map is split into two branches in a 3:7 ratio: a non-operating branch and an Omni branch. Within the Omni branch, the feature map undergoes a 1×1 convolution and is further divided into three sub-branches: the Local Branch, Region Branch, and Global Branch.

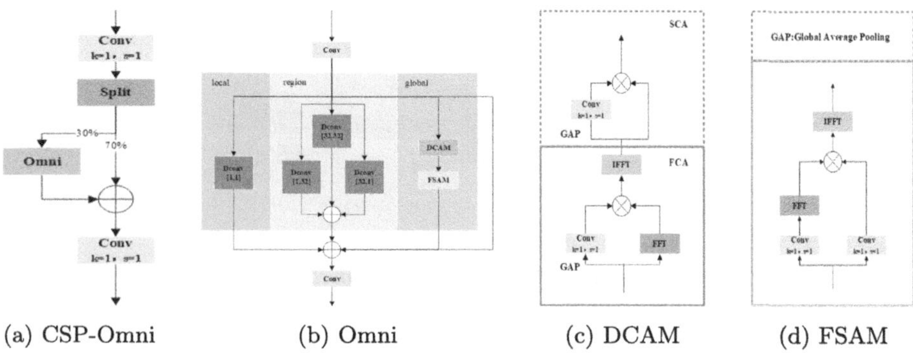

(a) CSP-Omni (b) Omni (c) DCAM (d) FSAM

Fig. 4. CSP-Omni module.

The proposed architecture integrates three complementary branches for multi-scale feature extraction. The local branch employs a 1 × 1 depthwise separable convolution to preserve fine-grained details with minimal computational overhead. The region branch combines a 32 × 32 large-kernel depthwise convolution with parallel 1 × 32 and 32 × 1 striped convolutions, efficiently capturing regional context while reducing computational complexity through directional decomposition. The global branch enhances global features using two modules: the Dual Channel Attention Module (DCAM) and the Frequency-Spatial Attention Module (FSAM). The DCAM module combines attention mechanisms in both the frequency domain and the spatial domain. It first applies a Fourier transform (FFT) to convert the feature map into the frequency domain, where global average pooling (GAP) and a 1×1 convolution are used to weight the frequency-domain features. An inverse Fourier transform ($IFFT$) is then applied to restore the spatial domain features. The enhancement of frequency domain information is achieved through the following formula:

$$X_{FCA} = \mathrm{IFFT}\left(\mathrm{FFT}\left(X_{Global}\right) \otimes W_{FCA}^{1\times1}\left(\mathrm{GAP}\left(X_{Global}\right)\right)\right) \tag{3}$$

In this context, X_{Global} represents the input feature map, and $W_{FCA}^{1\times1}$ denotes the weight information used during the convolution operation when performing feature weighting in the frequency domain. Subsequently, the feature representation is further enhanced through the channel attention mechanism in the spatial domain. The formula is as follows:

$$X_{DCAM} = X_{FCA} \otimes W_{SC4}^{1\times1}\left(\mathrm{GAP}\left(X_{FCA}\right)\right) \tag{4}$$

The FSAM module performs feature reconstruction between the frequency domain and the spatial domain, further enhancing the fine-grained expressive capability of the global features. The formula is as follows:

$$X_{FSAM} = \mathrm{IFFT}\left(\mathrm{FFT}\left(W^{1\times1}\left(X_{DCAM}\right)\right) \otimes W^{2\times1}\left(X_{DCAM}\right)\right) \tag{5}$$

Finally, The three branch outputs are fused by pointwise addition and concatenated with the non-operating branch's feature map, then output through a 1 × 1 convolution. This design enables multi-scale object detection while reducing computational overhead, improving model performance.

3.4 Dense Mosaic

To address the data scarcity issue in small object detection, we propose Dense-Mosaic, an enhanced data augmentation method. Unlike traditional Mosaic, Dense-Mosaic employs a fine-grained region selection strategy that prioritizes high-density small object areas during image stitching. Specifically, it calculates target density for each candidate image and places the densest one in the largest mosaic region, increasing the frequency of dense small object scenarios in training data. This optimization improves feature learning for small objects while maintaining computational efficiency. As shown in Fig. 5, the modified approach better preserves critical small object features compared to standard Mosaic, leading to more robust detection performance.

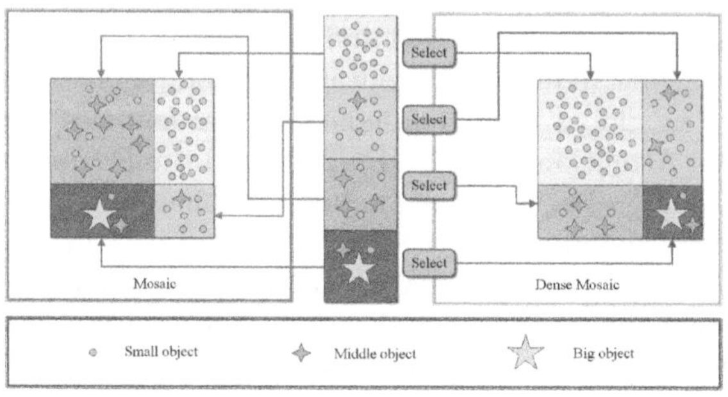

Fig. 5. Dense Mosaic.

4 Experiments and Analysis

4.1 Experimental Environment and Configuration

The experiment was conducted using Ubuntu 22.04, with an NVIDIA RTX 3090 GPU for acceleration. CUDA 12.1 and PyTorch 2.3 were used, and the development was done in Python 3.8.

4.2 Dataset

Existing aerial datasets often ignore weather effects and include many medium- and large-sized objects, making small-object detection challenging. To address this, the WeDrone dataset was created using drone-captured videos(Fig. 6).

WeDrone focuses on small-object detection under various weather conditions (sunny, rainy, snowy, foggy, and nighttime) in high-altitude environments. With 3,215 images and 31,614 annotated instances of pedestrians, riders, and umbrellas, the dataset has 94.3% of objects smaller than 32×32 pixels. It is split into 80% for training and 20% for testing. The dataset features a higher proportion of small objects compared to other datasets like VisDrone (94.3% vs. 80%).

The proposed algorithm's generalization capability was evaluated using two complementary drone-based datasets: the VisDrone2019 [9] dataset comprising 10,209 aerial images with diverse scenes, backgrounds, and weather conditions across 10 object categories, and the AI-TOD [10] high-resolution remote sensing dataset containing 28,036 images (1920×1080 pixels) specifically designed for small-object detection challenges, featuring an average object size of just 12.8 pixels across 700,000+ instances in complex urban and natural environments.

Together these datasets provide rigorous testing conditions encompassing varied object densities, challenging backgrounds, and different viewing perspectives to thoroughly assess detection performance.

(a) rainy (b) snowy and foggy (c) sunny (d) nighttime

Fig. 6. Ground Truth Visualization of the WeDrone Dataset.

4.3 Experimental Results Analysis

Ablation Experiment on Feature Pyramid. To evaluate the effectiveness of EMFPN, we replace the original FPN in YOLOv10 with alternative feature fusion structures (GFPN, BiFPN, CGRFPN) under identical settings. The experimental results are presented in Table 1.

Table 1. Ablation Study on Feature Pyramid

FPN	mAP@50(%)	mAP@50:95(%)	Params(M)	GFLOPs(G)
YOLOv10n	74.2	44.2	2.27	6.5
BiFPN [11]	74.7	44.6	**1.82**	**6.3**
yellowGFPN [12]	75.4	44.9	3.33	8.9
CGRFPN [13]	73.2	43.7	3.13	8.5
YOLOv10-EMFPN	**76**	**45.2**	3.05	7.9

EMFPN achieves 76% mAP@50 and 45.2% mAP@50:95, outperforming the baseline FPN (74.2%, 44.2%) while maintaining efficiency (3.05M parameters, 7.9 GFLOPs). BiFPN offers marginal gains (74.7%, 44.6%) with lower computational cost, while GFPN improves accuracy (75.4%, 44.9%) at higher resource demand (3.33M, 8.9 GFLOPs). CGRFPN underperforms, likely due to ineffective channel re-weighting in this architecture.

These results confirm that EMFPN optimally balances accuracy and efficiency, making it the best choice for YOLOv10.

Comparison Experiment on WeDrone Dataset. To validate the superiority of the improved We-YOLO algorithm compared to other methods, this paper conducts a series of comparative experiments on the custom WeDrone dataset.

Experimental results on the WeDrone dataset (Table 2) demonstrate We-YOLO's superior performance compared to state-of-the-art YOLO variants. The improved model achieves 79.6% mAP@50 and 48.1% mAP@50:95, representing gains of 5.4% and 3.9% over YOLOv10n baseline. With 3.91M parameters and 11.1 GFLOPs, We-YOLO maintains real-time capability at 74.9 FPS while showing 3% improvement in small-object detection (APs).

Table 2. Comparative Experiment on the WeDrone Dataset

Model	Category			mAP@50 (%)	mAP@50:95 (%)	APs (%)	Param (M)	GFLOPs (G)	FPS
	pedestrian	rider	umbrella						
yolov10n	73.3	71.7	78	74.2	44.2	27	2.7	8.4	122
yolov10s	76.7	74.8	81.6	77.7	48.6	29.7	7.22	21.4	106.3
yolov7tiny [14]	76.7	74.4	80.1	77	42.8	28.4	6	13	**294**
yolov8n	72.3	68.8	78.7	73.3	44	25.3	3.2	8.7	124
yolov8s	75.6	74.7	**82.2**	77.5	47.6	28.4	11.2	28.6	118
yolov5n	71.6	72.4	78.6	74.2	44.4	26.7	1.9	**4.5**	118.9
yolov5s	75.1	73	81.8	76.6	47.3	28.7	7.2	17	112
hyper-yolot [15]	72.1	69.4	78.4	73.3	44.5	25.9	4	11.4	96.4
hyper-yolo	72.9	71	80.6	74.9	45.2	27.2	14.8	39	78.9
yolo11n [16]	72.5	72.5	79.2	74.7	45	27.5	2.59	6.4	154.9
yolo11s	75.7	74.9	81.1	77.2	47.9	30.3	9.42	21.6	155.2
yolov9t [17]	71.7	72.2	78.1	74	44.9	27.6	**1.76**	6.7	80.5
yolov9s	75.5	73.8	81.6	77	48	29.8	6.31	22.7	99
yolov6	69.8	69.2	75.1	71.4	42.1	25.4	4.24	11.9	321
RCS-YOLO [18]	69.2	70	66.2	68.5	36.4	25.5	50.6	105.2	94.5
MAF-YOLOn [19]	–	–	–	77.4	46	28.4	3.8	10.5	100
MAF-YOLOs	–	–	–	78.1	47	29.9	8.6	25.5	80.9
Gold-YOLOs [20]	–	–	–	76.9	45.8	28.1	21.5	46	78.7
Gold-YOLOn	–	–	–	75.1	43.4	26	5.6	12.1	81.4
Ours	**77**	**80.5**	81.3	**79.6**	**48.1**	**31**	3.91	11.1	74.9

Generalization Experiment. To validate the model's generalization capability, we conducted experiments on multiple datasets. Experimental results (Table 3) demonstrate We-YOLO's superior performance in drone-based object detection. On the VisDrone2019 dataset, the model achieves 39.3% mAP@50 and 23.6% mAP@50:95, with small object detection (APs) reaching 13.8%. For the more challenging AI-TOD dataset (average object size: 12.8 pixels), We-YOLO attains even higher precision at 39.7% mAP@50 and 17.2% mAP@50:95.

By integrating multi-scale feature fusion and attention mechanisms, We-YOLO effectively reduces false positives/negatives for small objects while maintaining model efficiency. The system outperforms all YOLOv5-v11 variants and other state-of-the-art detectors, providing an optimal solution for real-time aerial vision tasks (Table 4).

Model Ablation Experiment. Ablation experiments on YOLOv10n show that each proposed module improves small-object detection. Adding EMFPN raised mAP@50 from 74.2% to 76%, with minimal cost. With CSP-OMni and C2f-TKSA, performance increased to 78.6%/47%. Finally, Dense-Mosaic pushed results to 79.6%/48.1%. Despite slight increases in parameters and GFLOPs, the model maintained real-time speed (74.9 FPS), confirming the modulesâĂŹ effectiveness and efficiency.

Table 3. Generalization Experiment

Model	VisDrone			AI-TOD		
	mAP@50(%)	mAP@50:95ïijĹ%ïijĽ	APs(%)	mAP@50(%)	mAP@50:95ïijĹ%ïijĽ	APs(%)
YOLOv5n	33.2	19.2	**9.1**	34.3	13.8	10.5
YOLOv8n	33.6	19.4	9.5	34.3	14.1	11.6
YOLOv8s	38	22.4	12.2	36.2	16.8	12.2
YOLOv9t	34.2	19.7	9.4	34.1	14	10.9
YOLOv10n	34.2	19.9	10.1	35.3	14.1	11.4
YOLOv11n	33.1	19.4	9.4	33.7	13.5	10.5
MAF-YOLOn	34.6	19.6	10.5	35.2	14	11
Gold-yolo	31.4	17.9	8.4	32.9	13.6	9.8
Ours	**39.3**	**23.6**	13.8	**39.7**	**17.2**	**13.5**

Table 4. Ablation Experiment

Dense-mosaic	EMFPN	CSP-OMni	C2fTKSA	mAP@50(%)	mAP@50:95(%)	Params(m)	GFLOPs(G)	inference(ms)	FPS	Weight(M)
				74.2	44.2	2.27	6.5	9.1	152	5.5
✓				75.3	44.9	2.27	6.5	9.1	152	5.5
	✓			76	45.2	3.05	7.9	14.7	126	7
✓	✓			76.7	46.3	3.05	7.9	14.7	126	7
	✓	✓		76.9	45.8	3.74	12.7	14.3	95.7	7.5
✓	✓	✓		77.3	47.9	3.74	12.7	14.3	95.7	7.5
	✓	✓	✓	78.6	47	3.91	11.1	17.7	74.9	8.7
✓	✓	✓	✓	79.6	48.1	3.91	11.1	17.7	74.9	8.7

4.4 Generalization Experiment Analysis

To provide more intuitive demonstration of the improvements, we present the visualization results. Figure 7 compares the detection performance of several YOLO models on the WeDrone dataset. The improved We-YOLO model shows higher target regression accuracy. It excels in detecting challenging targets like pedestrians with umbrellas, validating its superiority in aerial image object detection, especially in complex and small-object scenarios.

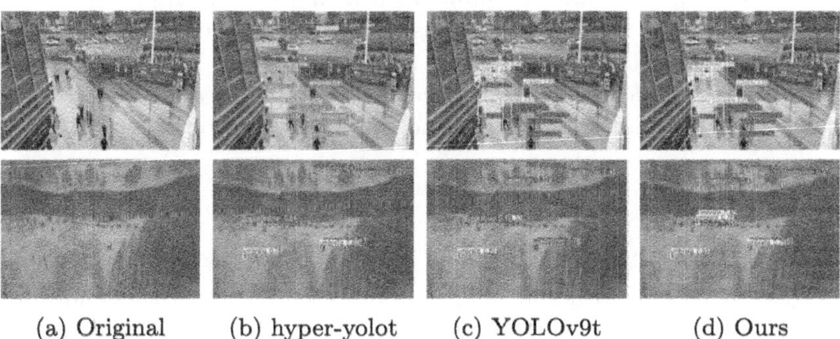

(a) Original (b) hyper-yolot (c) YOLOv9t (d) Ours

Fig. 7. Detection results of different models on the WeDrone dataset.

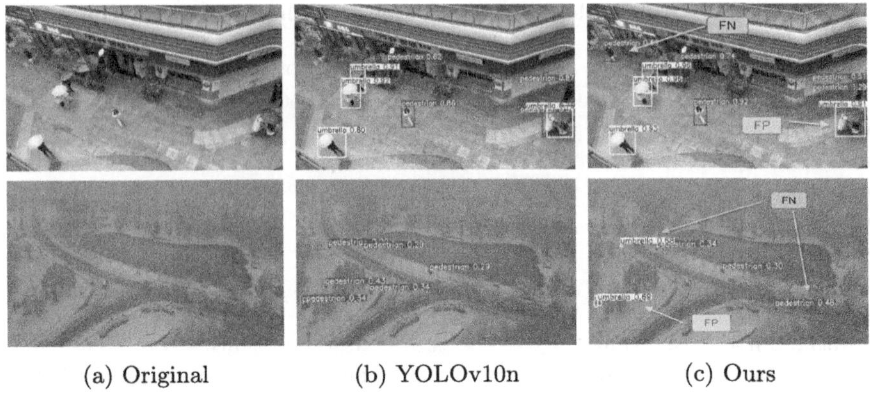

(a) Original (b) YOLOv10n (c) Ours

Fig. 8. Comparison of improved models through visual comparison.

(a) Original-Rainy (b) Ours-Rainy (c) Original-Snowy (d) Ours-Snowy

Fig. 9. Heatmap comparison of detection results.

Figure 8 shows detection results, with the original image on the left and We-YOLO's detections on the right. In rainy weather, We-YOLO handles raindrop noise better than YOLOv10n, especially for occluded pedestrians. In snowy/foggy conditions, We-YOLO detects more umbrella-wielding pedestrians and achieves better bounding box accuracy, demonstrating robustness in extreme weather.

This paper also presents the heatmap under different extreme weather conditions visualization, as illustrated in Fig. 9. (a) and (c) show the heatmaps of the baseline model, while (b) and (d) show the heatmaps of the improved We-YOLO model. Under various weather conditions, the baseline model exhibits more scattered and weaker responses in the target area, whereas We-YOLO shows stronger and more concentrated responses, indicating its superior ability to capture key target features, especially under extreme weather conditions.

5 Conclusion

This paper presents We-YOLO, an enhanced version of YOLOv10 designed for small-object detection in aerial images under complex weather conditions. By incorporating innovations like the EMFPN, C2f-TKSA module, CSP-OMni module, and Dense-Mosaic data augmentation, We-YOLO improves detection accuracy. Experimental results on WeDrone, VisDrone, and AI-TOD show mAP50 improvements of 5.5%, 5.1%, and 4.4%, respectively. While the model has a slight increase in computational cost (11.1 GFLOPs) and parameters (3.91M), it retains real-time performance with an average detection time of 21.8ms. These results validate We-YOLO's effectiveness for small-object detection, with future work focused on further optimization for broader real-world applications.

References

1. Redmon, J., Farhadi, A.: Yolov3: An incremental improvement. arXiv preprint arXiv:1804.02767 (2018)
2. Jiang, L., Zhan, P., Bai, T., Yu, H.: Yolo-cca: a context-based approach for traffic sign detection. arXiv preprint arXiv:2412.04289 (2024)
3. Kang, M., Ting, C., Ting, F., Phan, R.: Bgf-yolo: enhanced yolov8 with multiscale attentional feature fusion for brain tumor detection. arxiv arXiv preprint arXiv:2309.12585 (2023)
4. Wang, A., Chen, H., Liu, L., Chen, K., Lin, Z., Han, J., et al.: Yolov10: real-time end-to-end object detection. Adv. Neural Inform. Process. Syst. **37**, 107984–108011 (2024)
5. Lin, T.Y., DollÂťar, P., Girshick, R., He, K., Hariharan, B., Belongie, S.: Feature pyramid networks for object detection. In: Proceedings of the IEEE Conference on Computer Vision and Pattern Recognition, pp. 2117–2125 (2017)
6. Tian, Z., Shen, C., Chen, H., He, T.: Fcos: fully convolutional one-stage object detection. In: Proceedings of the IEEE/CVF International Conference on Computer Vision, pp. 9627–9636 (2019)
7. Bochkovskiy, A., Wang, C.Y., Li, H.: Yolov4: optimal speed and accuracy of object detection. arXiv preprint arXiv:2004.10934 (2020)
8. Cui, Y., Ren, W., Knoll, A.: Omni-kernel network for image restoration. In: Proceedings of the AAAI Conference on Artificial Intelligence, vol. 38, pp. 1426–1434 (2024)
9. Zhu, P., Wen, L., Bian, X., Ling, H., Hu, Q.: Vision meets drones: A challenge. arXiv preprint arXiv:1804.07437 (2018)
10. ang, J., Yang, W., Guo, H., Zhang, R., Xia, G.S.: Tiny object detection in aerial images. In: 2020 25th international conference on pattern recognition (ICPR), pp. 3791–3798. IEEE (2021)
11. Chen, J., Mai, H., Luo, L., Chen, X., Wu, K.: Effective feature fusion network in bifpn for small object detection. In: 2021 IEEE International Conference On Image Processing (ICIP), pp. 699–703. IEEE (2021)
12. Xu, X., Jiang, Y., Chen, W., Huang, Y., Zhang, Y., Sun, X.: Damo-yolo: a report on real-time object detection design. arXiv preprint arXiv:2211.15444 (2022)
13. Ni, Z., Chen, X., Zhai, Y., Tang, Y., Wang, Y.: Context-guided spatial feature reconstruction for efficient semantic segmentation. In: European Conference on Computer Vision, pp. 239–255. Springer (2024). https://doi.org/10.1007/978-3-031-72943-0_14
14. Wang, C.Y., Bochkovskiy, A., Liao, H.Y.M.: Yolov7: trainable bag-of- freebies sets new state-of-the-art for real-time object detectors. In: Proceedings of the IEEE/CVF Conference on Computer Vision and Pattern Recognition, pp. 7464–7475 (2023)
15. Feng, Y., et al.: Hyper-yolo: when visual object detection meets hypergraph computation. IEEE Trans. Pattern Analy. Mach. Intell. (2024)

16. Khanam, R., Hussain, M.: Yolov11: an overview of the key architectural enhancements. arXiv preprint arXiv:2410.17725 (2024)
17. Wang, C.Y., Yeh, I.H., Mark Liao, H.Y.: Yolov9: learning what you want to learn using programmable gradient information. In: European Conference on Computer Vision, pp. 1–21. Springer (2024). https://doi.org/10.1007/978-3-031-72751-1_1
18. Kang, M., Ting, CM., Ting, F.F., Phan, R.C.W.: RCS-YOLO: a fast and high-accuracy object detector for brain tumor detection. In: Greenspan, H., et al (eds.) MICCAI 2023. LNCS, vol. 14223. Springer, Cham (2023). https://doi.org/10.1007/978-3-031-43901-8_57
19. Xue, Y., Ju, Z., Li, Y., Zhang, W.: Maf-yolo: multi-modal attention fusion based yolo for pedestrian detection. Infrared Phys. Technol. **118**, 103906 (2021)
20. Wang, C., et al.: Gold-yolo: efficient object detector via gather-and-distribute mechanism. Adv. Neural. Inf. Process. Syst. **36**, 51094–51112 (2023)

Scale-Aware Guidance Network for SAR Ship Detection

Wenjing Jiang[1(✉)], Ming Liu[2], Yue Yu[1], and Qi Hu[1(✉)]

[1] College of Electronic and Information Engineering, Hebei University, Baoding 071002, China
wjjiang_hbu@163.com, qihu_hbu@163.com

[2] Information Technology Center, Hebei University, Baoding 071002, China

Abstract. In the ship detection task, synthetic aperture radar (SAR) is regarded as a powerful tool for obtaining data. However, the scale variation of ship objects in SAR images poses challenges during the detection process. To address it, we decouple the detection head and propose a new detection framework based on global precision optimization. The framework is composed of a scale-aware subnetwork and a detection subnetwork. During training, the scale-aware subnetwork guides the detection subnetwork, enhancing the extraction of multi-scale features. This approach optimizes detection precision across three scales, ensuring balanced performance. During inference, the scale-aware subnetwork is discarded to eliminate additional parameters and computation costs. Moreover, unlike Grad-CAM, this paper provides a more faithful post-hoc interpretability method based on hierarchical similarity. The proposed method improves the performance of six classical detectors on three widely used ship datasets.

Keywords: SAR · Multi-scale · Ship detection · Scale-aware · Post-hoc interpretability

1 Introduction

Synthetic aperture radar (SAR), as an effective tool to achieve high-resolution microwave imaging, has been widely used in many fields such as ocean monitoring [1, 2], terrain mapping [3], and object detection [4, 5].

Ship detection is a research hotspot in SAR image analysis and object detection. In the ship detection task, the sizes of ships are usually not fixed and can vary significantly. Figure 1 illustrates the distribution of large, medium, and small objects divided according to the COCO standard on two commonly used SAR ship datasets. These objects range from a few to thousands of pixels. While medium and large objects dominate the datasets, the problem of unbalanced object scales remains a significant challenge. Recently, significant research has focused on tackling the challenge of extreme variation in object size ratios in SAR ship detection, employing both traditional and deep learning methods. The traditional method mainly explores and finds solutions from the perspective of extracting scale-invariant features [6]. In the research based on deep learning, remarkable results have been achieved by using attention modules and feature pyramid

P. Li et al. (Eds.): CGI 2025, LNCS 16508, pp. 117–129, 2026.
https://doi.org/10.1007/978-3-032-22264-0_10

structures [7–10]. For example, deformable convolution is used to construct a local attention module and a non-local attention module to extract the local and non-local features of the image, respectively. The feature maps from both local and non-local attention form a feature pyramid, addressing the issue of detecting ships of various sizes in large-scale SAR images [8]. Some researchers have also combined traditional methods and deep learning methods to deal with the problem. They merge rotation-invariant features with advanced depth features extracted by CNN to adequately represent ship objects [11]. Additionally, the research on multi-scale object detection in optical images also provides a working idea [12–15]. They focus on the optimization of backbones and feature pyramid networks (FPN) structures of models. By designing the backbone to produce a unified feature map with specific scale capabilities and redesigning the FPN structure of the detector, the network's adaptability to scale variation is improved.

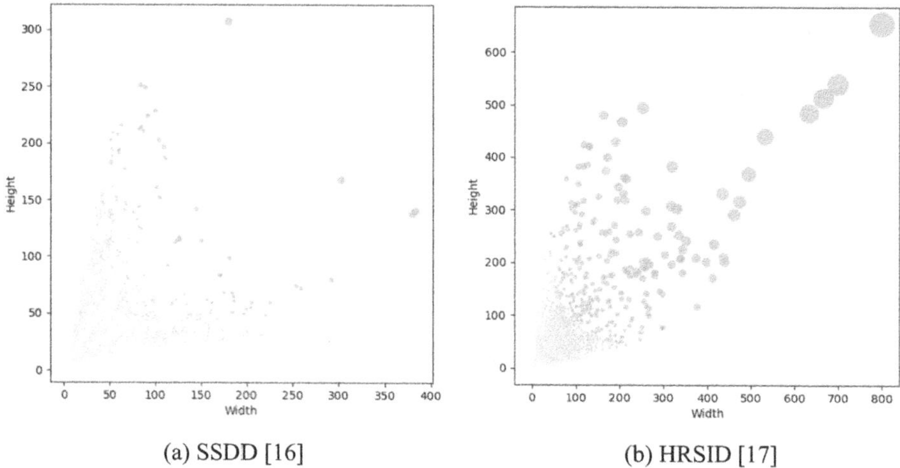

(a) SSDD [16] (b) HRSID [17]

Fig. 1. The object distribution of the SAR ship datasets. (a) SSDD [16] (b) HRSID [17]

The above-mentioned work has achieved surprising breakthroughs. However, most studies focus on designing enhancement modules for the backbone and FPN. The crucial role of the detection head has not been fully explored in existing research. Additionally, with the development of deep neural networks, the demand for interpretability has grown increasingly important. The abstract module structure design proves difficult to interpret and optimize. Although attention heatmaps can illustrate which areas the model focuses on, they cannot further reveal what feature information changes have driven the model's decisions. Therefore, this paper concentrates on multi-scale ship detection in SAR images and proposes a scale-aware guidance network with post-hoc interpretability. The main contributions of this paper are summarized as follows:

- This paper proposes a detection model based on global precision optimization to improve the performance in detecting large, medium, and small objects.

- To effectively extract multi-scale features, we design a scale-aware subnetwork that guides the detection subnetwork. This approach enhances feature extraction during training while eliminating additional computational costs during inference.
- For qualitative analysis, we propose a hierarchical similarity-based interpretation method, providing deeper insights into the model's internal mechanisms. For quantitative evaluation, experiments on two SAR ship datasets demonstrate the method's flexibility, while tests on an optical ship dataset confirm its extensibility.

2 Method

Convolutional neural network-based object detection algorithms generate feature maps from shallow to deep layers during the feature extraction process. The applicability of network depth varies when detecting small and large objects. Additionally, SAR ship objects have large scale variations, leading to poor detection performance. Although some pyramid-based network designs in recent years have addressed this issue to some extent, they often neglect the relationships between detection heads, limiting overall detection performance. To tackle this challenge, this paper proposes an innovative multi-scale ship detection network. The approach aims to improve the comprehensive detection capability for SAR objects by redesigning the structure of the detection head and introducing a scale-aware mechanism. Furthermore, this paper introduces an explanation method based on hierarchical similarity, which enhances the transparency and interpretability of the model design and optimization process through an analysis of the model's internal mechanisms.

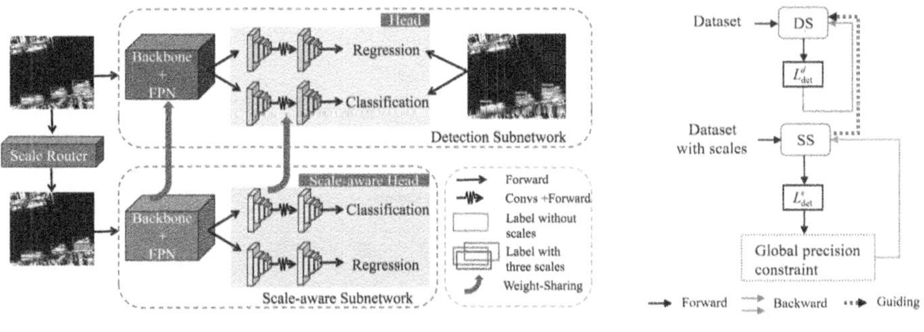

(a) Scale-guided network architecture (b) Scale-guided learning

Fig. 2. Overview of the architecture in this paper. There are two branches in (a): detection subnetwork and scale-aware subnetwork. These two branches feed the raw dataset and the dataset containing the scale label, respectively. DS and SS in (b) represent detection subnetwork and scale-aware subnetwork, respectively. In the training process, the scale-aware subnetwork guides the detection subnetwork to optimize the model.

2.1 Overall Architecture

As shown in Fig. 2(a), this paper presents a scale-aware guidance network. To reduce computational overhead and improve feature representation, a weight-sharing mechanism is used between the two subnetworks. The detection subnetwork takes the raw dataset as input and follows a classical object detection framework. Its main function is to perform object regression and classification tasks, outputting object bounding boxes and category predictions. The scale-aware subnetwork takes an enhanced dataset with scale annotations as input, which is processed by the scale router. This subnetwork learns the scale characteristics of various objects, extracts scale-related features, and produces a guiding signal to improve the performance of the detection subnetwork. As illustrated in Fig. 2(b), a scale-guided learning mechanism is incorporated during training. By adding global precision optimization constraints, the scale-dependent features generated by the scale-aware subnetwork effectively guide the detection subnetwork, improving its performance at different scales.

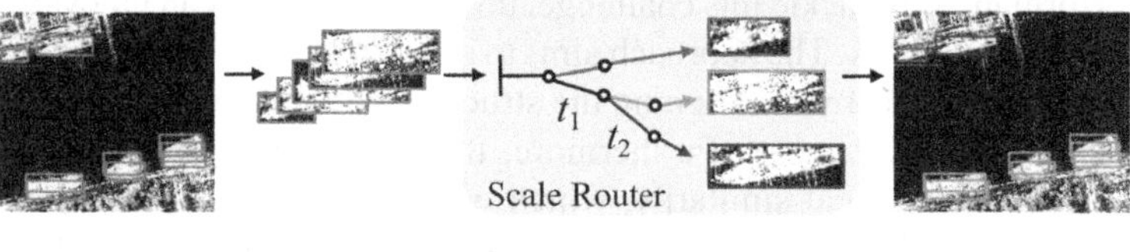

(a) Scale router

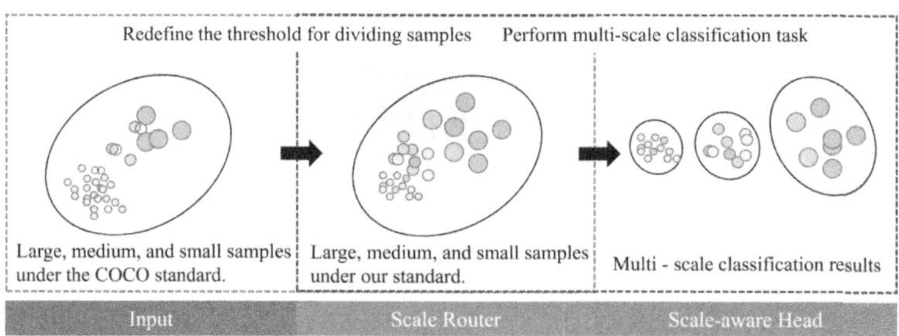

(b) Schematic of sample processing through the scale router and scale-aware head

Fig. 3. The principle of scale router and scale-aware head. (a) t_1 and t_2 are area thresholds. (b) The mechanism of the scale router working with the sensing head is demonstrated.

2.2 Scale-Aware Mechanism

The scale-aware subnetwork is developed to boost performance in multi-scale object detection tasks. Its key element is the decoupled head, which enhances detection accuracy by independently processing features at different scales. The input data for this subnetwork comes from the enhanced dataset processed by the scale router. This dataset includes not only the object's location information but also its scale. Figure 3 illustrates the process of input data generation and the functioning of the scale-aware head. Specifically, after initial screening by the scale router, the input data undergoes label reassignment, as shown in Fig. 3(a). t_1 and t_2 are redefined scale thresholds. The setting of the thresholds follows the empirical guidelines:

(1) Referencing the COCO standard, the initial setting is ${t_1}^2 = 32^2$, and the ratio r of the number of objects with an area smaller than t_1 to those larger than t_1 is calculated.
(2) Although the ideal ratio for the three classes is $r = \frac{1}{1+1} = 0.5$, the SAR ship dataset is dominated by small objects. Following Google Developer's criteria for imbalanced data partitioning [18], if the actual ratio $r > 4$, it indicates a moderate imbalance in the data distribution. In this case, t_1 should be dynamically adjusted in 8-pixel steps (e.g., from 32^2 to 24^2) until $r \leq 4$, achieving an acceptable balanced state.
(3) Once t_1 is determined, adjust t_2 with the same step size to ensure the quantity ratio between medium and large objects remains within the range of 1:1 to 2:1.

Figure 3(b) shows the schematic diagram of the sample processing through the scale router and aware head. The scale router adjusts the data distribution to handle extreme proportions. Based on the assigned scale information, the aware head focuses on feature extraction for a specific scale, refining the detection process. As the network structure is gradually trained and optimized, the traditional single-scale feature extraction evolves into more fine-grained multi-scale feature decoupling. This mechanism helps balance the recognition precision for various objects in the sample. It enables the network to maintain efficient object detection, even in complex scenes with multi-scale objects, ultimately improving overall detection accuracy and robustness.

2.3 Scale-Guided Learning

The core idea of scale-guided learning is to optimize and detect the performance of subnetworks through scale-aware subnetwork guidance. This paper divides the process into a self-updating phase and a guided updating phase. First, in the self-updating phase, the detection subnetwork $F_d(\theta_{fd})$ and scale sensing subnetwork $F_s(\theta_{f_s})$ are independently optimized, with the goal of:

$$\begin{cases} \min\limits_{\theta_{F_d}}(L_{\text{det}}^d(x^d, y^d \mid \theta_{F_d})) \\ \min\limits_{\theta_{F_s}}(\sum_{i=1}^{3} L_{\text{det}}^s(x^{s_i}, y^{s_i} \mid \theta_{F_s})) \end{cases} \tag{1}$$

where θ and L_{det} are the parameters and losses of the subnetwork, the sum of the classification loss and the regression loss. x and y are respectively the input image and Ground Truth. $i \in \{1, 2, 3\}$ representing three different scales. In this process, the two subnetworks gradually adjust their internal parameters to more accurately identify objects of different sizes.

For multi-scale ship detection, it is necessary to ensure the comprehensive detection precision of the model under different overlap degrees and object scales in the optimization process. Therefore, this paper proposes the global precision constraint (GPC):

$$\min_{\theta_{F_d},\theta_{F_s}} (L_{\det}^{d}(x^{d}, y^{d} \mid \theta_{F_d}, \sum_{i=1}^{3} L_{\det}^{s}(x^{s_i}, y^{s_i} \mid \theta_{F_s}) \mid \Psi(AP_s, AP_s^{*}))) \tag{2}$$

where $\Psi(AP_s, AP_s^{*}) = \prod_{t\in\{0,1,\ldots,9\}} \frac{\sum_{t=0}^{9} AP_{s,IoU=0.5+0.05t}}{\sum_{t=0}^{9} AP_{s,IoU=0.5+0.05t}^{*}}$ is the cooperative constraint term. AP_s and AP_s* is the precision before and after the optimization of the scale-aware subnetwork respectively. Intersection over union (IoU) is a measure of the overlap between the detection box and the real box. In this way, the scale-guided learning mechanism can maintain the coordination and balance of multi-scale information in the optimization process, so as to improve the overall performance of object detection tasks at different scales.

2.4 Hierarchical Similarity Measure

In multi-scale SAR image object detection tasks, hierarchical similarity measurement helps analyze the relationships between multi-level features. For instance, in convolutional neural networks, higher-level features typically contain more abstract semantic information, while lower-level features focus on finer details and local information. The model must effectively combine features from different scales. In this process, hierarchical similarity measurement allows us to quantify the correlation between the features at each layer, providing interpretability for the model's training and optimization process.

Centered kernel alignment (CKA) is a metric commonly used to analyze the similarity of layer representations both between and within networks. The center-core alignment is based on the Hilbert-Schmidt independence criterion, which evaluates the independence between random variables in a non-parametric manner [19]. The higher the value, the greater the similarity. Research by Wu et al. [20] demonstrates that, in prediction and anomaly detection tasks, higher similarity corresponds to better performance. In other words, networks with higher CKA values can detect objects more accurately. CKA takes the two-layer representations X and Y from the network as inputs and outputs a similarity score, ranging from 0 to 1, calculated as follows:

$$\mathrm{CKA}(K, L) = \frac{\mathrm{HSIC}(K, L)}{\sqrt{\mathrm{HSIC}(K, K) * \mathrm{HSIC}(L, L)}} \tag{3}$$

where $K = XX^T$ and $L = YY^T$ represents the two-layer Gram matrix. HSIC is the Hilbert-Schmidt independence criterion, calculated by the following formula:

$$HSIC(K, L) = \frac{1}{(n-1)^2} tr(KHLH) \tag{4}$$

where H is the central matrix and$H_n = I_n - \frac{1}{n} 11^T$.

Table 1. Scale router threshold settings

Threshold	SSDD	HRSID	HRSC2016
t_1	32	24	96
t_2	48	32	128

Table 2. Comparison of other state-of-the-art models and ours on SSDD

Detector	Note	AP	AP_S	AP_M	AP_L	AP_{50}
FCOS [23]	Baseline and other popular models	54.9	58.2	45.7	29.9	87.4
Faster R-CNN [24]		68.1	63.9	65.3	13.7	95.9
Cascade R-CNN [25]		70.5	71.8	66.7	41.4	95.5
RetinaNet [26]		60.3	62.2	55.0	31.2	90.6
GFL [27]		67.2	68.0	65.1	24.0	94.8
YOLOv8-MS [28]		72.6	72.0	78.6	70.0	97.2
ATSS [29]		65.4	66.6	61.8	16.2	95.7
DECA [30]		76.2	75.3	81.4	85.2	99.1
M^2S-DETR [31]		76.2	75.3	81.7	73.5	97.7
FINet [32]		87.7	89.0	83.2	47.7	99.0
PEGNet [33]		71.1	70.9	72.9	55.1	97.3
DFENet [34]		62.6	54.4	72.6	72.3	97.6
PFARN [35]		66.3	57.4	70.1	82.1	98.1
FCOS [23]	**Ours**	60.1	62.0	54.7	30.1	93.0
Faster R-CNN [24]		71.0	72.2	68.5	43.7	97.4
Cascade R-CNN [25]		72.6	73.0	71.6	53.0	97.1
YOLOv8-MS [28]		74.7	73.4	80.4	85.0	98.6
Mask-RCNN [36]*		**89.6**	**89.7**	**90.5**	**85.6**	**100.0**

[a]FINet is an improved detector based on Mask-RCNN, specifically designed for ship detection in SAR images. In experiments, we use the original Mask-RCNN as the baseline to compare with FINet, demonstrating its superiority over other popular detectors under the same benchmark.

3 Experiments

3.1 Datasets and Implementation Details

We conducted experiments on SSDD [16], HRSID [17] and HRSC2016 [21]. SSDD and HRSID are SAR ship datasets. To validate the flexibility of the proposed method, we also conducted experiments on the HRSC2016. AP metrics under COCO and PASCAL VOC

2012 metrics were used to evaluate detector performance. The proposed method was implemented based on the popular PaddleDetection. ResNet-50 is used as the backbone. The threshold settings of the scale router are shown in Table 1, set based on the rules mentioned in Sect. 2.2. With Momentum as the optimizer, the initial learning rate is 0.001 and the momentum value is 0.9. The experiments were conducted on the NVIDIA RTX A4000 GPU. Other unspecified configurations remain consistent with the baseline configuration.

Table 3. Comparison of other state-of-the-art models and ours on HRSID

Detector	Note	AP	AP_S	AP_M	AP_L	AP_{50}
FCOS [23]	Baseline and other popular models	54.8	55.9	59.4	9.5	80.9
Faster R-CNN [24]		62.6	64.0	61.3	12.2	87.6
Cascade R-CNN [25]		63.1	64.3	63.2	6.6	85.4
RetinaNet [26]		52.6	53.5	56.3	12.2	77.0
GFL [27]		51.9	51.5	59.6	10.5	72.9
YOLOv8-MS [28]		57.3	66.7	67.3	5.1	80.6
ATSS [29]		60.8	62.0	62.1	16.1	85.9
DECA [30]		69.5	**70.3**	73.9	37.6	92.9
OEGR-DETR [37]		64.9	66.7	62.6	34.1	90.5
FINet [32]		66.3	67.5	66.4	13.3	89.3
PEGNet [33]		67.9	57.4	80.6	45.2	90.5
Enhanced YOLO [38]		66.7	66.3	74.5	23.1	91.0
FCOS [23]	**Ours**	59.1	60.5	61.6	17.2	85.3
Faster R-CNN [24]		64.6	65.7	65.3	18.2	89.0
Cascade R-CNN [25]		64.8	66.0	65.3	12.3	87.1
YOLOv8-MS [28]		58.6	67.1	68.9	7.2	81.7
Mask-RCNN [36]*		**70.3**	**70.3**	**76.6**	**55.3**	**93.6**

[a]FINet is an improved detector based on Mask-RCNN, specifically designed for ship detection in SAR images. In experiments, we use the original Mask-RCNN as the baseline to compare with FINet, demonstrating its superiority over other popular detectors under the same benchmark.

3.2 Comparison with the Most Advanced Methods

Tables 2 and 3 show the results of the proposed method and other popular methods on two SAR datasets. It can be seen that the detectors guided by the proposed method consistently outperform the original detectors. For the AP of the detectors, the proposed method yields an improvement of 2.1%–5.2% on SSDD and 1.3%–4.3% on HRSID. It is worth noting that Mask-RCNN (ours) achieves SOTA performance across all metrics. Additionally, the values demonstrate strong competitiveness across the three scales.

To further validate the effectiveness and applicability of the proposed algorithm, we conducted experiments on optical remote sensing datasets. LSKNet [22] is a rotation-invariant remote sensing image object detection algorithm. The experimental results are presented in Table 4. In terms of the comprehensive evaluation index, the proposed method achieves an AP score of 73.6%, which is 1.1% higher than the baseline algorithm. Additionally, it can be observed that, under various IoU thresholds, the proposed method demonstrates distinct advantages in high-precision object detection. Specifically, when IoU $\geq$ 75, the performance of the proposed method surpasses that of the baseline.

Table 4. Implementation of our method on SOTA model of HRSC2016

Model	AP	AP_{50}	AP_{75}	AP_{80}	AP_{85}	AP_{90}
LSKNet [22]	72.5	**97.9**	90.3	81.5	57.0	15.6
Ours	**73.6**	97.5	**90.4**	**82.9**	**62.4**	**20.1**

3.3 Interpretability of the Proposed Model

In the process of feature extraction from shallow to deep layers, shallow features have higher resolution and can capture rich geometric details, but their receptive field is small and they lack semantic information. In contrast, deep features have a larger receptive field and contain more semantic information, but their resolution is lower, making it harder to capture fine geometric details. The analysis suggests that a feature extraction network with a fixed number of layers should be designed so that both shallow and deep features carry as much detailed and semantic information as possible. To evaluate this, we calculated the centered kernel alignment between the backbone network of the baseline and the proposed method, as shown in Fig. 4. The selected layers are the five-stage convolution layer and the maxpooling layer in ResNet-50, where the convolution layer contains four subsampled convolution layers, totaling 54 layers. From the figure, particularly the area inside the circular dashed line, it is evident that the baseline method exhibits clear stages in similarity structure, with a lower similarity score between high and low levels. The weak correlation between shallow and deep features may hinder effective information transfer when detecting multi-scale objects. In contrast, the proposed network shows a high similarity between shallow and deep features. This indicates that our optimization approach enables better cooperation between shallow and deep features, enhancing the ability to extract both detailed and semantic information.

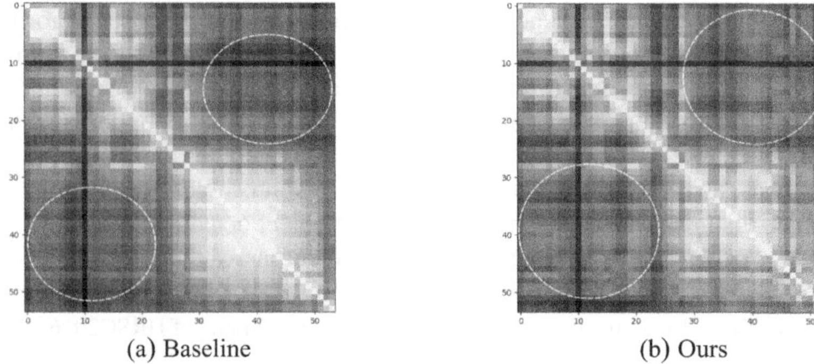

(a) Baseline (b) Ours

Fig. 4. The hierarchical similarity of the baseline and proposed method.

Table 5. Verification of the generalization ability of the proposed method. Bold font represents the best values, while blue font indicates the second-best values.

Detector	Note	Precision	Recall	F1	AP_{75}
FCOS [23]	Baseline	32.1	45.9	37.8	22.0
Faster R-CNN [24]		34.3	45.4	39.1	25.7
Cascade R-CNN [25]		31.1	42.2	35.8	23.2
FCOS [23]	Ours	33.2	47.4	39.0	26.8
Faster R-CNN [24]		**38.2**	**48.1**	**42.6**	28.0
Cascade R-CNN [25]		33.7	45.5	38.7	**28.7**

3.4 Generalization Verification of the Proposed Method

Hu [8] verified the generalization ability of the model by training on HRSID and testing on SSDD. We adopted this method to assess the generalization ability of our network, using the same evaluation metrics. We chose a representative detector for the experiment. Specifically, they are the one-stage detector FCOS, the two-stage detector Faster R-CNN, and the multi-stage detector Cascade R-CNN. The results are presented in Table 5. The detector guided by the method in this paper is superior to the baseline algorithm. Specifically, the Faster R-CNN detector guided by the proposed method has better overall performance, followed by Cascade R-CNN and FCOS. For example, in Precision and Recall, Faster R-CNN(Ours) achieves 38.2% and 48.1%, respectively, which is better than the baseline algorithm +3.9% and + 2.7%. Cascade R-CNN guided by scale sensing subnetwork has achieved the best performance among the three algorithms, but its generalization performance is still a certain gap compared with R-CNN. This means that the detection performance and generalization performance of SAR image detection algorithm are worthy of further study.

4 Conclusion

This paper proposes a multi-scale object detection model based on the principle of global precision optimization. By decoupling the model's head, a scale-aware subnetwork is designed to guide the detection subnetwork, enhancing the detector's ability to extract multi-scale features of remote sensing objects. Additionally, we propose an explanation method based on hierarchical similarity, which improves the understanding of the model's internal mechanisms.

While the scale-aware network effectively enhances multi-scale object detection performance, there remains room for improvement. To address the limitations of the current fixed-step threshold adjustment strategy, future work could explore more refined adaptive optimization based on clustering algorithms. This improvement direction would maintain compatibility with the existing architecture while further enhancing the method's practicality in complex scenarios.

References

1. Ma, X., Xu, J., Wu, P., Kong, P.: Oil spill detection based on deep convolutional neural networks using polarimetric scattering information from sentinel-1 SAR images. IEEE Trans. Geosci. Remote Sens. **60**, 1–13 (2022)
2. Mdakane, L.W.: Sentinel-1 Sar for operational monitoring of southern Africa oceans. Int. Arch. Photogramm. Remote. Sens. Spat. Inf. Sci. **XLIII-B3-2022**, 301–306 (2022)
3. He, P., Wen, Y., Xu, C., Chen, Y.: Complete three-dimensional near-field surface displacements from imaging geodesy techniques applied to the 2016 Kumamoto earthquake. Remote Sens. Environ. **232**, 111321 (2019)
4. Chen, S.-W., Cui, X.-C., Wang, X.-S., Xiao, S.-P.: Speckle-free SAR image ship detection. IEEE Trans. Image Process **30**, 5969–5983 (2021)
5. Ai, J., Pei, Z., Yao, B., Wang, Z., Xing, M.: AIS data aided Rayleigh CFAR ship detection algorithm of multiple-target environment in SAR images. IEEE Trans. Aerosp. Electron. Syst. **58**(2), 1266–1282 (2022)
6. Guiming, S., Jidong, S.: Multi-scale Harris corner detection algorithm based on canny edge-detection. In: 2018 IEEE International Conference on Computer and Communication Engineering Technology (CCET), pp. 305–309. IEEE (2018)
7. Cui, Z., Li, Q., Cao, Z., Liu, N.: Dense attention pyramid networks for multi-scale ship detection in SAR images. IEEE Trans. Geosci. Remote Sens. **57**(11), 8983–8997
8. Hu, Q., Hu, S., Liu, S.: BANet: a balance attention network for anchor-free ship detection in SAR images. IEEE Trans. Geosci. Remote Sens. **60**, 1–12 (2022)
9. Liu, N., Cui, Z., Cao, Z., Pi, Y., Lan, H.: Scale-transferrable pyramid network for multi-scale ship detection in Sar images. In: IGARSS 2019–2019 IEEE International Geoscience and Remote Sensing Symposium, pp. 1–4. IEEE (2019)
10. Zhang, Y., Wang, X., Jiang, Z., Li, G., He, Y.: An efficient center-based method with multilevel auxiliary supervision for multiscale SAR ship detection. IEEE J. Sel. Top. Appl. Earth Obs. Remote Sens. **15**, 7065–7075 (2022)
11. Ai, J., Tian, R., Luo, Q., Jin, J., Tang, B.: Multi-scale rotation-invariant Haar-like feature integrated CNN-based ship detection algorithm of multiple-target environment in SAR imagery. IEEE Trans. Geosci. Remote Sens. **57**(12), 10070–10087 (2019)
12. Cui, Z., et al.: Exploring Resolution and Degradation Clues as Self-Supervised Signal for Low Quality Object Detection. In: European Conference on Computer Vision Lecture Notes in Computer Science, pp. 473–491. Springer Nature Switzerland, Cham (2022)

13. Li, Y., Chen, Y., Wang, N., Zhang, Z.-X.: Scale-aware trident networks for object detection. In: 2019 IEEE/CVF International Conference on Computer Vision (ICCV), pp. 6053–6062. IEEE (2019)
14. Singh, B., Davis, L.S.: An analysis of scale invariance in object detection-SNIP. In: 2018 IEEE/CVF Conference on Computer Vision and Pattern Recognition, pp. 3578–3587. IEEE (2018)
15. Wang, X., Zhang, S., Yu, Z., Feng, L., Zhang, W.: Scale-equalizing pyramid convolution for object detection. In: 2020 IEEE/CVF Conference on Computer Vision and Pattern Recognition (CVPR), pp. 13356–13365. IEEE (2020)
16. Zhang, T., et al.: SAR ship detection dataset (SSDD): official release and comprehensive data analysis. Remote Sens. **13**(18), 3690 (2021)
17. Wei, S., Zeng, X., Qu, Q., Wang, M., Su, H., Shi, J.: HRSID: a high-resolution SAR images dataset for ship detection and instance segmentation. IEEE Access **8**, 120234–120254 (2020)
18. Google developers. Datasets: Imbalanced datasets. Retrieved from https://developers.google.cn/machine-learning/crash-course/overfitting/imbalanced-datasets.
19. Wang, S., Gao, J., Li, Z., Zhang, X., Hu, W.: A closer look at self-supervised lightweight vision transformers. In: International Conference on Machine Learning, pp. 35624–35641 (2023)
20. Wu, H., Hu, T., Liu, Y., Zhou, H., Wang, J., Long, M.: TimesNet: temporal 2D-variation modeling for general time series analysis. In: Proceedings of the International Conference Learning Represent (2023)
21. Liu, Z., Yuan, L., Weng, L., Yang, Y.: A high resolution optical satellite image dataset for ship recognition and some new baselines. In: Proceedings of the 6th International Conference on Pattern Recognition Applications and Methods, SCITEPRESS - Science and Technology Publications, pp. 324–331 (2017)
22. Li, Y., Hou, Q., Zheng, Z., Cheng, M.-M., Yang, J., Li, X.: Large selective kernel network for remote sensing object detection. In: 2023 IEEE/CVF International Conference on Computer Vision (ICCV), pp. 16748–16759. IEEE (2023)
23. Tian, Z., Shen, C., Chen, H., He, T.: FCOS: fully convolutional one-stage object detection. In: 2019 IEEE/CVF International Conference on Computer Vision (ICCV), pp. 9626–9635. IEEE (2019)
24. Ren, S., He, K., Girshick, R., Sun, J.: Faster R-CNN: towards real-time object detection with region proposal networks. IEEE Trans. Pattern Anal. Mach. Intell. **39**(6), 1137–1149 (2017)
25. Cai, Z., Vasconcelos, N.: Cascade R-CNN: delving into high quality object detection. In: 2018 IEEE/CVF Conference on Computer Vision and Pattern Recognition, pp. 6154–6162. IEEE (2018)
26. Lin, T.-Y., Goyal, P., Girshick, R., He, K., Dollar, P.: Focal loss for dense object detection. In: 2017 IEEE International Conference on Computer Vision (ICCV), pp. 2999–3007. IEEE (2017)
27. Li, X., Wang, W., Hu, X., Li, J., Tang, J., Yang, J.: Generalized focal loss V2: learning reliable localization quality estimation for dense object detection. In: 2021 IEEE/CVF Conference on Computer Vision and Pattern Recognition (CVPR), pp. 11627–11636. IEEE (2021)
28. Chen, Y., et al.: YOLO-MS: rethinking multi-scale representation learning for real-time object detection. IEEE Trans. Pattern Anal. Mach. Intell. **47**(6), 4240–4252 (2025)
29. Zhang, S., Chi, C., Yao, Y., Lei, Z., Li, S.Z.: Bridging the gap between anchor-based and anchor-free detection via adaptive training sample selection. In: 2020 IEEE/CVF Conference on Computer Vision and Pattern Recognition (CVPR), pp. 9756–9765. IEEE (2020)
30. Lin, H., et al.: DCEA: DETR with concentrated deformable attention for end-to-end ship detection in SAR images. IEEE J. Sel. Topics Appl. Earth Obs. Remote Sens. **17**, 17292–17307 (2024)

31. Guo, P., Li, H.-C., Liu, N., Lei, S., Geng, X., Pan, J.: M2S-DETR: a mixed receptive field and multiposition encoding for scale-sensitive SAR ship detection with transformer. IEEE Sensors J. **25**(7), 12184–12197 (2025)
32. Hu, Q., Hu, S., Liu, S., Xu, S., Zhang, Y.-D.: FINet: a feature interaction network for SAR ship object-level and pixel-level detection. IEEE Trans. Geosci. Remote Sens. **60**, 1–15 (2022)
33. Tang, X., Zhang, J., Xia, Y., Cao, K., Zhang, C.: PEGNet: an enhanced ship detection model for dense scenes and multiscale targets. IEEE Geosci. Remote Sens. Lett. **22**, 1–5 (2025)
34. Yang, C., Li, C., Zhu, Y.: Denoising and feature enhancement network for target detection based on SAR images. Remote Sens. **17**(10), 1739 (2025)
35. Li, K., Yu, H., Li, S., Chen, S., Wang, B.: PFARN: pyramid fusion attention and refinement network for multiscale ship detection in SAR images. IEEE J. Sel. Topics Appl. Earth Obs. Remote Sens. **18**, 9821–9836 (2025)
36. He, K., Gkioxari, G., Dollar, P., Girshick, R.: Mask R-CNN. In: 2017 IEEE International Conference on Computer Vision (ICCV), pp. 2980–2988. IEEE (2017)
37. Feng, Y., You, Y., Tian, J., Meng, G.: OEGR-DETR: A novel detection transformer based on orientation enhancement and group relations for SAR object detection. Remote Sens. **16**(1), 106 (2023)
38. Guan, T., Chang, S., Wang, C., Jia, X.: SAR small ship detection based on enhanced YOLO network. Remote Sens. **17**(5), 839 (2025)

Image Analysis and Processing

IMFDM: Improved Mamba-Based Feature Decomposition Model for Multi-Modality Image Fusion

Ziheng Ling[1], Hui Wang[2], Lina Chen[2(✉)], and Hong Gao[2]

[1] College of Physics and Electronic Information Engineering, Zhejiang Normal University, Jinhua 321004, China
hor1zon1zz@zjnu.edu.cn

[2] College of Computer Science and Technology, Zhejiang Normal University, Jinhua 321004, China
chenlina@zjnu.cn

Abstract. Multi-Modality Image Fusion (MMIF) aims to integrate complementary information from multiple source images into a single image while preserving the original highlights and detailed textures. To tackle the critical problem of cross-modality feature modeling and decomposition, an Improved Mamba-based Feature Decomposition Model (IMFDM) is proposed. Firstly, IMFDM extracts cross-modality shallow features using the Shallow Feature Encoder (SFE). Secondly, the dual-branch feature extractor decomposes these shallow features into low-frequency and high-frequency. Finally, the decomposed features are adaptively integrated by the Content-Guided Attention Fusion module (CGAFusion), and then the decoder outputs the fusion result. This method explores the application of Mamba in MMIF and proposes a dual-branch State-Space Model (SSM)-Convolutional Neural Network (CNN) encoder: the Base Feature Encoder (BFE) leverages Mamba's efficient long-range modeling for low-frequency features, while the Detail Feature Encoder (DFE) extracts high-frequency details by a multi-branch strategy. Extensive experiments show that IMFDM exhibits advanced performance in various fusion tasks. Furthermore, IMFDM also achieves satisfactory results in downstream Multi-modality object detection in subsequent unified benchmarks.

Keywords: Multi-Modality Image Fusion · Low-High Frequency Feature Decomposition · Improved Mamba-based Feature Decomposition Model · Dual-Branch SSM-CNN Feature Extractor

1 Introduction

Multi-modality image fusion is a digital image processing method for generating high-quality, information-rich images by integrating multiple modalities of the same target [16,18]. Our work considers that the input features are correlated at

P. Li et al. (Eds.): CGI 2025, LNCS 16508, pp. 133–145, 2026.
https://doi.org/10.1007/978-3-032-22264-0_11

low-frequency, representing the shared information between modalities; while at high-frequency are irrelevant, representing the specific information of modality. The Correlation Coefficient function is introduced to measure the linear relationship strength of cross-modality features. Moreover, to balance the efficiency and performance, the efficient selection mechanism and hardware awareness in Mamba [2] inspire us with potential solutions. Mamba and its variants have shown a deep influence on computer vision [3,20]. However, due to the lack of a similar cross-attention mechanism, the potential of Mamba has not been fully exploited for MMIF. Therefore, Improved Mamba-based Feature Decomposition Model (IMFDM) is proposed, the workflow is shown in Fig. 1. The specific contributions are as follows:

1) The dual-branch SSM-CNN extractor is proposed for feature modeling, in which BFE and DFE block process long-range and short-range dependencies in parallel for modality-shared and modality-specific features.
2) The CGAFusion and specific training paradigm are introduced to adaptively integrate useful information for deeper features, which improves the quality of the fusion images and enhances the robustness of the network.
3) IMFDM achieves more advanced performance in the three mainstream Infrared-Visible Image Fusion (IVF) datasets, and the trained model without fine-tuning can be directly applied to Medical Image Fusion (MIF). Experiments show advanced performance and excellent generalisation ability.

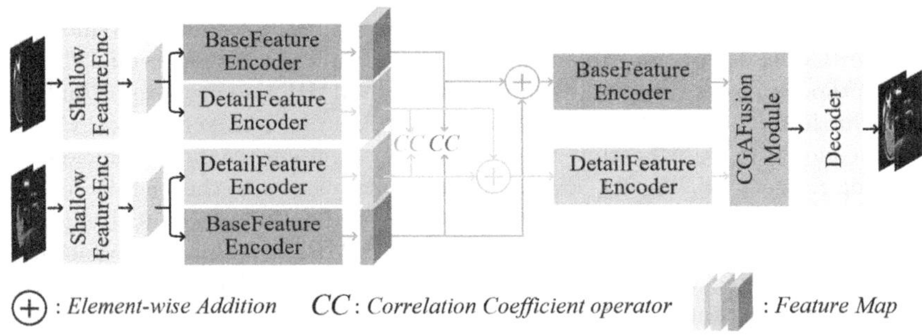

Fig. 1. The overall network architecture of IMFDM.

2 Related Work

2.1 Multi-Modality Image Fusion

In the field of deep learning, image fusion algorithm realizes effective feature extraction and information fusion by the powerful fitting ability of the neural network. These fusion images integrate complementary information from the source images, facilitating a wide range of applications [8]. Multi-Modality Image Fusion has made great breakthroughs in recent years. CDDFuse [17] combined with Transformer and CNN for cross-modality information extraction has impressed the field of general image fusion. At the same time, the method based on the diffusion model began to come into view. DDFM [19] used Bayesian theory and a pre-trained diffusion model to formalize the image fusion into a conditional generation problem and obtained high-quality fusion results. Recently, EMMA [18] sought a new training paradigm to solve the problem of a lack of ground-truth support in fusion model training. However, the current approaches are not yet able to achieve both robust performance and efficiency. Therefore, our work seeks to incorporate new backbones to drive the development and innovation.

2.2 State-Space Models

State-Space Models, originated from classical control theory. Due to the property of linearly scaling with sequence length in processing continuous long sequence data, it has become one of the hotspots for deep networks. Many studies about SSMs have been devoted to their structural improvement. Recently, Mamba [2] further improved S4 by constructing a data-dependent SSM layer, introducing an efficient selection mechanism and hardware-aware algorithm. In addition, Mamba has been applied to computer vision with remarkable success, such as image classification [20], image restoration [3], and medical image segmentation [13]. Overall, Mamba performs impressively in natural language processing and vision tasks, but its application in MMIF has been relatively understudied. This work investigates the suitability of Mamba for image fusion and designs specific structures that enable Mamba to realize its full potential.

3 Method

3.1 Encoder

As shown in Fig. 2, there are three different feature encoders in IMFDM: Restormer-based [15] SFE, SSM-Based BFE and CNN-Based DFE. BFE and DFE together constitute the dual-branch long-short range encoder. Here, the input infrared-visible image pairs are denoted as $\mathrm{I} \in \mathbb{R}^{H\times W\times 1}$ and $\mathrm{R} \in \mathbb{R}^{H\times W\times 3}$.

Shallow Feature Encoder. SFE is to preliminarily extract shallow features $\{\Phi_I^S, \Phi_V^S\}$ from the source images. As shown in Fig. 2(c), the Restormer block is introduced as the basic unit of the SFE. On the one hand, MDTA can efficiently process high-resolution images. On the other hand, the GDFN can retain more useful information for further decomposition. More detailed information about MDTA and GDFN within the Restormer can be found in the original paper [15].

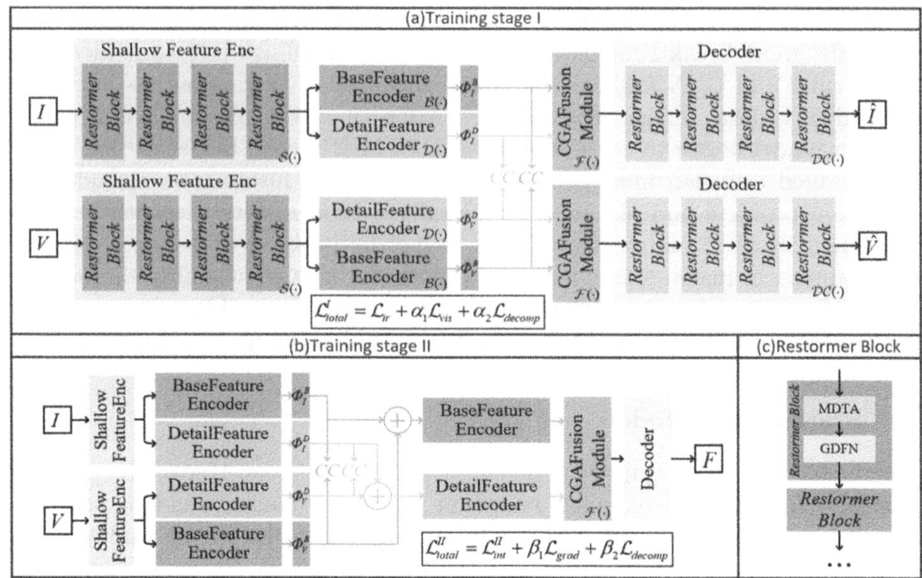

Fig. 2. The training paradigm of IMFDM. (a) The pipeline of stage I, whose purpose is to train the AE architecture for reconstructing images. (b) The pipeline of stage II, whose purpose is to output fusion image on the basis of the pre-trained AE architecture in training stage I. (c) The structure of Restormer.

Base Feature Encoder. Because extracting low-frequency features requires strong long-range dependency modeling performance. For the purpose of keeping both the long-range modeling and efficiency, this method is inspired by the Residual State-Space Block [3] and proposes the BFE block, as shown in Fig. 3. Due to the SSM layer having to flatten 2D features into 1D sequences, this may result in spatially close pixels being too far apart on 1D sequence. To address the inherent lack of spatial perception in SSM, the GSC [13] is designed to capture spatial relationships of 2D features. As shown in Fig. 3(a), given a 2D shallow feature $\Phi^s \in \mathbb{R}^{H \times W \times C}$ firstly after passing through two convolution blocks with convolution kernel sizes of 3×3 and 1×1, respectively, the information transfer is controlled by pixel-by-pixel multiplication. Finally, the convolution block further integrates the features and residual connections, as presented in Eq. (1):

$$\Phi^S_{GSC} = \Phi^S + C_{3\times3}(C_{3\times3}(\Phi^S) \cdot C_{1\times1}(\Phi^S)). \tag{1}$$

The VSSM [20] is introduced to capture the long-range dependencies, as shown in Fig. 3(c). 2D-Selective Scan as the core part can scan from four directions to spread 2D image features into 1D sequences by the discretised iterative formulation in spatial dimension, as shown in Fig. 3(b). Accompanied by a learnable scale factor s to adjust the weights from the residual connections, as presented in Eq. (2):

$$\Phi^B_{SSM} = \mathrm{VSSM}\left(\mathrm{LN}(\Phi^S_{GSC})\right) + s \cdot \Phi^S_{GSC}. \tag{2}$$

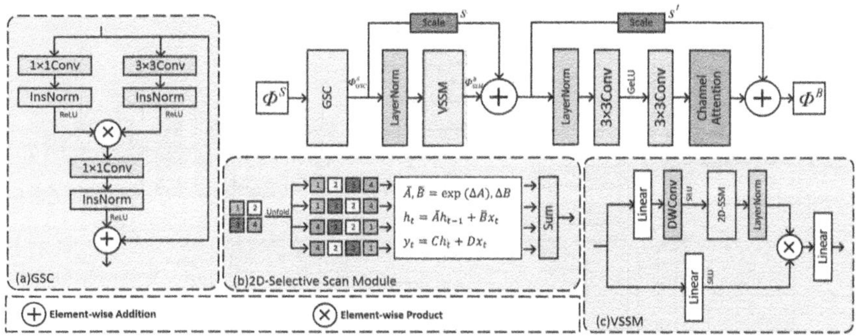

Fig. 3. The detailed structure of BFE. (a) Gated Spatial Convolution (GSC). (b) 2D-Selective Scan Module. (c) Visual State-Space Module (VSSM).

where LN(·) represents the layer normalized, and s represents the learnable scale factor.

In addition, since the SSM layer processes flattened feature maps in the form of 1D sequences, neighborhood pixels are susceptible to flattening strategies, leading to local information forgetting. Meanwhile, the state-space equation usually contains a large number of hidden states to remember long-sequence dependencies, which easily leads to channel redundancy. Therefore, triple local convolution and channel attention are designed to help complement the neighbor pixel similarity and spatial dimension interactions, as presented in Eq. (3):

$$\Phi^B = \mathrm{CA}(\mathrm{Convs}(\mathrm{L}(\Phi^{\mathrm{B}}_{\mathrm{SSM}}))) + s' \cdot \Phi^B_{SSM}. \quad (3)$$

where CA(·) represents a channel attention operation, Convs represents the local convolution block, and s' represents another learnable scaling factor.

Detail Feature Encoder. DFE is designed to extract high-frequency information from shallow features. Given that the edge and texture information is critical to the quality of fusion images, the high-frequency information faces the difficulties of easy loss and wide distribution. For this reason, a multi-branch parallel feature extraction strategy is adopted, and it helps DFE adapt to the multi-scale information of different targets so that it can focus on as much detailed texture information as possible, as shown in Fig. 4. Specifically, the parallel strategy of DFE involves the following branches: the local (P = 2), global (P = 4), convolutional, and dynamic branches. For the local and global branches, the patch-aware [14] mechanism is introduced to control non-overlapping patch aggregation and displacement to achieve the extraction and interaction of local and global information. For the Conv branch, DFE combines three 3×3 convolutional kernels to capture multi-level information, as shown in Fig. 4(a).

Unlike existing multi-branch strategies that often rely on global and local branches, the dynamic branch is designed for fusion images, and the LSK [7] block is introduced to adjust the weights of the large kernels, which helps DFE

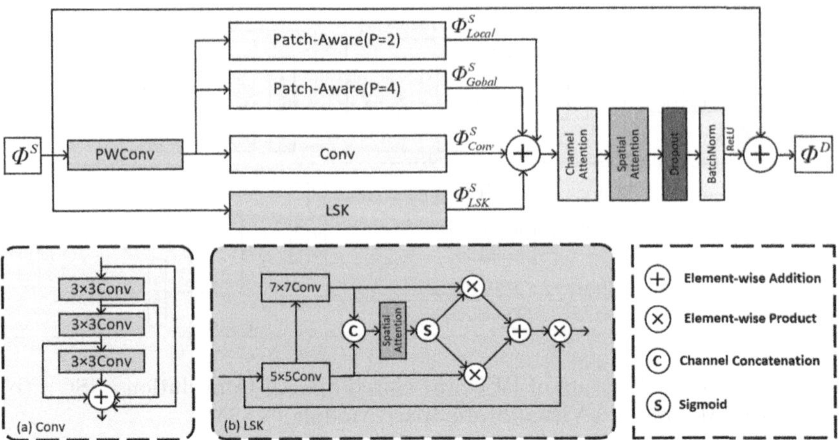

Fig. 4. The detailed structure of DFE. (a) Large Selective Kernel (LSK). (b) The Conv branch.

effectively adapt to the differences in the background information of different targets and preserve potential low-frequency features, as shown in Fig. 4(b). Given the DFE input $\Phi^S \in \mathbb{R}^{H\times W\times C}$, and then the Φ^S_{Local}, Φ^S_{Global}, Φ^S_{Conv}, and Φ^S_{LSK} are computed by the involved branches, respectively. The outputs from these four branches are then aggregated, as presented in Eq. (4):

$$\hat{\Phi^D} = \Phi^S_{Local} + \Phi^S_{Global} + \Phi^S_{Conv} + \Phi^S_{LSK}. \tag{4}$$

The gradient vanishing of neural networks is alleviated by residual connections after channel and spatial attention, as presented in Eq. (5) and Eq. (6):

$$\Phi^D_I = CA\left(\hat{\Phi^D}\right) \otimes \hat{\Phi^D}, \Phi^D_{II} = \mathrm{SA}(\Phi^D_I) \otimes \Phi^D_I. \tag{5}$$

$$\Phi^D = \sigma(BN(dropout(\Phi^D_{II}))) + \Phi^S. \tag{6}$$

where $\mathrm{SA}(\cdot)$ represents Spatial attention operation, $\sigma(\cdot)$ represents the activation function, and $BN(\cdot)$ represents BatchNorm.

3.2 CGAFusion Moduel

The low-frequency feature Φ^B is very different from the high-frequency feature Φ^D because they have completely different receptive fields. Simple addition or concatenation can not fully integrate the information comprehensively. To alleviate the receptive field mismatch, this method introduces the CGAFusion [1] for adaptively blending low-frequency and high-frequency features. CGAFusion is introduced to emphasise the integration of critical information and to reduce the redundancy of insignificant information. CGA black can learn the channel and spatial weights to adaptively fuse different level features, and output

$W \in \mathbb{R}^{H\times W\times C}$. After weighted summation and adding residual joins, the fusion feature $\Phi^F \in \mathbb{R}^{H\times W\times C}$ is obtained by the projection, as presented in Eq. (7):

$$\Phi^F = C_{1\times 1}(\Phi^B \cdot W + \Phi^D \cdot (1 - W) + \Phi^B + \Phi^D). \tag{7}$$

3.3 Decoder and Two-Stage Training

In the decoder, the decomposed features are processed by CGAFusion as input and output the reconstructed original image (stage I) and fusion image (stage II). The Restormer block is designed to be consistent with SFE, which aims to help a finer reconstruction of the fusion image.

Moreover, the lack of ground truth limits the role of advanced supervised learning methods in MMIF. The specific two-stage training is proposed for End-to-End training, as shown in Fig. 2. In stage I, firstly, SFE extracts shallow features $\{\Phi_I^S, \Phi_V^S\}$ from infrared-visible image pairs $\{I, V\}$. Then, the low-frequency global features $\{\Phi_I^B, \Phi_V^B\}$ and high-frequency local features $\{\Phi_I^D, \Phi_V^D\}$ are further obtained by BFE and DFE. After that, the low-high frequency features $\{\Phi_V^B, \Phi_V^D\}$ for the visible (or $\{\Phi_I^B, \Phi_I^D\}$ the infrared) are processed by CGAFusion for reconstructing visible images $\hat{V}$ (or infrared images $\hat{I}$). Similarly, in stage II, the AE trained in stage I for capturing the deeper features $\{\Phi^B, \Phi^D\}$ by additional BFE and DFE. Finally, the fusion feature Φ^F is obtained by CGAFusion and output fusion result F.

3.4 Training Loss Function

In stage I, the total $\mathcal{L}_{total}^I$ is Eq. (8):

$$\mathcal{L}_{total}^I = \mathcal{L}_{vis} + \alpha_1 \mathcal{L}_{ir} + \alpha_2 \mathcal{L}_{decomp}. \tag{8}$$

where α_1 and α_2 are the tuning parameters, $\mathcal{L}_{decomp}$ is the decomposition loss, $\mathcal{L}_{vis}$ and $\mathcal{L}_{ir}$ are the reconstruction losses for infrared and visible images, which aim to reduce the loss of image information, as presented in Eq. (9):

$$\mathcal{L}_{vis} = \mathcal{L}_{int}^I\left(I, \hat{I}\right) + \mu \mathcal{L}_{SSIM}\left(I, \hat{I}\right). \tag{9}$$

where $\mathcal{L}_{int}^I = \| I - \hat{I} \|_2^2, \mathcal{L}_{SSIM}(I, \hat{I}) = 1 - SSIM(I, \hat{I})$. $SSIM(\cdot,\cdot)$ is the structural similarity index, $\mathcal{L}_{ir}$ is obtained in the same way.

Following [17], the feature decomposition loss $\mathcal{L}_{decomp}$ is presented in Eq. (10):

$$\mathcal{L}_{decomp} = \frac{\left(\mathcal{L}_{CC}^D\right)^2}{\mathcal{L}_{CC}^B} = \frac{\left(CC(\Phi_I^D, \Phi_V^D)\right)^2}{CC\left(\Phi_I^B, \Phi_V^B\right) + \delta}. \tag{10}$$

where $CC(\cdot,\cdot)$ is presented in Eq. (11). Its solution space is restricted to $[-1, 1]$, where closer to 1 means more highly correlated, closer to -1 means more negatively correlated, and closer to 0 means more irrelevant. δ is set to 1.01 to ensure that $\mathcal{L}_{decomp}$ is meaningful.

$$CC(X,Y)=\sum_{i=1}^{M}\sum_{j=1}^{N}\frac{(X(i,j)-\overline{X})(Y(i,j)-\overline{Y})}{\sqrt{(X(i,j)-\overline{X})^2(Y(i,j)-\overline{Y})^2}}. \quad (11)$$

where M and N represent the width and height of the images, $\overline{X}$ and $\overline{Y}$ represent the pixel mean of X and Y, respectively. During the loss function guides model to training, $\mathcal{L}_{CC}^{B}$ gradually becomes larger and $\mathcal{L}_{CC}^{D}$ gradually approaches 0, and Fig. 5 shows the visualization of the feature decomposition.

In stage II, the total loss $\mathcal{L}_{decomp}^{II}$ is Eq. (12):

$$\mathcal{L}_{total}^{II}=\mathcal{L}_{int}^{II}+\beta_1\mathcal{L}_{grad}+\beta_2\mathcal{L}_{decomp}. \quad (12)$$

where β_1 and β_2 are the tuning parameters, $\mathcal{L}_{int}^{II}=\frac{1}{HW}\parallel I_f-max(I_{vis},I_{ir})\parallel_1$, $\mathcal{L}_{grad}=\frac{1}{HW}\parallel|\nabla I_f|-\max(|\nabla I_{vis}|,|\nabla I_{ir}|)\parallel_1$, ∇ represents the Sobel gradient.

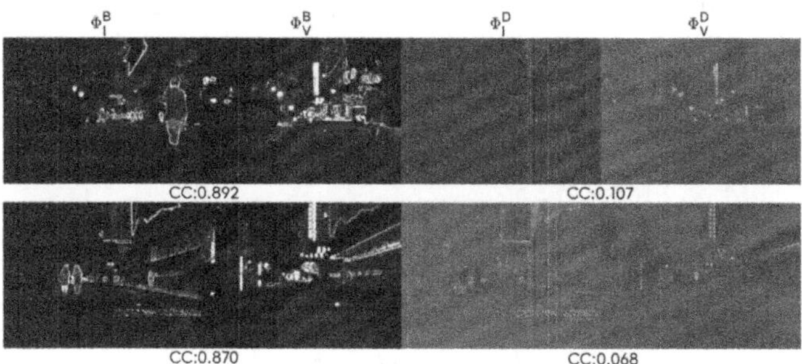

Fig. 5. Visualization results of the features decomposition.

4 Experiment

4.1 Infrared-Visible Image Fusion

Comparison with SOTA. Here IMFDM is compared qualitatively and quantitatively with SOTA methods: TarDAL [8], SwinFusion [9], LRRNet [6], MetaFusion [16], DDFM [19], CDDFuse [17] and EMMA [18] on three popular benchmarks: MSRS [11], M^{3}FD [8] and LLVIP [4]. To measure results more comprehensively and objectively, six common indices are utilized: Entropy (EN), Standard Deviation (SD), Spatial Frequency (SF), Average Gradient (AG), Structural Content Dissimilarity (SCD), and Visual Information Fidelity (VIF).

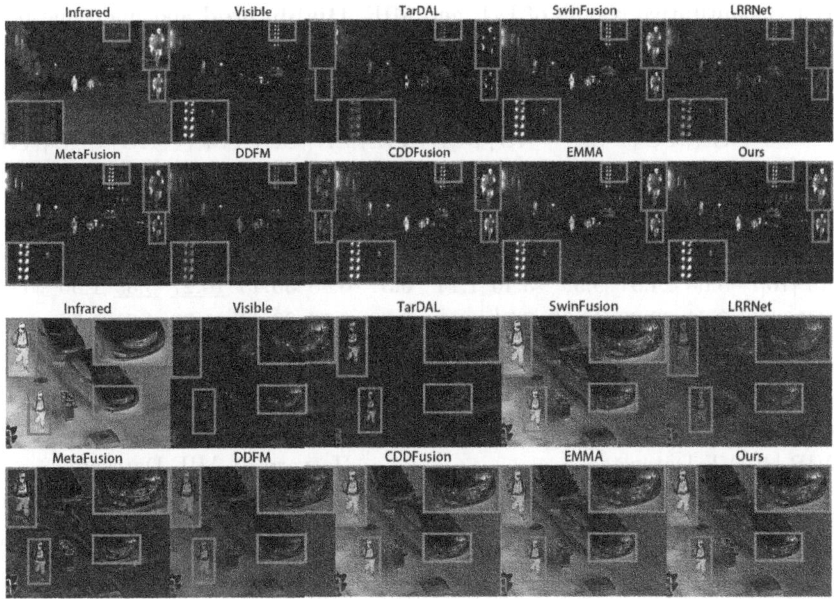

Fig. 6. Visual comparison of MSRS [11] and LLVIP [4] IVF dataset.

Qualitative Comparison. As shown in Fig. 6, the fusion results of IMFDM are qualitatively compared with SOTA. Compared to SOTA, IMFDM can complement information between different modalities more effectively, preserving the rich contours and edges in the background details while reducing redundant information and noise effects. The object is also clearly highlighted when the ambient lighting conditions are insufficient, which facilitates the distinction between the foreground objects and the background.

Quantitative Comparison. The six metric indicators are used for quantitative comparison, and the results are shown in Table 1. Evidently, IMFDM has leading performance on almost all the metrics, proving that IMFDM can cope with the challenges in various complex situations. In particular, IMFDM is only trained on MSRS dataset and directly applied to M^{3}FD and LLVIP test sets without fine-tuning, which showed the best performance in the vast majority of indicators, proving that IMFDM has outstanding generalization performance.

As shown in Table 2, given the same 256×256 image pair input in the test, the parameters, floating point operations (FLOPs) and frames per second (FPS) are three commonly used comparative computational efficiency metrics. Compared with CDDFuse [17], these results show that IMFDM effectively balances performance and efficiency, making it more suitable for resource-constrained environments while maintaining competitive fusion quality.

Table 1. Quantitative results of IVF and MIF. **Highlighted** and underline present the Best and second-best values, respectively.

MSRS [11] IVF Datasets							M^{3}FD [8] IVF Datasets					
	EN↑	SD↑	SF↑	AG↑	SCD↑	VIF↑	EN↑	SD↑	SF↑	AG↑	SCD↑	VIF↑
TarD [8]	5.28	25.22	5.98	1.81	0.71	0.42	6.84	**39.64**	7.51	2.64	1.30	0.54
SwinF [9]	6.07	27.47	10.79	3.46	1.32	0.72	6.79	35.84	13.29	4.60	1.56	0.77
LRR [6]	6.19	29.26	7.44	2.51	1.45	0.73	6.44	27.18	10.68	3.59	1.16	0.57
Meta [16]	5.65	24.97	9.99	3.40	1.14	0.31	6.88	35.45	<u>16.27</u>	<u>5.39</u>	1.55	0.65
DDFM [19]	6.82	32.68	10.07	3.71	1.35	0.60	6.72	32.49	11.79	4.31	<u>1.58</u>	0.75
CDDF [17]	6.70	43.48	11.56	3.73	1.62	**1.00**	6.90	37.24	14.78	4.86	1.57	**0.79**
EMMA [18]	<u>6.71</u>	<u>44.13</u>	<u>11.56</u>	<u>3.76</u>	<u>1.63</u>	0.97	<u>6.92</u>	38.26	15.23	5.33	1.49	<u>0.77</u>
Ours	**6.75**	**45.6**	**12.85**	**4.18**	**1.66**	<u>0.99</u>	**6.97**	<u>38.83</u>	**16.48**	**5.50**	**1.70**	0.75
LLVIP [4] IVF Datasets							Harvard [5] MIF Datasets					
	EN↑	SD↑	SF↑	AG↑	SCD↑	VIF↑	EN↑	SD↑	SF↑	AG↑	SCD↑	VIF↑
TarD [8]	6.31	37.27	7.42	2.20	1.01	0.54	4.08	53.09	19.05	5.78	0.77	0.30
SwinF [9]	7.16	<u>51.39</u>	<u>15.77</u>	4.54	1.55	0.84	4.38	57.66	20.71	5.55	1.20	0.56
LRR [6]	6.28	28.77	10.24	2.79	0.82	0.55	4.23	44.71	13.17	3.49	0.41	0.35
Meta [16]	7.02	47.19	11.33	4.16	1.30	0.53	4.04	56.11	19.81	5.42	1.01	0.47
DDFM [19]	7.01	38.91	7.47	2.53	1.35	0.62	3.93	59.91	17.01	4.45	1.51	0.59
CDDF [17]	7.19	49.26	15.48	4.14	1.56	**0.90**	4.06	<u>77.26</u>	<u>24.97</u>	<u>6.37</u>	<u>1.83</u>	<u>0.63</u>
EMMA [18]	<u>7.32</u>	49.60	15.20	<u>4.54</u>	<u>1.57</u>	0.86	**4.66**	70.83	20.50	5.64	1.68	0.55
Ours	**7.37**	**52.02**	**18.55**	**5.02**	**1.67**	<u>0.88</u>	<u>4.63</u>	**78.36**	**27.14**	**6.88**	**1.87**	**0.66**

Table 2. Quantitative comparison of computational efficiency with CDDFuse [17], which propose a two-stream Transformer-based SOTA.

	Parms↓	FLOPs↓	FPS↑
CDDF	1.19M	116.55G	15.93
Ours	**1.05M**	**90.168G**	**16.68**

Table 3. Ablation experiment results. **Highlighted** indicates the best value.

	Configuration	EN↑	SD↑	AG↑	VIF↑
I	DFE → BFE Block	6.69	43.98	3.68	0.95
II	BFE → DFE Block	6.69	43.10	3.77	**1.00**
III	LT → BFE Block	6.67	43.94	3.70	0.95
IV	w/o GSC Module	6.69	44.38	3.78	0.96
V	w/o CGAFusion	6.70	44.05	3.97	0.97
VI	w/o two-stage training	6.69	42.35	4.05	0.96
	Ours	**6.75**	**45.60**	**4.18**	0.99

4.2 Ablation Studies

In Exp. I and Exp. II, the result shows that the architectural fusion effect of using BFE or DFE block alone is lower than the proposed dual-branch architecture. In Exp. III, BFE is replaced by the efficient Transformer variant Lite-Transformer [12], which is also less effective than BFE. This result fully demonstrates that the SSM is competent in extracting long-distance dependencies for MMIF. In Exp. IV, the GSC module in BFE is removed, and the results indicate that the GSC module helps to capture spatial relations effectively. If there is no CGAFusion, but simply concatenation and compression, the result in Exp. V is not satisfactory. In Exp. VI, IMFDM only employs Stage II process (lacking self-supervised training of Stage I), and the result shows that the specific training strategy is meaningful. In summary, the result of the ablation experiments in Table 3 demonstrates the effectiveness and rationality of the structure.

4.3 Medical Image Fusion

The Harvard Medical dataset [5] includes 136 pairs of MRI-CT/MRI-PET/MRI-SPECT images that are used for MIF. The model trained on IVF dataset was directly applied to MIF without any fine-tuning. The results of quantitative and qualitative comparisons are shown in Table 1 and Fig. 7. IMFDM also achieves outstanding performance in MIF compared to SOTA. Therefore, it shows that IMFDM can extract efficient information and achieve a significant fusion effect for MIF, which proves its superiority and powerful generalization ability.

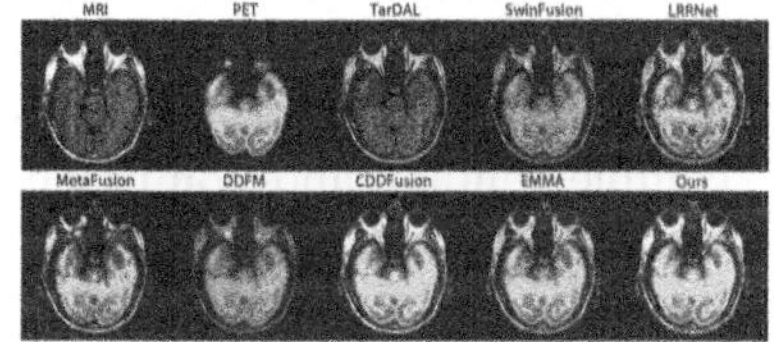

Fig. 7. Visual comparison of "MRI-PET" in Harvard dataset.

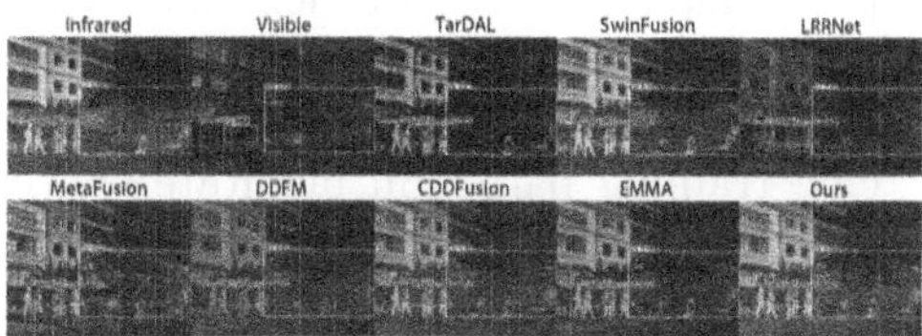

Fig. 8. Visual comparison of "230001" for MM object detection on M^3FD.

Table 4. mAP@0.5 values for MM object detection on M^3FD dataset. **Highlighted** and underline present the Best and second-best values, respectively.

	Peo	Car	Bus	Lam	Mot	Tru	All
IR	0.703	0.798	0.881	0.499	0.586	0.524	0.665
VI	0.586	0.838	0.892	0.753	0.627	0.545	0.707
TarD	0.708	0.833	0.798	0.729	0.627	<u>0.587</u>	0.714
SwinF	0.698	0.827	0.892	0.768	0.627	0.582	0.731
LRR	0.706	0.829	0.866	<u>0.770</u>	0.570	0.564	0.718
Meta	0.691	0.847	**0.940**	0.749	0.615	0.549	0.732
DDFM	0.703	<u>0.849</u>	0.882	0.768	0.627	**0.598**	<u>0.737</u>
CDDF	<u>0.708</u>	0.838	0.887	0.765	**0.648**	0.561	0.735
EMMA	0.690	**0.851**	0.882	0.757	<u>0.629</u>	0.555	0.727
Our	**0.709**	0.847	<u>0.905</u>	**0.778**	0.627	0.570	**0.740**

4.4 Downstream IVF Applications

To further demonstrate the effectiveness of our research, the fusion images generated by the SOTA method and IMFDM are applied to downstream vision tasks. A total of 420 image pairs are randomly selected from M^3FD [8], and 60 pairs are set as the validation set. Here, using the pre-trained YOLOv5 detector [10] for 300 epochs of training. Here, the value of mAP@0.5 can be compared to demonstrate the effectiveness of image fusion from a side perspective. As shown in Table 4, these results not only prove that image fusion is conducive to integrating different modalities, but also reflect the excellent detection performance of IMFDM. Figure 8 provides the visual comparison of MM object detection.

5 Conclusion

To balance performance and efficiency, a dual-branch SSM-CNN architecture is proposed for MMIF. On the one hand, the dual-branch feature extractor enhances the decomposition of shallow features, and the long-range modeling performance of the BFE demonstrates the potential of Mamba for image fusion. In contrast, the DFE with a multi-branch feature extraction strategy helps preserve modality-specific features. On the other hand, the CGAFusion and specific training paradigm facilitate synthesizing complementary and comprehensive fusion images. Experimental results show that IMFDM achieves advanced performance and generalization ability across various types of image fusion and improves the accuracy of downstream MM objective detection. This method provides a referenceable idea for Mamba in cross-modality applications.

Acknowledgments. This work was supported by the National Natural Science Foundation of China Regional Innovation Joint Fund Key Project (Grant U22A2025).

Disclosure of Interests. All authors declare that they have no conflict of interest.

References

1. Chen, Z., He, Z., Lu, Z.M.: DEA-Net: single image dehazing based on detail-enhanced convolution and content-guided attention. IEEE Trans. Image Process. **33**, 1002–1015 (2024)
2. Gu, A., Dao, T.: Mamba: linear-time sequence modeling with selective state spaces, arXiv preprint arXiv:2312.00752 (2023)
3. Guo, H., Li, J., Dai, T., Ouyang, Z., Ren, X., Xia, S.T.: MambaIR: a simple baseline for image restoration with state-space model. In: European Conference on Computer Vision, pp. 222–241. Springer (2024)
4. Jia, X., Zhu, C., Li, M., Tang, W., Zhou, W.: LLVIP: a visible-infrared paired dataset for low-light vision. In: Proceedings of the IEEE/CVF International Conference on Computer Vision, pp. 3496–3504 (2021)
5. Johnson, K.A., Becker.r, J.A.: Harvard medical website. http://www.med.harvard.edu/AANLIB/home.html

6. Li, H., Xu, T., Wu, X.J., Lu, J., Kittler, J.: LRRNet: a novel representation learning guided fusion network for infrared and visible images. IEEE Trans. Pattern Anal. Mach. Intell. **45**(9), 11040–11052 (2023)
7. Li, Y., Hou, Q., Zheng, Z., Cheng, M.M., Yang, J., Li, X.: Large selective kernel network for remote sensing object detection. In: Proceedings of the IEEE/CVF International Conference on Computer Vision, pp. 16794–16805 (2023)
8. Liu, J., et al.: Target-aware dual adversarial learning and a multi-scenario multi-modality benchmark to fuse infrared and visible for object detection. In: Proceedings of the IEEE/CVF Conference on Computer Vision and Pattern Recognition, pp. 5802–5811 (2022)
9. Ma, J., Tang, L., Fan, F., Huang, J., Mei, X., Ma, Y.: SwinFusion: cross-domain long-range learning for general image fusion via swin transformer. IEEE/CAA J. Automatica Sinica **9**(7), 1200–1217 (2022)
10. Redmon, J., Divvala, S., Girshick, R., Farhadi, A.: You only look once: unified, real-time object detection. In: Proceedings of the IEEE Conference on Computer Vision and Pattern Recognition, pp. 779–788 (2016)
11. Tang, L., Yuan, J., Zhang, H., Jiang, X., Ma, J.: PIAFusion: a progressive infrared and visible image fusion network based on illumination aware. Inf. Fusion **83**, 79–92 (2022)
12. Wu, Z., Liu, Z., Lin, J., Lin, Y., Han, S.: Lite transformer with long-short range attention. arXiv preprint arXiv:2004.11886 (2020)
13. Xing, Z., Ye, T., Yang, Y., Liu, G., Zhu, L.: SegMamba: long-range sequential modeling mamba for 3d medical image segmentation. In: International Conference on Medical Image Computing and Computer-Assisted Intervention, pp. 578–588. Springer (2024)
14. Xu, S., et al.: HCF-Net: hierarchical context fusion network for infrared small object detection. In: 2024 IEEE International Conference on Multimedia and Expo (ICME), pp. 1–6. IEEE (2024)
15. Zamir, S.W., Arora, A., Khan, S., Hayat, M., Khan, F.S., Yang, M.H.: Restormer: efficient transformer for high-resolution image restoration. In: CVPR (2022)
16. Zhao, W., Xie, S., Zhao, F., He, Y., Lu, H.: MetaFusion: infrared and visible image fusion via meta-feature embedding from object detection. In: Proceedings of the IEEE/CVF Conference on Computer Vision and Pattern Recognition, pp. 13955–13965 (2023)
17. Zhao, Z., et al.: CDDFuse: correlation-driven dual-branch feature decomposition for multi-modality image fusion. In: Proceedings of the IEEE/CVF Conference on Computer Vision and Pattern Recognition, pp. 5906–5916 (2023)
18. Zhao, Z., et al.: Equivariant multi-modality image fusion. In: Proceedings of the IEEE/CVF Conference on Computer Vision and Pattern Recognition, pp. 25912–25921 (2024)
19. Zhao, Z., et al.: DDFM: denoising diffusion model for multi-modality image fusion. In: Proceedings of the IEEE/CVF International Conference on Computer Vision, pp. 8082–8093 (2023)
20. Zhu, L., Liao, B., Zhang, Q., Wang, X., Liu, W., Wang, X.: Vision mamba: efficient visual representation learning with bidirectional state space model. arXiv preprint arXiv:2401.09417 (2024)

UTFusion: A General Image Fusion Framework with a Unified Transformer

Yong Peng[1,2], Zheyu Shi[1,2], and Yong Zhong[1,2](✉)

[1] University of Chinese Academy of Sciences, Beijing 100049, China
zhongyong@casit.com.cn
[2] Chengdu Institute of Computer Application, Chinese Academy of Sciences, Chengdu 610213, China

Abstract. The goal of image fusion tasks is to extract and integrate complementary information from multiple image sources to create a single image that captures the most relevant and salient features from each source. However, existing methods cannot often employ a single, unified model across various fusion tasks. In this paper, we introduce a novel unified model named UTFusion to handle different image fusion tasks. Our method uses patches as the fusion unit, adds an embedding of the fused scheme, and changes the fusion strategy by switching the embedding of the fused scheme. Qualitative and quantitative experiments show the competitiveness of our UTFusion compared to the state-of-the-art general image fusion models in terms of visual effects and quantitative metrics. Our code and pre-trained model weights are available at https://github.com/YPeng99/UTFusion.

Keywords: Image fusion · Unified model · Embedding of fused scheme

1 Introduction

Due to certain limitations in the hardware of imaging equipment, it is often difficult to use a single type of sensor or a single setup to fully and accurately represent the complex aspects of an imaging scene [1]. Different types of sensors, such as infrared, visible, and near-infrared, each have unique characteristics and advantages and can accurately capture specific information in the scene. Specifically, infrared sensors can highlight hot spots in a scene and effectively detect thermal signatures. Visible light sensors are good at capturing light information reflected by object surfaces and generating delicate and rich digital images. These images not only reveal the intricate texture details of the scene but also preserve its color information [2]. Furthermore, the near-infrared sensor can capture additional details that might otherwise be obscured in visible light images, thus offering complementary information [3]. Given these considerations, to achieve a comprehensive and detailed depiction of the imaging scene, a general image fusion strategy that can combine the advantages of different sensor types must

P. Li et al. (Eds.): CGI 2025, LNCS 16508, pp. 146–157, 2026.
https://doi.org/10.1007/978-3-032-22264-0_12

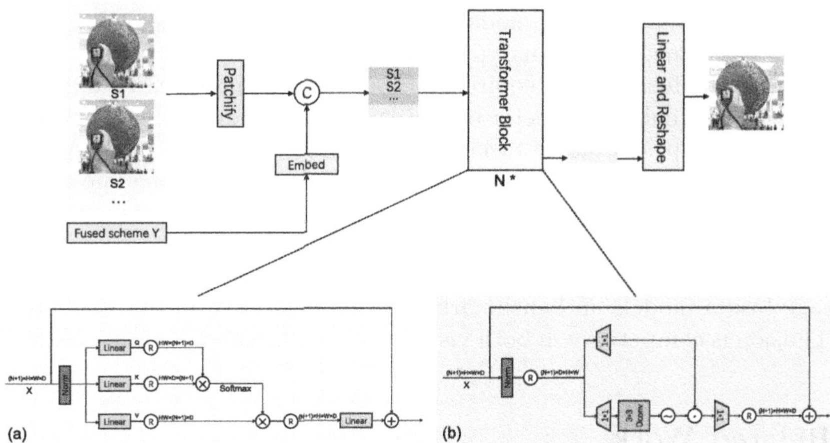

Fig. 1. The architecture of UTFusion, where $S1$, $S2$, and ... are the input images. Y is a fused scheme. (a) is attention layer, (b) is feed-forward layer.

be adopted. The single, unified image obtained in this way is not only superior in scene performance but also enhances the visual perception effect, thereby accurately and efficiently supporting a series of subsequent visual tasks.

Over the past decade, numerous techniques for image fusion have emerged, encompassing two primary categories: task-specific image fusion methods and general image fusion methods [4]. Both of them can be classified as two classes: traditional methods [5,6] and deep learning-based methods [7,8]. Traditional methods often require manual design of fusion regulations and are difficult to cope with complex fusion scenarios. Although deep learning-based methods for general image fusion have achieved acceptable fused results, they are unable to use a unified model across different tasks [4,9] or use continual learning methods [10], which results in poor performance on multiple tasks.

Therefore, we introduce a novel approach, a general image fusion framework with a unified transformer, term as UTFusion. In general image fusion tasks, different fusion regulations are often adopted according to different tasks, which leads to the previous general image fusion models containing multiple weight files or poor performance on multiple tasks. In addition, we believe that local cross-domain information is more important than global information in image fusion tasks. Therefore, we design an attention-based adaptive fusion module as shown in (a) in Fig. 1, which treats patches as fusion units. Thanks to the attention mechanism, our model can directly process image sequences without the need for fine-tuning. To adapt to different fusion tasks, we introduce a learnable embedding of the fused scheme. Different embeddings are selected according to different fused schemes. In addition, we also designed a gated feed-forward network for cross-patch information mixing.

To sum up, the key contributions of this work are outlined as follows:

- We design a unified fusion model and innovatively introduce the embedding of a fused scheme, which can dynamically adjust the fusion strategy according to the specific fusion task requirements so that the model can handle various tasks with negligible parameter increase and can achieve optimal performance for different types of fusion tasks.
- Our model is a sequence model, so our model can easily handle the fusion of image sequences without the need to fine-tune it for the image sequence fusion task.
- Qualitative and quantitative evaluations against the state-of-the-art general image fusion models on benchmark datasets demonstrate that our proposed UTFusion is competitive in both visual performance and quantitative metrics.

2 Related Work

Transformer [14]-based models have emerged as powerful contenders in the computer vision landscape, achieving remarkable performance in a wide array of vision tasks such as image classification, object detection, segmentation, and generation.

Transformer also shows promising prospects in the field of image fusion. TransMEF [15] uses a parallel Transformer and CNN structure to integrate global and local features for feature extraction and uses self-supervised multi-task learning for multi-exposure image fusion. SwinFusion [4] implements global interaction intra- and cross-domains in the fusion process based on SwinTransformer [16]. This method unifies digital photography image fusion and multi-modal image fusion into structural integrity, texture fidelity, and intensity adjustment. However, SwinFusion still needs to load corresponding weights for different fusion tasks. The above Transformer method focuses on mining global information, resulting in increased computational complexity. Local cross-domain interactions are more relevant to image fusion problems. Therefore, we introduce a general image fusion framework with a unified transformer, which treats image patches as fusion units and obtains cross-patch information through a gated feed-forward network.

3 Method

3.1 Overall Framework

The input of our model consists of $I \in \mathbb{R}^{N\times C\times H\times W}$ which are pairs of images produced by two different sensors or multiple source images produced by optical lenses and a scheme Y, the output is the fused images $f \in \mathbb{R}^{C\times H\times W}$. N, C, H, and W represent the number of fused images, the number of image channels, and the image size, respectively. For ease of understanding, batch size is ignored. The structure of our model is consistent with the transformer. Among them, the attention layer is shown in (a) in Fig. 1, and the feed-forward layer is shown in (b) in Fig. 1. Transformer block is composed of an attention layer and a feed-forward layer in series, and our model is a multi-layer transformer block stack. First, we reshape the model input $I \in \mathbb{R}^{N \times C \times H \times W}$ into a sequence of patches $I_p \in \mathbb{R}^{N \times H_p \times W_p \times D}$, $D = C * patch\_size * patch\_size$, $H_p = H/patch\_size$ and $W_p = W/patch\_size$. Then we add a trainable embedding vector representing the fused scheme Y to the patch sequence, so that I_p becomes $I_p \in \mathbb{R}^{(N+1) \times H_p \times W_p \times D}$. The complete process is shown in Fig. 1.

Previous transformer-based image fusion methods often used the attention mechanism to obtain global information. However, this resulted in unacceptable computational complexity. The objective of the image fusion task is to capture the salient features of different source images and generate a single high-quality image. It is more about comparing the local information of different source images. Therefore, our attention layer only performs attention calculation on the corresponding patches of different source images, as shown in (a) in Fig. 1. Our attention layer only focuses on local cross-domain information, so our computational complexity is only related to the number of source images. Specifically, we get Q, K, and V formulas as follows:

$$Q, K, V = (W^Q, W^K, W^V) \cdot LN(X) \tag{1}$$

where W^Q, W^K, and W^V are learnable weight matrices. Then we reshape Q, K, and V to $\mathbb{R}^{HW \times (N+1) \times D}$. We get attention score through QK^T. The full attention mechanism is as follows:

$$\widetilde{X} = W \cdot Attention(Q, K, V) + X \tag{2}$$

$$Attention(Q, K, V) = Softmax\left(\frac{QK^T}{\sqrt{D}}\right) \cdot V \tag{3}$$

Since our attention layer only focuses on local cross-domain information, we designed a gated feed-forward network to obtain the long-distance dependencies of the intra-domain. The gated feed-forward network consists of 1×1 convolution and 3×3 depth-wise convolution as shown in (b) in Fig. 1. The gated feed-forward network is as follows:

$$\widetilde{X} = W_2 Gating(X) + X \tag{4}$$

$$Gating(X) = W_1 LN(X) \odot Swish(W_3 LN(X)) \tag{5}$$

where $\odot$ represents point-wise multiply, $Swish$ represents activation function.

3.2 Loss Function

Inspired by SwinFusion, we reframe the image fusion challenge as texture preservation and appropriate intensity control. Therefore, we incorporate gradient loss and intensity loss as constraints within our network, guiding it toward these objectives.

The size of the image gradient represents the grayscale change rate of the image at that point, that is, the intensity of the edge. The direction of the image

Table 1. Quantitative evaluation results on image fusion tasks.

		IFCNN	SDNet	U2Fusion	SwinFusion	ZMFF	FusionDiff	MUfusion	Ours
Lytro	$PSNR$	74.8326	75.0523	72.8099	**75.6268**	74.4327	<u>75.5577</u>	72.4848	74.6568
	VIF	1.1707	1.0554	1.0204	1.1345	<u>1.1938</u>	1.1872	1.1524	**1.2614**
	$Q_{ab/f}$	<u>0.7107</u>	0.6500	0.6326	0.6945	0.7022	0.7060	0.6650	**0.7403**
	$SSIM$	0.6812	0.6658	0.6555	**0.6897**	0.6676	<u>0.6819</u>	0.6556	0.6739
		IFCNN	SDNet	U2Fusion	SwinFusion	DPE-MEF	FusionDN	HoLoCo	Ours
MEFB	$PSNR$	<u>59.0588</u>	58.5705	59.0280	57.7837	58.3577	58.3225	58.4507	**59.0879**
	VIF	1.0458	0.9204	1.0962	<u>1.1744</u>	1.1643	1.0634	1.0969	**1.2209**
	$Q_{ab/f}$	0.5695	0.4236	0.5617	0.3865	<u>0.6474</u>	0.5234	0.5100	**0.6955**
	$SSIM$	0.3601	0.3117	0.3773	0.3652	**0.4050**	0.3329	0.3645	<u>0.3986</u>
		IFCNN	SDNet	U2Fusion	SwinFusion	DIVFusion	PIAFusion	Diff-if	Ours
MSRS	$PSNR$	<u>66.0236</u>	61.4009	**66.5843**	64.4101	56.5309	64.3049	64.2854	64.2496
	VIF	0.8071	0.4356	0.5253	1.0003	0.7838	0.9876	**1.0417**	<u>1.0396</u>
	$Q_{ab/f}$	0.6127	0.2762	0.3973	0.6635	0.3407	<u>0.6871</u>	0.6851	**0.7116**
	$SSIM$	0.4862	0.2730	0.3847	**0.5070**	0.2501	0.4942	<u>0.5046</u>	0.4822
		IFCNN	SDNet	U2Fusion	SwinFusion	Diff-if	MSRPAN	EMFusion	Ours
CT-MRI	$PSNR$	62.9519	<u>63.3116</u>	**63.4743**	61.5049	61.3322	61.4189	62.5224	61.3603
	VIF	0.4424	0.3297	0.3455	0.5414	0.5348	0.4359	**0.5595**	<u>0.5570</u>
	$Q_{ab/f}$	0.5717	0.4466	0.4375	0.5548	**0.6048**	0.4546	0.4938	<u>0.5996</u>
	$SSIM$	<u>0.6797</u>	0.2373	0.2386	**0.6855**	0.6637	0.6532	0.6580	0.6247
		IFCNN	U2Fusion	SwinFusion	MSRPAN	EMFusion	Ours		
PET-MRI	$PSNR$	<u>62.2615</u>	**62.4236**	61.8109	61.1314	62.0406	61.0144		
	VIF	0.5595	0.4643	0.5455	0.5811	**0.6850**	<u>0.6779</u>		
	$Q_{ab/f}$	0.6756	0.2558	0.6694	0.6171	<u>0.7229</u>	**0.7525**		
	$SSIM$	**0.6288**	0.2202	0.3161	0.6098	<u>0.6286</u>	0.6025		

The highest and second highest scores are highlighted in **bold** and <u>underlined</u>.

gradient represents the edge direction of the image at that point. Therefore, we guide the network through Eq. (6) to save as many texture details as possible.

$$L_{gradient} = \frac{1}{HW}\||\nabla I_f| - max(|\nabla I_1|, |\nabla I_2|)\|_1 \tag{6}$$

where ∇ denotes the Sobel gradient operator. I_f is the fused image, I_1 and I_2 are the source images. $|\cdot|$ represents absolute operation, $\|\cdot\|_1$ represents l1-norm, and $max(\cdot)$ represents element-wise maximum selection.

In addressing intensity loss, we employ Eq. (7). Specifically, for situations that involve visible and infrared image fusion and multi-focus image fusion, we utilize the element-wise maximum operation. However, in the context of multi-exposure image fusion, we utilize the element-wise mean.

$$L_{intensity} = \frac{1}{HW}\|I_f - M(I_1, I_2)\|_1 \tag{7}$$

where $M(\cdot)$ represents an element-wise aggregation operation.

The total loss L_{total} as follows:

$$L_{total} = \lambda_1 L_{intensity} + \lambda_2 L_{gradient} \tag{8}$$

where λ is the hyper-parameter indicating the importance of each loss term, in this work, we set $\lambda_1 = 1$ and $\lambda_2 = 2$.

4 Experments

4.1 Datasets and Settings

On multi-modal image fusion, we have selected two primary areas of focus: visible and infrared image fusion, as well as medical image fusion. Where medical image fusion includes CT-MRI fusion and PET-MRI fusion. For digital photography image fusion, we chose multi-exposure image fusion and multi-focus image fusion. For the visible and infrared image fusion task, we employ the MSRS dataset [17, 18] for both training and evaluation. For medical image fusion, we utilize the Harvard medical dataset. The multi-focus image fusion task is trained utilizing the MFI-WHU dataset [19] and subsequently tested on the Lytro dataset [20]. Meanwhile, for multi-exposure image fusion, the MEF dataset [21] serves as the training set, while the MEF benchmark (MEFB) dataset [22] is used for testing. Notably, all of these training and testing datasets are publicly available, ensuring the reproducibility and comparability of our results.

During training, we randomly crop images to 224 ×224 as input. The patch size is set to 8×8. In this work, we use the AdamW optimizer, with the learning rate set to $1e-4$, weight decay set to $5e-2$, batch size set to 128, and epoch set to 3000. Our model comprises six transformer layers with 0.26M trainable parameters and is trained and tested on a Nvidia GPU 4070. During testing, fusing image pairs of size 520 × 520 took an average of 0.0057 s on Nvidia GPU 4070 and 0.07 s on Intel CPU i7-13600k.

4.2 Results

To make our comparisons more convincing, we selected four general image fusion SOTA models for comparison: IFCNN [7], SDNet [9], U2Fusion [15], and SwinFusion [4]. To comprehensively evaluate our method, we selected some specific image fusion algorithms for comparison [17,27–36]. For quantitative analysis, we used objective image quality assessment metrics to evaluate the fusion quality. In this paper, we use four of the most popular evaluation metrics: the peak signal-to-noise ratio ($PSNR$) [23], visual information fidelity (VIF) [24], edge-based similarity measurement ($Q_{ab/f}$) [25], and structural similarity index measure ($SSIM$) [26].

Table 1 shows the quantitative comparison results of our method UTFusion with other SOTA methods. We achieved top-2 results on VIF and $Q_(ab/f)$ in almost all tasks. The higher VIF and $Q_(ab/f)$ mean that our method transfers the most feature and edge information from the source images to the fused image.

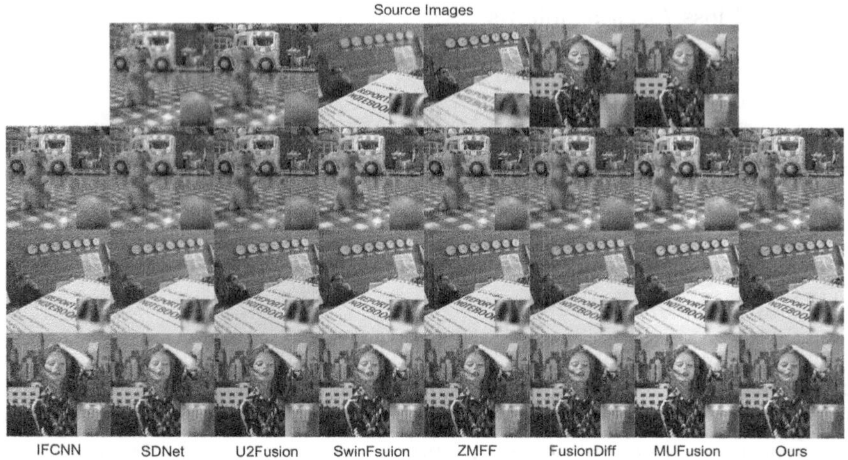

Fig. 2. Qualitative comparison results on Lytro dataset.

Our method still achieves good results on PSNR and SSIM metrics. Quantitative analysis shows that our method is comparable to the latest SOTA models.

Figure 2 shows that our method performs better than others in preserving details, particularly in the texture of the toy dog's feet and in the enlarged regions. From the last line of Fig. 2 that IFCNN, SDNet, U2Fusion, SwinFusion, and FusionDiff mistakenly saved the noise caused by foreground focus to the background. In Fig. 3, our method retains details better than others, while FusionDN and HoLoCo appear blurry. From the last row, IFCNN and DPE-MEF show weak detail retention for low-exposure images. IFCNN's fusion results also show clear color differences, and the outputs of SDNet and SwinFusion are darker. DPE-MEF includes a color enhancement module, which makes its images more vivid, but it leans toward overexposure and lacks detail in low-light areas. Figure 4 shows that the fusion result of SDNet is unacceptable. The fusion images of IFCNN, U2Fusion, and DIVFusion are overall darker, especially when the images contain the sky. As can be seen from the second row of the comparison figure, PIAFusion lacks information from infrared images of the headlights. Figure 5 shows that IFCNN, SDNet, and U2Fusion lack CT image information and have improper intensity control. EMFusion also lacks CT information, and Diff-IF has irregular black spots. SwinFusion, Diff-IF, and MSRPAN lack details in the enlarged area. Figure 6 shows an obvious color difference between IFCNN, U2Fusion, and SwinFusion. Our method performs the best in preserving MRI image details, while MSRPAN loses details, and the fused image of EMFusion lacks PET information.

Overall, U2Fusion's performance is extremely uneven due to the use of continuous learning. IFCNN does not perform well in complex scenes because the feature fusion strategy is too simple. SwinFusion uses transformers to obtain global information, which makes the computational complexity unacceptable.

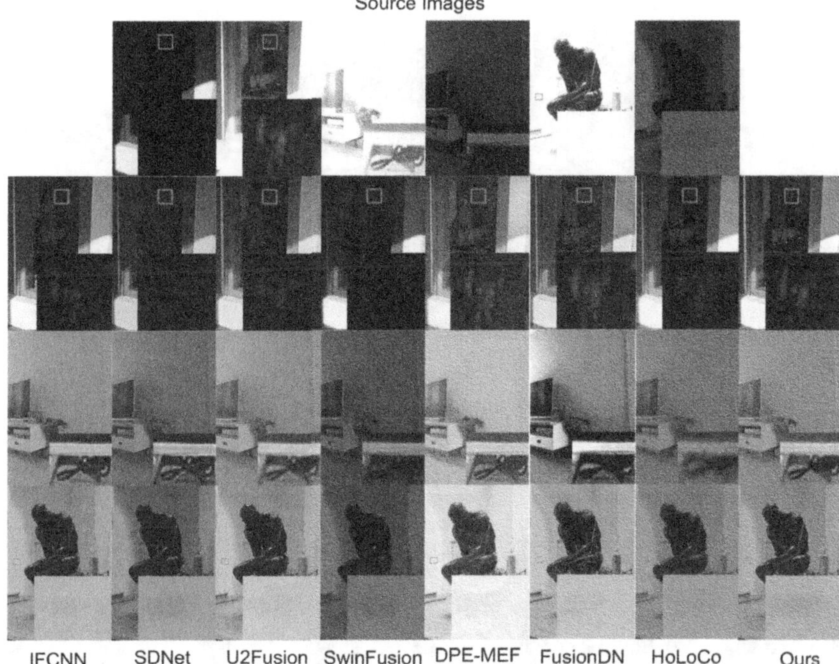

Fig. 3. Qualitative comparison results on MEFB dataset.

Compared with specific image fusion methods, our model is still competitive. The fusion results of our model are competitive in comprehensive comparison, which also shows that local cross-domain information is more important than global information in image fusion tasks.

4.3 Ablation Study and Discussion

We designed several ablation experiments to verify the role of different modules. Table 2 shows the quantitative analysis results of the ablation experiments, where $-nc$ means removing 3×3 depth-wise convolution, and $-l11$ means $\lambda_1 = 1$,$\lambda_2 = 1$, and $-p16$ means patch size is set to 16. From Table 2, we can see that the increase of λ_1 weight will increase the $PSNR$ value, but other evaluation indicators will decrease, especially VIF and $Q_{ab/f}$, which shows that gradient loss plays a significant role in preserving details. When we removed 3×3 depth-wise convolution or set the patch size to 16, all indicators decreased.

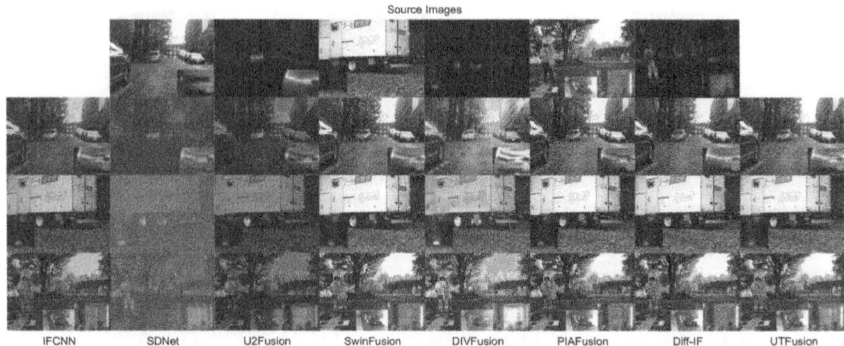

Fig. 4. Qualitative comparison results on MSRS dataset.

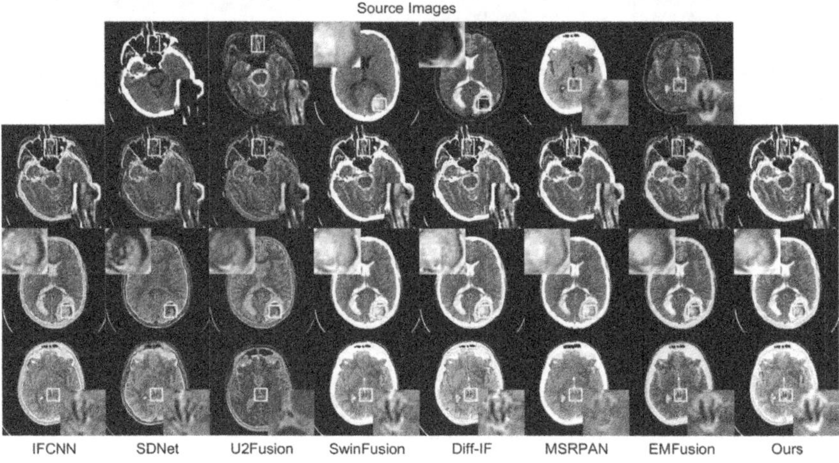

Fig. 5. Qualitative comparison on CT and MRI image fusion.

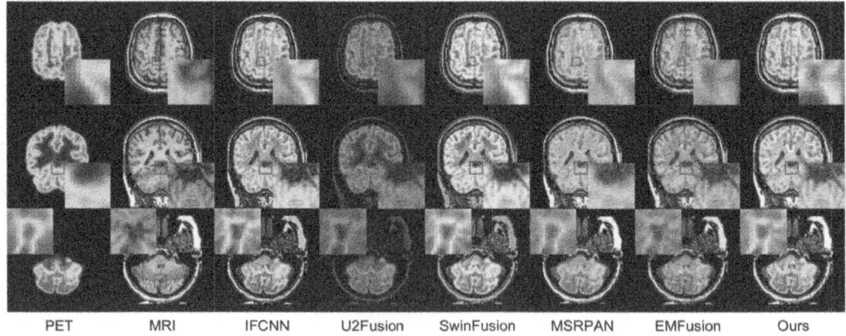

Fig. 6. Qualitative comparison on PET and MRI image fusion.

Fig. 7. Ablation study results.

As shown in Fig. 7, as the λ_1 weight increases, the image becomes increasingly blurred, and the details on the edge of the image are lost significantly. When we removed 3 × 3 depth-wise convolution, a checkerboard artifact appeared on the edge of the image, indicating that 3×3 depth-wise convolution can effectively integrate cross-patch information to make the image more consistent overall. When the patch size is set to 16, there is no obvious problem with the fusion result, but all objective evaluation indicators are reduced. The trainable parameters when the patch size is set to 8 are 0.26M, and when it is set to 16, the trainable parameters are 3.28M. The parameters are significantly increased. Setting the patch size to 8 is more effective without increasing the epoch.

Table 2. Quantitative evaluation of ablation study results.

	$PSNR$	VIF	$Q_{ab/f}$	$SSIM$
ours	74.6568	1.2594	0.7403	0.6739
$-l11$	75.0232	1.0381	0.6435	0.6618
$-l21$	75.5012	0.9906	0.5824	0.6645
$-nc$	74.9478	1.1652	0.7166	0.6674
$-p16$	74.751	1.1099	0.6792	0.6585

5 Conclusion

In this work, we introduce a general image fusion framework with a unified transformer, namely UTFusion. Our proposed UTFusion consists of an attention layer and a gated feed-forward network, which achieves universal image fusion by switching the embedding of the fused scheme. The attention layer is used for local cross-domain interaction, and the gated feed-forward network is used for cross-patch information mixing. Qualitative and quantitative experiments show that our model is competitive with state-of-the-art fusion models.

Acknowledgments. This research was supported by the Science and Technology Project of Sichuan (2024ZHCG0192).

References

1. Tang, L., Zhang, H., Xu, H., Ma, J.: Deep learning-based image fusion: a survey. J. Image Graph. **28**(1), 3–36 (2023)
2. Ma, J., Tang, L., Xu, M., Zhang, H., Xiao, G.: STDFusionNet: an infrared and visible image fusion network based on salient target detection. IEEE Trans. Instrum. Meas. **70**, 1–13 (2021)
3. Awad, M., Elliethy, A., Aly, H.A.: Adaptive near-infrared and visible fusion for fast image enhancement. IEEE Trans. Comput. Imaging **6**, 408–418 (2019)
4. Ma, J., Tang, L., Fan, F., Huang, J., Mei, X., Ma, Y.: SwinFusion: cross-domain long-range learning for general image fusion via swin transformer. IEEE/CAA J. Automatica Sinica **9**(7), 1200–1217 (2022)
5. Liu, Y., Liu, S., Wang, Z.: A general framework for image fusion based on multi-scale transform and sparse representation. Inf. Fus. **24**, 147–164 (2015)
6. Xu, H., Wang, X., Ma, J.: DRF: disentangled representation for visible and infrared image fusion. IEEE Trans. Instrum. Meas. **70**, 1–13 (2021)
7. Zhang, Y., Liu, Y., Sun, P., Yan, H., Zhao, X., Zhang, L.: IFCNN: a general image fusion framework based on convolutional neural network. Inf. Fus. **54**, 99–118 (2020)
8. Zhou, H., Wu, W., Zhang, Y., Ma, J., Ling, H.: Semantic-supervised infrared and visible image fusion via a dual-discriminator generative adversarial network. IEEE Trans. Multimedia **25**, 635–648 (2021)
9. Zhang, H., Ma, J.: SDNet: a versatile squeeze-and-decomposition network for real-time image fusion. Int. J. Comput. Vis. **129**(10), 2761–2785 (2021)
10. Xu, H., Ma, J., Jiang, J., Guo, X., Ling, H.: U2Fusion: a unified unsupervised image fusion network. IEEE Trans. Pattern Anal. Mach. Intell. **44**(1), 502–518 (2020)
11. Ram Prabhakar, K., Sai Srikar, V., Venkatesh Babu, R.: DeepFuse: a deep unsupervised approach for exposure fusion with extreme exposure image pairs. In: Proceedings of the IEEE International Conference on Computer Vision, pp. 4714–4722 (2017)
12. Li, H., Wu, X.-J.: DenseFuse: a fusion approach to infrared and visible images. IEEE Trans. Image Process. **28**(5), 2614–2623 (2018)
13. Huang, G., Liu, Z., Van Der Maaten, L., Weinberger, K.Q.: Densely connected convolutional networks. In: Proceedings of the IEEE Conference on Computer Vision and Pattern Recognition, pp. 4700–4708 (2017)
14. Vaswani, A., et al.: Attention is all you need. In: Advances in Neural Information Processing Systems, vol. 30 (2017)
15. Qu, L., Liu, S., Wang, M., Song, Z.: TransMEF: a transformer-based multi-exposure image fusion framework using self-supervised multi-task learning. In: Proceedings of the AAAI Conference on Artificial Intelligence **36**(2), 2126–2134 (2022)
16. Liu, Z., et al.: Swin transformer: hierarchical vision transformer using shifted windows. In: Proceedings of the IEEE/CVF International Conference on Computer Vision, pp. 10 012–10 022 (2021)
17. Tang, L., Yuan, J., Zhang, H., Jiang, X., Ma, J.: PIAFusion: a progressive infrared and visible image fusion network based on illumination aware. Inf. Fus. **83**, 79–92 (2022)

18. Ha, Q., Watanabe, K., Karasawa, T., Ushiku, Y., Harada, T.: MFNet: towards real-time semantic segmentation for autonomous vehicles with multi-spectral scenes. In: 2017 IEEE/RSJ International Conference on Intelligent Robots and Systems (IROS), pp. 5108–5115. IEEE (2017)
19. Zhang, H., Le, Z., Shao, Z., Xu, H., Ma, J.: MFF-GAN: an unsupervised generative adversarial network with adaptive and gradient joint constraints for multi-focus image fusion. Inf. Fus. **66**, 40–53 (2021)
20. Nejati, M., Samavi, S., Shirani, S.: Multi-focus image fusion using dictionary-based sparse representation. Inf. Fus. **25**, 72–84 (2015)
21. Cai, J., Gu, S., Zhang, L.: Learning a deep single image contrast enhancer from multi-exposure images. IEEE Trans. Image Process. **27**(4), 2049–2062 (2018)
22. Zhang, X.: Benchmarking and comparing multi-exposure image fusion algorithms. Inf. Fus. **74**, 111–131 (2021)
23. Jagalingam, P., Hegde, A.V.: A review of quality metrics for fused image. Aquatic Procedia **4**, 133–142 (2015)
24. Han, Y., Cai, Y., Cao, Y., Xu, X.: A new image fusion performance metric based on visual information fidelity. Inf. Fus. **14**(2), 127–135 (2013)
25. Xydeas, C.S., Petrovic, V., et al.: Objective image fusion performance measure. Electron. Lett. **36**(4), 308–309 (2000)
26. Wang, Z., Bovik, A.C., Sheikh, H.R., Simoncelli, E.P.: Image quality assessment: from error visibility to structural similarity. IEEE Trans. Image Process. **13**(4), 600–612 (2004)
27. Hu, X., Jiang, J., Liu, X., Ma, J.: ZMFF: zero-shot multi-focus image fusion. Inf. Fus. **92**, 127–138 (2023)
28. Li, M., Pei, R., Zheng, T., Zhang, Y., Fu, W.: FusionDiff: multi-focus image fusion using denoising diffusion probabilistic models. Expert Syst. Appl. **238**, 121664 (2024)
29. Cheng, C., Xu, T., Wu, X.-J.: MUFusion: a general unsupervised image fusion network based on memory unit. Inf. Fus. **92**, 80–92 (2023)
30. Han, D., Li, L., Guo, X., Ma, J.: Multi-exposure image fusion via deep perceptual enhancement. Inf. Fus. **79**, 248–262 (2022)
31. Xu, H., Ma, J., Le, Z., Jiang, Z., Guo, X.: FusionDN: a unified densely connected network for image fusion. In: Proceedings of the AAAI Conference on Artificial Intelligence, vol. 34, no. 07, pp. 12:484–12:491 (2020)
32. Tang, L., Xiang, X., Zhang, H., Gong, M., Ma, J.: DIVFusion: darkness-free infrared and visible image fusion. Inf. Fus. **91**, 477–493 (2023)
33. Yi, X., Tang, L., Zhang, H., Xu, H., Ma, J.: Diff-IF: multi-modality image fusion via diffusion model with fusion knowledge prior. Inf. Fus. **110**, 102450 (2024)
34. Fu, J., Li, W., Du, J., Huang, Y.: A multiscale residual pyramid attention network for medical image fusion. Biomed. Signal Process. Control **66**, 102488 (2021)
35. Xu, H., Ma, J.: EMFusion: an unsupervised enhanced medical image fusion network. Inf. Fus. **76**, 177–186 (2021)
36. Liu, J., Wu, G., Luan, J., Jiang, Z., Liu, R., Fan, X.: HoLoCo: holistic and local contrastive learning network for multi-exposure image fusion. Inf. Fus. **95**, 237–249 (2023)

DualShield: Dual-layer Protection for Secure and Robust Stable Diffusion Steganography

Kun Hu[1], Chen Tu[1], Guanghui Zhang[1], Zhibin Hao[1], Peiliang Guo[2], Hong Zou[3(✉)], and Xingjun Wang[1(✉)]

[1] Tsinghua Shenzhen International Graduate School, Tsinghua University, Shenzhen 518055, China
{huk22,tuc24,zgh24,hzb24}@mails.tsinghua.edu.cn,
wangxingjun@sz.tsinghua.edu.cn

[2] University of Technology Sydney, Untimo 2007, Australia
Peiliang.guo-1@student.uts.edu.au

[3] School of Computer Science and Engineering, South China University of Technology, Guangzhou 510006, China
202411090220@mail.scut.edu.cn

Abstract. Stable diffusion image steganography (SDIS) provides reliable protection for generating image traceability and secret transmission of information. However, existing SDISs still face challenges in achieving robust watermark traceability and secure secret information transmission. To address this problem, we propose DualShield, a dual-protection robust steganography for generating images based on a stable diffusion model. DualShield utilizes controllable public and private conditional texts as keys and embeds the preprocessed watermark into the reverse-encoded latent vectors in the latent space where the public key participates. To make the fusion of the watermark with the latent vectors more sufficient, we employ a U-Net network that can fuse low-level and high-level features as an encoder. To ensure the accuracy of the extracted watermark, we efficiently add random noise perturbations in the training phase. The design of the private key ensures that the receiver can reverse decode the high-value images transmitted in secret. Experimental results show that DualShield performs satisfactorily against common image attacks, steganalysis, and removal attacks.

Keywords: Image Steganography · Latent Diffusion Models · Robustness and Security

1 Introduction

Stable diffusion (SD) has made model-generated images more realistic and naturalistic. Meanwhile, easily disseminating the generated images raises significant concerns about data privacy, security, and protection [10,12]. An obvious solution is to watermark the model-generated images by post-processing [11,37].

P. Li et al. (Eds.): CGI 2025, LNCS 16508, pp. 158–172, 2026.
https://doi.org/10.1007/978-3-032-22264-0_13

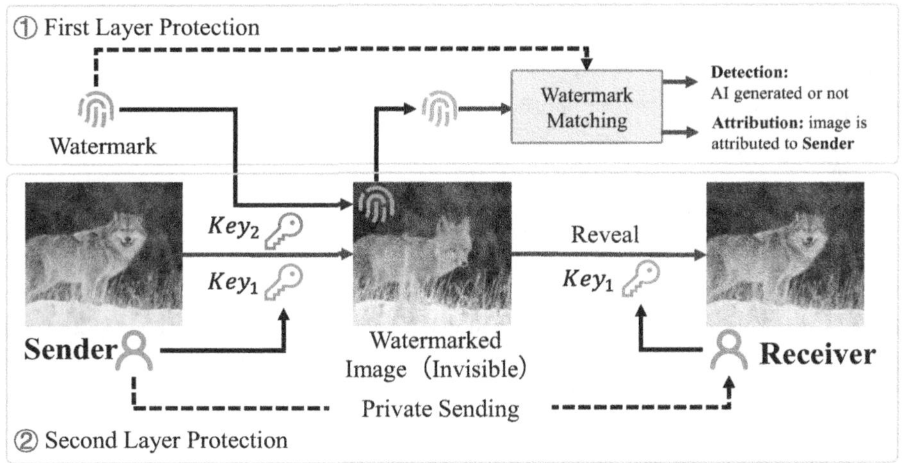

Fig. 1. An overview of DualShield. The first layer is watermark protection, and the second is secret image protection.

However, the watermark structure is not specifically designed to fully integrate the characteristics of the generated model, resulting in the performance of the watermark mainly relying on the post-processing model's ability and losing the model's flexibility. The flexibility is most fully utilized by fine-tuning the watermark into the SD model [13]. Nevertheless, different watermarks need to be trained on multiple models, and the watermark in the image generated by the same model is fixed, which seriously affects the practical application of the watermarking framework.

Recently, embedding watermark information in the latent space of SD has been widely investigated and enables the more flexible embedding of different watermarks. Tree-Ring [32] and LWMark [25] are two representative works that enable detecting whether AI-generated or not and confirming the identity of the image generator, respectively. However, their extraction accuracies under common image attacks are not satisfactory. Tree-Ring [32] has an average extraction accuracy of less than 50% under rotation attacks. Subsequently, Ring-ID [7] utilizes the multi-channel heterogeneous approach to achieve multi-key identification and further improve robustness. Nevertheless, its robustness to cropping and scaling attacks needs to be reconsidered. In addition to the research on robustness, the CRoSS [38] proposes a lossless SDIS, which seamlessly integrates a secret image of equal size into a produced stego image, realizing the secret transmission of images. However, since CRoSS [38] does not target the design of modules to resist attacks, the existing robustness can only rely on the stability of the latent vector in SD.

In this paper, we propose a framework named DualShield based on the SD model that can embed watermarks and transmit secret images concurrently. DualShield uses public and private conditional texts as keys to embed prepro-

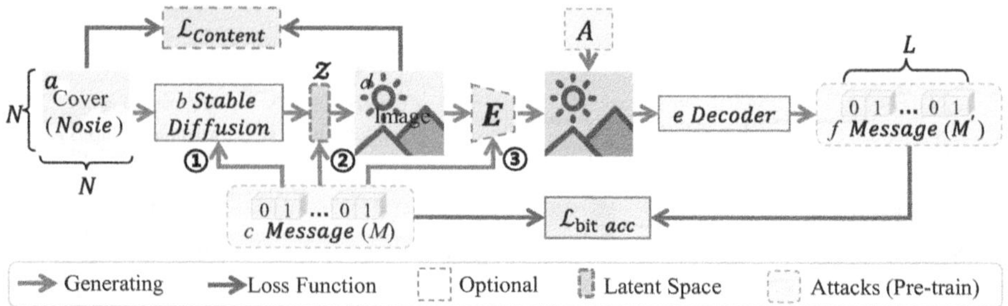

Fig. 2. A general framework for Stable Diffusion (SD) steganography. The ①②③ represents three embedding methods: pre-embedding through fine-tuning the SD model, joint generation embedding in the latent space, and post-embedding.

cessed watermarks into reverse-encoded latent vectors in the latent space. A U-Net encoder enhances watermark fusion by combining low- and high-level features. Random noise is added during training to improve extraction accuracy and robustness. The private key ensures secure reverse decoding of high-value images. Figure 1 demonstrates that our framework enables the covert transmission of more valuable images and copyright protection with anti-counterfeit traceability watermarks. Our contributions are summarized as follows:

- DualShield firstly introduces a dual-protection mechanism using public and private conditional texts as keys, enabling both secure transmission of high-value images and anti-counterfeit traceability of embedded watermarks.
- By leveraging a U-Net encoder, DualShield effectively combines low-level and high-level features, enhancing the integration of watermarks with latent vectors for improved robustness and stability.
- Random noise perturbations are added during training to enhance the accuracy and robustness of watermark extraction, ensuring strong resistance against common image attacks, and steganalysis.

2 Related Work

According to the position of watermark embedding, we divide the watermark generation methods of the model into three categories: pre-embedding watermark, embedding before image generation, post-embedding watermark, embedding after image generation, and a joint generation method that integrates watermark and image generation simultaneously, shown in Fig. 2.

2.1 Post-embedding SDIS

Post-embedding methods include traditional frequency domain transformation methods and watermark embedding methods based on deep learning. Classic methods, including HiDDeN [44], StegaEdge [15] SSL [14], FNNS [19], LISO [4],

DUAW [36], DiffusionShield [9] etc. can improve the robustness of watermark images against attacks or embed more information into the image. However, these methods directly embed watermarks in pixel space, which lacks flexibility and can affect image quality [16].

2.2 Pre-embedding SDIS

Wen et al. [32] embedded a watermark in the initial noise vector, varied it in the Fourier space, and then generated the image through a standard diffusion process. However, the watermark design still lacks robustness against image rotation attacks. Ci et al. [7] proposed a new multi-channel heterogeneous watermarking method, which integrates the advantages of each type by embedding multiple types of watermarks on different channels of the initial noise. Yang et al. [35] proposed Gaussian Shading, which maps watermarks to latent representations that follow a standard Gaussian distribution, achieving lossless watermark embedding. Lei et al. [20] trained an encoder-decoder model to establish a unified representation of the initial latent variables and watermark information. However, these methods require training multiple models for different watermarks, making it difficult to apply in real-world scenarios.

2.3 Mid-embedding SDIS

Zhang et al. [41] proposed a plug-in watermark framework to embed watermarks directly in the latent space without retraining the model. This method balances invisibility and extraction quality but relies on the architecture of SD. Meng et al. [25] improved watermark robustness while preserving image quality by embedding and detecting watermarks in the latent diffusion space, but struggled with larger rotation angles despite handling minor rotations. Rezaei et al. [26] optimized the latent space of the pre-trained autoencoder through the coarse-grained to fine-grained watermark embedding module LaWa, which significantly improved the robustness against various image transformations while ensuring the image perception quality. Lin et al. [22] embedded the watermark into the VAE decoder using low-rank adaptation with the minimum training parameters, and balanced the generation task with watermark embedding through a dynamic loss weight adjustment algorithm. Ci et al. [6] proposed a plug-and-play WMAdapter module that is directly connected to the VAE decoder of the latent diffusion model, and can dynamically label different watermarks for the diffusion model. However, the watermark image generated by this method has artifacts. Fernandez et al. [13] successfully integrated watermarks into the LDM generation process by fine-tuning the LDM decoder, maintaining high image quality. However, the approach depends heavily on the effectiveness of the watermark extractor.

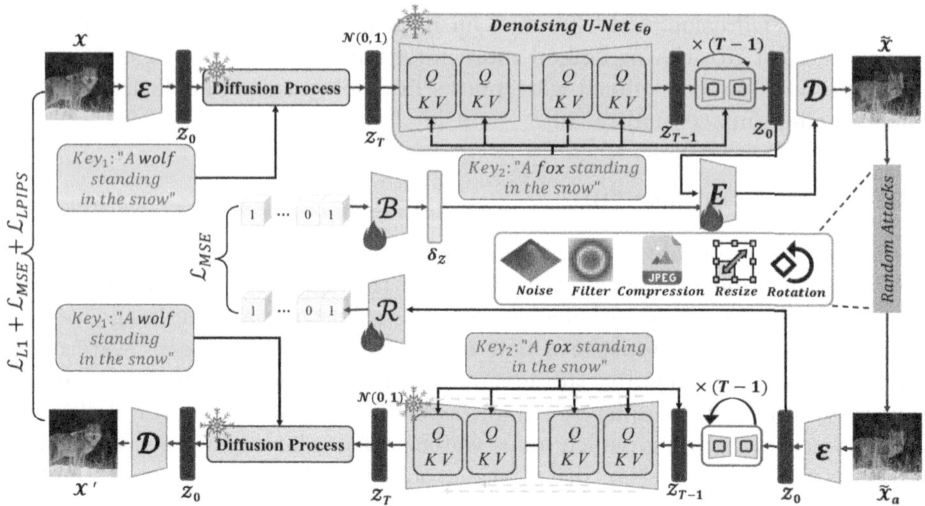

Fig. 3. Pipeline for DualShield steganography. The secretly transmitted images ensure the security of transmission under the control of public and private keys, and embedding secret information in the latent space enables effective tracking of puppet images. Message encoding network $\mathcal{B}$, embedding network $\mathcal{E}$, and recovery network $\mathcal{R}$ require training parameters, while SD models do not.

3 Method

3.1 Overview

Figure 3 shows the pipeline of Dualshield. We borrowed the design of CRoSS [38] framework, used Key1 and Key2 for secret transmission of secret high-value images after conversion, and added watermarks for anti-counterfeiting and traceability in the process.

Embedding Stage: Secret image $\mathrm{x} \in \mathbb{R}^{3\times H\times W}$, image encoder $\mathcal{E}$ is employed to map it into a latent space $\mathbf{z_0}$, expressed as $\mathbf{z_0} = \mathcal{E}(\mathbf{x}) \in \mathbb{R}^{C\times H\times W}$. Combined with the private key (Key_1), U-Net [28] is used to denoise, and the formula for the forward process is given by:

$$\mathbf{x}_t = \sqrt{\alpha_t}\mathbf{x}_{t-1} + \sqrt{1-\alpha_t}\boldsymbol{\epsilon}, \quad \boldsymbol{\epsilon} \sim \mathcal{N}(\mathbf{0}, \mathbf{I}), \tag{1}$$

where $\mathbf{x}_t$ denotes the noisy image in the t-th step, ϵ is sampled from a Gaussian distribution $\mathcal{N}(\mathbf{0}, \mathbf{I})$. During the training phase, LDM is trained to minimize the squared error loss $\mathcal{L}$, which is given by:

$$\mathcal{L} = \mathbb{E}_{\mathbf{z}_0,\epsilon,t,\mathbf{y}} \left[\|\boldsymbol{\epsilon}_\theta(\mathbf{z}_t, t, \mathbf{y}) - \epsilon\|_2^2 \right]. \tag{2}$$

This loss function is designed to ensure that the model effectively denoises the latent representations $\mathbf{z}_t := \alpha_t \mathbf{z}_0 + \sigma_t \epsilon$, where α_t and σ_t are parameters intrinsic to the diffusion process. The backward sampling process uses Eq. 4 to obtain the latent space z_0 by combining the public key (Key_2) and the denoised network.

$$\mathbf{z}_T \sim \mathcal{N}(\mathbf{0}, \mathbf{I}) \tag{3}$$

$$\mathbf{z}_{t-1} = \frac{1}{\sqrt{\alpha_t}}\left(\mathbf{z}_t - \frac{1-\alpha_t}{\sqrt{1-\bar{\alpha}_t}}\boldsymbol{\epsilon}_\theta\left(\mathbf{z}_t, t, \mathbf{y}\right)\right) + \sigma_t \boldsymbol{\epsilon}, \tag{4}$$

where $\bar{\alpha}_t := \Pi_{i=1}^t \alpha_i$. After backward sampling, messages $m \in \{0,1\}^L$ are sequentially passed through the binary message network ($\mathcal{B}$), including the linear layer, the expand and reshape layer and the convolution layer to acquire pre-processed messages $\delta_z \in \mathbb{R}^{3\times H\times W}$. We developed an embedding network $\mathcal{E}$ to fuse z_0 and δ_z, and the latent image obtained using network $\mathcal{D}$ is applied to obtain the container image $\widetilde{x} \in \mathbb{R}^{3\times H\times W}$. To allow a deeper fusion of information features with the latent space, we utilize a four-layer U-net network as a fusion network, drawing on stegastamp [29].

Noise Attacks: To improve the robustness effectively, we randomly select some images to simulate the attack to perturb $\widetilde{x}$ before extracting the watermark, which is given by: $\widetilde{x}_a = \mathit{Attacks}(\mathit{epoch}, \widetilde{x}) \in \mathbb{R}^{3\times H\times W}$, if epoch $\geq t$, where t is a threshold, and in this paper we choose to add noise after 25% of the

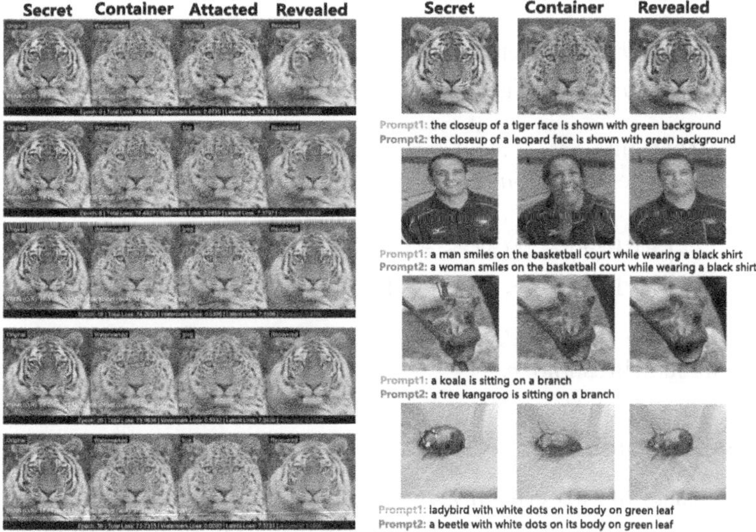

Fig. 4. Visual display of the training process. From top to bottom, the number of epochs gradually increases. The images in the third column are the watermark-embedded images after random attacks, and the images in the fourth column are the recovered secretly transmitted images. It can be observed that the container images exhibit a high degree of realism. In contrast, the revealed images demonstrate remarkable semantic consistency with the secret images, validating the effectiveness and fidelity of the DualShield method.

total training parameters. We choose five perturbations: brightness and contrast with parameters from 0.75 to 1.25, Gaussian noise with a kernel size of 5 and $\sigma \in [0.1, 1.5]$, hue with parameter 0.02, rotation from 1° to 10°, and JPEG compression with parameter $Q = 50$.

Detection Stage: Given a container image $\widetilde{x}_a \in \mathbb{R}^{3\times H\times W}$ subjected to random attacks, the image encoder $\mathcal{E}$ is used to map it into a latent space $\mathbf{z_0}$, mathematically expressed as $\mathbf{z_0} = \mathcal{E}(\widetilde{x}_a) \in \mathbb{R}^{C\times H\times W}$. The image decoder $\mathcal{R}$ decodes the latent space z_0 to extract messages $m \in \{0,1\}^L$. Combined with the public key (Key_2), the latent space z_0 is denoised by the forward process to obtain a latent space z_T using Eq. 1. The backward sampling process uses Eq. 4 to obtain the latent space z_0 by combining the private key (Key_1) and the denoised U-Net network. The obtained latent using network $\mathcal{D}$ is applied to get the revealed image x', mathematically expressed as $\mathbf{x}' = \mathcal{D}(z_0) \in \mathbb{R}^{3\times H\times W}$.

3.2 Watermark Matching

During the detection process, the model developer must determine whether the image is created by artificial intelligence, as shown in Fig. 1. $M(m, m') \geq \tau$, where $M(m, m') = \frac{1}{L}\sum_{i=1}^{L} \mathbb{I}(m_i = m'_i)$ and $\tau \in \{0, \ldots, L\}$. Following [13, 26, 39], the matching of the watermark for Alice boils essentially down to a hypothesis testing problem. Formally, we test the statistical hypothesis.

$$\begin{cases} H_0 : \widetilde{x}\,\text{was generated by Alice (Watermarked)}, \\ H_1 : \widetilde{x}\,\text{was not generated by Alice (Unwatermarked)}. \end{cases} \tag{5}$$

We assume that bits $m'_1, \ldots, m'_k$ are (i.i.d.). Bernoulli random variables with parameter 0.5. Then $M(m, m')$ follows a binomial distribution with parameters $(k, 0.5)$.

$$\begin{cases} \text{FPR}(\tau) = \mathbb{P}(M > \tau \mid H_0) & \text{if } \textit{detection}, \\ \text{FPR}(\tau, N) = 1 - (1 - \text{FPR}(\tau))^N & \text{if } \textit{attribution}. \end{cases} \tag{6}$$

The False Positive Rate (FPR) is the probability that $M(m, m')$ takes a value greater than the threshold τ.

3.3 Loss Functions

Our loss consists of two crucial aspects: image restoration loss and watermark information extraction loss, both of them are essential for maintaining the visual quality of original images and enhancing the robustness of embedded watermarks.

$$\mathcal{L}_{IR} = \gamma_1 |x(i) - x'(i)| + \gamma_2 \left(\|x, x'\|\right)^2, \tag{7}$$

$$\mathcal{L}_{All} = \mathcal{L}_{IR} + \gamma_3 \left\|\phi(x), \phi(x')\right\|^2 + \gamma_4 \left(\|m, m'\|^2\right), \tag{8}$$

where, $|\cdot|$ refers to the smooth-L1 loss, $\|\cdot,\cdot\|^2$ is the Mean Square Error (MSE) loss. $\gamma_i, i = 1, 2, 3, 4$ are the loss weights that control the trade-off between visual quality and extracted watermark quality. We choose $\gamma_1 = 0.1$, $\gamma_2 = 0.1$, $\gamma_3 = 0.01$, and $\gamma_4 = 1$, respectively. $\phi(x)$ represents the LPIPS [43] transformation of x, and we use the pre-trained VGG16 network [27].

4 Experiments

We utilize the dataset `stegaImage260` from CRoSS [38], which has already been generated with Prompt1 and Prompt2 by ChatGPT. Our network is implemented on the NVIDIA RTX 3090 GPU using the PyTorch framework, and the network input image resolution was fixed at (512×512) pixels. In this experiment, the Stable Diffusion V1.5[1] is used as the basic model to build a latent diffusion model framework from text to image. The evaluation metrics used include PSNR [31] and bit accuracy.

4.1 Visual Quality

Figure 4 illustrates the image quality at different training epochs on the left. As training progresses, the revealed images show noticeable improvements in quality, and the decoding accuracy steadily increases. On the right, the figure presents Key_1 and Key_2, corresponding to Prompt1 and Prompt2, along with the extracted watermarks. The resulting images exhibit excellent quality, and the watermarks are extracted with 100% accuracy under conditions without perturbation.

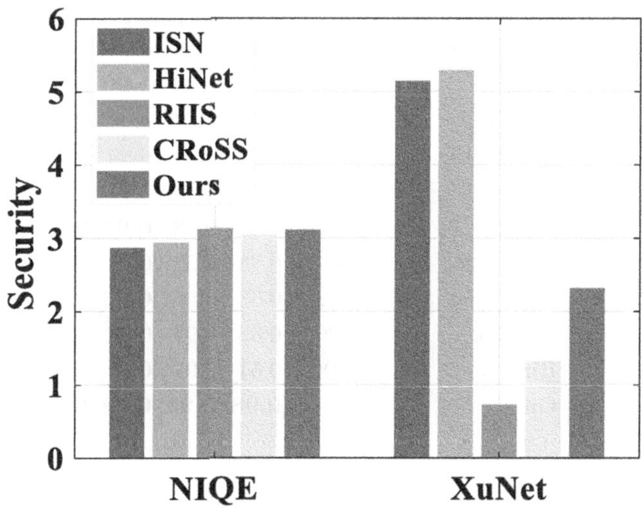

Fig. 5. Comparative NIQE and XuNet [33] results of different steganographic frameworks [18,23,34,38].

[1] https://huggingface.co/stable-diffusion-v1-5/stable-diffusion-v1-5.

4.2 Image Quality

Figure 5 of the NIQE results demonstrates the comparison of the naturalness of the images generated by the four methods with that of our method. As can be seen, the results of our framework are close to those of the other four methods. The values are slightly lower than those of RIIS and slightly higher than those of the other three algorithms, where the results are closer to those of CRoSS. Our framework still uses the same model of stable diffusion v1-5 for image generation as the CRoSS [38] framework uses, and there is no replacement, so the results of NIQE are also closer. However, our double-layer protection framework embeds watermark information in the generated images, so the quality of the images is slightly worse. By the same logic, our framework is improved in robustness while the image is more perturbed, so the XuNet [30] detection results are slightly lower than CRoSS [38], but better than those of ISN [23] and HiNet [18].

Table 1. Comparative analysis of robustness under different bits and different attacks.

# Bit	Methods	Rotate	C&S	Blur	Bri.	Avg
32	HiDDeN [44]	0.79	0.91	0.76	0.74	0.80
	SSL [14]	**0.99**	0.74	**1.00**	0.95	0.92
	RoSteALS [3]	0.47	0.50	**1.00**	0.86	0.71
	WMAdapter [6]	0.97	**0.99**	0.94	**0.99**	**0.97**
	Tree-Ring [13]	0.34	0.54	0.61	0.42	0.48
	Ring-ID [7]	**1.00**	0.53	**0.99**	0.96	0.87
	EW-LoRA [22]	0.55	0.89	0.78	0.95	0.79
	Training-Free [41]	0.95	0.97	0.98	0.95	**0.96**
	Ours	0.87	**0.98**	0.96	**1.00**	**0.95**
48	SSL [14]	**0.99**	0.72	**1.00**	0.94	**0.91**
	FNNS [19]	0.75	**0.98**	0.54	0.85	0.78
	RoSteALS [3]	0.50	0.51	**1.00**	0.85	0.72
	SS [13]	0.81	**0.95**	0.78	**0.96**	0.88
	LaWa [26]	0.84	0.83	0.92	0.95	0.89
	Tree-Ring [32]	0.32	0.53	0.56	**0.36**	0.44
	LW [25]	0.86	0.83	0.97	0.98	0.91
	Ring-ID [7]	**1.00**	0.51	0.97	0.95	0.86
	Ours	0.84	**0.98**	**0.99**	**0.98**	**0.94**

4.3 Robustness Results

Simulation Degradation: We conducted simulated degradation experiments (e.g., Gaussian noise and JPEG compression) to verify the robustness of our

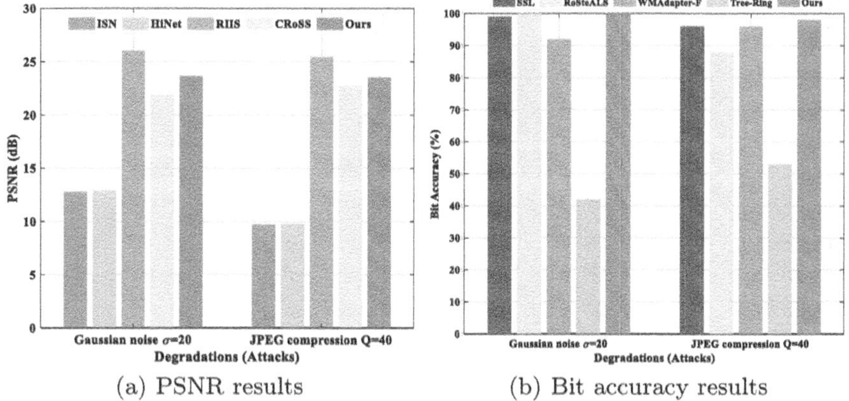

(a) PSNR results (b) Bit accuracy results

Fig. 6. Comparison results of simulation degradation PSNR of the five frameworks under two perturbation attacks, including Gaussian noise (σ = 20) and JPEG compression (Q = 20).

method. As shown in Fig. 6(a), our DualShield has the second best PSNR after RIIS [34] with Gaussian noise $\sigma = 20$, and the bit accuracy still reaches 100%. And at JPEG compression with $Q = 40$, the PSNR is still better, and the bit accuracy decreases, while still the highest among the five methods. It shows that the robustness of our extracted watermark information is better, this is since we introduced various attacks during the training process, which effectively improved the robustness of the model. But it is slightly lower than RIIS [34]. It is mainly because RIIS [34] uses a reversible network, which has a natural advantage in PSNR, but its robustness is not as good as ours.

Noise Attacks: Figure 6 (b) shows the bit accuracy of our algorithm under both attacks, and it can be seen that our method can reach 100% bit accuracy on Gaussian noise. It outperforms the four existing SOTA methods compared to the JPEG compression attack ($Q = 40$), reaching more than 98.5%. This is mainly because we add rich noise attack simulation in the training phase, making the network more noise-resistant. Since our framework adds a variety of analog noises after the embedded information image, the extraction network adapts to noise extraction for more stable features. Table 1 summarizes the robustness performance of the proposed method under various attacks, including rotation, cropping, blur, and brightness, for 32-bit and 48-bit cases. Notably, our approach demonstrates exceptional performance under random crop-and-scale (C&S) attacks, where 80% cropping and brightness levels [0, 6] are applied. This superior robustness is attributed to the embedding of information in the latent space, facilitated by U-Net's capability to effectively fuse low- and high-level features. Furthermore, including diverse attack scenarios during training significantly enhances the model's resilience to noise and perturbations, ensuring consistent performance across challenging conditions.

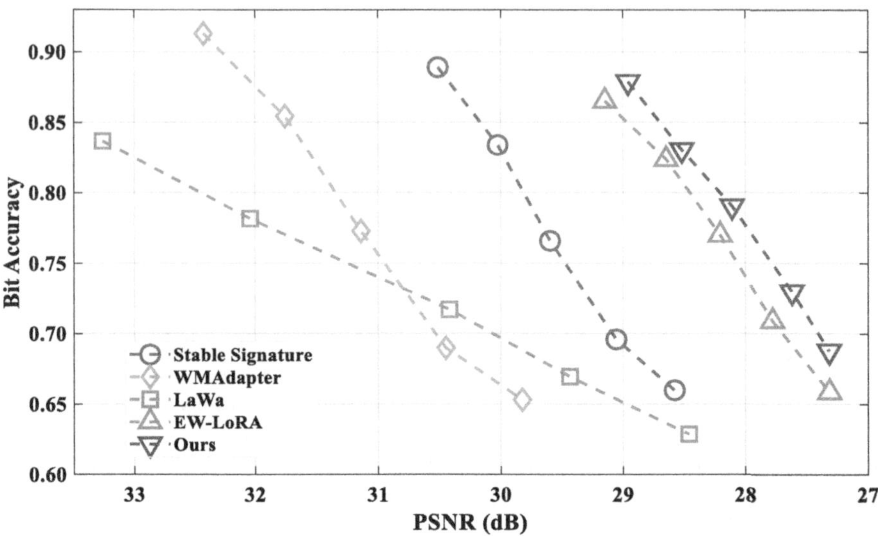

Fig. 7. Removal attacks comparison with four existing SOTA methods by Stable Signature [13], WMAdapter [6], LaWa [26], EW-LoRA [22] and Ours.

Watermark Removal Attacks: The watermark removal attack mainly process the watermarked images through image compression, aiming to destroy the embedded watermark information. We chose to test the auto-encoder image compression algorithm [5] based on several common SD-based watermarking methods. The results in Fig. 7 show that our method has higher robustness with the same PSNR value, indicating that the image compression attacks have less impact on the robustness of our method. This is mainly because the fusion network we designed and the added noise training play a decisive role.

4.4 Security Results

StegaExpose: To demonstrate the superiority of the proposed algorithm, we conducted a systematic comparative experiment with SOTA deep learning-based steganography algorithms, namely DDH [1], HCISNet [21], HiDDeN [44], HiNet [18], ISN [23], MIAIS [8], MS-HiDDeN [17], SteganoGan [42], UDH [40], FNNs [19], RIIS [34], S-FNNs [24] and CRoSS [38], using the StegaExpose benchmark [2]. As shown in Fig. 8(a), the AUC of our method approaches 0.5, indicating that the watermark embedded by DualShield is effectively concealed and resistant to steganographic analysis. Using U-Net for encoding enhances feature integration, enabling the effective fusion of δ_z and z_0, while embedding in the latent space improves invisibility. Using puppet images ensures the original secret image remains secure even if the watermark is leaked, further enhancing transmission security.

Size-Independent-Detector (SID) [30]: We evaluated several existing frameworks using the SID metric to demonstrate the security of our framework fur-

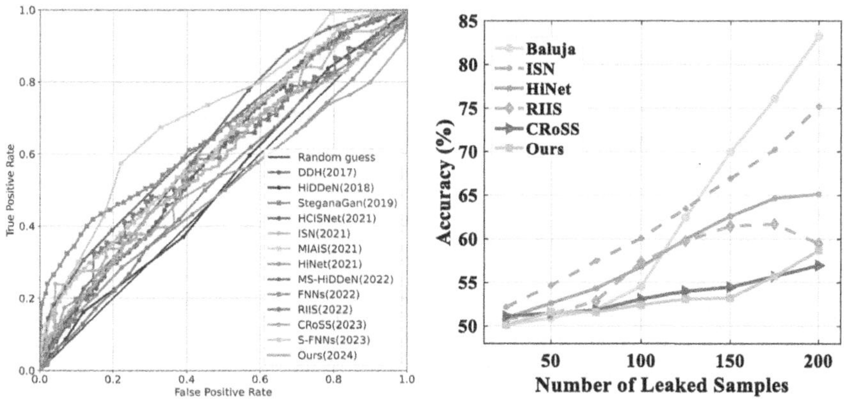

Fig. 8. Comparative security analysis results of different steganographic frameworks.

ther. As shown in Fig. 8(b), the comparison results indicate that with fewer than 150 leakage samples, our framework achieves accuracy comparable to or slightly lower than the SOTA CoRSS framework, demonstrating its strong security performance. When the sample size exceeds 150, although our method exhibits marginally lower accuracy than CoRSS [38], it still maintains a clear security advantage over other baseline frameworks, further validating the robustness and security of our approach. Overall, the security of our framework under the SID evaluation metric relies heavily on the security of the CRoSS [38], with no additional security enhancement design added.

5 Conclusion

We propose DualShield, an advanced robust steganography framework that effectively addresses the dual challenges of watermark traceability and secure secret information transmission in SDIS. Our framework incorporates a U-Net-based encoder architecture that optimizes the embedding process through enhanced fusion of low-level and high-level image features, along with a carefully designed noise injection mechanism during training that significantly improves robustness against various image distortions while maintaining high watermark extraction accuracy. Extensive experiments demonstrate DualShield's superior performance, showing strong resilience against common image attacks while preserving image quality. The framework also exhibits exceptional security characteristics, with low detection accuracy against SOTA steganalysis attacks and reliable watermark preservation. Furthermore, our innovative dual-key mechanism ensures secure transmission of high-value images, with the private key guaranteeing robust decoding even in adversarial scenarios, making DualShield particularly suitable for security-critical applications.

Acknowledgments. This study was funded by grants from the National Key R&D Program of China for International Science and Technology Innovation Cooperation "Home-based Wearable Multi-channel Monitor and AI-assisted Diagnostic System Development and Applications" (CN) (2023YFE0112600); the Sustainable Development Special Program of Shenzhen Municipal Science and Technology Innovation Commission "Development of a Medical-Prevention Integrated Chronic Disease Management Model with Hypertension as a Pilot" (CN) (KCXFZ202002011010487).

References

1. Baluja, S.: Hiding images in plain sight: deep steganography. Adv. Neural. Inf. Process. Syst. **30**, 2066–2076 (2017)
2. Boehm, B.: StegExpose-a tool for detecting LSB steganography. arXiv preprint arXiv:1410.6656 (2014)
3. Bui, T., Agarwal, S., Yu, N., Collomosse, J.: RoSteALS: robust steganography using autoencoder latent space. In: Proceedings of the IEEE/CVF Conference on Computer Vision and Pattern Recognition (CVPR) Workshops, pp. 933–942 (2023)
4. Chen, X., Kishore, V., Weinberger, K.Q.: Learning iterative neural optimizers for image steganography. In: The Eleventh International Conference on Learning Representations (2022)
5. Cheng, Z., Sun, H., Takeuchi, M., Katto, J.: Learned image compression with discretized gaussian mixture likelihoods and attention modules. In: Proceedings of the IEEE/CVF Conference on Computer Vision and Pattern Recognition, pp. 7939–7948 (2020)
6. Ci, H., Song, Y., Yang, P., Xie, J., Shou, M.Z.: WMAdapter: adding watermark control to latent diffusion models. arXiv preprint arXiv:2406.08337
7. Ci, H., Yang, P., Song, Y., Shou, M.Z.: RingID: rethinking tree-ring watermarking for enhanced multi-key identification. In: European Conference on Computer Vision, pp. 338–354. Springer (2025)
8. Cui, J., et al.: Multitask identity-aware image steganography via minimax optimization. IEEE Trans. Image Process. **30**, 8567–8579 (2021)
9. Cui, Y., et al.: DiffusionShield: a watermark for copyright protection against generative diffusion models. arXiv preprint arXiv:2306.04642 (2023)
10. Fang, H., Chen, K., Qiu, Y., Ma, Z., Zhang, W., Chang, E.C.: DERO: diffusion-model-erasure robust watermarking. In: Proceedings of the 32nd ACM International Conference on Multimedia, pp. 2973–2981 (2024)
11. Fei, J., Xia, Z., Tondi, B., Barni, M.: Supervised GAN watermarking for intellectual property protection. In: 2022 IEEE International Workshop on Information Forensics and Security (WIFS), pp. 1–6. IEEE (2022)
12. Feng, Z., et al.: ERNIE-ViLG 2.0: improving text-to-image diffusion model with knowledge-enhanced mixture-of-denoising-experts. In: Proceedings of the IEEE/CVF Conference on Computer Vision and Pattern Recognition, pp. 10,135–10,145 (2023)
13. Fernandez, P., Couairon, G., Jégou, H., Douze, M., Furon, T.: The stable signature: rooting watermarks in latent diffusion models. arXiv preprint arXiv:2303.15435 (2023)
14. Fernandez, P., Sablayrolles, A., Furon, T., Jégou, H., Douze, M.: Watermarking images in self-supervised latent spaces. In: ICASSP 2022 - 2022 IEEE International Conference on Acoustics, Speech and Signal Processing (ICASSP), pp. 3054–3058 (2022)

15. Hu, K., Huang, Z., Wang, X., Wang, X.: StegaEdge: learning edge-guidance steganography. Vis. Comput. **39**(8), 3319–3331 (2023)
16. Hu, K., Wang, M., Ma, X., Chen, J., Wang, X., Wang, X.: Learning-based image steganography and watermarking: a survey. Expert Syst. Appl., 123715 (2024)
17. Huang, C.H., Wu, J.L.: Image data hiding with multi-scale autoencoder network. arXiv preprint arXiv:2201.06038 (2022)
18. Jing, J., Deng, X., Xu, M., Wang, J., Guan, Z.: HiNet: deep image hiding by invertible network. In: Proceedings of the IEEE/CVF International Conference on Computer Vision (CVPR), pp. 4733–4742 (2021)
19. Kishore, V., Chen, X., Wang, Y., Li, B., Weinberger, K.Q.: Fixed neural network steganography: train the images, not the network. In: International Conference on Learning Representations (2021)
20. Lei, L., Gai, K., Yu, J., Zhu, L.: DiffuseTrace: a transparent and flexible watermarking scheme for latent diffusion model. arXiv preprint arXiv:2405.02696 (2024)
21. Li, Y., Liu, J., Liu, X., Wang, X., Gao, X., Zhang, Y.: HCISNet: higher-capacity invisible image steganographic network. IET Image Proc. **15**(13), 3332–3346 (2021)
22. Lin, D., Li, Y., Tondi, B., Li, B., Barni, M.: An efficient watermarking method for latent diffusion models via low-rank adaptation. arXiv preprint arXiv:2410.20202
23. Lu, S.P., Wang, R., Zhong, T., Rosin, P.L.: Large-capacity image steganography based on invertible neural networks. In: Proceedings of the IEEE/CVF Conference on Computer Vision and Pattern Recognition (CVPR), pp. 10,816–10,825 (2021)
24. Luo, Z., Li, S., Li, G., Qian, Z., Zhang, X.: Securing fixed neural network steganography. In: Proceedings of the 31st ACM International Conference on Multimedia, pp. 7943–7951 (2023)
25. Meng, Z., Peng, B., Dong, J.: Latent watermark: inject and detect watermarks in latent diffusion space. arXiv preprint arXiv:2404.00230 (2024)
26. Rezaei, A., Akbari, M., Alvar, S.R., Fatemi, A., Zhang, Y.: LaWa: using latent space for in-generation image watermarking. arXiv preprint arXiv:2408.05868
27. Simonyan, K., Zisserman, A.: Very deep convolutional networks for large-scale image recognition. arXiv preprint arXiv:1409.1556
28. Song, J., Meng, C., Ermon, S.: Denoising diffusion implicit models. arXiv preprint arXiv:2010.02502 (2020)
29. Tancik, M., Mildenhall, B., Ng, R.: StegaStamp: invisible hyperlinks in physical photographs. In: Proceedings of the IEEE/CVF Conference on Computer Vision And Pattern Recognition, pp. 2117–2126 (2020)
30. Tsang, C.F., Fridrich, J.: Steganalyzing images of arbitrary size with CNNs. Electron. Imaging **30**, 1–8 (2018)
31. Wang, Z., Bovik, A.C., Sheikh, H.R., Simoncelli, E.P.: Image quality assessment: from error visibility to structural similarity. IEEE Trans. Image Process. **13**(4), 600–612 (2004)
32. Wen, Y., Kirchenbauer, J., Geiping, J., Goldstein, T.: Tree-ring watermarks: fingerprints for diffusion images that are invisible and robust. arXiv preprint arXiv:2305.20030
33. Xu, G., Wu, H.Z., Shi, Y.Q.: Structural design of convolutional neural networks for steganalysis. IEEE Signal Process. Lett. **23**(5), 708–712 (2016)
34. Xu, Y., Mou, C., Hu, Y., Xie, J., Zhang, J.: Robust invertible image steganography. In: Proceedings of the IEEE/CVF Conference on Computer Vision and Pattern Recognition, pp. 7875–7884 (2022)
35. Yang, Z., Zeng, K., Chen, K., Fang, H., Zhang, W., Yu, N.: Gaussian shading: provable performance-lossless image watermarking for diffusion models. In: Proceedings

of the IEEE/CVF Conference on Computer Vision and Pattern Recognition, pp. 12,162–12,171 (2024)
36. Ye, X., Huang, H., An, J., Wang, Y.: DUAW: data-free universal adversarial watermark against stable diffusion customization. arXiv preprint arXiv:2308.09889 (2023)
37. Yin, Z., Yin, H., Zhang, X.: Neural network fragile watermarking with no model performance degradation. In: 2022 IEEE International Conference on Image Processing (ICIP), pp. 3958–3962. IEEE (2022)
38. Yu, J., Zhang, X., Xu, Y., Zhang, J.: Cross: diffusion model makes controllable, robust and secure image steganography. Adv. Neural Inf. Process. Syst. **36** (2024)
39. Yu, N., Skripniuk, V., Abdelnabi, S., Fritz, M.: Artificial fingerprinting for generative models: rooting deepfake attribution in training data. In: Proceedings of the IEEE/CVF International Conference on Computer Vision, pp. 14,448–14,457 (2021)
40. Zhang, C., Benz, P., Karjauv, A., Sun, G., Kweon, I.S.: UDH: universal deep hiding for steganography, watermarking, and light field messaging. Adv. Neural. Inf. Process. Syst. **33**, 10223–10234 (2020)
41. Zhang, G., Wang, L., Su, Y., Liu, A.A.: A training-free plug-and-play watermark framework for stable diffusion. arXiv preprint arXiv:2404.05607
42. Zhang, K.A., Cuesta-Infante, A., Xu, L., Veeramachaneni, K.: SteganoGAN: high capacity image steganography with GANs. arXiv preprint arXiv:1901.03892 (2019)
43. Zhang, R., Isola, P., Efros, A.A., Shechtman, E., Wang, O.: The unreasonable effectiveness of deep features as a perceptual metric. In: Proceedings of the IEEE Conference on Computer Vision and Pattern Recognition, pp. 586–595 (2018)
44. Zhu, J., Kaplan, R., Johnson, J., Fei-Fei, L.: Hidden: hiding data with deep networks. In: Proceedings of the European Conference on Computer Vision (ECCV), pp. 657–672 (2018)

VS-DSN: Variable-Speed Dual-Stream Network for Continuous Sign Language Recognition

Guang Zhou[1], Bo Yang[1,2(✉)], Wan Tang[3], and Jixing Yang[1]

[1] College of Computer Science, South-Central Minzu University, Wuhan 430074, China

[2] Key Laboratory of Cyber-Physical Fusion Intelligent Computing (South-Central Minzu University), State Ethnic Affairs Commission, Wuhan 430074, China
yangbo@mail.scuec.edu.cn

[3] School of Mathematics and Statistics, South-Central Minzu University, Wuhan 430074, China

Abstract. Continuous Sign Language Recognition (CSLR) requires modeling both spatial and temporal semantics, such as handshape, facial expressions, motion trajectories, and hand orientation. Despite the rich visual cues provided by RGB inputs, they often struggle to capture fine-grained temporal dynamics. To bridge this gap, we propose a novel Variable-Speed Dual-Stream Network (VS-DSN) that fuses spatial features from RGB sequences with motion cues from optical flow. We introduce a semantic-aware variable-speed sampling strategy that adaptively selects key frames from the RGB stream and compresses the optical flow sequence, effectively balancing recognition accuracy and computational cost. Additionally, we design a Spatio-Temporal Interaction Module (STIM) to enhance cross-modal fusion by modeling dependencies between spatial appearance and temporal motion. Extensive experiments on CSL-Daily, PHOENIX14, and PHOENIX14-T demonstrate that VS-DSN achieves state-of-the-art performance, reducing Word Error Rates (WER) to 27.5%, 19.4%, and 19.4%, respectively. Moreover, our method reduces FLOPs by at least 36%, validating its efficiency. These results highlight the effectiveness of VS-DSN as a lightweight yet accurate framework for CSLR.

Keywords: Continuous sign language recognition · Variable-speed Sampling · Dual-Stream

1 Introduction

Sign Language Recognition (SLR) aims to translate sign language into text using computational methods. It comprises Isolated SLR (ISLR) [13], which recognizes individual signs, and Continuous SLR (CSLR) [10], which handles unsegmented sign sequences. As shown in Fig. 1, sign language conveys meaning through

P. Li et al. (Eds.): CGI 2025, LNCS 16508, pp. 173–185, 2026.
https://doi.org/10.1007/978-3-032-22264-0_14

spatial cues (e.g., hand shapes, facial expressions) and temporal dynamics (e.g., movement trajectories). Effective CSLR models must capture both spatial details and temporal dependencies to accurately interpret continuous sign streams.

RGB have become the predominant input modality due to their rich visual information. Traditional methods using Dynamic Time Warping (DTW) [11] and Hidden Markov Models (HMMs) [16] processed temporal information through hand-crafted features but struggled with long-term dependencies. Deep learning approaches integrating Convolutional Neural Networks (CNN) with Long Short-Term Memory (LSTM) [9] improved spatio-temporal modeling. However, SLR uniquely requires capturing both local dynamic changes and global action coherence. While 3D CNNs perform better than 2D CNNs at capturing dynamic changes, RGB alone cannot effectively represent subtle changes in fast or complex gestures. Multi-modal methods can address this limitation but introduce higher computational costs and feature fusion challenges.

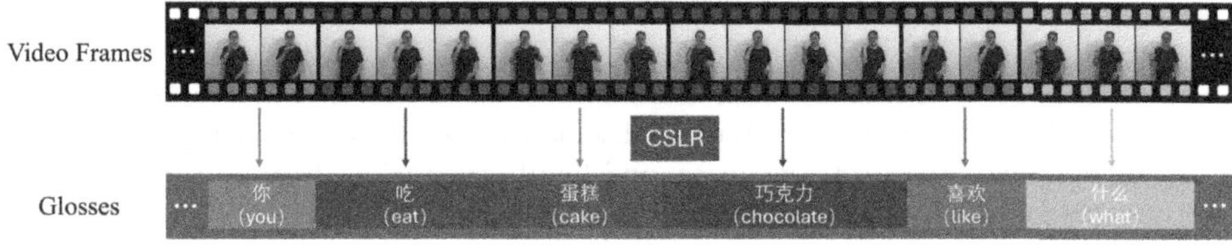

Fig. 1. Continuous sign language recognition.

To address these challenges, this paper proposes the Variable-Speed Dual-Stream Network for Continuous Sign Language Recognition (VS-DSN), combining RGB and optical flow modalities to capture spatial semantics and dynamic trajectory information. The contribution of this paper can be summarized as follows:

(1) A dual-stream feature extraction architecture that exploits the complementary strengths of RGB and optical flow modalities.
(2) A variable-speed sampling strategy based on semantic importance, where the RGB path uses keyframe sampling to reduce redundancy, while the optical flow path reduces spatial dimensions for computational efficiency.
(3) A multi-stage Spatio-Temporal Interaction Module (STIM) that integrates RGB and optical flow features through feature alignment and bidirectional attention mechanisms.

2 Related Work

SLR has shifted from hand-crafted features to deep learning. Early methods like DTW and HMMs handled gesture variation but relied on manual features.

Deep learning, especially CNNs, enables automatic feature extraction. Cheng et al. [2] proposed a Fully Convolutional Network (FCN) for pixel-level spatial features. Connectionist Temporal Classification (CTC) [7] supports end-to-end sequence learning. Min et al. [12] addressed CTC's alignment issues with a Visual Alignment Constraint (VAC). Hu et al. [5] introduced CorrNet to model spatio-temporal body motion. 3D CNNs also improve short-term temporal modeling.

Single-modality methods remain limited for CSLR. Multimodal strategies offer better representations. STMC [17] fuses features from RGB, hands, face, and pose. C2SLR [18] combines RGB and skeleton data to boost accuracy. Optical flow captures motion between frames, providing dense temporal cues. Although optical flow has been widely used in action recognition, it remains underexplored in SLR. Most works focus on RGB or skeletal data, lacking systematic integration of optical flow for fast and subtle movements.

3 Approach

3.1 Dual-Modal Visual Backbone

The goal of the CSLR task is to translate a video sequence $\mathbf{x}_v = \{x_t^v\}_{t=1}^T \in \mathbb{R}^{T\times 3\times H\times W}$ into its corresponding annotation sequence $\mathbf{y} = \{y_i\}_{i=1}^N$, where T is the number of frames and N denotes the output sequence length. The overall structure of the proposed VS-DSN is shown in Fig. 2. It comprises a Dual-Modal Visual Backbone and a Temporal Head Module.

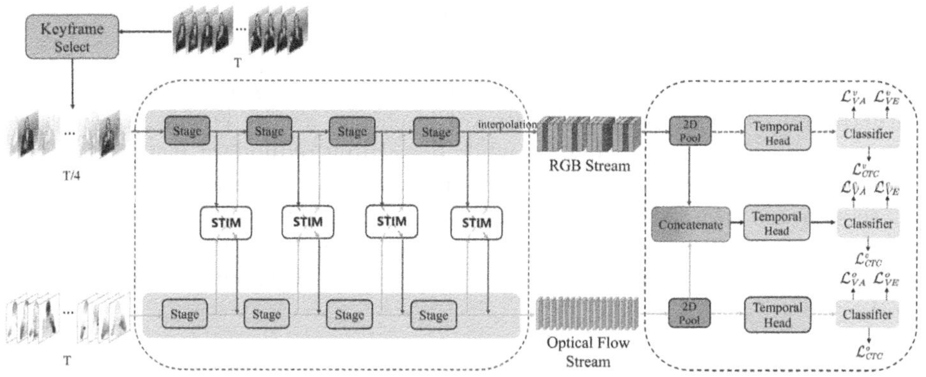

Fig. 2. Architecture of the proposed VS-DSN framework.

The Dual-Modal Visual Backbone includes two parallel branches for RGB frames and optical flow inputs, respectively, along with STIM. The RGB stream focuses on extracting spatial semantic features (e.g., hand shapes, positions), while the optical flow stream emphasizes motion dynamics across frames. STIM modules facilitate bidirectional feature enhancement by transferring motion cues into the RGB stream and injecting spatial context into the optical flow stream. Optical flow is computed using the RAFT algorithm [15], which provides dense motion estimation between adjacent frames. The resulting flow sequence $X_o =$

$\{x_t^o\}_{t=1}^T \in \mathbb{R}^{T\times 3\times H\times W}$ is stored in an image-like format to align with the RGB input structure, ensuring consistency across modalities during processing. The fused features from both streams are passed to the temporal head for sequence modeling and transcription, enabling accurate recognition of continuous sign language gestures.

3.2 Variable-Speed Sampling

Feature extraction plays a crucial role in the performance of SLR systems. Traditional approaches often face a trade-off between computational efficiency and semantic preservation. A sign language video sequence contains *keyframes*, which carry essential semantic information, and *transition frames*, which capture smooth action transitions but are largely redundant. These redundant frames increase computational costs with minimal recognition gains. Although optical flow encodes detailed motion trajectories and richer temporal cues, Incorporating it as a dual-modal input substantially increases computational overhead.

To alleviate these issues, we propose a variable-speed sampling strategy guided by semantic importance. Specifically, the RGB stream is downsampled by selecting one representative frame every four frames. The video is partitioned into intervals of length α, within which candidate frames are evaluated by inter-frame difference:

$$D(t) = \sum_{x,y} |I_t(x,y) - I_{t-1}(x,y)|\,, \quad (1)$$

where $I_t(x,y)$ denotes the grayscale intensity at pixel (x,y) in frame t. The frame with the maximal $D(t)$ in each interval is chosen as the keyframe, effectively retaining salient semantic changes while discarding redundant frames.

For the optical flow stream, to preserve continuous motion trajectories, the full sequence is retained. Since optical flow predominantly captures motion rather than spatial detail, its feature channels are reduced to β times that of the RGB stream ($\beta < 1$), thus lowering computational cost without sacrificing critical motion information.

3.3 Spatio-Temporal Interaction Module(STIM)

The RGB and optical flow features exhibit substantial complementarity in spatio-temporal dimensions. The RGB feature stream offers rich spatial semantic expressions, yet its temporal information is sparse due to the implementation of the keyframe sampling strategy. Conversely, the optical flow feature stream preserves continuous motion trajectory information, but lacks fine-grained spatial semantic expressions. Given the distinct differences between these two modal features, using straightforward methods like feature splicing or element-by-element summation for intermodal information integration may result in inadequate fusion or feature imbalance. Hence, as depicted in Fig. 3, the STIM designed in this paper achieves complementary enhancement of intermodal features at multiple feature extraction stages via feature projection and a bidirectional attention mechanism.

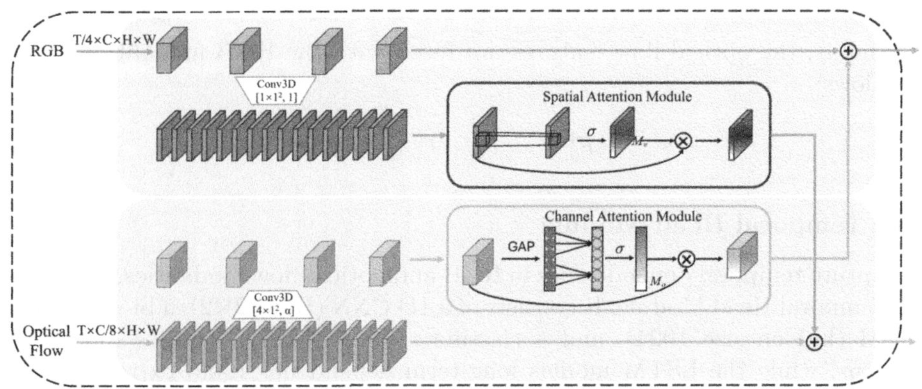

Fig. 3. Spatio-Temporal Interaction Module(STIM).

Specifically, for the features $F_v \in \mathbb{R}^{T/\alpha \times C \times H \times W}$ and $F_o \in \mathbb{R}^{T \times \beta C \times H \times W}$ extracted at each stage of the backbone network, we propose a bidirectional interaction pathway. First, we apply 3D convolution with a temporal stride of α and a kernel size of $4 \times 1 \times 2$ to the optical flow features for temporal downsampling and feature projection, resulting in $F_o' \in \mathbb{R}^{T/\alpha \times C \times H \times W}$. A channel attention mechanism is then applied to model inter-channel dependencies and enhance the feature representations. This mechanism uses Global Average Pooling (GAP) to obtain a global descriptor for each channel:

$$z = \mathrm{GAP}(F_o') = \frac{1}{T \cdot H \cdot W} \sum_{t=1}^{T} \sum_{h=1}^{H} \sum_{w=1}^{W} F_o'(t, h, w) \tag{2}$$

Local channel dependencies are further captured using a 1D convolution with kernel size k, followed by a sigmoid activation to produce normalized channel weights:

$$M_o = \sigma(\mathrm{Conv1D}(z)) \tag{3}$$

The final fused features are obtained by channel-wise weighting and integration with the RGB features:

$$F_v^{\mathrm{fuse}} = F_v \odot F_o' \odot M_o \tag{4}$$

To enhance the spatial representation capability of the optical flow modality, we apply a $1 \times 1 \times 1$ convolution to F_v, adjust its output channels to βC, and expand the temporal dimension via trilinear interpolation, resulting in $F'_v \in \mathbb{R}^{T\times \beta C\times H\times W}$. A spatial attention mechanism is employed to generate spatial attention weights M_v, which emphasize salient regions associated with sign language gestures:

$$M_v = \sigma(\text{Conv3D}_{1\times 3\times 3}(F'_v)) \tag{5}$$

Finally, the optical flow features are fused with the RGB modality features as follows:

$$F_o^{\text{fuse}} = F_o + F'_v \odot M_v \tag{6}$$

3.4 Temporal Head Module

To capture temporal dependencies in RGB and optical-flow modalities, we design the Temporal Head Module. It consists of a 1D CNN (K5, P2×2), a bi-directional LSTM (hidden size 1024), and a classifier. The 1D CNN handles short-term patterns, while the LSTM models long-term dependencies and extracts global sequence features. Each branch feature is first reduced via 2D pooling to reduce spatial dimensions, thereby decreasing computational complexity. To fully utilize multimodal information, we designate RGB and optical-flow as auxiliary paths while their concatenated features form a joint path that serves as our main pathway. This principal path undergoes temporal modeling through the Temporal Head. Finally, the features from all paths are mapped to the word-list space through a linear classifier and Softmax to generate frame-level probability distributions:

$$P^{v,o,c} = [\text{Softmax}(f_t^{v,o,c})]_{t=1}^{T} \in \mathrm{R}^{T\times V} \tag{7}$$

Where $P^{v,o,c}$ is a probability matrix of size $T \times V$, with each time step t corresponding to a probability distribution in the lexicon space V. These distributions are used to compute the CTC loss $\mathcal{L}_{CTC}^{v,o,c}$, modeling the alignment between input features and the target sequence. All three Temporal Head Modules are used only during training to contribute to the loss calculation. we discard the auxiliary modules and rely solely on the main Temporal Head Module for classification results.

3.5 Loss Design

In the CSLR task, establishing a direct mapping between the input and output is challenging due to varying input sequence lengths. To address this, we introduce the CTC loss function, which handles unclear output-symbol boundaries and repeated symbols by using blank symbols and intermediate alignment paths.

CTC calculates the sum of probabilities of all possible alignment paths using dynamic programming. Given an input sequence $F = \{f_i\}_{i=1}^{T}$ and a target sequence $S = \{s_i\}_{i=1}^{L}$, CTC extends the output space to $V \cup \{\text{blank}\}$, where V represents the vocabulary, and 'blank' indicates no symbol at that time step. For each time step t, CTC generates a probability distribution $p(\pi_t|F)$, where

$\pi_t \in V \cup \{\text{blank}\}$ represents the predicted character at time t. The probability of a path is calculated as:

$$p(\pi|F) = \prod_{t=1}^{T} p(\pi_t|F) \tag{8}$$

The conditional probability of the target sequence S is the sum of all possible mapping paths, which are folded into the target sequence by removing blanks and repeated symbols:

$$p(S|F) = \sum_{\pi \in B^{-1}(S)} p(\pi|F) \tag{9}$$

The CTC loss is the negative log-likelihood between the target sequence and the predicted output:

$$\mathcal{L}_{\text{CTC}} = -\ln p(S|F) \tag{10}$$

To enhance the model's visual feature understanding, we introduce the visual alignment loss (λ_{VA}) and visual enhancement loss (λ_{VE}). The visual alignment loss improves the model's perception of sign language details by increasing the similarity of similar features and reducing the discrepancy between dissimilar ones. The visual enhancement loss strengthens feature correlation via contrastive learning while suppressing irrelevant noise, improving semantic discrimination of sign language actions. The relative importance of these losses is controlled by the hyperparameters λ_{VA} and λ_{VE}. Together with the base CTC loss $\mathcal{L}_{\text{CTC}}$, they form the total loss function for a single pathway:

$$\mathcal{L}^{\{v,o,c\}} = \mathcal{L}_{\text{CTC}}^{\{v,o,c\}} + \lambda_{\text{VA}}\mathcal{L}_{\text{VA}}^{\{v,o,c\}} + \lambda_{\text{VE}}\mathcal{L}_{\text{VE}}^{\{v,o,c\}} \tag{11}$$

Total Loss. The total training loss is computed as a weighted sum of the losses from the RGB and optical flow modalities. Here, λ_{video} and λ_{optical} represent the respective loss weights for the RGB and optical flow losses. The total loss function is given by:

$$\mathcal{L} = \mathcal{L}_{\text{concat}} + \lambda_{\text{video}}\mathcal{L}_{\text{video}} + \lambda_{\text{optical}}\mathcal{L}_{\text{optical}} \tag{12}$$

4 Experiments

4.1 Dataset

We evaluate our CSLR approach using three widely adopted datasets: CSL-Daily, PHOENIX14, and PHOENIX14-T. CSL-Daily is a large-scale SLR corpus focusing on daily life scenarios, featuring 10 performers. It contains 20,654 sentences (18,401 training, 1,077 development, and 1,176 test samples), with each sentence interpreted by one to four performers. PHOENIX14 is a German sign language corpus of weather forecasts interpreted by nine actors. It comprises 6,841 sentences with 1,295 vocabulary items, split into 5,672 training, 540 development, and 629 test samples, with a resolution of 210 $\times$ 260 pixels. PHOENIX14-T, an extended version of PHOENIX14, contains 8,257 sentences and 1,085 vocabulary items, divided into 7,096 training, 519 development, and 642 test samples.

4.2 Evaluation Metric

Word Error Rate (WER) [9] is adopted as the primary evaluation metric to evaluate the recognition performance of the CSLR system. It measures the minimum number of edit operations—substitutions, insertions, and deletions—required to convert a predicted text sequence into the ground-truth reference. The WER is calculated as follows:

$$\text{WER} = \frac{\#\text{sub} + \#\text{ins} + \#\text{del}}{\text{reference}} \times 100\% \tag{13}$$

4.3 Training Details

We adopt 3D ResNet101 [4], pre-trained on the Kinetics dataset, as the backbone for feature extraction, followed by task-specific fine-tuning. During data preprocessing, input frames are resized to 256$\times$256 pixels. In the training phase, we employ several data augmentation techniques, including random cropping to 224$\times$224 pixels, horizontal flipping with a probability of 50%, and temporal augmentation with frame rate variations within $\pm$20%. During inference, only center cropping to 224$\times$224 pixels is applied. The model is trained for 60 epochs using the Adam optimizer [8]. The initial learning rate is set to 0.0001 and decayed to 20% of its initial value after the 40th epoch, following an exponential decay strategy. In the loss function, the weighting parameters λ are treated as hyperparameters. Specifically, based on the VAC method, λ_{VA} and λ_{VE} are set to 25 and 1, respectively. For the PHOENIX datasets, λ_{video} and λ_{optical} are set to 0.3, while for the CSL-Daily dataset, they are set to 0.1 and 0.4, respectively, based on empirical results. All experiments are conducted on an NVIDIA RTX 3090 GPU with 24 GB of memory.

4.4 Model Comparison

Table 1 presents a comprehensive comparison between our proposed VS-DSN and state-of-the-art methods across three benchmark datasets: CSL-Daily, PHOENIX14, and PHOENIX14-T. VS-DSN consistently achieves competitive accuracy while offering superior computational efficiency. On the CSL-Daily dataset, VS-DSN obtains WERs of 27.3% (Dev) and 27.5% (Test), outperforming CorrNet and AdaSize by 2.6% and 4.4%, respectively, on the Test set. For PHOENIX14 and PHOENIX14-T, our method achieves 19.4% WER on both test sets, matching or exceeding leading baselines. In terms of efficiency, VS-DSN records the lowest FLOPs (632.6G) among all compared models, clearly demonstrating its advantage in computational cost. This makes our approach particularly suitable for real-time applications and deployment in resource-constrained environments.

Table 1. Comparison with state-of-the-art methods on CSL-Daily, PHOENIX14, and PHOENIX14-T (WER %).

Method	Pre	FLOPs(G)	CSL-Daily		PHOENIX14		PHOENIX14-T	
			Dev (WER↓)	Test (WER↓)	Dev (WER↓)	Test (WER↓)	Dev (WER↓)	Test (WER↓)
DNF [3]	✓	1487.3	32.8	32.4	23.1	22.9	-	-
Joint-SLRT [1]	×	-	33.1	32.0	-	-	24.6	24.5
FCN [2]	×	983.0	33.2	33.5	23.7	23.9	23.3	25.1
VAC [12]	✓	1120.4	-	-	21.2	22.3	-	-
STMC [17]	✓	1742.1	-	-	19.6	21.1	19.6	21.0
C2SLR [18]	✓	1124.6	-	-	20.5	20.4	20.2	20.4
CorrNet [5]	✓	1035.4	30.6	30.1	18.8	19.4	18.9	20.5
AdaSize [6]	✓	-	31.3	31.9	19.7	20.9	19.7	21.2
VS-DSN (Ours)	✓	632.6	27.3	27.5	19.1	19.4	18.7	19.4

4.5 Ablation Studies

To verify the effectiveness of each component in our model, we conduct a series of ablation experiments on the PHOENIX14 dataset, using WER as the evaluation metric. The experiments focus on three aspects: the variable-speed sampling strategy, the bimodal feature fusion and loss design, and the contributions of key architectural modules.

Analysis of Performance-Efficiency Trade-off. We evaluated our variable-speed sampling strategy on the PHOENIX14 dataset by varying the time-step parameter α. As shown in Table 2, higher α values significantly reduce computational overhead and memory usage with moderate performance impact, while lower values yield only marginal performance improvements at substantially increased computational costs. Based on this analysis, we selected $\alpha = 4$ as the optimal configuration.

Table 2. Ablation study on variable-rate sampling for PHOENIX14 (WER %).

α	Dev(WER↓)	Test(WER↓)	Memory usage (MB)	FLOPs(G)
8	22.6	22.8	13049	351.3
4	19.1	19.4	22134	623.6
2	18.7	18.9	40356	1034.8

Ablation Study on Fusion Strategies and Loss Functions. Table 3 presents ablation results on the PHOENIX14 dataset. Among the fusion strategies, STIM achieves the lowest Test WER (19.4%), demonstrating superior cross-modal integration over Concat and Add. For loss functions, the combination of $\mathcal{L}_{\text{CTC}}$, $\mathcal{L}_{\text{VA}}$, and $\mathcal{L}_{\text{VE}}$ yields the best performance, enhancing both temporal alignment and semantic representation. These findings underscore the effectiveness of principled fusion design and joint optimization in CSLR.

Table 3. Ablation study on fusion strategies and loss functions on PHOENIX14 (WER %).

Ablation Domain	Strategy	Dev (WER↓)	Test (WER↓)
Fusion	Concat	20.7	20.5
	Add	20.4	20.3
	STIM	**19.1**	**19.4**
Loss	$\mathcal{L}_{\text{VA}}$	22.4	21.8
	$\mathcal{L}_{\text{CTC}} + \mathcal{L}_{\text{VA}}$	19.8	20.2
	$\mathcal{L}_{\text{CTC}} + \mathcal{L}_{\text{VE}}$	20.6	20.9
	$\mathcal{L}_{\text{CTC}} + \mathcal{L}_{\text{VA}} + \mathcal{L}_{\text{VE}}$	**19.1**	**19.4**

Contribution Analysis of Key Components. Table 4 shows the ablation results on the PHOENIX14 dataset. Single-modality models yield higher WER, indicating limited spatio-temporal modeling. Adding the STIM module improves performance by integrating bimodal features. Further gains are achieved by introducing the combined prediction head. These results confirm the effectiveness of each component in our framework.

Table 4. Key component ablation study on PHOENIX14 (WER %).

RGB	Optical Flow	STIM	Combined Head	Dev (WER↓)	Test (WER↓)
✓	×	×	×	22.8	23.5
×	✓	×	×	23.9	24.3
✓	✓	×	×	19.6	19.8
✓	✓	✓	×	19.4	19.6
×	✓	✓	✓	19.3	19.5
✓	✓	✓	✓	**19.1**	**19.4**

4.6 Visualizations

To illustrate the differences in feature extraction between model branches, we employ Gradient-weighted Class Activation Mapping (Grad-CAM) [14] to generate spatial heat maps. Grad-CAM computes gradients of the target class with respect to convolutional feature maps, which are weighted and aggregated to highlight regions of interest. As shown in Fig. 4, the RGB branch emphasizes facial features and hand contours, while the optical flow branch focuses on limb motion trajectories. This complementary mechanism allows the model to jointly exploit spatial and temporal cues, enhancing recognition performance.

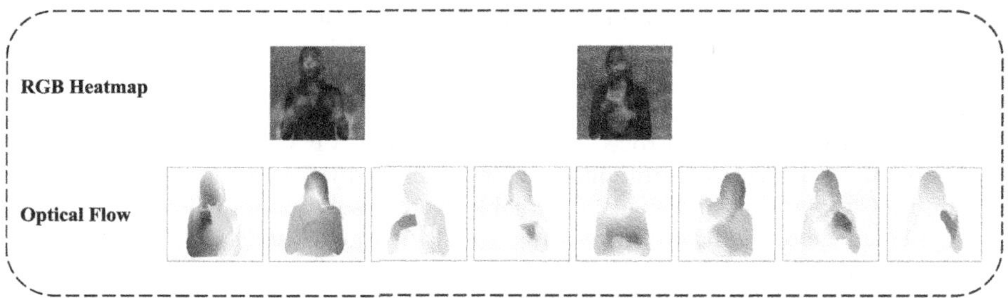

Fig. 4. Dual-Stream Visualization Analysis Based On Grad-CAM.

5 Conclusion

CSLR poses significant challenges in capturing both spatial and temporal semantics. While RGB-based models provide rich spatial features, they often fail to capture fine-grained motion patterns essential for temporal understanding. To address this, we introduce optical flow as an auxiliary modality. To reduce the resulting computational overhead, we propose a variable-speed sampling strategy that suppresses redundancy while preserving motion continuity. Additionally, we design a STIM with bidirectional attention to enable fine-grained multimodal fusion. Experiments show that our method achieves a favorable trade-off between recognition accuracy and efficiency, demonstrating its potential for lightweight, high-performance CSLR systems.

Acknowledgments. This study was funded by the National Natural Science Foundation of China (NSFC) under grant No. 61976226, and the Hubei Provincial Natural Science Foundation General Project No. 2022CFB469.

References

1. Camgoz, N.C., Koller, O., Hadfield, S., Bowden, R.: Sign language transformers: joint end-to-end sign language recognition and translation. In: Proceedings of the IEEE/CVF Conference on Computer Vision and Pattern Recognition, pp. 10023–10033 (2020)
2. Cheng, K.L., Yang, Z., Chen, Q., Tai, Y.-W.: Fully convolutional networks for continuous sign language recognition. In: Vedaldi, A., Bischof, H., Brox, T., Frahm, J.-M. (eds.) ECCV 2020. LNCS, vol. 12369, pp. 697–714. Springer, Cham (2020). https://doi.org/10.1007/978-3-030-58586-0_41
3. Cui, R., Liu, H., Zhang, C.: A deep neural framework for continuous sign language recognition by iterative training. IEEE Trans. Multimedia **21**, 1880–1891 (2019)
4. He, K., Zhang, X., Ren, S., Sun, J.: Deep residual learning for image recognition. In: Proceedings of the IEEE Conference on Computer Vision and Pattern Recognition, pp. 770–778 (2016)
5. Hu, L., Gao, L., Liu, Z., Feng, W.: Continuous sign language recognition with correlation network. In: Proceedings of the IEEE/CVF Conference on Computer Vision and Pattern Recognition, pp. 2529–2539 (2023)
6. Hu, L., Gao, L., Liu, Z., Feng, W.: Scalable frame resolution for efficient continuous sign language recognition. Pattern Recogn. **145**, 109903 (2024)
7. Huang, D.-A., Fei-Fei, L., Niebles, J.C.: Connectionist temporal modeling for weakly supervised action labeling. In: Leibe, B., Matas, J., Sebe, N., Welling, M. (eds.) ECCV 2016. LNCS, vol. 9908, pp. 137–153. Springer, Cham (2016). https://doi.org/10.1007/978-3-319-46493-0_9
8. Kingma, D.P., Ba, J.: Adam: a method for stochastic optimization (2014). arXiv preprint arXiv:1412.6980
9. Koller, O., Camgoz, N.C., Ney, H., Bowden, R.: Weakly supervised learning with multi-stream CNN-LSTM-HMMs to discover sequential parallelism in sign language videos. IEEE Trans. Pattern Anal. Mach. Intell. **42**, 2306–2320 (2019)
10. Koller, O., Forster, J., Ney, H.: Continuous sign language recognition: towards large vocabulary statistical recognition systems handling multiple signers. Comput. Vis. Image Underst. **141**, 108–125 (2015)
11. Lichtenauer, J.F., Hendriks, E.A., Reinders, M.J.: Sign language recognition by combining statistical DTW and independent classification. IEEE Trans. Pattern Anal. Mach. Intell. **30**, 2040–2046 (2008)
12. Min, Y., Hao, A., Chai, X., Chen, X.: Visual alignment constraint for continuous sign language recognition. In: Proceedings of the IEEE/CVF International Conference on Computer Vision, pp. 11542–11551 (2021)
13. Sarhan, N., Frintrop, S.: Unraveling a decade: a comprehensive survey on isolated sign language recognition. In: Proceedings of the IEEE/CVF International Conference on Computer Vision, pp. 3210–3219 (2023)
14. Selvaraju, R.R., Cogswell, M., Das, A., Vedantam, R., Parikh, D., Batra, D.: Grad-CAM: visual explanations from deep networks via gradient-based localization. In: Proceedings of the IEEE International Conference on Computer Vision, pp. 618–626 (2017)
15. Teed, Z., Deng, J.: RAFT: recurrent all-pairs field transforms for optical flow. In: Vedaldi, A., Bischof, H., Brox, T., Frahm, J.-M. (eds.) ECCV 2020. LNCS, vol. 12347, pp. 402–419. Springer, Cham (2020). https://doi.org/10.1007/978-3-030-58536-5_24

16. Zhang, J., Zhou, W., Xie, C., Pu, J., Li, H.: Chinese sign language recognition with adaptive hmm. In: 2016 IEEE International Conference on Multimedia and Expo (ICME), pp. 1–6 (2016)
17. Zhou, H., Zhou, W., Zhou, Y., Li, H.: Spatial-temporal multi-cue network for continuous sign language recognition. In: Proceedings of the AAAI Conference on Artificial Intelligence, pp. 13009–13016 (2020)
18. Zuo, R., Mak, B.: C2SLR: consistency-enhanced continuous sign language recognition. In: Proceedings of the IEEE/CVF Conference on Computer Vision and Pattern Recognition, pp. 5131–5140 (2022)

Hierarchical Action Recognition: A Contrastive Video-Language Approach with Hierarchical Interactions

Rui Zhang[1], Shuailong Li[2], Junxiao Xue[2(✉)], Diying Yan[2], Feng Lin[3,4], Qing Zhang[2], Xiao Ma[2], and Xiaoran Yan[2]

[1] Alibaba, Hangzhou 310000, China
[2] Zhejiang Lab, Hangzhou 310000, China
xuejx@zhejianglab.cn
[3] Fuyao University of Science and Technology, Fuzhou 350000, China
[4] Xianghu Lab, Hangzhou 310000, China

Abstract. Video recognition, while fundamental to computer vision, faces significant challenges in identifying diverse content categories. Traditional flat classification approaches fail to capture the inherent hierarchical relationships among categories, particularly crucial in fine-grained tasks like medical rehabilitation assessment. We address this limitation by introducing a novel hierarchical video recognition framework based on video-language learning. Our approach explicitly models semantic dependencies across hierarchical levels through a structured loss function and employs a top-down constraint mechanism to ensure cross-level prediction consistency. To evaluate our method, we develop a new fine-grained dataset from stroke rehabilitation assessments, featuring hierarchically annotated body movements. Extensive experiments demonstrate our method's superiority over conventional flat classification baselines, particularly in fine-grained subcategory recognition. By integrating contrastive learning with structured hierarchical constraints, our method advances video recognition beyond traditional flat categorization, showing particular promise in healthcare applications where precise, interpretable recognition is essential. This work not only establishes a new paradigm for hierarchical video understanding but also provides a robust foundation for future applications requiring fine-grained, multi-level video analysis.

Keywords: Action recognition · Video-language learning · Contrastive learning

1 Introduction

Human action recognition is fundamental to video understanding [9]. While early attempts relied on unimodal methods [8], recent advances leverage vision-language models (VLMs) to reframe action recognition as video-text matching [16]. CLIP-based architectures [12] have emerged as powerful tools for multi-modal learning, with several approaches [11] adapting them for video recognition through contrastive training on video-prompt pairs. However, despite their success, these methods focus primarily on flat classification, overlooking hierarchical relationships that are well-established in natural language processing and increasingly relevant in computer vision.

P. Li et al. (Eds.): CGI 2025, LNCS 16508, pp. 186–198, 2026.
https://doi.org/10.1007/978-3-032-22264-0_15

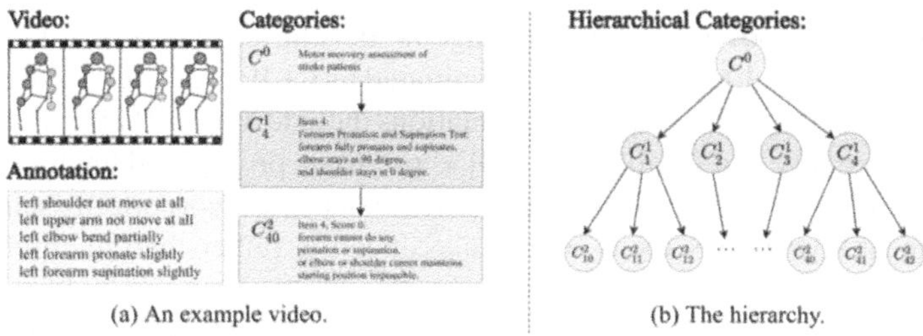

(a) An example video. (b) The hierarchy.

Fig. 1. An illustrated example of a stroke patient undergoing motor recovery assessment in a hierarchical video recognition problem.

Hierarchical action recognition enables fine-grained categorical distinctions essential for real-world applications, where objects naturally organize into super-classes and subclasses. Medical video-language understanding exemplifies this need, supporting clinical decision-making and patient care. Figure 1a illustrates this through a stroke patient's motor recovery assessment, where the video contains three hierarchical levels: assessment summary, items, and scores. As shown in Fig. 1b, these categories form a tree structure where the root node (level 0) represents the overall summary, level 1 contains assessment item descriptions, and level 2 specifies corresponding scores. This hierarchical approach surpasses flat classification by better reflecting human knowledge organization through explicit parent-child relationships and granular distinctions. The result is enhanced video understanding that aligns with human cognition and enables precise analysis in human-centric applications.

Hierarchical action recognition in computer vision faces two fundamental challenges: leveraging hierarchical category structures and modeling inter-level dependencies for knowledge fusion. While natural language processing has developed solutions for similar hierarchical tasks [6], computer vision lacks effective methods for modeling complex video-category relationships and dependencies. The challenges span temporal video modeling, visual-textual alignment, and cross-level category interactions, all while maintaining computational efficiency. Despite these complexities, hierarchical approaches show particular promise for fine-grained applications in healthcare and education, where precise categorical distinctions are essential.

2 Related Work

Video Recognition: Video recognition has evolved significantly through large-scale datasets like UCF101 [15], ActivityNet [3], and Kinetics [4]. The field progressed from two-stream networks [14] incorporating optical flow to 3D convolutional architectures [7] for spatio-temporal feature extraction, and recently to transformer-based approaches [1] for long-range dependency modeling. Despite these advances, challenges persist in hierarchical recognition, fine-grained analysis, and computational efficiency, suggesting the need for more sophisticated approaches incorporating relational knowledge and multimodal grounding.

Vision Language Models: Vision-language models have transformed video recognition through joint visual-textual modeling, initiated by CLIP [12]'s successful large-scale image-text pretraining. Video-specific adaptations include X-CLIP [11] with cross-frame information exchange and ActionCLIP [18]'s "pre-train, prompt and finetune" paradigm. Recent works like ASU [5] have enhanced performance by incorporating semantic units. However, most approaches focus on flat classification rather than hierarchical understanding. While HierVL [2] explores hierarchical video-language embeddings, it emphasizes scene graphs over human actions, leaving room for advancement in hierarchical action recognition systems.

Hierarchical Action Recognition: Early hierarchical vision research emerged from competitive sports video analysis [10]. However, these differ fundamentally from our proposed hierarchical action recognition task. While sports analysis focuses on evaluating performance sequences, hierarchical video recognition aims to categorize content within a taxonomic structure, progressing from coarse to fine-grained levels. This novel approach addresses unique challenges in: (1) modeling inter-level dependencies, (2) fusing motion and language cues, (3) capturing fine-grained semantics. These capabilities have broad applications in healthcare diagnostics, human-robot interaction, and multimedia retrieval.

3 Preliminary

3.1 Dataset Preparation

Category Construction: We focus on the Fugl-Meyer Assessment (FMA), a standardized medical evaluation protocol for post-stroke patients, as our primary application of hierarchical video recognition. The FMA employs a systematic approach to evaluate motor impairment across multiple body parts using a 3-point scoring scale. We restructure the FMA into a hierarchical tree, selecting four representative upper limb assessment categories. Each category is evaluated on a three-level scoring system: 0 (unable to perform), 1 (partial completion), and 2 (full completion). Table 1 outlines this hierarchical structure and statistics.

Data Construction: We collected a comprehensive video dataset from 28 adult volunteers performing selected FMA assessment tasks. Multiple camera angles were used to capture diverse perspectives. Following quality control measures to eliminate occlusion, motion blur, and poor framing, we curated 1,257 high-quality videos spanning the complete FMA hierarchy. The dataset encompasses four assessment categories focusing on upper extremity evaluation, each with three ordered scores (0–2) indicating task completion levels. To enable detailed analysis, we manually annotated eight key body parts (bilateral shoulders, elbows, and forearms) with fine-grained state descriptions. These annotations combine verbs describing motions and adverbs indicating completeness, synthesized into natural language sentences that comprehensively describe the demonstrated actions. This unique dataset combines standardized assessments, videos, and detailed natural language annotations.

Table 1. Description of hierarchical FMA categories

Fugl-Meyer Assessment		num
Item 1: Shoulder Flexion to 180° Test: shoulder flexes from 90° to 180°, elbow stays at 0°, and forearm does not pronate or supinate.		
Scores	S0: shoulder abduction or elbow flexion happens immediately when shoulder flexion starts.	110
	S1: shoulder abduction or elbow flexion happens during movement.	114
	S2: shoulder flex to 180°, no shoulder abduction or elbow flexion.	112
Item 2: Shoulder Flexion to 90° Test: shoulder flexes from 0° to 90°, elbow stays at 0°, and forearm does not pronate or supinate.		
Scores	S0: shoulder abduction or elbow flexion happens immediately when shoulder flexion starts.	109
	S1: shoulder abduction or elbow flexion happens during movement.	112
	S2: shoulder can flex to 90°, no shoulder abduction or elbow flexion.	112
Item 3: Shoulder Abduction to 90° Test: shoulder spreads out from 0° to 90°, elbow stays at 0°, and foream keeps neutral.		
Scores	S0: shoulder supination or elbow flexion happens immediately when shoulder abduction starts.	85
	S1: shoulder supination or elbow flexion happens during movement.	84
	S2: shoulder spread out 90°, and maintains extension and pronation.	85
Item 4: Forearm Pronation and Supination Test: forearm fully pronates and supinates, elbow stays at 90°, and shoulder stays at 0°.		
Scores	S0: forearm cannot do any pronation or supination, or elbow or shoulder cannot maintain starting position impossible.	112
	S1: forearm can do limited pronation and supination, and elbow and shoulder maintain starting position.	111
	S2: forearm can pronate and supinates fully, and elbow and shoulder maintain starting position.	111

3.2 Problem Formulation

We formalize our hierarchical video recognition framework as follows: let $V = \{v_1, v_2, \ldots, v_n\}$ be a set of videos, where each video v_i consists of frames $\left\{f_{v_i,1}, f_{v_i,2}, \ldots, f_{v_i,n_{v_i}}\right\}$. Each video is associated with a natural language description a_i from the set $A = \{a_1, a_2, \ldots, a_n\}$. The hierarchical taxonomy $C = \{C^0, C^1, C^2\}$ comprises three levels: $C^0 = \{c^0\}$ high-level assessment summary (fixed as "motor recovery assessment of stroke patients"), $C^1 = \{I1, I2, I3, I4\}$ assessment items, $C^2 = \{I1S0, I1S1, \ldots, I4S2\}$ assessment scores. For notation simplicity, C^1_* and C^2_* denote individual elements within C^1 and C^2 respectively (e.g., C^1_1 represents $I1$, and C^2_{10} represents $I1S0$). Importantly, hierarchical constraints exist between C^1 and C^2, where sub-categories under any C^1 item are restricted to its corresponding score set. The dataset can be represented as:

$$\mathcal{X} = \left\{ \left(v_1, a_1, c_1^1, c_1^2 \right), \ldots, \left(v_n, a_n, c_n^1, c_n^2 \right) \right\} \tag{1}$$

where $c_i^1 \in C^1$ and $c_i^2 \in C^2$ are the assigned categories. The objective is to learn a multi-modal recognition model Φ that predicts hierarchical action labels:

$$\Phi(v, a, C, \Theta) \rightarrow \left(c^1, c^2 \right) \tag{2}$$

where Θ denotes model parameters.

4 Methods

We propose H-CLIP, a contrastive video-language learning framework for hierarchical Fugl-Meyer assessment. Built upon CLIP's multi-modal architecture, our model leverages cross-category knowledge interaction to capture hierarchical relationships between assessment categories. H-CLIP jointly processes video inputs, annotations, and categorical text descriptions to generate aligned representations while enforcing top-down hierarchical constraints across assessment levels (Figs. 2 and 3).

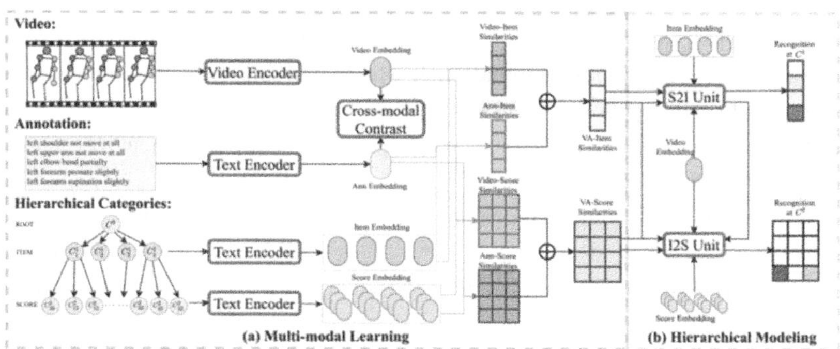

Fig. 2. An overview of our proposed framework.

4.1 Multi-modal Learning

Knowledge Encoding: For multi-modal knowledge acquisition, we employ CLIP's image encoder (f_{img}) and text encoder (f_{txt})). The image encoder is augmented with a temporal encoder (f_{tem})—implemented as a mean pooling function—to process video temporal information. This yields the following normalized embeddings: video embedding $H_V = f_{tem}(f_{img}(V)) \in R^{n \times d}$, annotation embedding $H_A = f_{txt}(A) \in R^{n \times d}$, C^1-level category embedding $H_{C^1} = f_{txt}(C^1) \in R^{|C^1| \times d}$, and C^2-level category embedding $H_{C^2} = f_{txt}(C^2) \in R^{|C^1| \times 3 \times d}$, where n denotes sample count, d represents embedding dimension, and $\mathrm{H}_{\mathrm{C}^2}$ is three-dimensional to accommodate upper-level assessment dependencies. The multi-modal embedding space is optimized using symmetric InfoNCE loss on similarity matrices between video and annotation representations:

$$S_{V-A} = H_V \cdot H_A^{\mathsf{T}} \quad \in \quad R^{n\times n} \tag{3}$$

$$\mathcal{L}_{]\nabla\wr ff} = -\frac{1}{n}\sum_{i=1}^{n} \log \frac{\exp(S_{V-A}(i,i))}{\sum_{j=1}^{n}\exp(S_{V-A}(i,j))} \tag{4}$$

Knowledge Fusion: We evaluate hierarchical interactions by calculating similarities between learning objects and categories at each hierarchical level. For category level C^*, the similarity matrices between video representations H_V and category representations $\mathrm{H}_{\mathrm{C}^*}$ are computed as:

$$S_{V-C^*} = H_V \cdot H_{C^*}^{\mathsf{T}} \tag{5}$$

This yields C^1-level similarity matrix $\mathrm{S}_{\mathrm{V-C}^1}\mathrm{R}^{\mathrm{n}\times|\mathrm{C}^1|}$ and C^2-level similarity matrix $\mathrm{S}_{\mathrm{V-C}^2}\mathrm{R}^{\mathrm{n}\times|\mathrm{C}^1|\times 3}$. Similarly, for annotation representations H_A:

$$S_{A-C^*} = H_A \cdot H_{C^*}^{\mathsf{T}} \tag{6}$$

generating $\mathrm{S}_{\mathrm{A-C}^1}\mathrm{R}^{\mathrm{n}\times|\mathrm{C}^1|}$ and $\mathrm{S}_{\mathrm{A-C}^2}\mathrm{R}^{\mathrm{n}\times|\mathrm{C}^1|\times 3}$. The final assessment results at level C^* are represented by averaged similarity matrices:

$$S_{VA-C^*} = (S_{V-C^*} + S_{A-C^*})/2 \tag{7}$$

These independent level-specific similarity matrices $\mathrm{S}_{\mathrm{VA-C}^1} \in \mathrm{R}^{\mathrm{n}\times|\mathrm{C}^1|}$ and $\mathrm{S}_{\mathrm{VA-C}^2} \in \mathrm{R}^{\mathrm{n}\times|\mathrm{C}^{\nVdash}|\times\nVdash}$ form the foundation for subsequent hierarchical interaction modeling.

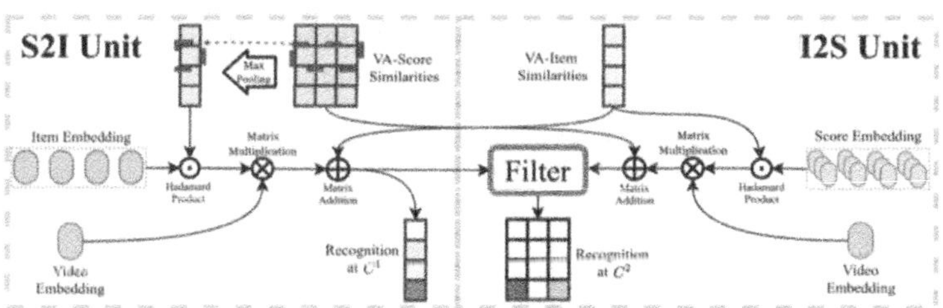

Fig. 3. An illustration of S2I unit (left) and I2S unit (right).

4.2 Hierarchical Modeling

S2I Unit: The Score-to-Item (S2I) unit integrates fine-grained C^2-level relevance with independent C^1-level matching information S_{VA-C^1} to generate final C^1-level recognition outputs. The process involves:

$$MS_{C^2} = MaxPooling(S_{VA-C^2}) NS_{C^1} = H_{C^1} \odot MS_{C^2} \tag{8}$$

where $\odot$ is the Hadamard product between H_{C^1} and MS_{C^2} based on the C^1 dimension. Similarity re-computation for video-label connections:

$$S'_{C^1} = NS_{C^1} \cdot H_V \quad \in \quad R^{n \times |C^1|} \tag{9}$$

Final C^1-level prediction through convex combination:

$$\hat{S_{C^1}} = \left[\delta\left(S_{VA-C^1}\right) + \delta\left(S'_{C^1}\right)\right]/2 \tag{10}$$

where δ denotes softmax normalization along rows.

I2S Unit: We incorporate both bottom-up (S2I) and top-down (I2S, item-to-score) interactions, allowing C^1 predictions to influence C^2 scoring. The C^1 similarities $SVA - C^1 \in R^{n \times |C^1|}$ are mapped to the C^2 level by triplicating each row along the C^1 dimension, creating $MSC^1 \in R^{n \times |C^1| \times 3}$ to match the C^2 tensor 's shape. This is then integrated with C^2-level embeddings H_{C^2} through element-wise multiplication:

$$NS_{C^2} = H_{C^2} \odot MS_{C^1} \tag{11}$$

Video-oriented information matching during hierarchical interaction generates the C^2-level recognition result:

$$S'_{C^2} = NS_{C^2} \cdot H_V \quad \in \quad R^{n \times |C^1| \times 3} \tag{12}$$

The C^2 level scores are computed by fusing independent and interactive terms:

$$\hat{S_{C^2}} = \left[\delta\left(S_{VA-C^2}\right) + \delta\left(S'_{C^2}\right)\right]/2 \tag{13}$$

Given the inherent hierarchical constraints between category levels, we introduce a filter Ω in the I2S unit to enforce top-down constraints, preserving only lower-level categories corresponding to the highest-scoring parent item:

$$\hat{S'_{C^2}} = \Omega\left(\hat{S_{C^2}}\right) \odot \hat{S_{C^2}} \tag{14}$$

The filter Ω is defined as:

$$\Omega\left(\hat{S_{C^2}}(i,j,k)\right) = \begin{cases} 1 & if\ j = \underset{u}{argmax}\left(\hat{S_{C^1}}(i,u)\right) \\ 0 & otherwise \end{cases} \tag{15}$$

This filtering mechanism ensures that lower-level predictions are only considered when the upper-level recognition is accurate, maintaining taxonomical coherence in the hierarchical recognition process. The combined bidirectional I2S and S2I units enable comprehensive hierarchical interactions between video-label matching rounds.

4.3 Optimization

We optimize KG-CLIP using Kullback-Leibler (KL) divergence as the video-text contrastive loss across category levels. Ground-truth matrices G_{C^1} and G_{C^2} are constructed with binary similarities: 1 for positive pairs and 0 for negative pairs. The hierarchical loss is formulated as:

$$\mathcal{L}^1_{\langle\rangle\rceil\nabla} = \mathcal{D}_{\mathcal{KL}}\left(\delta(\hat{S_{C^1}})\,\middle\|\,\delta(G_{C^1})\right) \qquad \mathcal{L}^2_{\langle\rangle\rceil\nabla} = \mathcal{D}_{\mathcal{KL}}\left(\delta\left(\hat{S_{C^2}}\right)\,\middle\|\,\delta(G_{C^2})\right) \tag{16}$$

where δ represents softmax, and $\mathcal{D}_{\mathcal{KL}}$ computes the KL divergence between predicted and target similarity distributions. This loss function optimizes the model to maximize similarities for positive pairs while minimizing them for negative pairs. The complete hierarchical recognition loss combines cross-modal and hierarchical components:

$$\mathcal{L} = \mathcal{L}_{\rfloor\nabla\wr ff} + \lambda_1 \mathcal{L}^1_{\langle\rangle\rceil\nabla} + \lambda_2 \mathcal{L}^2_{\langle\rangle\rceil\nabla} \tag{17}$$

where $\lambda_{1,2}$ weight the influence of assessment item and scoring level losses. These can be tuned for optimal taxonomy-structured prediction.

5 Experiments

5.1 Experimental Setup

Baselines: As our proposed method is the first work on hierarchical video recognition with a cross-modal contrastive framework, we compare against several recent CLIP-based multi-modal baselines and a different version of our approach: X-CLIP [11], ViFi-CLIP [13] and H-CLIP-t (a variant of H-CLIP).

Implementation Details: All CLIP-based methods utilize public CLIP checkpoints (ViT-B/32 and ViT-B/16) for initialization. Training employs AdamW optimizer with learning rates of 1e-5 for CLIP encoders and 1e-4 for new modules, incorporating a 5-epoch warmup followed by cosine decay. Models are trained for 30 epochs with 0.2 weight decay. Video frames are processed to 224 $\times$ 224 resolution following standard sampling [17] and augmentation [18] protocols.

Evaluation Protocols: Following established video recognition protocols [5, 13], we use Top-1 and Top-3 accuracy metrics for C^1. For C^2, which contain only three possible scores per item, we report solely Top-1 accuracy. For baseline models, which process assessment items and scores independently, we calculate accuracy separately across 4 assessment items and 12 assessment scores.

5.2 Overall Performance

Fully-Supervised Recognition: We compared H-CLIP against two CLIP-based baselines (X-CLIP and ViFi-CLIP) and our variant (H-CLIP-t) on the FMA dataset, which features two category levels (C^1 and C^2). Since the baselines aren't designed for hierarchical recognition, we separated C^1 and C^2 categories into distinct tasks for their evaluation. Table 2 presents the comparative results, revealing several key findings: **1)** H-CLIP significantly outperforms baselines across both category levels, demonstrating approximately 8% improvement at C^1 and 36% at C^2. While baselines show acceptable performance on C^1 -level recognition, they struggle considerably with the more fine-grained C^2 categories. This performance gap highlights the effectiveness of our hierarchical interaction modeling, where upper and lower-level predictions mutually inform each other. **2)** Interestingly, H-CLIP-t, which replaces mean pooling with a Transformer for temporal information encoding, performs slightly below H-CLIP. We attribute this to limited training data, which constrains the complex Transformer's training potential. However, based on existing research, we believe H-CLIP-t could achieve superior performance with sufficient training samples (Fig. 4).

Table 2. Performance (%) comparison on each category level (C^1 level and C^2 level) with state-of-the-art on FMA dataset.

Methods	Backbones	Frames	C^1 (Item)		C^2 (Score)
			Top-1	Top-3	Top-1
X-CLIP	ViT-B/32	8	84.92	100.00	50.00
		16	88.49	100.00	55.16
	ViT-B/16	8	89.68	99.60	58.33
		16	88.49	99.60	58.33
ViFi-CLIP	ViT-B/32	8	83.73	99.21	43.65
		16	82.54	99.60	41.67
	ViT-B/16	8	86.11	99.60	48.41
		16	83.72	99.60	48.41
H-CLIP-t	ViT-B/32	8	96.83	100.00	92.06
		16	97.22	100.00	93.25
	ViT-B/16	8	98.02	100.00	94.05
		16	97.22	100.00	93.65
H-CLIP	ViT-B/32	8	98.02	100.00	92.46
		16	98.02	100.00	94.05
	ViT-B/16	8	98.02	100.00	94.44
		16	98.02	100.00	95.24

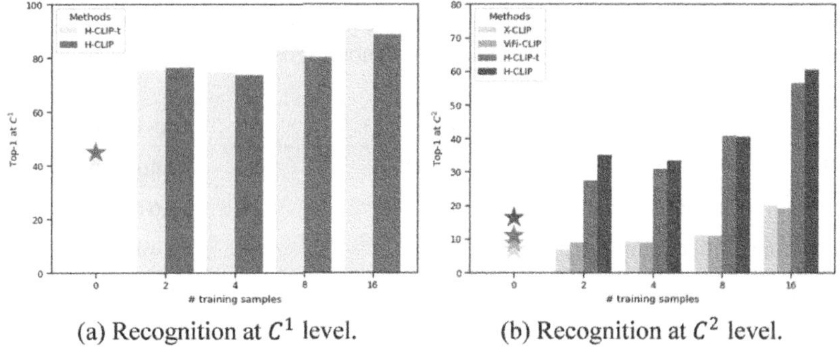

(a) Recognition at C^1 level. (b) Recognition at C^2 level.

Fig. 4. Zero−/few-shot results under 8 video frames with ViT-B/32 as the backbone.

Zero-/Few-Shot Recognition: We evaluated H-CLIP's zero/few-shot capabilities using 8-frame inputs, with training samples based on C^2-level labels. Our hierarchical approach significantly outperformed baseline models at the C^2 level, where traditional non-hierarchical methods were limited to flat classification. At the C^1 level, H-CLIP-t matched or exceeded H-CLIP's performance, leveraging the Transformer's natural ability to capture relationships beyond mean pooling's capabilities. These results demonstrate how our structured hierarchical modeling enhances transfer learning and generalization, particularly valuable for real-world applications where comprehensive labeling is impractical. The model's strong performance under limited data validates the effectiveness of our hierarchical approach for practical deployment scenarios.

5.3 Model Analysis

Ablation Study: Our ablation studies evaluated H-CLIP's components under full supervision using 8 frames per video. The complete H-CLIP achieved optimal results across all metrics, maintaining robust performance even without cross-modal contrast due to its pre-trained knowledge base. Removing S2I and I2S units decreased performance by 1–4%, validating our hierarchical interaction mechanism's effectiveness. Single modality tests showed reduced accuracy, especially at C^2 level, with textual annotations proving more critical than visual information alone - reflecting the subtle distinctions in medical assessment videos. Notably, KL divergence significantly outperformed cross-entropy loss, showing 10% and 40% improvements at C^1 and C^2 levels respectively, demonstrating its superior capability in distribution modeling and confidence handling. These results comprehensively validate the effectiveness of our design choices and hierarchical approach (Table 3).

Table 3. Ablation study on the effect of proposed components under 8 frames of each video (ViT-B/32), where KLL denotes KL loss and CEL denotes cross-entropy loss.

Methods	Top-1 at C^1	Top-1 at C^2
H-CLIP	98.02	92.46
-w/o cross-modal contrast	97.22	91.67
-w/o hierarchical interactions	94.44	88.49
-w/o annotations	77.78	38.89
-w/o videos	86.51	82.54
-replaced KLL with CEL	83.33	41.67

Efficiency Study: We present the results of Floating Point Operations (FLOPs) and the number of parameters in Table 4. The results indicate that although H-CLIP has slightly more parameters than ViFi-CLIP, it has fewer FLOPs. Even the variant based on a multi-layer Transformer has significantly lower FLOPs than the baselines. This demonstrates that H-CLIP not only overcomes the limitations of existing flat learning methods in handling hierarchical video recognition tasks but also represents a cost-effective and efficient approach for video recognition.

Table 4. Model efficiency analysis under 8 frames of each video, ViT-B/32.

Methods	FLOPs (G)	# params (M)
X-CLIP	106.96	196.6
ViFi-CLIP	106.07	126
H-CLIP-t	84.59	170.2
H-CLIP	84.44	151.2

5.4 Visualization

We illustrate H-CLIP's hierarchical recognition capabilities through two cases from our medical assessment dataset, featuring video-text pairs of upper limb movements (Fig. 5). H-CLIP processes these inputs through a two-stage recognition pipeline: **1)** C^1 classification: the model first identifies the correct assessment item category, demonstrating effective context understanding. **2)** C^2 classification: through cross-hierarchy interactions, it then refines predictions to specific assessment scores. This coarse-to-fine recognition process aligns with human cognitive patterns in understanding hierarchical concepts, demonstrating the advantage of our approach over traditional flat classification methods for complex medical assessment tasks.

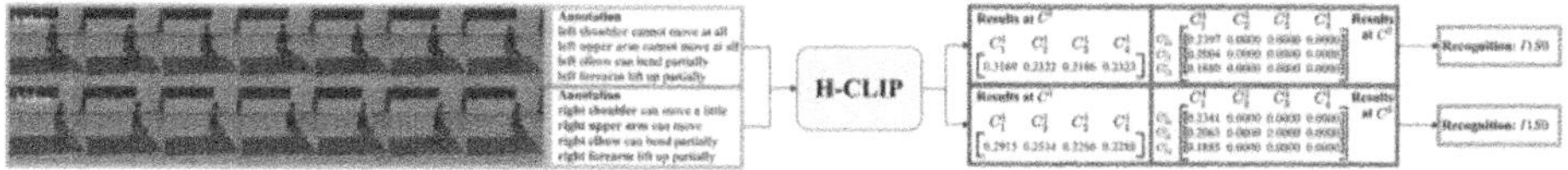

Fig. 5. Demonstration of H-CLIP for hierarchical video recognition.

6 Discussion and Conclusions

Medical video understanding presents unique challenges that distinguish it from mainstream tasks, particularly in detecting subtle action differences that define assessment scores (e.g., timing and completeness of shoulder or elbow movements). Our proposed contrastive video-language approach with hierarchical modeling demonstrates effectiveness in capturing these fine-grained distinctions while maintaining assessment precision. While our work focuses on stroke rehabilitation assessment, the principles of hierarchical modeling have broader implications across video understanding domains. Applications extend to video retrieval, recommendation systems, temporal localization, and video captioning, where hierarchical structures can refine searches from coarse to fine-grained descriptors and support generalization through parent-child relationships.

This paper introduces hierarchical video recognition as a novel computer vision task, addressing the limitations of existing models in multi-level semantic labeling. Our approach uniquely integrates inter-level interactions between objects, actions, and hierarchical text descriptors, while incorporating dependencies between labels for coherent top-down reasoning. We further design a filter mechanism that enforces taxonomic constraints for category predictions based on the affiliations between hierarchical categories. To validate our approach and foster research in this direction, we developed a comprehensive medical assessment dataset comprising over 1,200 annotated videos. While experimental results demonstrate the effectiveness of our method, future work should explore additional datasets beyond the medical domain, integration of domain-specific knowledge, advanced architectures for improved spatio-temporal modeling, and enhanced interpretability of hierarchical predictions.

References

1. Arnab, A., Dehghani, M., Heigold, G., Sun, C., Lucic, M., Schmid, C.: Vivit: a video vision transformer. In: 2021 IEEE/CVF International Conference on Computer Vision, ICCV 2021, Montreal, QC, Canada, pp. 6816–6826 (2021)
2. Ashutosh, K., Girdhar, R., Torresani, L., Grauman, K.: Hiervl: learning hierarchical video-language embeddings. In: Proceedings of the IEEE/CVF Conference on Computer Vision and Pattern Recognition, p. 23,066–23,078
3. Caba Heilbron, F., Escorcia, V., Ghanem, B., Carlos Niebles, J.: Activitynet: a large-scale video benchmark for human activity understanding. In: Proceedings of the IEEE Conference on Computer Vision and Pattern Recognition, pp. 961–970
4. Carreira, J., Zisserman, A.: Quo vadis, action recognition? A new model and the kinetics dataset. In: Proceedings of the IEEE Conference on Computer Vision and Pattern Recognition, pp. 6299–6308

5. Chen, Y., Chen, D., Liu, R., et al.: Video action recognition with attentive semantic units. In: Proceedings of the IEEE/CVF International Conference on Computer Vision, pp. 10170–10180 (2023)
6. Huang, W., et al.: Hierarchical multi-label text classification: an attention-based recurrent network approach. In: Proceedings of the 28th ACM International Conference on Information and Knowledge Management, pp. 1051–1060
7. Karpathy, A., Toderici, G., Shetty, S., Leung, T., Sukthankar, R., Fei-Fei, L.: Large-scale video classification with convolutional neural networks. In: 2014 IEEE Conference on Computer Vision and Pattern Recognition, pp. 1725–1732
8. Kong, Y., Fu, Y.: Human action recognition and prediction: a survey. Int. J. Comput. Vis. **130**(5), 1366–1401 (2022)
9. Li, K.: et al.: Videochat: Chat-centric video understanding. arXiv preprint https://arxiv.org/abs/2305.06355
10. Li, T., et al.: Dynamic spatio-temporal specialization learning for fine-grained action recognition. In: European Conference on Computer Vision, pp. 386–403
11. Ni, B., et al.: Expanding language-image pretrained models for general video recognition. In: European Conference on Computer Vision, pp. 1–18. Springer Nature Switzerland, Cham (2022)
12. Radford, A., et al.: Learning transferable visual models from natural language supervision. In: Meila, M., Zhang, T. (eds.) Proceedings of the 38th International Conference on Machine Learning, ICML 2021, pp. 18–24
13. Rasheed, H.A., Khattak, M.U., Maaz, M., Khan, S., Khan, F.S.: Fine-tuned CLIP models are efficient video learners. In: Proceedings of the IEEE/CVF Conference on Computer Vision and Pattern Recognition, pp. 6545–6554 (2023)
14. Simonyan, K., Zisserman, A.: Two-stream convolutional networks for action recognition in videos. Adv. Neural Inf. Proces. Syst. **27** (2014)
15. Soomro, K., Zamir, A.R., Shah, M.: Ucf101: A dataset of 101 human actions classes from videos in the wild. arXiv preprint https://arxiv.org/abs/1212.0402
16. Sun, Z., Ke, Q., Rahmani, H., Bennamoun, M., Wang, G., Liu, J.: Human action recognition from various data modalities: a review. IEEE Trans. Pattern Anal. Mach. Intell. **45**(3), 3200–3225
17. Wang, L., et al.: Temporal segment networks for action recognition in videos. IEEE Trans. Pattern Anal. Mach. Intell. **41**(11), 2740–2755
18. Wang, M., Xing, J., Liu, Y.: Actionclip: A new paradigm for video action recognition. arXiv preprint. (2021). https://arxiv.org/abs/2109.08472

MIGEdit: Multimodal Interactive Garment Editing

Sicheng Zheng[1], Bangchao Wang[1], Jinxing Liang[1], Li Li[1], Tao Peng[1], Kai He[1], Junping Liu[1(✉)], Ping Li[3], and Xinrong Hu[1,2(✉)]

[1] School of Computer Science and Artificial Intelligence, Wuhan Textile University, Wuhan 430200, China
jpliu@wtu.edu.cn
[2] Engineering Research Center of Hubei Province for Clothing Information, Wuhan Textile University, Wuhan 430200, China
hrx@wtu.edu.cn
[3] Department of Computing, The Hong Kong Polytechnic University, Hong Kong, China

Abstract. Existing clothing image editing methods typically rely on single-modal traditional models. However, as user demands evolve, these methods still face challenges in global consistency, fine-grained control, and intuitive interaction. Traditional GAN-based approaches produce limited editing effects, while current diffusion-based methods struggle with region-aware editing. To address these issues, we propose MIGEDIT, a multimodal interactive clothing editing process framework. It integrates potential spatial optimization, inversion guidance, and region aware editing into a pre trained diffusion model. MIGEDIT supports the generation of clothing images from clothing sketches and supports point based interactive editing as well as text or region guided modifications, enabling precise and flexible clothing adjustments. Experimental results demonstrate that MIGEDIT outperforms existing methods in visual quality and editing accuracy, making it well-suited for intelligent fashion design and virtual try-on applications.

Keywords: Multi-modal · Interactive editing · Image generation · Diffusion model · Garment editing

1 Introduction

With the growing fashion industry and rising consumer demand for personalization, clothing image editing has become increasingly vital in design, marketing, and virtual try-on. The rapid advancement of generative models and multimodal fusion technologies has brought generative model-based editing to the forefront of research. DragGAN [20] pioneered drag-based point-level editing, though its effectiveness is constrained by the limitations of GANs [4,13]. DragDiffusion [23] addresses these issues by combining interactive editing with pre-trained diffusion

P. Li et al. (Eds.): CGI 2025, LNCS 16508, pp. 199–210, 2026.
https://doi.org/10.1007/978-3-032-22264-0_16

models [11,19,24–27], enabling more robust editing performance. While diffusion models benefit from large-scale parameters and training data to produce diverse, high-quality images, clothing image editing still faces the following challenges:

- Poor global consistency between the original and edited images, affecting overall visual coherence.
- The complexity and variability of clothing styles exceed the capabilities of existing models for fine-grained editing.
- Limited interaction modes hinder the execution of more sophisticated editing tasks (Figs. 1 and 2).

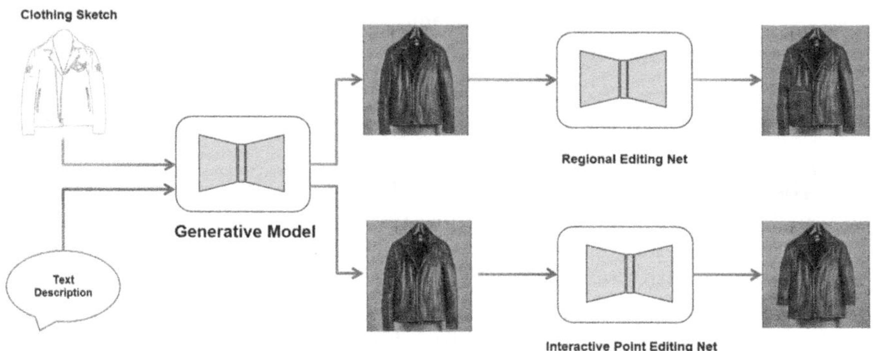

Fig. 1. The flowchart illustrates the fashion design and editing process of MIGEdit. Clothing images can be generated from either clothing sketches or descriptive text using generative models. Personalized edits are then applied through interactive point editing and region-based editing modules. The blue-green gradient line in the diagram represents the workflow of generating clothing from sketches followed by region editing. In contrast, the yellow-blue gradient line below demonstrates the process of generating clothing from text and applying interactive point editing. (Color figure online)

To address these issues, we propose MIGEDIT, a novel multimodal interactive clothing editing framework. Our approach leverages clothing images, text, masks, and user interaction points to perform high-quality editing. By integrating latent optimization, inversion guidance, and region-based editing into a pre-trained diffusion model, MIGEDIT supports both precise point-based and flexible regional edits.

Our main contributions include:

1. A comprehensive editing pipeline tailored for clothing, supporting sketch-to-image generation, point editing, and region editing to accommodate diverse user requirements.
2. Introduction of latent optimization (including motion supervision and point tracking) and inversion guidance to enhance global consistency in edited images.

Fig. 2. Our interactive point editing feature enables changes in clothing collars that can meet users' different needs in various situations. We show an example of dragging and editing to adjust the v-neck and round neck of clothing in the figure.

3. A region-editing module that enables automatic or manual region specification (e.g., adding a pocket), facilitating complex and targeted modifications.
4. Refinement of the SimpleFashion dataset by removing low-quality samples and performing relabeling, leading to improved model performance in interactive editing tasks.

2 Related Work

The research in the field of garment editing primarily focuses on achieving efficient and precise garment image editing through interactive approaches between users and generative models. Current popular deep learning-based garment editing methods can be categorized into three main types.

2.1 Generative Model-Based Image Editing Methods

In recent years, generative models such as GANs and diffusion models have made significant strides in image editing. As foundational models, GANs have been widely applied in clothing image generation. CycleGAN [32] introduced Cycle Consistency Loss, enabling style transfer and facilitating clothing style migration. Text2LIVE [3] proposed a zero-shot, text-driven editing method for natural images and videos. The DeepFashion dataset [15] and related models have further advanced the field.

High-quality clothing images generated by GANs support style and color editing, but still suffer from issues like limited global consistency and lack of fine detail. To overcome these challenges, diffusion models such as DDPM [11], DDIM [24], and Stable Diffusion [22], along with related methods [5,9,16], have become widely used. These models generate images through progressive denoising, offering improved fidelity and stability.

However, despite their strengths, diffusion models still face challenges in domains like clothing editing, where the diversity and intricacy of garments limit the performance of pre-trained models.

2.2 Interactive Image Editing Methods

Interactive image editing allows users to guide generative models via clicks, drags, or drawings, offering greater flexibility and precision than traditional methods. DragGAN is a notable example that enables efficient point-based editing by linking drag operations with network optimization, eliminating the need for model retraining. DragDiffusion builds on this by combining interactive editing with powerful diffusion models, yielding better results in complex tasks.

However, these methods still struggle with clothing image editing due to the wide variety and complexity of garments. Simple interactions are often insufficient. Traditional approaches tend to focus on single operations like warping or texture changes, while clothing editing demands more—such as generating new styles or finely adjusting colors and structures based on user input.

2.3 Multimodal Fusion-Based Editing Methods

Multimodal fusion techniques integrate diverse inputs—such as images, text [8,23], masks [18], and interaction points [17,20]—to improve editing performance. Recently, their application in clothing editing has shown promising results. The CLIP model [21], which fuses visual and textual information, enables more expressive and precise image edits. Based on CLIP, models like [12,28,29] support natural language-driven editing of clothing styles and designs, allowing users to directly input instructions via text.

The integration of mask mechanisms with diffusion models further enhances editing precision and flexibility. Mask-guided diffusion models [1,5,31] allow users to define editable regions while preserving unmasked areas. This approach is widely applied to tasks such as local inpainting, object replacement, and style transfer, offering fine control and high visual fidelity.

Moreover, combining multiple user inputs—images, interaction points, masks, and text—enables customizable and intuitive editing workflows, supporting applications like virtual try-on and personalized design. While early efforts have demonstrated the potential of multimodal fusion in clothing editing, achieving efficient and fine-grained interaction remains a key challenge.

3 Method

This paper introduces latent optimization and inversion guidance to enhance the global consistency between the original and edited garment images. Subsequently, a region-based editing module is incorporated to improve the diversity of edits. Our editing module enables text-controlled garment image editing by automatically generating mask regions corresponding to the specified edits.

3.1 Latent Optimization

Based on user-provided handle points, target points, and a specified editable region mask M, we optimize the latent diffusion to achieve interactive point-based editing. Initially, we perform DDIM inversion on the input real image to obtain the latent diffusion at a specific step t (denoted as z_t). This latent diffusion serves as the initial value for our latent optimization process. Drawing inspiration from the method proposed in DragGAN, we divide the latent optimization process into two sequential steps: motion supervision and point tracking. These two steps are iteratively executed until all handle points reach their targets or the maximum number of iterations is reached (Fig. 3).

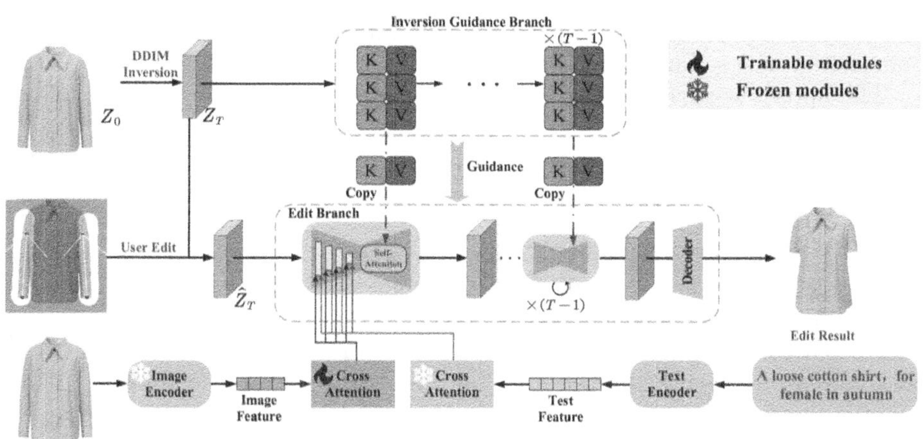

Fig. 3. Our clothing interactive point editing network structure diagram uses inversion information to guide the diffusion step. We replace the keys and values in the self attention module of the UNet decoder with the corresponding keys and values collected in the DDIM inversion.

Motion Supervision. The motion supervision loss during the motion supervision phase is defined as:

$$\mathcal{L}_{ms}\left(\tilde{z}_t^k\right) = \sum_{i=1}^{n} \sum_{q \in \Omega\left(h_i^k, r_1\right)} ||F_{q+d_i}\left(\tilde{z}_t^k\right) - sg\left(F_q\left(\tilde{z}_t^k\right)\right)||_1 + \lambda||\left(\tilde{z}_t^k - sg\left(\tilde{z}_{t-1}^0\right)\right) \odot (1 - M)||_1 \tag{1}$$

where $\tilde{z}_t^k$ denotes the t-th step latent after the k-th update,r_1 denotes the *radius* of the local neighborhood around the keypoint h_i^k, within which pixel positions q are sampled to form the set $\Omega(h_i^k, r_1)$. sg$(\cdot)$ represents the stop gradient operator and $d_i = \frac{(g_i - h_i^k)}{||g_i - h_i^k||_2}$is the normalized vector pointing from h_i^k to g_i. The term $F_{q+d_i}\left(\tilde{z}_t^k\right)$ is computed using bilinear interpolation.To minimize L_{ms}, we update $\hat{z}_t^k$ using the gradient descent step:

$$\hat{z}_t^{k+1} = \hat{z}_t^k - \eta \cdot \frac{\partial L_{ms}(\hat{z}_t^k)}{\partial \hat{z}_t^k}. \tag{2}$$

where η is the learning rate of the latent optimization process.We empirically set $\eta = 1 \times 10^{-3}$ to ensure a stable and smooth update in the latent space.

Point Tracking. During the point tracking step, we use U-Net feature maps $F\left(\tilde{z}_t^{k+1}\right)$ and $F\left(\tilde{z}_t\right)$ to track new handle points. Each handle point is updated within a square region defined as:

$$\Omega\left(h_i^k, r_2\right) = \{(x, y) : |x - x_i^k| \leq r_2, |y - y_i^k| \leq r_2\} \tag{3}$$

where:$\Omega\left(h_i^k, r_2\right)$ is a square region centered around the handle point h_i^k with radius r_2. h_i^k is the position of the i-th handle point at iteration k. r_2 is the given radius that defines the size of the region.(x, y) are the coordinates of any point within the square region.

The update is performed as follows:

$$h_i^{k+1} = \underset{q \epsilon \Omega\left(h_i^k, r_2\right)}{\text{arg min}} \left\| F_q\left(\tilde{z}_t^{k+1}\right) - \left(F_{h_i^o}\left(z_t\right)\right) \right\|_1 \tag{4}$$

where h_i^{k+1} represents the updated position of the i-th handle point at iteration $k+1$. The operation $\underset{q \in \Omega\left(h_i^k, r_2\right)}{\arg\min}$ finds the point q within the region $\Omega\left(h_i^k, r_2\right)$, which is a square region centered at the position of the i-th handle point h_i^k with radius r_2, that minimizes the following expression. The term $F_q\left(\tilde{z}_t^{k+1}\right)$ denotes the feature map value at point q from the U-Net at iteration $k+1$, based on the input $\tilde{z}_t^{k+1}$, while $F_{h_i^o}\left(z_t\right)$ represents the feature map value at the original handle point h_i^o from the U-Net at time t, based on the input z_t. The L_1-norm, denoted by $\|\cdot\|_1$, measures the sum of absolute differences between the feature maps, ensuring that the updated handle point position minimizes the discrepancy between the two feature maps.

3.2 Inversion Information Guidance

In the image editing process, the initial latent z_T, generated through DDIM inversion and guided by the prior introduced by [27], ensures alignment with the original image. However, relying exclusively on the final step of this approximate inversion process proves inadequate for providing precise guidance in generating clothing images. To overcome this limitation, we construct a repository to fully harness the information derived from the DDIM inversion process. This repository stores the latent variables z_t^{gud}at each inversion step, along with the corresponding keys $K_t^{\text{gud}}$and values V_t^{gud} extracted from the self-attention modules of the U-Net decoder. By reusing these intermediate features stored in the repository, we substitute the keys and values in the self-attention modules of the U-Net decoder with those collected during the DDIM inversion. The visual cross-attention at each timestep is subsequently defined as follows:

$$\mathrm{Q}_t = \mathrm{Q}_t^{\text{gen}}, \quad \mathrm{K}_t = \mathrm{K}_t^{\text{gud}}, \quad \mathrm{V}_t = \mathrm{V}_t^{\text{gud}} \tag{5}$$

$$\text{Att}\left(\mathrm{Q}_t, \mathrm{K}_t, \mathrm{V}_t\right) = \text{softmax}\left(\frac{\mathrm{Q}_t \mathrm{K}_t^{\top}}{\sqrt{d}}\right) \mathrm{V}_t \tag{6}$$

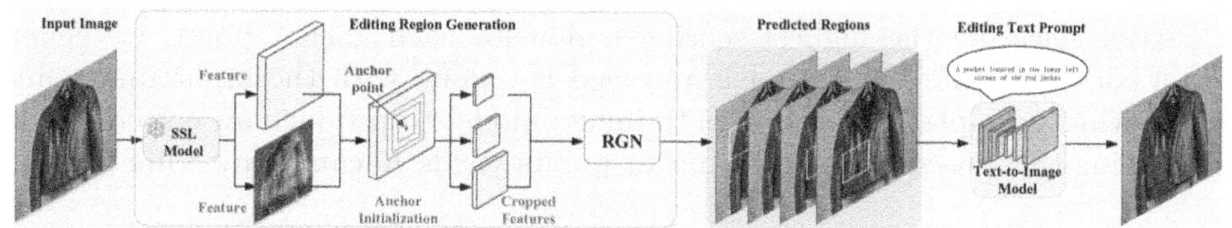

Fig. 4. Our regional editing network structure diagram is controlled by text to automatically generate editing areas and perform editing operations corresponding to the text. In the structure diagram, a pocket is generated for the red jacket. (Color figure online)

3.3 Region Edit

Given an input image $X \in R^{3\times H\times W}$ and a text prompt consisting of p words, represented as $T \in Z^p$, we first extract features using a pre-trained ViT-B/16 [7] visual transformer. This model is trained with the DINO [30] self-supervised learning objective. The resulting feature map $F \in \mathbb{R}^{d\times h\times w}$ from the final transformer layer has been shown to capture object-level semantics and thus serves as a valuable prior in our task (Fig. 4).

We begin by selecting K anchor points $\{C_i\}_{i=1}^K$, located at the top-K scoring patches in the self-attention map produced by querying the [CLS] token of the DINO transformer. Since the [CLS] token aggregates high-level semantic cues, it effectively identifies informative object regions.

For each anchor point C_i, we define a set of bounding box proposals $\mathcal{B}_i = \{B_j\}_{j=1}^M$, where each B_j is a square box of size $j\times j$ centered at C_i. To simplify the representation, each bounding box is parameterized by a single scalar indicating its size.

Next, we train a region generation network that explicitly evaluates all candidate boxes associated with the same anchor point. For each C_i, the process is defined as:

$$f_j = \text{RoI-pool}(F, B_j), \tag{7}$$

$$S([f_1, \ldots, f_M]) = [\pi_1, \ldots, \pi_M], \tag{8}$$

where $[\cdot]$ denotes concatenation along the channel dimension, and RoI pooling extracts a fixed-size feature $f_j \in R^{d\times 1\times 1}$ from F for each bounding box B_j.

In our setup, we set the RoI pooled size to $l = 7$. The scoring function S is implemented using two convolutional layers followed by two fully connected layers, with ReLU activations in between. The final output logits $\{\pi_j\}_{j=1}^M$ are passed through a softmax layer to produce a distribution over box sizes: $\text{Softmax}([\pi_1, \ldots, \pi_M])$.

To enable differentiable selection during training, we use the GumbelSoftmax trick by reparameterizing each logit as $g_j = -\log(-\log(u_j))$, where $u_j \sim \mathcal{U}(0, 1)$. We apply the straight-through estimator, using softmax in the backward pass and argmax in the forward pass.

After selecting the highest-scoring region for each anchor point, we generate a corresponding binary mask and feed it—along with the input image and the editing prompt—into the text-to-image model to produce an edited result. Repeating this process for all K anchor points yields K candidate edits (Fig. 5).

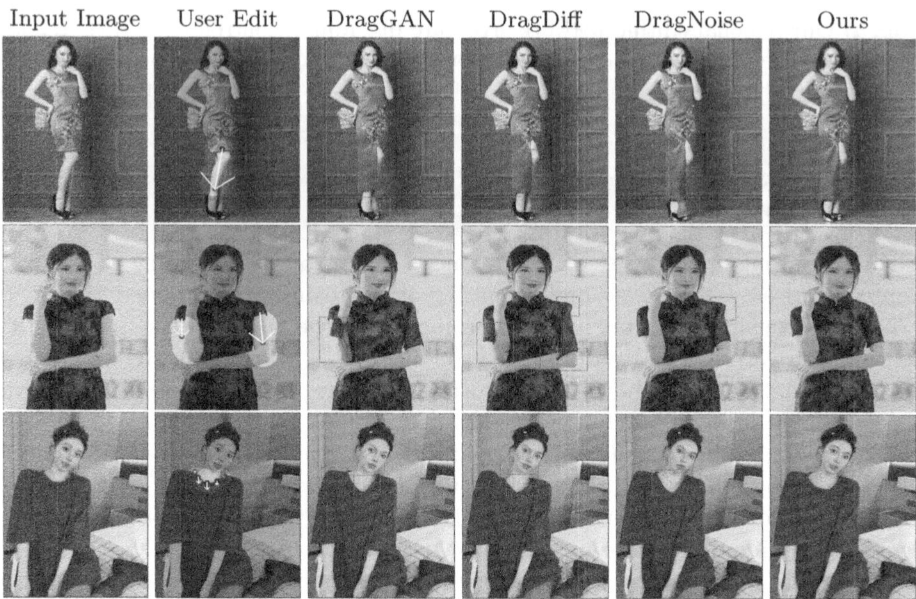

Fig. 5. Displayed a comparison of visualization effects of different methods in interactive image editing tasks. Compared with existing methods, our MIGEdit method can achieve more accurate matching of the target deformation set by the user while maintaining the overall structural consistency of the image. Our method demonstrates better robustness, making the final result more in line with human visual perception.

4 Experiments

In experiments, we use StableDiffusion-V1.5 [22] as the base model. The inference adopts DDIM sampling with 50 steps, and we set the classifier-free guidance scale as 5. the graphics processing unit was NVIDIA GeForce RTX 3090 24GB. For comparison, we selected DragGAN, DragDiffusion, and Drag Noise [14] to evaluate the clothing interactive point editing performance of the proposed model and selected Blended Diffusion, GLIDE, Stable Diffusion, Stable Inpainting, and DiffEdit [6] to evaluate the region editing function in the model.

Table 1. Comparison of different methods in terms of complexity, alignment, and evaluation metrics. Lower values are better.

Method	Complexity ↓		Regional editing function	Evaluation Metrics		
	Preparing (s)	Inference (s)		LPIPS ↓	PSNR ↑	FID ↓
DragGAN [20]	62.45	**10.71**	✗	0.28	27.13	39.12
DragDiffusion [23]	52.33	31.71	✗	0.15	29.22	38.32
DragNoise [14]	63.67	22.67	✗	0.13	28.74	39.74
MIGEdit (ours)	**50.23**	18.46	✓	**0.11**	**30.44**	**35.55**

Table 2. Comparison of different methods on SimpleFashion dataset. Lower FID and Local FID are better, while higher CLIP Score is better.

Method	SimpleFasion		
	Local FID ↓	CLIP Score ↑	FID ↓
Blended Diffusion [2]	26.71	0.261	10.83
GLIDE [18]	20.27	0.249	9.67
Stable Diffusion [22]	13.21	0.252	9.05
Stable Inpainting [22]	10.57	0.268	7.01
DiffEdit [6]	10.32	0.268	6.88
MIGEdit (Ours)	**9.51**	**0.272**	**6.12**

4.1 Dataset

To enhance the quality of clothing image generation, this study refines the multimodal clothing dataset, SimpleFashion, by addressing certain limitations. Specifically, images featuring multiple overlapping clothing items were identified and removed, along with the corresponding sketch images originally used to construct the dataset. The dataset now encompasses 23 distinct clothing categories, with the total number of clothing images exceeding 39,000.

4.2 Experimental Evaluation

To comprehensively evaluate the performance of different methods in image editing, we employ the following quantitative metrics: Computational Complexity,Fréchet Inception Distance (FID), Local FID, CLIP Score [10], PSNR and LPIPS. Computational Complexity measures the time required for preparing and inference. A lower value indicates a more efficient algorithm. FID, Local FID are used to measure the perceptual realism of generated images by comparing them to real images. A lower FID score indicates better image quality. CLIP Score measures the semantic consistency between the generated image and the original input. A higher score suggests better semantic preservation.

Table 1 presents a comparison of different methods in terms of computational complexity and editing functionality. DragGAN achieves the fastest inference time (10.71 s), but it lacks a regional editing function, making it less suitable for localized modifications. DragNoise achieves fast inference (22.67 s) but fails to produce high-quality modifications, as indicated by its high FID score .Our proposed MIGEdit achieves a favorable balance between computational efficiency and editing accuracy, with a preparation time of 50.23 s, inference time of 18.36 s, and the lowest FID score 35.55.

Table 2 presents a quantitative comparison of different methods on the SimpleFashion dataset, where lower FID and Local FID scores indicate better realism, and a higher CLIP Score represents better semantic alignment. MIGEdit outperforms all competing methods across all metrics. Specifically, MIGEdit achieves the lowest Local FID of 9.51, demonstrating superior local consistency in the edited regions compared to the other methods. Additionally, our method attains the highest CLIP Score of 0.272, indicating better semantic alignment with the desired textual descriptions. Furthermore, MIGEdit achieves the lowest FID of 6.12, highlighting its ability to generate high-quality images that are more consistent with the original data distribution.

5 Conclusion

Our quantitative results indicate that our proposed MIGEdit achieves state-of-the-art performance in both computational efficiency and image quality. We have achieved an excellent balance between efficiency and accuracy, significantly improving the realism of the restoration, achieving the lowest FID and highest CLIP scores, ensuring perceptual and semantic quality. However, challenges remain when dealing with complex fabric textures and substantial structural transformations, such as converting long pants into shorts or preserving fabric relief details. In future work, we plan to further refine and enhance our method to better address these issues.

Acknowledgments. This work was supported by the Applied Basic Research Project of China National Textile and Apparel Council (Project No. J202209) and the CCF Industry-Academia Research Fund (CCF-Zhipu AI Large Model OF 2022).

Disclosure of Interests. The authors declare that they have no known competing financial interests or personal relationships that could have appeared to influence the work reported in this paper.

References

1. Avrahami, O., et al.: Spatext: spatio-textual representation for controllable image generation. In: Proceedings of the IEEE/CVF Conference on Computer Vision and Pattern Recognition, pp. 18370–18380 (2023)
2. Avrahami, O., Lischinski, D., Fried, O.: Blended diffusion for text-driven editing of natural images. In: Proceedings of the IEEE/CVF Conference on Computer Vision and Pattern Recognition, pp. 18208–18218 (2022)

3. Bar-Tal, O., Ofri-Amar, D., Fridman, R., Kasten, Y., Dekel, T.: Text2live: TextDriven layered image and video editing. In: European Conference on Computer Vision, pp. 707–723. Springer (2022). https://doi.org/10.1007/978-3-031-19784-0_41
4. Brock, A., Donahue, J., Simonyan, K.: Large scale GAN training for high fidelity natural image synthesis. arXiv preprint arXiv:1809.11096 (2018)
5. Brooks, T., Holynski, A., Efros, A.A.: Instructpix2pix: learning to follow image editing instructions. In: Proceedings of the IEEE/CVF Conference on Computer Vision and Pattern Recognition, pp. 18392–18402 (2023)
6. Couairon, G., Verbeek, J., Schwenk, H., Cord, M.: DiffeDit: diffusion-based semantic image editing with mask guidance. arXiv preprint arXiv:2210.11427 (2022)
7. Dosovitskiy, A., et al.: An image is worth 16x16 words: transformers for image recognition at scale. arXiv preprint arXiv:2010.11929 (2020)
8. Esser, P., Rombach, R., Ommer, B.: Taming transformers for high-resolution image synthesis. In: Proceedings of the IEEE/CVF Conference on Computer Vision and Pattern Recognition, pp. 12873–12883 (2021)
9. Hertz, A., Mokady, R., Tenenbaum, J., Aberman, K., Pritch, Y., Cohen-Or, D.: Prompt-to-prompt image editing with cross attention control. arXiv preprint arXiv:2208.01626 (2022)
10. Hessel, J., Holtzman, A., Forbes, M., Bras, R.L., Choi, Y.: ClipScore: a reference free evaluation metric for image captioning. arXiv preprint arXiv:2104.08718 (2021)
11. Ho, J., Jain, A., Abbeel, P.: Denoising diffusion probabilistic models. Adv. Neural. Inf. Process. Syst. **33**, 6840–6851 (2020)
12. Huang, N., Zhang, Y., Tang, F., Ma, C., Huang, H., Dong, W., Xu, C.: DiffStyler: Controllable dual diffusion for text-driven image stylization. IEEE Trans. Neural Netw. Learn. Syst. (2024)
13. Karras, T., Laine, S., Aila, T.: A style-based generator architecture for generative adversarial networks. In: Proceedings of the IEEE/CVF Conference on Computer Vision and Pattern Recognition, pp. 4401–4410 (2019)
14. Liu, H., Xu, C., Yang, Y., Zeng, L., He, S.: Drag your noise: interactive point based editing via diffusion semantic propagation. In: Proceedings of the IEEE/CVF Conference on Computer Vision and Pattern Recognition, pp. 6743–6752 (2024)
15. Liu, Z., Luo, P., Qiu, S., Wang, X., Tang, X.: DeepFashion: powering robust clothes recognition and retrieval with rich annotations. In: Proceedings of the IEEE Conference on Computer Vision and Pattern Recognition, pp. 1096–1104 (2016)
16. Meng, C., Song, Y., Song, J., Wu, J., Zhu, J.Y., Ermon, S.: SDEDIT: image synthesis and editing with stochastic differential equations. arXiv preprint arXiv:2108.01073 (2021)
17. Mou, C., Wang, X., Song, J., Shan, Y., Zhang, J.: DragonDiffusion: enabling dragstyle manipulation on diffusion models arXiv preprint. arXiv:2307.02421 (2023)
18. Nichol, A., et al.: Glide: towards photorealistic image generation and editing with text-guided diffusion models. arXiv preprint arXiv:2112.10741 (2021)
19. Nichol, A.Q., Dhariwal, P.: Improved denoising diffusion probabilistic models. In: International Conference on Machine Learning, pp. 8162–8171. PMLR (2021)
20. Pan, X., Tewari, A., Leimkühler, T., Liu, L., Meka, A., Theobalt, C.: Drag your GAN: interactive point-based manipulation on the generative image manifold. In: ACM SIGGRAPH 2023 Conference Proceedings, pp. 1–11 (2023)
21. Radford, A., et al.: Learning transferable visual models from natural language supervision. In: International Conference on Machine Learning, pp. 8748–8763. PmLR (2021)

22. Rombach, R., Blattmann, A., Lorenz, D., Esser, P., Ommer, B.: High-resolution image synthesis with latent diffusion models. In: Proceedings of the IEEE/CVF Conference on Computer Vision and Pattern Recognition, pp. 10684–10695 (2022)
23. Shi, Y., et al.: DragDiffusion: harnessing diffusion models for interactive point-based image editing. In: Proceedings of the IEEE/CVF Conference on Computer Vision and Pattern Recognition, pp. 8839–8849 (2024)
24. Song, J., Meng, C., Ermon, S.: Denoising diffusion implicit models. arXiv preprint arXiv:2010.02502 (2020)
25. Song, Y., Ermon, S.: Generative modeling by estimating gradients of the data distribution. In: Advances in Neural Information Processing Systems, p. 32 (2019)
26. Song, Y., Ermon, S.: Improved techniques for training score-based generative models. Adv. Neural. Inf. Process. Syst. **33**, 12438–12448 (2020)
27. Song, Y., Sohl-Dickstein, J., Kingma, D.P., Kumar, A., Ermon, S., Poole, B.: Score-based generative modeling through stochastic differential equations. arXiv preprint arXiv:2011.13456 (2020)
28. Starodubcev, N., Baranchuk, D., Khrulkov, V., Babenko, A.: Towards real-time text-driven image manipulation with unconditional diffusion models. arXiv preprint arXiv:2304.04344 (2023)
29. Wang, Z., Zhao, L., Xing, W.: StyleDiffusion: controllable disentangled style transfer via diffusion models. In: Proceedings of the IEEE/CVF International Conference on Computer Vision, pp. 7677–7689 (2023)
30. Zhang, H., et al.: DINO: DETR with improved denoising anchor boxes for end-to-end object detection. arXiv preprint arXiv:2203.03605 (2022)
31. Zhang, L., Rao, A., Agrawala, M.: Adding conditional control to text-to-image diffusion models. In: Proceedings of the IEEE/CVF International Conference on Computer Vision, pp. 3836–3847 (2023)
32. Zhu, J.Y., Park, T., Isola, P., Efros, A.A.: Unpaired image-to-image translation using cycle-consistent adversarial networks. In: Proceedings of the IEEE International Conference on Computer Vision, pp. 2223–2232 (2017)

WA-FDNet: A Unified Weight Adaptation Network for Multimodal Image Fusion and Object Detection

Yanyin Guo[1], Ying Luo[1], Junwei Li[1,2](✉), and Zhiyuan Zhang[3]

[1] College of Information Science and Electronic Engineering, Zhejiang University, Hangzhou 310027, China
{guoyanyin,22431035,lijunwei7788}@zju.edu.cn
[2] Ningbo Global Innovation Center, Zhejiang University, Ningbo 315100, China
[3] School of Computing and Information Systems, Singapore Management University, Singapore 178902, Singapore
cszyzhang@gmail.com

https://github.com/Yanyin-Guo/WA-FDNet

Abstract. Multimodal image fusion and object detection are critical tasks in computer vision, particularly in scenarios requiring robust perception under low illumination conditions. Existing approaches that attempt to combine these tasks often rely on cascaded or loosely coupled designs, which can result in suboptimal performance due to gradient conflicts and task imbalance. In this paper, we propose WA-FDNet, a novel Weight Adaptation Fusion Detection Network that unifies multimodal image fusion and object detection into a single end-to-end framework. WA-FDNet adopts a shared encoderprivate decoder architecture, enabling efficient feature sharing while preserving task-specific characteristics. The image fusion branch employs a spatial attention-based feature reconstruction module to generate high-quality fused images by emphasizing semantically important regions. Meanwhile, the detection branch introduces a dual-cross attention feature interaction module that enhances inter-modal representation learning for accurate object detection. To address training instability caused by conflicting objectives, we propose a Dynamic Task Weight Adaptation (DTWA) strategy that dynamically balances gradient contributions across tasks based on optimization feedback. Extensive experiments on public benchmarks demonstrate that WA-FDNet achieves state-of-the-art performance in both fusion quality and detection accuracy, validating the effectiveness of our unified multitask learning approach.

Keywords: Image fusion · Object detection · Multimodal · Attention

---

Supplementary Information The online version contains supplementary material available at https://doi.org/10.1007/978-3-032-22264-0_17.

P. Li et al. (Eds.): CGI 2025, LNCS 16508, pp. 211–223, 2026.
https://doi.org/10.1007/978-3-032-22264-0_17

1 Introduction

Multimodal image fusion and object detection have received increasing attention due to their pivotal role in applications such as autonomous driving [19], video surveillance [1], and intelligent monitoring systems [7]. These applications require visual perception systems that can operate reliably under poor illumination, adverse weather, and complex scenes. Infrared imaging performs well in low-light and nighttime conditions but lacks rich textural details [4]. In contrast, visible imaging provides high-resolution detail under good lighting, but its performance degrades in darkness or when occluded [12]. Therefore, integrating these complementary modalities through image fusion offers an effective strategy to overcome the inherent limitations of unimodal systems.

Traditional image fusion methods rely on handcrafted fusion rules [9]. While effective in some cases, these methods often lack theoretical rigor and limit model generalization [18]. Recent efforts have been devoted to deep learning-based image fusion with numerous methods proposed, including autoencoder (AE)-based [8], convolutional neural network (CNN)-based [11], and generative adversarial network (GAN)-based [6] methods. However, these methods often overlook the impact of fusion quality on high-level vision tasks such as object detection, which limits their practical value in real-world systems.

To bridge this disconnect, recent works advocate for task-driven fusion-detection frameworks that jointly optimize both tasks. Pioneering efforts like TarDAL [7] introduced bi-level optimization and the M3FD benchmark, while MetaFusion [20] leveraged meta-feature embedding to align fusion with detection semantics. Most recently, E2E-MFD [19] proposed a synchronous learning framework with gradient alignment to harmonize fusion and detection objectives. Despite these promising advances, two key challenges remain unresolved. The existing methods often fail to dynamically balance competing optimization objectives between the fusion and detection tasks, especially in shared-parameter architectures. Fixed or heuristic loss weighting can lead to gradient conflicts and task dominance, hampering convergence and stability.

To address these challenges, we propose WA-FDNet (Weight Adaptation Fusion Detection Network) tailored for end-to-end multimodal multitask learning within a unified, single-stage pipeline. Specifically, WA-FDNet adopts an encoderdecoder architecture, where the Multitask Shared Encoder (MSE) extracts hierarchical and modality-aware features from registered visible and infrared image pairs. These shared features are then processed by two task-specific decoder branches: a Multimodal Image Fusion (MIF) branch with bottom-up spatial attention, and the Cross-Attention Detector (CTD) branch, which refines detection features via a novel Dual-Cross Attention Feature Interaction (DCAFI) module. To further promote balanced optimization between the pixel-level fusion task and the high-level semantic detection task, WA-FDNet incorporates a Dynamic Task Weight Adaptation (DTWA) strategy. This mechanism continuously monitors task-specific learning progress and adaptively adjusts the gradient contributions of each task during backpropagation, effectively mitigating gradient conflicts and preventing task dominance. By dynamically tuning the task priorities based on the rate of loss descent and task difficulty, WA-FDNet encourages cooperative multitask learning, resulting in more stable training and improved overall performance. In summary, our main contributions include:

- **End-to-End Fusion Detection Framework**: We propose WA-FDNet, an encoder (shared)-decoder (private) architecture that integrates multimodal fusion and object detection into a unified framework. This design facilitates efficient feature sharing while preserving task-specific characteristics, significantly enhancing the performance of both tasks.
- **Spatial Attention-Based Feature Reconstruction**: For multimodal image fusion, We design a spatial attention-guided feature reconstruction module. This module reconstructs multiscale fused features in a bottom-up manner, leveraging spatial attention to prioritize high-semantic object regions, thereby producing higher-quality fused images.
- **Dual-Cross Attention Feature Interaction**: For object detection, we introduce a dual-cross attention module to refine inter-modal feature representations. By combining self-attention and cross-attention mechanisms, it dynamically weights features from different modalities, improving discriminative power and detection accuracy.
- **Dynamic Task Weight Adaptation Optimization**: To mitigate gradient conflicts in multitask learning, we propose a dynamic task weight adaptation technique to adaptively adjust gradient updates based on task-specific contributions, preventing imbalance and enhancing training stability.

2 Method

2.1 Overview

The proposed architecture, illustrated in Fig. 1, comprises three main components: the Multitask Shared Encoder (MSE), the Multimodal Image Fusion (MIF) branch, and the Cross-Attention Detector (CTD) branch. Furthermore, Dynamic Task Weight Adaptation (DTWA) optimization is employed to balance potential gradient conflicts between the fusion and detection tasks. The network takes as input a pair of registered visible image I_{vi} and infrared image I_{ir}. A dense residual block-based MSE module extracts multiscale features F_{vi}^k and F_{ir}^k (where $k = 0, 1, \ldots, 5$) from both modalities. These features are then shared between the fusion and detection tasks. The network adopts a dual-path parallel design for the fusion and detection branches. Specifically, the MIF branch leverages dense multimodal feature fusion to obtain fused features F_f^k, followed by a spatial attention-based decoder for feature reconstruction. The CTD branch, on the other hand, fuses multimodal features F_{det}^k via a dual cross-attention-based feature interaction module and feeds them into a detection network to complete the detection task. This encoder(shared)decoder(private) design, along with dynamic task weight optimization, allows us to achieve both visually appealing fusion results and superior detection performance.

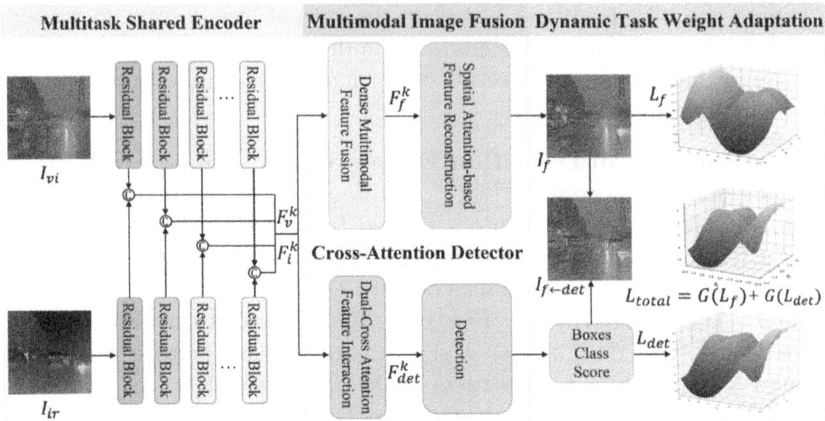

Fig. 1. Overview of the proposed WA-FDNet. WA-FDNet comprises a shared encoder, a fusion task branch, and a detection task branch.

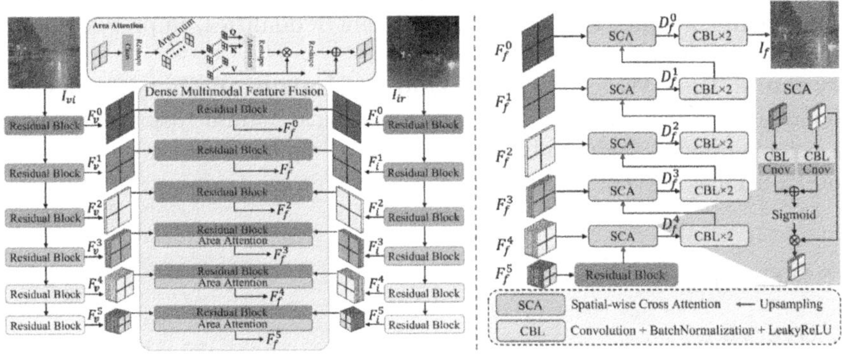

Fig. 2. Network details: Multitask Shared Encoder with Dense Multimodal Feature Fusion (Left) and Spatial Attentionbased Feature Reconstruction (Right).

2.2 Multimodal Image Fusion

The Multitask Shared Encoder (MSE) module needs to provide sufficient features to accomplish both fusion and detection tasks. Therefore, we adopt dense residual blocks to generate multiscale features F_{vi}^k and F_{ir}^k. Since the fusion task is a pixel-level generation task, in the shallow modules of the encoder, we significantly increase the number of channels while keeping the image resolution unchanged, which can be represented as $F_{v/i}^1 \in \mathbb{R}^{H\times W\times 32}$. In the deep feature extraction modules, the number of channels is increased while the spatial resolution is decreased, which can be expressed as $F_{v/i}^k \in \mathbb{R}^{\frac{H}{2^k}\times\frac{W}{2^k}\times(32\times 2^k)}$. Using dense residual blocks is crucial for extracting rich multiscale features from both modalities. This satisfies the detailed information requirements for both the fusion and detection branches. Figure 2 illustrates the details of multiple residual blocks extracting features from visible and infrared images.

The multiscale features extracted from visible and infrared images are subsequently processed by a dense multimodal feature fusion module. As illustrated in Fig. 2, this module is composed of several residual blocks that progressively integrate features, resulting in a series of fused feature maps, represented as F_f^k (where $k = 0, 1, \ldots, 5$). Subsequently, we employ a Spatial Attention-based Feature Reconstruction module to generate the fused image. This approach utilizes a half U-Net architecture, featuring a bottom-up information fusion framework. For the fused features, we perform progressive upsampling at each layer, enabling cross-level interaction and integration through the Spatial-wise Cross Attention (SCA) module. The output of the SCA module is then passed through two sequential Convolution+BatchNormalization+LeakyReLU (CBL) units, further boosting feature representation capabilities. By repeating this process across layers, we obtain features $F_f^{5'}, F_f^{4'}, F_f^{3'}, F_f^{2'}, F_f^{1'}$ and I_f. This design balances multiscale feature fusion and effectively strengthens the expressiveness of the fused features, ultimately producing visually superior fusion images. The specific implementation details are shown in Fig. 2. **Please refer to the supplementary materials for details of the SCA module**.

2.3 Cross-Attention Detector

In the detection branch, we design a Cross-Attention Detector. It leverages the Dual-Cross Attention Feature Interaction (DCAFI) module to fuse multiscale visible and infrared features, denoted as F_{vi}^{k+3} and F_{ir}^{k+3}, and generate detection features at different scales, F_f^k, where $k = 0, 1, 2$. Subsequently, we utilize the Detection network from YOLO [16] to perform the downstream detection tasks.

Inspired by [3], we apply adaptive pooling to both the infrared and visible features to reduce computational overhead. Next, we flatten each set of features and embed a learnable positional encoding of size $H \times W \times C$. This results in two groups of tokens, F_{vi}^p and F_{ir}^p, which serve as inputs for modality interaction. First, we apply self-attention to obtain $\overline{F}_{vi}^p$ and $\overline{F}_{ir}^p$. Afterwards, to supplement information for each modality, we employ cross-attention to achieve further refinement and get $\overline{\overline{F}}_{vi}^p$ and $\overline{\overline{F}}_{ir}^p$. We then perform weighted residual connections and gain $\tilde{F}_{vi}^p$ and $\tilde{F}_{ir}^p$. They are then reshaped to match the feature spaces of F_{vi}^{k+3} and F_{ir}^{k+3}, and residual connections are applied accordingly. This process can be written as:

$$\tilde{F}_{vi}^{k+3} = F_{vi}^{k+3} + Reshape(\tilde{F}_{vi}^p), \tag{1}$$

$$\tilde{F}_{ir}^{k+3} = F_{ir}^{k+3} + Reshape(\tilde{F}_{ir}^p). \tag{2}$$

Finally, the enhanced features $\tilde{F}_{vi}^{k+3}$ and $\tilde{F}_{ir}^{k+3}$ are concatenated and further refined by a 3×3 convolutional layer, resulting in the detection features F_f^k at the corresponding scale. **Please refer to the supplementary materials for details of the DCAFI module.**

2.4 Dynamic Task Weight Adaptation

The multimodal image fusion task is a pixel-level generation task, while the detection task captures the semantic information of objects in a scene. A natural conflict of objectives exists between these two tasks. If the network is trained directly, the detection loss, which has a large gradient variation, causes the network to focus on optimizing the detection task, resulting in poor performance for the fusion task. To address the optimization challenges in fusion-detection tasks, we introduce dynamic adaptive task weights to efficiently mitigate gradient conflicts.

Let L_f represent the loss for the fusion network and L_{det} represent the loss for the detection network. We aim to balance the losses of the two tasks so that they can be optimized at a similar rate. In the parameter space θ, we define the improvement rate of the i-th task as follows:

$$r(\alpha, d_t) = (\frac{L_{f,t} - L_{f,t+1}}{L_{f,t}}, \frac{L_{det,t} - L_{det,t+1}}{L_{det,t}}), \tag{3}$$

where α represents the step size, d_t is the update direction at time t.To determine the update direction for the fusion-detection task, when α is very small, we seek to maximize the minimum improvement rate of the two tasks, which can be expressed as:

$$\max_{d_t} min(\frac{\nabla log L_{f,t}^T d_t}{L_{f,t}} - \frac{||d_t||^2}{2}, \frac{\nabla log L_{det,t}^T d_t}{L_{det,t}} - \frac{||d_t||^2}{2}), \tag{4}$$

where $\nabla log L_{f,t}$ and $\nabla log L_{det,t}$ denote the log gradient of the loss function for the fusion and detection tasks, L_f, t and L_det, t are the current loss, d_t is the update direction, and the penalty term $||d_t||^2$ is introduced to control the extent of the updates, ensuring a relatively balanced reduction in losses for each task.

As learned from FAMO, task weights can be computed using the Softmax function, dynamically updating at each time step based on the loss history. This approach enables the assignment of higher weights to tasks with smaller losses. Specifically, a vector ξ of length equal to the number of tasks (in this case, 2) is constructed, where the learnable parameters ξ are used to allocate weights to the task losses. ξ is updated directly according to the logarithmic change of loss, reflecting the rate at which each task's loss decreases. The update process can be expressed as:

$$\mathbf{z}_t = softmax(\xi_t), \tag{5}$$

$$\xi_{t+1} = \xi_t - \beta\, \delta_t, \tag{6}$$

where

$$\delta_t = \nabla_{\mathbf{z}} \left(\frac{1}{2} \left\| \sum_{i=1}^{2} z_{i,t} \nabla \log \ell_{i,t} \right\|^2 \right) \Bigg|_{\mathbf{z}=softmax(\xi_t)} \tag{7}$$

and $\ell_{1,t}$ denotes the loss of task i at time step t, β is the learning rate for updating ξ. In this case, $\ell_{1,t}$ denotes $L_{f,t}$, and $\ell_{2,t}$ denotes $L_{det,t}$. After that, we can get the overall weighted loss function:

$$L_{total} = \sum_{i=1}^{k} z_{i,t+1} \cdot \ell_{i,t+1}. \tag{8}$$

Finally, we determine the d_t and use an optimizer to update the model parameters again. By continuously repeating the above steps during training, we achieve dynamic adaptive weights, encouraging the model to focus on more challenging tasks.

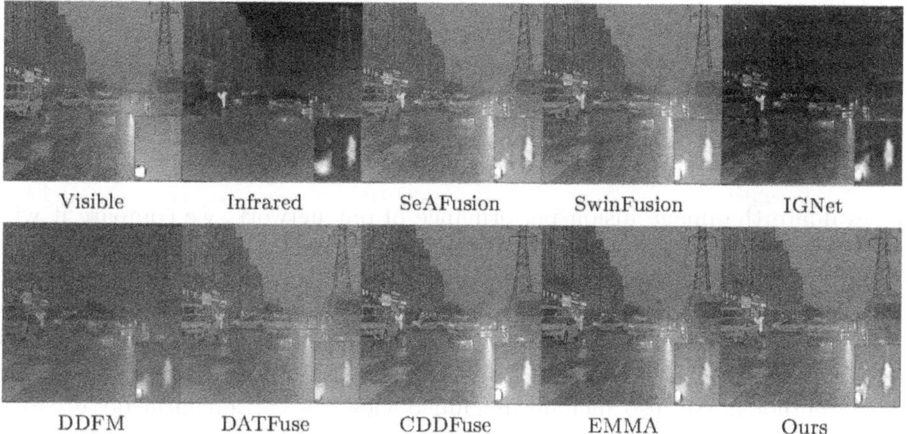

Fig. 3. Qualitative comparisons between our WA-FDNet algorithm and other SOTA methods in the M3FD dataset.

3 Experiment

3.1 Dataset and Implementation Details

Datasets and Evaluation Metrics. We conduct experiments on two benchmark datasets: M3FD [7] and MSRS [14]. Both datasets are used to evaluate the image fusion and object detection performance of our network.

Implementation Details. All experiments are conducted on NVIDIA GeForce RTX 4090 GPUs. Images in the M3FD dataset are cropped into 768 × 768 patches, while images in the MSRS dataset are cropped into 480× 480 patches. The network is trained for 300 epochs with a batch size of 4. The Adam optimizer is employed, with an initial learning rate of 1×10^{-4} for the MSE and MIF networks, and 1×10^{-3} for the CAD network. A warm-up strategy is used during the first 50 epochs. **Please refer to the supplementary materials for more qualitative and Quantitative results.**

Table 1. Quantitative comparison of SOTA fusion methods on the M3FD and MSRS datasets. The best and second-best are highlighted in deep red and blue respectively.

Methods	M3FD				MSRS			
	$IF\uparrow$	$MI\uparrow$	$Q_{abf}\uparrow$	$PSNR\uparrow$	$IF\uparrow$	$MI\uparrow$	$Q_{abf}\uparrow$	$PSNR\uparrow$
SeAFusion (IF2022)	0.726	3.724	0.612	61.072	0.949	**4.101**	0.663	64.153
SwinFusion (JAS2022)	0.761	**4.111**	0.616	61.103	0.960	4.075	0.614	64.294
IGNet (ACMMM2023)	0.607	2.442	0.414	60.077	0.680	1.992	0.468	64.127
DDFM (ICCV2023)	0.468	2.940	0.348	**63.500**	0.604	2.538	0.372	**66.459**
DATFuse (TCSVT2023)	0.646	4.083	0.510	61.095	0.875	3.861	0.626	63.172
CCDFuse (CVPR2023)	**0.787**	4.081	**0.624**	61.092	**0.962**	4.036	**0.675**	64.244
EMMA (cvpr2024)	0.760	3.895	0.611	60.792	0.951	4.007	0.631	64.236
WA-FDNet (ours)	**0.867**	**4.606**	**0.689**	**61.123**	**0.970**	**4.115**	**0.691**	**64.443**

3.2 Results of Image Fusion

To evaluate the image fusion performance of our network, we compare it with several state-of-the-art (SOTA) visible and infrared image fusion algorithms from recent years [5,10,13,15,21–23]. All methods are tested under the same experimental settings.

Qualitative Results. Figure 3 presents the fused images of RGB and infrared image pairs from the M3FD dataset, obtained using our algorithm and seven other methods. We also include magnified views of certain local details for a more thorough comparison. There are two people highlighted by a red box. All methods successfully capture the right-side target with strong intensity, but only our WA-FDNet and IGNet are able to adequately present the features of the left-side target, whose information is more limited. DDFM and DATFuse even lose some target detail altogether. Compared to IGNet, our approach better preserves the visible image information, resulting in higher visual fidelity. This advantage can be attributed to our fusion network's spatial attention-based multi-scale U-Net architecture, which effectively retains both visible and infrared information and avoids feature loss.

Quantitative Results. The quantitative results of different fusion methods on the M3FD and MSRS datasets are shown in Table 1. The results indicate that our WA-FDNet achieves the highest performance in terms of IF, MI, and Q_{abf}. Our method also attains the second-best performance in PSNR. This is primarily due to DDFM employing a powerful diffusion model, which results in overall lower noise in the images. Notably, our method significantly outperforms others in the Qabf metric, demonstrating its strong capability for texture information preservation.

3.3 Results of Multimodal Object Detection

We employed several approaches to comprehensively evaluate the detection performance of our WA-FDNet, including single-modal object detection (OD) on

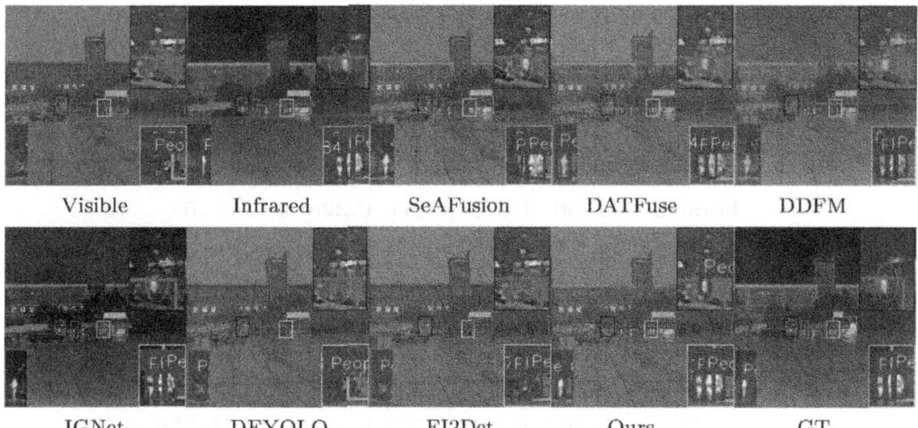

Fig. 4. Qualitative comparison results of our proposed WA-FDNet algorithm and other detection methods on detection task in the M3FD datasets.

visual (VI) and infrared (IR) images, object detection on fused images (FOD), and multimodal object detection (MOD) using state-of-the-art algorithms [1,3]. Our proposed WA-FDNet, which integrates both multimodal fusion and detection (MFOD), is built upon the YOLO detector framework. To ensure a fair comparison, we also conducted experiments using YOLO12s for VI/IR OD and FOD tasks.

Qualitative Results. The visualization results of different detection methods on the M3FD dataset are shown in Fig. 4. The yellow box indicates that our algorithm successfully detected three people standing closely together, whereas most fusion detection methods performed suboptimally in this scenario. For small and distant targets within the brown box, only a few methods were able to detect them. Overall, our method-along with algorithms specifically designed for dual-modal object detection-demonstrates robust and comprehensive detection capabilities. Notably, only our model detected the target outlined by the black box in the image. This target was not annotated in the ground truth (GT), and after reviewing the images before and after, we confirmed that it was a moving person. This highlights the excellent generalization and robustness of our WA-FDNet, which we attribute to dense feature extraction and rich intra-modal feature interaction. Overall, WA-FDNet outperforms the SOTA EI2Det method and achieves cutting-edge detection performance.

Quantitative Results. Table 2 presents the quantitative detection performance of various methods on the M3FD and MSRS datasets. It can be observed that dedicated multimodal object detection algorithms generally outperform methods that perform detection on fused images. Among these methods, our approach achieves the best performance. This is because, similar to MOD-based methods, WA-FDNet can effectively extract useful semantic features from both modalities.

Table 2. Quantitative comparisons of the detection performance on M3FD and MSRS datasets. We mark the best result in deep red, the second-best result in deep blue.

Task	Method	M3FD		MSRS				
		mAP$_{50}$	mAP$_{95}$	People	Bicycle	Car	mAP$_{50}$	mAP$_{95}$
VI/IR OD	Visible	0.837	0.661	0.276	0.184	0.562	0.645	0.341
	Infrared	0.850	0.672	0.454	**0.228**	0.529	0.706	0.404
FOD	SeAFusion	0.879	0.703	0.520	0.165	0.550	0.695	0.412
	DATFuse	0.875	0.684	0.518	0.176	**0.571**	0.697	**0.422**
	DDFM	0.851	0.687	0.503	0.188	0.455	0.688	0.390
	IGNet	0.892	0.668	0.497	0.188	0.458	0.709	0.381
MOD	DEYOLO	0.898	0.701	0.516	0.184	0.552	0.707	0.417
	EI2Det	**0.904**	**0.710**	**0.521**	0.168	**0.564**	**0.726**	0.418
MFOD	WA-FDNet	**0.919**	**0.736**	**0.524**	**0.198**	0.551	**0.733**	**0.424**

Table 3. Quantitative ablation experiment results of the proposed SCA and DCAFI modules. The best results and second-best are highlighted in deep red, while the second-best results are highlighted in deep blue.

Model	Module		M3FD					
	SCA	DCAFI	$IF \uparrow$	$MI \uparrow$	$Q_{abf} \uparrow$	$PSNR \uparrow$	$mAP_{50} \uparrow$	$mAP_{50:95} \uparrow$
M1	×	×	0.751	3.762	0.563	59.538	0.841	0.663
M2	×	✓	0.760	3.817	0.594	59.438	**0.914**	**0.725**
M3	✓	×	**0.858**	**4.469**	**0.679**	**61.354**	0.839	0.664
M4(WA-FDNet)	✓	✓	**0.867**	**4.606**	**0.689**	**61.123**	**0.919**	**0.736**

3.4 Ablation Studies

Effect of SCA and DCAFI Modules. To verify the effectiveness of the SCA module, we removed SCA from the network. For the DCAFI module, we replaced it with a simple CBL module to perform multimodal feature aggregation. Table 3 presents the results conducted on the M3FD dataset. The comparison between M2 and M4 shows that removing the SCA module leads to a significant drop in fusion performance, while the detection network's performance changes only slightly. This suggests that SCA strengthens the network's semantic representation, thereby enhancing the visual quality of the fused images. The comparison between M3 and M4 indicates that the DCAFI module has a substantial impact on detection performance, highlighting that effective multimodal feature aggregation is key for multimodal object detection.

Effect of DTWA. To validate the effectiveness of DTWA, we separately trained the fusion network, the detection network, and other optimization methods (GradNorm [2] and PGGrad [17]), along with both networks using simple synchronous optimization without DTWA. Table 4 compares these approaches,

Table 4. Quantitative ablation experiment results of DTWA. MF refers to the visible and infrared image fusion, and OD represents the detection task. The best results are highlighted in deep red, while the second-best results are highlighted in deep blue.

Task	$IF\uparrow$	$MI\uparrow$	$Q_{abf}\uparrow$	$mAP_{50}\uparrow$	$mAP_{50:95}\uparrow$	$Params(M)$	$FLOPs(G)$
MF	**0.875**	**4.565**	**0.694**	-	-	18.17	93.88
OD	-	-	-	**0.921**	**0.740**	21.17	62.48
GradNorm	0.844	4.257	0.627	0.903	0.694	-	-
PGGrad	0.835	4.126	0.609	0.914	0.726	-	-
w/o DTWA	0.825	3.928	0.631	0.895	0.685	-	-
WA-FDNet	**0.867**	**4.606**	**0.689**	**0.919**	**0.736**	32.23	114.01

revealing that using DTWA for synchronous optimization outperforms simple synchronous training and other optimization methods on both tasks. This improvement is due to the fact that, without proper constraints, the stronger network is prone to getting stuck in local optima and is affected by the optimization disturbances from the weaker network. Such conflicts prevent both networks from achieving optimal performance, resulting in a noticeable performance gap compared to single-task training. Comparative experiments also show that the performance of WA-FDNet closely matches that of the MF and OD baseline models, indicating that the use of DTWA effectively balances the optimization of the two tasks, allowing the network to approach single-task performance. Furthermore, with input images of resolution 768×768, WA-FDNet has approximately $32.23M$ parameters and $114.01G$ FLOPs (using the M3FD dataset as an example). Compared to the baseline methods for separate visible-infrared image fusion ($18.17M$ parameters and $93.88G$ FLOPs) and joint detection ($21.17M$ parameters and $62.48G$ FLOPs), our method demonstrates greater efficiency.

4 Conclusion

This paper presents WA-FDNet, an end-to-end multimodal multitask learning framework for joint image fusion and object detection. By adopting a shared encoderprivate decoder architecture, WA-FDNet effectively leverages shared representations while preserving task-specific processing. The introduction of a spatial attention-based fusion decoder and a dual-cross attention detection branch enhances the quality of fused images and improves detection accuracy. To address task conflicts during training, a dynamic task weight adaptation strategy is proposed, enabling stable and balanced optimization. Experimental results demonstrate that WA-FDNet achieves state-of-the-art performance on benchmark datasets, highlighting the advantages of unified training and adaptive task coordination in multimodal perception tasks.

Acknowledgments. This research is supported by the Ningbo 2025 Science & Technology Innovation Major Project (No. 2023Z044).

References

1. Chen, Y., et al.: Deyolo: dual-feature-enhancement yolo for cross-modality object detection. In: International Conference Pattern Recognition, pp. 236–252 (2025)
2. Chen, Z., Badrinarayanan, V., Lee, C.Y., Rabinovich, A.: Gradnorm: Gradient normalization for adaptive loss balancing in deep multitask networks. In: International Confernence Machine Learning, pp. 794–803 (2018)
3. Hu, K., He, Y., Li, Y., Zhao, J., Chen, S., Kang, Y.: Ei 2 det: Edge-guided Illumination-aware Interactive Learning For Visible-infrared Object Detection. IEEE Trans. Circuit Syst, Video Technol (2025)
4. Kim, J.U., Park, S., Ro, Y.M.: Uncertainty-guided cross-modal learning for robust multispectral pedestrian detection. IEEE Trans. Circuit Syst. Video Technol. **32**(3), 1510–1523 (2021)
5. Li, J., Chen, J., Liu, J., Ma, H.: Learning a graph neural network with cross modality interaction for image fusion. In: ACM International Conference Multimedia, pp. 4471–4479 (2023)
6. Li, J., Huo, H., Li, C., Wang, R., Feng, Q.: Attentionfgan: Infrared and visible image fusion using attention-based generative adversarial networks. IEEE Trans. Multimedia **23**, 1383–1396 (2020)
7. Liu, J., et al.: Target-aware dual adversarial learning and a multi-scenario multi-modality benchmark to fuse infrared and visible for object detection. In: IEEE Conference Computer Vision Pattern Recognition, pp. 5802–5811 (2022)
8. Long, Y., Jia, H., Zhong, Y., Jiang, Y., Jia, Y.: Rxdnfuse: a aggregated residual dense network for infrared and visible image fusion. Infom. Fusion **69**, 128–141 (2021)
9. Ma, J., Chen, C., Li, C., Huang, J.: Infrared and visible image fusion via gradient transfer and total variation minimization. Infom. Fusion **31**, 100–109 (2016)
10. Ma, J., Tang, L., Fan, F., Huang, J., Mei, X., Ma, Y.: Swinfusion: cross-domain long-range learning for general image fusion via swin transformer. IEEE/CAA J. Autom. Sinica **9**(7), 1200–1217 (2022)
11. Ma, J., Tang, L., Xu, M., Zhang, H., Xiao, G.: Stdfusionnet: an infrared and visible image fusion network based on salient target detection. IEEE Trans. Instru. Measure. **70**, 1–13 (2021)
12. Song, Z., et al.: An infrared dataset for partially occluded person detection in complex environment for search and rescue. Sci. Data **12**(1), 300 (2025)
13. Tang, L., Yuan, J., Ma, J.: Image fusion in the loop of high-level vision tasks: A semantic-aware real-time infrared and visible image fusion network. Infom. Fusion **82**, 28–42 (2022)
14. Tang, L., Yuan, J., Zhang, H., Jiang, X., Ma, J.: Piafusion: A Progressive Infrared and Visible Image Fusion Network Based on Illumination Aware. Infom, Fusion (2022)
15. Tang, W., He, F., Liu, Y., Duan, Y., Si, T.: Datfuse: infrared and visible image fusion via dual attention transformer. IEEE Trans. Circuit Syst. Video Technol. **33**(7), 3159–3172 (2023)
16. Tian, Y., Ye, Q., Doermann, D.: Yolov12: Attention-centric real-time object detectors, (2025). arXiv:2502.12524v1 arXiv preprint
17. Yu, T., Kumar, S., Gupta, A., Levine, S., Hausman, K., Finn, C.: Gradient surgery for multi-task learning. Adv. Neural Inform. Process. Syst. **33**, 5824–5836 (2020)
18. Zhang, H., Xu, H., Tian, X., Jiang, J., Ma, J.: Image fusion meets deep learning: a survey and perspective. Infom. Fusion **76**, 323–336 (2021)

19. Zhang, J., et al.: E2e-MFD: Towards end-to-end synchronous multimodal fusion detection. Adv. Neural Inform. Process. Syst. **37**, 52296–52322 (2024)
20. Zhao, W., Xie, S., Zhao, F., He, Y., Lu, H.: Metafusion: Infrared and visible image fusion via meta-feature embedding from object detection. In: IEEE Conference Computer Vision Pattern Recognition, pp. 13955–13965 (2023)
21. Zhao, Z., et al.: CDDFuse: Correlation-driven dual-branch feature decomposition for multi-modality image fusion. In: IEEE Conference Computer Vision Pattern Recognition, pp. 5906–5916 (2023)
22. Zhao, Z., et al.: Equivariant multi-modality image fusion. In: IEEE Conference Computer Vision Pattern Recognition, pp. 25912–25921 (2024)
23. Zhao, Z., et al.: DDFM: denoising diffusion model for multi-modality image fusion. In: International Conference Computer Vision, pp. 8082–8093 (2023)

Generating Multi-illumination Leaf Images Through Single-Image Material Estimation for Robust Disease Recognition

Jiahui Chen, Yu Zhang, and Xiaogang Wang(✉)

College of Computer and Information Science, Southwest University, Chongqing, China
wangxiaogang@swu.edu.cn

Abstract. Visual conditions are critical for vision-based smart agricultural production tasks. However, traditional field acquisition methods struggle to capture complex illumination variations and are often time-consuming, labor-intensive, and expensive. In this work, we propose an innovative method for generating datasets of crop leaf images under diverse visual conditions, which synthesizes high-fidelity leaf data through physics-based simulation of realistic agricultural illumination variations. Our methodology comprises three stages. First, we use advanced techniques to estimate depth from the input image and reconstruct accurate leaf geometry. Second, we employ a physics-based inverse rendering framework to estimate the material and illumination characteristics of leaf surfaces. Finally, high dynamic range (HDR) environment maps are utilized to achieve photorealistic relighting across diverse agricultural conditions. Extensive experiments conducted on the AppleLeaf9 dataset validate the effectiveness of the proposed image generation method for leaf disease classification across various deep learning architectures. The synthesized images achieved classification accuracies of 97.10% with MobileNetV2, 95.65% with DenseNet121, 96.62% with ResNet50, and 98.07% with VGG16. These results underscore the strong potential of the proposed method in agricultural vision applications, particularly in addressing domain-specific challenges that are often insufficiently handled by existing image generation approaches.

Keywords: Image synthesis · Inverse rendering · Relighting · Crop disease classification

1 Introduction

Advances in computer vision have significantly enhanced smart agricultural systems. While dataset construction remains fundamental to these developments,

Supplementary Information The online version contains supplementary material available at https://doi.org/10.1007/978-3-032-22264-0_18.

P. Li et al. (Eds.): CGI 2025, LNCS 16508, pp. 224–236, 2026.
https://doi.org/10.1007/978-3-032-22264-0_18

current agricultural image collections face critical limitations. Most existing datasets are captured under controlled experimental conditions, lacking sufficient illumination diversity to represent dynamic field environments affected by seasonal variations, weather fluctuations, and diurnal changes. These environmental dynamics lead to significant variations in leaf color, surface texture, and the visual manifestation of disease symptoms. Large-scale image collection and annotation require substantial human and financial investment, making it difficult to comprehensively address practical agricultural scenarios [29]. Therefore, expanding crop leaf image datasets incorporating a variety of visual conditions is essential for advancing vision-based research in smart agricultural production.

Recent advancements in generative adversarial networks (GANs) [8] and diffusion models have demonstrated remarkable capabilities in photorealistic image synthesis, emerging as powerful tools for agricultural vision research [22,34]. To improve feature richness and image fidelity, Liu [20] proposed LeafGAN, incorporating a densely connected architecture to capture finer details. Conditional GANs [1] have been employed to synthesize tomato leaf images, leading to substantial improvements in classification accuracy. Despite these successes, GANs still face several challenges, including training instability, mode collapse, and reliance on large-scale datasets [6,7]. Li [17] introduced Denoising Diffusion Probabilistic Models [11] for data augmentation, demonstrating their effectiveness in citrus disease diagnosis under limited data conditions. Furthermore, diffusion models were applied to weed identification tasks, significantly improving the quality of generated weed images [5]. Nevertheless, diffusion models often produce images that lack physical realism and offer limited controllability over specific visual attributes.

Specifically in this work, we introduce a simple yet effective image generation method for synthesizing crop leaf images, which simulates various typical visual conditions in agricultural environments to enhance the diversity and realism of leaf disease datasets. Starting from a single image, our approach reconstructs the 3D leaf geometry and estimates material and lighting properties using advanced physics-based inverse rendering techniques. To faithfully simulate the diverse and naturally occurring illumination scenarios found in outdoor agricultural scenes, we incorporate high dynamic range (HDR) environment maps during the relighting process. Our analysis involves training classification models on various combinations of real and synthetic datasets, accompanied by quantitative performance comparisons across multiple deep learning architectures. The results demonstrate that our synthetic images not only enhance classification accuracy but also contribute to more diverse and representative training data. Through this work, we validate the effectiveness of our synthetic generation method in capturing complex illumination scenarios and faithfully replicating real-world conditions, thereby supporting the development of more accurate and robust vision systems for agricultural applications.

2 Related Work

2.1 Inverse Rendering

Inverse rendering aims to decompose the visual appearance of an image into its underlying geometric structure, material properties, and illumination [3,28,38], and has become a foundational problem in both computer vision and graphics. Early work such as [19] introduced the first single-image inverse rendering framework under unknown environmental illumination. With the emergence of differentiable renderers, inverse rendering has been successfully applied to various domains, including human face reconstruction [30] and photorealistic indoor scene modeling [18]. Despite these advancements, the application of inverse rendering in agriculture remains largely unexplored. In this study, we adapt and extend differentiable inverse rendering techniques to the context of crop leaf image enhancement.

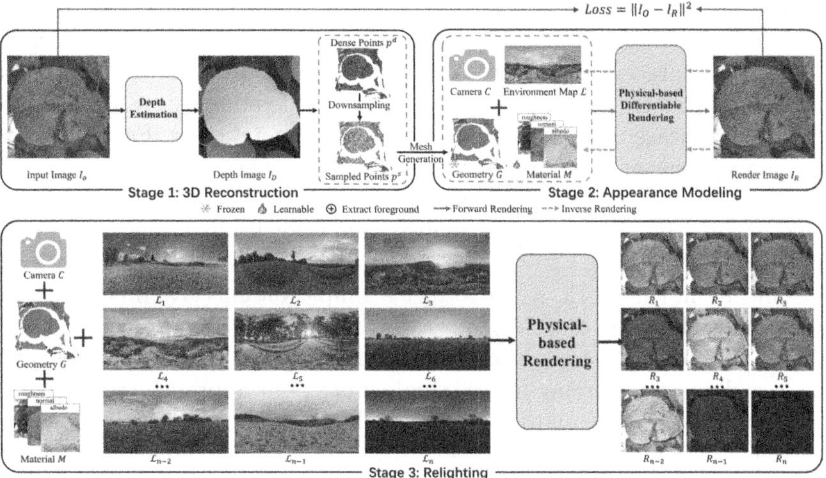

Fig. 1. The pipeline of the proposed framework. Given a single-view image, we first reconstruct the leaf geometry as a 3D mesh by generating a point cloud and performing surface reconstruction. Next, physics-based inverse rendering is employed to jointly optimize the leaf's material properties and scene illumination. Finally, the reconstructed scene is relit under HDR environment maps to achieve photorealistic appearance synthesis.

2.2 Generative Adversarial Networks (GANs)

GANs consist of two core components: a generator and a discriminator. The generator aims to produce images that closely resemble real samples, while the discriminator evaluates whether the input images are real or generated. GANs have been widely employed for synthesizing crop disease images. These studies [36,37] modified the original GAN architecture, effectively generating more realistic images and improving the performance of leaf disease classification. AR-GAN extends traditional GAN-based image-to-image translation methods, producing visually realistic tomato leaves and enhancing disease recognition in data-scarce environments [24]. Despite their ability to generate high-fidelity images, GAN-based methods require large-scale training datasets and often underperform when trained on limited data. Furthermore, the joint training of the generator and discriminator is computationally intensive and time-consuming.

2.3 Diffusion Models

Diffusion models involve a forward process that adds noise to images and a reverse process that removes the noise to generate samples approximating the original data distribution [32]. Leveraging their strong generative stability, diffusion models have recently emerged as powerful alternatives to GANs [7], particularly in the context of agricultural image synthesis. TomatoDIFF [13] was introduced for the semantic segmentation of tomatoes in complex environments. Stable Diffusion is a text-to-image generation model [25], which was adopted by Moreno [23] to synthesize weed images within tomato crops. However, due to substantial variation in lighting conditions among collected images, multiple models had to be trained separately for different image categories.

3 Method

Our pipeline for generating synthetic images of leaves is illustrated in Fig. 1. In Sect. 3.1, we reconstruct 3D models of leaves. In Sect. 3.2, we refine leaf material parameters through physics-based differentiable rendering. Section 3.3 leverages HDR environment maps to simulate dynamic illumination conditions inherent to agricultural ecosystems, enabling scalable generation of diverse and photorealistic leaf images.

3.1 Geometry Modeling

Given a single-view leaf image I_O, we reconstruct its geometry as a triangular mesh G. Using a pre-trained Depth Anything V2 network [33], we first predict the depth map I_D. Each pixel (u, v) is then back-projected to a 3D point p, forming a dense point cloud $p^d = \{p_1^d, p_2^d, \ldots, p_n^d\}$. To reduce computation cost while preserving geometric features, we apply farthest point sampling to obtain a uniformly distributed subset $p^o = \{p_1^s, p_2^s, \ldots, p_m^s\}$ $(m < n)$. Finally, we reconstruct the triangular mesh G using the Ball Pivoting algorithm [2].

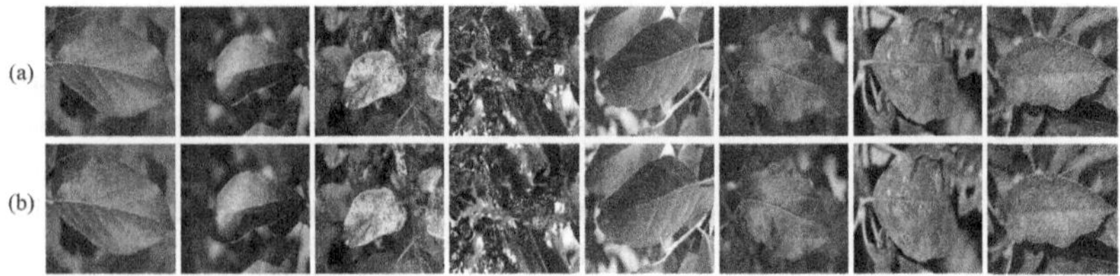

Fig. 2. Qualitative comparison of inverse rendering and real images. (a) Input reference images; (b) Re-rendered results using estimated illumination and material parameters.

3.2 Appearance Modeling

Camera Parameters Accurate camera parameter specification constitutes a critical prerequisite for precise scene inference in inverse rendering pipelines. Nevertheless, agricultural leaf datasets frequently lack camera metadata. We propose an automated camera estimation framework grounded in geometric normalization. Assuming the camera is an orthographic camera positioned directly above the leaf at coordinates (0, 0, 1) and oriented toward (0, 0, 0), our method first computes the minimum bounding box R_b surrounding each leaf, where W_b and H_b represent the width and height of R_b. The geometric center of R_b is translated to the image center, ensuring that the camera remains directly above the leaf. To guarantee that the entire leaf remains visible within the rendered frame, we adjust the orthographic scale based on the ratio between the normalized model space and its actual size in image pixels. The orthographic camera's scale s in Mitsuba3 [14] specifies the half-height of the projection plane. When the leaf's geometric model is normalized to $[-n, n]^3$, the camera scale for a rendered image with resolution $W_r \times W_r$ is computed as:

$$C_{scale} = \frac{W_r}{\max(W_b, H_b)} \times n \tag{1}$$

In our implementation, we set $n = 0.5$. Following the above procedure, the estimated camera parameters C can be directly used as known inputs in the inverse rendering process.

Material Estimation Based on Differentiable Rendering Rendering can be defined as a complex function g that maps a set of scene parameters θ to output imagery, formally expressed as:

$$I_R = \mathrm{g}(\theta) = \mathrm{g}(G, M, L, C) \tag{2}$$

where G, M, L, C represent geometry, materials, illumination, and camera parameters. The function g involves solving rendering equations by various numerical methods such as ray tracing or path tracing. The rendering equation follows the physical law of energy conservation and was proposed by Kajiya

[15] to be a mathematical model to describe light propagation and interaction in a scene:

$$L_o(\omega_o, x) = \int_\Omega L_i(\omega_i, x) f_r(\omega_o, \omega_i, x)(\omega_i \cdot n) d\omega_i \tag{3}$$

where x denotes surface position, n is the surface normal, Ω represents the hemisphere space in the direction of incident light, ω_i and ω_o are the directions of incoming and outgoing light, L_i and L_o denote the radiance corresponding to those directions, f_r is the Spatially Varying Bidirectional Reflectance Distribution Function describing how different materials reflect the incident light. Our methodology follows Eq. (3) and uses radiance to calculate pixel values of the rendered image. For material modeling, we implement the Disney microfacet BRDF [4] as f_r in the rendering equation:

$$f_r(\omega_i, \omega_o) = \frac{f \cdot d \cdot g}{4(\omega_i \cdot n)(\omega_o \cdot n)} \tag{4}$$

where f is the Fresnel reflection coefficient, d is the microfacet distribution function, and g is the geometric attenuation factor. We encode material parameters (albedo, roughness) as spatially varying texture maps UV-mapped onto leaf geometry, with refractive indices stored as scalar values. The estimated material is saved as a 512 × 512 resolution texture map, and the whole process, including all 1000 iterations, is completed in about 5 minutes on an NVIDIA RTX3090 GPU. This representation enables efficient material estimation in complex scenes.

Loss Function. Our goal is to calculate the gradient with respect to scene parameters and optimize the environment illumination L and materials M by minimizing the difference between the rendered image I_R and the reference image I_O:

$$\mathcal{L}_{IR} = \lambda_{RGB}\mathcal{L}_{RGB} + \lambda_M\mathcal{L}_M + \lambda_{TV}\mathcal{L}_{TV} \tag{5}$$

where $\mathcal{L}_{RGB} = \|I_O - \mathrm{g}(\theta)\|^2$ is the pixel-wise RGB loss, $\mathcal{L}_M$ is defined as the mean square error loss between the true mask and generated mask, $\mathcal{L}_{TV}$ is the image total variation loss, which is a commonly used regularization technique in image processing. λ_{RGB}, λ_M and λ_{TV} represent the coefficient weights of each loss term.

3.3 Relighting

Natural illumination predominantly originates from skylight and ambient sources, so we use HDR environment maps to simulate the appearance variations of leaves under real agricultural conditions. The incident radiance at a given surface point can be derived from the environment map by evaluating it along the corresponding reflection vector. Specifically, the incident radiance in the direction ω_i is given by:

$$L_i(\omega_i) = L_{env}(N(\omega_i)) \tag{6}$$

where $N(\omega_i)$ denotes the reflection direction of the incident vector ω_i about the surface normal, and L_{env} represents the radiance function defined by the environment map.

A set of diverse environment maps $\{E_i\}_{i=1}^{n}$ can be employed to simulate a variety of natural illumination conditions. Using ray tracing, we compute the intersection point x between each camera ray ω_i and the leaf geometry surface G to determine the corresponding surface interaction. Given the surface normal n at the intersection point, the material properties M, and the illumination defined by E, the outgoing radiance along the viewing direction ω_o is evaluated using the Eq. (3).

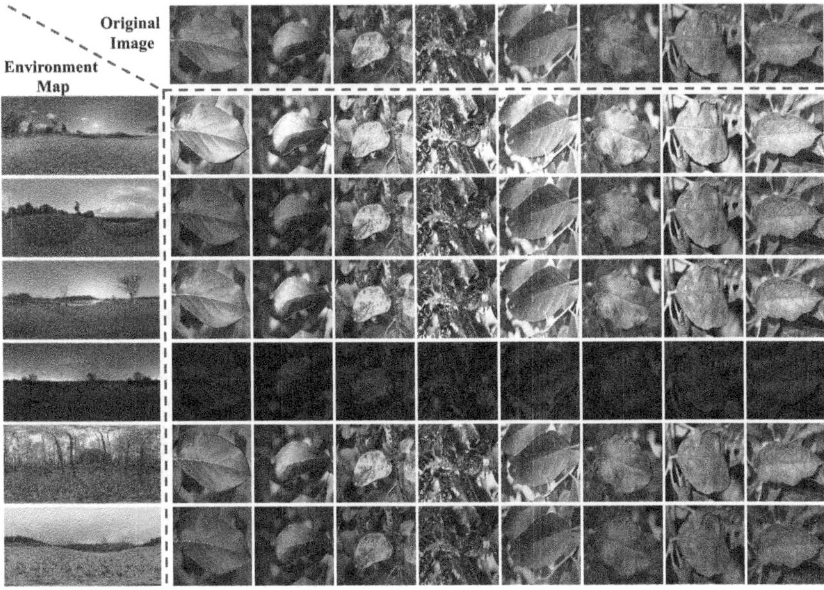

Fig. 3. Our method re-renders leaves under various illumination conditions using different environment maps. Specifically, the second to the seventh rows correspond to sunny, cloudy, evening, night, autumn, and winter lighting, respectively.

4 Experiments and Results

4.1 Dataset

To evaluate the effectiveness of our method, we conducted comparative experiments on the AppleLeaf9 dataset [35], which includes 14,582 images spanning healthy leaves and eight disease categories. Approximately 94% of the samples were collected in the wild, while the remaining 6% were obtained indoors under controlled settings, with an imbalanced distribution across categories. To simulate data scarcity scenarios, we selected four representative categories (healthy, mosaic, rust, and scab) and excluded all indoor-acquired samples. Through random sampling, we constructed a baseline dataset comprising 643 field-collected images: 169 healthy, 132 mosaic, 186 rust, and 156 scab, which was partitioned into 70% training-validation and 30% testing subsets. The training-validation set served as the foundation for generating synthetic images, with each synthesis method used to produce a 10-fold expansion of the dataset. All images were standardized to a resolution of 512×512.

4.2 Experiment Setup and Evaluation Metrics

We evaluated the effectiveness of our multi-illumination synthetic images by training four advanced classification models to distinguish between healthy and diseased leaves, including MobileNetV2 [27], DenseNet121 [12], ResNet50 [10], and VGG16 [31]. All models were trained under identical conditions on an NVIDIA RTX 3090 GPU for 30 epochs, with a batch size of 16, a learning rate of 0.001, and a momentum of 0.9. Classification performance was evaluated using four standard metrics: recognition accuracy, precision, recall, and F1 score.

4.3 Evaluation of Inverse Rendering and Relighting Results

Our method demonstrates the robustness of inverse rendering results. As shown in Fig. 2, the synthetic image generated with optimized material and illumination parameters is nearly indistinguishable from the real reference image. Table 1 provides quantitative evidence of this fidelity through standard image quality metrics (SSIM, PSNR, and MSE), showing consistently high scores across different categories. The qualitative results in Fig. 3 further validate our approach, where the scene is relit using multiple distinct HDR environment maps to simulate complex outdoor illumination scenarios, including direct sunlight, overcast skies, and other natural lighting conditions. These results indicate that the estimated leaf materials from the inverse rendering stage exhibit high fidelity and generalize well to novel lighting conditions, producing visually realistic renderings. The rendered leaf images preserve fine geometric and textural details and accurately capture the effects of varying illumination conditions.

Table 1. Quantitative comparison of image quality metrics across different categories

Categories	SSIM	PSNR	MSE
Healthy	0.9804	34.9075	0.0004
Mosaic	0.9598	31.7933	0.0008
Rust	0.9834	34.4767	0.0004
Scab	0.9836	35.0356	0.0003

4.4 Performance Evaluation of Classification Task

To more comprehensively validate the advantages of our approach, we compared it with several existing approaches. StyleGAN2-ADA [16] and FastGAN [21]

are GAN-based models that can be applied to few-shot image generation tasks. DreamBooth [26] and SVDiff [9] are diffusion-based fine-tuning methods that can acquire novel concepts from just 35 images, while maintaining diversity in the generated outputs under different lighting-related prompts.

Table 2 presents the classification performance comparison of four models on the original dataset and various synthesized datasets. The boldfaces show the best evaluation metric for each classification model. Using the original unenhanced dataset as the baseline, all image generation methods demonstrate significant performance improvements. Both StyleGAN2-ADA and FastGAN notably enhance classification accuracy, while diffusion-based methods DreamBooth and SVDiff show limited performance gains due to instability in structural consistency and quality control of generated images. In contrast, our proposed method achieves substantially greater advancements.

Table 2. Performance comparison of classification models with different methods

Model	Method	Accuracy(%)	Precision(%)	Recall(%)	F1 Score(%)
MobileNetV2	None	77.29	79.50	77.31	77.61
	StyleGan2-ADA	95.17	95.40	95.30	95.20
	FastGan	96.62	96.62	96.91	96.73
	DreamBooth	91.30	91.54	91.55	91.47
	SVDiff	86.96	87.82	86.97	87.21
	Ours	**97.10**	**97.09**	**97.37**	**97.21**
DenseNet121	None	81.64	82.55	82.52	82.50
	StyleGan2-ADA	94.69	95.02	95.11	95.04
	FastGan	94.20	94.63	94.69	94.61
	DreamBooth	89.37	89.38	89.51	89.17
	SVDiff	93.72	93.97	93.59	93.72
	Ours	**95.65**	**95.84**	**95.78**	**95.72**
ResNet50	None	70.53	71.78	72.67	71.44
	StyleGan2-ADA	93.72	93.91	93.98	93.79
	FastGan	94.69	94.80	95.02	94.89
	DreamBooth	79.71	80.35	80.91	80.59
	SVDiff	91.30	92.01	91.70	91.80
	Ours	**96.62**	**96.50**	**96.83**	**96.64**
VGG16	None	77.29	78.82	78.10	78.25
	StyleGan2-ADA	96.62	96.61	96.76	96.65
	FastGan	94.20	94.23	94.56	94.04
	DreamBooth	81.64	87.59	80.78	82.19
	SVDiff	90.82	90.76	91.45	90.88
	Ours	**98.07**	**98.10**	**98.16**	**98.11**

Taking VGG16 as an example, its test accuracy on the DreamBooth enhanced dataset reaches 81.64%, representing only a 4.35% improvement over the baseline. However, with our approach, the accuracy surges to 98.07%, marking a 20.78% increase from the baseline and outperforming all comparative methods. Similar trends emerge across other models: MobileNetV2 achieves 97.10% accuracy with our method, DenseNet121 reaches 95.65%, and ResNet50 shows remarkable improvement from 70.53% on the baseline dataset to 96.62%. Across all four classification models, our approach achieves better performance in all metrics. Fig. 4 illustrates the confusion matrices of VGG16 across different methods. The classification network trained on original data struggles to distinguish between Healthy and Scab disease categories, whereas our method effectively resolves this issue, with only 4 misclassified samples in the test set. More results can be found in the supplementary materials.

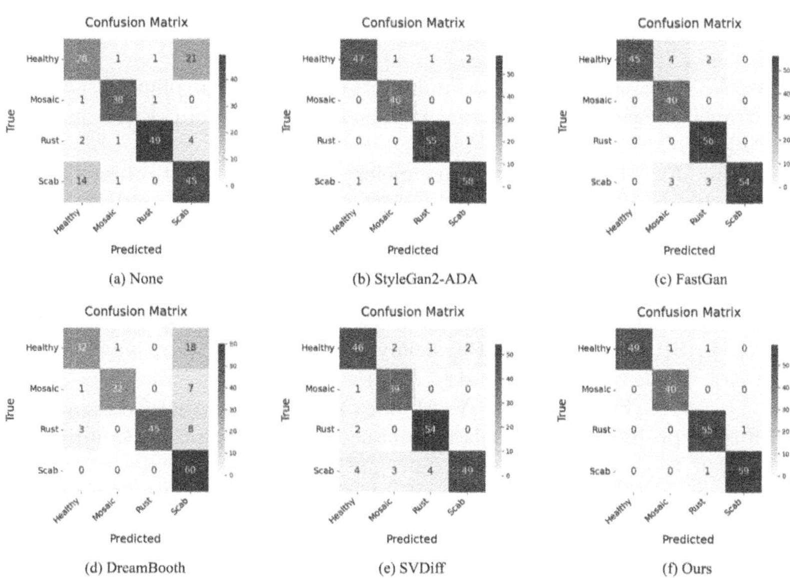

Fig. 4. Confusion matrices of the VGG16 classification model with different data augmentation methods.

Experimental results demonstrate that our proposed method enhances the illumination diversity of the leaves, enabling deep neural networks to better extract leaf features during training. The quantitative improvements across multiple architectures and metrics confirm the effectiveness of our approach in addressing critical challenges in real-world agricultural vision tasks.

5 Discussion and Conclusion

Collecting a large number of crop leaf images under diverse illumination conditions is a complex and costly task. Although contemporary generative models are capable of synthesizing high-fidelity image datasets, these models still rely on a substantial amount of agricultural data for training and face difficulties in generating leaf images under varying lighting conditions. In this study, we propose a simple yet efficient new method that learns the material parameters and lighting information of the leaves through inverse rendering, and then uses HDR environment maps for relighting to simulate the visual changes of the leaves under different illumination conditions. Our method demonstrates significant value in realistic smart agriculture tasks, particularly in the analysis of diseased leaves.

Acknowledgments. This work was supported in part by the Chongqing Natural Science Foundation (CSTB2024NSCQ-MSX1026), in part by the Fundamental Research Funds for the Central Universities (No. SWU-KT25012).

References

1. Abbas, A., Jain, S., Gour, M., Vankudothu, S.: Tomato plant disease detection using transfer learning with c-gan synthetic images. Comput. Electron. Agric. **187**, 106279 (2021)
2. Bernardini, F., Mittleman, J., Rushmeier, H., Silva, C., Taubin, G.: The ball-pivoting algorithm for surface reconstruction. IEEE Trans. Visual Comput. Graphics **5**(4), 349–359 (2002)
3. Boss, M., Braun, R., Jampani, V., Barron, J.T., Liu, C., Lensch, H.: Nerd: Neural reflectance decomposition from image collections. In: Proceedings of the IEEE/CVF International Conference on Computer Vision, pp. 12684–12694 (2021)
4. Burley, B., Studios, W.D.A.: Physically-based shading at disney. In: ACM Siggraph. vol. 2012, pp. 1–7 vol. 2012 (2012)
5. Chen, D., Qi, X., Zheng, Y., Lu, Y., Huang, Y., Li, Z.: Synthetic data augmentation by diffusion probabilistic models to enhance weed recognition. Comput. Electron. Agric. **216**, 108517 (2024)
6. Creswell, A., White, T., Dumoulin, V., Arulkumaran, K., Sengupta, B., Bharath, A.A.: Generative adversarial networks: an overview. IEEE Signal Process. Mag. **35**(1), 53–65 (2018)
7. Dhariwal, P., Nichol, A.: Diffusion models beat GANs on image synthesis. Adv. Neural. Inf. Process. Syst. **34**, 8780–8794 (2021)
8. Goodfellow, I., et al.: Generative adversarial nets. In: Advances in Neural Information Processing Systems, p. 27 (2014)
9. Han, L., Li, Y., Zhang, H., Milanfar, P., Metaxas, D., Yang, F.: SVDIFF: compact parameter space for diffusion fine-tuning. In: Proceedings of the IEEE/CVF International Conference on Computer Vision, pp. 7323–7334 (2023)
10. He, K., Zhang, X., Ren, S., Sun, J.: Deep residual learning for image recognition. In: Proceedings of the IEEE Conference on Computer Vision and Pattern Recognition, pp. 770–778 (2016)
11. Ho, J., Jain, A., Abbeel, P.: Denoising diffusion probabilistic models. Adv. Neural. Inf. Process. Syst. **33**, 6840–6851 (2020)
12. Huang, G., Liu, Z., Van Der Maaten, L., Weinberger, K.Q.: Densely connected convolutional networks. In: Proceedings of the IEEE Conference on Computer Vision and Pattern Recognition, pp. 4700–4708 (2017)

13. Ivanovska, M., Štruc, V., PerŠ, J.: Tomatodiff: On-plant tomato segmentation with denoising diffusion models. In: 2023 18th International Conference on Machine Vision and Applications (MVA), pp. 1–6 IEEE (2023)
14. Jakob, W., et al.: Mitsuba 3 renderer (2022). https://mitsuba-renderer.org
15. Kajiya, J.T.: The rendering equation. In: Proceedings of the 13th Annual Conference on Computer Graphics and Interactive Techniques, pp. 143–150 (1986)
16. Karras, T., Aittala, M., Hellsten, J., Laine, S., Lehtinen, J., Aila, T.: Training generative adversarial networks with limited data. Adv. Neural. Inf. Process. Syst. **33**, 12104–12114 (2020)
17. Li, Y., Guo, J., Qiu, H., Chen, F., Zhang, J.: Denoising diffusion probabilistic models and transfer learning for citrus disease diagnosis. Front. Plant Sci. **14**, 1267810 (2023)
18. Li, Z., Shafiei, M., Ramamoorthi, R., Sunkavalli, K., Chandraker, M.: Inverse rendering for complex indoor scenes: Shape, spatially-varying lighting and svbrdf from a single image. In: Proceedings of the IEEE/CVF Conference on Computer Vision and Pattern Recognition, pp. 2475–2484 (2020)
19. Li, Z., Xu, Z., Ramamoorthi, R., Sunkavalli, K., Chandraker, M.: Learning to reconstruct shape and spatially-varying reflectance from a single image. ACM Trans. Graph. (TOG) **37**(6), 1–11 (2018)
20. Liu, B., Tan, C., Li, S., He, J., Wang, H.: A data augmentation method based on generative adversarial networks for grape leaf disease identification. IEEE Access **8**, 102188–102198 (2020)
21. Liu, B., Zhu, Y., Song, K., Elgammal, A.: Towards faster and stabilized GAN training for high-fidelity few-shot image synthesis, p. iclr (2021)
22. Lu, Y., Chen, D., Olaniyi, E., Huang, Y.: Generative adversarial networks (GANs) for image augmentation in agriculture: a systematic review. Comput. Electron. Agric. **200**, 107208 (2022)
23. Moreno, H., Gómez, A., Altares-López, S., Ribeiro, A., Andújar, D.: Analysis of stable diffusion-derived fake weeds performance for training convolutional neural networks. Comput. Electron. Agric. **214**, 108324 (2023)
24. Nazki, H., Yoon, S., Fuentes, A., Park, D.S.: Unsupervised image translation using adversarial networks for improved plant disease recognition. Comput. Electron. Agric. **168**, 105117 (2020)
25. Rombach, R., Blattmann, A., Lorenz, D., Esser, P., Ommer, B.: High-resolution image synthesis with latent diffusion models. In: Proceedings of the IEEE/CVF Conference on Computer Vision and Pattern Recognition, pp. 10684–10695 (2022)
26. Ruiz, N., Li, Y., Jampani, V., Pritch, Y., Rubinstein, M., Aberman, K.: Dreambooth: fine tuning text-to-image diffusion models for subject-driven generation. In: Proceedings of the IEEE/CVF Conference on Computer Vision and Pattern Recognition, pp. 22500–22510 (2023)
27. Sandler, M., Howard, A., Zhu, M., Zhmoginov, A., Chen, L.C.: Mobilenetv 2: Inverted residuals and linear bottlenecks. In: Proceedings of the IEEE Conference on Computer Vision and Pattern Recognition, pp. 4510–4520 (2018)
28. Sang, S., Chandraker, M.: Single-shot neural relighting and SVBRDF estimation. In: Computer Vision-ECCV 2020: 16th European Conference, Glasgow, UK, August 23-28, 2020, Proceedings, Part XIX 16, pp. 85–101 Springer (2020)
29. Sarkar, C., Gupta, D., Gupta, U., Hazarika, B.B.: Leaf disease detection using machine learning and deep learning: Review and challenges. Appl. Soft Comput. **145**, 110534 (2023)

30. Sengupta, S., Kanazawa, A., Castillo, C.D., Jacobs, D.W.: SfSNet: learning shape, reflectance and illuminance of facesin the wild. In: Proceedings of the IEEE Conference on Computer Vision and Pattern Recognition, pp. 6296–6305 (2018)
31. Simonyan, K., Zisserman, A.: Very deep convolutional networks for large-scale image recognition, (2014). arXiv:1409.1556 arXiv preprint
32. Song, J., Meng, C., Ermon, S.: Denoising diffusion implicit models, (2020). arXiv:2010.02502 arXiv preprint
33. Yang, L., et al.: Depth anything v2. arXiv preprint arXiv:2406.09414 (2024)
34. Yang, L., et al.: Diffusion models: a comprehensive survey of methods and applications. ACM Comput. Surv. **56**(4), 1–39 (2023)
35. Yang, Q., Duan, S., Wang, L.: Efficient identification of apple leaf diseases in the wild using convolutional neural networks. Agronomy **12**(11) (2022). https://doi.org/10.3390/agronomy12112784, https://www.mdpi.com/2073-4395/12/11/2784
36. Yilma, G., Belay, S., Qin, Z., Gedamu, K., Ayalew, M.: Plant disease classification using two pathway encoder GAN data generation. In: 2020 17th International Computer Conference on Wavelet Active Media Technology and Information Processing (ICCWAMTIP), pp. 67–72. IEEE (2020)
37. Zhang, L., et al.: MMDGAN: a fusion data augmentation method for tomato-leaf disease identification. Appl. Soft Comput. **123**, 108969 (2022)
38. Zhang, Y., Sun, J., He, X., Fu, H., Jia, R., Zhou, X.: Modeling indirect illumination for inverse rendering. In: Proceedings of the IEEE/CVF Conference on Computer Vision and Pattern Recognition, pp. 18643–18652 (2022)

Enhancing Nvshu Recognition Based on Polarity-Aware Linear Attention and Learnable Local Salient Kernel

Guiren Zhou[1,2], Meng Sun[1,2], Yuxin Hong[1,2], Xiao Zhang[1,2,3], Jianlin Zhu[1,2](✉), and Bo Yang[1,2]

[1] School of Computer Science (School of Artificial Intelligence), South-Central Minzu University, Wuhan 430074, China

[2] Hubei Provincial Engineering Research Center for Intelligent Management of Manufacturing Enterprises, South-Central Minzu University, Wuhan 430074, China

Jianlin.Zhu@mail.scuec.edu.cn

[3] School of Computer Science and Technology, University of Science and Technology of China, Hefei 230026, China

Abstract. Nvshu is a unique Chinese writing system and a gender-specific script in the world. Its characters feature rich variations in stroke direction, numerous intersecting and decorative strokes, and specific writing rules. These characteristics often lead to inaccurate recognition and poor robustness when processed by traditional methods. To address these challenges, this paper proposes a new Nvshu recognition model, Polarity-aware Linear Attention and Learnable Local Salient Kernel (PALLS), which incorporates collaborative optimization of multiple modules in its network architecture. The PALLS model enhances feature extraction by introducing a Learnable Local Salient Kernel Module (LLSKM) after traditional convolution. This module performs multi-scale feature extraction, significantly improving the model's ability to capture the edges and texture details of Nvshu strokes. Additionally, the model replaces traditional linear attention with a Polarity-aware Linear Attention (PLAttention) module. By decomposing and interactively modeling positive and negative directional features, this module enhances the model's discriminative power in identifying stroke directions. Furthermore, a Multi-scale Feature Fusion Module (MSFFM) is constructed to integrate semantic information from different levels, enhancing the model's adaptability to diverse samples. Experiments prove that the PALLS model achieves a recognition accuracy of 92.2% on a self-built Nvshu dataset, representing a significant improvement of 4.6% to 6.8% over baseline models. This enhanced precision and robustness fill the gap in deep learning-based research on Nvshu recognition and provide crucial technical support for the preservation and dissemination of Nvshu culture.

Keywords: Nvshu Recognition · Polarity-Aware · Local Salient Kernel · Multi-Scale Fusion · Channel Attention

P. Li et al. (Eds.): CGI 2025, LNCS 16508, pp. 237–248, 2026.
https://doi.org/10.1007/978-3-032-22264-0_19

1 Introduction

The film *Snow Flower and the Secret Fan*, adapted from Lisa See's novel, depicts the bond between two women, Lily and Snow Flower, through Nvshu. Set in Jiangyong County, Hunan, China, Nvshu is the world's sole female script [1], reflecting millennia of women's thoughts and a distinctive Eastern aesthetic [2]. It features a diamond shape with a left-low and right-high structure; its strokes are thin, smooth arcs-pointed at the ends and thicker in the middle-giving it a symbolic appearance [3].

As a precious intangible cultural heritage, Nvshu faces transmission challenges due to modern civilization, making its preservation essential [4]. Accurate recognition and display of Nvshu characters can introduce this unique culture to broader audiences, fostering cultural exchange and understanding.

Traditional Nvshu recognition methods encompass data preprocessing, feature extraction, matching, and classification [5]. However, these approaches have shortcomings in capturing stroke direction, representing local details, and handling fuzzy samples. Existing deep learning techniques also struggle to adapt to Nvshu's complex structure and diversity.

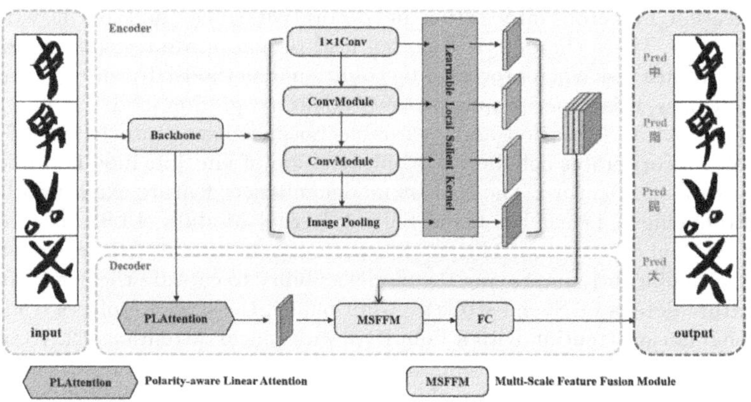

Fig. 1. PALLS Model Architecture. Arrows indicate key data flows between components.

As shown in Fig. 1, to address these limitations, this paper introduces a Nvshu recognition method leveraging polarity-aware linear attention [6] and local salient kernels [7]. This approach enhances recognition accuracy by modeling stroke direction features, dynamically emphasizing local details, and integrating multi-scale semantic information. The proposed PALLS model extracts features using a local salient kernel module, models features through polarity-aware linear attention, and fuses information via a multi-scale feature fusion module.

The main contributions of this paper include:

1) Creating the first dataset for Nvshu character recognition with 2,000 annotated samples across 200 categories. It covers normal images, blurred/degraded samples, and decorative strokes.
2) Proposing the PLAttention and LLSKM modules to address the insensitivity of traditional methods to stroke directions and local details.
3) Conducting extensive experiments on the self-built Nvshu dataset. Results show the PALLS model achieves 92.2% accuracy, a 4.6%–6.8% improvement over baseline models.

2 Related Work

Optical Character Recognition (OCR), a key pattern recognition method, has advanced significantly over three decades and is widely applied. Text recognition methods can be categorized into traditional and deep learning-based approaches. Traditional methods rely on manual feature extraction and shallow models. While effective in simple scenarios, they struggle with complex strokes and diverse writing styles. For example, template matching methods compare input text with predefined templates pixel by pixel but are highly sensitive to variations in stroke intersections and writing styles.

In recent years, CNNs have advanced text recognition, especially in complex backgrounds and diverse fonts. ResNet tackles the vanishing gradient problem via residual learning, boosting model performance. YOLO [8], with its end-to-end framework and efficiency, is great for real-time text recognition. Transformers, successful in natural language processing, have also been applied to image recognition. Dosovitskiy et al. introduced ViT [9], and Li Minghao et al. proposed the TrOCR [10] encoder-decoder model. Researchers have combined CNNs and Transformers for feature extraction [11]. These methods have worked well in text recognition.

In China, minority scholars have used computer tech to protect their languages. Research has moved from traditional to deep learning methods. Huang et al. used KPCA and wavelet transform for Tibetan features. Chen et al. expanded CNN models for ancient Yi script recognition [12]. Wang et al. used attention-based vectors in a Bi-LSTM-CRF network for Uyghur entity recognition, hitting a 90.13% F-measure [13]. Tang used Faster R-CNN with different backbone networks for Shui Manuscripts feature extraction, achieving 87.8% average accuracy [14]. Cai proposed a Tibetan character recognition method based on RCNN, attaining 91.43% average accuracy on a single Tibetan character test dataset [15].

3 PALLS Model

The PALLS model proposed in this paper is based on an encoder-decoder structure, integrating the PLAttention module and the LLSKM module to address the challenges in Nvshu recognition. The network architecture is divided into two parts: the Encoder and the Decoder. The Encoder uses the Residual Network (ResNet) as its backbone. In the feature decomposition part, we combine traditional fixed convolutional kernels with the Learnable Local Salient Kernel Module (LLSKM). This allows the model to dynamically adjust convolutional kernel weights, enhancing its ability to capture local details and edge information of Nvshu characters.

The Decoder part employs the PLAttention module instead of the traditional attention mechanism. By decomposing and interactively modeling the positive and negative direction features, it significantly strengthens the discriminative power of stroke direction. Meanwhile, a Multi-Scale Feature Fusion Module (MSFFM) is constructed in the Decoder to integrate semantic information from different levels, improving the model's adaptability to complex samples.

3.1 Polarity-Aware Linear Attention Model

Traditional attention mechanisms struggle to capture the direction of strokes and global features in Nvshu characters due to their unique characteristics and the ignoring of interactions between positive and negative directional features. The Polarity-aware Linear Attention (PLAttention) module proposed in this paper explicitly models these interactions and combines learnable dynamic weights to enhance the model's ability to discern stroke directionality and local details in Nvshu characters, as shown in Fig. 2.

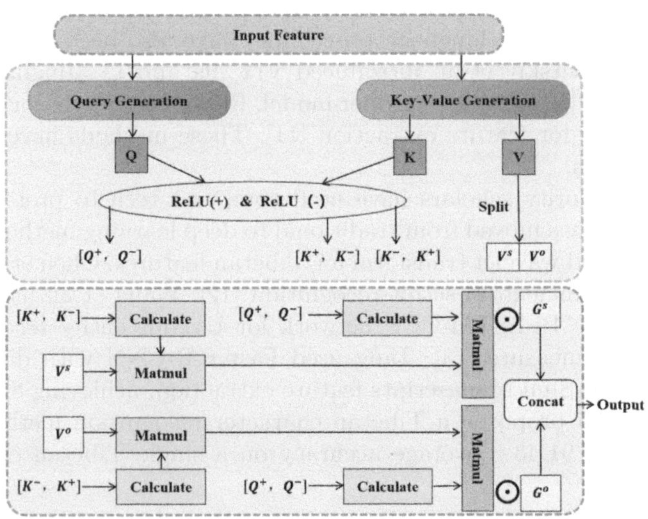

Fig. 2. Polarity-aware Linear Attention Structure with Decomposed Key-Query-Value.

The core design of PLAttention includes the following steps:

Step 1: Positive and Negative Directional Feature Decomposition. Nvshu characters have diverse stroke directions, often involving intersections of positive and negative directions. This module decomposes query and key vectors into positive and negative components to independently model their interactions, enhancing the capture of complex stroke directionality. The decomposition is as follows:

$$\mathbf{X}^{\pm} = \begin{cases} \max(\mathbf{X}, 0), & \text{for } \mathbf{X}^{+} \\ -\min(\mathbf{X}, 0), & \text{for } \mathbf{X}^{-} \end{cases} \quad \text{where } \mathbf{X} \in \{\mathbf{Q}, \mathbf{K}\} \tag{1}$$

Step 2: Adaptive Nonlinear Scaling. To address the varying visual importance of decorative strokes in Nvshu characters, a channel-wise learnable power function is introduced for nonlinear feature scaling. This allows the model to adaptively enhance strong response channels and suppress noise areas. The scaling is performed as:

$$\mathbf{F}_{\text{scaled}} = \mathbf{F}^{\gamma} \tag{2}$$

Step 3: Homogeneous and Heterogeneous Interaction Modeling. The value vector is split into positive and negative flows to capture similarities in the same direction and contrasts in opposite directions. Learnable matrices $\mathbf{G}^s$ and $\mathbf{G}^o$ dynamically balance these interactions:

$$O^{\varsigma} = \frac{\phi(\mathbf{Q}^{\varsigma})[\phi(\mathbf{K}^{\varsigma})^{\top}\mathbf{V}^{\varsigma}]}{\Sigma\phi(\mathbf{K}^{\varsigma})} \odot \mathbf{G}^{\varsigma}, \quad \varsigma \in \{s, o\} \tag{3}$$

Step 4: Local Enhancement and Residual Connection. To address low signal-to-noise ratio features in Nvshu stroke intersections, depthwise separable convolution is used for local enhancement, improving edge continuity and suppressing background noise. The final output is fused with original and attention features via a residual connection.

Through positive-negative decomposition and interaction modeling, the module reduces misrecognition in intersecting areas, enhances stroke directionality, and preserves decorative details. The polarity-aware coefficient matrix dynamically adjusts to suppress noise from irregular writing.

3.2 Learnable Local Salient Kernel

To address challenges like intersecting strokes and blurred edges in Nvshu characters, this paper introduces the Learnable Local Salient Kernel Module (LLSKM), which merges convolutional neural networks with attention mechanisms. This module integrates traditional saliency models into neural networks, enhancing the capture of Nvshu stroke features and strengthening stroke edges and texture details using channel attention. The core formula of the learnable kernel in the LLSKM module is as follows:

$$\mathbf{F}_{\text{out}} = \mathbf{W}_g * \mathbf{F}_{\text{in}} + \mathbf{W}_c * \mathbf{F}_{\text{in}} + \mathbf{W}_a \odot (\mathbf{W}_l * \mathbf{F}_{\text{in}}) \tag{4}$$

Here, $\mathbf{W}_g * \mathbf{F}_{\text{in}}$ captures overall features after background suppression, $\mathbf{W}_c * \mathbf{F}_{\text{in}}$ retains the original feature response, $\mathbf{W}_l * \mathbf{F}_{\text{in}}$ focuses on local salient regions, and $\mathbf{W}_a$ is the dynamic weight coefficient generated by channel attention.

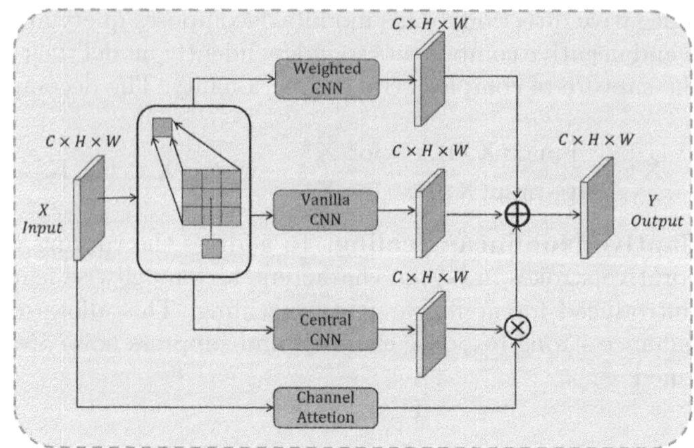

Fig. 3. LLSKM architecture: Standard convolution, center-weighted convolution, and attention-weighted convolution. Channel attention generates adaptive weights $\alpha \in [0, 1]$.

The basic structure of the LLSKM model is shown in Fig. 3. The LLSKM integrates three CNN components: Vanilla CNN for basic feature extraction, Central CNN for enhancing central region responses, and Weighted CNN for adaptive enhancement via channel attention. The channel attention mechanism dynamically adjusts convolution kernel weights by generating a channel descriptor through global average pooling and producing attention coefficients via a multilayer perceptron. These coefficients scale the convolution kernel weights to enhance important features and suppress noise. This design effectively boosts the model's ability to recognize complex and degraded Nvshu characters.

3.3 Multi-scale Feature Fusion

To address Nvshu characters with multi-scale stroke details and degraded samples, this paper employs a multi-scale feature fusion technique. This technique integrates high-resolution features from shallow layers (layer1 and layer2) and high-level semantic features from deep layers (layer3 and layer4), achieving complementary enhancement of multi-scale semantic information and improving the model's robustness. Shallow feature maps capture local details but lack semantic information, while deep feature maps possess rich semantics but may lose small stroke details. By fusing features across layers, the model balances local precision and global discriminative power, restoring stroke edges and suppressing background noise in blurred or damaged samples.

The implementation involves 1×1 convolution operations to unify the channel number of features from each network stage to 256. A nearest-neighbor upsampling and layer-by-layer residual addition strategy progressively injects high-level semantics into shallow features. This enhances the semantic expression of shallow features and makes the fused feature suitable for classification tasks.

3.4 Training Strategy

This paper employs a three-tier progressive optimization architecture for model training, combining a multi-task loss function and a dynamic learning rate strategy to enhance model robustness. The loss function is composed of cross-entropy loss ($\mathcal{L}_{\text{CE}}$) and direction consistency constraint loss ($\mathcal{L}_{\text{DC}}$), defined as:

$$\mathcal{L}_{\text{total}} = \mathcal{L}_{\text{CE}} + \lambda \mathcal{L}_{\text{DC}} \tag{5}$$

where $\mathcal{L}_{\text{CE}}$ measures the difference between predicted classes and true labels, and $\mathcal{L}_{\text{DC}}$ enforces stroke direction coherence using the mean squared error (MSE) of positive and negative feature maps:

$$\mathcal{L}_{\text{DC}} = \frac{1}{2}\left(\|\mathbf{F}^{+} - \mathbf{F}^{-}\|^{2}\right) \tag{6}$$

Here, $\mathbf{F}^{+}$ and $\mathbf{F}^{-}$ are the positive and negative direction feature maps from the polarity-aware module, and λ is the balancing weight set to 1.0 and 0.5 in experiments. This strategy enhances stroke direction consistency while ensuring classification accuracy.

4 Experiments

The experiments were conducted using the PyTorch 2.0 framework, CUDA 11.8, CUDNN 8.9, Ubuntu 20.04, and an RTX 4060 GPU. The Adam optimizer was used with an initial learning rate of 0.0001, and a cosine annealing strategy dynamically adjusted the learning rate. The weight decay coefficient was set to 0.01 to prevent overfitting. Input images were resized to 64×64 and normalized. Automatic mixed precision training was implemented to reduce GPU memory usage and increase training speed.

4.1 Dataset

To verify the PALLS model's effectiveness in Nvshu recognition, a self-built dataset with 2000 annotated samples across 200 categories was constructed. The dataset was divided into training (1600 images), validation (200 images), and testing (200 images) sets in an 8:1:1 ratio. Data augmentation strategies such as random rotation, horizontal flipping, and Gaussian noise injection were used to enhance model robustness. The dataset distribution is shown in Table 1.

Table 1. Distribution of data sets

Category	Training Set	Validation Set	Test Set
Normal Samples	960	120	120
Blurred Samples	640	80	80

4.2 Experimental Results

To ensure fairness and comparability, all baseline models used the same data augmentation and training framework, with identical input image format and size. The proposed PALLS model excelled in Nvshu character recognition, achieving a test accuracy of 92.2%, significantly outperforming other models. The results are detailed in Table 2.

YOLOv11-cls and YOLOv12-cls offer fast recognition but show lower accuracy with stroke adhesion and decorative elements. ResNet50 performs well in general image classification but lacks the detail capture needed for Nvshu recognition. ViT-Base improves accuracy with its long-range dependency modeling but lacks directional feature modeling, leading to shortcomings in complex stroke directions. In contrast, PALLS enhances stroke direction and local detail recognition through Polarity-aware Linear Attention, showing excellent performance in challenging stroke areas and high consistency with ground-truth images (Fig, 4).

Table 2. Comparison of different methods of Nvshu Recognition

Method	Accuracy↑	F1-Score↑	Blurred Sample Accuracy↑
YOLOv11-cls	85.4%	0.83	78.1
YOLOv12-cls	85.4%	0.83	79.1
ResNet50	87.6%	0.86	83.2
ViT-Base	89.3%	0.88	85.6
PALLS	92.2%	0.91	89.5

The PALLS model proves highly effective for Nvshu character recognition. Its Polarity-aware Linear Attention module enables accurate stroke direction capture, solving recognition issues in stroke adhesion and decorative elements. In "picking and pressing" stroke cross-hatching areas, PALLS shows remarkable accuracy, aligning well with ground-truth images. The Learnable Local Salient Kernel module further boosts local detail recognition, while the Multi-scale Feature Fusion Module enhances adaptability to complex samples. The Nvshu recognition results are shown in Fig. 5.

Figure 6 offers a comprehensive evaluation of PALLS' performance. Subfigure (a) shows the synchronized decrease of training and validation losses, indicating stable convergence and good generalization. Subfigure (b) highlights PALLS' consistent accuracy improvement over the baseline model across all training stages, confirming the effectiveness of our architectural innovations.

4.3 Ablation Analysis

To verify the effectiveness of the PALLS model, ablation experiments were conducted with different model configurations to analyze the impact of each module on performance.

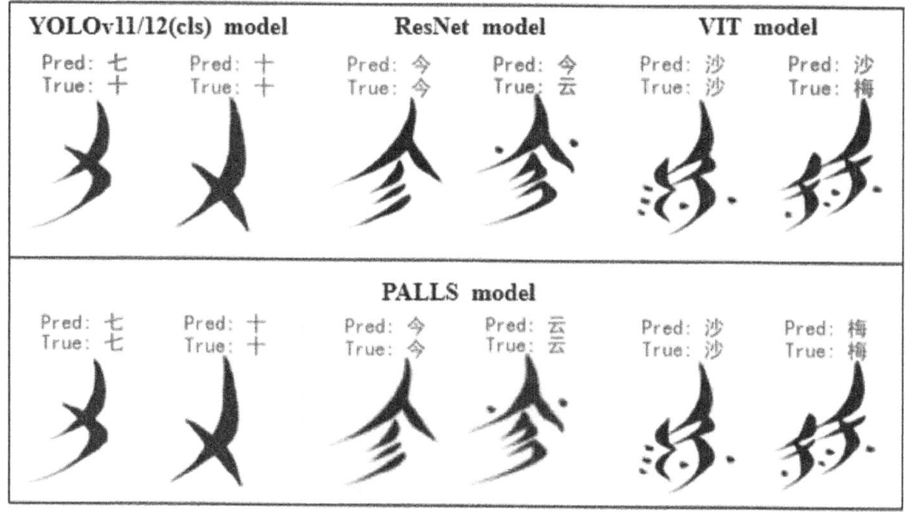

Fig. 4. Comparison of Nvshu character recognition performance between baseline models (top) and the proposed PALLS method (bottom). PALLS achieves excellent recognition accuracy, correctly identifying different strokes.

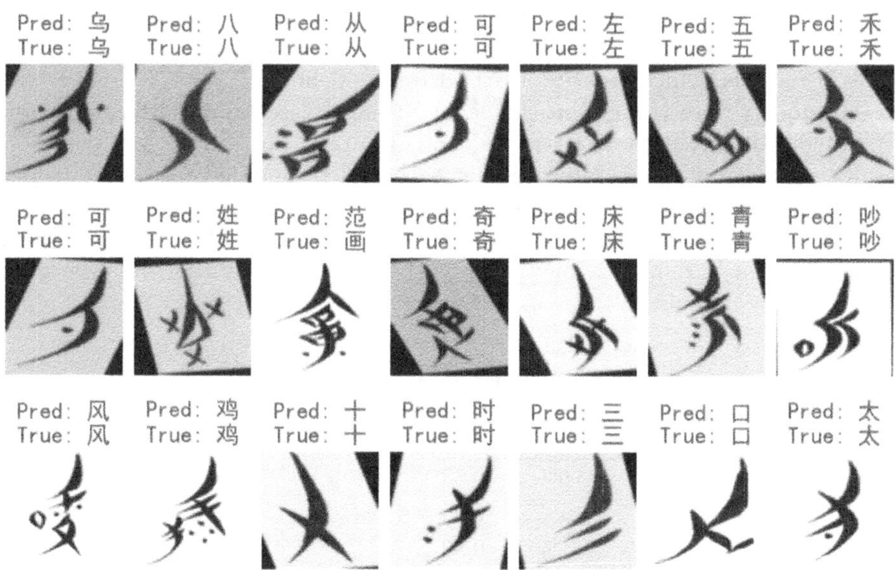

Fig. 5. Nvshu recognition results.

Variant A retains only the basic network architecture and uses conventional attention mechanisms instead of the proposed PLAttention module. Variant B

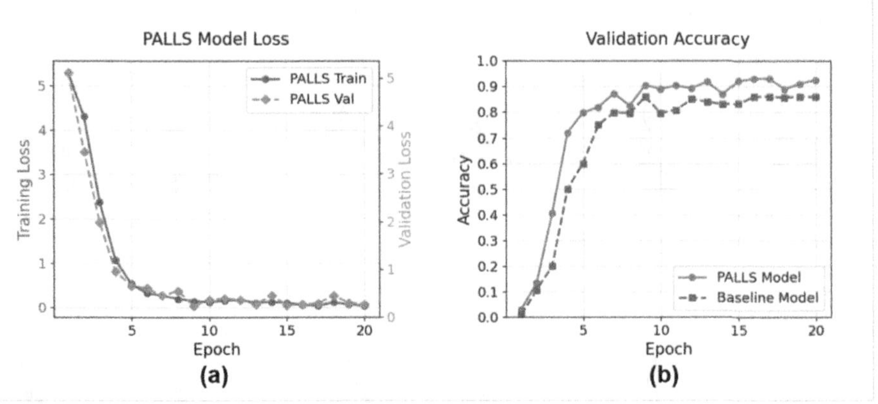

Fig. 6. Performance comparison between PALLS and baseline models: (a) Training and validation loss curves of the PALLS model showing convergence behavior, (b) Validation accuracy comparison demonstrating the performance gap.

incorporates the LLSKM module into Variant A while keeping the standard attention mechanisms. Variant C adds the polarity-aware PLAttention module to the backbone but excludes the LLSKM component. Variant D integrates both the PLAttention module, designed for directional feature learning, and the LLSKM module, which focuses on structural modeling.

All models were trained on the same Nvshu dataset, and performance was evaluated using Accuracy, F1-Score, and accuracy on blurred samples. The results, shown in Table 3, indicate that each added module contributes to performance improvement. The PLAttention module enhances stroke direction discrimination, while the LLSKM module improves local detail recognition. Their combination in Variant D achieves the best results, highlighting the synergistic effect of these modules.

Table 3. Ablation Analysis Results

Method	Accuracy↑	F1-Score↑	Blurred Sample Accuracy↑
Variant A	85.9%	0.83	78.1
Variant B	87.1%	0.85	81.2
Variant C	89.7%	0.88	85.4
Variant D(PALLS)	92.2%	0.91	89.5

Figure 7 illustrates the ablation study results for four model configurations. Only the complete architecture (Variant D) achieves optimal recognition performance, confirming the effectiveness of both modules.

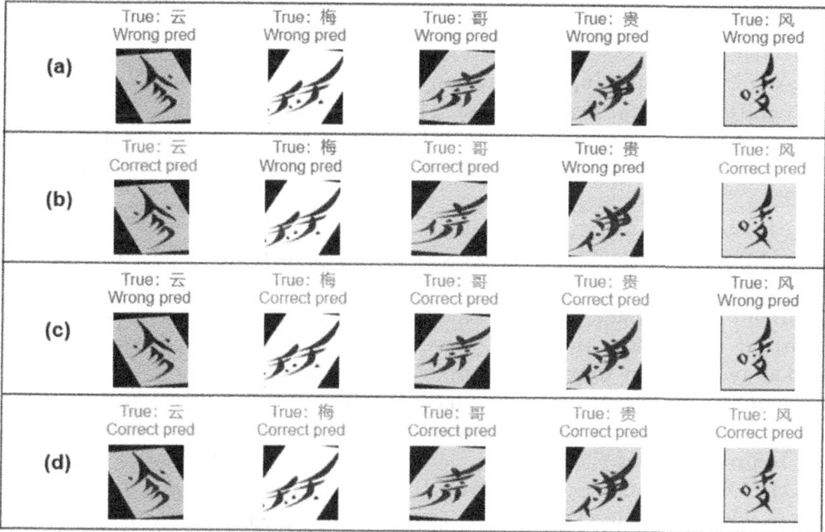

Fig. 7. Ablation study results: (a–d) Variants A–D. Our proposed method (D) stands as the sole architecture delivering excellent recognition accuracy.

5 Conclusion

The proposed PALLS model has significantly improved Nvshu character recognition accuracy to 92.2%, surpassing existing methods by 4.6% to 6.8%. Ablation experiments confirm the effectiveness of each module, and error analysis provides direction for future optimization. This study demonstrates the feasibility of the method in handling complex Nvshu recognition tasks and offers technical support for preserving and disseminating Nvshu cultural heritage.

Acknowledgments. I would like to acknowledge and thank Sun Meng and Zhang Haobo for their support in data collection. I'm also grateful to Zhu Jianlin, Yang Bo and Zhang Xiao for their guidance. This work was supported in part by the Fundamental Research Funds for the Central Universities, South-Central Minzu University (Grant Numbers: CZQ25015, PTZ25002, XTZ24003).

References

1. Zhu, Z., Wang, J., Xie, Z., et al.: Protection and inheritance of Nü Shu in the information age. Microcomput. Appl. **30**(23), 94–97+100 (2011)
2. Bai, P.: Jiang Yong Nv Shu Cultural and Creative Product Design. University of South China (2023)
3. Xiang, M.: Font design based on morphological characteristics of Nvshu calligraphy and performance method research. Lanzhou University (2021)

4. Wang, L.: Based on the Nvshu design and its derivatives design research. Hebei University (2014)
5. Li, Y.: Design and Implementation of Online Handwritten Nüshu Characters Recognition System. South-Central Minzu University (2013)
6. Meng, W., Luo, Y., Li, X., et al.: PolaFormer: polarity-aware linear attention for vision transformers. In: International Conference on Learning Representations (2025)
7. Wu, F., Liu, A., Zhang, T., Zhang, L., Luo, J., Peng, Z.: Saliency at the helm: steering infrared small target detection with learnable kernels. In: IEEE Trans. Geosci. Remote Sens. **63**, 1–14 (2025). Art no. 5000514
8. Redmon, J., Divvala, S., Girshick, R., Farhadi, A.: You only look once: unified, real-time object detection. In: Proceedings of the IEEE Conference on Computer Vision and Pattern Recognition, pp. 779–788. (2016)
9. Dosovitskiy, A., Beyer, L., Kolesnikov, A., et al.: An image is worth 16x16 words: transformers for image recognition at scale. In: International Conference on Learning Representations (2021)
10. Li, M., Lv, T., Chen, J., et al.: TrOCR: transformer-based optical character recognition with pre-trained models. In: International Conference on Learning Representations (2021)
11. Fang, S., Xie, H., Wang, Y., et al.: Read like humans: autonomous, bidirectional and iterative language modeling for scene text recognition. In: 2021 I EEE/CVF Conference on Computer Vision and Pattern Recognition, Nashville, TN, USA, pp. 7094–7103 (2021)
12. Chen, S., Wang, X., Han, X., et al.: A deep learning-based recognition method for ancient Yi script. J. Zhejiang Univ. (Sci. Edn.) **46**(03), 4–12 (2019)
13. Wang, L., Ai, S.: Research on Uyghur named entity recognition based on deep neural networks. J. Chinese Inf. Process. **033**(003), 64–70 (2019)
14. Tang, M.: Handwritten Character Recognition of Ancient Shui Manuscripts Based on Deep Learning. Xiamen University (2022)
15. Cai, R.: Research on Detection and Recognition of Printed Tibetan Cursive Script. Qinghai Normal University (2024)

DAN: Dual-Attention Network for Occlusion-Robust 3D Hand Pose Estimation

Qi Zhang and Lunke Fei(✉)

School of Computer Science and Technology, Guangdong University of Technology, Guangzhou, China
yy1787017@163.com, flksxm@126.com

Abstract. Accurate 3D hand pose estimation from depth images remains challenging due to self-occlusion and complex joint dependencies. To address this, we propose a Dual Attention Network (DAN) that captures joint-discriminative features in a coarse-to-fine manner. First, using a ResNet backbone, we extract multi-scale features refined by spatial and channel attention modules to highlight joint-related regions. Then, a two-branch decoder regresses coarse 3D joint positions and depth offsets for refinement. Experiments on NYU and ICVL datasets show our method achieves competitive performance by focusing on informative regions and improving joint localization.

Keywords: Hand pose estimation · Hand depth images · Attention mechanism · Human-computer interaction

1 Introduction

3D hand pose estimation, which predicts 3D joint coordinates from RGB or depth images, is fundamental to applications like virtual reality, sign language recognition, and human-computer interaction [14,18]. Among input modalities, depth images stand out for their robustness to illumination changes and explicit spatial cues.

Depth-based methods generally fall into regression, detection, and hybrid categories. Regression approaches [16,33] directly predict joint positions, detection methods [13,23,29] estimate heatmaps or offsets, and hybrids [1,9,10] combine both strategies. Despite advances, challenges such as self-occlusion and high articulation variability persist, often causing accuracy degradation. Moreover, many existing solutions rely on computationally intensive models, hindering real-time deployment.

To overcome these issues, we propose DAN, a Dual-Attention Network that follows a coarse-to-fine pipeline. DAN first extracts multi-scale features using ResNet50, then refines these features via a dual-attention module that sequentially applies channel and spatial attention to emphasize joint-related information. Finally, a two-branch regression module performs global localization and

P. Li et al. (Eds.): CGI 2025, LNCS 16508, pp. 249–260, 2026.
https://doi.org/10.1007/978-3-032-22264-0_20

local depth refinement, adaptively fusing predictions for improved accuracy. Our framework is lightweight yet effective, balancing precision and efficiency.

The main contributions of this work are:

- A novel dual-attention module that enhances occlusion-aware hand features by combining channel-wise and spatial attention.
- A coarse-to-fine regression design that decouples global pose estimation from local refinement to improve joint localization.
- Extensive evaluation on public benchmarks demonstrating superior accuracy and robustness compared to state-of-the-art methods.

The rest of the paper is organized as follows: Sect. 2 reviews related work, Sect. 3 details our approach, Sect. 4 presents experimental results, and Sect. 5 concludes the paper.

2 Related Work

In this section, we briefly review prior works related to three key aspects of our method, including depth-based hand pose estimation, attention mechanisms, and coarse-to-fine regression strategies in 3D hand pose estimation.

2.1 Depth-Based 3D Hand Pose Estimation

Depth images offer pixel-wise spatial information, making them robust to lighting variations and background clutter [33]. Unlike RGB images, depth maps preserve geometric structure and are invariant to appearance changes, making them well-suited for 3D hand pose estimation [9,10,16]. While RGB-D methods [24] provide complementary cues, they often rely on expensive sensors. In this work, we focus on depth-only input and design a framework to fully exploit its geometric richness through hierarchical feature learning.

2.2 Attention Mechanisms in Hand Pose Estimation

Attention mechanisms help emphasize informative regions and suppress noise, which is vital for handling occlusions and ambiguities in hand pose estimation [2]. Prior works have introduced Transformer-based models [11], topology-aware attention [31], and graph-integrated attention [34], all demonstrating improved robustness. Inspired by these, we propose a dual-attention mechanism that sequentially applies channel and spatial attention to progressively enhance features in a lightweight manner.

2.3 Coarse-to-Fine Regression for 3D Hand Pose

Coarse-to-fine strategies enable accurate pose estimation by separating global structure modeling from fine joint refinement [8,20]. While cascaded or hierarchical methods [3,22,25] improve accuracy, they often involve complex pipelines. Our approach integrates coarse and fine predictions within a unified design: the coarse branch captures holistic features, the fine branch refines local details, and an adaptive fusion module combines them for precise joint localization.

3 Method

In this section, we first present the overall architecture of our proposed Dual-Attention Network(DAN), and then elaborate the main components of the DAN.

3.1 DAN Architecture

Our Dual-Attention Network (DAN) employs a three-stage pipeline for robust 3D hand pose estimation. As illustrated in Fig. 1, first, a ResNet50 backbone extracts multi-scale features (F_1, F_2, F_3) from the input depth image. These features are refined via a dual-attention mechanism(i.e. channel attention and spatial attention). The channel attention enhances discriminative patterns, while spatial attention focuses on joint regions. Finally, a coarse-to-fine regression module predicts initial 3D joint positions and refines them with local offsets, fused adaptively for the final pose.

3.2 Occlusion-Robust Feature Enhancement

To address the dual challenges of multi-scale feature integration and partial occlusion in 3D hand pose estimation, we propose an occlusion-robust feature enhancement sub-network that processes multi-scale features through sequential channel and spatial attention modules, as illustrated in Fig. 2.

Given the input pyramid $F_1 \in \mathbb{R}^{256\times32\times32}, F_2 \in \mathbb{R}^{256\times8\times8}, F_3 \in \mathbb{R}^{256\times16\times16}$ extracted from different ResNet50 layers, we first compress the spatial dimensions via global average pooling (GAP), producing channel-wise descriptors:

$$g_i = GAP(F_i) \in \mathbb{R}^{256\times1\times1}, \quad fori \in \{1,2,3\}, \tag{1}$$

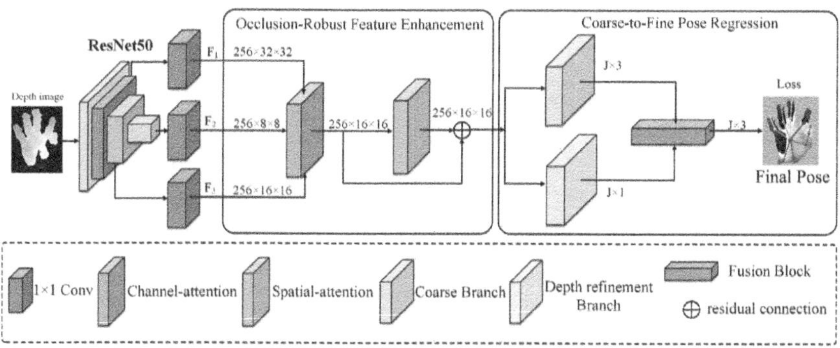

Fig. 1. The overall architecture of the proposed DAN for 3D hand pose estimation from hand depth images, which consists of a ResNet50-based shallow feature extraction backbone, occlusion-robust feature enhancement subnetwork and coarse-to-fine pose regression subnetwork.

Rather than processing each scale independently, we model cross-resolution relationships by concatenating the descriptors and generating resolution-specific weights:

$$g = [g_1; g_2; g_3] \in \mathbb{R}^{768\times1\times1}, \ W_c^i \qquad = \sigma(Conv1D(g)) \in \mathbb{R}^{256\times1\times1},$$

Each input feature is then enhanced via element-wise multiplication:

$$\tilde{F}_i = F_i \odot W_c^i \in \mathbb{R}^{256\times H_i\times W_i}, \tag{2}$$

This design enables the network to emphasize or suppress channels based on complementary information across scales, which is particularly beneficial when joint visibility varies due to perspective or occlusion.

To enable cross-resolution fusion, we align spatial dimensions: $\tilde{F}_1$ is downsampled to $\mathbb{R}^{256\times16\times16}$ via a 3×3 convolution (stride=2, padding=1), $\tilde{F}_2$ is upsampled via bilinear interpolation, and $\tilde{F}3$ retains its original size. The aligned features are then fused by:

$$F_{fused} = BN(ReLU(Down(\tilde{F}_1) + Up(\tilde{F}_2) + \tilde{F}_3)) \in \mathbb{R}^{256\times16\times16} \tag{3}$$

Building upon the fused features, we apply spatial attention to address occlusion. The module computes both max and average pooling maps across channels:

$$M_{max} = max_c(F_{fused}) \in \mathbb{R}^{1\times16\times16}, \ M_{avg} \qquad = avg_c(F_{fused}) \in \mathbb{R}^{1\times16\times16},$$

These maps capture different spatial cues. The max pooling highlights salient visible joints, while average pooling retains context from occluded regions. They are fused via a 7×7 convolution to yield the spatial attention mask:

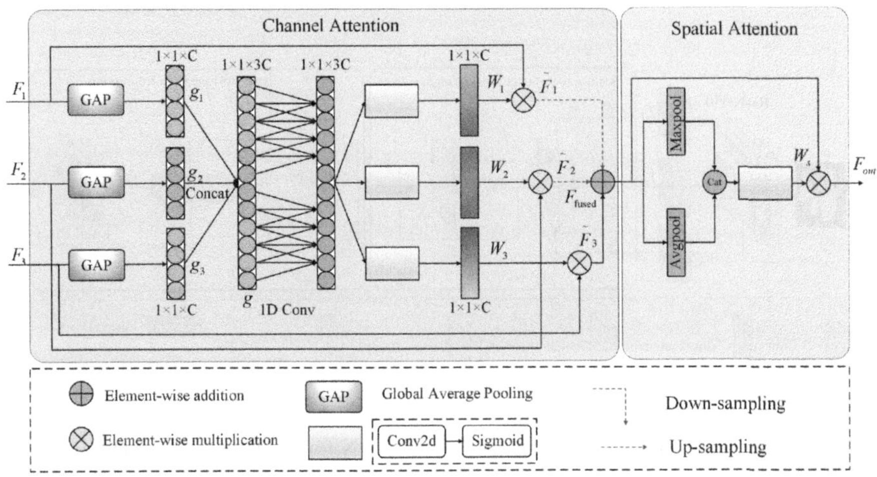

Fig. 2. Architecture of our occlusion-robust feature enhancement subnetwork with dual-attention mechanism, which combine the channel attention and spatial attention to explore the multi-scale features.

$$W_s = \sigma(Conv7 \times 7([M_{max}; M_{avg}])) \in \mathbb{R}^{1\times 16\times 16}, \tag{4}$$

Finally, we apply residual learning to combine both attention mechanisms:

$$F_{out} = (F_{fused} \otimes W_s) + F_{fused} \in \mathbb{R}^{256\times 16\times 16} \tag{5}$$

Our dual-attention design integrates channel attention for multi-scale fusion and spatial attention for occlusion robustness, enhanced with residual connections for stable optimization. This approach enables accurate 3D pose estimation even under complex articulations and occlusions.

3.3 Coarse-to-Fine Pose Regression

Our framework adopts a hierarchical dual-branch strategy for 3D hand pose estimation, as illustrated in Fig. 3. The coarse prediction branch processes occlusion-aware features through three sequential bottleneck blocks (ResBlocks), each composed of a 1×1 channel reduction (256→128), a 3×3 convolution, and a 1×1 channel restoration (128→256), with residual connections to preserve fine-grained joint features. The resulting features are passed through channel-wise fully connected layers implemented via 1×1 convolutions and global average pooling to yield the initial 3D joint positions $\mathbf{P}_{\text{coarse}} \in \mathbb{R}^{J\times 3}$.

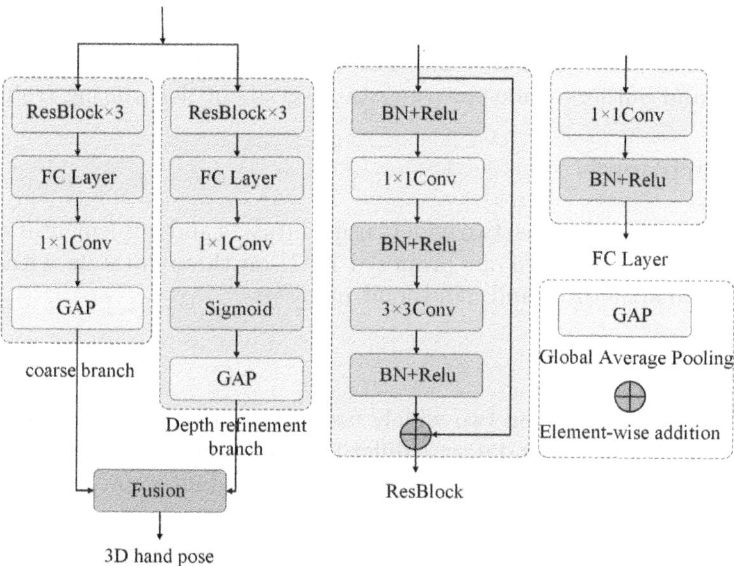

Fig. 3. Detailed architecture of our coarse-to-fine regression. Coarse branch predicts initial 3D coordinates via ResBlocks and depth refinement branch estimates normalized offsets, finally the coordinates are fused adaptively.

In parallel, the depth refinement branch employs a symmetric architecture for consistency, but predicts normalized depth offsets $\Delta\mathbf{z} \in [0,1]^J$ via sigmoid-activated 1×1 convolutions. These offsets refine the coarse depth predictions through learnable adaptive fusion:

$$\mathbf{z}^* = \mathbf{z}_{\text{coarse}} + \boldsymbol{\alpha} \odot \Delta\mathbf{z}, \tag{6}$$

where $\boldsymbol{\alpha} \in \mathbb{R}^J$ are trainable weights that adapt to occlusion severity—larger values indicate greater reliance on local corrections. The final 3D hand pose is then:

$$\mathbf{P}^* = [\mathbf{x}_{\text{coarse}}, \mathbf{y}_{\text{coarse}}, \mathbf{z}^*] \tag{7}$$

This dual-branch design combines global structure understanding with local refinement, enabling accurate pose prediction even under occlusion.

3.4 Loss Function

We train the network using a robust L1 loss between predicted joint positions $\mathbf{P}^*$ and ground truth $\mathbf{P}^{\text{gt}}$:

$$\mathcal{L}_{3\text{D}} = \frac{1}{J}\sum_{j=1}^{J} \left\| \mathbf{p}_j^* - \mathbf{p}_j^{\text{gt}} \right\|_1 \tag{8}$$

where $\mathbf{p}_j^* = (x_j^*, y_j^*, z_j^*)$ and $\mathbf{p}_j^{\text{gt}} = (x_j^{\text{gt}}, y_j^{\text{gt}}, z_j^{\text{gt}})$ denote the predicted and ground truth coordinates of the j-th joint. The L1 norm improves robustness against occlusions and outliers while ensuring stable gradient flow during training.

4 Experiments

In this section, we introduce two widely used datasets and implementation details of our model, and evaluate our proposed DAN on these datasets with different hand-skeleton structures and hand-joint numbers.

4.1 Datasets

We conduct experiments on two widely used hand pose estimation benchmarks, i.e. NYU and ICVL. These datasets differ in aspects such as hand-skeleton structures, joint annotations, and capture settings, providing a comprehensive evaluation platform.

The NYU dataset [28] includes 240,000 depth images captured using a Kinect sensor from multiple views. Following standard protocol [28], we use the frontal view, with 72,000 training samples from one subject and 8,000 testing samples from two subjects. Fourteen joints are selected for evaluation.

The ICVL dataset [26] consists of 331,600 images from 10 subjects. For fair comparison, we use the 22,000 unaugmented training images and 1,600 testing images. Each image contains 16 annotated joint positions.

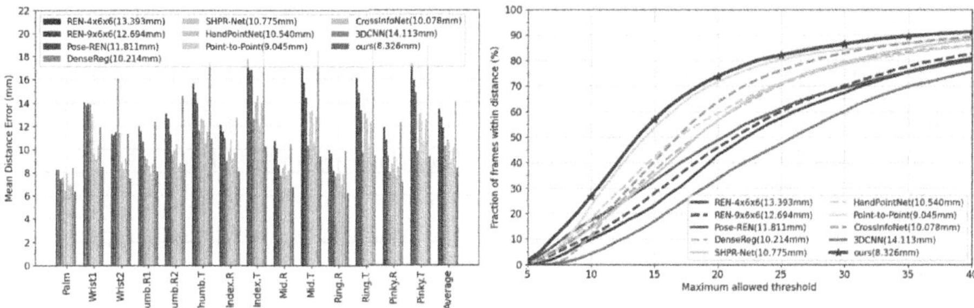

Fig. 4. The 3D hand pose estimation results of (a) the mean distance errors, and (b) the fraction of successful frames with different thresholds, obtained by different methods on the NYU database.

4.2 Implementation Details

Our method is implemented using the PyTorch framework and trained end-to-end with the Adam optimizer on an NVIDIA GeForce RTX 3080 GPU. To focus on relevant regions, each hand depth image is cropped to a fixed-size cube containing the hand and resized to 256×256 with normalized values in the range of [-1, 1].

Considering the differences between datasets, we set learning rates 0.001 for NYU and 0.0005 for ICVL empirically. The model is trained for 70 epochs with a batch size of 64 on both datasets.

4.3 3D Hand Pose Estimation Results on the NYU

We evaluate our method on the NYU dataset and compare it with recent state-of-the-art approaches. We use mean distance error (MDE) and fraction of successful frames (FSF) [31] as metrics. MDE measures the average Euclidean distance between predicted and ground-truth joints, while FSF reflects the percentage of frames with MDE below a threshold. We report both joint-wise and average MDEs for 14 joints.

As shown in Fig. 4, our method achieves lower MDEs for most joints, outperforming most baselines. By leveraging 2D cross-channel interactions and modeling joint dependencies, our approach enables accurate and structurally guided estimation. The slightly higher error on Thumb. R1 likely results from its broader region and joint-balanced loss design.

Figure 4(b) shows higher FSF under strict thresholds, indicating robustness to occlusion. Table 1 confirms our competitive average MDE, though TriHorn-Net, AWR, and Virtual View Selection achieve marginally better results due to richer depth modeling.

Table 1. The overall MDEs obtained by different methods on the NYU dataset

Method	HandPointNet [12]	Pose-REN [3]	TriHorn-Net [23]	V2V-PoseNet [1]
MDE	10.54	11.81	7.95	8.41
Method	MuTr [21]	A2J [33]	HandfoldingNet [6]	DRN [32]
MDE	8.71	8.61	8.58	8.40
Method	CrossInfoNet [9]	AWR [17]	HandDiff [7]	MH-Net [27]
MDE	10.08	7.75	7.38	6.039
Method	SHPR-Net [4]	VVS [5]	A2J Trans. [19]	DAN (Ours)
MDE	10.78	**6.40**	8.43	8.33

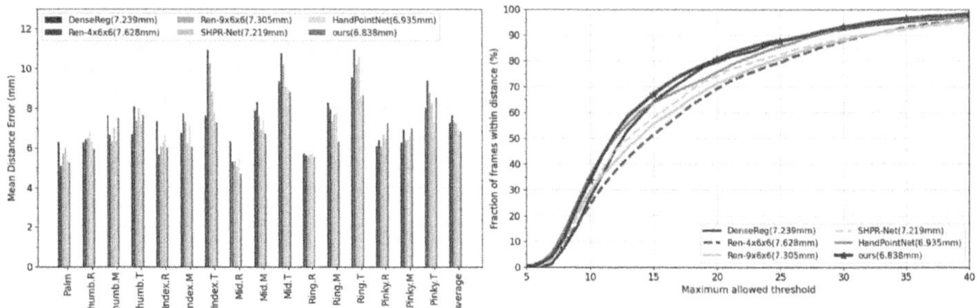

Fig. 5. The 3D hand pose estimation results of (a) the mean distance errors, and (b) the fraction of successful frames with different thresholds, achieved by different methods on the ICVL database.

4.4 3D Hand Pose Estimation Results on the ICVL

The ICVL dataset includes 16 annotated hand joints. We compare our method with five representative baselines, evaluating mean distance error (MDE) and fraction of successful frames (FSF) under various thresholds.

As shown in Fig. 5, our approach achieves lower MDE and higher FSF than most baselines, benefiting from effective joint learning of 2D spatial and 3D depth features in a coarse-to-fine manner. Although improvements over HandPointNet are modest, our method shows more consistent performance across thresholds.

Table 2 reports an average MDE of 6.838 mm, outperforming most existing methods, indicating that even with a simple, compact design, our model delivers competitive results on datasets with limited pose variability like ICVL.

4.5 Ablation Analysis

Our proposed network consists of the occlusion-robust feature enhancement subnetwork and the coarse-to-fine pose regression subnetwork. To validate their effectiveness, we conduct systematic ablation studies on the NYU dataset, with results shown in Tables 3 and 4.

Table 2. Comparison of MDEs (in mm) on the ICVL dataset

Method	DenseReg [29]	REN-4 x 6 x 6 [15]	REN-9 x 6 x 6 [30]
MDE (mm)	7.239	7.628	7.305
Method	SHPR-Net [4]	HandPointNet [12]	**Ours**
MDE	7.219	6.935	**6.838**

Table 3. Ablation study of attention modules in the Occlusion-Robust Feature Enhancement subnetwork

Spatial Attention	Channel Attention	MDE
×	√	8.604
√	×	8.420
√	√	**8.326**

Table 4. Impact of depth refinement in the Coarse-to-Fine Pose Regression

Depth Refinement Branch	MDE
×	8.576
√	**8.326**

Occlusion-Robust Feature Enhancement. As shown in Table 3, removing the spatial attention module increases the MDE by 0.278 (8.604 vs 8.326), demonstrating its crucial role in handling occluded joints through spatial reasoning. Conversely, ablating the channel attention results in a 0.094 MDE degradation (8.420 vs 8.326), indicating its importance for cross-scale feature integration. The full model achieves the best performance by synergizing both attention mechanisms.

Coarse-to-Fine Pose Regression. Table 4 reveals that removing the depth refinement branch degrades performance by 0.250 MDE (8.576 vs 8.326). This verifies our coarse branch provides robust initial estimates while the refinement branch recovers precise depth details, particularly for occluded joints where the initial z-coordinate predictions may be unreliable.

4.6 Visualization

Figure 6 presents representative 3D hand pose results on the NYU dataset. Our method accurately localizes joints even under self-occlusion, thanks to the dual-channel attention that highlights important spatial and channel features, and the dual-branch regression that progressively refines predictions.

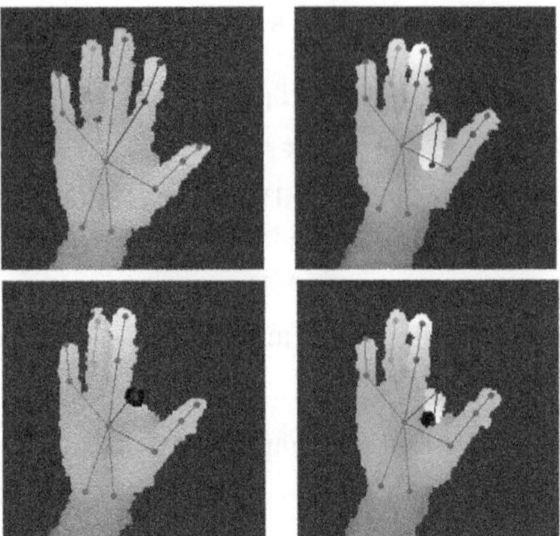

Fig. 6. The estimated 3D hand joint positions on the NYU samples with self-occlusions.

5 Conclusion

We propose DAN, a dual-attention guided coarse-to-fine 3D hand pose estimation network based on depth images. DAN employs a dual-attention module to sequentially enhance channel and spatial features, helping the network focus on key joints under occlusions and background clutter. A coarse-to-fine regression module combines global and local predictions to refine joint positions with improved accuracy and efficiency. Experiments show that DAN achieves competitive results with lower computational cost.

Although effective, DAN currently works on single frames. Future work includes extending it to video-based hand pose estimation using temporal modeling, and exploring its application to two-hand or hand-object interactions under complex occlusions.

References

1. Chang, J.Y., Moon, G., Lee, K.M.: V2V-PoseNet: voxel-to-voxel prediction network for accurate 3D hand and human pose estimation from a single depth map. In: Proceedings of the IEEE Conference on Computer Vision and Pattern Recognition (CVPR), pp. 5079–5088 (2018)
2. Chen, G., et al.: A survey of the four pillars for small object detection: multiscale representation, contextual information, super-resolution, and region proposal. IEEE Trans. Syst. Man Cybern. Syst. **52**(2), 936–953 (2022)
3. Chen, X., Wang, G., Guo, H., Zhang, C.: Pose guided structured region ensemble network for cascaded hand pose estimation. Neurocomputing **395**, 138–149 (2020)
4. Chen, X., Wang, G., Zhang, C., Kim, T.K., Ji, X.: SHPR-net: deep semantic hand pose regression from point clouds. IEEE Access **6**, 43425–43439 (2018)
5. Cheng, J., et al.: Efficient virtual view selection for 3D hand pose estimation. In: Proceedings of the Thirty-Sixth AAAI Conference on Artificial Intelligence, pp. 419–426 (2022)

6. Cheng, W., Park, J., Ko, J.: HandFoldingNet: a 3D hand pose estimation network using multiscale-feature guided folding of a 2D hand skeleton. In: Proceedings of the IEEE/CVF International Conference on Computer Vision (ICCV), pp. 11260–11269 (2021)
7. Cheng, W., Tang, H., Gool, L., Ko, J.: Handdiff: 3D hand pose estimation with diffusion on image-point cloud. In: Proceedings of the IEEE/CVF Conference on Computer Vision and Pattern Recognition (CVPR), pp. 2274–2284 (2024)
8. Doosti, B., Naha, S., Mirbagheri, M., Crandall, D.J.: HOPE-net: a graph-based model for hand-object pose estimation. In: Proceedings of the IEEE/CVF Conference on Computer Vision and Pattern Recognition (CVPR), pp. 6608–6617 (2020)
9. Du, K., Lin, X., Sun, Y., Ma, X.: CrossInfoNet: multi-task information sharing based hand pose estimation. In: Proceedings of the IEEE Conference on Computer Vision and Pattern Recognition (CVPR), pp. 9896–9905 (2019)
10. Fang, L., Liu, X., Liu, L., Xu, H., Kang, W.: JGR-P2O: joint graph reasoning based pixel-to-offset prediction network for 3D hand pose estimation from a single depth image. In: Proceedings of the European Conference on Computer Vision (ECCV), pp. 120–137 (2020)
11. Fu, Q., Liu, X., Xu, R., Niebles, J., Kitani, K.M.: Deformer: dynamic fusion transformer for robust hand pose estimation. In: Proceedings of the IEEE/CVF International Conference on Computer Vision (ICCV), pp. 23600–23611 (2023)
12. Ge, L., Cai, Y., Weng, J., Yuan, J.: Hand PointNet: 3D hand pose estimation using point sets. In: Proceedings of the IEEE Conference on Computer Vision and Pattern Recognition (CVPR), pp. 8417–8426 (2018)
13. Ge, L., Ren, Z., Yuan, J.: Point-to-point regression PointNet for 3D hand pose estimation. In: Proceedings of the European Conference on Computer Vision (ECCV), pp. 475–491 (2018)
14. Guleryuz, O.G., Kaeser-Chen, C.: Fast lifting for 3D hand pose estimation in AR/VR applications. In: Proceedings of IEEE International Conference on Image Processing (ICIP), pp. 106–110 (2018)
15. Guo, H., et al.: Region ensemble network: improving convolutional network for hand pose estimation. In: Proceedings of the IEEE International Conference on Image Processing (ICIP), pp. 4512–4516 (2017)
16. Huang, L., Tan, J., Liu, J., Yuan, J.: Hand-transformer: non-autoregressive structured modeling for 3D hand pose estimation. In: Proceedings of the European Conference on Computer Vision (ECCV), pp. 17–33 (2020)
17. Huang, W., Ren, P., Wang, J., Qi, Q., Sun, H.: AWR: adaptive weighting regression for 3D hand pose estimation. In: Proceedings of the AAAI Conference on Artificial Intelligence, pp. 11061–11068 (2020)
18. Hwang, C.L., Liao, G.H.: Real-time pose imitation by mid-size humanoid robot with servo-cradle-head RGB-D vision system. IEEE Trans. Syst. Man Cybern. Syst. **49**(1), 181–191 (2019)
19. Jiang, C., et al.: A2J-transformer: anchor-to-joint transformer network for 3D interacting hand pose estimation from a single RGB image. In: Proceedings of the IEEE Conference on Computer Vision and Pattern Recognition (CVPR), pp. 8846–8855 (2023)
20. Jiang, X., Tao, H., Hwang, J.N., Fang, Z.: A multiscale coarse-to-fine human pose estimation network with hard keypoint mining. IEEE Trans. Syst. Man Cybern. Syst. **54**(3), 1730–1741 (2024)
21. Kanis, J., et al.: MuTr: multi-stage transformer for hand pose estimation from full-scene depth image. Sensors, 5509 (2023)

22. Ren, P., et al.: Pose-guided hierarchical graph reasoning for 3-D hand pose estimation from a single depth image. IEEE Trans. Cybern., 315–328 (2023)
23. Rezaei, M., Rastgoo, R., Athitsos, V.: TriHorn-Net: a model for accurate depth-based 3D hand pose estimation. Expert Syst. Appl. **223**, 119922 (2023)
24. Sinha, A., Choi, C., Ramani, K.: DeepHand: robust hand pose estimation by completing a matrix imputed with deep features. In: Proceedings of the IEEE Conference on Computer Vision and Pattern Recognition (CVPR), pp. 4150–4158 (2016)
25. Sun, X., Wei, Y., Liang, S., Tang, X., Sun, J.: Cascaded hand pose regression. In: Proceedings of the IEEE Conference on Computer Vision and Pattern Recognition (CVPR). pp. 824–832 (2015)
26. Tang, D., Chang, H.J., Tejani, A., Kim, T.K.: latent regression forest: structured estimation of 3D articulated hand posture. In: Proceedings of the IEEE Conference on Computer Vision and Pattern Recognition (CVPR), pp. 3786–3793 (2014)
27. Tewolde, T., Manjotho, A., Niu, Z.: MH-net: multiheaded 3D hand pose estimation network with 3d anchorsets and improved multiscale vision transformer. IEEE Trans. Intell. Veh., 1–12 (2024)
28. Tompson, J., Stein, M., Lecun, Y., Perlin, K.: Real-time continuous pose recovery of human hands using convolutional networks. ACM Trans. Graph. **33**(5), 1–10 (2014)
29. Wan, C., Probst, T., Gool, L.V., Yao, A.: Dense 3D regression for hand pose estimation. In: Proceedings of the IEEE Conference on Computer Vision and Pattern Recognition (CVPR), pp. 5147–5156 (2018)
30. Wang, G., Chen, X., Guo, H., Zhang, C.: Region ensemble network: towards good practices for deep 3D hand pose estimation. J. Vis. Commun. Image Represent. **55**, 404–414 (2018)
31. Wang, Y., Chen, L., Li, J., Zhang, X.: HandGCNFormer: a novel topology-aware transformer network for 3D hand pose estimation. In: Proceedings of the IEEE/CVF Winter Conference on Applications of Computer Vision (WACV), pp. 5675–5684 (2023)
32. Xing, H., Yang, J., Xiao, Y.: Learning dynamic relationship between joints for 3D hand pose estimation from single depth map. J. Vis. Commun. Image Represent. **92**, 103803 (2023)
33. Xiong, F., et al.: A2J: anchor-to-joint regression network for 3D articulated pose estimation from a single depth image. In: Proceedings of the IEEE International Conference on Computer Vision (ICCV), pp. 793–802 (2019)
34. Zhao, W., Wang, W., Tian, Y.: GraFormer: graph-oriented transformer for 3D pose estimation. In: Proceedings of the IEEE/CVF Conference on Computer Vision and Pattern Recognition (CVPR), pp. 20438–20447 (2022)

Image Attention and Perception

Attention-Enhanced 3D Craniomaxillofacial Anatomical Landmark Detection Based on Projection

Junyi Liu[1], Yuyou Zhong[1], Peng Yu[1], Xi Fu[2], Ruilin Zhao[2], Feng Niu[2], Qiyuan Chen[3], Jian Zhang[4], and Junjun Pan[1(✉)]

[1] State Key Laboratory of Virtual Reality Technology and Systems, Beihang University, Beijing, China
{junyi.liu,junjun.pan}@email.placeholder

[2] The Craniofacial Center One, Plastic Surgery Hospital, Chinese Academy of Medical Sciences and Peking Union Medical College, Beijing, China

[3] The High School Affiliated Renmin University of China, Beijing, China

[4] National Centre for Computer Animation, Bournemouth University, Bournemouth, UK

Abstract. Craniomaxillofacial deformities can substantially disrupt the quality of life, and treatments for these conditions present considerable complexity and risk. Intelligent surgical planning systems hold the potential to address these challenges effectively, and one key aspect lies in the accurate detection of anatomical landmarks within the craniomaxillofacial region. However, in clinical applications, landmark detection based on 2D images does not adequately represent the structural details of the craniomaxillofacial region. Landmark detection utilizing 3D models is largely confined to CBCT datasets, which exhibits a deficiency in adaptability to more general modeling platforms. We propose an attention-enhanced method based on common 3D models for automatically detecting craniomaxillofacial anatomical landmarks. The approach relies on the dimensional reduction of a 3D craniomaxillofacial model achieved through multi-angle projections under multi-light conditions. To enhance the robustness of our method, an attention module is introduced to integrate detection results from projections under diverse lighting conditions. Our method has undergone evaluation using data from professional surgeons at the Chinese Academy of Medical Sciences and Peking Union Medical College. The average error in landmark localization on the 3D model is successfully constrained to approximately 2.51 mm. From experimental evaluations and the user study, both the qualitative and quantitative results consistently indicate that our techniques can accurately detect 3D craniomaxillofacial anatomical landmarks.

Keywords: 3D Craniomaxillofacial Model · Landmark Detection · Attention Module · Projection Method

P. Li et al. (Eds.): CGI 2025, LNCS 16508, pp. 263–275, 2026.
https://doi.org/10.1007/978-3-032-22264-0_21

1 Introduction

Craniomaxillofacial(CMF) deformities are common diseases involving both bone and overlying soft tissue, which can be effectively treated through surgery. However, craniomaxillofacial surgery faces substantial complexities and heightened surgical risks when addressing severe deformities. By providing comprehensive surgical design, surgical path planning helps surgeons enhance surgical precision [14] and becomes an effective measure to deal with complex craniomaxillofacial deformities. Moreover, the craniomaxillofacial orthopedic surgical pathways can be deconstructed into anatomical landmarks and the curves connecting these point. Therefore, the accurate detection of anatomical landmarks has become a key part of the craniomaxillofacial clinical workflow.

Table 1. Description of craniomaxillofacial anatomical landmarks [5].

Landmark	Description
N	**Nasion**: Midsagittal point at the junction of frontal and nasal bones at the nasofrontal suture.
Or	**Orbitale**: The most inferior point on the infraorbital rim.
ANS	**Anterior Nasal Spine**: The most anterior limit of the floor of the nose at the tip of the anterior nasal spine.
A	**A-Point**: The most concave point of the anterior maxilla.
B	**B-Point**: The most concave point on mandibular symphysis.
Go	**Gonion**: The point in the middle of the curvature at the left and right angles of the mandible.
Pg	**Pogonion**: The most anterior point along the curvature of the chin.
Me	**Menton**: The most inferior point along the curvature of the chin.

Nowadays, the accurate detection of anatomical landmarks still mainly relies on manual techniques. However, manual marking is not only time-consuming and labor-intensive but also highly dependent on the doctor's clinical experience and prone to errors [9]. In the past few years, many automatic landmark detection methods, including two-dimensional(2D) image detection [1,4] and three-dimensional(3D) model detection [3,7,15,17], have been proposed and applied. The methods based on 2D images have become the primary technical approaches for clinical applications due to their precision and robustness. Compared with conventional 2D images, 3D models provide a more accurate representation of complex 3D craniomaxillofacial anatomical structures [10]. Up to now, automated detection of anatomical landmarks within 3D models has fulfilled the clinical requirements in terms of precision. Various technologies based on 3D models can assist clinicians in making critical decisions preoperatively and help them achieve favorable results across various surgical stages [10].

However, landmark detection based on 3D models still faces the following problems: 1. Most existing methods for detecting 3D craniomaxillofacial anatomical landmarks rely on CBCT imaging, indicating a lack of detection techniques based on more common 3D models. 2. The huge data volume in 3D medical models impedes the efficiency of landmark detection processes. 3. Existing methods have not sufficiently utilized the unique morphological characteristics of various landmarks on the models.

In this paper, we introduce an effective methodology for the detection of certain critical anatomical landmarks on 3D craniomaxillofacial models. The annotated landmarks include 10 key points: N point, Or-left point, Or-right point, ANS point, A point, Go-left point, Go-right point, Me point, Pg point, and B point. These landmarks are detailed in Table 1. The main contributions of this article are summarized as follows:

- We propose an attention-enhanced automatic detection system that achieves the transition from high-precision detection of landmarks in 2D images to those on 3D models, thereby improving the precision of landmark detection within the generic 3D context.
- We devise the projection method to achieve dimensionality reduction on the 3D model, improving computational efficiency. Afterward, we introduce an attention module to integrate detection results derived from 2D images under disparate conditions, which can decrease the information loss associated with dimensionality reduction.
- Our proposed attention module considers the varied projections of each landmark under diverse lighting conditions. This module employs the morphological features of the landmarks to compute their definitive positions, improving the precision of landmark detection.

The performance of our method is evaluated on data from professional surgeons at the Chinese Academy of Medical Sciences and Peking Union Medical College. We achieve an average error constrained to approximately 2.51 mm, better than the baselines [7,11,12,17]. This proves that our method achieves promising results.

2 Methods

2.1 Overview

Figure 1 illustrates the overview of our method. Our method involves a multi-step process. Initially, we project the 3D skull model from various angles and

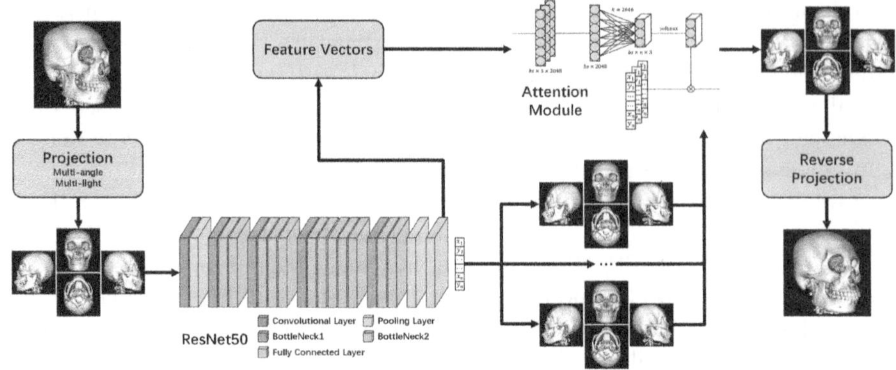

Fig. 1. Overview of our method.

under different lighting conditions to generate a series of 2D images. These 2D images are processed using a ResNet50 convolutional neural network [6] to compute the 2D coordinates of all landmarks. An attention module is designed to integrate detection results derived from 2D images under disparate conditions. These integrated 2D coordinates are then reversely projected to compute their corresponding 3D coordinates.

2.2 Projection

Owing to the high resolution of medical images, the resulting data volume for 3D models constructed from these images becomes considerably huge. According to the theory in the research of Berrone et al. [2], for a common class of artificial neural networks, the mean integrated squared error between the estimated network and a target function f can be estimated as follows:

$$E\|f - \hat{f}_{n,N}\|^2 \leq O\left(\frac{C_f^2}{n}\right) + O\Big(\frac{nd}{N}\log N\Big) \tag{1}$$

where n is the number of nodes, d is the input dimension of the function, N is the number of training observations, and C_f is the first absolute moment of the Fourier magnitude distribution of f.

According to Equation (1), the increase in network complexity and the expansion of data dimensions will degrade model accuracy under conditions of fixed dataset scale. Therefore, the direct training of neural networks employing 3D model data for anatomical landmark detection appears to be an enormous challenge, which not only affects computational efficiency but also detection precision. As a solution, we engage in a dimensionality reduction process aimed at transforming the complex 3D data into a 2D format. It is important to acknowledge that this transformation will result in the loss of some of the 3D features present in the original data. Although Su et al. [13] proposed the multi-view convolutional neural network to analyze 3D models through two-dimensional images, they focus on classification tasks rather than regression tasks. Therefore, there exists a need to devise strategies that enable the preservation of a maximal portion of the original 3D features within the 2D representation.

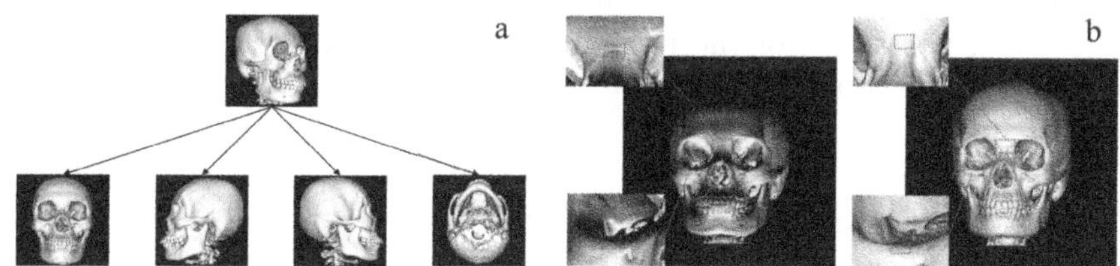

Fig. 2. (a) Projection through different angles. (b) Projection under different lighting conditions.

Taking advantage of planar projection [8] through multi-angle projection under multi-light conditions, we aim to preserve as many 3D features as possible in the 2D data, thereby enabling the neural network to operate with higher accuracy and precision. The critical aspect of this approach lies in its capacity to reconstitute the essential 3D features of the skull model through reference to the model's multi-angle projections acquired under multi-light conditions.

Multi-angle projection involves selecting appropriate projection directions to generate comprehensive 2D images of the skull model. The objective is to ensure that these 2D images contain all relevant anatomical landmarks. In this paper, our chosen multi-angle projection strategy entails projecting the 3D skull model along several key axes. Specifically, these axes include the positive x-axis, negative x-axis, positive y-axis, and positive z-axis directions. As shown in Fig. 2 (a), each of these projections captures different sides of the skull model, including its frontal view, left profile view, right profile view, and basilar view. Notably, our selection of projection directions omits projections in the extended negative y-axis direction and negative z-axis direction, as the anatomical landmarks of interest in this study reside in regions other than the posterior and superior sides of the skull. This simplification aligns with the focus of our research and the specific anatomical regions under examination.

Multi-light condition refers to the effect of lighting conditions on the projection. By changing the position of the point light source, the original 3D features are displayed in the 2D images. When a point light source is introduced, it casts shadows on the surface of the skull model. These shadows serve to demonstrate the potential geometric features of the 3D models within the resulting 2D images, as shown in Fig. 2 (b). In our approach, we conduct projections under three distinct lighting conditions for each selected projection direction. This method results in the generation of a total of 12 projected images, each presenting the skull model under different lighting conditions. The marked variations in these projections under different lighting conditions are visually shown in Fig. 2 (b), providing a clear representation of the influence of lighting on the generated images. Different lighting conditions can highlight the 3D geometric structure of different landmarks, thus enabling more precise detection of them.

The projection process is as follows: for each pixel s on the projection plane, a ray d is made perpendicular to the projection plane starting from point s and intersecting with the 3D skull model. The first intersection point is the corresponding point $p(s)$ of the projected point, and its corresponding normal vector $n(p(s))$ is computed. In the presence of light q, the gray value of point s can be calculated as:

$$Gray\_value(s) = \max\left(\frac{n(p(s)) \cdot (q - p(s))}{||q - p(s)||}, 0\right) \tag{2}$$

2.3 Attention Module

As shown in Fig. 3 (a), we employ ResNet50 to perform detection and localization of the landmarks visible within that particular orientation for each projection direction. Subsequently, we extract the 2048-dimensional feature vectors computed from the fully connected layer and serve these vectors as input for the subsequent attention module. The computation of the loss function is executed based on the actual 2D coordinates of all landmarks. The formulation of the loss function is expressed as follows:

$$Loss = \sum_{k=1}^{M}\sum_{i=1}^{n} ||Pred_k(s_i) - True_k(s_i)||^2 \tag{3}$$

where M denotes the size of the training set, n denotes the number of landmarks, $Pred_k(s_i)$ denotes the predicted 2D coordinates of the ith landmark of the kth data, and $True_k(s_i)$ denotes the true value of the corresponding landmark.

Given the inherent variability in landmark clarity under diverse lighting conditions, it is expected that the calculated 2D coordinates for the same landmark will exhibit some degree of deviation when computed under different conditions. To solve this challenge and make use of the potential geometric features, we introduce an attention module. This module selectively emphasizes reliable features and suppresses noise-corrupted estimations through context-aware feature fusion, dynamically generating confidence weights for multi-light predictions. These weighted results are subsequently integrated to produce the final predicted values of the 3D coordinates [16]. As shown in Fig. 3 (b), the attention module within this study consists of four primary steps.

In the first step of our method, we input three 2D projected images into the ResNet50 convolutional neural network. These images share identical conditions, except for variations in illumination. As a result, the network generates corresponding 2048-dimensional feature vectors for each of the three images, along with predicted 2D coordinate values for the landmarks within them. It is important to note that for each landmark, there currently exist three different coordinate predictions. To consolidate these multiple predictions, we proceed to

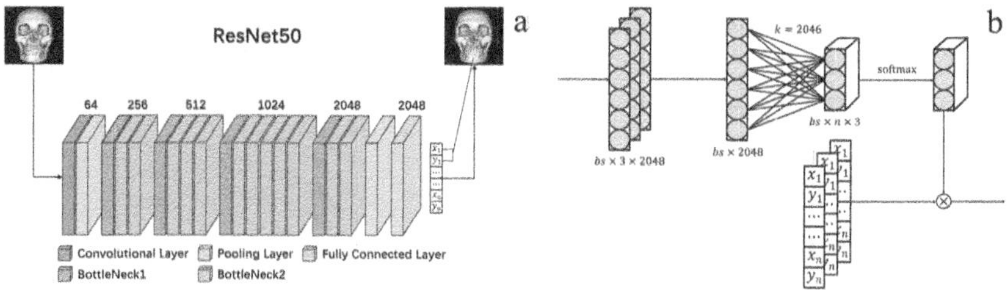

Fig. 3. (a) Framework of ResNet50. (b) Attention module.

calculate the average of the three feature vectors. The resulting 2048-dimensional feature vector computed through this averaging process contains the composite features derived from the three projected images. This step facilitates the amalgamation of information from different illumination conditions, ultimately contributing to a more comprehensive representation of the landmarks.

In the second step of our procedure, we execute a one-dimensional convolution operation on the previously computed average feature vector. The number of convolution kernels corresponds to the total count of landmarks slated for detection. Each convolution kernel is configured with a size parameter set to 2046. The convolution process for each individual kernel can be expressed mathematically through Equation (4):

$$a_k = \sum_{i=1}^{2046} \omega_{i+k}\gamma_i \tag{4}$$

where a_k denotes the value of the kth dimension in the computed result, ω_k denotes the value of the kth dimension in the average feature vector, and γ_k denotes the value of the kth dimension in the convolution kernel.

In the third step of our process, the tensor resulting from the convolution operation transforms the softmax activation function. This transformation yields corresponding weights assigned to different components of the tensor, with the constraint that the sum of these three weight values equals 1.

Subsequently, in the fourth step, these computed weights are used to modulate and aggregate the predicted 2D coordinates of the landmarks. The outcome of this computation will be the final detection result.

2.4 Reverse Projection

After the integration of 2D coordinates from projection images captured under diverse lighting conditions through an attention module, a reverse projection process is employed. The comprehensive process of reverse projection is executed across projection images captured at multiple angles, ensuring that the entire set of 2D coordinates is accurately reconstructed into the 3D landmarks.

The reverse projection is implemented similarly to the projection. For each 2D coordinate s_i, the reverse projection operation is conducted by extending a ray d perpendicular to the projection plane from the point s_i, intersecting with the 3D model. The first intersection point is then identified as the corresponding point $p(s_i)$ on the 3D model, providing the 3D coordinates for the corresponding landmark.

3 Experiments

3.1 Datasets

We use a dataset that includes 145 generic 3D craniomaxillofacial models of real patients, which are provided by the Chinese Academy of Medical Sciences and Peking Union Medical College. Professional doctors annotate the craniomaxillofacial anatomical landmarks on each model using Mimics software. For our method, 100 samples of the data are designed as the training set, while the remaining 45 samples constitute the test set, promoting the assessment of the proposed method's feasibility and precision.

Table 2. Modifications of ResNet50.

Network	Type	Parameter	Original Value	Modified Value
conv1	convolutional layer	in_channels	3	1
fc	fully connected layer	out_features	1000	$2 \times landmark\_num$

3.2 Experiment Details

Given the higher spatial complexity of 3D models compared to 2D images, a direct application of conventional 2D image landmark detection evaluation metrics is unsuitable. Therefore, a more fundamental evaluation metric for coordinates was adopted in these experiments. Specifically, we relied on the Euclidean distance between the predicted positions of landmarks and their corresponding real-world positions as the principal criterion for evaluating the method's precision:

$$Error = ||X_{Predict} - X_{Truth}||. \quad (5)$$

In this research, we employed the Adam optimizer with default parameters to minimize the loss function outlined in Equation (3). The $batch\_size$ was configured at 4, and the number of iterations was set to 200. The light sources are arranged in a plane containing both the centroid of the model and the central axis of the projection plane, with angular configurations established at 45° above the horizontal plane, directly on the horizontal plane, and 45° below the horizontal plane. At the same time, we modified the input and output layers of ResNet50 to accomplish landmark detection. The specific modifications are shown in Table 2, where $landmark\_num$ denotes the number of landmarks to be detected.

Table 3. Comparison among our method and baselines(mm).

Landmark	Kang's [7]	Zhang's [17]	Template Matching [11,12]	Ours
N	8.33	3.39	3.59	**3.21**
Or-left	9.36	3.32	3.70	**2.73**
Or-right	8.36	3.88	4.19	**2.53**
ANS	5.24	3.20	1.80	**1.78**
A	7.41	2.79	3.66	**2.43**
B	7.65	2.77	2.94	**2.31**
Go-left	9.74	4.42	4.86	**2.76**
Go-right	8.85	4.50	5.35	**2.97**
Pg	6.51	2.89	2.84	**2.32**
Me	11.40	3.04	3.15	**2.07**
Mean Error	8.28	3.42	3.61	**2.51**

3.3 Comparison Experiments

We employed the Euclidean distance between the predicted and true positions of the anatomical landmarks to evaluate the performance of automatic detection of craniomaxillofacial anatomical landmarks on the validation set. Our method can achieve a mean error of 2.51 mm on the dataset, and most of the landmarks are located within 4 mm away from the ground truth. Furthermore, we employed Kang's [7], Zhang's [17], and Template Matching (implemented according to Sipiran et al. [12] and Myronenko et al. [11]) to serve as baselines for comparison with our method. A comparative analysis of all methods was conducted for each landmark, with the results detailed in Table 3 and Fig. 4.

The results reveal that the ANS points have the lowest error rates, while the N points have the highest. This can be attributed to the distinct geometric features of the ANS points, which are markedly different from those in their neighborhood. Consequently, the model can efficiently capture these characteristics and achieve lower mean errors during training. In contrast, the N points, which exhibit a high degree of similarity with nearby points, pose a challenge for the model to distinguish them from adjacent landmarks.

Our method demonstrates a marked improvement over the methods proposed by Kang et al. [7] and Zhang et al. [17]. This might be because the prevalent reliance on the voxelization of 3D models in current deep learning methods may lead to the incorrect detection of landmarks within the interior of models. In comparison, our method utilizes projection and reverse projection, which ensure that the landmarks are precisely located on the surface. This approach also protects the detection process from the influence of irrelevant internal structures of models.

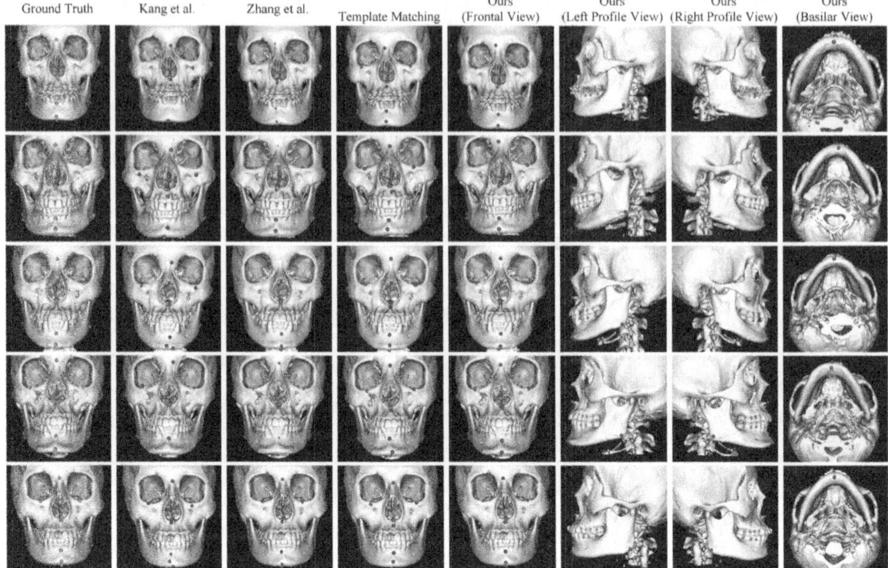

Fig. 4. Results among our method and baselines.

3.4 Ablation Experiments

We evaluated the effectiveness of each module through ablation experiments. The results of the ablation experiments are presented in Table 4. We evaluated our method in single lighting conditions on the dataset by designing a new training set. We selected projection images under consistent lighting conditions to train the ResNet50 convolutional neural network. A comparative analysis was conducted between the test results under multiple lighting conditions and those under single lighting conditions. We further verified the effectiveness of the proposed attention module. In the absence of the attention module, the ResNet50 convolutional neural network yielded three distinct localizations for the same landmark, and the average error across all localizations was considered the final result.

Ablation experiments have confirmed the effectiveness of both the multi-light module and the attention module. The projection process deprives 2D images of depth information, thereby necessitating the reconstruction of this information based on shadows cast under varying lighting conditions. The attention module plays a key role in addressing the variability in landmark detection accuracy under different lighting conditions, which is because it can reduce the influence of inaccurate localizations and enhance the weights of precise detection outcomes.

Table 4. Ablation experiments(mm).

Landmark	Ours with All	W/O Multi-Light	W/O Attention Module
N	**3.21**	4.36	3.48
Or-left	**2.73**	4.28	3.81
Or-right	**2.53**	4.74	3.55
ANS	**1.78**	3.36	3.43
A	**2.43**	4.10	5.11
B	**2.31**	3.48	3.02
Go-left	**2.76**	4.59	5.10
Go-right	**2.97**	4.83	5.49
Pg	**2.32**	3.58	2.60
Me	2.07	3.62	**1.93**
Mean Error	**2.51**	4.09	3.75

3.5 User Study

We invited 7 surgeons and related practitioners to test and evaluate our method. After evaluation, all participants were asked to complete a survey for feedback. We designed a questionnaire that contains six evaluation items: (1) The precision of landmark detection; (2) The guidance of surgical planning; (3) The efficiency of the method; (4) The smoothness of operation; (5) The convenience of operation. The scores for these items range from 0 to 10, where 0 represents the worst and 10 represents the most satisfactory. As shown in Table 5, the precision of landmark detection, the guidance of surgical planning, the smoothness of operation, and the convenience of operation have reached a good level (8.1 or higher on average). The lowest score is the efficiency of the method. The reason lies in the extremely high resolution of medical imaging, resulting in the huge scale of datasets for 3D models reconstructed from medical images. Efficiently handling such large-scale datasets requires additional effort. One potential solution is to simplify the model through corner detection or filtering techniques, aiming to reduce the data scale while maintaining nearly unchanged detection precision.

Table 5. Statistics of the questionnaire.

Item	1	2	3	4	5
Mean	8.14	8.29	7.29	8.43	8.14
Standard deviation	0.69	0.76	0.49	0.53	0.90

4 Conclusions

We introduce an attention-enhanced 3D craniomaxillofacial anatomical landmark automatic detection method based on common models, aiming to assist surgeons in surgical path planning. We employ multi-angle projection under multi-light conditions for dimensionality reduction and utilize a reverse projection method to restore 2D results to 3D space. An attention module is introduced to decrease information loss and collect morphological features. Experimental results indicate that this method can precisely and automatically detect craniomaxillofacial anatomical landmarks.

We believe that there is room for improvement in this method. Regarding framework enhancements, we plan to employ neural networks for feature extraction from the model, serving as a reference for subsequent landmark detection and the attention module to further improve the method's precision. Furthermore, we also intend to extend the automated path planning based on landmark detection, advancing research in the field of intelligent surgery.

Acknowledgments. This study is funded by Beijing Municipal Science & Technology Commission (No. Z221100007422005), Natural Science Foundation of China (No. U20A20195, 62272017, 62172437), and Beijing Natural Science Foundation (No. L232065, L232135).

Disclosure of Interests. The authors declare no conflict of interest.

References

1. Arık, S.Ö., Ibragimov, B., Xing, L.: Fully automated quantitative cephalometry using convolutional neural networks. J. Med. Imaging **4**(1), 014501–014501 (2017)
2. Barron, A.R.: Approximation and estimation bounds for artificial neural networks. Mach. Learn. **14**, 115–133 (1994)
3. Chen, R., et al.: Structure-aware long short-term memory network for 3D cephalometric landmark detection. IEEE Trans. Med. Imaging **41**(7), 1791–1801 (2022)
4. Favaedi, L., Petrou, M.: Cephalometric landmarks identification using probabilistic relaxation. In: 2010 Annual International Conference of the IEEE Engineering in Medicine and Biology, pp. 4391–4394. IEEE (2010)
5. Greenberg, A.M., Schmelzeisen, R.: Craniomaxillofacial reconstructive and corrective bone surgery. Springer, New York (2019)
6. He, K., Zhang, X., Ren, S., Sun, J.: Deep residual learning for image recognition. In: Proceedings of the IEEE Conference on Computer Vision and Pattern Recognition, pp. 770–778. (2016)
7. Kang, S.H., Jeon, K., Kim, H.J., Seo, J.K., Lee, S.H.: Automatic three-dimensional cephalometric annotation system using three-dimensional convolutional neural networks: a developmental trial. Comput. Methods Biomech. Biomed. Eng. Imaging Vis. **8**(2), 210–218 (2020)
8. Lee, S.M., Kim, H.P., Jeon, K., Lee, S.H., Seo, J.K.: Automatic 3D cephalometric annotation system using shadowed 2D image-based machine learning. Phys. Med. Biol. **64**(5), 055002 (2019)

9. Lin, Z., et al.: Augmented-reality-based surgical navigation for endoscope retrograde cholangiopancreatography: a phantom study. Int. J. Med. Robot. Comput. Assist. Surg. **20**(3), e2649 (2024)
10. Lo, L.J., Lin, H.H.: Applications of three-dimensional imaging techniques in craniomaxillofacial surgery: a literature review. Biomed. J. **46**(4), 100615 (2023)
11. Myronenko, A., Song, X.: Point set registration: coherent point drift. IEEE Trans. Pattern Anal. Mach. Intell. **32**(12), 2262–2275 (2010)
12. Sipiran, I., Bustos, B.: Harris 3D: a robust extension of the harris operator for interest point detection on 3D meshes. Vis. Comput. **27**, 963–976 (2011)
13. Su, H., Maji, S., Kalogerakis, E., Learned-Miller, E.: Multi-view convolutional neural networks for 3D shape recognition. In: 2015 IEEE International Conference on Computer Vision, pp. 945–953. (2015)
14. Tel, A., Arboit, L., De Martino, M., Isola, M., Sembronio, S., Robiony, M.: Systematic review of the software used for virtual surgical planning in craniomaxillofacial surgery over the last decade. Int. J. Oral Maxillofac. Surg. **52**(7), 775–786 (2023)
15. Topsakal, O., Akinci, T.C., Murphy, J., Preston, T.L.J., Celikoyar, M.M.: Detecting facial landmarks on 3D models based on geometric properties–a review of algorithms, enhancements, additions and open-source implementations. Ieee Access **11**, 25593–25603 (2023)
16. Wang, Q., Wu, B., Zhu, P., Li, P., Zuo, W., Hu, Q.: ECA-Net: Efficient channel attention for deep convolutional neural networks. In: Proceedings of the IEEE/CVF Conference on Computer Vision and Pattern Recognition, pp. 11534–11542. (2020)
17. Zhang, Y., et al.: An automated method of 3D facial soft tissue landmark prediction based on object detection and deep learning. Diagnostics **13**(11), 1853 (2023)

A Visual Self-Attention Mechanism Facial Expression Recognition Network Beyond ConvNeXt

Bingyu Nan[1], Feng Liu[2(✉)], Xuezhong Qian[1(✉)], and Wei Song[1]

[1] Jiangnan University, Wuxi 214122, China
xzqian@jiangnan.edu.cn
[2] Shanghai Jiao Tong University, Shanghai 200062, China
1sttoy@163.com

Abstract. Facial expression recognition is an important research direction in the field of artificial intelligence. Although new breakthroughs have been made in recent years, the uneven distribution of datasets and the similarity between different categories of facial expressions, as well as the differences within the same category among different subjects, remain challenges. This paper proposes a visual facial expression signal feature processing network based on truncated ConvNeXt approach (Conv-cut), to improve the accuracy of FER under challenging conditions. The network uses a truncated ConvNeXt-Base as the feature extractor, and then we designed a Detail Extraction Block to extract detailed features, and introduced a Self-Attention mechanism to enable the network to learn the extracted features more effectively. To evaluate the proposed Conv-cut approach, we conducted experiments on the RAF-DB and FERPlus datasets, and the results show that our model has achieved state-of-the-art performance. Our code could be accessed at https://github.com.

Keywords: Facial Expression Recognition · Visual Self-attention Mechanism · Extract Detailed · Truncated Network · Computational Perception

1 Introduction

Facial expression recognition (FER) is one of the hot topics in the field of artificial intelligence research today. As a component of basic emotion recognition, facial expression recognition can effectively capture and analyze subtle changes in facial expressions, thereby determining a person's emotional and psychological [9] state. Accurate facial expression recognition [18] not only provides deep insights into human emotions [8], but also lays a solid foundation for developing interactive systems with engineering ethics [23]. However, unlike other image segmentation tasks, the challenge for Facial Expression Recognition (FER) mainly lies in the similarities between different categories of expressions [6] and the differences among different subjects within the same category [21]. For example,

P. Li et al. (Eds.): CGI 2025, LNCS 16508, pp. 276–287, 2026.
https://doi.org/10.1007/978-3-032-22264-0_22

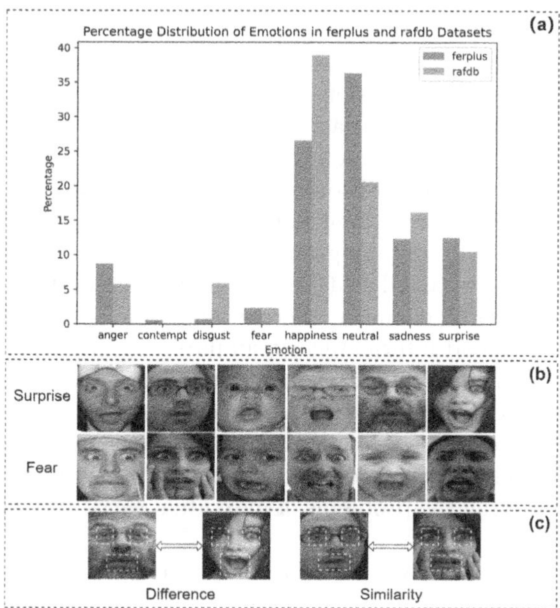

Fig. 1. This article attempts to address the variability between the expressions of different subjects in the field of FER. (a) Uneven distribution of data in public datasets between FERPlus and RAF-DB. (b) Similarities between expression categories. (c) Differences between different contributors in the same category.

in Fig. 1B, surprise and fear are quite similar, while in 1C, even though it is the same expression of surprise, there is a noticeable difference between the expressions of the elderly and the young girl. Additionally, uneven data distribution is also one of the challenges faced [25]. We have demonstrated the data distribution of commonly used datasets in Fig. 1A.

In the feature extraction stage, traditional FER methods usually use machine learning algorithms such as FERM [2], MLP [1], etc. However, these methods are difficult to overcome the detail feature extraction of facial expressions and lack robustness to facial poses or occlusions. Therefore, more and more researchers are turning their attention to deep learning models, such as convolutional neural networks and ViT models. Wang et al. [17] proposed the Information Reuse Attention Module, a CNN based FER method for extracting attention perception features of faces. Ma et al. [11] applied the Transformer model to facial expression recognition, designed the VTFF model, and designed the ASF module to fuse global and local facial information. Although these works have achieved good results, they still have not effectively addressed the challenges faced by FER, namely the uneven distribution of facial expression datasets and the differences and similarities between expressions.

In order to address the challenges previously mentioned, a convolutional neural network with a ConvNeXt network as the backbone is proposed. This is known as Conv-Cut and it combines the strengths of convolutional neural networks and Transformer architectures. The aim of this is to improve the recognition accuracy of different expression categories. Specifically, the truncated ConvNeXt network is utilised as the backbone network, with the objective of reducing the number of network parameters to address the issue of the small sample problem in the FER task. In addition, inspired by the contemplation of attention mechanisms in [13], an independent detail extraction module has been devised for the purpose of extracting fine-grained facial features. The model's capacity to attend to facial fine-grained feature regions is enhanced through the utilisation of a self-attention mechanism, thereby addressing the challenges posed by individual variability and inter-category similarity.

Overall, our contributions can be summarized as follows.

(1) The Detail Extraction Block has been designed for the purpose of extracting fine-grained features in conjunction with the self-attention mechanism. This ensures that the model pays more attention to the fine-grained feature region of the face, thereby solving the problems of individual variability and inter-category similarity.

(2) A convolutional network, Conv-cut, is proposed, based on ConvNeXt-Base. This uses truncated ConvNeXt as a feature extractor, and solves the problem of small samples in FER tasks by reducing the number of network parameters. The application of a Detail Extraction Block is intended to extract detailed features, thereby reducing the risk of overfitting due to the limited number of parameters. The experimental results demonstrate the efficacy of Conv-cut in challenging conditions.

(3) This Conv-Cut method achieved a success rate of 97.33% on the RAF-DB dataset and 95.69% on the FERPlus dataset, thereby demonstrating superiority over existing State-Of-The-Art methods.

2 Related Work

The conventional techniques for expression recognition primarily depend on manual features, categorised as low-level features, for identification. These features encompass geometric, texture, and motion characteristics.For instance, Tian et al. [16] have proposed a geometric feature-based expression recognition (FER) method for expression classification, which involves the identification and analysis of facial action units. In contrast, Shan et al. [14] have employed local binary patterns (LBP) as texture features for expression recognition. In addition, Bartlett et al. [4] proposed an expression recognition method combining geometric and dynamic features, which achieved good results in practical applications. Despite the success of these traditional methods in the field of expression recognition, they often lack sufficient robustness in the face of complex environmental factors such as changing lighting conditions, differences in facial poses, and occlusion.

The remarkable accomplishments of deep learning in numerous domains have prompted researchers to explore its application in the domain of expression recognition. For instance, Wang et al. [17] have proposed an expression recognition method based on convolutional neural networks (CNNs), with a focus on information reuse and attention mechanisms. Addressing the challenge of label uncertainty in expression recognition, Wang et al. [19] relabelled samples with low classification confidence. Liu et al. [10] They then focused on extracting different fine-grained features to learn the underlying diversity and key information of facial expressions. Ma et al. [11] applied the Transformer model to facial expression recognition, designed the VTFF model, and designed the ASF module to fuse global and local facial information. Xue et al. [22] proposed the APP and ATP modules, where the APP is used to select the CNN feature information patches with the highest content and ATP is used to discard unimportant tokens in ViT. These works have achieved good results but still failed to effectively address the challenges faced by FER, i.e., the uneven distribution of facial expression datasets and dissimilarities between expressions.

In contrast to the aforementioned studies, the present study employs a truncated ConvNeXt network to extract facial expression features. This is achieved by reducing the number of network parameters in order to address the issue of the small sample size that is prevalent in expression recognition tasks. In addition, in order to reduce the risk of overfitting, a separate detail extraction module has been designed to extract fine-grained facial features, thereby enabling the accurate learning of the key information contained within facial expressions.

3 Methodology

The truncated ConvNext is utilised as the fundamental framework for feature extraction, with subsequent refinement via the implementation of Detail Extraction. The overall structure of Conv-cut is illustrated in Fig. 2.

Truncated Convnext. In comparison to other visual tasks, FER tasks are distinguished by their utilisation of small sample sizes and the presence of subtle variations in facial expressions. This characteristic poses a significant challenge in the training of even small parameter versions of the model on the available dataset. To address this challenge, a truncated network is devised, drawing upon the principles of ConvNeXt-Base. Specifically, we construct a powerful feature extraction network by truncating the third and fourth stages of ConvNeXt-Base.

It is noteworthy that ConvNeXt-Base was originally divided into four stages. In the initial two phases, the model extracts low-level features and progressively reduces the resolution of the image to one-half of the original. In the subsequent phases, the network typically extracts more high-level semantic features, with the structure of these phases primarily designed for compatibility with downstream tasks (e.g. target detection).

In order to address the characteristics of the FER task, the third and fourth stages of ConvNeXt-Base are truncated, with the feature extraction capability of the first three stages being retained and the irrelevant part of the high-level semantic extraction being removed. This approach serves to reduce the complexity and the number of model parameters, thereby enabling the model to

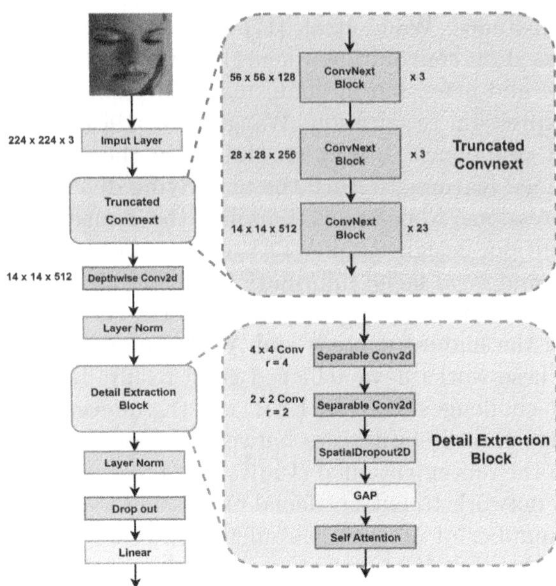

Fig. 2. The truncated ConvNext is utilised as the foundational framework for feature extraction, with the subsequent extraction of fine-grained features being achieved via the detail extraction module. The employment of the attention mechanism serves to enhance the model's focus on fine-grained feature regions.

focus on the low-level and intermediate-level features of facial expressions. This, in turn, leads to enhanced training efficiency and generalisation ability of the model when working with a limited sample size.

Detail Extraction. The truncated Convnext has been demonstrated to be capable of extracting low and medium-level features of facial expressions with a reasonable degree of proficiency. However, it is observed to be deficient in its ability to extract fine-grained features. To address this limitation, a detail extraction module has been designed, consisting of a combination of convolutional network and self-attention mechanism to further extract fine-grained features of facial expressions. As illustrated in Algorithm 1, we employ two depth-separable convolutional layers to extract fine-grained features from low-level features.The first depth-separable convolutional layer possesses a convolutional kernel size of 4 X 4 and a step size of 4, which is designed to learn fine-grained features from a broader perspective and capture complete contextual relationships. The second depth-separable convolutional layer, with a convolutional kernel size of 2 X 2 and a step size of 2, is employed to further learn more detailed information. Subsequent to this, the model is enhanced through the implementation of pooling operations, with the objective of focusing on fine-grained feature regions of facial expressions, such as the corners of the eyes and mouth, in conjunction with the self-attention mechanism. Assuming the input vector is denoted by X, the query vector by Q, the key vector by K, and the value vector by V, the pooling operation and the attention operation can be expressed as follows:

$$x_{\text{pool}} = \frac{1}{H \times W} \sum_{i=1}^{H} \sum_{j=1}^{W} x_{i,j,:} \tag{1}$$

$$Attention(Q, K, V) = \text{softmax}(\frac{QK}{\sqrt{d_q}})V. \tag{2}$$

Algorithm 1 Pseudo code for Detail Extraction.

Input: $X \in \mathbb{R}^{B \times H \times W \times C}$
Output: f: feature
$Y = \gamma\left(\frac{X-\mu}{\sqrt{\sigma^2+\epsilon}}\right) + \beta$
$Y = SeparableConv(Y, kernelsize = 4, strides = 4)$
$Y = SeparableConv(Y, kernelsize = 2, strides = 2)$
$Y = SpatialDropout(Y, p = 0.1)$
$y_c = \frac{1}{H \times W} \sum_{i=1}^{H} \sum_{j=1}^{W} Y_{ijc}$
$Y = [y_1, y_2, ...y_c]$
$f = \text{softmax}\left(\frac{YY^T}{\sqrt{d}}\right) Y$
return f

4 Experiments

4.1 Implementation Details

A pre-trained Convnext-Base model is employed, with the weights being truncated and frozen. The hyperparameters were set as follows: batch size of 16, epoch of 50, initial learning rate of 1e-3, augmented dataset using random level-flip, sparse classification cross entropy as loss function and Adam as optimiser. All models were trained using a 16GB 4060Ti GPU.

4.2 Datasets

RAF-DB (The Real-world Affective Faces Database) [7] is a widely used in-the-wild dataset, containing over 30,000 distinct facial expression images downloaded from the internet, with both single-label and compound-label types. In our experiments seven basic expressions were used, namely, anger, disgust, fear, happiness, neutral, sadness and surprise. 12,271 of these images were used for training and 3,068 images were used for testing.
FERPlus [3] is an extension of FER2013 [5], collected by Google search engine, which includes 28,709 training images, 3,589 validation images, and 3,589 test images. Eight expressions (seven basic expressions plus contempt) were used in our experiments. Of these, 28,709 images were used for training and 3,589 images were used for testing.

4.3 Comparison with the State-of-the-Art Methods

As illustrated in Table 1, the performance of our Conv-cut is demonstrated on the RAF-DB and FERPlus datasets, with a comparison to other methods over the past three years. The Conv-cut demonstrates notable efficacy in the 7-classification task, exhibiting substantial superiority over competing methods and attaining optimal outcomes. Specifically, on the RAF-DB dataset, Conv-cut demonstrates superior performance in comparison to the second-ranked PAtt-Lite method, exhibiting an enhancement of 2.28% points on the ACC metric. This superiority is further substantiated in the FERPlus dataset, where an enhancement of 1.97% points on the ACC metric is observed. The best results are highlighted in bold. The PAtt Lite result is obtained by replicating the original author's steps on a Nvidia 4090 GPU.

Table 1. Comparing accuracy of our models with the state-of-the-art methods in RAF-DB and FERPlus datasets.† is Results based on local reproduction.

Method	Year	**Acc**↑(%)	
		RAF-DB	FERPlus
DMUE [15]	2021	88.76	-
VTFF [11]	2021	88.14	-
EAC [26]	2022	90.35	90.05
POSTER [27]	2023	92.05	91.62
CLEF [24]	2023	90.09	89.74
APViT [22]	2023	91.98	-
PAtt-Lite† [12]	2023	**95.05**	**93.72**
LNSU-Net [25]	2024	89.77	88.81
MGR^{3}Net [20]	2024	91.05	-
CEPrompt [28]	2024	92.43	-
Conv-cut(Ours)		**97.33**(+2.28)	**95.69**(+1.97)

4.4 Ablation Studies

The full ConvNeXt Base, pre-trained on the ImageNet dataset, is utilised as the baseline model, and it is trained employing the same training method. A comparison of the detail extraction module with attention to the baseline model is then made in order to evaluate their effectiveness. The outcomes of this investigation are presented in Table 2. The findings reveal that employing attention alone results in a modest enhancement in model performance. The enhancement observed is approximately 3%, as compared to the benchmark model. This finding suggests that self-attention facilitates the model's comprehension of contextual information. Conversely, the application of the Detail Extraction (DET)

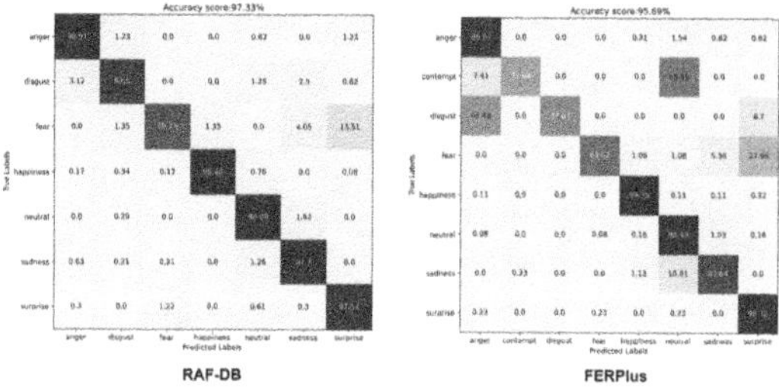

Fig. 3. The confusion matrix of our proposed Conv-cut evaluated on RAF-DB and FERPlus.

module without attention enhances the model's accuracy by nearly 10%. As illustrated in Figure 4, the features extracted from the baseline model are almost indistinguishable from those extracted from the truncated model. In addition, an investigation was conducted into the effect of the convolutional network layer of the detail extraction module on the model accuracy and F1 score. The experimental results are presented in Table 3, which indicates that the module demonstrates optimal fine-grained feature extraction capability when the number of convolutional layers is two.

Table 2. Ablation studies on the accuracy of proposed method in the RAF-DB and FERPlus datasets.

Self-Attention	Detail Extraction	RAF-DB↑(%)	FERPlus↑(%)
×	×	75.62	75.71
✓	×	78.65(+3.03)	78.31(+2.6)
×	✓	84.24(+5.59)	82.46(+4.15)
✓	✓	**97.33**(+13.09)	**95.69**(+13.23)

Table 3. Comparison of different convolutional layers in the Detail Extraction module.

Detail Extraction	Acc↑(%)	F1↑(%)
One layer	92.86	86.84
Three layers	95.24(+2.38)	90.91(+4.07)
Two layers	**97.33**(+2.09)	**94.69**(+3.78)

4.5 Visualization

Attention Visualization. In order to further investigate the effectiveness of Conv-cut, Grad-CAM was utilised to visualise randomly sampled attention maps

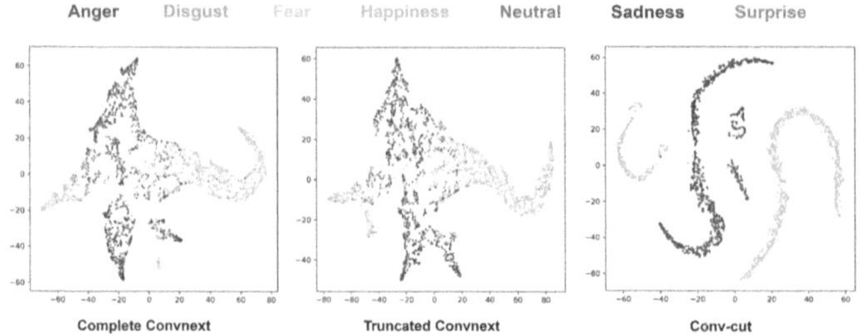

Fig. 4. 2D t-SNE visualization of facial expression features obtained through different models, including baseline model, truncated ConvNext model, Conv-cut. These features were extracted from the RAF-DB dataset.

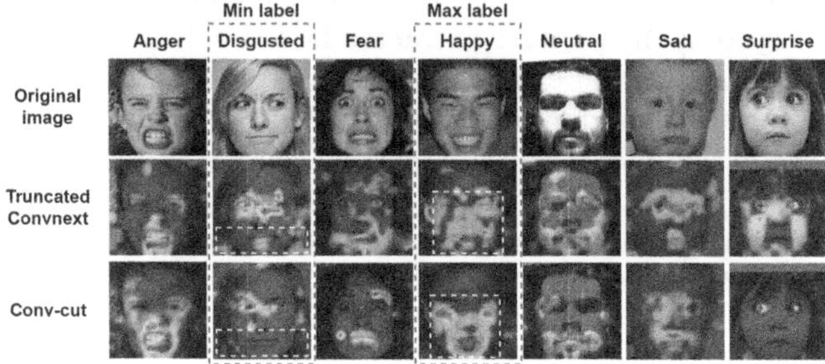

Fig. 5. Attention visualization for images from RAF-DB dataset. The min label and max label represent the average minimum and average maximum number of categories, respectively.

from the RAF-DB dataset.As illustrated in Figure 5, the initial row depicts the original image from left to right, with 'angry', 'disgusted', 'fearful', 'happy', 'neutral', 'sad' and 'surprised' from left to right. A comparison of the second and third rows reveals that the truncated Convnext focuses predominantly on expression-related regions, yet still focuses on redundant features (e.g., the attention to hair in 'disgust').Con-cut eliminates redundant features and accurately focuses on expression-related regions (e.g., the corners of the eyes in 'neutral' and the lips in 'sad'). In the case of category imbalance, the average minimum number of samples is shown to be as good as the average maximum number of samples for focusing on(e.g., the average maximum sample size category "Happy" focuses as well as the average minimum sample "Disgusted").

Feature Visualization .We use T-SNE to visualize the distribution of facial expression features extracted from our benchmark model and Conv-cut. We also visualize the confusion matrix of our proposed CFER model evaluated on the RAF-DB and FERPlus datasets to analyze the results. In Fig. 3, we observe that the model evaluated on RAF-DB had a lower prediction accuracy for negative emotions such as fear, with only 79.73%. This is because the proportion of such negative emotions in the RAF-DB dataset is relatively low, with fear accounting for only 2.28%, resulting in poor performance of the model for such emotions. In addition, we also observe that the models evaluated on FERPlus had lower accuracy in predicting contemper, disgust, and fear. The models frequently incorrectly predict contemper as neutral because contemper and disgust have a relatively low proportion in FERPlus, with contemper accounting for 0.58%, disgust accounting for 0.67%, and fear accounting for 2.29%. Therefore, the models are more inclined to predict these negative emotions as other emotions.

5 Conclusion

In this paper, we propose a convolutional neural network with ConvNeXt as the backbone, namely Conv-Cut. by using truncated ConvNeXt as the feature extraction backbone, the small sample problem is solved by reducing the network parameters. An independent detail extraction block is also designed to extract fine-grained features by conjunction with the self-attention mechanism to ensure that the model pays more attention to the fine-grained feature regions of the face, thus solving the problem of individual variability and inter-category similarity. Experimental results show that Conv-Cut still performs well under challenging conditions.

However, due to the more severe category imbalance problem in the FERPlus dataset compared to the RAF-DB dataset, our model performs poorly in predicting negative expressions (e.g.,empt, disgust, fear) on FERPlus. Also, the training stability is poor compared to RAF-DB. Our subsequent work will focus on addressing this issue.

Acknowledgments. This work is supported by the National Key R&D Program"Active Health and Aging Population Technology Response" Key Project (No.2024YFC3606802) and also supported by Beijing Key Laboratory of Behavior and Mental Health, Peking University.

Disclosure of Interests. The authors have no competing interests to declare that are relevant to the content of this article.

References

1. Akhtar, M.S., Ekbal, A., Cambria, E.: How intense are you? Predicting intensities of emotions and sentiments using stacked ensemble [application notes]. IEEE Comput. Intell. Mag. **15**(1), 64–75 (2020)
2. Alhussan, A., Talaat, F.M., El-kenawy, E.S., Abdelhamid, A., Ibrahim, A., Khafaga, D., Alnaggar, M.: Facial expression recognition model depending on optimized support vector machine. Comput. Mater. Continua **76**, 499–515 (2023). https://doi.org/10.32604/cmc.2023.039368
3. Barsoum, E., Zhang, C., Canton-Ferrer, C., Zhang, Z.: Training deep networks for facial expression recognition with crowd-sourced label distribution. In: Proceedings of the 18th ACM International Conference on Multimodal Interaction (2016). https://api.semanticscholar.org/CorpusID:3080611

4. Bartlett, M.S., Littlewort, G., Frank, M.G., Lainscsek, C., Fasel, I.R., Movellan, J.R., et al.: Automatic recognition of facial actions in spontaneous expressions. J. Multim. **1**(6), 22–35 (2006)
5. Goodfellow, I.J., et al.: Challenges in representation learning: a report on three machine learning contests. Neural Netw. Official J. Int. Neural Netw. Soc. **64**, 59–63 (2013). https://api.semanticscholar.org/CorpusID:1103216
6. Li, H., Wang, N., Yang, X., Wang, X., Gao, X.: Towards semi-supervised deep facial expression recognition with an adaptive confidence margin. In: 2022 IEEE/CVF Conference on Computer Vision and Pattern Recognition (CVPR), pp. 4156–4165 (2022). https://api.semanticscholar.org/CorpusID:247618790
7. Li, S., Deng, W.: Reliable crowdsourcing and deep locality-preserving learning for unconstrained facial expression recognition. IEEE Trans. Image Process. **28**(1), 356–370 (2019). https://doi.org/10.1109/TIP.2018.2868382
8. Liu, F.: Artificial intelligence in emotion quantification : a prospective overview. CAAI Artif. Intell. Res. **3**, 9150040 (2024).https://doi.org/10.26599/AIR.2024.9150040, https://www.sciopen.com/article/10.26599/AIR.2024.9150040
9. Liu, F., et al.: OPO-FCM: a computational affection based occ-pad-ocean federation cognitive modeling approach. IEEE Trans. Comput. Soc. Syst. **10**(4), 1813–1825 (2023). https://doi.org/10.1109/TCSS.2022.3199119
10. Liu, H., Cai, H., Lin, Q., Li, X., Xiao, H.: Adaptive multilayer perceptual attention network for facial expression recognition. IEEE Trans. Circ. Syst. Video Technol. **32**(9), 6253–6266 (2022)
11. Ma, F., Sun, B., Li, S.: Facial expression recognition with visual transformers and attentional selective fusion. IEEE Trans. Affect. Comput. (2021)
12. Ngwe, J.L., Lim, K.M., Lee, C.P., Ong, T.S., Alqahtani, A.: PAtt-Lite: Lightweight patch and attention MobileNet for challenging facial expression recognition. IEEE Access **12**, 79327–79341 (2024). https://doi.org/10.1109/ACCESS.2024.3407108
13. Qian, B., et al.: Deep contour attention learning for scleral deformation from OCT images. Vis. Comput. 1–16 (2024)
14. Shan, C., Gong, S., McOwan, P.W.: Facial expression recognition based on local binary patterns: a comprehensive study. Image Vis. Comput. **27**(6), 803–816 (2009)
15. She, J., Hu, Y., Shi, H., Wang, J., Shen, Q., Mei, T.: Dive into ambiguity: latent distribution mining and pairwise uncertainty estimation for facial expression recognition. In: 2021 IEEE/CVF Conference on Computer Vision and Pattern Recognition (CVPR), pp. 6244–6253 (2021).https://doi.org/10.1109/CVPR46437.2021.00618
16. Tian, Y.I., Kanade, T., Cohn, J.F.: Recognizing action units for facial expression analysis. IEEE Trans. Pattern Anal. Mach. Intell. **23**(2), 97–115 (2001)
17. Wang, C., Hu, R.: Information reuse attention in convolutional neural networks for facial expression recognition in the wild. In: International Joint Conference on Neural Networks (2021)
18. Wang, H., et al.: Rethinking the learning paradigm for dynamic facial expression recognition. In: Proceedings of the IEEE/CVF Conference on Computer Vision and Pattern Recognition (CVPR), pp. 17958–17968 (2023)
19. Wang, K., Peng, X., Yang, J., Lu, S., Qiao, Y.: Suppressing uncertainties for large-scale facial expression recognition. In: 2020 IEEE/CVF Conference on Computer Vision and Pattern Recognition (CVPR), pp. 6896–6905 (2020), https://api.semanticscholar.org/CorpusID:211258635
20. Wang, Y., et al.: Mgr3net: multigranularity region relation representation network for facial expression recognition in affective robots. IEEE Trans. Ind. Inf. **20**(5), 7216–7226 (2024). https://doi.org/10.1109/TII.2024.3353912

21. Wu, Z.F., Cui, J.: La-net: landmark-aware learning for reliable facial expression recognition under label noise. In: 2023 IEEE/CVF International Conference on Computer Vision (ICCV), pp. 20641–20650 (2023). https://api.semanticscholar.org/CorpusID:259951174
22. Xue, F., Wang, Q., Tan, Z., Ma, Z., Guo, G.: Vision transformer with attentive pooling for robust facial expression recognition. IEEE Trans. Affect. Comput. 3244–3256 (2022)
23. Zhang, S., Pan, Y., Wang, J.Z.: Learning emotion representations from verbal and nonverbal communication. In: 2023 IEEE/CVF Conference on Computer Vision and Pattern Recognition (CVPR), pp. 18993–19004 (2023).https://doi.org/10.1109/CVPR52729.2023.01821
24. Zhang, X., Wang, T., Li, X., Yang, H., Yin, L.: Weakly-supervised text-driven contrastive learning for facial behavior understanding. In: 2023 IEEE/CVF International Conference on Computer Vision (ICCV), pp. 20694–20705 (2023). https://api.semanticscholar.org/CorpusID:257912613
25. Zhang, Y., Li, Y., Qin, L., Liu, X., Deng, W.: Leave no stone unturned: Mine extra knowledge for imbalanced facial expression recognition. ArXiv ArXiv:abs/2310.19636 (2023). https://api.semanticscholar.org/CorpusID:264828859
26. Zhang, Y., Wang, C., Ling, X., Deng, W.: Learn from all: erasing attention consistency for noisy label facial expression recognition. In: European Conference on Computer Vision (2022). https://api.semanticscholar.org/CorpusID:250921004
27. Zheng, C., Mendieta, M., Chen, C.: Poster: a pyramid cross-fusion transformer network for facial expression recognition. In: 2023 IEEE/CVF International Conference on Computer Vision Workshops (ICCVW), pp. 3138–3147 (2022). https://api.semanticscholar.org/CorpusID:248069142
28. Zhou, H., Huang, S., Zhang, F., Xu, C.: Ceprompt: cross-modal emotion-aware prompting for facial expression recognition. IEEE Trans. Circ. Syst. Video Technol. 1–1 (2024).https://doi.org/10.1109/TCSVT.2024.3424777

Enhancing Vision Transformer for Fine-Grained Visual Classification with Selective Attention Aggregation and Multi-Head Noise Suppression

TianRong Chen[1], JuanDong Huang[2], YaoSen Huang[2], Xiang Luo[3](✉), and Hua Tang[2](✉)

[1] School of Artificial Intelligence, South China Normal University, FoShan, China
2023025160@m.scnu.edu.cn
[2] School of Computer Science, South China Normal University, GuangZhou, China
tanghua@m.scnu.edu.cn
[3] Guangdong Tabacco Meizhou Ltd, Mei Zhou, China
57105275@qq.com

Abstract. Fine-grained visual classification (FGVC) is a challenging task that requires distinguishing between visually similar subcategories by capturing subtle local differences. The constrained receptive field and translation-insensitive nature of CNNs hinder their ability to capture detailed features. Vision Transformers (ViTs) have recently achieved impressive results by utilizing self-attention mechanisms to model long-range interactions and global information. However, ViTs often emphasize global coarse features while underutilizing critical local details, limiting their effectiveness in FGVC tasks. To mitigate this limitation, we introduce SaM, a novel FGVC approach that incorporates Selective Attention Aggregation and Multi-Head Noise Suppression. Specifically, we design a Selective Attention Aggregation (SAA) module that fuses both shallow and deep semantic cues to enhance hierarchical feature representation. Additionally, a Multi-Head Noise Suppression (MHNS) module is introduced to suppress irrelevant background noise and enhance local structural cues, ensuring robust token selection. Comprehensive evaluations across diverse FGVC datasets show that SaM delivers performance on par with or exceeding current state-of-the-art approaches, confirming its reliability and effectiveness.

Keywords: Vision Transformer · Attention · Fine-Grained · Image Classification · Neural Networks

1 Introduction

Fine-grained visual classification (FGVC) focuses on distinguishing visually similar subcategories within the same superclass—such as bird species [21], car models [11], or dog breeds [10]—by identifying subtle, localized differences. FGVC

P. Li et al. (Eds.): CGI 2025, LNCS 16508, pp. 288–299, 2026.
https://doi.org/10.1007/978-3-032-22264-0_23

is particularly challenging because of limited inter-class separability, high intra-class diversity induced by environmental and pose changes, and the requirement to recognize subtle visual cues like feather textures or facial features. These nuances are often obscured by noise and difficult to capture without compromising global context. Moreover, FGVC typically relies on costly, labor-intensive annotations (e.g., part locations), which limit scalability and hinder generalization.

Early CNN-based FGVC methods can be broadly categorized into localization-classification frameworks [8,9,18] and end-to-end feature encoding approaches [6,30]. The former focuses on detecting semantic parts to guide classification, while the latter integrates discriminative features directly through unified architectures. Both significantly advanced fine-grained recognition by improving feature representation. However, they often rely on large-scale annotated data, incur high computational costs, and struggle to effectively balance fine local details with global semantic context, limiting their scalability and robustness in real-world applications.

In recent years, Vision Transformers (ViT) [4] have shown strong potential in fine-grained visual classification (FGVC), with multi-head self-attention (MHSA) [20] effectively modeling global dependencies among image patches. To solve the problem of the limited ability of ViT to capture local features in the FGVC task, recent works [7,22,23] have enhanced local representation learning by selecting discriminative patches or fusing features across layers. Despite these advances, two key issues remain: (1) inconsistent discriminative ability across attention heads and layers, and (2) lack of modeling for the spatial coherence of discriminative regions, which tend to cluster, unlike dispersed noise regions. Existing methods often overlook these aspects, limiting their effectiveness.

In this paper, we address key challenges in fine-grained visual classification (FGVC) by proposing a novel fine-grained feature learning framework that enhances computational efficiency while reducing model complexity. Our approach introduces an attention weight aggregation strategy based on feature selection, which refines the raw attention weights of Vision Transformer (ViT) into structured attention maps. These maps effectively capture discriminative regions via self-attention. To further suppress background noise, we incorporate a noise reduction module based on a multi-head selection mechanism, enhancing the model's focus on critical areas while filtering out irrelevant information.This work makes the following key contributions: 1) An framework that improves fine-grained feature extraction with high computational efficiency. 2) An attention aggregation strategy that integrates low-level details and high-level semantics for richer representations. 3) A background suppression module using multi-head attention to enhance region focus and reduce noise. 4) Our approach demonstrates competitive results across three FGVC benchmarks, highlighting its robustness and strong generalization capabilities.

2 Related Work

2.1 Fine-Grained Visual Classfication

Fine-grained image recognition has been a central focus in fine-grained image analysis (FGIA), yet it remains a highly challenging task due to the difficulty in accurately localizing discriminative regions and effectively learning fine-grained features. To address these challenges, researchers have developed various approaches, which can be broadly categorized into two paradigms: part-based recognition frameworks and unified feature learning.

Recognition by part-based recognition frameworks. The core idea of part-based recognition approaches [3,8,9,12,18,24,25,27–29] is to localize discriminative regions of fine-grained entities and establish transitional representations for categorization. A localization subnetwork detects key regions (e.g., bird head or torso), extracts local features, and combines them with global features to form a comprehensive representation, which is then processed by a classification subnetwork. This two-stage framework—first locating parts, then comparing their attributes—effectively captures shared structural components and subtle differences across subcategories, leading to notable success in fine-grained tasks.

Recognition by unified feature learning. A second paradigm is the unified feature learning approach like [2,5,6,14,15,30], which eliminates explicit localization modules and instead focuses on progressively refining feature representations within a unified deep neural network framework. Unified feature learning aims to enhance fine-grained feature learning by integrating multi-scale representations and high-order semantic information. Unlike part-based recognition frameworks, this approach learns global and local features simultaneously in a streamlined architecture, reducing complexity while achieving improved recognition performance.

2.2 Vision Transformer

Transformer-based models offer an innovative solution to fine-grained visual classification by capturing both global and local image features through self-attention. The Vision Transformer (ViT) splits images into patches of a fixed size and processes each patch as a token, and models their relationships using a Transformer to extract contextual and fine-grained information. DeiT [19] (Data-efficient Image Transformer) improves upon ViT by introducing a distillation token and applying knowledge distillation, enabling strong performance without large-scale pretraining. The Swin Transformer [13] further enhances efficiency through a hierarchical design and shifted window attention, balancing local feature extraction with global context integration. Its scalability makes it effective for FGVC and broader vision tasks.

Building on these foundational architectures, a series of advanced Transformer-based methods have been proposed to further improve FGVC performance. TransFG [7] refines ViT by integrating raw attention weights into attention maps to highlight discriminative regions and applies contrastive loss to improve inter-class separability, though with added computational cost. SIM-Trans [17] models spatial structures through self-attention and enhances robustness via multi-level feature fusion, albeit with increased architectural complexity. AA-Trans [23] introduces an attention aggregator and entropy-based region selector for more precise localization, while IELT [26] optimizes multi-head attention through dynamic cross-layer feature selection and noise suppression. Collectively, these works highlight ongoing efforts to balance accuracy, efficiency, and model complexity in Transformer-based FGVC frameworks.

3 Methods

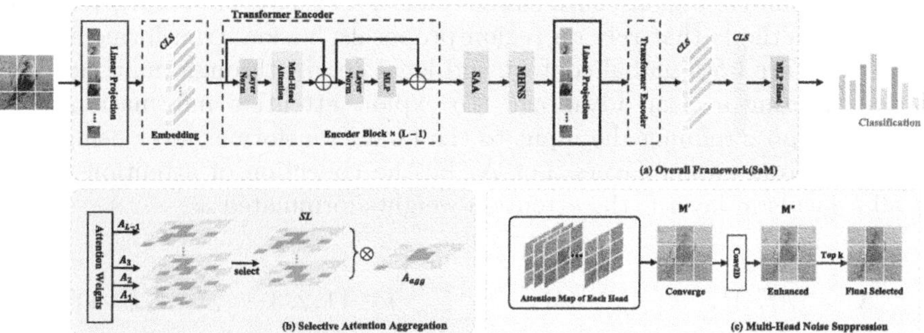

Fig. 1. (a) Overall framework of the proposed SaM network for FGVC. (b) Selective Attention Aggregation (SAA) integrates optimal attention maps to retain discriminative features. (c) Multi-Head Noise Suppression (MHNS) enhances region focus while reducing background noise.

3.1 Vision Transformer Architecture

Building upon the Vision Transformer (ViT) framework, we employ a sliding window mechanism with controlled overlap to preserve local structural continuity. For the input image $x \in \mathbb{R}^{H\times W\times C}$, we partition it into $N = \lfloor \frac{H-P+S}{S} \rfloor \times \lfloor \frac{W-P+S}{S} \rfloor$ patches using a convolution kernel of size P and stride S. Through linear transformation matrix $E \in \mathbb{R}^{(P^2\cdot C)\times d}$, each patch $x_i \in \mathbb{R}^{P\times P\times C}$ is mapped to a d-dimensional space, then concatenated with a learnable class token $x_{[\mathrm{CLS}]}$ to form the initial sequence:

$$\mathbf{z}_0 = [x_{[\mathrm{CLS}]}; x_1E, ..., x_NE] + E_{\mathrm{pos}} \tag{1}$$

where positional encoding $E_{\mathrm{pos}} \in \mathbb{R}^{(N+1)\times d}$ encodes spatial information.

This sequence is processed through L-layer Transformer encoders for feature evolution. Every layer comprises both multi-head self-attention (MHSA) and multi-layer perceptron (MLP) blocks, interconnected with residual skip connections:

$$\begin{aligned} \mathbf{z}'_l &= \mathrm{MHSA}(\mathrm{LN}(\mathbf{z}_{l-1})) + \mathbf{z}_{l-1}, & l &= 1, \ldots, L \\ \mathbf{z}_l &= \mathrm{MLP}(\mathrm{LN}(\mathbf{z}'_l)) + \mathbf{z}'_l, & l &= 1, \ldots, L \end{aligned} \tag{2}$$

layer normalization ($\mathrm{LN}(\cdot)$) ensures training stability. The global features extracted from the class token $x_{[\mathrm{CLS}]}$ are ultimately utilized for downstream classification tasks.

3.2 Selective Attention Aggregation

In fine-grained visual classification (FGVC), a key challenge lies in identifying subtle discriminative regions, such as the color of a bird's eyes or feathers. Unlike CNN-based methods that rely on region proposals, Vision Transformers (ViTs) naturally capture both global context and local details through multi-head self-attention, offering a clear advantage. To exploit attention information across layers, we propose refining the input to the final Transformer layer using attention weights from earlier layers. Let $\mathbf{A}_l$ be the collection of attention weights from all k heads in layer l, the attention weights formulated as:

$$\mathbf{A}_l = [A_l^0, A_l^1, \cdots, A_l^{k-1}, A_l^k] \qquad l \in \{1, 2, 3 \cdots, L-2, L-1\} \tag{3}$$

$$A_l^i = [a_l^{i_0}; a_l^{i_1}, \cdots, a_l^{i_{N-1}}, a_l^{i_N}] \qquad i \in \{0, 1, 2 \cdots, k-1, k\} \tag{4}$$

Prior studies [1,16] have shown that in deeper layers of Vision Transformers (ViTs), the original attention weights may no longer reflect the true semantic importance of input tokens. This is due to the progressive blending of token information across layers, which can lead to a loss of discriminative specificity. To address this, we propose aggregating attention weights from multiple Transformer layers to better preserve discriminative features, as illustrated in Fig. 1(b).

Unlike TransFG [7], which assumes equal importance across all layers, our method recognizes that different layers capture varying degrees of semantic relevance. Some may focus on background or redundant patterns, potentially impairing classification. Therefore, we selectively integrate attention weights from a subset of salient layers (SL) identified as critical for fine-grained differentiation. The aggregation process is defined as:

$$\mathbf{A}_{\mathrm{agg}} = \prod_{l \in \mathcal{SL}} \mathbf{A}_l \qquad \mathcal{SL} \subseteq \{1, 2, \ldots, L\} \tag{5}$$

where $\mathbf{A}_l$ represents the attention weights in layer l, $\mathcal{SL}$ represents the selected subset of k salient layers, $\mathbf{A}_{\mathrm{agg}}$ is to selectively aggregate the attention weights of key layers, which has prominent discriminant characteristics compared with the original attention weights, and realize effective fusion of cross-layer information.

3.3 Multi-Head Noise Suppression

Building upon the aggregated attention map $\mathbf{A}_{\text{agg}}$ derived from multi-layer Transformer encoders, we observe persistent noise originating from the MHSA mechanism. While diverse attention heads capture complementary features, certain heads may inadvertently focus on non-discriminative background regions. To mitigate this issue, inspired by [26], we propose a Multi-Head Noise Suppression (MHNS) module as shown in Fig. 1 part (c), which identifies and retains tokens critical for fine-grained classification.

Let $\mathbf{A}_{\mathbf{agg}} = [\mathbf{A}^1; \mathbf{A}^2; \cdots ; \mathbf{A}^k]$ denoted the aggregated attention weight, where A^k is the k-th head's attention score matrix in $\mathbb{R}^N$. To preserve spatial relationships, the attention score matrix $\mathbf{A}^k$ is reshaped into a 2D matrix $\mathbf{A}^{k'}$. Next, we select the indices of the most valuable tokens from $\mathbf{A}^{k'}$. To measure the frequency of token indices across all attention heads, we define a counting matrix $\mathrm{M}^k(i, j)$ as follows:

$$\mathrm{M}^k(i,j) = \begin{cases} 1, & \text{if } \mathrm{A}^{k'}(i,j) \text{ is top} - e \text{ value} \\ 0, & \text{otherwise} \end{cases} \tag{6}$$

where the hyper-parameter **e** determines the number of tokens selected per attention head. The score maps from all attention heads are aggregated to produce the final composite score map. To further highlight informative spatial areas, we apply a filtering process to the aggregated score representation using a convolution kernel **K**, producing the enhanced score map $\mathbf{M}^*$, computed as::

$$\mathrm{M}^* = \left(\sum_{k=0}^{K} \mathrm{M}^k \right) * \mathrm{K} \tag{7}$$

By sorting M^*, we define a hyperparameter **t** for the final selection of the **t** tokens with the highest saliency scores. These tokens are retrieved from the previous layer $\mathbf{z}_{l-1}$ via their indices and combined with the class token $x_{[\text{CLS}]}$ to constitute the input $\mathbf{z}_{local}$ of the final layer. This process is formally defined as:

$$\mathbf{z}_{local} = \left[x_{[\text{CLS}]}, x_{i_1}, x_{i_2}, \ldots, x_{i_t} \right] \tag{8}$$

where $\{i_1, i_2, \ldots, i_t\}$ are the indices of the selected tokens. This approach effectively suppresses noise while emphasizing the most discriminative regions, thereby improving the model's overall performance in fine-grained classification tasks.

4 Experiments

4.1 Experiments Setup

We evaluated our method using the following fine-grained benchmarks: CUB-200-2011, Stanford Dogs and NABirds.All experiments are implemented using PyTorch with APEX for mixed-precision FP16 training on two NVIDIA RTX

3090 GPUs. Unless otherwise specified, the CUB dataset is used by default. All input images are resized to 448 × 448. During training, random cropping is applied, while center cropping is used at test time. Each image is partitioned into 16 × 16 patches via a sliding window with a stride of 12. Data augmentation strategies include random horizontal flipping and automated augmentation techniques. The model is initialized from the ViT-B/16 pre-trained on ImageNet-21k. We use SGD with a momentum of 0.9, a batch size of 16, and a cosine annealing scheduler. The initial learning rate is 0.03 for all datasets, except 0.003 for Stanford Dogs.

4.2 Comparison with State-of-the-Arts

We conducted experiments on three fine-grained classification benchmarks—CUB, Stanford Dogs, and NABirds—using ViT-B/16 as the unified backbone. As shown in Table 1, our method consistently outperforms or matches state-of-the-art approaches. On CUB, it achieves 91.8% accuracy, surpassing TransFG (91.6%), SIM-Trans (91.5%), and IELT (91.4%), highlighting its ability to capture subtle discriminative features. On Stanford Dogs, our method reaches 90.8%, closely trailing the best-performing IELT (90.9%) while maintaining robust performance under high inter-class similarity. For NABirds, it achieves 90.7%, outperforming IELT (90.4%) and TransFG (90.5%), demonstrating strong generalization across diverse fine-grained tasks.

Table 1. Accuracy (%) of different methods on CUB, Dogs and Nabirds.

Method	Backbone	CUB-200–2011	Stanford Dogs	Nabirds
GCL [25]	ResNet-50+BN	88.3	-	-
FDL [12]	ResNet-50	88.6	85.0	-
S3N [3]	ResNet-50	88.5	87.1	-
PA-CNN [29]	VGG-19	87.8	87.3	-
MOMN [15]	VGG-16	87.3	-	-
CIN [6]	ResNet-101	88.1	87.6	-
API-Net [30]	DenseNet-161	87.8	89.4	88.5
DCL [2]	ResNet-50	87.8	-	
Cross-X [14]	ResNet-50	87.7	88.9	88.6
PMG [5]	ResNet-50	89.6	-	-
ViT [4]	ViT-B/16	90.9	90.5	89.9
TransFG [7]	ViT-B/16	91.6	90.6	90.5
SIM-Trans [17]	ViT-B/16	91.5	-	-
AA-Trans [23]	ViT-B/16	91.2	90.7	90.5
IELT [26]	ViT-B/16	91.4	90.9	90.4
SaM(Ours)	ViT-B/16	**91.8**	90.8	**90.7**

4.3 Ablation Studies

Effectiveness of the Proposed Modules. We analyzed the effectiveness of each module through ablation studies. As shown in Table 2, the baseline model achieves a strong accuracy of 90.93%. Adding the Selective Attention Aggregation (SAA) module improves accuracy to 91.62%, while introducing the Multi-Head Noise Suppression (MHNS) module raises it to 91.47%. When both modules are applied together, the accuracy further increases to 91.85%, demonstrating their complementary effects.

Effectiveness of Kernel Types. As shown in Table 3, the Box Blur Variant-like kernel consistently outperforms the Gaussian Blur-like kernel, particularly at a kernel size of 3 × 3, where the model achieves the highest accuracy of 91.85%. This indicates that the Box Blur Variant is more effective in enhancing local features while preserving critical details, making it well-suited for fine-grained recognition. Notably, changing the kernel size from 3 × 3 to 5 × 5 in the Box Blur Variant leads to a decline in accuracy, suggesting that smaller kernels better capture fine-grained patterns, while larger ones may introduce excessive smoothing. In contrast, the Gaussian kernel shows minimal sensitivity to kernel size, with a slight performance gain from 3 × 3 to 5 × 5, likely due to improved noise suppression.

Table 2. Effectiveness of the Modules

Baseline	SAA	MHNS	Acc (%)
✓			90.93
✓	✓		91.62
✓		✓	91.47
✓	✓	✓	**91.85**

Table 3. Effectiveness of kernel type.

kernel_type	kernel_size	Acc (%)
Box Blur Variant	3×3	**91.85**
	5×5	91.45
Gaussian Blur	3×3	91.43
	5×5	91.50

Effectiveness of Aggregation Methods. We evaluate various layer selection strategies for feature aggregation in Table 4. The Even-layer strategy achieves the highest accuracy (91.85%) with moderate training time (3h 18min), indicating that even-indexed layers offer more stable and discriminative features. The Fibonacci-like strategy (91.62%, 3h 42min) also performs well by balancing local and global information. In contrast, the Triangular-like (91.45%) and Odd-layer (91.56%) strategies yield lower accuracy, likely due to uneven coverage or reduced global context. Compared to baseline methods such as PSM [7] (91.59%, 4h 35min) and CAA [23] (91.24%, 4h 24min), our SAA-based methods maintain or exceed accuracy with significantly reduced training time. These results validate the effectiveness of selective layer aggregation and suggest its potential for efficient fine-grained classification.

Table 4. Effectiveness of Different Aggregation Methods.

type	Aggregation_method	layer_number	Accuracy (%)	Train Time (h)
baseline	PSM	11	91.59	4h 35min
	CAA	11	91.24	4h 24min
SAA	Odd	5	91.56	3h 07min
	Even	6	**91.85**	3h 18min
	Triangular-like	6	91.45	3h 27min
	Fibonacci-like	6	91.62	3h 42min

4.4 Qualitative Analysis

In order to prove the validity and interpretability of our method, we present a visual analysis in Fig. 2. The first row shows the input images, followed by our attention maps, and the selected tokens from PSM and SaM. Our method produces more focused and coherent attention, accurately highlighting discriminative regions. In contrast, PSM suffers from scattered activation due to the limitations of multi-head self-attention. SaM effectively suppresses noise and emphasizes key areas, leading to more relevant token selection. Additionally, it preserves feature diversity while capturing fine-grained details, enabling a richer and more robust representation.

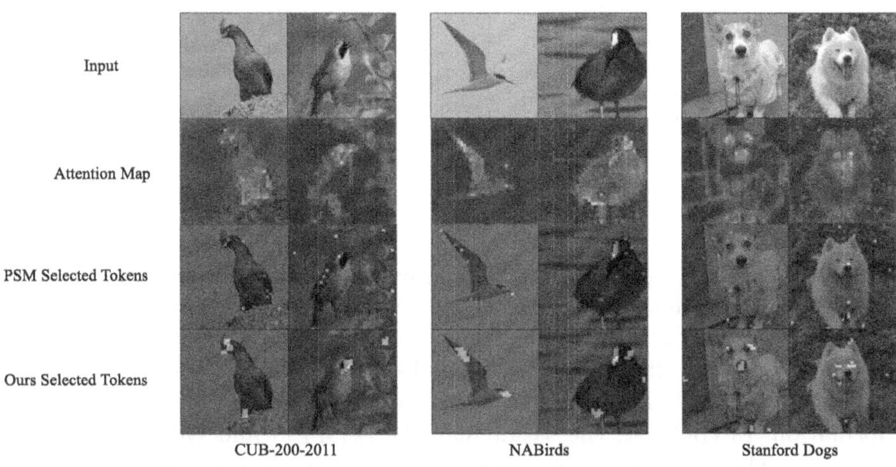

Fig. 2. Visualization results across datasets. The first row shows input images, the second displays attention maps from our method, where brighter areas indicate stronger responses. The third and fourth rows compare token selections by PSM and our method, with selected regions highlighted.

4.5 Hyperparameter Analysis

The Number of Selected Patches. We investigate how patch selection affects model performance, focusing on the number of patches selected per head ($\mathbf{e}$) and the total number of selected patches(t). As shown in Fig. 3, both factors significantly influence accuracy. The model achieves peak accuracy (91.85%) at $\mathbf{e} = 6$, suggesting that selecting six patches per head effectively captures key local features. Performance improves from $\mathbf{e} = 2$ to 6 but drops at $\mathbf{e} = 10$ due to redundant or noisy patches. Likewise, selecting $\mathbf{t} = 16$ patches in total yields the best results, while further increasing the count introduces redundancy and degrades performance. These results highlight the need to balance information richness and noise in patch selection for optimal fine-grained classification.

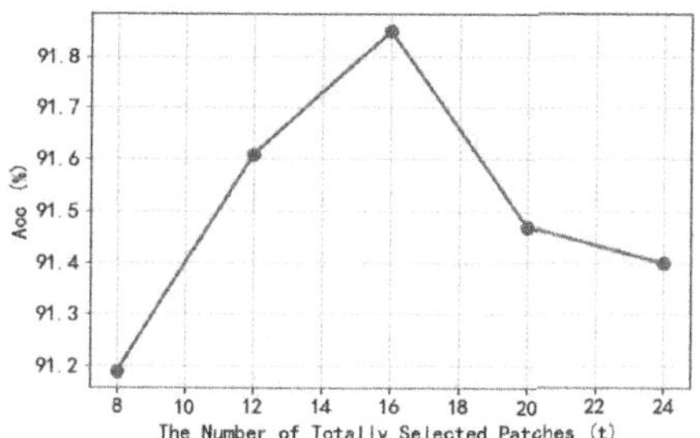

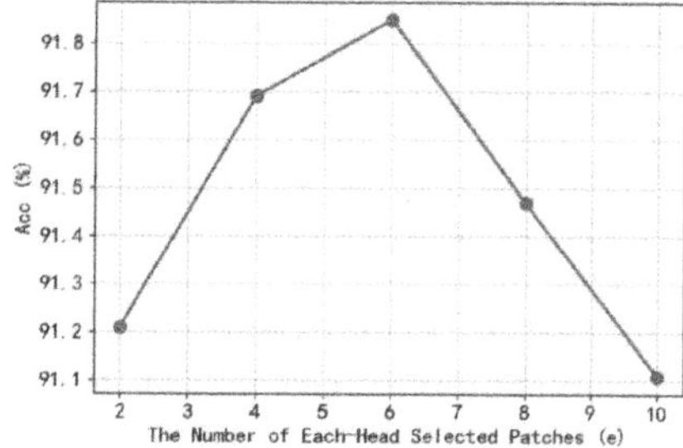

Fig. 3. Effect of patch selection on model performance. Accuracy vs. total number of selected patches(left). Accuracy vs. number of selected patches per head(right).

Conclusion

This paper presents SaM, an innovative Vision Transformer (ViT) architecture tailored for fine-grained visual classification tasks. To address ViT's limited focus on key local regions, we first analyze the layer-wise contribution to classification. Based on this insight, we introduce a Selective Attention Aggregation (SAA) module to extract and fuse informative hierarchical features. Additionally, we design a Multi-Head Noise Suppression (MHNS) module to refine local representations by integrating multi-head attention outputs and enhancing structural detail. Rigorous experiments conducted on the standard benchmark have shown that SaM demonstrates competitive performance, proving the credibility and interpretability of our method.

Acknowledgment. This work was partially supported by the National Natural Science Foundation of China under Grant No. 82271267, and the Guangdong Tobacco (Meizhou) Company Technology Project under Grant No. 2024441400240135.

References

1. Abnar, S., Zuidema, W.: Quantifying attention flow in transformers. arXiv: Learning, arXiv: Learning (2020)
2. Chen, Y., Bai, Y., Zhang, W., Mei, T.: Destruction and construction learning for fine-grained image recognition. In: Proceedings of the IEEE/CVF Conference on Computer Vision and Pattern Recognition, pp. 5157–5166 (2019)
3. Ding, Y., Zhou, Y., Zhu, Y., Ye, Q., Jiao, J.: Selective sparse sampling for fine-grained image recognition. In: Proceedings of the IEEE/CVF International Conference on Computer Vision, pp. 6599–6608 (2019)
4. Dosovitskiy, A.: An image is worth 16x16 words: transformers for image recognition at scale (2020). arXiv:2010.11929 arXiv preprint
5. Du, R., et al.: Fine-grained visual classification via progressive multi-granularity training of jigsaw patches. In: European Conference on Computer Vision, pp. 153–168. Springer (2020)
6. Gao, Y., Han, X., Wang, X., Huang, W., Scott, M.: Channel interaction networks for fine-grained image categorization. In: Proceedings of the AAAI Conference on Artificial Intelligence, vol. 34, pp. 10818–10825 (2020)
7. He, J., et al.: Transfg: a transformer architecture for fine-grained recognition. In: Proceedings of the AAAI Conference on Artificial Intelligence, vol. 36, pp. 852–860 (2022)
8. Huang, Z., Li, Y.: Interpretable and accurate fine-grained recognition via region grouping. In: Proceedings of the IEEE/CVF Conference on Computer Vision and Pattern Recognition, pp. 8662–8672 (2020)
9. Ji, R., et al.: Attention convolutional binary neural tree for fine-grained visual categorization. In: Proceedings of the IEEE/CVF Conference on Computer Vision and Pattern Recognition, pp. 10468–10477 (2020)
10. Khosla, A., Jayadevaprakash, N., Yao, B., Li, F.F.: Novel dataset for fine-grained image categorization: stanford dogs. In: Proceedings CVPR workshop on fine-grained visual categorization (FGVC), vol. 2, (2011)
11. Krause, J., Stark, M., Deng, J., Fei-Fei, L.: 3D object representations for fine-grained categorization. In: Proceedings of the IEEE International Conference on Computer Vision Workshops, pp. 554–561 (2013)
12. Liu, C., Xie, H., Zha, Z.J., Ma, L., Yu, L., Zhang, Y.: Filtration and distillation: enhancing region attention for fine-grained visual categorization. In: Proceedings of the AAAI Conference on Artificial Intelligence, vol. 34, pp. 11555–11562 (2020)
13. Liu, Z., Lin, Y., Cao, Y., Hu, H., Wei, Y., Zhang, Z., Lin, S., Guo, B.: Swin transformer: hierarchical vision transformer using shifted windows. In: Proceedings of the IEEE/CVF International Conference on Computer Vision, pp. 10012–10022 (2021)
14. Luo, W., et al.: Cross-x learning for fine-grained visual categorization. In: Proceedings of the IEEE/CVF International Conference on Computer Vision, pp. 8242–8251 (2019)
15. Min, S., Yao, H., Xie, H., Zha, Z.J., Zhang, Y.: Multi-objective matrix normalization for fine-grained visual recognition. IEEE Trans. Image Process. **29**, 4996–5009 (2020)
16. Serrano, S., Smith, N.A.: Is attention interpretable? In: Proceedings of the 57th Annual Meeting of the Association for Computational Linguistics (2019). https://doi.org/10.18653/v1/p19-1282, http://dx.doi.org/10.18653/v1/p19-1282

17. Sun, H., He, X., Peng, Y.: Sim-trans: structure information modeling transformer for fine-grained visual categorization. In: Proceedings of the 30th ACM International Conference on Multimedia, pp. 5853–5861 (2022)
18. Sun, M., Yuan, Y., Zhou, F., Ding, E.: Multi-attention multi-class constraint for fine-grained image recognition. In: Proceedings of the European Conference on Computer Vision (ECCV), pp. 805–821 (2018)
19. Touvron, H., Cord, M., Douze, M., Massa, F., Sablayrolles, A., Jégou, H.: Training data-efficient image transformers & distillation through attention. In: International Conference on Machine Learning, pp. 10347–10357. PMLR (2021)
20. Vaswani, A., et al.: Attention is all you need. Neural Information Processing Systems, Neural Information Processing Systems (2017)
21. Wah, C., Branson, S., Welinder, P., Perona, P., Belongie, S.: The caltech-ucsd birds-200-2011 dataset (2011)
22. Wang, J., Yu, X., Gao, Y.: Feature fusion vision transformer for fine-grained visual categorization. arXiv preprint arXiv:2107.02341 (2021)
23. Wang, Q., Wang, J., Deng, H., Wu, X., Wang, Y., Hao, G.: Aa-trans: Core attention aggregating transformer with information entropy selector for fine-grained visual classification. Pattern Recogn. **140**, 109547 (2023)
24. Wang, Z., Wang, S., Yang, S., Li, H., Li, J., Li, Z.: Weakly supervised fine-grained image classification via guassian mixture model oriented discriminative learning. In: Proceedings of the IEEE/CVF Conference on Computer Vision and Pattern Recognition, pp. 9749–9758 (2020)
25. Wang, Z., Wang, S., Li, H., Dou, Z., Li, J.: Graph-propagation based correlation learning for weakly supervised fine-grained image classification. In: Proceedings of the AAAI Conference on Artificial Intelligence, vol. 34, pp. 12289–12296 (2020)
26. Xu, Q., Wang, J., Jiang, B., Luo, B.: Fine-grained visual classification via internal ensemble learning transformer. IEEE Trans. Multimedia **25**, 9015–9028 (2023)
27. Zhang, L., Huang, S., Liu, W., Tao, D.: Learning a mixture of granularity-specific experts for fine-grained categorization. In: Proceedings of the IEEE/CVF International Conference on Computer Vision, pp. 8331–8340 (2019)
28. Zheng, H., Fu, J., Zha, Z.J., Luo, J.: Looking for the devil in the details: learning trilinear attention sampling network for fine-grained image recognition. In: Proceedings of the IEEE/CVF Conference on Computer Vision and Pattern Recognition, pp. 5012–5021 (2019)
29. Zheng, H., Fu, J., Zha, Z.J., Luo, J., Mei, T.: Learning rich part hierarchies with progressive attention networks for fine-grained image recognition. IEEE Trans. Image Process. **29**, 476–488 (2019)
30. Zhuang, P., Wang, Y., Qiao, Y.: Learning attentive pairwise interaction for fine-grained classification. In: Proceedings of the AAAI Conference on Artificial Intelligence, vol. 34, pp. 13130–13137 (2020)

Multi-scale Attention and Adaptive Self-attention for Occlusion-Aware Depth Estimation in Light Field

Zhineng Zhang, Tao Yan(✉), Chenglong Wang, Xianglong Chen, Jinsheng Liu, and Weilong Huang

Jiangnan University, Wuxi 214122, China
yantao.ustc@gmail.com

Abstract. Light field depth estimation is a fundamental and hot research topic, which aims to exploiting angular and spatial information for estimating the depth of object surfaces. Though a lot of methods have been proposed for the light field depth estimation task, few methods can effectively capture depth information in challenging scenes, especially for occluded scenes. Meanwhile, these methods rarely reduce the impact of occluded pixels on the cost values in the cost construction stage of depth estimation. In this paper, we propose a novel Occlusion-Aware Depth Estimation Network, named *OADENet*, for light field image depth estimation. Specifically, to capture the depth variations between distant backgrounds and foreground objects, which are challenging to represent using single-scale feature extraction, we propose a Multi-Scale Attention Fusion Module (MSAFM) for capturing and integrating features across different scales. Subsequently, we propose a cost constructor based on an adaptive self-attention mechanism to adaptively capture global pixel-wise matching costs and reduce the impact of occluded pixels, improving the reliability of the cost volume. Finally, we also propose an occlusion mask supervision strategy to effectively learn our network, enhancing the network's depth estimation capability in occluded regions. Extensive experiments on synthetic and real light field datasets demonstrate that our method achieves good performance in both accuracy and efficiency.

Keywords: Light field image · Depth estimation · Occlusion mask · Adaptive self-attention mechanism

1 Introduction

Light Field (LF) images record both the position and direction of incoming light rays, providing richer spatial and angular information compared to single-lens reflex (SLR) images, which facilitates scene depth estimation. Building upon this, LF depth estimation, a critical task in computer vision, aims to infer the depth information of objects within a scene from LFs.

P. Li et al. (Eds.): CGI 2025, LNCS 16508, pp. 300–312, 2026.
https://doi.org/10.1007/978-3-032-22264-0_24

This task has numerous applications, including refocusing, super-resolution, view synthesis, virtual reality, and three-dimensional reconstruction. Depth estimation methods can be broadly categorized into several methods. Multi-View Stereo (MVS) based methods [8,13] construct a cost volume using traditional stereo matching techniques. Epipolar Plane Image (EPI) based methods [25] focus on analyzing linear structures in the EPI, while defocus-based methods [17] leverage focal stack information for depth estimation. Despite their effectiveness, these methods are sensitive to noise and occlusion regions and often require significant computational resources.

To address the challenges of occlusion in light field depth estimation, we propose *OADENet*, an Occlusion-Aware Depth Estimation Network with several key innovations. We introduce a Multi-Scale Attention Fusion Module (MSAFM) that extracts global, local, and fine-grained features using attention to enhance depth perception in complex scenes. An adaptive self-attention-based cost volume models long-range pixel dependencies and mitigates occlusion effects during matching. To further improve occlusion handling, we design a Mask Refinement Block (MRB) and an occlusion mask loss. Additionally, we adopt a disparity regression strategy with more predefined disparity labels to better capture wide depth ranges and enhance generalization.

In summary, the main contributions of our work presented in this paper are as follows:

- First, we propose an effective and efficient deep learning-based network, called Occlusion-Aware Depth Estimation Network *(OADENet)*, for light field image depth estimation.
- Second, we propose a Multi-Scale Attention Fusion Module (MSAFM) to extract multi-scale features and fuse them according to the importance of different scale features.
- Third, we construct a cost volume based on an adaptive self-attention mechanism to adaptively capture global pixel-wise matching costs and assign higher weights to the matching costs of pixels in non-occluded regions, enabling the network to accurately capture cost volume from these regions.
- Finally, we propose a Mask Refine Block (MRB) to enable the network to refine occlusion masks for better localization of the occluded regions and an occlusion mask supervision strategy for effective network learning.

2 Related Work

2.1 Traditional Methods in LF Depth Estimation

Traditional depth estimation methods can be divided into three categories. Multi-View Stereo (MVS) based methods [8,14] use disparity cues by performing stereo matching from the LFs for depth estimation. Jeon *et al.*[8] used phase shift theory for sub-pixel translation and stereo matching of sub-aperture images. Epipolar plane image (EPI) based methods estimate depth [23,25] by analyzing the slope of lines in EPIs, which correspond to the depth of points in the scene.

Wang *et al.*[23] used variational optimization on epipolar plane images (EPIs) to simultaneously estimate disparity. Zhang *et al.*[25] proposed the Spinning Parallelogram Operator (SPO) to estimate the EPI image by its slope of the depth. Defocus-based methods [17] estimate depth by analyzing the amount of blur at different focal planes to infer depth information. Tao *et al.*[17] combined defocus and correspondence information through a joint optimization framework to achieve robust and accurate depth estimation. However, these methods rely on traditional optimization algorithms and predefined disparity priors, which make depth estimation challenging in complex and occluded scenes, while also incurring high computational costs.

2.2 Deep Learning-Based Methods in LF Depth Estimation

Currently, there are two main categories of learning-based depth estimation methods. Some representative methods [3,16,18] explore the correspondence between views for better inferring spatial information. Tsai *et al.*[18] used attention mechanisms to dynamically adjust its attention to different views, optimizing the combination of these views. For instance, Chen *et al.*[3] proposed intra-branch and inter-branch fusion strategies and introduced an attention mechanism to select texture-rich feature views within and between branches. Zhao *et al.*[26] propose a method for sparse feature matching to dense pixel-level matching, accurately capturing the geometric features of the scene.

other representative methods [11,19,21,24] focus on occlusion-aware depth estimation. For instance, Wang *et al.*[21] proposed a cost volume composed of a series of convolutions with specially designed expansion rates to perceive occlusion information. Yang *et al.*[24] proposed a hybrid cost volume, integrating global and local features with an occlusion perception loss to enhance depth estimation quality. Li *et al.*[11] proposed a method that learns occlusion patterns through unsupervised loss to improve disparity accuracy. Although these methods achieve promising results in depth estimation tasks for occluded scenes, they fail to effectively capture the dependencies between pixels and suppress the impact of occluded pixels on depth estimation.

3 Method

In this section, we first propose a learning-based occlusion mask generation method. Second, we introduce our network architecture for LF depth estimation. Finally, we describe our occlusion-aware loss function.

3.1 Occlusion Mask Method

Occlusion masks are typically binary or probabilistic representations that distinguish visible regions from occluded ones. These masks guide the network to focus on valid, non-occluded regions and alleviate the ambiguity introduced by

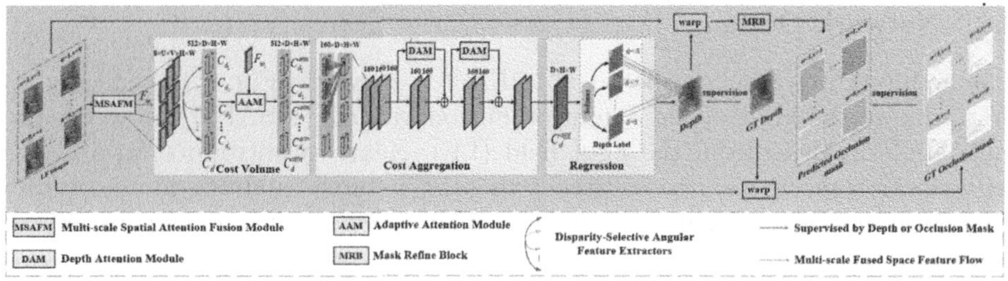

Fig. 1. The overview of our proposed depth estimation method mainly consists of five parts: multi-scale feature extraction and fusion, cost volume construction, cost volume aggregation, depth regression, and mixed supervision based on depth and occlusion information.

occluded pixels during the cost construction phase, thereby improving the accuracy and robustness of depth predictions.

The process of the generation of an occlusion mask has two steps. First, we warp each view to the center view through a depth map of the center view. The warping process can be mathematically represented as:

$$\mathcal{V}_{k\to c} = \mathcal{W}_{k\to c}^{\hat{\mathcal{D}}_c}(\mathcal{V}_k), \quad k = 1, 2, \cdots, UV, \tag{1}$$

where $\mathcal{W}_{k\to c}^{\hat{\mathcal{D}}_c}$ denotes the warping operation that projects the k-th view $\mathcal{V}_k$ to the center view $\mathcal{V}_c$ depend on the predicted depth map $\hat{\mathcal{D}}_c$, UV represents the number of sub-aperture images (SAIs). Second, the occlusion map is derived by calculating the absolute difference between the warped sub-view and the central view. The process of generating occlusion maps can be formulated as follows:

$$\begin{aligned} \mathcal{V}_{k\to c}^{res} &= \left|\mathcal{V}_{k\to c} - \mathcal{V}_c\right|, \\ \hat{\mathcal{M}}_k &= |1 - \mathcal{V}_{k\to c}^{res}|^2, \end{aligned} \tag{2}$$

where $\mathcal{V}_{k\to c}$ denotes the warped center sub-view, $\mathcal{V}_c$ denotes the center sub-view, $\mathcal{V}_{k\to c}^{res}$ is the difference between $\mathcal{V}_{k\to c}$ and $\mathcal{V}_c$, $\hat{\mathcal{M}}_k$ is the initial occlusion mask. Specifically, the projected view $\mathcal{V}_{k\to c}$ should have identical values to the center view V_c at non-occluded regions. Therefore, we use the absolute error between $\mathcal{V}_{k\to c}$ and $\mathcal{V}_c$ to locate the occluded region initially. Then, we propose a Mask Refine Block (MRB) to get the learning-based occlusion mask $\hat{\mathcal{M}}_k^r$ for more accurate localization of the occluded region. The process is as follows:

$$\hat{\mathcal{M}}_k^r = \mathrm{MRB}(\hat{\mathcal{M}}_{\mathrm{k}}), \tag{3}$$

the detail of MRB is in Sect. 3.3. the MRB further refines the occlusion mask by mitigating the physical influences of illumination on photometric consistency, enabling more accurate localization of occluded regions. Using this method, the more accurate occlusion mask for each view can be obtained.

3.2 Network Design

The architecture of our proposed *OADENet* is shown in Fig. 1. Specifically, we first propose the Multi-Scale Attention Fusion Module (MSAFM) for extracting multi-scale features from the light field (LF). Next, we introduce an adaptive self-attention mechanism to construct the cost volume, enabling more accurate pixel-level matching. Then, we aggregate the cost volume using 3D convolutions and the Depth Attention Module (DAM) [21] to learn the confidence of depth labels. Additionally, we regress the depth labels to obtain the depth map. Finally, we propose an MRB and an occlusion mask supervision strategy to accurately locate occlusion regions and learn our network easily, respectively.

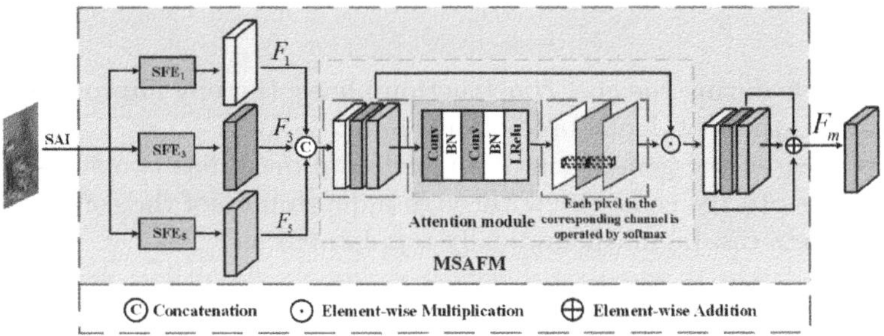

Fig. 2. Our Multi-Scale Attention Fusion Module (MSAFM) primarily consists of three parts: multi-scale spatial feature extraction, spatial attention, and multi-scale feature fusion.

Feature Extraction. To extract multi-scale features from SAIs, we propose the Multi-Scale Attention Fusion Module (MSAFM), which shares weights across views to reduce the number of parameters, as illustrated in Fig. 2. Specifically, each SAI is fed into the Spatial Feature Extraction module (SFE_i) [21] to get spatial feature $F_i \in \mathbb{R}^{C\times U\times V\times H\times W}$, and $i \in \{1,3,5\}$ denotes the scale of feature extractor is $i \times i$. Subsequently, we concatenate the spatial features F_1, F_3, and F_5 for getting the attention maps through an attention module, where we use the softmax operation to obtain $\mathrm{Att}(F_i)$ to perceive the importance of the three-scale spatial features. After that, we multiply $\mathrm{Att}(F_i)$ with F_i separately and then add them to obtain the multi-scale fused feature $F_m \in \mathbb{R}^{C\times U\times V\times H\times W}$. F_m is defined as:

$$F_m = \sum_i \mathrm{Att}(F_i) * F_i. \tag{4}$$

Cost Volume Based on Adaptive Self-attention Mechanism. Cost volume is typically constructed by comparing pixel similarities [7,26] across different views to compute matching costs. Traditional methods achieve this by shifting the features of each pixel according to specific disparity values and combining them to build the cost volume. However, these methods rely on predefined disparity labels for feature shifting, making it difficult to capture long-range dependencies between pixels. In occluded regions, feature shifting fails to leverage contextual information, leading to inaccurate matching costs.

To address this limitation, we propose a cost volume based on adaptive self-attention. The detailed process is illustrated in Fig. 3. First, we perform feature shifting based on a wide range of predefined disparity hypotheses (covering the maximum scene depth) to capture long-range dependencies between pixels. Then, we employ an adaptive self-attention mechanism (as shown in Fig. 4) to reduce the impact of feature shifting from occluded points on the matching cost volume. The shifted feature (also referred to as the initial cost volume) process can be formulated as follows:

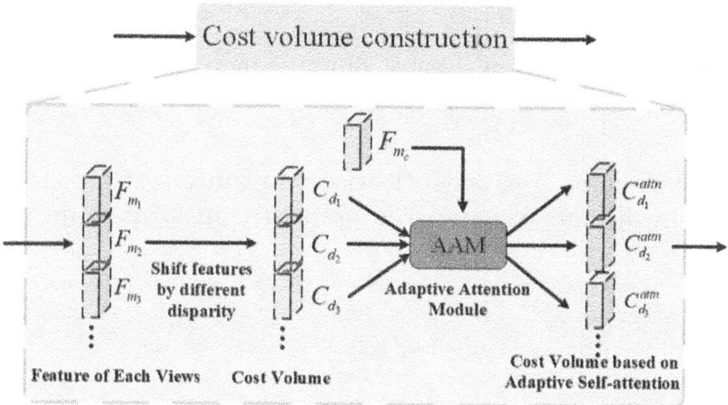

Fig. 3. The architecture of our cost volume. It contains two parts: feature shifting by disparity and an adaptive attention mechanism for capturing the long-range dependencies between matching pixels.

$$C_d = F_m(u, v, x + (u - u_c) \cdot d, y + (v - v_c) \cdot d), \tag{5}$$

where $C_d \in \mathbb{R}^{C \times D \times H \times W}$ is the initial cost volume obtained by shifting the feature by a predefined disparity $d \in \{d_1, \cdots, d_n\}$. C, D, H, and W represent the channel, disparity, height, and width dimensions, respectively.

To capture the dependency between each pair of pixels, every shifted feature $C_{d_i} \in \mathbb{R}^{C \times H \times W}$ is first reshaped into $C^s_{d_i} \in \mathbb{R}^{HW \times C}$, where HW represents the number of tokens and C represents the token dimension. Next, $C^s_{d_i}$ is multiplied by the matrices $W_Q \in \mathbb{R}^{C \times C}$ and $W_K \in \mathbb{R}^{C \times C}$ respectively, to map it into the richer feature space, producing $Q \in \mathbb{R}^{HW \times C}$ and $K \in \mathbb{R}^{HW \times C}$. Additionally, Q and K^T are multiplied to obtain an score map $S_{d_i} \in \mathbb{R}^{HW \times HW}$, representing the cost relationship between any two pixels in shifted feature C_{d_i}. The process can be formulated as follows:

$$
\begin{aligned}
Q &= W_Q C_{d_i}, K = W_K C_{d_i}, V = W_V C_{d_i}, \\
S_{d_i} &= \text{Softmax}(\frac{QK^T}{\sqrt{C}}),
\end{aligned} \tag{6}
$$

where W_Q, W_K, W_V are represent feature space transformation.

Then, to suppress the influence of occluded pixels on others in score map S_{d_i}, we propose a dynamic adjustment mechanism to refine the score map S_{d_i}. Specifically, First, we use the central view feature $F_{m_c} \in \mathbb{R}^{C \times H \times W}$ from the MSAFM to pass through a depth-wise separable convolution to extract edge information $F_{m_c}^d \in \mathbb{R}^{C \times H \times W}$. Second, $F_{m_c}^d$ is processed with point-wise convolution for channel interaction, producing the edge feature map $F_{m_c}^{d,p} \in \mathbb{R}^{1 \times H \times W}$, where the edge regions correspond to occlusion regions. Third, $F_{m_c}^{d,p}$ is reshaped to obtain $F_{m_c}^{d,p,s} \in \mathbb{R}^{1 \times HW}$. Finally, $F_{m_c}^{d,p,s}$ and S are element-wise multiplied to produce the refined score map $S_r \in \mathbb{R}^{HW \times HW}$. The formula is as follows:

$$
\begin{aligned}
F_{m_c}^{d,p,s} &= \text{reshape}(\text{Conv}_\text{p}(\text{Conv}_\text{d}(F_{m_c}))), \\
S_r &= S \cdot F_{m_c}^{d,p,s},
\end{aligned} \tag{7}
$$

where $\text{Conv}_\text{d}(\cdot)$ denotes 3×3 depth-wise convolution, $\text{Conv}_\text{p}(\cdot)$ denotes 1×1 point-wise convolution. reshape$(\cdot)$ is used to transform shape $\mathbb{R}^{1 \times H \times W}$ into shape $\mathbb{R}^{1 \times HW}$.

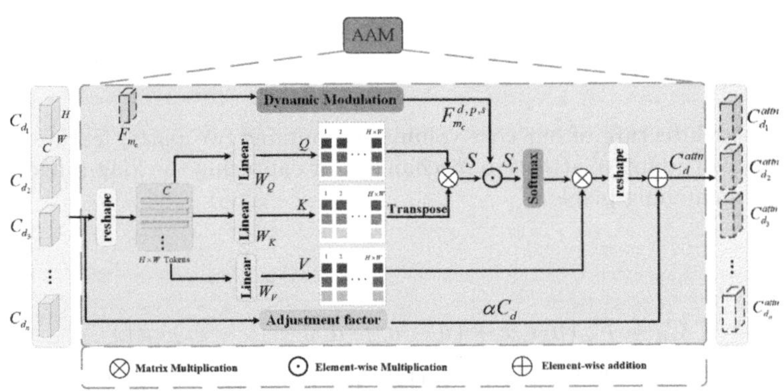

Fig. 4. Adaptive Attention Module(AAM) contains three parts: The first part is self-attention for capturing the matching cost between any two pixels. The second is the dynamic modulation mechanism for adaptively adjusting the attention distribution across different pixels. The third is the adjustment factor α for Adjusting the impact of the self-attention module on the output result.

Finally, to adjust the contribution ratio of the initial cost volume in the output, we set an adjustment factor α. The cost volume based on adaptive self-attention is denoted as $C_{d_i}^{attn} \in \mathbb{R}^{C \times H \times W}$. The process can be formulated as follows:

$$C_{d_i}^{attn} = \text{reshape}(\text{Softmax}(S_r)V) + \alpha C_{d_i}, \tag{8}$$

reshape$(\cdot)$ is used to transform shape $\mathbb{R}^{HW \times C}$ into shape $\mathbb{R}^{C \times H \times W}$.

Table 1. Mean square error (multiplied with 100) achieved by different methods on the 4D LF benchmark [5]. The best results are in red, the second best results are in blue and the third best results are in light blue.

Category	Method	Bg.	Dots	Pyramids	Stripes	Boxes	Cotton	Dino	Sideboard	Time(s)
Traditional	SPO[25]	4.587	5.238	0.043	6.955	9.107	1.313	0.310	1.024	2115
	OBER-cross-ANP[15]	4.700	1.757	0.008	1.435	4.750	0.555	0.336	0.941	183
	OAVC[4]	3.835	16.58	0.040	1.316	6.988	0.598	0.267	1.047	19.41
learning-based	EPN+OS+GC[12]	3.699	22.37	0.018	8.731	9.314	1.406	0.565	1.744	274.7
	Epinet-fcn-9 × 9[16]	3.909	1.980	0.007	0.915	6.036	0.223	0.151	0.806	2.041
	EPI_Shift[9]	12.79	13.15	0.037	1.686	9.790	0.475	0.392	1.261	22.57
	EPI_ORM[10]	3.411	14.48	0.016	1.744	4.189	0.287	0.336	0.778	76.61
	LFAttNet[18]	3.648	1.425	0.004	0.892	3.996	0.209	0.093	0.530	5.862
	FastLFNet[6]	3.986	3.407	0.018	0.984	4.395	0.322	0.189	0.747	0.624
	DistgDisp[22]	4.542	1.525	0.005	0.924	3.743	0.225	0.132	0.578	2.788
	Wang *et al.*[20]	3.040	2.570	0.020	6.580	8.080	0.290	0.740	0.630	205.5
	OADENet(ours)	4.177	1.395	0.006	0.819	4.085	0.132	0.092	0.517	3.02

Cost Volume Aggregation and Depth Regression. We aggregate cost volume $C_d^{attn} \in \mathbb{R}^{C \times D \times H \times W}$ using 3D convolution, the method consists of two steps: Firstly, a $1 \times 1 \times 1$ 3D convolution is introduced to reduce the number of channel C from 512 to 160. Then, following [18], spatial features are fully integrated using nine cascaded 3D convolutions, generating the aggregated cost volume $C_d^{agg} \in \mathbb{R}^{D \times H \times W}$. During the cascading process, we follow [21] to use a Depth Attention Module (DAM) to highlight important depth channels. Finally, the disparity is regressed as follows:

$$\hat{d} = \sum_{d_i \in D} d_i \times \text{Softmax}(C_{d_i}^{agg}), \tag{9}$$

where $\hat{d}$ denotes the final estimated disparity, $D = \{-8, -7, -6, \cdots, 6, 7, 8\}$ is the set of the predefined disparity labels. $C_{d_i}^{agg} \in \mathbb{R}^{1 \times H \times W}$ is the aggregated cost of predefined disparity d_i. Softmax operation is used to get the probability of the disparity label.

3.3 Mask Refine Block and Occlusion Aware Loss Function

In fact, the generation of occlusion masks requires the depth map as input, but depth information is unreliable during the network inference stage. To address this issue, we propose a Mask Refine Block (MRB). Specifically, our MRB consists of several convolutional layers, BatchNorm, and Leaky ReLU. We apply MRB to fully integrate and interact the occlusion information across all views, yielding refined occlusion maps. We then use a combined loss function that incorporates both depth and occlusion mask supervision to improve depth estimation accuracy described as follows:

$$\mathcal{L}_m = \sum_{k=1}^{UV} \|\hat{\mathcal{M}}_k - \mathcal{M}_k\|_1, \mathcal{L}_d = \|\hat{\mathcal{D}}_c - \mathcal{D}_c\|_1, \mathcal{L}_{total} = \mathcal{L}_m + \mathcal{L}_d, \tag{10}$$

where $\mathcal{M}_k$ and $\hat{\mathcal{M}}_k$ are the GT and predicted occlusion mask of k-th SAI, respectively. $\mathcal{D}_c$ and $\hat{\mathcal{D}}_c$ are the GT and predicted depth map of the center view, respectively. UV represents the number of SAIs.

4 Experiments

We evaluate our method on both synthetic and real-world Light Field (LF) datasets. For the 4D LF benchmark [5], which consists of 9×9 angular and 512×512 spatial resolution synthetic LFs, we follow existing methods [2,3,6,16, 18,21,22] by training on 16 "Additional" scenes, validating on 8 "Stratified" and "Training" scenes, and testing on 4 "Testing" scenes. To assess generalization, we use the real-world (New) Stanford LF dataset [1], which lacks ground truth depth. During training, 32×32 grayscale patches are cropped and augmented via flipping, rotation, refocusing, and downsampling. The model is optimized using Adam ($\beta_1 = 0.9$, $\beta_2 = 0.999$) with a batch size of 16 and a learning rate of 1×10^{-3}, implemented in PyTorch and trained on an NVIDIA RTX 4090 GPU. Evaluation is based on Mean Square Error (MSE) and Bad Pixel ratio (BP), where lower values indicate better performance.

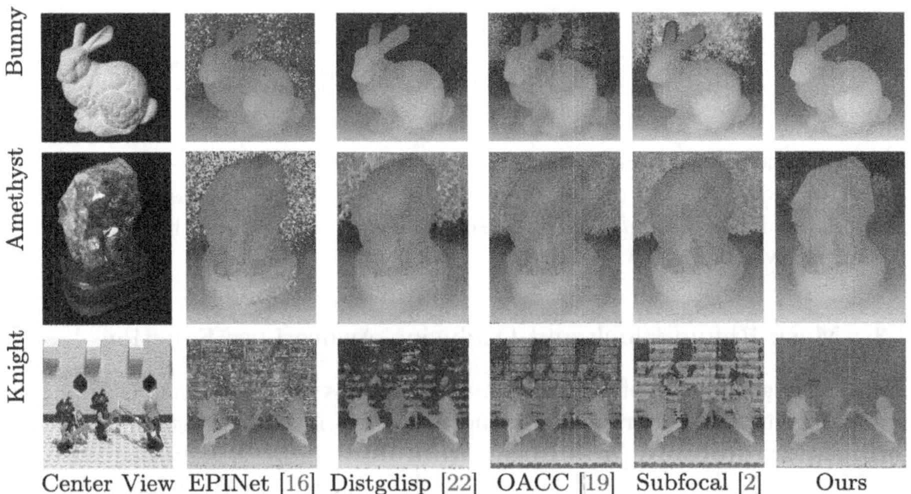

Fig. 5. Comparison of the state-of-the-art depth estimation methods on the challenging real-world LFs from The (New) Stanford Light Field Archive [1].

4.1 Comparison to the State-of-the-Art Methods

We compare our *OADENet* to the state-of-the-art methods, including three traditional methods [4,7,15] and eight deep learning-based methods [6,9,10,12, 16,18,20,22]. Table 1 presents the MSE and average running time achieved by various methods. Our method demonstrates the lowest MSE in five scenes, indicating superior accuracy. Furthermore, our method requires only approximately 3 s per scene on average, outperforming many other methods. As shown in Fig. 5, our *OADENet* accurately estimates the disparity between the background and foreground regions in the Bunny, Amethyst, and Knight scenes.

Table 2. Ablation study on MASFM, MRB, Occlusion Mask Loss on eight scenes of 4D LF Benchmark [5]. Due to space limitations, only four scenes are presented in the table, while the average values are computed based on the metrics over all eight scenes. "MASFM→SSF" represents replacing MASFM with SSF. "w/o-AAM" represents that our model removes Adaptive Attention Module. "w/o-Mask Refine" represents that our model removes Mask Refine Module. "w/o-Mask Loss" represents that our model removes Occlusion Mask Loss Function.

Models	Boxes		Cotton		Dino		Sideboard		Average	
	MSE	BP007	MSE	BP007	MSE	BP007	MSE	BP007	MSE	BP007
MASFM→SSF	4.398	12.660	0.173	0.374	0.103	1.329	0.598	3.581	1.484	3.484
w/o-AAM	4.922	13.112	0.206	0.363	0.147	1.427	0.588	3.524	1.572	3.999
w/o-Mask Refine	**4.031**	12.365	0.228	0.376	0.132	1.395	0.551	3.466	1.593	3.534
w/o-Mask Loss	4.808	12.741	0.199	0.376	0.112	1.251	0.575	3.518	1.606	3.407
Ours	4.085	**11.714**	**0.132**	**0.372**	**0.092**	**1.096**	**0.517**	**3.096**	**1.403**	**3.201**

4.2 Ablation Study

In this subsection, we evaluate variants of our *OADENet* to demonstrate the effectiveness of the Multi-Scale Attention Fusion Module (MSAFM), Mask Refine Block (MRB), and Adaptive Attention Module (AAM). Additionally, we observe that varying disparity ranges significantly impact the performance of the LF depth estimation network. To ensure the validity of the experiments and the adaptability of the model, all ablation studies are performed by retraining the entire network after removing each individual module.

To evaluate the effectiveness of each component in our proposed network, we conduct a series of ablation studies, as shown in Table 2. Replacing the Multi-Scale Attention Fusion Module (MSAFM) with a Single-Scale Feature Extraction Module (SSF) leads to increases of 0.08 and 0.28 in MSE and BadPix0.07, respectively, indicating the importance of multi-scale feature extraction for handling complex depth variations. Removing the Adaptive Attention Module (AAM) results in larger performance degradation (MSE ↓ 0.17, BadPix0.07

$\downarrow$ 0.8), showing its crucial role in accurately computing matching costs, especially in occluded regions. Excluding the Mask Refine Block (MRB) and Mask Loss Function further degrades performance, suggesting that both are essential for improving occlusion localization and enhancing overall network learning. Finally, as shown in 3, we explore the impact of disparity range and find that a range of $[-8, 8]$ achieves the best trade-off between accuracy and computational cost.

Table 3. Ablation study on disparity range on eight scenes (Backgammon, Dots, Pyramids, Stripes, Boxes, Cotton, Dino, and Sideboard) of 4D LF Benchmark [5]. "Running time" and "FLOPs" are tested on the LFs with a size of 32×32.

Disparity range	Running time↓	FLOPs↓	Avg MSE↓	Avg BP007↓
$[-4, 4]$	**25.334ms**	**52.38G**	1.54	3.44
$[-8, 8]$	29.731ms	93.10G	**1.40**	**3.20**
$[-12, 12]$	36.766ms	133.83G	1.63	3.71
$[-16, 16]$	44.488ms	174.56G	1.72	4.00

5 Conclusion

In this paper, we present a novel network *OADENet* for occlusion-aware light field depth estimation. First, to effectively capture information from both foreground objects and the background, we propose a Multi-Scale Attention Fusion Module (MSAFM) to fuse features based on their importance across different scales. Second, to reduce the impact of occluded pixels, we construct a cost volume based on an adaptive self-attention mechanism, enhancing the reliability of the cost volume. Third, we propose a Mask Refine Block (MRB) and an occlusion mask supervision strategy to effectively locate occluded regions and facilitate learning for our network, respectively. Finally, we introduce an LF depth estimation method with a wide disparity range to provide more predefined disparity labels for disparity regression, thereby enhancing the network's generalization to real-world scenes. In the future, we will further enhance the network's performance in real-world scenes and apply it to other LF tasks.

References

1. Bok, Y., Jeon, H.G., Kweon, I.S.: Geometric calibration of micro-lens-based light field cameras using line features. IEEE Trans. Pattern Anal. Mach. Intell. **39**(2), 287–300 (2016)
2. Chao, W., Wang, X., Wang, Y., Wang, G., Duan, F.: Learning sub-pixel disparity distribution for light field depth estimation. IEEE Trans. Comput. Imag. **9**, 1126–1138 (2023)

3. Chen, J., Zhang, S., Lin, Y.: Attention-based multi-level fusion network for light field depth estimation. In: Proceedings of the AAAI Conference on Artificial Intelligence, vol. 35, pp. 1009–1017 (2021)
4. Han, K., Xiang, W., Wang, E., Huang, T.: A novel occlusion-aware vote cost for light field depth estimation. IEEE Trans. Pattern Anal. Mach. Intell. **44**(11), 8022–8035 (2021)
5. Honauer, K., Johannsen, O., Kondermann, D., Goldluecke, B.: A dataset and evaluation methodology for depth estimation on 4d light fields. In: Computer Vision–ACCV 2016: 13th Asian Conference on Computer Vision, Taipei, Taiwan, November 20-24, 2016, Revised Selected Papers, Part III 13, pp. 19–34. Springer (2017). https://doi.org/10.1007/978-3-319-54187-7_2
6. Huang, Z., Hu, X., Xue, Z., Xu, W., Yue, T.: Fast light-field disparity estimation with multi-disparity-scale cost aggregation. In: Proceedings of the IEEE/CVF International Conference on Computer Vision, pp. 6320–6329 (2021)
7. Jeon, H.G., et al.: Depth from a light field image with learning-based matching costs. IEEE Trans. Pattern Anal. Mach. Intell. **41**(2), 297–310 (2018)
8. Jeon, H.G., et al.: Accurate depth map estimation from a Lenslet light field camera. In: Proceedings of the IEEE Conference on Computer Vision and Pattern Recognition, pp. 1547–1555 (2015)
9. Leistner, T., Schilling, H., Mackowiak, R., Gumhold, S., Rother, C.: Learning to think outside the box: wide-baseline light field depth estimation with epi-shift. In: 2019 International Conference on 3D Vision (3DV), pp. 249–257. IEEE (2019)
10. Li, K., Zhang, J., Sun, R., Zhang, X., Gao, J.: Epi-based oriented relation networks for light field depth estimation. arXiv preprint arXiv:2007.04538 (2020)
11. Li, P., et al.: Opal: occlusion pattern aware loss for unsupervised light field disparity estimation. IEEE Trans. Pattern Anal. Mach. Intell. (2023)
12. Luo, Y., Zhou, W., Fang, J., Liang, L., Zhang, H., Dai, G.: Epi-patch based convolutional neural network for depth estimation on 4D light field. In: Neural Information Processing: 24th International Conference, ICONIP 2017, Guangzhou, China, November 14-18, 2017, Proceedings, Part III 24, pp. 642–652. Springer (2017). https://doi.org/10.1007/978-3-319-70090-8_65
13. Park, I.K., Lee, K.M., et al.: Robust light field depth estimation using occlusion-noise aware data costs. IEEE Trans. Pattern Anal. Mach. Intell. **40**(10), 2484–2497 (2017)
14. Peng, R., Wang, R., Wang, Z., Lai, Y., Wang, R.: Rethinking depth estimation for multi-view stereo: a unified representation. In: Proceedings of the IEEE/CVF Conference on Computer Vision and Pattern Recognition, pp. 8645–8654 (2022)
15. Schilling, H., Diebold, M., Rother, C., Jähne, B.: Trust your model: light field depth estimation with inline occlusion handling. In: Proceedings of the IEEE Conference on Computer Vision and Pattern Recognition, pp. 4530–4538 (2018)
16. Shin, C., Jeon, H.G., Yoon, Y., Kweon, I.S., Kim, S.J.: EpiNet: a fully-convolutional neural network using epipolar geometry for depth from light field images. In: Proceedings of the IEEE Conference on Computer Vision and Pattern Recognition, pp. 4748–4757 (2018)
17. Tao, M.W., Hadap, S., Malik, J., Ramamoorthi, R.: Depth from combining defocus and correspondence using light-field cameras. In: Proceedings of the IEEE International Conference on Computer Vision, pp. 673–680 (2013)
18. Tsai, Y.J., Liu, Y.L., Ouhyoung, M., Chuang, Y.Y.: Attention-based view selection networks for light-field disparity estimation. In: Proceedings of the AAAI Conference on Artificial Intelligence, vol. 34, pp. 12095–12103 (2020)

19. Wang, T.C., Efros, A.A., Ramamoorthi, R.: Occlusion-aware depth estimation using light-field cameras. In: Proceedings of the IEEE International Conference on Computer Vision, pp. 3487–3495 (2015)
20. Wang, X., Chao, W., Wang, L., Duan, F.: Light field depth estimation using occlusion-aware consistency analysis. Vis. Comput. **39**(8), 3441–3454 (2023)
21. Wang, Y., Wang, L., Liang, Z., Yang, J., An, W., Guo, Y.: Occlusion-aware cost constructor for light field depth estimation. In: Proceedings of the IEEE/CVF Conference on Computer Vision and Pattern Recognition, pp. 19809–19818 (2022)
22. Wang, Y., et al.: Disentangling light fields for super-resolution and disparity estimation. IEEE Trans. Pattern Anal. Mach. Intell. **45**(1), 425–443 (2022)
23. Wanner, S., Goldluecke, B.: Variational light field analysis for disparity estimation and super-resolution. IEEE Trans. Pattern Anal. Mach. Intell. **36**(3), 606–619 (2013)
24. Yang, X., Deng, J., Chen, R., Cong, R., Ke, W., Sheng, H.: Disentangling local and global information for light field depth estimation. In: Proceedings of the IEEE/CVF Conference on Computer Vision and Pattern Recognition, pp. 3418–3426 (2023)
25. Zhang, S., Sheng, H., Li, C., Zhang, J., Xiong, Z.: Robust depth estimation for light field via spinning parallelogram operator. Comput. Vis. Image Underst. **145**, 148–159 (2016)
26. Zhao, Y., Zhang, H., Lu, P., Li, P., Wu, E., Sheng, B.: DSD-MatchingNet: deformable sparse-to-dense feature matching for learning accurate correspondences. Virtual Reality Intell. Hardw. **4**(5), 432–443 (2022)

DOMVS: Unsupervised Multi-view Stereo for Dealing With Occlusion Scenes

Mingwei Cao[1,2](✉), Qiuju Wang[1,2], Ning Li[1,2], and Haifeng Zhao[1,2]

[1] Anhui Provincial Key Laboratory of Multimodal Cognitive Computation, Anhui University, Hefei 230601, China
caomw@hfut.edu.cn

[2] School of Computer Science and Technology, Anhui University, Hefei 230601, China

Abstract. Deep learning-based multi-view stereo (MVS) methods have made significant progress in recent years. Due to limited access to large-scale annotated datasets, researchers explore unsupervised MVS methods that do not require ground-truth depth data. However, unsupervised MVS methods struggle with occluded or texture-less regions, as they rely on the assumption of photometric consistency. To address these issues, we propose an unsupervised MVS method named Unsupervised Multi-View Stereo for Dealing With Occlusion Scenes (DOMVS). We first propose a feature-level perceptual consistency module that minimizes reconstruction errors by comparing the differences in high-level semantic features between images. Meanwhile, we propose a structured occlusion generation module. It improves the accuracy and completeness of depth estimation by generating augmented samples for contrastive learning. Moreover, we propose the DLA-Net module for normalization to address the limitations of the receptive field. It enhances the accuracy of the depth map through the aggregation of global information. We test DOMVS on the DTU and Tanks&Temples datasets. Results demonstrate that DOMVS achieves an overall score of 0.339 on the DTU dataset, it is higher than RC-MVSNet. On the Tanks & Temples dataset, DOMVS outperforms ADR-MVSNet and JDACS-MS by 4.31% and 20.34%, respectively. Code is available at https://github.com/caomw/domvs.

Keywords: Multi-view Stereo · Unsupervised Learning · Perceptual Consistency · Structured Occlusion · Depth Estimation

1 Introduction

Multi-view stereo(MVS) [16] reconstructs a dense point cloud model from multi-view images [21]. It has been widely used in applications such as robotics, autonomous driving, and the preservation of cultural heritage. With the development of deep learning (DL) technology, DL-based MVS methods have gained considerable attention from researchers. For example, MVSNet [27] leveraged convolutional neural networks (CNNs) to extract image features and build a

P. Li et al. (Eds.): CGI 2025, LNCS 16508, pp. 313–325, 2026.
https://doi.org/10.1007/978-3-032-22264-0_25

cost volume using the plane-sweep algorithm. It regularized the cost volume to obtain a probability volume and used a regression operation to compute depth maps. However, cost volume regularization requires a substantial amount of GPU memory space. To address this issue, some supervised learning-based MVS methods [6,26] utilized cascaded cost volumes for the coarse-to-fine depth estimation task, which produced a multi-scale depth map during the training stage.

Fig. 1. Qualitative comparison of 3D reconstruction of previous state-of-the-art methods [3,6] and our DOMVS.

Supervised MVS methods rely on ground truth depth, thus limiting their generalization due to the difficulty of large-scale data acquisition. Unsupervised methods, like Unsup_MVSNet [9], avoid this by using photometric consistency, but still struggle in occlusion or textureless regions.

To address these challenges, we propose a new unsupervised MVS method called DOMVS. As shown in Fig. 1, compared to CasMVSNet [6] and RC-MVSNet [3], DOMVS shows significant advantages in occluded areas, such as building structures, textural details, and roof shadows. DOMVS comprises three essential components. First, we design a structured occlusion generation module to simulate occlusions and produce augmented samples whose depth maps serve as pseudo-ground truth, guiding the model to distinguish valid depth from occlusion-induced errors. Then, we introduce a perceptual consistency module that combines geometric and semantic features to enhance depth estimation in occluded regions. Furthermore, we propose DLA-Net, a deformable large-kernel attention module that performs global feature normalization, improving depth prediction under occlusions. Finally, we evaluate DOMVS and make a comparison with the state-of-the-art MVS methods on the DTU [1] and Tanks&Temples [11] datasets.

In summary, the contributions of this paper are as follows:

- We propose a novel unsupervised MVS method, called DOMVS, which recovers high-quality point cloud models from multi-view images without requiring ground truth depth.

- We propose a structured occlusion generation module to generate augmented samples for contrastive learning. It helps distinguish correct and incorrect depth estimates.
- We propose a perceptual consistency module that utilizes feature semantic similarity as a pseudo supervisory signal. It guides the depth estimation task and enhances the accuracy of depth maps.
- We propose a novel normalization module, namely DLA-Net, which solves the limitations of traditional CNNs in global information integration. It further improves the ability of DOMVS for occluded scenes.

2 Related Works

2.1 Supervised MVS Methods

Compared to traditional methods, DL-based MVS methods can handle complex scenes, such as occlusions, lighting variations, and large disparities. For example, MVSNet [27] introduced a plane-sweeping algorithm for depth estimation but required significant GPU memory due to large-scale cost volume processing. To mitigate this, the following researchers have optimized and improved the regularization process. R-MVSNet [28] adopted Gated Recurrent Units (GRU) to process the cost space instead of regularizing the whole 3D cost volume. Another work provided a coarse-to-fine framework [6], which processed information at multi-scale by using a staged approach. It first generated a coarse depth map from the roughest feature maps to guide depth hypotheses, then progressively refined the hypothesis range to produce high-quality depth maps of varying resolutions for supervised training. Several works have further improved DL-based MVS methods. P-VSNet [14] explored a feature representation method. PatchmatchNet [19] integrates information from multi-viewpoint for feature volume aggregation. Moreover, TransMVSNet [15] utilizes attention mechanisms to enhance feature representation capability. Go-MVSNet [23] optimized the cost volume aggregation process by introducing Geometrically Consistent Cost Aggregation (GCA). CT-MVSNet [20] combines coarse-grained global semantic information with fine-grained local texture details to construct the cost volume. Recently, MSP-MVS [29] introduces edge-aware patch deformation guided by multi-granularity segmentation priors. VMVS [12] enhances occlusion robustness by leveraging inter and intra-view visibility with surface normal priors to suppress mismatches and guide accurate depth estimation.

However, these methods heavily dependent on high-quality ground truth depth maps as supervisory signals, they are costly to obtain in practical deployments and often suffer from performance degradation in occluded or texture-poor regions.

2.2 Unsupervised and Self-Supervised MVS Methods

To reduce the reliance on ground-truth depth, self-supervised and unsupervised MVS methods have obtained much attention in recent years. Self-supervised approaches, such as CVP-MVSNet [26], first train a supervised model to generate pseudo labels and then iteratively refine the model to enhance generalization. However, such methods remain limited by the quality of the initial supervised model. Unsupervised methods, like Unsup_MVSNet [9], it dependents on the photometric consistency assumption and are trained using image reconstruction losses, with additional image gradient constraints introduced to improve edge perception. Nevertheless, in real-world scenes having occlusion, lighting variation, and textureless regions, the photometric assumption often fails, leading to degraded depth estimation. Subsequent works, such as MVS2 [5] incorporate cross-view consistency losses, M3VSNet [8] combines normal-depth consistency with multi-scale features, JDACS-MS [25] introduces semantic priors and data-cooperative segmentation, and RC-MVSNet [3] enhances supervision through depth re-rendering. CL-MVSNet [24] introduces a dual-level contrastive learning strategy that enhances robustness to indistinguishable regions.

In summary, existing unsupervised methods generally face performance bottlenecks when handling occlusion regions, and the supervisory signals still heavily dependent on photometric consistency assumptions.

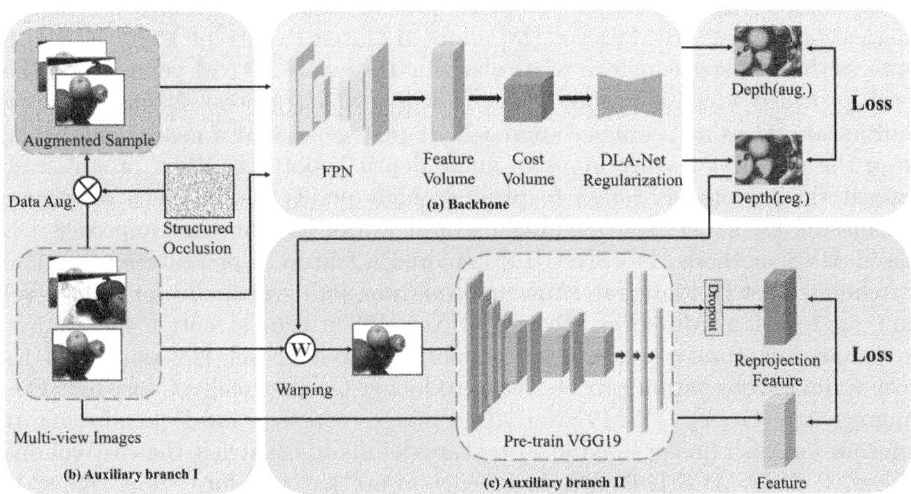

Fig. 2. Flowchart of the DOMVS. It consists of a backbone branch and two auxiliary branches. Specifically, (a) the backbone branch is used for depth prediction, (b) the first auxiliary branch provides pseudo-supervisory signals through augmented samples, and (c) the second auxiliary branch employs a pretrained model to extract high-level semantic features.

3 Our Method

Figure 2 illustrates the framework of DOMVS. The input includes multi-view images $\{I_i\}_{i=1}^N$ and their camera parameters $\{K_i, [R_i|t_i]\}_{i=1}^N$, where K_i is the intrinsic matrix, R_i is the rotation matrix, and t_i is the translation vector. N denotes the number of multi-view images.

Next, the input images are passed through the backbone network (Fig. 2(a)) to obtain the predicted depth maps, and the auxiliary branches are used for subsequent optimization. Specifically, the input image is fed into the Feature Pyramid Network (FPN) [13] to obtain features. Then, a cost function is constructed based on these features. Subsequently, regularization is implemented on the constructed cost volume and again, the regularized cost volume is used to infer the optimal depth value corresponding to each pixel through a depth regression stage to generate a depth map of the scene. Finally, the optimization of the depth map is carried out through the auxiliary branch.

This section is organised as follows, with auxiliary branch **I** presented in Sect. 3.1, using the structured occlusion generation module. Auxiliary branch **II**, presented in Sect. 3.2, demonstrates the perception consistency. In Sect. 3.3, we present a novel normalization module DLA-Net. Finally, Sect. 3.4 discusses the overall loss function of DOMVS.

3.1 Structured Occlusion Generation Module

To improve reconstruction quality under lighting variations and occlusions, we simulate real-world conditions during training process by introducing structured occlusions. Specifically, we use connected component analysis [7] to generate block-wise occlusions, avoiding fragmented patterns.

Meanwhile, we introduce these structured occlusions into the input images. This encourages the model to learn how to identify and avoid unreliable regions during training process, while focusing more on valid geometric and semantic cues. As shown in Fig. 3, connected component analysis (ECCA) creates regions by randomly selecting a center point within the image and defining its size within a predetermined range. Thus, it ensures that the regions remain inside the image boundaries. Subsequently, binary erosion is applied to preserve the continuity of these regions. This technique is utilized in the initial occlusion mask, which marks the pixels within these regions as zero to represent occlusion and dynamically updates the count of occluded pixels. Finally, the generated occlusion mask M_{cca} maintains the coherence of the occlusion while reflecting the spatial distribution characteristics of occlusions in real-world scenes.

In the following stages, as shown in Fig. 3, the multi-view images are multiplied (element by element) with the corresponding structured occlusion masks to generate a set of augmented samples. To further enhance the feature consistency between the regular samples and the augmented samples, we use the smooth **L1** loss to measure the contrastive consistency of data augmentation between the two samples. Avoid over-penalizing outliers for squared errors to improve the accuracy of depth estimation.

$$L_{\text{Aug}} = \begin{cases} 0.5 \times (\mathrm{D}_r - \mathrm{D}_a)^2, & \text{if } |\mathrm{D}_r - \mathrm{D}_a| < 1 \\ |\mathrm{D}_r - \mathrm{D}_a| - 0.5, & \text{otherwise} \end{cases} \tag{1}$$

where D_r represents the predicted depth of the regular samples, D_a represents the predicted depth of the augmented samples, and all of them lie in the discrete depth assumption space. This depth assumption space defines an effective depth interval for model predictions.

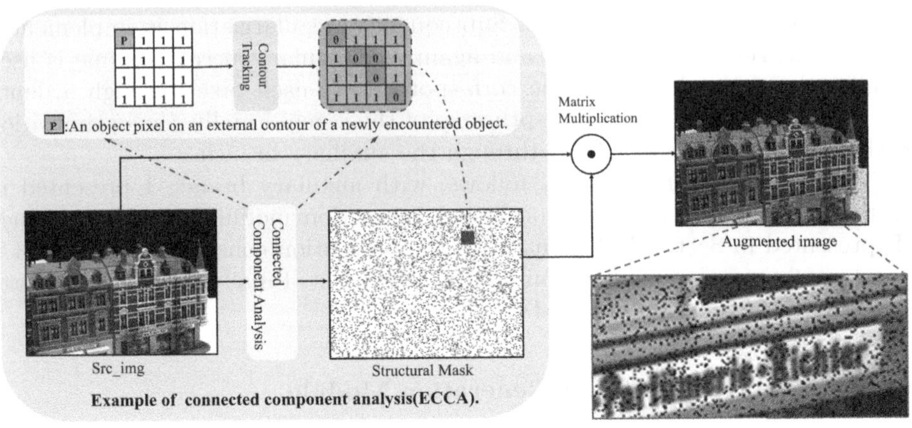

Fig. 3. Structured occlusion generation module. Build structured masks based on connected component analysis (CCA) to generate augmented samples.

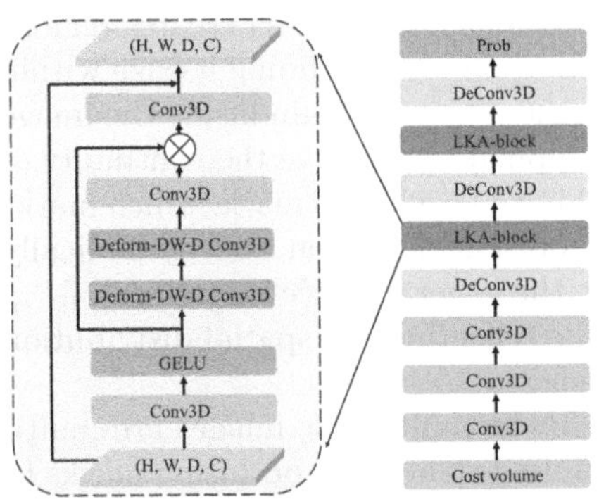

Fig. 4. The DLA-Net module. LKA block is on the left, which contains a residual-connected 3D convolutional encoder.

Fig. 5. Visualization results of DOMVS on the DTU dataset.

3.2 Perceptual Consistency Module

Based on the depth map by the backbone network, we warp each pixel in the reference view to a different viewpoint to generate a reprojected view corresponding to the target view. As shown in Fig. 2(c), we use a feature extraction network (VGG-19) [17] to extract the feature F_1 of the reference image and the features F_j' of the reprojected images. By selecting features from multiple layers, we maximize feature similarity while retaining important details and maintaining the consistency of the overall structure. Thus, it prevents the model from focusing too much on specific aspects of the image. Features were extracted for each pair of reference and reprojected views using the mean square error (MSE), which is used to quantify the differences between the extracted feature maps on different layers in order to compute the loss of perceptual consistency.

$$L_{\text{perc}} = \beta \cdot \frac{1}{N-1} \cdot \left(\sum_{j=2}^{N} \|(F_1 - F_j')\|^2 \right) \tag{2}$$

where β is the weight of the perceptual consistency loss.

By calculating the mean of these losses, DOMVS does not focus on a single image during the training process. It attempts to minimize the perceptual differences across all images for high-quality consistent depth maps.

The feature extraction network utilizes an uncertainty mechanism to enhance the generality of DOMVS. The model learns diverse feature representations by randomly dropping a fraction of neurons during training process. Dropout and weight initialization during loss calculation alter neuron activations, reducing feature co-adaptation. This enhances the ability of the model to process diverse features and contributes to a deep understanding of input variability. Thus, the model avoids relying on fixed feature combinations, which enables more flexible decision-making. It ensures accurate recognition and adaptability to variations in multi-view images.

3.3 DLA-Net Module

To enhance the spatial awareness of depth estimation, we propose a Deformable Large Kernel Attention Network (DLA-Net) for the regularization in DOMVS. Figure 4 illustrates the architecture of DLA-Net. This module captures global contextual information through a large receptive field attention mechanism, then helping the model understand the structural relationships behind occlusions and maintain the consistency of depth predictions in complex scenes. Additionally, DLA-Net combines deformable convolutions to adaptively build spatial offset features, enhancing adaptability to occlusion boundaries and non-rigid regions. Through multi-level feature fusion and deconvolution upsampling, the module further integrates local details with global semantics, effectively repairing occluded regions in depth maps, thereby improving the integrity of reconstruction models.

DLA-Net consists of two components: the large kernel attention block (LKA) [2] and the feature fusion module. As shown in the left of Fig. 4, the input features are first processed through a 3D convolution to extract preliminary features. Then we use an activation function to enhance non-linearity. Next, two deformable depth convolutions are adopted to capture spatial-offset features. Subsequently, a 3D convolution fuses multi-branch features, while residual connections are utilized to preserve the original input features while enhancing the representation ability of the module. Finally, another 3D convolution merges the features for the feature map.

Constructed feature maps are up-sampled by 3D deconvolution during the feature fusion process. The LKA block enhances the ability to capture global background information. The combination of up-sampling and LKA blocks gradually recovers the spatial resolution of the feature map through a deconvolution operation. At each up-sampling stage, the skip connection is used to merge low-level features and high-level features to improve the quality of the reconstructed point-cloud model. Finally, the DLA-Net outputs the normalized probability volume through a 1×1 convolutional kernel.

3.4 Overall Loss

The overall loss of DOMVS consists of several components, including data augmentation, perceptual consistency, structural similarity, and smoothness. It is defined as follows:

$$L = \lambda_1 L_{Aug} + \lambda_2 L_{Perc} + \lambda_3 L_{SSIM} + \lambda_4 L_{Smooth} \tag{3}$$

where L_{Aug} represents the data augmentation contrastive consistency loss, L_{Perc} represents the perceptual consistency loss, and L_{SSIM} and L_{Smooth} represent the structural similarity loss and depth smoothness loss, respectively. The weights for each loss term are empirically set as $\lambda_1 = 0.01$, $\lambda_2 = 0.01$, $\lambda_3 = 0.2$, $\lambda_4 = 0.0067$.

Fig. 6. Visualization results of DOMVS on the intermediate subset of the Tanks and Temples dataset.

Fig. 7. Visualization results of DOMVS on the advanced subset of the Tanks and Temples dataset.

4 Experiment

4.1 Implementation Details

We implement DOMVS using PyTorch and train the model on the machine equipped with 4 NVIDIA GeForce RTX 4090 GPUs. During the training stage, we use Adam [10] to optimize our model with an initial learning rate of 0.0005, which decayed by half after the *9*th, *11*th, and *13*th epochs. We conduct 16 epochs on the DTU [1] training set to obtain a pre-trained model and evaluate the trained model on the DTU test set and the Tanks and Temples [11] dataset.

4.2 Datasets

The DTU [1] is a benchmark dataset used to evaluate the performance of MVS methods, consisting of 128 scenes with 79 training sets and 22 test sets. Each of the sets has 7 lighting conditions and a ground truth model.

The Tanks and Temples [11] dataset is a widely used benchmark, which is composed of intermediate and advanced subsets. The intermediate subset has 8 scenes, while the advanced subset has 6 scenes.

4.3 Evaluation on DTU

Table 1 presents the quantitative results of the DTU test set, and all of the above indicators are measured in millimetres, and the statistical methods and calculation details follow the classic standards in the field of multi-view stereo methods [6,9,27]. DOMVS outperforms state-of-the-art methods in terms of the overall score, thus the effectiveness of the proposed DOMVS for handling occlusion scenes is proved. Figure 5 illustrates visualization results of DOMVS on the DTU dataset, in which each scene maintains a high level of geometric consistency.

4.4 Evaluation on Tanks and Temples

Similar to the RC-MVSNet [3], we conduct a test on the Tanks and Temples dataset using the trained model on the DTU dataset. Table 2 presents the quantitative results of DOMVS, and comparison with state-of-the-art methods on the subset of Tanks and Temples in terms of F-score. DOMVS achieves better performance than that of others, which indicates that DOMVS has superior robustness and generality. Figure 6 and Fig. 7 present the visualization results on the subset and the advanced subset of the Tanks and Temples dataset, respectively. We can see that these point-cloud models produced by DOMVS have high completeness and few noises.

Table 1. Evaluation results of point-cloud models on the evaluation set of DTU. **Bold** indicates the best result.

Class	Method	Acc↓	Comp↓	Overall↓
Supervised	MVSNet [27]	0.396	0.527	0.462
	CasMVSNet [6]	0.325	0.385	0.355
	CVP-MVSNet [26]	0.296	0.406	0.351
	UCSNet [4]	0.338	0.349	**0.344**
Unsupervised	Unsup_MVSNet [9]	0.881	1.073	0.977
	M3VSNet [8]	0.636	0.531	0.583
	JDACS-MS [25]	0.398	0.318	0.358
	RC-MVSNet [3]	0.396	0.295	0.345
	ACL-MVS [22]	0.341	0.356	0.349
	LargescaleAS [18]	0.397	0.305	0.351
	DOMVS(Ours)	0.366	0.313	**0.339**

Table 2. Comparison with state-of-the-art methods on the Tanks and Temples dataset. **Bold** indicates the best result.

Class	Method	Mean↑	Fam.↑	Fra.↑	Hor.↑	Lig.↑	M60↑	Pan.↑	Pla.↑	Tra.↑
Supervised	MVSNet [27]	43.48	55.99	28.55	25.07	50.79	53.96	50.86	47.90	34.69
	CVP-MVSNet [26]	**54.03**	76.50	47.74	36.34	55.12	57.28	54.28	57.43	47.50
	UCS-Net [4]	43.48	55.99	28.55	25.07	50.79	53.96	50.86	47.90	47.89
	PatchmatchNet [19]	53.15	66.99	52.64	43.24	54.87	52.87	49.54	54.21	50.81
Unsupervised	MVS2 [5]	37.21	47.74	21.55	19.50	44.54	44.86	46.32	43.38	29.72
	M3VSNet [8]	37.67	47.74	24.38	18.74	44.42	43.45	44.9	47.39	30.31
	JDACS-MS [25]	45.48	66.62	38.25	36.11	46.12	46.66	45.25	47.69	37.16
	LargescaleAS [18]	47.18	70.06	44.95	37.24	46.63	46.28	49.27	45.97	37.04
	DOMVS(Ours)	**54.73**	74.84	52.67	44.54	53.37	55.38	52.53	55.36	49.15

4.5 Ablation Study

We conduct an ablation study on the DTU dataset. Table 3 presents the quantitative results, and Fig. 8 shows the depth maps produced with independent modules.

Evaluation of the Data Augmentation Contrastive Consistency Loss. We introduce the data augmentation contrastive consistency loss L_{Aug} for the baseline, and the overall score of the model improved by 11.4%. Figure 8(b) presents some depth maps produced by the baseline with this loss.

Evaluation of the Perceptual Consistency Loss. Statistical results in Table 3 show that the overall score of the model increased by 13.7% when incorporating the perceptual consistency loss L_{Perc}. Figure 8(c) presents the depth maps produced by the perceptual consistency loss.

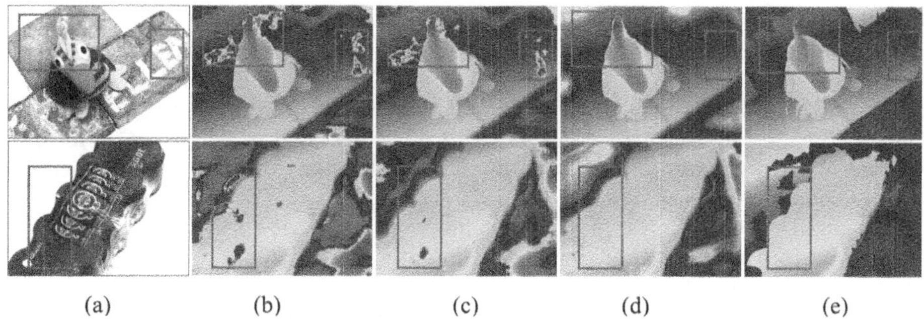

(a) (b) (c) (d) (e)

Fig. 8. Depth maps of the ablation study on the DTU dataset. (a) reference image; (b) depth maps produced by the trained model with the data augmentation contrastive consistency loss; (c) depth maps produced by the trained model with the perceptual consistency loss; (d) depth map produced by the trained model with all the proposed loss; (e) ground truths.

Table 3. Quantitative results of ablation study on the DTU dataset for the proposed DOMVS. **Bold** indicates the best result.

L_{PC}	L_{Aug}	L_{Perc}	$DLA-Net$	Acc↓	Comp↓	Overall↓
√				0.462	0.328	0.395
√			√	0.369	0.369	0.369
√	√		√	0.363	0.338	0.350
√		√	√	**0.359**	0.324	0.341
√	√	√	√	0.366	**0.313**	**0.339**

Evaluation of the Normalization Module. Statistical results in Table 3 show that the overall score increased by 6.6% when the model integrated with DLA-Net. Figure 8(d) shows some depth maps obtained by using the DLA-Net module.

5 Conclusion

In this paper, we present a novel unsupervised MVS method, namely DOMVS. It defends the weakness of existing MVS methods for occlusion and texture-less regions. First, the structured occlusion generation module effectively enhances the robustness of DOMVS in occluded scenes by generating high-quality positive samples. Second, the perceptual consistency loss provides novel pseudo-supervisory signals for depth map estimation by leveraging high-level semantic features. Finally, the DLA-Net module efficiently aggregates global information, particularly when handling occlusion scenes. Experiments on DTU and Tanks & Temples datasets demonstrates that DOMVS achieves excellent performance in terms of accuracy and completeness. In the future, we will focus on optimizing the proposed DOMVS to boost the robustness to strong reflections and explore its application in dynamic scene 3D reconstruction.

References

1. Aanæs, H., Jensen, R.R., Vogiatzis, G., Tola, E., Dahl, A.B.: Large-scale data for multiple-view stereopsis. Int. J. Comput. Vision **120**, 153–168 (2016)
2. Azad, R., et al.: Beyond self-attention: deformable large kernel attention for medical image segmentation. In: 2024 IEEE/CVF Winter Conference on Applications of Computer Vision (WACV), pp. 1276–1286 (2023)
3. Chang, D., et al.: RC-MVSNET: unsupervised multi-view stereo with neural rendering. In: European Conference on Computer Vision (2022)
4. Cheng, S., et al.: Deep stereo using adaptive thin volume representation with uncertainty awareness. 2020 IEEE/CVF Conference on Computer Vision and Pattern Recognition (CVPR), pp. 2521–2531 (2019)
5. Dai, Y., Zhu, Z., Rao, Z., Li, B.: MVS2: deep unsupervised multi-view stereo with multi-view symmetry. In: 2019 International Conference on 3D Vision (3DV), pp. 1–8 (2019)
6. Gu, X., Fan, Z., Zhu, S., Dai, Z., Tan, F., Tan, P.: Cascade cost volume for high-resolution multi-view stereo and stereo matching. 2020 IEEE/CVF Conference on Computer Vision and Pattern Recognition (CVPR), pp. 2492–2501 (2019)
7. He, L., Ren, X., Gao, Q., Zhao, X., Yao, B., Chao, Y.: The connected-component labeling problem: a review of state-of-the-art algorithms. Pattern Recognit. **70**, 25–43 (2017)
8. Huang, B., Huang, C., He, Y., Liu, J., Liu, X.: M3VSNet: unsupervised multi-metric multi-view stereo network. 2021 IEEE International Conference on Image Processing (ICIP), pp. 3163–3167 (2020)
9. Khot, T., Agrawal, S., Tulsiani, S., Mertz, C., Lucey, S., Hebert, M.: Learning unsupervised multi-view stereopsis via robust photometric consistency. ArXiv abs/1905.02706 (2019)
10. Kingma, D.P., Ba, J.: Adam: a method for stochastic optimization. CoRR abs/1412.6980 (2014)
11. Knapitsch, A., Park, J., Zhou, Q.Y., Koltun, V.: Tanks and temples. ACM Trans. Graph. (TOG) **36**, 1–13 (2017)
12. Lee, H., Lee, S., Lee, S.: Visibility-aware multi-view stereo by surface normal weighting for occlusion robustness. IEEE Trans. Pattern Anal. Mach. Intell., 1–17 (2025). https://doi.org/10.1109/TPAMI.2025.3568447
13. Lin, T.Y., Dollár, P., Girshick, R.B., He, K., Hariharan, B., Belongie, S.J.: Feature pyramid networks for object detection. 2017 IEEE Conference on Computer Vision and Pattern Recognition (CVPR), pp. 936–944 (2016)
14. Luo, K., Guan, T., Ju, L., Huang, H., Luo, Y.: P-MVSNET: learning patch-wise matching confidence aggregation for multi-view stereo. 2019 IEEE/CVF International Conference on Computer Vision (ICCV), pp. 10451–10460 (2019)
15. Luo, K., Guan, T., Ju, L., Wang, Y., Chen, Z., Luo, Y.: Attention-aware multi-view stereo. 2020 IEEE/CVF Conference on Computer Vision and Pattern Recognition (CVPR), pp. 1587–1596 (2020)
16. Seitz, S.M., Curless, B., Diebel, J., Scharstein, D., Szeliski, R.: A comparison and evaluation of multi-view stereo reconstruction algorithms. In: IEEE Computer Society Conference on Computer Vision and Pattern Recognition (CVPR 2006), vol. 1, pp. 519–528 (2006)
17. Simonyan, K., Zisserman, A.: Very deep convolutional networks for large-scale image recognition. CoRR abs/1409.1556 (2014)

18. Tong, K.W., et al.: Large-scale aerial scene perception based on self-supervised multi-view stereo via cycled generative adversarial network. Inf. Fus. **109**, 102399 (2024)
19. Wang, F., Galliani, S., Vogel, C., Speciale, P., Pollefeys, M.: PatchMatchNet: learned multi-view PatchMatch stereo. 2021 IEEE/CVF Conference on Computer Vision and Pattern Recognition (CVPR), pp. 14189–14198 (2020)
20. Wang, S., Jiang, H., Xiang, L.: CT-MVSNET: efficient multi-view stereo with cross-scale transformer. ArXiv abs/2312.08594 (2023)
21. Wang, X., Guo, Y., Yang, Z., Zhang, J.: Prior-guided multi-view 3D head reconstruction. IEEE Trans. Multimedia **24**, 4028–4040 (2021)
22. Wang, Z., Luo, H., Wang, X., Zheng, J., Ning, X., Bai, X.: A contrastive learning based unsupervised multi-view stereo with multi-stage self-training strategy. Displays **83**, 102672 (2024)
23. Wu, J., et al.: GOMVS: geometrically consistent cost aggregation for multi-view stereo. In: 2024 IEEE/CVF Conference on Computer Vision and Pattern Recognition (CVPR), pp. 20207–20216 (2024)
24. Xiong, K., et al.: Cl-MVSNET: unsupervised multi-view stereo with dual-level contrastive learning. In: IEEE/CVF International Conference on Computer Vision (ICCV), pp. 3746–3757 (2023)
25. Xu, H., Zhou, Z., Qiao, Y., Kang, W., Wu, Q.: Self-supervised multi-view stereo via effective co-segmentation and data-augmentation. In: AAAI Conference on Artificial Intelligence (2021)
26. Yang, J., Mao, W., Álvarez, J.M., Liu, M.: Cost volume pyramid based depth inference for multi-view stereo. In: 2020 IEEE/CVF Conference on Computer Vision and Pattern Recognition (CVPR), pp. 4876–4885 (2019)
27. Yao, Y., Luo, Z., Li, S., Fang, T., Quan, L.: MVSNet: depth inference for unstructured multi-view stereo. In: European Conference on Computer Vision (2018)
28. Yao, Y., Luo, Z., Li, S., Shen, T., Fang, T., Quan, L.: Recurrent MVSNET for high-resolution multi-view stereo depth inference. In: IEEE/CVF Conference on Computer Vision and Pattern Recognition (CVPR), pp. 5520–5529 (2019)
29. Zhang, Z., Hu, Y., Gao, H., Wang, R.: Bi-CluemvsNet: learning bidirectional occlusion clues for multi-view stereo. In: 2023 International Joint Conference on Neural Networks (IJCNN), pp. 1–8 (2023). https://doi.org/10.1109/IJCNN54540.2023.10191325

Dynamic Prompting and Cross-Modal Attention for Context-Aware Multimodal Emotion Recognition

Guangzi Zhang, Yupeng Zhang, Shanshan He, Haoyu Song, and Xingquan Cai(✉)

School of Information Science and Technology, North China University of Technology, Beijing 100144, China
caixingquan@ncut.edu.cn

Abstract. Multimodal emotion recognition is crucial for applications like human-computer interaction (HCI) and mental health, but capturing fine-grained emotions from complex scenes remains challenging. Existing methods often generate descriptions lacking context-specific emotional nuance, struggle to effectively fuse visual and textual cues, and may suffer from inconsistencies between explanations and predictions. This paper proposes CARE (Context-Aware Reasoning for Emotion), a novel framework that dynamically integrates scene-level context and textual reasoning. CARE first generates emotion-guided prompts by combining predicted affective cues with structured scene features, guiding a vision-language model to produce contextually rich descriptions. It then applies a targeted cross-modal attention mechanism that aligns visual observations with relevant semantic details. Finally, a consistency loss enforces agreement between the predicted emotion distribution and that inferred from the generated text, improving robustness and interpretability. Experiments show our framework achieves state-of-the-art results with 36.82% mAP on EMOTIC and 90.17% Accuracy on CAER-S, while also significantly improving description quality. These results underscore the framework's effectiveness in modeling complex scene-emotion interactions for context-aware emotion recognition.

Keywords: Emotion Recognition · Multimodal Learning · Cross-Modal Attention · Context-Aware

1 Introduction

Emotion recognition is pivotal in advancing human-computer interaction (HCI), mental health monitoring, and social media analysis [5,23]. While significant research has focused on discerning emotions from isolated cues like facial expressions [18], such approaches often overlook the crucial role of context inherent in real-world emotional expression and perception [15]. Understanding emotions in context has gained traction [17], yet remains less explored than traditional

P. Li et al. (Eds.): CGI 2025, LNCS 16508, pp. 326–337, 2026.
https://doi.org/10.1007/978-3-032-22264-0_26

tasks like Facial Expression Recognition (FER), despite being more reflective of genuine human experience. This gap stems partly from the task's inherent complexity: emotional displays can be ambiguous and heavily influenced by the surrounding environment, social interactions, and cultural norms, making interpretation challenging even for humans [4]. For instance, a smile at a birthday party signifies joy, whereas a similar expression at a funeral might indicate relief or sad reminiscence.

Context, while vital, introduces significant challenges for automated systems. This is exacerbated by the high intra-class variance (e.g., 'happiness' can be expressed in myriad ways) and low inter-class variance (e.g., 'fear' and 'surprise' often share similar facial cues) of emotional expressions. Previous attempts to incorporate context often relied on complex pipelines, domain-specific prior knowledge, or predefined feature extraction that might struggle with diverse real-world scenes [19,40]. While some works have explored vision and language for emotion recognition [36,41], they often depend on existing descriptions or use text primarily for retrieval, not actively leveraging generated textual reasoning to inform the final classification.

To address these challenges, we propose CARE, a novel framework integrating dynamic textual reasoning with targeted multimodal fusion. The main contributions of CARE can be summarized as follows:

- **Dynamic Emotion Prompt Generation:** We utilize zero-shot emotion pre-prediction derived from CLIP, alongside structured scene features, to dynamically construct context-aware natural language prompts. This targeted guidance steers the Vision-Language Model away from generic descriptions towards generating narratives rich in the specific affective signals required for the downstream task.
- **Cross-Modal Attention Fusion:** A tailored attention mechanism is employed where image features, obtained from InstructBLIP, query token-level textual features derived from the generated description. This enables the model to precisely ground visual observations in the most relevant semantic details identified within the text, facilitating finer-grained integration than typical fusion methods.
- **Emotion Consistency Loss:** An explicit consistency loss enforces semantic alignment between the final prediction and the emotion distribution inferred from the description, achieved using KL divergence. This ensures the model's output aligns with its textual reasoning, enhancing robustness and interpretability.

This framework is designed to model nuanced scene-emotion interactions, providing a promising foundation for context-aware affective computing.

2 Related Work

2.1 Multimodal Emotion Recognition in Context

Recognizing emotions in context is essential for real-world applications, yet remains challenging due to the limitations of traditional methods that rely on isolated cues such as facial expressions [1,18]. Existing strategies often involve explicitly separating subject and context features [3,35], extracting features based on prior knowledge about emotional expression (e.g., body pose [24]), or examining label relationships using techniques like Graph Neural Networks (GNNs) [9,40]. For instance, Zhang et al. [40] utilized a GNN to explicitly model the relationships between different emotion labels, but this approach can be sensitive to the predefined label taxonomy. While these methods demonstrate improvements over unimodal baselines [11,37], effectively leveraging diverse contextual information remains challenging. Methods relying on predefined context features might miss crucial interactive or environmental cues [24], while attempts to categorize broad visual context [35] may yield coarse representations insufficient for nuanced understanding.

2.2 Vision-Language Models and Description Generation

Recent advances in Vision-Language Models (VLMs), such as CLIP [27] and generative models like LLaVA [21], have significantly advanced tasks requiring joint visual and textual understanding. These models exhibit strong capabilities in generating natural language descriptions of visual content [30] and performing zero-shot reasoning. In tasks such as Visual Question Answering (VQA), integrating large language models (LLMs) within VLMs has led to notable performance improvements [31,33]. However, applying these generative capabilities effectively for affective understanding, particularly for generating descriptions tailored to emotion recognition, is less explored [32,38]. Standard VLMs often produce generic captions focusing on objects and actions, potentially overlooking the subtle affective signals relevant for emotion [8,41]. This highlights the need for strategies that can steer VLMs toward generating emotionally salient, task-specific descriptions to better support affective understanding [34,39].

2.3 Cross-Modal Fusion Strategies

Integrating information from different modalities is a core challenge in multimodal learning. Effective strategies must go beyond simple concatenation and often involve attention mechanisms [29] to selectively weigh information. While various fusion approaches exist (e.g., early, late, hybrid fusion), the optimal strategy for emotion recognition—where cues are often subtle and highly context-dependent—remains an open question. Generic fusion mechanisms, even those in powerful VLMs like InstructBLIP [6], are not specifically optimized to align fine-grained visual features with the nuanced semantic cues in text [4]. Developing fusion strategies that can robustly integrate such disparate signals is essential for achieving accurate and context-aware emotion recognition [16]. Our work proposes a targeted attention mechanism specifically for this purpose.

3 Proposed Method

As illustrated in Fig. 1, CARE integrates three core components: (1) dynamic prompt generation to guide LLaVA toward context-aware description generation;

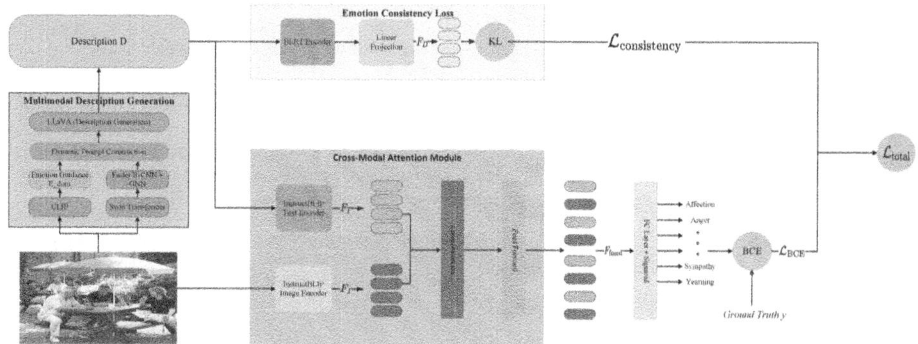

Fig. 1. Overview of the proposed CARE framework. An input image I undergoes: 1) Dynamic Prompt Generation using CLIP-based emotion pre-prediction and Swin+GNN scene features to guide LLaVA for description D generation. 2) Feature Extraction using InstructBLIP for image features F_I and BERT for text features $F_{T,\text{token}}$. 3) Cross-Modal Attention Fusion where F_I queries text token features. 4) Emotion Prediction yielding $\hat{y}$. 5) An Emotion Consistency Loss aligns D and $\hat{y}$.

(2) cross-modal attention fusion to align visual evidence with textual reasoning; and (3) an emotion consistency loss to enforce semantic agreement between predictions and explanations.

3.1 Multimodal Description Generation Guided by Context

To overcome the generic nature of VLM descriptions, we dynamically construct an informative, emotion-guided prompt P to steer LLaVA toward generating a relevant description D.

Emotion Pre-prediction and Scene Feature Extraction. To supply initial affective cues, we leverage the zero-shot capabilities of CLIP [27] for a preliminary emotion prediction. Image features F_{CLIP} are compared against text embeddings for each emotion category $E = \{e_1, \ldots, e_K\}$ to find the dominant emotion e_{dom}.

$$s_k = \frac{F_{\text{CLIP}} \cdot F_E[k]}{||F_{\text{CLIP}}|| \, ||F_E[k]||} \tag{1}$$

$$p_{\text{pre}} = \text{softmax}(\mathbf{s}), \quad \text{where } \mathbf{s} = [s_1, ..., s_K] \tag{2}$$

$$e_{\text{dom}} = E[\text{argmax}_k(p_{\text{pre}})] \tag{3}$$

To capture scene context, we extract global features using a Swin Transformer [22] and local object relations using Faster R-CNN [28] plus a GNN [14]. These features are fused and classified to yield a discrete scene label s (e.g., ‘park’, ‘home’).

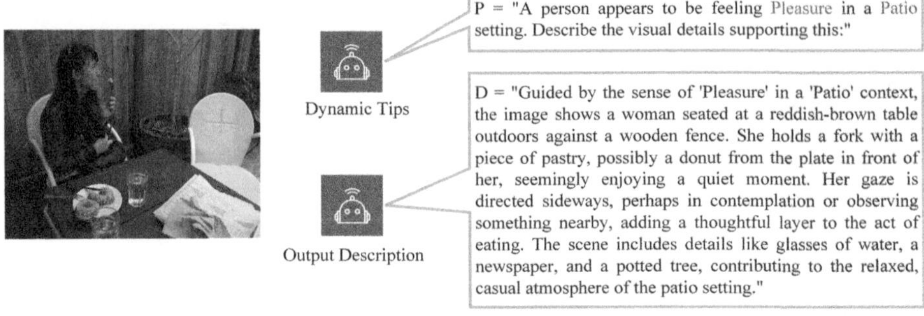

Fig. 2. Illustration of the dynamic prompt (P) generation process and the resulting description (D) for a sample image. This visualizes the core mechanism described in Sect. 3.1.

Dynamic Prompting and Guided Description Generation. Armed with e_{dom} and s, we dynamically construct a prompt P by formatting a predefined template string: *"A person appears to be feeling {e_ dom} in a {s} setting. Describe the visual details supporting this:"*. This prompt explicitly directs LLaVA to focus on relevant visual evidence. LLaVA then generates the description $D = \text{LLaVA}(I, P)$, for which we use LoRA [10] for efficient fine-tuning. This guided generation process, illustrated in Fig. 2, yields descriptions that are richer in relevant affective and contextual details compared to unguided generation.

3.2 Cross-Modal Attention Fusion

We introduce a targeted cross-modal attention where visual features query textual reasoning. Visual features $F_I \in \mathbb{R}^{N \times d_{img}}$ are extracted using InstructBLIP's [6] visual encoder, while the description D is encoded into token-level embeddings $F_{T,\text{token}} \in \mathbb{R}^{L \times d_t}$ using BERT [7].

We employ multi-head cross-modal attention [29], where visual features F_I act as the Query, while textual features $F_{T,\text{token}}$ provide the Key and Value.

$$Q_I = \text{Linear}_Q(F_I) \in \mathbb{R}^{N \times d_k} \tag{4}$$

$$K_T = \text{Linear}_K(F_{T,\text{token}}) \in \mathbb{R}^{L \times d_k} \tag{5}$$

$$V_T = \text{Linear}_V(F_{T,\text{token}}) \in \mathbb{R}^{L \times d_v} \tag{6}$$

This is performed in parallel across 8 heads. The resulting attention output F_{att} is pooled and combined with the original pooled visual features through a residual connection and layer normalization to produce the final fused representation:

$$F_{\text{fused}} = \text{LayerNorm}(F_{\text{att}} + \text{Linear}_{\text{res}}(\text{MeanPool}(F_I))) \tag{7}$$

This is fed to the emotion classifier to yield logits $\hat{y}$.

3.3 Emotion Consistency Loss

To enhance robustness, we introduce a loss term that encourages consistency between the final prediction $\hat{y}$ and the emotional content of the description D. We project the sentence-level embedding of D (F'_D) to obtain a text-implied probability distribution P_D.

$$P_D = \text{softmax}(\text{Linear}_{\text{consist}}(F'_D)) \tag{8}$$

The consistency loss is the KL divergence between this distribution and the one derived from the final prediction. The total loss combines the primary classification loss and the consistency loss:

$$\mathcal{L}_{\text{consistency}} = D_{\text{KL}}(P_D \| \text{softmax}(\hat{y})) \tag{9}$$

$$\mathcal{L}_{\text{total}} = \mathcal{L}_{\text{emotion}}(\hat{y}, y) + \lambda \mathcal{L}_{\text{consistency}} \tag{10}$$

where we set $\lambda = 0.1$ based on validation experiments.

4 Experiments

4.1 Datasets and Implementation Details

We evaluate CARE on two benchmarks: **EMOTIC** [15], a multi-label dataset with 26 emotion categories, and **CAER-S** [17], a single-label dataset with 7 basic emotions. We report mean Average Precision (mAP) on EMOTIC and Top-1 Accuracy on CAER-S.

We use AdamW with an initial learning rate of 1e−4, a weight decay of 0.01, and a cosine annealing schedule. For LLaVA-13B, we use LoRA with a rank of 8, alpha of 16, and dropout of 0.05, inserted into the query and value projection matrices of the self-attention layers. All experiments were performed on a single NVIDIA A100 GPU.

4.2 Comparison with State-of-the-Art Methods

Tables 1 and 2 show that CARE achieves new state-of-the-art results on both datasets. On EMOTIC, CARE achieves **36.82% mAP**, outperforming strong context-augmented methods like EmotiCon [24] (35.28%). This improvement is consistent across most categories, as shown in the per-category analysis in Fig. 3. On CAER-S, CARE achieves **90.17% accuracy**, surpassing the previous best by +1.52%. This demonstrates the superiority of leveraging dynamically generated, context-aware textual descriptions over relying on visual cues or retrieved text.

Table 1. Comparison with state-of-the-art methods on EMOTIC (mAP %).

Category	Method	Modalities	mAP (%)
Vision-Only	CAER-Net [17]	Vision	23.85
	EMOTNet [15]	Vision	27.93
Context-Aug.	EmotiCon [24]	Vision + Context	35.28
Vision-Lang.	InstructBLIP [6]	Vision + Text (retrieval)	34.10
	CARE (Ours)	**Vision + Text (generated)**	**36.82**

Table 2. Comparison with state-of-the-art methods on CAER-S (Accuracy %).

Category	Method	Modalities	Accuracy (%)
Vision-Only	CAER-Net [17]	Vision	73.47
Context-Aug.	RRLA [19]	Vision + Context	84.82
	EmotiCon [24]	Vision + Context	88.65
Vision-Lang.	InstructBLIP [6]	Vision + Text (retrieval)	87.80
	CARE (Ours)	**Vision + Text (generated)**	**90.17**

4.3 Ablation Study and Analysis

Our ablation study, with results detailed in Table 3 and visualized in Fig. 4, validates the contribution of each component. This study also serves as a comparison

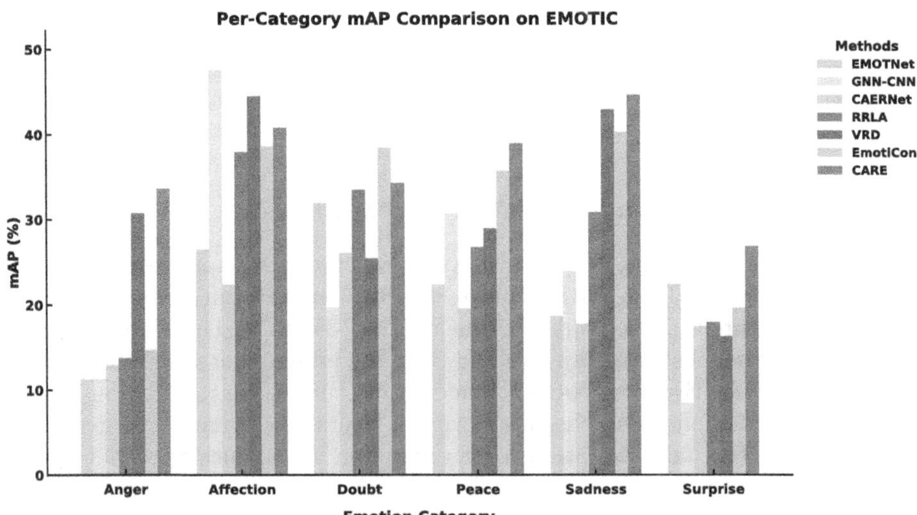

Fig. 3. Per-Category mAP comparison on the EMOTIC dataset, comparing CARE against representative baselines. Our method shows strong and consistent performance across diverse emotional categories.

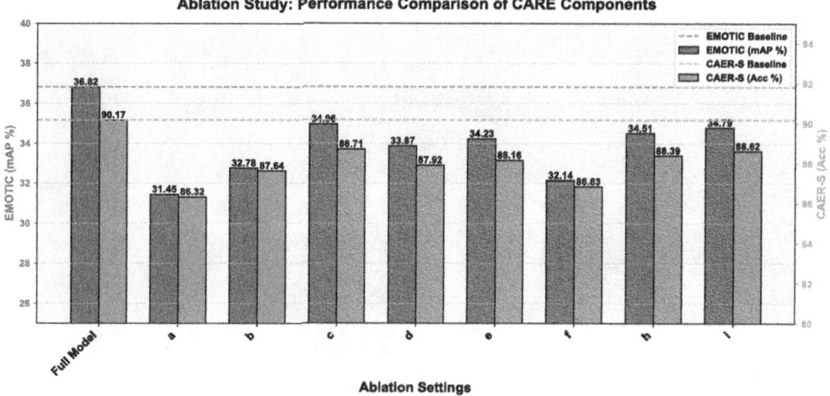

Fig. 4. Ablation study results of CARE components on EMOTIC (mAP %) and CAER-S (Acc %), visually demonstrating the impact of key modules on performance.

Table 3. Ablation Study of CARE components on EMOTIC (mAP %)

ID	Setting	mAP (%)
(0)	Full CARE Model (Ours)	**36.82**
(a)	w/o Dynamic Prompting (Static)	31.45 (−5.37)
(b)	w/o Cross-Modal Attention (Concat)	32.78 (−4.04)
(c)	w/o Consistency Loss ($\lambda = 0$)	34.96 (−1.86)
(d)	w/o Emotion Pre-prediction in Prompt	33.87 (−2.95)
(e)	w/o Scene Label in Prompt	34.23 (−2.59)
(f)	w/o LoRA (Frozen LLaVA)	32.14 (−4.68)

Table 4. Analysis of computational cost and model parameters.

Component	Parameters (M)	Time (ms)
Prompt Generation		
CLIP ViT-L/14	∼304	∼25
Swin-T + GNN	∼87	∼30
Description Generation		
LLaVA-13B (LoRA)	∼13,000 (∼20 trainable)	∼350
Fusion & Prediction		
InstructBLIP VE	∼1,100	∼40
BERT-base + Attention	∼110	∼15
Total (CARE)	**∼14,600**	**∼460**

against simpler baselines derived from our own framework, as the ablated versions represent simpler deep learning models.

(a) Input Image

(b) Dynamic Prompt (P):
"A person appears to be feeling Confidence in a Stadium setting. Describe the visual details supporting this:"

(c) Generated Description (D):
"Guided by the sense of 'Confidence' in a 'Stadium' context, the image captures a baseball pitcher wearing an Orioles jersey #64 at the crucial moment of throwing. His body exhibits the power pose of pitching, eyes sharply focused forward, face taut with concentration and determination. The blurred stadium background confirms the competitive setting, reinforcing the professionalism and confidence displayed by the pitcher amidst the game's intensity."

(d) Emotion Labels:
Ground Truth (y): ['Confidence']
Our Prediction ($\hat{y}$): ['Confidence']

Fig. 5. A detailed qualitative example for the baseball pitcher case, showing: (a) the input image, (b) the dynamically generated prompt, (c) the resulting context-aware description, and (d) the final emotion labels.

The most significant performance drop was observed when dynamic prompting was removed (a). This setting, which uses a static, generic prompt, resulted in a 5.37% mAP decrease, demonstrating that without specific guidance, the VLM defaults to generic descriptions that lack the emotional nuance crucial for this task. Replacing our targeted cross-modal attention with simple feature concatenation (b) resulted in the second-largest decline (4.04% mAP). This suggests that merely combining features is insufficient; the alignment provided by our image-querying-text attention is vital for grounding visual evidence in its semantic explanation. Other components, including the consistency loss (c), individual prompt elements (d, e), and LoRA fine-tuning (f), all proved beneficial, validating their inclusion in the final framework.

4.4 Qualitative and Computational Cost Analysis

To provide a concrete illustration of our framework in action, Fig. 5 presents a complete walkthrough of a single example. It showcases how the dynamically generated prompt (b), informed by the initial prediction of 'Confidence' and the 'Stadium' context, steers the VLM to produce a highly relevant and detailed description (c). The model's final prediction (d) aligns perfectly with both the ground truth and the generated rationale, demonstrating the end-to-end effectiveness and interpretability of our approach. In another case (not shown due to space constraints), the model demonstrated robustness by correctly identifying 'Fatigue' even when guided by an imperfect initial prompt of 'Affection', highlighting the strength of the fusion mechanism.

While qualitatively effective, CARE's integration of large models incurs significant computational cost, as detailed in Table 4. The LLaVA-13B generator is the primary bottleneck, reflecting a trade-off between performance and efficiency.

5 Conclusion and Future Work

This work introduced CARE, a framework demonstrating that explicitly generating context-aware textual descriptions, guided by both scene and preliminary emotion cues, significantly enhances multimodal emotion recognition. By coupling this dynamic prompt generation with a targeted cross-modal attention mechanism and enforcing prediction-explanation consistency, CARE achieves state-of-the-art performance on the challenging EMOTIC and CAER-S benchmarks. The quantitative improvements and ablation studies validate the effectiveness of CARE's core components.

Despite its strong performance, CARE has limitations that open avenues for future research. Firstly, the dynamic prompt relies on a fixed template. Future work could explore more flexible strategies, such as using another LLM to generate the prompt itself or employing prompt-tuning. Secondly, the initial emotion cue from zero-shot CLIP prediction may struggle with highly nuanced or culturally-specific emotions (e.g., 'nostalgia'). Finally, as analyzed, the model's computational cost is high; future efforts will focus on model compression techniques to make the framework more practical for real-world deployment.

Acknowledgments. This work was supported by the Funding Project of Humanities and Social Sciences of the Ministry of Education in China (22YJAZH002).

References

1. Abdul-Mageed, M., Ungar, L.: EmoNet: fine-grained emotion detection with gated recurrent neural networks. In: Proceedings of the ACL, vol. 1, pp. 718–728 (2017)
2. Ba, J.L., Kiros, J.R., Hinton, G.E.: Layer Normalization, arXiv preprint arXiv:1607.06450 (2016)
3. Bhattacharya, U., Mittal, T., Chandra, R., et al.: Step: spatial temporal graph convolutional networks for emotion perception from gaits. In: Proceedings of the AAAI, vol. 34 (2020)
4. Chen, Y., Wang, Z., Peng, H., et al.: Multimodal emotion recognition with temporal and contextual consistency. IEEE Trans. Affect. Comput. **14**(4), 2408–2420 (2023)
5. Cohn, J.F., Kruez, T.S., Matthews, I., et al.: Detecting depression from facial actions and vocal prosody. In: Proceedings of the ACII, pp. 1–8 (2009)
6. Dai, W., Li, J., Li, D., et al.: InstructBLIP: towards General-purpose Vision-Language Models with Instruction Tuning. arXiv preprint arXiv:2305.06500 (2023)
7. Devlin, J., Chang, M.W., Lee, K., et al.: BERT: pre-training of deep bidirectional transformers for language understanding. In: Proceedings of the NAACL-HLT, vol. 1, pp. 4171–4186 (2019)
8. Fu, C., Qian, F., Su, K., et al.: HiMul-LGG: a hierarchical decision fusion-based local–global graph neural network for multimodal emotion recognition in conversation. Neural Netw. **181**, 106764 (2025)
9. Gao, Q., Zeng, H., Li, G., Tong, T.: Graph reasoning-based emotion recognition network. IEEE Access **3**
10. Hu, E.J., Shen, Y., Wallis, P., et al.: LoRA: low-rank adaptation of large language models. In: Proceedings of the ICLR (2022)
11. Jaiswal, S., Misra, S., Nandi, G.: Attention-guided context-aware emotional state recognition. In: Proceedings of the UPCON (2020)
12. Jeong, M., Lee, H.: LaERC-S: improving LLM-based emotion recognition in conversation with speaker characteristics, arXiv preprint arXiv:2501.02164 (2025)
13. Kingma, D.P., Ba, J.: Adam: a method for stochastic optimization. In: Proceedings of the ICLR (2015)
14. Kipf, T.N., Welling, M.: Semi-supervised classification with graph convolutional networks. In: Proceedings of the ICLR (2017)
15. Kosti, R., Alvarez, J.M., Recasens, A., et al.: EMOTIC: emotions in context dataset. In: Proceedings of the CVPRW, pp. 61–69 (2017)
16. Lee, D.H., Lee, G.S.: Gated cross-modal fusion mechanism for audio-video-based emotion recognition. Electronics **13**(7), 1367 (2024)
17. Lee, J., Kim, S., Kim, S., et al.: Context-aware emotion recognition networks. In: Proceedings of the ICCV, pp. 9363–9372 (2019)
18. Levi, G., Hassner, T.: Emotion recognition in the wild via convolutional neural networks and mapped binary patterns. In: Proceedings of the ICMI Workshops, pp. 503–510 (2015)
19. Li, W., Dong, X., Wang, Y.: Human emotion recognition with relational region-level analysis. IEEE Trans. Affect Comput. (2021)
20. Lin, C.Y.: ROUGE: a package for automatic evaluation of summaries. In: Proceedings of the ACL Workshop on Text Summarization, pp. 74–81 (2004)
21. Liu, H., Li, C., Wu, Q., et al.: Visual instruction tuning (LLaVA), arXiv preprint arXiv:2304.08485 (2023)
22. Liu, Z., Lin, Y., Cao, Y., et al.: Swin transformer: hierarchical vision transformer using shifted windows. In: Proceedings of the ICCV, pp. 10012–10022 (2021)

23. McDuff, D., Picard, R.W.: A review of remote physiological measurement using imaging methods. Behav. Res. Methods **48**, 1186–1206 (2016)
24. Mittal, T., Guhan, P., Bhattacharya, U., et al.: EmotiCon: context-aware multimodal emotion recognition using Frege's principle. In: Proceedings of the CVPR, pp. 14234–14243 (2020)
25. Papineni, K., Roukos, S., Ward, T., et al.: BLEU: a method for automatic evaluation of machine translation. In: Proceedings of the ACL, pp. 311–318 (2002)
26. Paszke, A., Gross, S., Massa, F., et al.: PyTorch: an imperative style, high-performance deep learning library. In: Proceedings of the NeurIPS, vol. 32, pp. 8024–8035 (2019)
27. Radford, A., Kim, J.W., Hallacy, C., et al.: Learning transferable visual models from natural language supervision. In: Proceedings of the ICML, PMLR 139, pp. 8748–8763 (2021)
28. Ren, S., He, K., Girshick, R., et al.: Faster R-CNN: towards real-time object detection with region proposal networks. In: Proceedings of the NeurIPS, vol. 28, pp. 91–99 (2015)
29. Vaswani, A., Shazeer, N., Parmar, N., et al.: Attention is all you need. In: Proceedings of the NeurIPS, vol. 30, pp. 5998–6008 (2017)
30. Vinyals, O., Toshev, A., Bengio, S., et al.: Show and tell: a neural image caption generator. In: Proceedings of the CVPR, pp. 3156–3164 (2015)
31. Wang, J., Chen, D., Luo, C., et al.: Chatvideo: a tracklet-centric multimodal and versatile video understanding system (2023)
32. Wang, Z., Wang, L., Wu, X., et al.: Multimodal emotion recognition with vision-language prompting and modality dropout. arXiv preprint arXiv:2409.07078 (2024)
33. Xenos, A., Stafylakis, T., Patras, I., Tzimiropoulos, G.: A simple baseline for knowledge-based visual question answering. In: Proceedings of the EMNLP, pp. 14871–14877 (2023)
34. Yang, Q., Wang, W., Wang, L., et al.: EmoVIT: revolutionizing emotion insights with visual instruction tuning. In: Proceedings of the CVPR (2024)
35. Yang, D., Chen, Z., Wang, Y., et al.: Context de-confounded emotion recognition. In: Proceedings of the CVPR, pp. 19005–19015 (2023)
36. Yu, P., He, X., Li, H., et al.: FMLAN: a novel framework for cross-subject and cross-session EEG emotion recognition. Biomed. Signal Process. Control **100**, 106912 (2025)
37. Zhao, Z., Liu, Q., Zhou, F.: Robust lightweight facial expression recognition network with label distribution training. In: Proceedings of the AAAI, vol. 35, pp. 3510–3519 (2021)
38. Zheng, L., Tian, J., She, J., et al.: VLLMs provide better context for emotion understanding through common sense reasoning, arXiv preprint arXiv:2404.11636 (2024)
39. Zhang, H., Jiang, Y., Liu, Z., et al.: Contrastive language-image learning with augmented textual prompts for 3D/4D FER using vision-language model, arXiv preprint arXiv:2404.02537 (2024)
40. Zhang, M., Liang, Y., Ma, H.: Context-aware affective graph reasoning for emotion recognition. In: Proceedings of the ICME, pp. 151–156 (2019)
41. Zhang, S., Pan, Y., Wang, J.Z.: Learning emotion representations from verbal and nonverbal communication. In: Proceedings of the CVPR, pp. 18993–19004 (2023)

SigNet-TAM: Indian Sign Language Recognition with ResNet50-BiLSTM and Temporal Attention Mechanism

Abraham Vellaiparambil Jose[1], Aditya Pal[1], Vaibhav Prajapati[1], K. Rangachary[2], Mrinmoy Ghorai[1], and Himangshu Sarma[1(✉)]

[1] Human Computer Interaction Lab, Department of Computer Science and Engineering, Indian Institute of Information Technology Sri City, Sricity, India
himangshu.tezu@gmail.com, himangshu.sarma@iiits.in
[2] School of Data Science, Krea University, Sricity, India

Abstract. We present SigNet-TAM, a model for isolated Indian Sign Language (ISL) recognition, evaluated on a custom dataset of 20 location-based signs from 50 signers. It combines a ResNet-50 backbone for spatial feature extraction, bidirectional LSTMs for temporal modeling, and a temporal attention module to weight key frames. SigNet-TAM achieves 81.5% top-1 accuracy and 81.0% macro F1-score, balancing efficiency and accuracy. Ablation studies assess the impact of each component, while confusion matrix analysis identifies common misclassifications and difficult sign categories. The dataset's signer diversity and varied lighting make it a valuable ISL benchmark.

Keywords: Sign Language Recognition · Indian Sign Language · Temporal Attention · ResNet50 · BiLSTM

1 Introduction

Sign languages are the primary communication medium for Deaf and Hard-of-Hearing (DHH) communities. Automatic Sign Language Recognition (ASLR) systems [1] aim to bridge communication gaps between DHH individuals and the hearing population. However, robust ASLR remains challenging due to the complex spatio-temporal nature of sign languages, encompassing hand gestures, facial expressions, and body movements. These challenges are compounded by the limited availability of high-quality datasets—particularly for Indian Sign Language (ISL)—hindering the development of scalable and accurate models.

Large-scale datasets for American Sign Language (ASL), such as WLASL [4] and MS-ASL [5], have advanced ASLR research. In contrast, ISL datasets remain scarce, often lacking signer diversity, environmental variability, and standardized annotations. Most focus on continuous signing or gloss-level annotation, with limited benchmarks for isolated sign classification—a key task for scalable and efficient SLR systems.

P. Li et al. (Eds.): CGI 2025, LNCS 16508, pp. 338–350, 2026.
https://doi.org/10.1007/978-3-032-22264-0_27

To address existing gaps, we introduce a new ISL video dataset specifically for isolated sign classification. It comprises 20 location-based signs performed by 50 signers under varied lighting and environmental conditions. By emphasizing signer diversity and realistic settings, the dataset serves as a valuable benchmark for robust ISL recognition. Beyond sign language, it also aligns with broader research trends in gesture modeling, particularly for location-specific signs [2].

For recognition, we propose SigNet-TAM (Sign Language Network with Temporal Attention Mechanism), a hybrid architecture that captures spatial and temporal dynamics. It combines a ResNet-50 backbone for spatial feature extraction, a bidirectional LSTM (BiLSTM) for temporal modeling, and a temporal attention module that highlights informative frames for improved classification.

In SigNet-TAM, spatial features are extracted per frame using a ResNet-50 (pre-trained on ImageNet, fine-tuned from stage 4), then processed by a BiLSTM to capture bidirectional temporal dependencies. The temporal attention module learns a weight distribution over frames, allowing the model to focus on salient segments while reducing redundancy.

Our key contributions are:

- A publicly available ISL dataset with rich signer and environmental diversity for isolated sign classification.
- SigNet-TAM: a ResNet-BiLSTM-Attention model that effectively captures spatio-temporal structure in sign videos.
- Comprehensive evaluation with ablation and confusion analyses to assess the impact of each architectural component.

2 Related Work

Modern SLR systems typically consist of: (i) diverse and representative datasets, (ii) effective spatio-temporal feature extraction architectures, and (iii) mechanisms to dynamically focus on salient temporal information. Based on these functions, we organize prior work into three categories below.

2.1 Sign Language Datasets

Effective SLR depends on high-quality, diverse data. In ASL, datasets like WLASL [4] (2,000+ signs, 100+ signers) and MS-ASL [5] (25,000+ videos, 1,000 classes) have enabled large-scale benchmarking under signer-independent settings.

For other sign languages, datasets remain relatively limited. LSA64 [8] contains 3,200 samples of Argentinian Sign Language. AUTSL [9] includes 38,000 RGB-D samples from 43 signers across 226 Turkish signs. ISL also remains relatively under-resourced, with most datasets showing low signer diversity and constrained environments.

To bridge this gap, we introduce a 20-class ISL dataset with recordings from 50 signers across varied lighting and backgrounds. It improves ecological validity and supports generalized learning via diverse signer and environment conditions.

2.2 Spatio-Temporal Feature Extraction Strategies

2D CNN-Based Models. Initial SLR approaches used 2D CNNs like VGG [10] and ResNet [11] for per-frame spatial features. Though effective for static gestures, they lack temporal modeling. Kaushik et al. [6] report 99.92% and 99.95% accuracy with VGG16 and ResNet50, respectively. Khatawate et al. [7] show improvements using dropout and custom dense layers for better generalization.

CNN-RNN Hybrid Architectures. To add temporal context, CNNs are combined with LSTMs or BiLSTMs. Frame-wise CNN features are passed to recurrent layers. Huang et al. [12] demonstrate this architecture's effectiveness in isolated sign recognition. These models offer strong performance with moderate computational cost.

3D Convolutional Networks. 3D CNNs jointly model spatial and temporal features using spatiotemporal convolutions. I3D [13] inflates 2D filters for video modeling and excels on UCF-101 and HMDB-51. For SLR, I3D reaches 65.89% accuracy on WLASL100 [14]. However, these models are compute-heavy and rely on large datasets like Kinetics-400. We use I3D as a baseline to benchmark trade-offs.

Transformer-Based Models. Transformers use self-attention to model long-range dependencies. ViViT [15] tokenizes spatio-temporal inputs, achieving strong performance on Kinetics-400. VideoMAE [16] improves this via masked autoencoding. Brettmann et al. [14] show VideoMAE outperforms I3D with 75.58% on WLASL100. Despite their promise, transformers require substantial compute and pretraining. While promising, these models require extensive pre-training and are computationally intensive. We include them as baselines in our comparative analysis to validate the efficacy of our attention-augmented hybrid model.

2.3 Attention Mechanisms for Temporal Modeling

Temporal attention assigns relevance weights to frames—crucial in sign language where only some frames are informative. Kumari and Anand [17] show attention-based CNN-LSTM hybrids yield improved accuracy with lower cost.

In gesture modeling, Habibie et al. [3] use spatio-temporal attention in a motion-matching gesture synthesis framework. Although their focus is generation, their approach supports our attention-based design for improved sign classification.

3 Proposed Dataset and SigNet-TAM

We introduce a new ISL video dataset and the SigNet-TAM model. The dataset provides a diverse and realistic set of signs to support the development of robust recognition systems.

Fig. 1. Data Collection Setup: Image showing the data collection environment.

3.1 ISL Dataset for Location-Based Signs

The dataset contains 20 frequently used signs (cities, states, countries), performed by 50 unique signers, ensuring a wide range of demographic and expressive variation essential for generalizable models.

Recordings were captured using a Microsoft Kinect sensor, which provides RGB and depth data. In this study, only RGB frames are used, aligning with standard model inputs and real-world deployment conditions where depth data may be unavailable.

To enhance diversity, videos were recorded under varied lighting and indoor settings. Signers performed gestures naturally, without restrictions on speed or expressiveness, introducing variability across individuals and environments—beneficial for real-world generalization.

Table 1 highlights the diversity of the dataset by categorizing signs by handedness, gesture type (static/dynamic), and motion complexity. This provides a broad evaluation range across both simple and complex gestures.

The data collection setup is depicted in Fig. 1, which shows the camera position, lighting, signer, and background.

Preprocessing. Each video was trimmed and temporally interpolated to 32 frames. Frames were resized to 224×224 pixels, center-cropped, and normalized using ImageNet statistics. Each video was manually annotated with one of 20 predefined location-based sign labels.

The dataset was divided into training (80%) and validation (20%) sets, with no signer overlap to ensure a signer-independent evaluation protocol.

Table 1. Linguistic Properties of the 20 ISL Place Name Signs.

Place Name	Handedness	Gesture Type	Notes
Afghanistan	Two-handed	Dynamic	Letter-based gesture
Africa	Two-handed	Dynamic	Letter + rotation motion
Andhra Pradesh	Two-handed	Mixed	Letters + place indicator
Argentina	One-handed	Dynamic	Repeated hand movement
Bihar	Two-handed	Mixed	Letters + place indicator
Czech Republic	One-handed	Dynamic	Facial-adjacent motion
Delhi	One-handed	Dynamic	Letter repetition + place
Denmark	One-handed	Dynamic	Lateral hand movement
England	One-handed	Dynamic	Vibratory face movement
Gangtok	Two-handed	Dynamic	Hand twist + place sign
Gujarat	Two-handed	Mixed	Letters + place indicator
Haryana	Two-handed	Mixed	Letters + place indicator
Himachal Pradesh	Two-handed	Dynamic	Letters + cold + place indicator
Jaipur	Two-handed	Mixed	Hand gesture + place indicator
Jammu & Kashmir	Two-handed	Dynamic	Letters + cold + place indicator
Kenya	One-handed	Dynamic	Signaling-type movement
Kuwait	Two-handed	Dynamic	Repeated crossing motion
Maharashtra	One-handed	Dynamic	Chest tap + place sign
Mali	Two-handed	Dynamic	Palm-based gesture

Training and Evaluation Preprocessing. Input videos were uniformly sampled to extract 60-frame sequences. The preprocessing differed slightly across phases:

- **Training:** Frames were resized, randomly flipped horizontally, and color-jittered (brightness, contrast, saturation), then converted to tensors and normalized using ImageNet statistics.
- **Validation/Testing:** Frames were resized, converted to tensors, and normalized, without applying augmentation.

Figure 2 illustrates a sample 9-frame sequence from the "JAMMU AND KASHMIR" sign, capturing the temporal gesture flow.

3.2 Proposed Framework

This section details SigNet-TAM, our proposed framework for Indian Sign Language (ISL) recognition. It combines spatial feature extraction, temporal modeling, attention-based weighting, and classification into a unified pipeline. The full architecture is shown in Fig. 3, illustrating the model's design and data flow.

Fig. 2. Sample sequence showing the temporal evolution of Jammu & Kashmir.

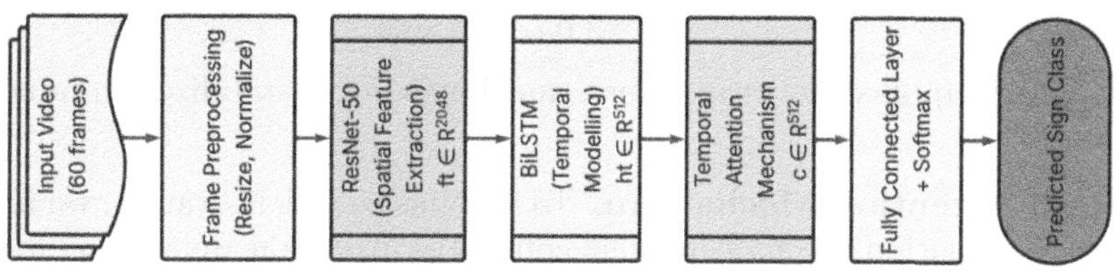

Fig. 3. SigNet-TAM architecture.

Overview of SigNet-TAM. SigNet-TAM is a hybrid architecture comprising the following modules:

1. **Frame Extraction**: Extracts frames from video sequences.
2. **Spatial Feature Extraction**: Uses a pre-trained ResNet-50 to encode spatial features from each frame.
3. **Temporal Modeling**: Employs a bidirectional LSTM (BiLSTM) to capture temporal relationships across frames.
4. **Temporal Attention**: Assigns adaptive weights to frames, highlighting those most relevant to the final prediction.
5. **Classification**: Outputs predicted sign classes via a fully connected layer followed by a softmax activation function.

By learning spatio-temporal patterns and selectively emphasizing key frames, SigNet-TAM enables robust and interpretable sign recognition.

Feature Extraction. We use a ResNet-50 pretrained on ImageNet to extract spatial features. Its 25M parameters and residual connections make it efficient and suitable for fine-tuning. The final classification layer is removed, and only the last convolutional block is fine-tuned; earlier layers remain frozen to preserve pretrained representations. Dropout ($p = 0.5$) is added for regularization.

Each frame I_t is passed through ResNet-50 to yield a 2048-dimensional feature:

$$\mathbf{f}_t = \text{ResNet50}(I_t), \quad \mathbf{f}_t \in \mathbb{R}^{2048}, \quad t = 1, \ldots, 60 \tag{1}$$

ResNet-50 matches deeper models like VGG16 in accuracy while offering better generalization and compute efficiency [18].

Temporal Modeling. We employ a 2-layer BiLSTM with hidden size $h = 256$ to capture temporal dependencies. BiLSTM processes both past and future context—key for gesture interpretation.

Given input features $\mathbf{f}_t$, forward and backward hidden states are computed and concatenated:

$$\begin{aligned} \overrightarrow{\mathbf{h}}_t, \overleftarrow{\mathbf{h}}_t &= \text{LSTM}(\mathbf{f}_t) \\ \mathbf{h}_t &= [\overrightarrow{\mathbf{h}}_t, \overleftarrow{\mathbf{h}}_t] \in \mathbb{R}^{512} \end{aligned} \tag{2}$$

Dropout is applied between layers, and LayerNorm stabilizes training.

Temporal Attention Mechanism. To emphasize salient frames, we integrate a temporal attention mechanism that computes attention weights α_t from BiLSTM outputs $\mathbf{h}_t$:

$$e_t = \mathbf{v}^\top \tanh(\mathbf{W}_a \mathbf{h}_t + \mathbf{b}_a) \tag{3}$$

where $\mathbf{W}_a$, $\mathbf{b}_a$, and $\mathbf{v}$ are learnable parameters.
Attention weights are normalized using softmax:

$$\alpha_t = \frac{\exp(e_t)}{\sum_{k=1}^{60} \exp(e_k)} \tag{4}$$

A context vector $\mathbf{c}$ is computed as the weighted sum of hidden states:

$$\mathbf{c} = \sum_{t=1}^{60} \alpha_t \mathbf{h}_t \in \mathbb{R}^{512} \tag{5}$$

Final Classification. The context vector $\mathbf{c}$ is passed through a dense layer and softmax to generate final class probabilities:

$$\hat{y} = \text{softmax}(\mathbf{W}_c \mathbf{c} + \mathbf{b}_c) \tag{6}$$

SigNet-TAM contains 28M parameters—substantially fewer than VGG16 (138M) or 3D/transformer models—making it well-suited for efficient deployment in constrained environments.

4 Results and Discussion

This section reports SigNet-TAM's performance against baseline and state-of-the-art ISL recognition models. We also present ablation studies and evaluate class-wise trends and computational efficiency.

4.1 Comparative Analysis and Contextual Benchmarking

Table 2 presents performance on the ISL dataset. SigNet-TAM achieves the highest accuracy (81.5%) and macro-F1 score (81.6%), outperforming all baselines—2D CNNs (VGG16, ResNet50), CNN+LSTM hybrids, and advanced models like I3D and ViViT. Accuracy improves with stronger temporal modeling: VGG16 and ResNet50 score 65–74%, while ResNet50+LSTM, I3D, and ViViT reach 78.2%–80.3%. SigNet-TAM's integration of BiLSTM and attention leads to the best performance, with a 4.2% gain over ResNet50+LSTM and a further 1.7% improvement over BiLSTM alone—highlighting the effectiveness of attention-enhanced temporal modeling.

To contextualize these results, we decouple model accuracy from dataset complexity. Table 3 compares existing sign language datasets, and Table 4 shows reported results on those datasets (not retrained on ours). Despite using a smaller but more diverse ISL dataset, SigNet-TAM remains competitive with state-of-the-art methods, underscoring its efficiency and generalization ability.

Table 2. Model-wise recognition results on the ISL dataset.

Model	Accuracy (%)	Macro-F1 (%)
VGG16 (2D CNN)	65.0	64.5
ResNet50 (2D CNN)	74.0	73.8
ResNet50 + LSTM	78.2	78.0
I3D (3D CNN)	79.5	79.4
ViViT/VideoMAE	80.3	80.2
SigNet-TAM (Ours)	**81.5**	**81.6**

Table 3. Comparison of Dataset Properties for Sign Language Recognition.

Dataset	#Signs	#Signers	Modality	Notes
ASL Alphabet	26	30+	RGB	Static, fingerspelling only
LSA64	64	10	RGB	Indoor, controlled lighting
WLASL100	100	119	RGB	Unconstrained, diverse
AUTSL	226	43	RGB+D	Ensemble, multimodal
ISL (Ours)	20	50	RGB	Signer-independent, varied scenes

4.2 Ablation Study

To assess the contribution of each SigNet-TAM component, we conducted an ablation study (Fig. 4). Results show that adding a bidirectional LSTM (BiLSTM) and attention significantly boosts performance. ResNet50+LSTM improves accuracy by 4.2% over ResNet50, while adding attention provides an additional 1.7% gain, underscoring the impact of these design choices.

Table 4. Accuracy on benchmark datasets.

Model	Dataset	Accuracy (%)
VGG16/ResNet50	ASL Alphabet	99.92/99.95
ResNet50 + LSTM	LSA64	86.25
I3D (3D CNN)	WLASL100	65.89
ViViT/VideoMAE	WLASL100	75.58
SOTA (AUTSL)	AUTSL	~96.0
SigNet-TAM	ISL (Ours)	**81.5**

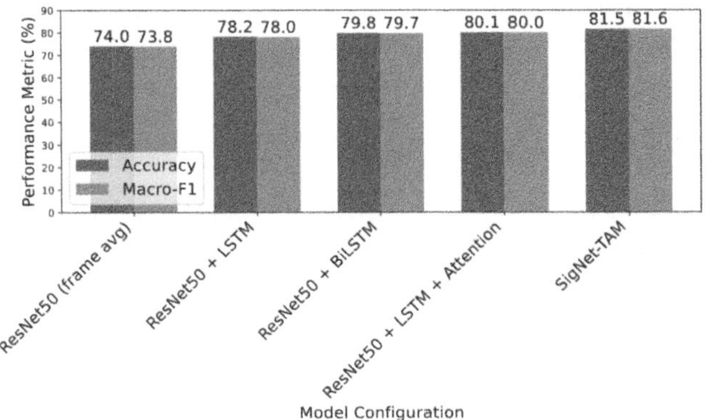

Fig. 4. Ablation study of SigNet-TAM components.

4.3 Training Dynamics

SigNet-TAM shows stable convergence, reaching peak performance around 50 epochs. Validation accuracy plateaus near 82%, with a 3–4% gap from training accuracy, indicating good generalization to unseen signers. Dropout, layer normalization, and early stopping help mitigate overfitting despite the limited dataset size. The learning rate scheduler aids efficient optimization, with improvements observed after each warm restart.

4.4 Class-Wise Performance and Confusion Analysis

Most classes achieve F1 scores above 85%, though some signs remain challenging. As shown in Fig. 5, misclassifications often occur between signs with similar hand trajectories or subtle orientation differences. The confusion matrix offers insight into these errors and highlights overlapping gesture patterns.

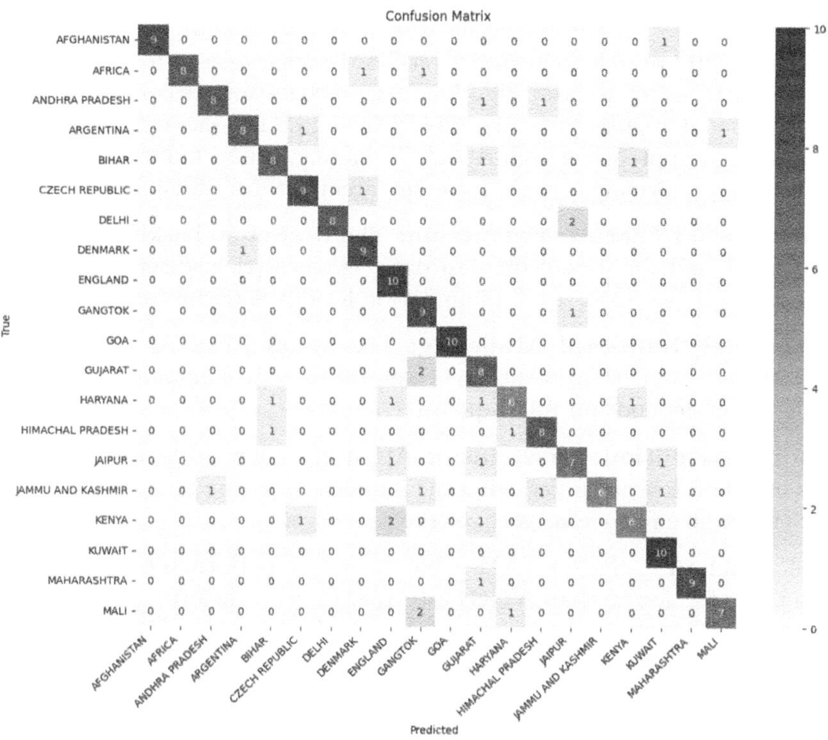

Fig. 5. Confusion matrix for SigNet-TAM on the ISL dataset.

On the other hand, certain signs such as "GOA," "MAHARASHTRA," and "ENGLAND" achieve perfect classification accuracy due to distinctive motion patterns that are consistently performed across signers.

4.5 Deployment Feasibility and Efficiency Considerations

SigNet-TAM, with approximately 28M parameters and RGB-only input, offers a lightweight alternative to most spatio-temporal models. On an NVIDIA RTX A4000 GPU, it achieves an average inference time of ~65 ms per 60-frame video ($\rightarrow$15 FPS) and peak memory usage under 450 MB, indicating its potential for near-real-time deployment in moderately powered environments. In comparison, heavier models like I3D and ViViT incur over 100 ms latency and require more than 1 GB memory due to their 3D and transformer-based computations. While SigNet-TAM strikes a strong balance between accuracy and efficiency, further evaluation on edge devices (e.g., Jetson Nano) is necessary. Future work will focus on model pruning and quantization to enhance its deployment in low-resource settings.

5 Discussion

The experimental results confirm SigNet-TAM's effectiveness in modeling spatio-temporal patterns for isolated sign language recognition. It consistently outperforms traditional architectures like 2D CNNs and LSTM-based models, as well as more advanced approaches such as 3D CNNs (e.g., I3D) and transformer-based models. This performance stems from key architectural decisions:

Robust Spatial Feature Extraction: The ResNet-50 backbone, pre-trained on ImageNet and fine-tuned on sign data, extracts rich, discriminative frame-level features. These form a solid foundation for downstream temporal modeling.

Bidirectional Temporal Modeling: The use of BiLSTM enables learning from both past and future context—essential for sign language, where gesture meaning often depends on full sequence context.

Temporal Attention Mechanism: Attention allows dynamic weighting of frames based on relevance, reducing the influence of redundant frames and focusing on the most informative parts of the sequence.

Model Efficiency: SigNet-TAM achieves strong performance with only 28M parameters—far fewer than VGG16 (∼138M) or transformer-based models—making it suitable for real-time or resource-limited settings (Table 5).

Table 5. Misclassification patterns for challenging signs.

True Class	Predicted Classes	Likely Reason
KENYA	DENMARK, GANGTOK, J&K	Similar circular hand trajectories
GUJARAT	GOA	Starting sign is same
HARYANA	ANDHRA, BIHAR, HP, MALI	Inconsistent elbow articulation
JAIPUR	CZECH, ENGLAND, HARYANA	Ambiguous finger spacing
GANGTOK	GOA	Similar to GUJARAT (all start with G)

Limitations and Future Enhancements: Despite its strengths, SigNet-TAM has scope for improvement:

- *Fine-grained hand modeling:* Current features may miss subtle finger movements. Integrating hand keypoints or localized attention could boost fine gesture recognition.

- *Multi-modal integration:* Adding depth, optical flow, or skeletal data could enhance temporal-spatial cues and overall performance.
- *Temporal augmentation:* Techniques like temporal jittering, playback speed variation, or synthetic data could improve robustness to signer variability.

In summary, SigNet-TAM provides an accurate and efficient solution for ISL recognition, showing that hybrid architectures can effectively balance performance and deployment feasibility.

6 Conclusion

This work introduces SigNet-TAM, an architecture for isolated Indian Sign Language recognition. Evaluated on a curated 20-class dataset with 50 diverse signers, the model processes 60-frame videos using spatial feature learning, temporal modeling, and adaptive attention. SigNet-TAM uses a ResNet-50 backbone for frame-level feature extraction, a BiLSTM for capturing bidirectional temporal dynamics, and a temporal attention module to emphasize informative frames. It achieves 81.5% accuracy and 81.6% macro F1-score, outperforming 2D CNNs, RNN-based models, and transformer variants. Ablation studies and qualitative analyses confirm the effectiveness of each component. Future work includes enhancing fine-grained hand modeling, integrating multi-modal inputs, and improving signer-independent generalization. We also aim to benchmark SigNet-TAM on larger, public datasets to test its scalability and adaptability.

Acknowledgment. This work was supported by the project titled "Design and Development of a Communication System for the Speech and Hearing Disorder Persons" under the grant OO/ISI/IDEAS-TIH/2023-24/85, and IIIT-H/IHub/Project/Healthcare|2025-26/H2-013 (PH). The authors sincerely thank the funding agencies and associated institutions for their valuable support and resources that contributed to the successful execution of this research.

References

1. Prakash, V., Tripathy, B.K.: Recent advancements in automatic sign language recognition (SLR). In: Computational Intelligence for Human Action Recognition, pp. 1–24. Chapman and Hall/CRC (2020)
2. Zhou, Y., Park, J., Lee, M.: Finger-pointing interface for human gesture recognition based on real-time geometric comprehension. In: SIGGRAPH Asia Posters (2024)
3. Habibie, I., et al.: A motion matching-based framework for controllable gesture synthesis from speech. In: ACM SIGGRAPH Conference Proceedings, pp. 1–9 (2022)
4. Li, D., Opazo, C., Yu, X., Li, H.: Word-level deep sign language recognition from video: a new large-scale dataset and methods comparison. In: WACV (2020)
5. Joze, M.V., Koller, O.: MS-ASL: a large-scale data set and benchmark for understanding American Sign Language. In: CVPR Workshops (2019)

6. Kaushik, P., et al.: Deep learning for sign language recognition utilizing VGG16 and ResNet50 models. In: 2nd Int. Conf. on Sustainable Computing and Smart Systems (ICSCSS). IEEE (2024)
7. Khatawate, P., et al.: A comprehensive analysis of VGG16 and ResNet50 models in sign language recognition. In: 5th Int. Conf. for Emerging Technology (INCET). IEEE (2024)
8. Ronchetti, F., Quiroga, F., Estrebou, C.A., Lanzarini, L.C., Rosete, A.: LSA64: an Argentinian Sign Language dataset. In: XXII Congreso Argentino de Ciencias de la Computación (CACIC) (2016)
9. Sincan, O.M., Keles, H.Y.: AUTSL: a large scale multi-modal Turkish Sign Language dataset and baseline methods. IEEE Access **9**, 130142–130161 (2021)
10. Simonyan, K., Zisserman, A.: Very deep convolutional networks for large-scale image recognition. In: ICLR (2015)
11. He, K., Zhang, X., Ren, S., Sun, J.: Deep residual learning for image recognition. In: CVPR (2016)
12. Huang, J., Chouvatut, V.: Video-based sign language recognition via ResNet and LSTM network. J. Imaging **10**(1), 12 (2024)
13. Carreira, J., Zisserman, A.: Quo vadis, action recognition? A new model and the Kinetics dataset. In: CVPR (2017)
14. Brettmann, A., Gravinghoff, J., Rüschoff, M., Westhues, M.: Breaking the barriers: video vision transformers for word-level sign language recognition. In: Computer Graphics International (2025)
15. Arnab, A., Dehghani, M., Heigold, G., Sun, C., Lučić, M., Schmid, C.: ViViT: a video vision transformer. In: ICCV (2021)
16. Tong, Z., Song, Y., Wang, J., Wang, L.: VideoMAE: masked autoencoders are data-efficient learners for self-supervised video pre-training. In: NeurIPS (2022)
17. Kumari, D., Anand, R.S.: Isolated video-based sign language recognition using a hybrid CNN-LSTM framework based on attention mechanism. Electronics **13**(1), 121 (2024)
18. Sharma, J., Gill, K.S., Kumar, M., Rawat, R.: Deep learning for sign language recognition: exploring VGG16 and ResNet50 capabilities. In: Applied Intelligence and Computing, pp. 115–124 (2024)
19. Raheja, J.L., Mishra, A., Chaudhary, A.: Indian sign language recognition using SVM. Pattern Recognit. Image Anal. **26**, 434–441 (2016)

Reconstruction

Dynamic Voxel Grid Optimization for High-Fidelity RGB-D Supervised Surface Reconstruction

Xiangyu Xu[1], Qingan Yan[2(✉)], Changjiang Cai[1], Huangying Zhan[2], Pan Ji[3], Yang Zhou[1], Junsong Yuan[4], and Yi Xu[2]

[1] OPPO US Research Center, Palo Alto, CA, USA
{xiangyu.xu,changjiang.cai,yang.zhou}@oppo.com
[2] Goertek Alpha Labs, Santa Clara, CA, USA
yanqinganssg@gmail.com
[3] Tencent, Shanghai, China
[4] University at Buffalo, Buffalo, NY, USA
jsyuan@buffalo.edu

Abstract. Direct optimization of interpolated features on multi-resolution voxel grids has emerged as a more efficient alternative to MLP-like modules. However, this approach is constrained by higher memory expenses and limited representation capabilities. In this paper, we introduce a novel dynamic grid optimization method for high-fidelity 3D surface reconstruction that incorporates both RGB and depth observations. Rather than treating each voxel equally, we optimize the process by dynamically modifying the grid and assigning more finer-scale voxels to regions with higher complexity, allowing us to capture more intricate details. Furthermore, we develop a scheme to quantify the dynamic subdivision of voxel grid during optimization without requiring any priors. The proposed approach is able to generate high-quality 3D reconstructions with fine details on both synthetic and real-world data, while maintaining computational efficiency, which is substantially faster than the baseline method NeuralRGBD [1].

Keywords: NeRF · surface reconstruction · dynamic voxel grid · RGB-D

1 Introduction

3D scene reconstruction plays an essential role in a variety of virtual reality, augmented reality, and robotics applications. Although low-cost depth sensors have proven to be an efficient tool for capturing 3D geometries, relying exclusively on range measurements, such as in the case of KinectFusion [13], may result in incomplete or incorrect reconstructed geometry due to deficiencies in depth data. To address this issue, radiance-based scene representations [1,19] offer a powerful way to incorporate spatial context from color observations for more high-quality RGB-D reconstruction.

P. Li et al. (Eds.): CGI 2025, LNCS 16508, pp. 353–366, 2026.
https://doi.org/10.1007/978-3-032-22264-0_28

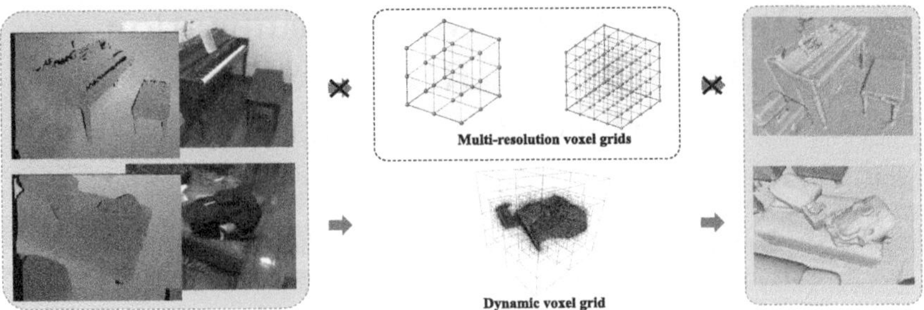

Fig. 1. Our dynamic voxel grid optimization method can generate high-fidelity 3D reconstructions from RGB-D data. Instead of relying on fixed multi-resolution voxel grids, the idea is to dynamically refine the grid representation during optimization by assigning more finer-scale voxels to regions with higher complexity, and efficiently regress 3D structures via interpolation rather than MLPs.

Drawing from [12], NeuralRGBD [1] employs two multi-layer perceptrons (MLP) to learn the mapping from a 3D query to its corresponding signed distance function (SDF) and color value. Despite the effectiveness of scene reconstruction, this comes at the cost of hours of training time. While Go-Surf [19] cuts the runtime into minutes, it can not well preserve high-frequency details since the limited multi-scale resolution.

Taking inspiration from the recent success [15,30] that uses voxel grid to explicitly store rendering properties, we introduce a dynamic voxel grid optimization for fine-scale RGB-D supervised surface reconstruction. Rather than employing multiple voxel grids in various scales, expanding each voxel uniformly, our approach dynamically partition some voxels within one grid during iteration according to local scene complexity. In this way, regions with more geometric and textural information would be represented by voxels of higher resolution, while surfaces with simple details remain in relatively low resolution. Divergent from Octree structure [26] which relies on a pretrained geometric prior, our scheme adaptively select certain voxels for subdivision during optimization without priors. To address this challenge, we measure depth and color inconsistency with the corresponding references as a means of quantification. It is intuitive that complex structures and textures with higher losses usually deserve more primitive samples to approximate. Furthermore, we showed that using grayscale instead of RGB can improve efficiency with minimal impact on reconstruction quality.

The proposed hierarchical representation has three merits. First, it improves scalability. While voxel-based architectures [19] lead to super-efficient convergences, such structures entail high memory consumption as the size of the scene grows. In contrast, our representation achieves better memory efficiency thanks to selective partitioning. Second, the representation has an inherent advantage in recovering geometric details. Specifically, with lower memory cost, our method is able to divide complex regions into voxels with higher resolution under the same hardware configuration, which accordingly alleviates suboptimal solutions and results in finer reconstructions. Moreover, unlike previous radiance-based 3D reconstruction methods [1,19], the proposed representation can be optimized simply via gradient descents and regularization without any MLPs and pre-training. Evaluations on both synthetic and real-world datasets show that our proposed method achieves similar runtime compared to [19]. Meanwhile, our method produces 3D reconstruction with finer geometric details, as shown in Fig. 1.

To summarize, our contributions are the following:

- A novel 3D surface reconstruction method that regresses SDF from the supervision of color and depth images without leveraging MLP components;
- A hierarchical structure that enables highly efficient scene representation and detailed geometry recovery;
- A well-designed partitioning strategy for dynamic voxel subdivision during optimization.

2 Related Work

2.1 Neural RGB-D Surface Reconstruction

Neural surface reconstruction [1,3,5,9–11,14,17,19–25,27], which reduces artifacts from traditional 3D reconstruction through training end-to-end networks, has been a trend for high-fidelity 3D surface reconstruction. In particular, for RGB-D reconstruction, NeuralRGBD [1] first couples the merit of SDF representation and volume rendering to jointly leverage the context in color and depth. While it is able to reconstruct high-quality metrical 3D geometries, due to the similar network architecture to NeRF, NeuralRGBD takes hours to converge. GO-Surf [19] proposes a learned hierarchical feature voxel grid to represent the scene and achieves a substantial speedup over NeuralRGBD. Since it favors scene completeness, the reconstructed result is prone to lose some high-frequency details. InFusionSurf [8] improves neural RGB-D surface reconstruction by combining per-frame intrinsic refinement with learned Truncated Signed Distance Function (TSDF) fusion priors. In the field of SLAM research, NiceSLAM [30] introduces a real-time dense RGB-D SLAM system that optimizes a multi-level feature grid representation with pre-trained geometric priors. NicerSLAM [29] alleviates the requirement for depth images. Instead, it is enhanced with an additional monocular depth estimation module and a normal calculation module. Co-SLAM [18] integrates coordinate-based and sparse parametric methods to enhance SLAM in neural networks. GO-SLAM [28] excels in real-time 3D reconstruction with robust pose estimation and versatile input compatibility, yet may face challenges in computational efficiency due to its global optimization approach, while ESLAM [6] employs a hybrid representation of signed distance fields to balance accuracy and efficiency in dense SLAM systems.

2.2 Direct Voxel Grid Optimization

Directly optimizing interpolated features recorded in a voxel grid leads to orders of magnitude faster training and inference time than querying MLPs. To accelerate the training of NeRF models, DirectVoxGO [15,16] methods use a dense voxel grid to directly model volume density and optimize view-dependent colors in a hybrid way by incorporating a voxel grid with shallow MLP. PlenOctrees [26] adopts an Octree structure to exclude redundant queries, however, an additional conversion step from a pretrained model is required to serve as the prior for structure generation. Plenoxel [4] utilizes multi-resolution voxel grids to model the scene with additional spherical harmonic coefficients at each voxel replacing view direction information.

Our proposed method is also based on the voxel grid representation and can be optimized directly by gradient back-propagation. What sets it apart is that our algorithm can dynamically enlarge certain voxel resolutions to fit local scene complexity during optimization, without requiring any pretrained geometric priors, unlike [26]. Compared to the coarse-to-fine manner of DirectVoxGO [15,16], it is more efficient in memory.

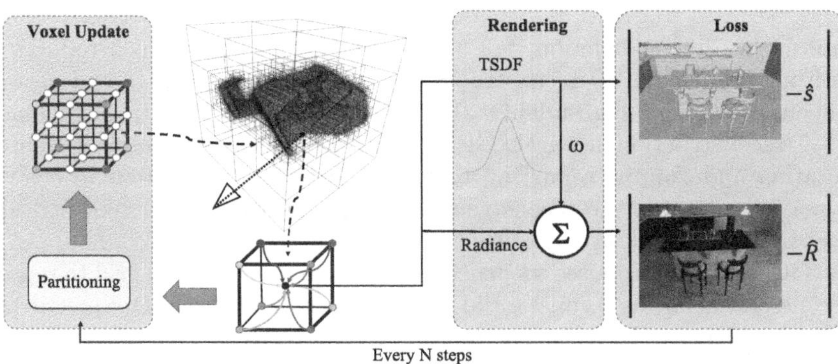

Fig. 2. Our proposed pipeline utilizes a single dynamic voxel grid to efficiently store both Signed Distance Function (SDF) and color values. At each sample point along a ray, we trace the terminal voxel and compute the corresponding feature using trilinear interpolation of the voxel's eight corners. Loss terms are then applied to both the SDF values and color, and the voxel grid is updated based on the corresponding loss values after a specified number of steps.

3 Method

In this work, we represent the 3D scene by using a dynamically partitioned grid structure. With such a representation, complex areas can be adaptively approximated by finer-scale voxels in iteration, while leaving well-fitted voxels unchanged. Moreover, with modalities of interest explicitly in its grid cells, we conduct reconstruction by jointly optimizing values stored on each vertex under the self-supervision of both color $\mathcal{I}$ and depth observations $\mathcal{D}$. Camera poses $\mathcal{T}$ can be acquired by SLAM or SfM. As illustrated in Fig. 2, we query arbitrary 3D radiance samples directly through interpolation based on current voxel partitioning, and dynamically update the grid representation according to the voxel split metrics in Sect. 3.3.

3.1 Volumetric Rendering in Voxel Grid

A voxel grid representation approximates the scene geometry by a uniform 3D grid with different modalities of interest stored in each voxel node. For our RGB-D fusion task, the modalities correspond to SDF and radiance values. With such representation, it is efficient to query for 3D positions $\mathbf{x}$ via interpolation:

$$s = interp(\mathbf{x}, \mathbf{G}^{(s)}(\mathbf{x})), \tag{1}$$

$$\mathbf{r} = interp(\mathbf{x}, \mathbf{G}^{(r)}(\mathbf{x})), \tag{2}$$

where s and $\mathbf{r}$ are the SDF and radiance value. $\mathbf{G} \in \mathbb{R}^{C \times N_x \times N_y \times N_z}$ is the voxel grid and $\mathbf{G}(\mathbf{x})$ returns the voxel in which $\mathbf{x}$ is allocated. C is the dimension of modalities and (N_x, N_y, N_z) indicates the grid resolution. Higher resolutions contribute to better representation ability. In our implementation, we utilize trilinear interpolation due to the trade-off between simplicity and stability.

Leveraging this property, it is thus easy to integrate volumetric rendering. Along each viewing ray, N_k points are sampled and optimized for their corresponding SDF and radiance. We approximate the color $\mathbf{R}$ along the viewing ray as a weighted sum of these samples:

$$\mathbf{R} = \frac{1}{\sum_{i=0}^{N_k-1} w_i} \sum_{i=0}^{N_k-1} w_i \cdot \mathbf{r}_i, \tag{3}$$

where w is the weight gauging the visibility of current sample on the ray given by $w_i = T_i \alpha_i$. T_i is the *accumulated transmittance* and α is the *opacity value*:

$$T_i = \prod_{j=1}^{i-1} (1 - \alpha_j), \tag{4}$$

$$\alpha_i = \max\left(\frac{\sigma_b(\phi(\mathbf{x}_i)) - \sigma_b(\phi(\mathbf{x}_{i+1}))}{\sigma_b(\phi(\mathbf{x}_i))}, 0\right), \tag{5}$$

$\sigma_b(x) = (1+e^{-bx})^{-1}$ is the transition smoothness and b is a learnable parameter.

The predicted color serves as an important auxiliary to depth regulations. Note that in contrast to NeRF models [1,12,15] which need another round of optimization by incorporating view direction, we solely focus here on exploiting only view-invariant colors. We found that it is able to generate similar reconstructed geometries under sufficient grid resolutions. This modification contributes a further boost to our runtime and makes the entire optimization independent of any MLP components.

3.2 Hierarchical Representation

A big limitation of the voxel grid structure is its cubic memory consumption. We address this by introducing a hierarchical structure to avoid excessively partitioning in regions that are able to be well-represented in their present resolutions. Additionally, the saved resource can further benefit those parts requiring finer cells in the following iteration.

For the sake of clarity, we denote our hierarchically split grid as $\mathbf{H}$. It allows the 3D points bounded by different-sized voxels. For an arbitrary 3D query, we first locate its terminal node that has the finest split. Since now it is unable to trace it directly from the coordinate, therefore a recursive search is needed. Next, after getting the bounding voxel, modalities can be estimated via interpolation based on the distances to its eight vertices:

$$\mathbf{V}_x = trace(\mathbf{x}, \mathbf{H}), \tag{6}$$

$$\mathbf{m} = interp(\mathbf{x}, \mathbf{V}_x^{(m)}), \tag{7}$$

where $\mathbf{V}$ is the terminal voxel of current query point, $\mathbf{m}$ corresponds to either the SDF or radiance value.

The grid is first initialized as a uniform voxel grid $\mathbf{H}^{[0]} \in \mathbb{R}^{N_x \times N_y \times N_z}$ at a coarse resolution. During the optimization, it will be updated every S_u steps by adaptively subdividing certain voxels into eight more cells, until all voxels sufficiently split or reach the predefined deepest layer.

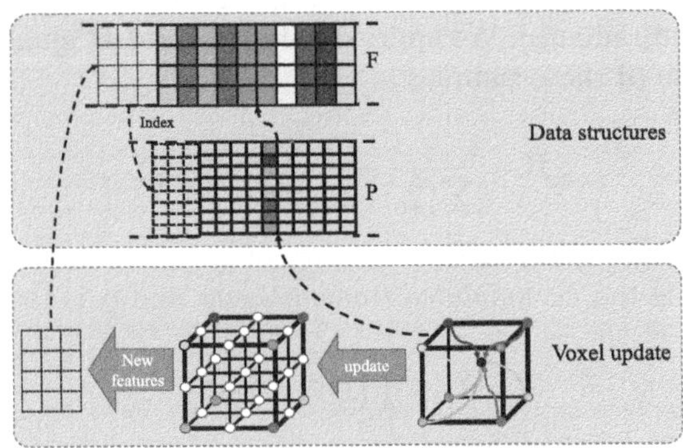

Fig. 3. When a voxel being subdivided, new modalities and pointers will be added to **F** and **P**. The original voxel will be deactivated and removed from **P**.

Data Structure. Our method optimizes storage and access of voxel node modalities by consolidating them into a matrix, $\mathbf{F} \in \mathbb{R}^{N_n^{[l]} \times C}$, where $l \in [0, L_{max}]$ represents the subdivision level and $N_n^{[l]}$ the node count at this level. Each node references its modalities via pointers, organized in a matrix $\mathbf{P} \in \mathbb{Z}_+^{N^{[l]} \times 8}$, as shown in Fig. 3. This arrangement captures the grid's detailed information and improves training and traversal efficiency.

To track terminal voxels and modalities, we employ a list $\mathbf{K}$. Starting with $\mathbf{K}^{[0]} \in \mathbb{Z}_{+}^{N^{[0]}}$, which indexes voxels in $\mathbf{P}$, this list updates with each subdivision, adding new features to $\mathbf{F}$ and $\mathbf{P}$, and removing inactive voxel information (see Fig. 3). A new $\mathbf{K}^{[l]} \in \mathbb{Z}_{+}^{N^{[l]}}$ is created for each level l, assigning a unique key to each voxel based on its midpoint $\mathbf{x}$, calculated as:

$$key^{[l]} = (\overline{x}_2 \times 2^l N_x \times 2^l N_y + \overline{x}_1 \times 2^l N_x + \overline{x}_0), \tag{8}$$

with $\mathbf{K}(key)$ storing the index to $\mathbf{P}$.
Voxel Tracing. By virtue of this design, we can extract the corresponding terminal corner modalities of arbitrary node keys through a set of operations as:

$$\begin{aligned} (s, \mathbf{r}) &= \mathbf{F}(\mathbf{P}(\mathbf{K}^{[l]}(key^{[l]}))), \\ \text{w.r.t.}, \mathbf{K}^{[l+1]}(key^{[l+1]}) &== None. \end{aligned} \tag{9}$$

Since there usually are more than two levels, we thus trace the terminal voxels in a recursive manner. It is worth noting that index values without gradients during training, such as $\mathbf{P}$, can be stored in CPU memory. This allocation strategy helps manage the memory requirements efficiently.

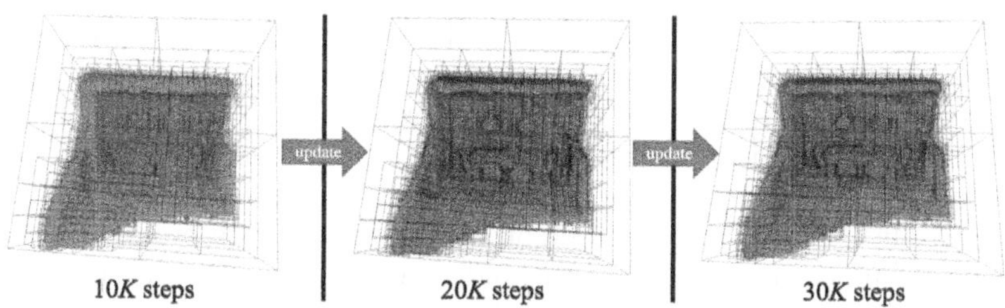

Fig. 4. Our proposed updating strategy focuses on identifying and subdividing voxels in areas of high loss, which are typically indicative of complex structures. As the scene becomes better trained, our approach automatically narrows the updating area, prioritizing thin objects and detailed surfaces to avoid wasting computational resources on unnecessary areas.

3.3 Optimization

We first estimate the bounding box based on the camera frustums. Then we randomly sample the pixels $\mathbf{I}$ from the input images and sample 3D points $\mathbf{X}$ along viewing ray between intersects with the bounding box. We directly use grayscale images instead of full RGB values, as it would weaken the impact from non-Lambertian materials and it is more computational-friendly.

With all 3D points sampled, we optimize our grid structure by minimizing the objective function with respect to node modalities $\mathbf{F}$ and camera poses $\mathcal{T}$.

We define the truncation distance as $tr = 5\,\text{cm}$ and scale the scene to bound the truncation region in range $[-1, 1]$.

Loss Function. Our object function consists of three terms: image loss, free space loss, and SDF loss referring to [1]. The image loss measures the pixel-wise color difference between the rendered image and the ground-truth image:

$$L_{image}(\mathbf{I}) = \frac{1}{|\mathbf{I}|} \sum_{i \in \mathbf{I}} (\mathbf{R}_i - \hat{\mathbf{R}}_i)^2, \tag{10}$$

where $\hat{\mathbf{R}}$ is the observed image. The free space loss term enforces the SDF value between the truncation region and the camera origin to be tr as follows:

$$L_{fs}(\mathbf{X}) = \frac{1}{|\mathbf{X}_i^{fs}|} \sum_{\mathbf{x} \in \mathbf{X}_i^{fs}} (s_{\mathbf{x}} - tr)^2, \tag{11}$$

where $\mathbf{X}^{fs}$ denotes the set of samples belonging to the free space. For the samples lay in the truncation area, we use L_{sdf} to encourage estimated SDF values to be equal to the ones computed from depth observations:

$$L_{sdf}(\mathbf{X}) = \frac{1}{|\mathbf{X}_i^{sdf}|} \sum_{\mathbf{x} \in \mathbf{X}_i^{sdf}} (s_{\mathbf{x}} - \hat{s}_{\mathbf{x}})^2. \tag{12}$$

where $\mathbf{X}^{sdf}$ denote samples belonging to the truncated region. For the weight applied to each loss, please kindly refer to the supplementary material.

Dynamic Partitioning. After some steps, we review the representing capability of our voxel grid and perform a further subdivision for certain voxels if necessary. Our dynamic partitioning metrics are subject to two criteria:

1) We only split voxels whose eight corner SDF values cross the surface—*i.e.*, at least one corner is less than 0 and at least one is greater 1. This keeps refinement focused on voxels that actually sit near the object's boundary.

2) During training we keep two per-voxel scoreboards: one for image loss, one for SDF loss. If either score rises above a set threshold, that voxel is marked for splitting, because high loss usually means the current voxel is too coarse to capture the texture or geometry inside it.

As illustrated in Fig. 4, the proposed voxel refinement technique selectively subdivides voxels with higher loss values, labeled in color red, to achieve higher resolution representation. With iterating, the scheme gradually narrows the area and focuses on some really challenging parts.

4 Experiments

We validated the performance of our method on both synthetic and real datasets. We first presented the quantitative results on the synthetic dataset to demonstrate the accuracy of our reconstruction. We then showed the advantage of our method in reconstructing fine details on both synthetic and real datasets. Finally, we provided results that demonstrate our efficiency, as well as an ablation study to analyze the contribution of each key component in our method.

4.1 Synthetic Dataset

We conducted a comprehensive quantitative evaluation of our method using 10 synthetic scenes provided by [1]. To simulate realistic conditions, noise and artifacts were added to depth observations and camera poses.

We compare our approach with baseline methods, such as NeuralRGB-D [1], GO-Surf [19] and InFusionSurf [8], using four different evaluation metrics: the Chamfer ℓ_1 distance, normal consistency, intersection-over-union (IoU) and the F-score. As demonstrated in Table 1, our method outperforms all the others in both Chamfer ℓ_1 distance and IoU. While our F-score of is lower than that of InFusionSur, the overall performance of our method is still superior. We observed that GO-Surf achieves the best normal consistency, which can be attributed to its enforcement of normal smoothness during training.

Furthermore, we provide comparisons of the reconstructed 3D scenes using our method, NeuralRGBD, InFusionSur and GO-Surf in Fig. 5. Notable that our method shows superiority in terms of recovering fine details and complex structures, as the closeup figures. While GO-Surf exhibits the most completed meshes, it fails to recover complicated structures due to its smoothness enforcement.

Table 1. To evaluate the reconstruction performance of our method, we conduct a quantitative analysis on 10 synthetic scenes provided by [1]. We directly cite the results reported in [1] and compare the performance of GO-Surf [19], InFusionSurf [8] and our method under the same metrics. We compute the Chamfer ℓ_1 distance, normal consistency, and the F-score [7] between point clouds sampled with a density of 1 point per cm^2, with a threshold of 5 cm for the F-score. Moreover, we voxelize the mesh to compute the intersection-over-union (IoU) between predictions and ground truth.

Method	C-ℓ_1 ↓	IoU ↑	NC ↑	F-score ↑
NeuralRGBD [1]	0.044	0.747	0.918	0.924
GO-Surf [19]	0.041	0.916	**0.920**	0.907
InFusionSurf [8]	0.038	0.737	0.904	**0.929**
Ours	**0.037**	**0.923**	0.902	0.920

4.2 Real Dataset

We also conducted experiments on the real-world RGB-D dataset ScanNet [2], which presents difficulties due to noisy depth, missing observations, and image blur. Figure 6 exhibits the reconstruction results from the proposed method and GO-Surf. Similar to the synthetic scenes, our method demonstrates good performance in recovering complex structures and details of objects, such as the shape of shoes, wrinkles on bags, and laces around chairs. In contrast, GO-Surf emphasizes smoother surfaces at the cost of losing finer details. Our results suggest that the proposed method is well-suitable for real-world applications, where the accurate reconstruction of complex objects with fine details is crucial.

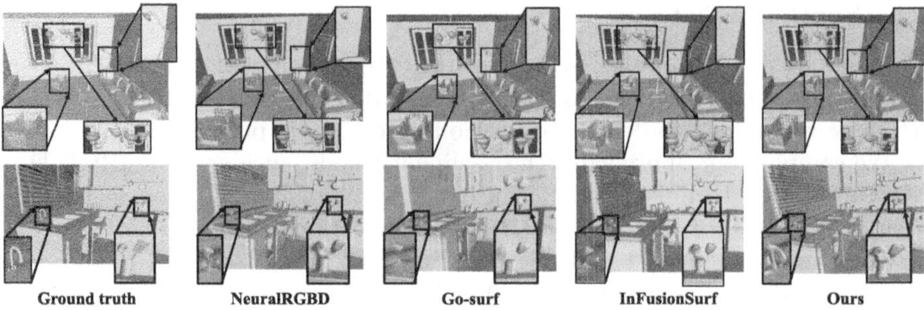

Fig. 5. We compare our method with SOTA techniques, NeuralRGBD [1], GO-Surf [19] and InFusionSurf [8] on - Complete Green Room - from 10 synthetic scenes [1]. Our qualitative results demonstrate that our method outperforms both methods in terms of reconstruction completion and detail recovery.

Fig. 6. We conducted a comparative evaluation of our method and GO-Surf [19] on scenes 0014 from the ScanNet dataset [2]. The results demonstrate that our method is highly effective in recovering thin objects and complex surfaces, while GO-Surf often over-smooths the surfaces.

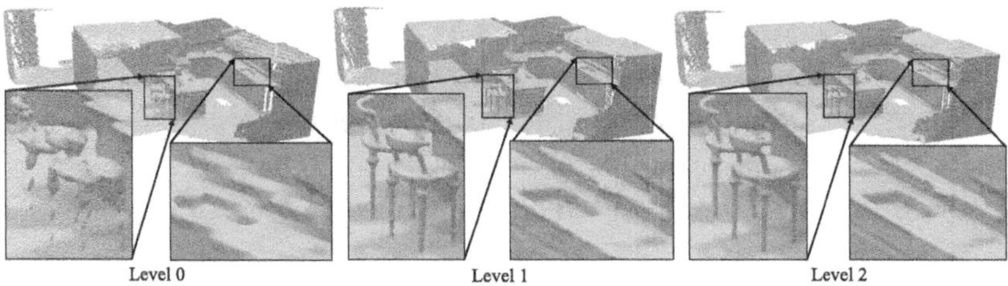

Fig. 7. We present the reconstruction results obtained with varying subdivision level of our voxel grid. We demonstrate that increasing the subdivision level of the structure results in superior reconstruction quality.

4.3 Ablaition Study

Voxel Subdivision Level. We first investigated the impact of different subdivision levels of voxel grid on the quality of reconstructed 3D scenes. We initialized the voxel grid with a resolution of 128^3 and train it for $30K$ steps. To examine the effect of the subdivision level, we performed three experiments. In the first experiment, we did not subdivide the voxel during the entire training process, so the subdivision level $L_{max} = 1$. In the second experiment, we subdivided the voxel once at 10K steps, resulting in $L_{max} = 2$. Finally, in the third experiment, we subdivided the voxel at $10K$ and $20K$ steps, leading to $L_{max} = 3$.

The reconstruction results shown in Fig. 7 demonstrate that a higher level of subdivision contributes to better reconstruction quality. Specifically, the model trained with a non-subdivided structure exhibits the lowest quality, with missing structures and coarse details.

Table 2. Ablation study result

Method	C-ℓ_1 ↓	IoU ↑	NC ↑	F-score ↑
Ours(surf+loss)	0.03654	0.923	0.9017	0.9195
Ours(surf)	0.03836	0.9229	0.9013	0.9196

(a) Results updating on the surface with large loss and on the whole surface.

Method	C-ℓ_1 ↓	IoU ↑	NC ↑	F-score ↑	PSNR
Ours(64^3, grayscale)	0.03921	0.9170	0.9136	0.9103	27.59
Ours(64^3, rgb)	0.03920	0.9119	0.9143	0.9103	26.94
Ours(64^3, grayscale+SH)	0.03905	0.9255	0.9125	0.9102	30.55
Ours(64^3, rgb+SH)	0.03929	0.9212	0.9143	0.9098	29.61

(b) Results rendering with different color strategies.

Voxel Subdivision Criterion. We conducted an extensive investigation into the impact of our voxel subdivision strategies on the proposed method. We compared the performance of subdividing the voxels naively on the entire surface versus selectively in areas with larger loss values, as described in Sect. 3.3. Our experimental results, summarized in Table 2(a), demonstrate that the reconstruction results are comparable between the two strategies. This indicates that our strategy, which focuses on high-loss areas, is effective in reconstructing surfaces.
Image Color. Here we investigated the impact of color formats on our method. We compared the performance of four models which are initialized with 64^3 resolution. The first two are trained with view-independent grayscale and RGB values directly stored in voxel nodes. Another two are computed based on spherical harmonic coefficients (SH), as [26], in order to preserve view-dependent information. We keep all other parameters constant to isolate the effect of different color strategies on reconstruction accuracy. As illustrated in Table 2(b), the grayscale shows an overall balance among the five metrics. Moreover, while the view-dependent information helps to yield higher peak signal-to-noise ratio (PSNR) scores, it does not significantly affect the quality of 3D reconstruction.
Initial Resolution. We further performed two tests to investigate the effect of initialization resolution on our structure. They are initialized respectively using 256^3 and 64^3 and running for $60K$ steps. The structures were then updated separately by twice and four times, to reach the same resolution level. The results in Table 1 and Table 2(b), show that our approach, denoted as $Ours$, outperforms the variant initialized with lower resolution, $Ours(64^3, grayscale)$. Initializing with lower resolution results in a deeper structure, leading to a longer search time for terminal nodes. Conversely, the lower resolution initialization would provide a more memory-efficient solution by leaving most free-space voxels undivided, which could lead to fewer voxels.

4.4 Memory and Runtime

Compared to voxel-based methods [15,16], our method can refine local areas without increasing the resolution of the entire space. We reconstructed *complete kitchen* in the synthetic dataset, starting at a resolution of 128^3. We performed the dynamic partitioning every $10K$ steps until the CUDA memory ran out. As shown in Table 3(a), directly increasing the entire grid resolution only goes to level 2 before running out of memory. In contrast, our method can keep updating until reaching level 4. For runtime, as demonstrated in Table 3(b), our method offers a significant improvement in terms of training time compared to NeuralRGBD [1]. By reducing the total sampling number to 128 and running iterations to $30K$, our method can further reduce the training time which is comparable to GO-Surf [19] while maintaining high reconstruction quality as shown in Fig. 6.

Table 3. Memory and runtime.

Method	level 0	level 1	level 2	level 3	level 4
Dynamic voxel grid	3,747 MB	4,249 MB	5,967 MB	12,771 MB	32,023 MB
Voxel grid	3,245 MB	4,263 MB	10,983 MB	OOM	OOM

(a) GPU memory consumption between full-size and dynamize voxel grid. Our structure is more GPU-efficient. OOM stands for out-of-memory

Method	scene0014	scene0360	scene0600	average
NeuralRGBD [1]	20 h14 min19 s	20 h10 min21 s	20 h6 min51 s	20 h10 min30 s
GO-Surf [19]	19 min25 s	17 min3 s	20 min45 s	19 min4 s
Ours	47 min43 s	49 min52 s	45 min55 s	47 min50 s
Ours*	22 min33 s	21 min28 s	21 min41 s	21 min54 s

(b) Running time among NeuralRGBD [1], GO-Surf [19], and ours. Ours* reducing the sampling number and iterations.

5 Conclusions

In this work, we have presented a new RGB-D surface reconstruction method by exploring dynamic voxel grid optimization. It takes both color and depth observations as guidance. By directly storing and regressing modalities on grid voxels, the entire reconstruction converges fast and requires no MLP structures. Meanwhile, our selective subdivision strategy can dynamically represent complex objects during optimization without any pretrained geometric priors, refraining from naively holistic resolution expansion. The comprehensive evaluation demonstrates the effectiveness of our approach in generating high-quality 3D reconstructions with fine details, while maintaining computational efficiency. The proposed method may still fail in cases of inaccurate depth or camera pose, which we plan to address in future work.

References

1. Azinović, D., Martin-Brualla, R., Goldman, D.B., Nießner, M., Thies, J.: Neural RGB-D surface reconstruction. In: Proceedings of the IEEE/CVF Conference on Computer Vision and Pattern Recognition, pp. 6290–6301 (2022)

2. Dai, A., Chang, A.X., Savva, M., Halber, M., Funkhouser, T., Nießner, M.: ScanNet: richly-annotated 3D reconstructions of indoor scenes. In: CVPR (2017)
3. Feng, Z., Yang, L., Guo, P., Li, B.: CVRecon: rethinking 3D geometric feature learning for neural reconstruction. In: Proceedings of the IEEE/CVF International Conference on Computer Vision, pp. 17750–17760 (2023)
4. Fridovich-Keil, S., Yu, A., Tancik, M., Chen, Q., Recht, B., Kanazawa, A.: Plenoxels: radiance fields without neural networks. In: Proceedings of the IEEE/CVF Conference on Computer Vision and Pattern Recognition, pp. 5501–5510 (2022)
5. Guo, H., et al.: Neural 3D scene reconstruction with the Manhattan-world assumption. In: Proceedings of the IEEE/CVF Conference on Computer Vision and Pattern Recognition, pp. 5511–5520 (2022)
6. Johari, M.M., Carta, C., Fleuret, F.: ESLAM: efficient dense slam system based on hybrid representation of signed distance fields. In: Proceedings of the IEEE/CVF Conference on Computer Vision and Pattern Recognition, pp. 17408–17419 (2023)
7. Knapitsch, A., Park, J., Zhou, Q.Y., Koltun, V.: Tanks and temples: benchmarking large-scale scene reconstruction. ACM Trans. Graph. **36**(4) (2017). https://doi.org/10.1145/3072959.3073599
8. Lee, S., Park, G., Son, H., Ryu, J., Chae, H.J.: InfusionSURF: refining neural RGB-D surface reconstruction using per-frame intrinsic refinement and TSDF fusion prior learning. arXiv preprint arXiv:2303.04508 (2023)
9. Li, H., Yang, X., Zhai, H., Liu, Y., Bao, H., Zhang, G.: Vox-Surf: voxel-based implicit surface representation. IEEE Trans. Vis. Comput. Graph. (2022)
10. Li, K., Tang, Y., Prisacariu, V.A., Torr, P.H.: BNV-Fusion: dense 3D reconstruction using bi-level neural volume fusion. In: Proceedings of the IEEE/CVF Conference on Computer Vision and Pattern Recognition (CVPR) (2022)
11. Li, Z., et al.: Neuralangelo: high-fidelity neural surface reconstruction. In: Proceedings of the IEEE/CVF Conference on Computer Vision and Pattern Recognition, pp. 8456–8465 (2023)
12. Mildenhall, B., Srinivasan, P.P., Tancik, M., Barron, J.T., Ramamoorthi, R., Ng, R.: NeRF: representing scenes as neural radiance fields for view synthesis. Commun. ACM **65**(1), 99–106 (2021)
13. Newcombe, R.A., et al.: KinectFusion: real-time dense surface mapping and tracking. In: 2011 10th IEEE International Symposium on Mixed and Augmented Reality, pp. 127–136 (2011)
14. Niemeyer, M., Mescheder, L., Oechsle, M., Geiger, A.: Differentiable volumetric rendering: learning implicit 3d representations without 3d supervision. In: Proceedings of the IEEE/CVF Conference on Computer Vision and Pattern Recognition, pp. 3504–3515 (2020)
15. Sun, C., Sun, M., Chen, H.T.: Direct voxel grid optimization: super-fast convergence for radiance fields reconstruction. In: Proceedings of the IEEE/CVF Conference on Computer Vision and Pattern Recognition, pp. 5459–5469 (2022)
16. Sun, C., Sun, M., Chen, H.T.: Improved direct voxel grid optimization for radiance fields reconstruction. arXiv preprint arXiv:2206.05085 (2022)
17. Sun, J., Xie, Y., Chen, L., Zhou, X., Bao, H.: NeuralRecon: real-time coherent 3D reconstruction from monocular video. In: Proceedings of the IEEE/CVF Conference on Computer Vision and Pattern Recognition, pp. 15598–15607 (2021)
18. Wang, H., Wang, J., Agapito, L.: Co-SLAM: joint coordinate and sparse parametric encodings for neural real-time SLAM. In: Proceedings of the IEEE/CVF Conference on Computer Vision and Pattern Recognition, pp. 13293–13302 (2023)

19. Wang, J., Bleja, T., Agapito, L.: Go-SURF: neural feature grid optimization for fast, high-fidelity RGB-D surface reconstruction. arXiv preprint arXiv:2206.14735 (2022)
20. Wang, P., Liu, L., Liu, Y., Theobalt, C., Komura, T., Wang, W.: NeuS: learning neural implicit surfaces by volume rendering for multi-view reconstruction. arXiv preprint arXiv:2106.10689 (2021)
21. Wei, Y., Liu, S., Rao, Y., Zhao, W., Lu, J., Zhou, J.: NerfingMVS: guided optimization of neural radiance fields for indoor multi-view stereo. In: Proceedings of the IEEE/CVF International Conference on Computer Vision, pp. 5610–5619 (2021))
22. Wu, T., et al.: Voxurf: voxel-based efficient and accurate neural surface reconstruction. arXiv preprint arXiv:2208.12697 (2022)
23. Yariv, L., Gu, J., Kasten, Y., Lipman, Y.: Volume rendering of neural implicit surfaces. Adv. Neural. Inf. Process. Syst. **34**, 4805–4815 (2021)
24. Yariv, L., et al.: Multiview neural surface reconstruction by disentangling geometry and appearance. Adv. Neural. Inf. Process. Syst. **33**, 2492–2502 (2020)
25. Ye, B., Liu, S., Li, X., Yang, M.H.: Self-supervised super-plane for neural 3D reconstruction. In: Proceedings of the IEEE/CVF Conference on Computer Vision and Pattern Recognition, pp. 21415–21424 (2023)
26. Yu, A., Li, R., Tancik, M., Li, H., Ng, R., Kanazawa, A.: Plenoctrees for real-time rendering of neural radiance fields. In: Proceedings of the IEEE/CVF International Conference on Computer Vision, pp. 5752–5761 (2021)
27. Yu, Z., Peng, S., Niemeyer, M., Sattler, T., Geiger, A.: MonoSDF: exploring monocular geometric cues for neural implicit surface reconstruction. Adv. Neural. Inf. Process. Syst. **35**, 25018–25032 (2022)
28. Zhang, Y., Tosi, F., Mattoccia, S., Poggi, M.: Go-SLAM: global optimization for consistent 3D instant reconstruction. In: Proceedings of the IEEE/CVF International Conference on Computer Vision, pp. 3727–3737 (2023)
29. Zhu, Z., et al.: Nicer-SLAM: neural implicit scene encoding for RGB SLAM. arXiv preprint arXiv:2302.03594 (2023)
30. Zhu, Z., et al.: Nice-SLAM: neural implicit scalable encoding for slam. In: Proceedings of the IEEE/CVF Conference on Computer Vision and Pattern Recognition, pp. 12786–12796 (2022)

Te3DFR: Texture-Enabled 3D Face Reconstruction from Monocular Image via Self-supervised Learning

Yishen Bi[1], Chen Wang[1], Lei Li[2(✉)], Yiran Shen[1], and Yuanfeng Zhou[1(✉)]

[1] School of Software, Shandong University, Jinan 250101, China
{yishen.bi,chen.wang}@mail.sdu.edu.cn, {yiran.shen,yfzhou}@sdu.edu.cn

[2] School of Computer Science and Technology, Shandong University of Finance and Economics, Jinan 250101, China
lilei@sdufe.edu.cn

Abstract. Reconstructing high-fidelity 3D faces from monocular RGB images has garnered significant research interest, with most approaches relying on 3D Morphable Models (3DMM). However, the capabilities of 3DMM-based methods are often constrained by the limited dimensionality of the representation space, leading to inaccuracies in detailed facial shapes and realistic skin textures. While several recent works aim to enhance 3DMM-based face reconstruction, many focus on fine-tuning the outputs of pre-trained 3DMM models—such as estimating offset maps—rather than improving the underlying pre-trained model itself, which is the root of these inaccuracies.

To address this gap, we propose a Visual Transformer (ViT)-based framework for predicting 3DMM coefficients for face reconstruction, thereby creating a new pre-trained model that improves reconstruction performance. Additionally, our model incorporates an optimization module with innovative filter constraints for face textures, significantly enhancing the high-frequency components that correspond to fine details in facial textures. Extensive experiments conducted on publicly available face reconstruction datasets, including SCUT-FBP5500 and FaceScape, demonstrate that our method achieves promising generalization performance and markedly improves the precision of texture details compared to state-of-the-art techniques.

Keywords: 3D face modeling · Monocular reconstruction · Self-supervised learning

1 Introduction

The reconstruction of high-fidelity 3D human faces from monocular images has become a prominent research focus in computer graphics and vision, aiming to recover precise 3D facial shapes and realistic textures using only monocular

P. Li et al. (Eds.): CGI 2025, LNCS 16508, pp. 367–379, 2026.
https://doi.org/10.1007/978-3-032-22264-0_29

images. This technique has been successfully applied in a wide range of fields, including digital human modeling, face editing, face recognition, and facial animation, among others.

Achieving high-quality 3D face models still largely depends on the use of specialized equipment [1,7]. However, such equipment is typically available only in specialized facilities, limiting its broader accessibility. To address this, researchers have developed a range of face reconstruction methods that eliminate the need for costly hardware. These approaches primarily rely on parametric face morphable models, such as 3DMM [12,28], combined with deep learning and computer graphics. Although these methods offer the advantages of minimal input requirements and ease of use, their reconstruction accuracy, especially in capturing high-frequency texture details, often falls short compared to professional-grade equipment.

To bridge this gap, we propose a texture-enabled, high-fidelity 3D face reconstruction approach (Te3DFR), which integrates a novel 3D face reconstruction module based on 3DMM and coefficient prediction, alongside a texture fitting module to enhance fine-grained texture recovery (as shown in Fig. 1). The contributions of this paper can be summarized as follows:

- To address the limitations of previous backbones in capturing features at the pixel level, we adopt the Vision Transformer (ViT) framework as the new backbone to predict 3DMM coefficients for the first time. This approach yields a new pre-trained model with promising data efficiency.
- To generate fine-grained 3D face textures, we designed a texture fitting module incorporating an innovate filtering loss that constrains errors in high-frequency details. This approach significantly enhances the visual quality of the reconstruction with minimal computational cost.
- We conducted extensive experimental analysis on publicly available face reconstruction datasets, demonstrating that our Te3DFR approach delivers superior generalization and texture detail performance.

The rest of this paper is organized as follows: Sect. 2 describes the related works about 3D face reconstruction. Section 3 gives the details of our proposed Te3DFR. Section 4 analyzes the obtained results by evaluating and comparing. Section 5 concludes this paper and finally discusses some problems and directions for our future work.

2 Related Work

3D Morphable Model. The 3D Morphable Model (3DMM) is a widely used parametric template model for face reconstruction from RGB images, capable of generating 3D face models based on the given coefficients. The pioneering method [3] organized data from 200 face scans and employed PCA [5] to generate the shape and texture PC bases, finally forming a static linear template model. Over the decades, this idea has developed continuously, leading to the generation of various 3DMMs such as BFM [22], FLAME [18], LSFM [4], HiFi3D [2], and etc. The comprehensive review [8] has recorded their development in detail.

Traditional Monocular Face Reconstruction. With the advent of 3DMM and advancements in neural networks, viable solutions for monocular face reconstruction have emerged. For representation, Ref. [11] creates a well pre-trained model by leveraging vast training datasets and innovative loss function constraints, and remains the best method for a certain time. Ref. [24] employs similar techniques, incorporating spatial consistency constraints in multi-view images when training to address monocular occlusion issues. The methods above are in self-supervision mode, while Ref. [32] organizes a series of topologically consistent 3D faces for directly supervision on vertexes, resulting in a little improved shape accuracy.

Improved Monocular Face Reconstruction. Recent researches like Ref. [10,21] indicate that the traditional methods are confined within the limited space of the 3DMM. Consequently, methods building upon initial reconstruction have emerged. An excellent work [17] proposes a hierarchical approach, which applies deformation and displacement maps for shape optimization. Ref. [9] extends the 3DMM conception, incorporating PC bases of displacement map to construct a more expressive parametric model. As for texture, there are methods Ref. [13,31] focusing on training models to predict fine UV texture maps. Besides, Ref. [20] trains all vertex colors of the face shape directly. Though improvement has been made, the textures produced by these models are still not real enough.

3 Methods

3.1 Overview

In this paper, a novel method for 3D face reconstruction named Te3DFR is proposed, which includes a face reconstruction module based on the parameterized model and a texture fitting module carried out in the UV space. As shown in Fig. 1, the face reconstruction module uses the idea of 3DMM and the ViT-RecNet to produce coarse reconstruction results. Then the texture fitting module improves the visual effect greatly and produces the fine results by optimizing maps in the ED-OptNet. Combining the two modules closely, our proposed Te3DFR achieves monocular face reconstruction with high reality.

3.2 Parameterized Model

Morphable Model. With the idea of 3D morphable model, our method applies the adjusted BFM [22] with 35709 vertexes. The model includes three PC bases: identity(B_{id}), expression(B_{exp}) and albedo(B_{alb}), corresponding to the first three types of coefficients produced by the ViT-RecNet: $\alpha \in \mathbb{R}^{80}$, $\beta \in \mathbb{R}^{64}$ and $\delta \in \mathbb{R}^{80}$. Subsequently, a simple face geometry model can be obtained by combining the PC basis and the corresponding coefficients:

$$\begin{aligned} S &= \overline{S} + \alpha B_{id} + \beta B_{exp} \\ A &= \overline{A} + \delta B_{alb} \end{aligned} \tag{1}$$

where S represents the face shape and A is the albedo color without illumination. $\overline{S}$ and $\overline{A}$ are the average shape and albedo color provided by BFM.

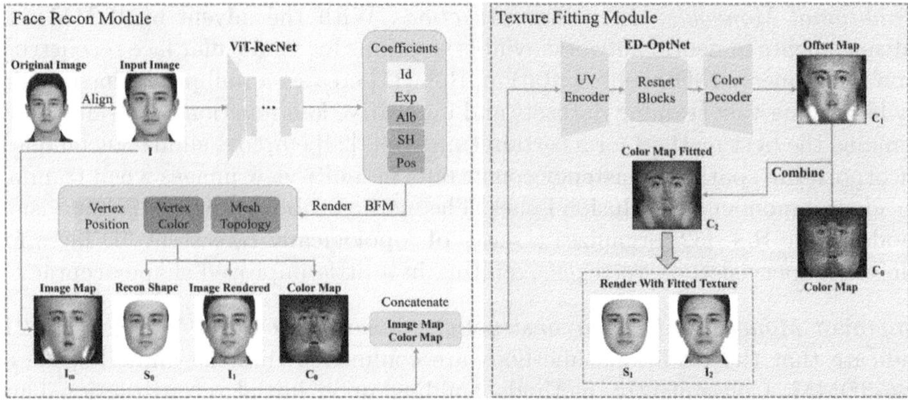

Fig. 1. Overview of the proposed Te3DFR. The left is our face-recon module, which regresses the coefficients about 3DMM, illumination, and pose using the ViT-RecNet, then produces a series of information for 3D face. The right is the texture fitting module, organizing two UV maps as input and producing the offset map with details by the ED-OptNet to realize vivid visual effect of the reconstructed face.

Camera Model. To map the reconstructed 3D face to 2D image, a perspective camera with pre-defined focal length is applied. At the same time, in order to use the input image as self-supervised information, it is necessary to estimate the pose of the reconstructed face for aligning the 3D face to the 2D input. So the $P = (T, t)$ is used to represent the face pose, where $T \in SO(3)$ defines the 3D rotation and $t \in \mathbb{R}^3$ represents the translation vector.

Illumination Model. Similar to the previous works [11,17], the Spherical Harmonics(SH) is used to represent the scene illumination. Specifically, the coefficient $\gamma \in \mathbb{R}^9$ is used in the SH model [23].

3.3 Methodology Module

Face Reconstruction Module. As described in Sect. 3.2, the face reconstruction module needs to predict five types of coefficients: $(\alpha, \beta, \delta, P, \gamma) \in \mathbb{R}^{239}$, and then the coarse 3D face can be reconstructed with the thought of 3DMM. In order to predict the coefficients above, the ViT-RecNet is got by combining the ViT Framework with the wrapper layers corresponding to the five coefficients together. After getting the coefficients, performing pose adjustment and light rendering, a 3D face similar to the input image can be obtained finally. During the whole training process, the image I_1 is synthesized continuously with the help of a differentiable rendering tool [16] to support self-supervision.

Texture Optimization Module. Aiming to refine the visual effect of coarse result, the texture fitting module is carried out. Optimizing the 3D data in the form of 2D UV map is more suitable for the processing in network [13,30]. So we firstly map the input image and the coarse vertex colors predicted by 3DMM method into 3-channel image map [17] and color map (texture), which are denoted as I_m and C_0 respectively. And then, the ED-OptNet is applied to generate the color map bias C_1 through optimization. Lastly, the C_1 and C_0 are combined in proportion to generate the final color map C_2, which contains more texture details compared with the original C_0.

3.4 Key Loss Functions

Pixel Loss. For comparing the rendered image with the input image, directly measuring the difference of pixels is an effective way:

$$L_{pix}(I, I^{'}) = \frac{||Skin_a \odot (I - I^{'})||^2}{Max(Sum(Skin_a), 1)} \tag{2}$$

where I is the input image, $I^{'}$ denotes the rendered coarse or fine image (such as the I_1 and I_2 in Fig. 1), and $\odot$ is defined as element-wise multiplication. As for $Skin_a$, the specific values can be computed as follows:

$$Skin_a(I_i) = \begin{cases} P_i & \text{if } P_i < 0.5 \\ 1 & \text{otherwise} \end{cases} \tag{3}$$

where P_i can be predicted by Ref. [11], denoting the probability of skin area pixel.

Landmark Loss. Given an image, by using FaceAlignment [6], the accurate 68 landmarks can be detected as the ground truth. Additionally, the BFM can define the vertex indexes of the corresponding 68 landmarks in advance. Based upon the two sets of landmarks, the reconstructed face can conform to the input image well both in shape and pose:

$$L_{lm} = \frac{1}{N} \sum_{i=1}^{N} W_i \times ||lm_i^{GT} - lm_i^{BFM}||^2 \tag{4}$$

where $N = 68$ indicates the number of landmarks, lm^{GT} and lm^{BFM} represent the coordinates of landmarks above, W denotes the weights, which are predefined as 15 for the points of nose and inner mouth, and 1 for the other points.

Filter Loss. We carry out the 8-neighborhood image filtering to concerning the high frequency details. This scheme concentrates on pixels that change heavily in 8 directions, so as to highlights the differences in high frequency details between the input image and the optimized rendered image:

$$L_{filter} = \sum_{k=1}^{K} \frac{Sum(|F_k(I) - F_k(I^{'})|)}{w \times h \times c} \tag{5}$$

where $K = 8$ represents the filter number, $w \times h \times c$ denotes the number of pixels, F_k stands for 8-neighborhood filter functions.

3.5 Implementation Details

Data Preparation. In the face reconstruction module, a large dataset is required. Otherwise, the monocular reconstruction method is naturally not suitable for the extreme images. So we'd better like to focus more on the normal images to gain the improvement. We manually remove the particularly obscured data from the CelebA [26] and FFHQ [15] datasets, and carefully select a total of about 75k images as our training dataset. After that, data pre-processing is performed: landmark prediction [6,14] and skin attention mask generation [11].

Training Strategy. The ViT-RecNet is trained for 50 epochs on a dataset of 75k images, with an initial learning rate empirically set to 1e−4 and reduced to half every 5 epochs. Working on the RTX 3090 GPU, the training time is about 22 h, and the referencing time for a single image is about 2 s. Then the image is optimized for 60 epochs through the ED-OptNet with a learning rate set to 2e−4, and a whole optimization takes about 12 min.

4 Experiments

To analyze the effectiveness of our proposed Te3DFR, 300 monocular images are collected from two datasets: SCUT-FBP5500 [19] and FaceScape [29], which are used as our test datasets. Then, for comparing the effectiveness of our work, we collect and achieve two representative methods Deep3D [11] and HRN [17]. They produce the widely-used model and still have enormous influence in the filed. Furthermore, for comparing with the methods that extremely concentrate on optimizing the facial textures, we choose the method 3DDFA-v3 [27]. In addition, two excellent works [20,31] are collected, as the supplement value comparison for rough reference.

4.1 Qualitative Comparison

As for qualitatively evaluating, we run four methods on the test datasets. As displayed in Fig. 2, 7 facial examples aligned to the input images are shown, together with the side view. Generally, our Te3DFR shows the finest results, successfully maintaining the high-frequency facial details.

4.2 Quantitative Comparison

For quantitatively evaluating the visual effect of the methods above, we compute 4 criteria for each method. As shown in Table 1, other than two rows marked with '*', the values are all computed using the same test datasets with their pre-trained models. Generally, our fine results gain the best values in all the four criteria, which demonstrate the effectiveness of our proposed method.

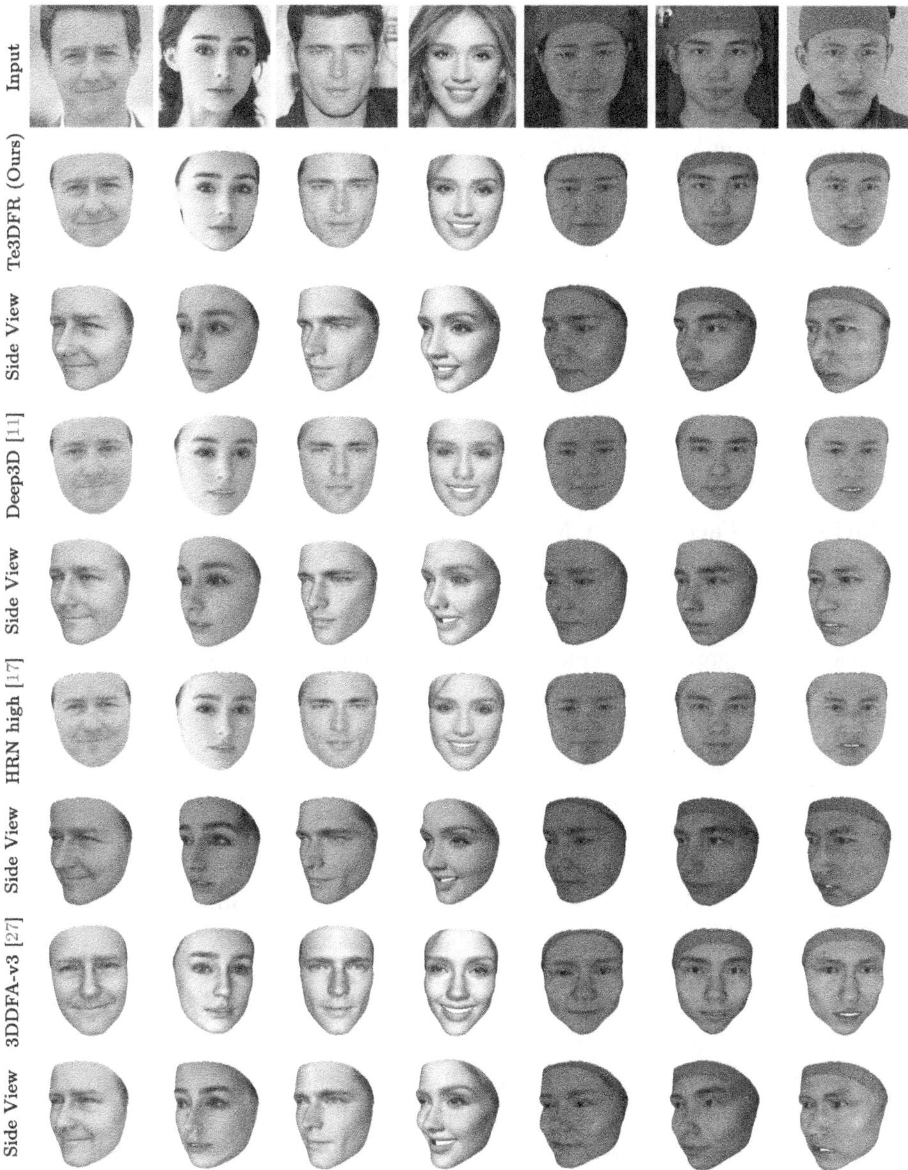

Fig. 2. Qualitative Comparison. The first row shows 7 input images. The following are the reconstructed 3D faces aligned to the input images and the faces from side view.

Table 1. The experiment results of quantitative comparison.

Method	L1 ↓	LPIPS ↓	SSIM ↑	PSNR ↑	Training Data Scale
Deep3d [11]	0.022	0.095	0.862	25.490	25w images
HRN mid [17]	0.020	0.102	0.883	26.291	26w images + 15w GT maps
HRN high [17]	0.018	0.096	0.895	26.883	–
3DDFA-v3 [27]	0.016	0.146	0.915	26.547	60w images
Lin et al. [20]*	0.034	–	0.894	29.690	–
Yin et al. [31]*	0.021	–	0.915	–	–
Ours Course	0.022	0.095	0.861	25.602	7.5w images
Ours Fine	**0.004**	**0.025**	**0.976**	**38.650**	–

4.3 Ablation Study

Ablation for Face Recon Module. For the backbone of predicting 3DMM coefficients, the previous works [11,24] usually use the ResNet-50, while the latter works [17,25] always stand on the off-the-shelf methods with the backbone not updated. In our work, we firstly use the ViT to rebuild the backbone for 3DMM coefficients and gain the decent efficiency. To show this, we separately train the ViT-Net and ResNet-50 using the same datasets. Then we test the two kinds of pre-trained models on our test datasets and compute 4 criteria in Table 2.

Table 2. Quantitatively comparison of the pre-trained models.

Model	L1 ↓	LPIPS ↓	SSIM ↑	PSNR ↑
ViT-Net	**0.0216**	**0.095**	0.861	**25.602**
ResNet-50	0.0347	0.144	0.788	21.925
ResNet-50 [11]	0.0221	**0.095**	**0.862**	25.490

It can be seen that, the testing results of ViT backbone is similar to the full trained ResNet-50 model (last row), whose training datasets are more than 3 times of ours. When using the same training sources, the re-trained ResNet-50 (second row) is heavily worse than our used ViT backbone, and even fails to reconstruct the basic face shapes for 52% examples (in Fig. 3). One important fact is that, the ViT-Net can attain the satisfied ability only using the smaller training datasets, which highlights its superior ability of data efficiency.

Ablation for Texture Fitting Module. Then the second main study is for the texture fitting module, including the whole module and the filter operation. For the whole module, visual examples are displayed in Fig. 4, in which the second column without texture fitting module shows visually fewer facial details

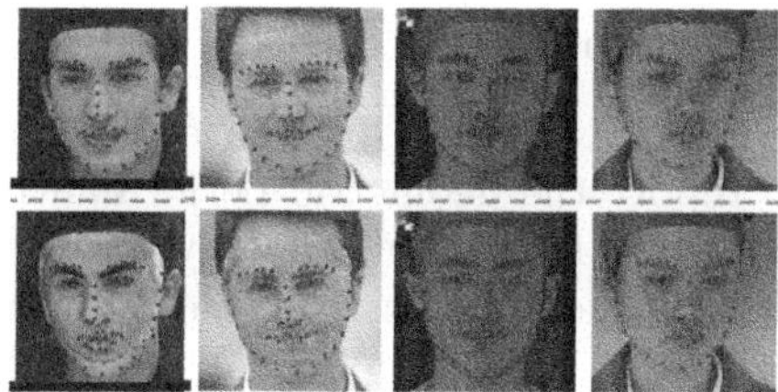

Fig. 3. Qualitatively comparison of the pre-trained models. The rows show 4 reconstructed faces using ViT-Net (first row) and ResNet-50, together with the 68 key-points.

compared with the last column. In addition, the values without this module (the seventh row in Table 1) are obviously worse than the fine results. The above two aspects demonstrate that our texture fitting module improves the details greatly both in visual quality and value quantity.

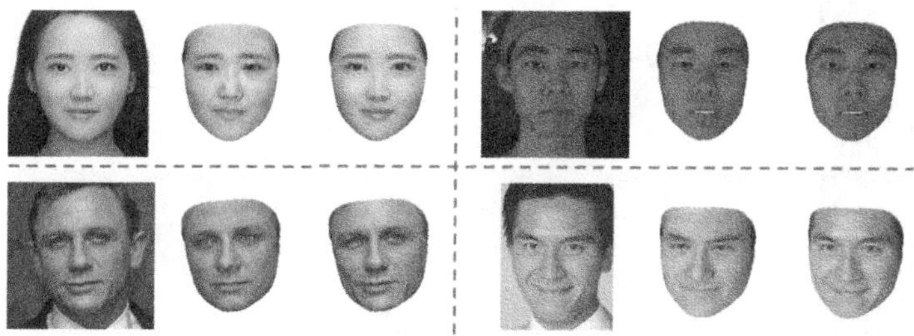

Fig. 4. Ablation for texture module. For each of the 4 items, the last two columns are our reconstructed results without texture module and the fine results.

Besides, we also take out the ablation study for filter loss. In detail, we conduct experiments among three different filter methods: the 8-neighbor filter, the 4-neighbor filter and the Sobel filter. The results are compiled in first three rows in Table 3, which indicates the superiority of our chosen 8-neighbor filter.

Table 3. Ablation for filter loss in texture fitting module.

Filter Type	L1 ↓	LPIPS ↓	SSIM ↑	PSNR ↑
8-nbr Filter	**0.004**	**0.025**	**0.976**	**38.650**
4-nbr Filter	0.007	0.048	0.951	33.504
Sobel Filter	0.008	0.047	0.950	32.907
w/o Filter	0.007	0.030	0.958	36.080

4.4 Geometric Evaluation

Although our primary objective is not to precisely reconstruct facial shapes, it remains essential to report the geometric performance of our reconstructed meshes as a fundamental 3D facial methodology. We compute the Euclidean distance per vertex between the reconstructed mesh and the re-topologized GT mesh. After mapping the distance into a color-bar, the geometric error can be visualized. As shown in Fig. 5, the 3D shapes of our results are in the same level of Deep3D [11] and a little worse compared with HRN [17]. Because HRN especially concentrates on shape optimization, this result is within our expectation.

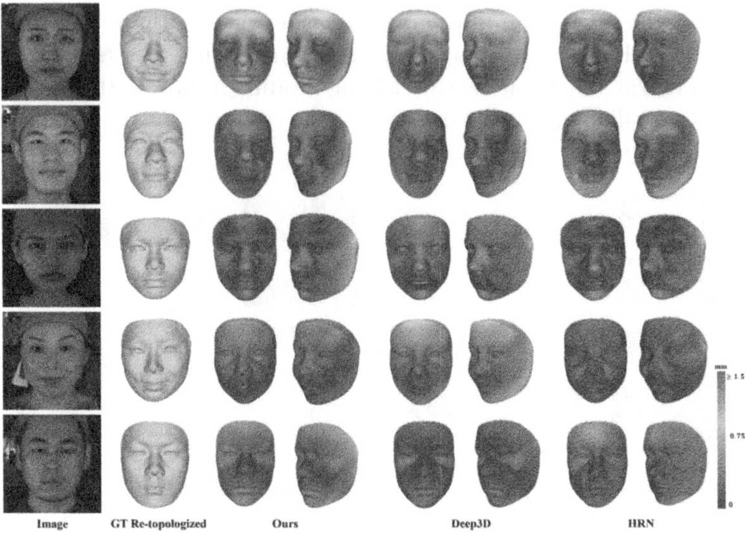

Fig. 5. Error-map for geometric evaluation.

5 Conclusion

In this paper, we introduce Te3DFR, a novel method for face reconstruction with vivid visual effects from a monocular image. Te3DFR consists of two key modules: the first module reconstructs a coarse 3D face using 3DMM and the ViT-RecNet framework. The second module then refines the vertex colors by optimizing the UV texture map with ED-OptNet. This process results in a high-fidelity 3D face that visually aligns closely with the original image. Extensive experimental results demonstrate that our proposed Te3DFR method offers promising generalization performance and significantly enhances the precision of texture details compared to state-of-the-art methods.

Although our Te3DFR gains satisfactory results in the task of monocular face reconstruction, mainly for predicting coefficients and optimizing facial colors, it is still challenging to recover the facial colors of the unviewable areas. A proper strategy for this problem may be using the multi-view information or a certain kind of constrain for colors. Besides, we don't realize the shape optimization, which is a more meaningful task. In this case, organizing more sufficient datasets for color and shape supervision to further enhance the fidelity of reconstructed digital faces may be our future work.

Acknowledgments. This research was supported by the National Natural Science Foundation of China under Grant, No.62172257, the Science and Technology Plan for Young Talents in Colleges and Universities of Shandong Province (2023KJ221) and the Shandong Provincial Science Foundation, Grant 2022HWYQ040.

Disclosure of Interests. The authors have no competing interests to declare that are relevant to the content of this article.

References

1. Alexander, O., Rogers, M., Lambeth, W., Chiang, M., Debevec, P.: The digital emily project: photoreal facial modeling and animation. ACM (2009)
2. Bao, L., et al.: High-fidelity 3D digital human head creation from RGB-D selfies. ACM Trans. Graph. (TOG) **41**(1), 1–21 (2021)
3. Blanz, V., Vetter, T.: A morphable model for the synthesis of 3D faces. In: 26th Annual Conference on Computer Graphics and Interactive Techniques (SIGGRAPH 1999). pp. 187–194. ACM Press (1999)
4. Booth, J., Roussos, A., Zafeiriou, S., Ponniah, A., Dunaway, D.: A 3D morphable model learnt from 10,000 faces. In: Proceedings of the IEEE Conference on Computer Vision and Pattern Recognition, pp. 5543–5552 (2016)
5. Bryant, F.B., Yarnold, P.R.: Principal-components analysis and exploratory and confirmatory factor analysis (1995)
6. Bulat, A., Tzimiropoulos, G.: How far are we from solving the 2D & 3D face alignment problem?(and a dataset of 230,000 3D facial landmarks). In: Proceedings of the IEEE International Conference on Computer Vision, pp. 1021–1030 (2017)
7. Cao, X., Chen, Z., Chen, A., Chen, X., Li, S., Yu, J.: Sparse photometric 3D face reconstruction guided by morphable models. In: Proceedings of the IEEE Conference on Computer Vision and Pattern Recognition, pp. 4635–4644 (2018)
8. Chai, Z., et al.: Realy: rethinking the evaluation of 3d face reconstruction. In: European Conference on Computer Vision, pp. 74–92. Springer (2022)
9. Chai, Z., et al.: HiFace: high-fidelity 3d face reconstruction by learning static and dynamic details. In: Proceedings of the IEEE/CVF International Conference on Computer Vision, pp. 9087–9098 (2023)
10. Chen, Y., Wu, F., Wang, Z., Song, Y., Ling, Y., Bao, L.: Self-supervised learning of detailed 3D face reconstruction. IEEE Trans. Image Process. **29**, 8696–8705 (2020)
11. Deng, Y., Yang, J., Xu, S., Chen, D., Jia, Y., Tong, X.: Accurate 3D face reconstruction with weakly-supervised learning: from single image to image set. In: Proceedings of the IEEE/CVF Conference on Computer Vision and Pattern Recognition Workshops, pp. 0–0 (2019)
12. Feng, Y., Feng, H., Black, M.J., Bolkart, T.: Learning an animatable detailed 3d face model from in-the-wild images. ACM Trans. Graph. (ToG) **40**(4), 1–13 (2021)

13. Gecer, B., Ploumpis, S., Kotsia, I., Zafeiriou, S.: Fast-GANFIT: generative adversarial network for high fidelity 3d face reconstruction. IEEE Trans. Pattern Anal. Mach. Intell. **44**(9), 4879–4893 (2021)
14. Guo, J., Zhu, X., Yang, Y., Yang, F., Lei, Z., Li, S.Z.: Towards fast, accurate and stable 3d dense face alignment. In: European Conference on Computer Vision, pp. 152–168. Springer (2020)
15. Karras, T., Laine, S., Aila, T.: A style-based generator architecture for generative adversarial networks. In: Proceedings of the IEEE/CVF Conference on Computer Vision and Pattern Recognition, pp. 4401–4410 (2019)
16. Laine, S., Hellsten, J., Karras, T., Seol, Y., Lehtinen, J., Aila, T.: Modular primitives for high-performance differentiable rendering. ACM Trans. Graph. **39**(6) (2020)
17. Lei, B., Ren, J., Feng, M., Cui, M., Xie, X.: A hierarchical representation network for accurate and detailed face reconstruction from in-the-wild images. In: Proceedings of the IEEE/CVF Conference on Computer Vision and Pattern Recognition, pp. 394–403 (2023)
18. Li, T., Bolkart, T., Black, M.J., Li, H., Romero, J.: Learning a model of facial shape and expression from 4d scans. ACM Trans. Graph. **36**(6), 194–1 (2017)
19. Liang, L., Lin, L., Jin, L., Xie, D., Li, M.: SCUT-FBP5500: a diverse benchmark dataset for multi-paradigm facial beauty prediction. In: 2018 24th International Conference on Pattern Recognition (ICPR), pp. 1598–1603. IEEE (2018)
20. Lin, J., Yuan, Y., Shao, T., Zhou, K.: Towards high-fidelity 3d face reconstruction from in-the-wild images using graph convolutional networks. In: Proceedings of the IEEE/CVF Conference on Computer Vision and Pattern Recognition, pp. 5891–5900 (2020)
21. Ling, J., Wang, Z., Lu, M., Wang, Q., Qian, C., Xu, F.: Structure-aware editable morphable model for 3d facial detail animation and manipulation. In: European Conference on Computer Vision, pp. 249–267. Springer (2022)
22. Paysan, P., Knothe, R., Amberg, B., Romdhani, S., Vetter, T.: A 3d face model for pose and illumination invariant face recognition. In: 2009 Sixth IEEE International Conference on Advanced Video and Signal Based Surveillance, pp. 296–301. IEEE (2009)
23. Ramamoorthi, R., Hanrahan, P.: A signal-processing framework for inverse rendering. In: Proceedings of the 28th Annual Conference on Computer Graphics and Interactive Techniques, pp. 117–128 (2001)
24. Shang, J., et al.: Self-supervised monocular 3d face reconstruction by occlusion-aware multi-view geometry consistency. In: European Conference on Computer Vision, pp. 53–70. Springer (2020)
25. Wang, X., Guo, Y., Deng, B., Zhang, J.: Lightweight photometric stereo for facial details recovery. In: Proceedings of the IEEE/CVF Conference on Computer Vision and Pattern Recognition, pp. 740–749 (2020)
26. Wang, Y., Gan, W., Yang, J., Wu, W., Yan, J.: Dynamic curriculum learning for imbalanced data classification. In: Proceedings of the IEEE/CVF International Conference on Computer Vision, pp. 5017–5026 (2019)
27. Wang, Z., Zhu, X., Zhang, T., Wang, B., Lei, Z.: 3D face reconstruction with the geometric guidance of facial part segmentation. In: Proceedings of the IEEE/CVF Conference on Computer Vision and Pattern Recognition, pp. 1672–1682 (2024)
28. Wood, E., et al.: 3d face reconstruction with dense landmarks. In: European Conference on Computer Vision, pp. 160–177. Springer (2022)

29. Yang, H., et al.: FaceScape: a large-scale high quality 3d face dataset and detailed riggable 3D face prediction. In: Proceedings of the IEEE/CVF Conference on Computer Vision and Pattern Recognition, pp. 601–610 (2020)
30. Yang, W., Chen, Z., Chen, C., Chen, G., Wong, K.Y.K.: Deep face video inpainting via UV mapping. IEEE Trans. Image Process. **32**, 1145–1157 (2023)
31. Yin, X., Huang, D., Fu, Z., Wang, Y., Chen, L.: Weakly-supervised photo-realistic texture generation for 3D face reconstruction. In: 2023 IEEE 17th International Conference on Automatic Face and Gesture Recognition (FG), pp. 1–8. IEEE (2023)
32. Zielonka, W., Bolkart, T., Thies, J.: Towards metrical reconstruction of human faces. In: European Conference on Computer Vision, pp. 250–269. Springer (2022)

MC-Gaussian: 3D Gaussian Splatting with Multi-camera Setup in Autonomous Driving

Chenwei Zhang, Kai Cheng, and Xuejin Chen(✉)

University of Science and Technology of China, Hefei 230026, Anhui, China
{cw_zhang,chengkai21}@mail.ustc.edu.cn, xjchen99@ustc.edu.cn

Abstract. Novel view synthesis is essential for closed-loop autonomous driving simulation. The modern autonomous driving system typically employs multiple cameras to achieve wide-field perception. However, this also introduces challenges for neural rendering, i.e., the color inconsistency among different cameras and the sparse observation in the side cameras. While NeRF-based methods offer solutions, their inefficiencies in rendering speed limit practical applications in simulation. We propose a real-time rendering solution, MC-Gaussian, for multi-camera settings based on 3D Gaussian representation. We introduce separate Gaussian models for the foreground and sky background, applying a pose-conditioned color correction to resolve color inconsistencies from different cameras. Additionally, we introduce the regularization terms of geometric consistency across cameras to alleviate the overfitting from sparse view observations. Our method achieves state-of-the-art results on static scenes from the Waymo and NuScenes datasets, producing high-fidelity and real-time rendering.

Keywords: Novel view synthesis · Autonomous Driving Scenes · 3D Gaussian Splatting

1 Introduction

Neural rendering is a breakthrough technique that learns 3D scenes from differentiable rendering processes and generates highly realistic images from novel viewpoints. It plays an increasingly important role in autonomous driving, eliminating the need for the costly manual construction in traditional methods [8,18]. In the past few years, series of works [21,25–27] explore the use of Neural Radiance Fields (NeRF) [15] to build driving simulators, which are further advanced in efficiency by the real-time rendering technique 3D Gaussian splatting (3DGS) [12] recently. These simulators provide vast amounts of training and testing data for perception models in autonomous driving, enabling closed-loop simulation to improve system performance.

Multi-camera system [4,19] is an advanced setup commonly used in autonomous driving and surveillance to capture comprehensive and detailed information about a scene from multiple perspectives. These systems involve strategically placing several

P. Li et al. (Eds.): CGI 2025, LNCS 16508, pp. 380–392, 2026.
https://doi.org/10.1007/978-3-032-22264-0_30

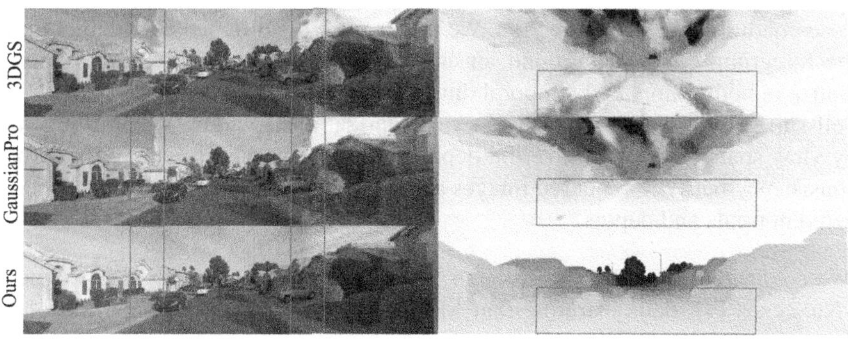

Fig. 1. The rendering quality of 3DGS and GaussianPro degrades dramatically in multi-camera systems, because of noticeable color inconsistencies (in red boxes) and inaccurate scene geometry (in blue boxes). Our MC-Gaussian generates higher-quality renderings while accurately maintaining geometric consistency in these challenging scenes. (Color figure online)

cameras on a vehicle to cover specific areas of interest. Due to the under-calibration of multiple cameras [6, 17], training directly with images captured by multi-camera systems often leads to serious degradation of rendering quality, as shown in the first two lines of Fig. 1. Although UC-NeRF [6] alleviates the camera's under-calibration within the NeRF's framework, naively transferring the solutions in multi-camera setups from NeRF to 3DGS for real-time rendering poses new challenges.

Firstly, previous NeRF methods [6, 17] employ per-image learnable latent codes independently for color calibration, neglecting spatial relationships between images and leading to the overfitting of each latent code to the specific view's color. Secondly, compared to NeRF's continuous density fields, the discrete nature of 3D Gaussians often leads to less smooth geometric modeling of surfaces. In multi-camera systems with sparse observations, particularly for side cameras, discontinuities tend to be amplified due to the overfitting problem of sparse training views. Additionally, overfitting of the sky region in the Gaussian representation causes floaters over the foreground in new viewpoints, further compromising rendering realism.

To address these issues, we propose a novel 3D Gaussian-based rendering framework for multi-camera setups. Unlike NeRF, which alters sampling strategies to model the sky, we establish a separate model for the sky region in 3DGS. We further address color inconsistency by applying pose-conditioned color calibration separately to the foreground and background. To avoid overfitting to sparse views, previous works [7, 33, 34] incorporate external depth estimation models or LiDAR priors to correct depths in 3DGS. However, we aim to avoid reliance on strong external priors and instead ensure geometric consistency through self-supervised depth correction.

Overall, we propose MC-Gaussian to address the challenges posed by multi-camera systems in 3DGS. Our work introduces three key innovations:

- Explicit sky modeling. We model sky Gaussians separately to prevent them from floating above foreground Gaussians.

- Pose-conditioned color correction. We utilize pose-conditioned color calibration for the foreground and background, ensuring the continuity of the color calibration matrix in both spatial and temporal dimensions.
- Self-supervised geometry consistency regularization. To address overfitting caused by view sparsity, we optimize the depth in a self-supervised manner by enforcing consistency between rendered images and rendered depths, as well as between rendered normals and depths.

We conducted extensive experiments on multi-camera datasets, i.e., Waymo [19] and NuScenes [4], demonstrating that MC-Gaussian achieves real-time high-fidelity rendering in static multi-camera scenes.

2 Related Work

2.1 Traditional Autonomous Driving Simulation

Autonomous driving simulators create virtual environments to test and refine self-driving systems, enabling safe and controllable performance evaluation. Simulators like CARLA [8] and AirSim [18] based on traditional graphics engines suffer from the high cost of manual effort and unrealistic simulation results. AADS [13] utilizes conventional graphics engines as well but achieves remarkable photorealism through carefully selected assets. Recently, significant progress has been made in developing sensor simulations using real-world autonomous driving data. Some approaches [10,29] focus on 3D reconstruction by combining LiDAR data to create textured geometric primitives. However, these methods mainly simulate LiDAR and struggle with the processing of high-resolution images. Several methods [9,28] utilize CAD models to generate the final asset either via feed-forward prediction or through optimization on real-world data. However, these methods are restrained by the limited amount of available CAD models. CADSim [20] integrates part-aware object-class priors from limited CAD models to automatically reconstruct vehicle models. Nonetheless, these techniques are limited by the reliance on pre-defined assets and cannot generate rendering from novel viewpoints.

2.2 Neural Rendering for Autonomous Driving Simulation

NeRF [15] is a groundbreaking technology that implicitly reconstructs 3D models and renders photorealistic images from given viewpoints. Numerous works [6,11,17,21,23] have further explored the application of NeRFs in reconstructing street scenes. For static urban scenes, Urban Radiance Fields [17] incorporate LiDAR data to produce higher-quality novel views. Streetsurf [11] decomposes the scene based on the distance from the camera and independently models each segment, thereby facilitating the reconstruction of urban environments. UC-NeRF [6] introduces color calibration and pose correction, effectively addressing issues of photometric inconsistency in multi-camera systems. For dynamic urban scenes, S-NeRF [23] achieves high-quality reconstruction of moving vehicles by using the proposed virtual camera transformation.

MARS [21] employs separate networks for dynamic instances and background, allowing independent control over the environment and dynamic properties. However, NeRF-based methods suffer from low rendering speed, restricting their practical application in autonomous driving simulators.

3DGS [12] makes remarkable breakthroughs in real-time novel view synthesis, demonstrating strong performance in urban street environments. StreetGaussian [24] models dynamic vehicles as 3D Gaussians with time-varying poses, optimized via a pose-tracking framework and enhanced with 4D spherical harmonics for appearance variation. Similarly, DrivingGaussian [33] integrates LiDAR-derived priors with a composite dynamic Gaussian graph, which enables effective management of moving objects in a multi-camera environment. In contrast, our approach addresses the photometric inconsistencies in rendering images and eliminates the degradation of geometry quality without LiDAR information for multi-camera static autonomous driving scenarios. Ultimately, this enables us to achieve real-time and high-quality rendering.

3 Our Method

Given the image sequences captured from multi-camera setups in urban street scenes, our MC-Gaussian method generates realistic images in realtime for any specified input time step and viewpoint. Figure 2 shows the framework of MC-Gaussian. After the preliminary introduction of 3DGS, we introduce our separate modeling of the sky within 3DGS in Sect. 3.2 and the pose-conditioned color calibration to address color supervision inconsistencies in Sect. 3.3. In Sect. 3.4, we introduce the self-supervised geometry

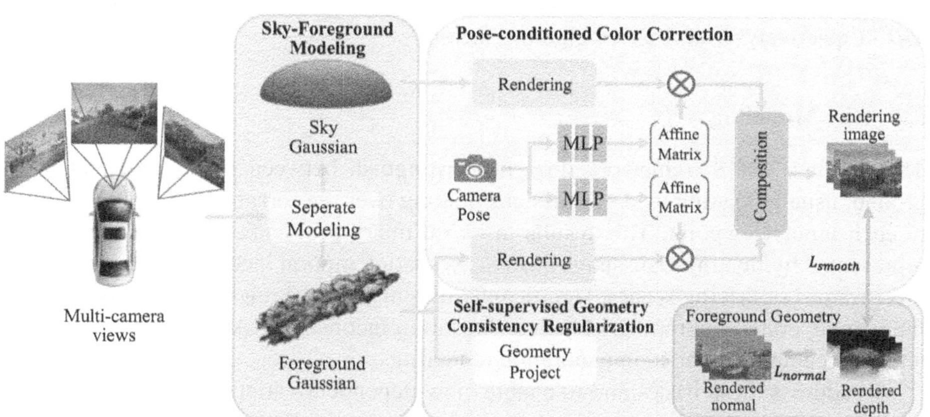

Fig. 2. Overview of MC-Gaussian framework. We separately model the foreground and sky for urban street scenes. Building on this, we utilize two independent MLPs to obtain color calibration matrices from the camera poses, addressing color inconsistencies across multiple cameras. To ensure reliable rendering from free viewpoints, we improve the geometric accuracy by enforcing consistency between rendered images and depths, as well as between rendered normals and depths.

consistency regularization module designed to tackle overfitting issues in sparse viewpoints.

3.1 Preliminary

3D Gaussian Splatting represents a scene with a set of anisotropic 3D Gaussians $G = \{G_i \mid i = 1, \ldots, N\}$, where N denotes the number of Gaussians used to represent the scene. Each 3D Gaussian primitive G_i is represented by a center point $\mu_i \in \mathbb{R}^{3\times 1}$ and a covariance matrix $\Sigma_i \in \mathbb{R}^{3\times 3}$ as:

$$G_i(\mathbf{x}) = e^{-\frac{1}{2}(\mathbf{x}-\mu_i)^T \Sigma_i^{-1}(\mathbf{x}-\mu_i)}. \tag{1}$$

For a given pixel p, the 3D Gaussians are projected into the image space for alpha-blending to get the color map $\mathbf{C}$:

$$\mathbf{C}(p) = \sum_{i=1}^{N} \mathbf{c}_i \alpha_i \prod_{j=1}^{i-1} (1 - \alpha_j), \tag{2}$$

where $\mathbf{c}_i \in \mathbb{R}^3$ denotes the RGB color vector of the i-th Gaussian G_i, and $\alpha_i \in [0, 1]$ represents its opacity. Differentiable rendering techniques allow end-to-end optimization of all Gaussian attributes (including center, covariance matrix, color, and opacity) through the reconstruction loss of training views, denoted as

$$L_{pho} = L_{rgb} + \lambda L_{ssim}, \tag{3}$$

where L_{rgb} and L_{ssim} denote the RGB reconstruction loss and the structural similarity loss, respectively, with λ as a weighting factor.

3.2 Sky Modeling

The original 3DGS framework does not distinguish between foreground and background, usually leading to sky Gaussians floating over the foreground while overfitting to each input viewpoint. This results in two primary problems. First, the sky region, represented by floating Gaussians, introduces spatiotemporal inconsistencies in consecutive frames of driving scenes, significantly diminishing the rendering quality. Second, the varying color calibrations of cameras result in inconsistent sky color representation and noticeable boundaries in panoramic renderings.

To address these issues and to enable view-dependent variation in sky appearance, we separately model the sky region by initializing a set of 3D Gaussians with a particular half-sphere dome. We initialize a sky dome centered at the origin of the scene $\mathbf{o}$ with a radius r. By tracing all camera rays, we determine the visible region of the sky from all cameras. We randomly initialize N_{sky} sky Gaussians within the visible area of the sky dome. The color of pixel p is computed as a weighted combination of the rendering colors from the foreground Gaussians and the sky Gaussians, as illustrated in Eq. 4:

$$\mathbf{C}(p) = \mathbf{C}^{fg}(p) + (1 - o^{fg})\mathbf{C}^{sky}(p), \tag{4}$$

where $o^{fg} = \sum_{i=1}^{N} \alpha_i^{fg} \prod_{j=1}^{i-1} \left(1 - \alpha_j^{fg}\right)$ is the accumulated opacity of foreground Gaussians at pixel p. To enforce o^{fg} approaching 1 in the foreground region and 0 in the sky region, a binary cross-entropy loss is applied:

$$L_{sky}(o^{fg}, m^{sky}) = -m^{sky} \log(1 - o^{fg}) - (1 - m^{sky}) \log(o^{fg}), \quad (5)$$

where m^{sky} is the sky mask generated from a pretrained segmentation model [22].

3.3 Pose-Conditioned Color Correction

In multi-camera systems, varying Image Signal Processing (ISP) configurations, which include white balance, tone mapping, and color correction, cause color inconsistencies across images. These color inconsistencies result in poor rendering quality when optimizing 3D Gaussians via rendering loss. Vast-Gaussian [14] addresses the issue of color discrepancies across different views due to lighting changes in single-camera setups. It introduces decoupled appearance modeling, generating a pixel-level transformation map to adjust the rendered images. However, this pixel-level transformation is inefficient and usually leads to overfitting in color correction, ultimately failing to learn a consistent color representation across the scene. Moreover, because the sky background and the foreground have different ISP imaging effects, a single global compensation transformation cannot eliminate color differences between different cameras.

Therefore, we propose a new pose-conditioned affine transformations to the foreground and sky for color correction. Unlike the color correction in UC-NeRF [6], we use the camera pose $P_{t,k}$ at timestamp t from camera k as a correction code to represent the image-related color changes, considering the color variations due to different cameras and timestamps. $P_{t,k} = [\mathbf{o}, \mathbf{q}]$, where $\mathbf{o} \in \mathbb{R}^3$ represents the camera's position, and $\mathbf{q} \in \mathbb{R}^4$ is the quaternion of the camera's rotation matrix. This approach ensures that color calibration is consistent for temporally and spatially nearby cameras, preventing abrupt changes and mitigating overfitting. The correction codes $P_{t,k}$ for each spatiotemporal camera are processed through multi-layer perceptrons (MLPs), resulting in separate affine transformations $[\mathbf{A}^{fg}, \mathbf{b}^{fg}]$ and $[\mathbf{A}^{sky}, \mathbf{b}^{sky}]$ (t, k are abridged for simplicity) for the foreground and sky regions for each camera. Here $\mathbf{A}^{fg}, \mathbf{A}^{sky} \in \mathbb{R}^{3\times3}$ and $\mathbf{b}^{fg}, \mathbf{b}^{sky} \in \mathbb{R}^{3\times1}$. The final color for the rendered pixel p in Eq. 4 can be rewritten as:

$$\mathbf{C}(p) = (\mathbf{A}^{fg}\mathbf{C}^{fg}(p) + \mathbf{b}^{fg}) + (1 - o^{fg})(\mathbf{A}^{sky}\mathbf{C}^{sky}(p) + \mathbf{b}^{sky}). \quad (6)$$

3.4 Self-supervised Geometry Consistency Regularization

In autonomous driving scenarios, the view direction of side cameras is generally orthogonal to the driving direction, causing rapid scene changes from the side views. This results in a sparsity of side-view cameras. 3D Gaussian Splatting (3DGS) often overfits the training views in sparse-view settings, leading to geometric ambiguities and a significant decline in rendering quality under free viewpoints.

We propose to enforce depth consistency by leveraging color consistency in the rendered images. Specifically, we define an adaptive smoothing loss L_{smooth} to promote depth smoothness in regions of image color smoothness (i.e., low-texture or homogeneous areas).

$$L_{smooth} = \sum_{p} |\nabla_x D(p)| e^{-|\nabla_x I(p)|} + |\nabla_y D(p)| e^{-|\nabla_y I(p)|}, \tag{7}$$

where $\nabla_x D(p)$ and $\nabla_y D(p)$ are the gradients of the depth map D at pixel p in the horizontal and vertical directions, $\nabla_x I(p)$ and $\nabla_y I(p)$ are the gradients of the input image I at pixel p in the horizontal and vertical directions. This adaptive smoothing loss, in conjunction with color calibration, constrains the depth more effectively and eliminates the rendering artifacts in regions with inconsistent color supervision.

In addition, we enforce depth consistency by leveraging the consistency of rendered normals. The depth-to-normal conversion [30] computes normal vectors using pixel position differences and cross products. This conversion often reveals significant discrepancies in flat regions due to holes and irregularities in the depth map. These discrepancies result in distorted and noisy normal vectors, which compromise the coherence of surfaces that should otherwise appear smooth. This issue highlights that the depth map inadequately represents surface geometry, leading to suboptimal normal reconstruction and degraded rendering quality. Although the color-guided depth smoothing alleviates this issue to some extent, we introduce a stronger constraint to enforce consistency between the depth-derived normal map and the rendered normal map by adding the normal loss

$$L_{normal} = \sum_{p} |1 - \mathbf{n}_{render}(p) \cdot \mathbf{n}_{conv}(p)|, \tag{8}$$

where $\mathbf{n}_{render}$ is the rendered normal at pixel p and $\mathbf{n}_{conv}$ is the normal converted from the rendered depths.

The final self-supervision geometric optimization loss L_{depth} is as follows:

$$L_{depth} = L_{smooth} + L_{normal}. \tag{9}$$

3.5 Optimization

While modeling the sky with a specific shape separately and applying the pose-conditioned color correction for sky and foreground regions, the whole set of 3D Gaussians is optimized by combining both the rendering and geometric loss:

$$L = L_{pho} + \lambda_1 L_{sky} + \lambda_2 L_{depth}, \tag{10}$$

where λ_1 and λ_2 are the weight of L_{sky} and L_{depth} respectively.

4 Experiments

4.1 Experimental Settings

Datasets and Metrics. We conduct experiments on two autonomous driving datasets, Waymo [19] and NuScenes [4], featuring diverse street scenes from multi-camera

Table 1. Quantitative comparison on the Waymo and NuScenes datasets.

Type	Method	Waymo			NuScenes		
		PSNR ↑	SSIM ↑	LPIPS ↓	PSNR ↑	SSIM ↑	LPIPS ↓
Offline Rendering	Mip-NeRF [1]	22.42	0.698	0.471	23.31	0.758	0.489
	Mip-NeRF 360 [2]	24.46	0.769	0.406	25.15	0.809	0.436
	Instant-NGP [16]	23.84	0.702	0.494	23.81	0.777	0.476
	S-NeRF [23]	24.89	0.772	0.401	26.02	0.824	0.415
	Zip-NeRF [3]	26.21	0.815	0.389	27.06	0.831	0.435
	UC-NeRF [6]	28.13	0.842	0.356	30.20	0.876	0.374
Online Rendering	3DGS [12]	29.26	0.873	0.264	29.90	0.919	0.246
	GaussianPro [5]	29.50	0.880	**0.240**	29.93	0.925	**0.222**
	Ours	**29.58**	**0.881**	0.241	**31.17**	**0.926**	0.225

setups. We evaluate 10 static scenes from Waymo and 3 from NuScenes. For novel view synthesis, we select every eighth frame as the test image, with the remaining frames used for training. We use Peak Signal-to-Noise Ratio (PSNR), Structural Similarity Index (SSIM), and Learned Perceptual Image Patch Similarity (LPIPS) [32] for quantitative evaluation.

Implementation Details. Our method is built upon the open-source GaussianPro [5] code base. Due to changes in camera sampling rates at higher resolutions, we applied the Mip-splatting 2D smoothing filter [31] in all experiments to achieve better sampling quality. All experiments are conducted on a single RTX 3090 GPU.

4.2 Quantitative and Qualitative Results

We compare our MC-Gaussian method with recent state-of-the-art approaches such as GaussianPro [5] and UC-NeRF [6], focusing on static street scene reconstruction under multi-camera setups without relying on LiDAR supervision, to ensure a fair comparison under consistent assumptions. The quantitative comparison is presented in Table 1. Our MC-Gaussian outperforms other methods on both datasets, with particularly notable improvements on the NuScenes dataset. Additionally, it significantly exceeds UC-NeRF [6], which addresses multi-camera calibration inconsistencies in NeRF. Figure 3 shows a set of novel view rendering results of different methods. Our method effectively eliminates rendering artifacts and maintains color consistency. Additionally, our approach provides more accurate 3D reconstruction, with smoother surfaces in textureless areas, as illustrated in the depth map of Fig. 3.

4.3 Ablation Study

We conduct ablation studies on 10 static scenes from the Waymo dataset to evaluate the contribution of each module in the MC-Gaussian framework: **Sky Modeling** (SKY),

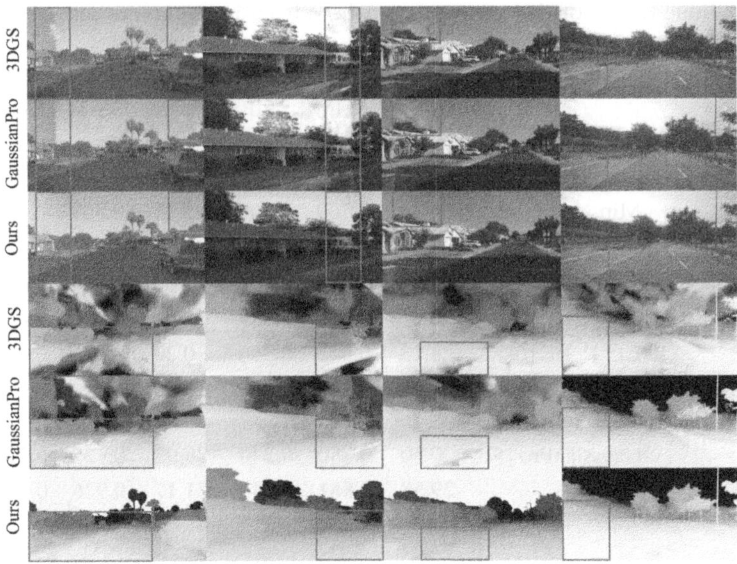

Fig. 3. Synthesized novel view images from the Waymo and NuScenes datasets. Compared to other methods, our results demonstrate consistent colors (red boxes) and better geometric structures (blue boxes). (Color figure online)

Pose-conditioned Color Correction (PCC), and **Self-supervised Geometry Consistency Regularization** (SGCR). Our baseline is GaussianPro [5], with all three modules removed. Additionally, we evaluate the geometric reconstruction accuracy using Relative Error (Rel) that captures proportional deviation in depth estimation, Absolute Error (Abs) that measures the overall accuracy by calculating the absolute difference, and Threshold Accuracy (σ) that reflects the percentage of pixels with depth errors below a specified threshold. The results are shown in Table 2.

Table 2. Ablation Study.

SKY	PCC	SGCR	**PSNR** ↑	**SSIM** ↑	**LPIPS** ↓	**Rel** ↓	**Abs** ↓	σ ↑
×	×	×	29.50	0.880	**0.240**	0.122	2.12	0.888
✓	×	×	29.39	0.878	0.243	——	——	——
✓	✓	×	**29.63**	**0.882**	<u>0.241</u>	<u>0.092</u>	<u>1.66</u>	<u>0.923</u>
✓	✓	✓	<u>29.58</u>	<u>0.881</u>	<u>0.241</u>	**0.084**	**1.54**	**0.933**

Sky Modeling. As shown in the first and second rows of Table 2, compared to the baseline, our separate sky modeling results in a slight performance drop when evaluated on the test views, which are close to the training views. However, separate sky modeling remains essential. In the baseline model, the sky Gaussians are overfitted to specific viewpoints, resulting in noticeable floating artifacts in the foreground region during free-viewpoint rendering, as shown in the blue box of Fig. 4 (a). Our separate sky model effectively resolves this issue, as demonstrated in Fig. 4 (b).

Pose-Conditioned Color Correction. The third row in Table 2 shows improvements with the PCC module. As indicated by the red and yellow arrows in Fig. 4(a) and Fig. 4(b), inconsistent color supervision across training views leads to incorrect rendering in the same 3D region. The proposed PCC module corrects these color inconsistencies, as shown by the red arrow in Fig. 4(c), where the sky colors become more consistent. Moreover, the yellow arrow in Fig. 4(c) demonstrates that the PCC module effectively alleviates the blurry artifacts caused by inconsistent color supervision.

Self-supervised Geometry Consistency Regularization. The last two rows in Table 2 demonstrate that our SGCR module effectively enhances geometric properties. Although the rendering quality remains unchanged in test views close to the training views, the geometric improvements further improve the rendering performance in free viewpoints with larger differences. As indicated by the yellow arrows in Fig. 4(c) and Fig. 4(d), rendering artifacts are further mitigated.

Fig. 4. Effectiveness validation of each MC-Gaussian module from a new free-view perspective. Enhancements are highlighted with blue boxes, red and yellow arrows. (Color figure online)

Efficiency Analysis. We test the efficiency of different methods on the same scene with image resolution 1920 $\times$ 1280 using an NVIDIA RTX 3090 GPU and compare them with NeRF-based off-line rendering methods. Although 3DGS achieves high PSNR and rendering efficiency, as shown in Table 3 and Fig. 3, it does not adequately address the inherent challenges of multi-camera systems, which can lead to artifacts due to inconsistent calibration or appearance variations across views. Our method consumes a bit more time than GaussianPro, but further corrects the geometry and resolves color inconsistency issues in multi-camera systems, as evidenced by the higher PSNR and comprehensive visual comparisons. Our MC-Gaussian is 100 times faster in rendering speed compared to UC-NeRF, advancing the practical application of novel view synthesis in multi-camera systems for autonomous driving simulation.

Table 3. Efficiency Analysis.

Method	Training	Inference	PSNR
Mip-NeRF [1]	20h	70s	22.42
Mip-NeRF-360 [2]	14h	42s	24.46
Instant-NGP [16]	**30min**	0.35s	23.84
S-NeRF [23]	15h	80s	24.89
Zip-NeRF [3]	2h	2s	26.21
UC-NeRF [6]	3h	3.2s	28.13
3DGS [12]	**30min**	**0.02s**	29.26
GaussianPro [5]	1h	**0.02s**	29.50
Ours	2h	0.03s	**29.58**

5 Conclusions

In summary, we introduce a reconstruction method that separately models the foreground and sky regions with 3DGS under the multi-camera setup in autonomous driving scenes. We propose pose-conditioned color calibration to address inconsistent color supervision from multiple cameras. Additionally, we introduce self-supervised geometric consistency optimization to mitigate overfitting from sparse side views. Our method achieves state-of-the-art performance on multi-camera datasets such as Waymo and NuScenes, enabling real-time and high-fidelity rendering.

Nevertheless, our method currently faces limitations in handling dynamic scenes, which restricts its applicability in real-time autonomous driving scenarios. Additionally, the inability to reconstruct occluded regions further constrains the method's performance in comprehensive scene understanding. Moreover, we observe that the PCC and SGCR modules increase the number of Gaussians while correcting the scene geometry, which leads to a substantial rise in training time and rendering time. These challenges hinder the full potential of autonomous driving simulations, and addressing them will be a key focus for future improvements in our approach.

References

1. Barron, J.T., Mildenhall, B., Tancik, M., Hedman, P., Martin-Brualla, R., Srinivasan, P.P.: Mip-NeRF: a multiscale representation for anti-aliasing neural radiance fields. In: ICCV, pp. 5855–5864 (2021)
2. Barron, J.T., Mildenhall, B., Verbin, D., Srinivasan, P.P., Hedman, P.: Mip-NeRF 360: unbounded anti-aliased neural radiance fields. In: CVPR, pp. 5470–5479 (2022)
3. Barron, J.T., Mildenhall, B., Verbin, D., Srinivasan, P.P., Hedman, P.: Zip-NeRF: anti-aliased grid-based neural radiance fields. In: CVPR, pp. 19697–19705 (2023)
4. Caesar, H., et al.: nuscenes: A multimodal dataset for autonomous driving. In: CVPR, pp. 11621–11631 (2020)
5. Cheng, K., et al.: GaussianPro: 3D Gaussian splatting with progressive propagation. In: ICML (2024)

6. Cheng, K., et al.: UC-NeRF: neural radiance field for under-calibrated multi-view cameras in autonomous driving. arXiv preprint arXiv:2311.16945 (2023)
7. Chung, J., Oh, J., Lee, K.M.: Depth-regularized optimization for 3D Gaussian splatting in few-shot images. In: CVPR, pp. 811–820 (2024)
8. Dosovitskiy, A., Ros, G., Codevilla, F., Lopez, A., Koltun, V.: Carla: an open urban driving simulator. In: CoRL, pp. 1–16. PMLR (2017)
9. Duggal, S., et al.: Secrets of 3D implicit object shape reconstruction in the wild, **1**. arXiv preprint arXiv:2101.06860 (2021)
10. Fang, J., et al.: Augmented lidar simulator for autonomous driving. IEEE RA-L **5**(2), 1931–1938 (2020)
11. Guo, J., et al.: StreetSuRF: extending multi-view implicit surface reconstruction to street views. arXiv preprint arXiv:2306.04988 (2023)
12. Kerbl, B., Kopanas, G., Leimkühler, T., Drettakis, G.: 3D Gaussian splatting for real-time radiance field rendering. ACM Trans. Graph. **42**(4), 139–1 (2023)
13. Li, W., et al.: AADS: augmented autonomous driving simulation using data-driven algorithms. Sci. Robot. **4**(28), eaaw0863 (2019)
14. Lin, J., et al.: VastGaussian: vast 3D Gaussians for large scene reconstruction. In: CVPR, pp. 5166–5175 (2024)
15. Mildenhall, B., Srinivasan, P.P., Tancik, M., Barron, J.T., Ramamoorthi, R., Ng, R.: NeRF: representing scenes as neural radiance fields for view synthesis. Commun. ACM **65**(1), 99–106 (2021)
16. Müller, T., Evans, A., Schied, C., Keller, A.: Instant neural graphics primitives with a multiresolution hash encoding. ACM Trans. Graph. **41**(4), 1–15 (2022)
17. Rematas, K., et al.: Urban radiance fields. In: CVPR, pp. 12932–12942 (2022)
18. Shah, S., Dey, D., Lovett, C., Kapoor, A.: AirSim: high-fidelity visual and physical simulation for autonomous vehicles. In: Hutter, M., Siegwart, R. (eds.) Field and Service Robotics. SPAR, vol. 5, pp. 621–635. Springer, Cham (2018). https://doi.org/10.1007/978-3-319-67361-5_40
19. Sun, P., et al.: Scalability in perception for autonomous driving: Waymo open dataset. In: CVPR, pp. 2446–2454 (2020)
20. Wang, J., et al.: Cadsim: robust and scalable in-the-wild 3D reconstruction for controllable sensor simulation. arXiv preprint arXiv:2311.01447 (2023)
21. Wu, Z., et al.: Mars: an instance-aware, modular and realistic simulator for autonomous driving. In: Fang, L., Pei, J., Zhai, G., Wang, R. (eds.) CICAI 2023. LNCS, vol. 14473, pp. 3–15. Springer, Singapore (2023). https://doi.org/10.1007/978-981-99-8850-1_1
22. Xie, E., Wang, W., Yu, Z., Anandkumar, A., Alvarez, J.M., Luo, P.: Segformer: simple and efficient design for semantic segmentation with transformers. NeurIPS **34**, 12077–12090 (2021)
23. Xie, Z., Zhang, J., Li, W., Zhang, F., Zhang, L.: S-NeRF: neural radiance fields for street views. arXiv preprint arXiv:2303.00749 (2023)
24. Yan, Y., et al.: Street Gaussians: modeling dynamic urban scenes with gaussian splatting. In: Leonardis, A., Ricci, E., Roth, S., Russakovsky, O., Sattler, T., Varol, G. (eds.) ECCV 2024. LNCS, vol. 15131, pp. 156–173. Springer, Cham (2024). https://doi.org/10.1007/978-3-031-73464-9_10
25. Yang, J., et al.: EmerNeRF: emergent spatial-temporal scene decomposition via self-supervision. arXiv preprint arXiv:2311.02077 (2023)
26. Yang, Z., et al.: UniSim: a neural closed-loop sensor simulator. In: CVPR, pp. 1389–1399 (2023)
27. Yang, Z., Manivasagam, S., Chen, Y., Wang, J., Hu, R., Urtasun, R.: Reconstructing objects in-the-wild for realistic sensor simulation. In: ICRA, pp. 11661–11668. IEEE (2023)

28. Yang, Z., Manivasagam, S., Liang, M., Yang, B., Ma, W.C., Urtasun, R.: Recovering and simulating pedestrians in the wild. In: CoRL, pp. 419–431. PMLR (2021)
29. Yang, Z., et al.: SurfelGAN: synthesizing realistic sensor data for autonomous driving. In: CVPR, pp. 11118–11127 (2020)
30. Yin, W., Liu, Y., Shen, C.: Virtual normal: enforcing geometric constraints for accurate and robust depth prediction. IEEE TPAMI **44**(10), 7282–7295 (2021)
31. Yu, Z., Chen, A., Huang, B., Sattler, T., Geiger, A.: Mip-splatting: alias-free 3D Gaussian splatting. In: CVPR, pp. 19447–19456 (2024)
32. Zhang, R., Isola, P., Efros, A.A., Shechtman, E., Wang, O.: The unreasonable effectiveness of deep features as a perceptual metric. In: CVPR, pp. 586–595 (2018)
33. Zhou, X., Lin, Z., Shan, X., Wang, Y., Sun, D., Yang, M.H.: DrivingGaussian: composite Gaussian splatting for surrounding dynamic autonomous driving scenes. In: CVPR, pp. 21634–21643 (2024)
34. Zhu, Z., Fan, Z., Jiang, Y., Wang, Z.: FSGs: real-time few-shot view synthesis using Gaussian splatting. In: Leonardis, A., Ricci, E., Roth, S., Russakovsky, O., Sattler, T., Varol, G. (eds.) ECCV 2024. LNCS, vol. 15097, pp. 145–163. Springer, Cham (2024). https://doi.org/10.1007/978-3-031-72933-1_9

Efficient Modeling of Long-Range Morphology for 3D Neuron Reconstruction from Electron Microscopy Images

Chenxuan Wang[1,2], Miaomiao Cai[1,2], Qihua Chen[1,2], and Xuejin Chen[1,2](✉)

[1] MoE Key Laboratory of Brain-inspired Intelligent Perception and Cognition, University of Science and Technology of China, Hefei, China
{wangcx01,mmcai,cqh}@mail.ustc.edu.cn

[2] Institute of Artificial Intelligence, Hefei Comprehensive National Science Center, Hefei 230088, China
xjchen99@ustc.edu.cn

Abstract. Reconstructing 3D neurons from large-scale electron microscopy images is crucial for brain connectomics. Existing 3D neuron reconstruction pipelines typically rely on labor-intensive manual proofreading to merge neuron fragments generated by automated image segmentation algorithms. To facilitate the proofreading process, we propose a novel neuron tracing framework based on point cloud representations. We formulate neuron reconstruction as a binary classification task that predicts whether a pair of segments should be merged into the same neuron based on their 3D morphology. Inspired by selective state space models (SSMs) that offer sequence modeling capabilities similar to transformers but with linear time complexity, we propose MambaTracingNet to integrate the growth direction of neuron segments into the dependency learning for neuron tracing. Our MambaTracingNet provides robust long-range dependency for neuron segments while maintaining superior computational efficiency based on the selective SSM architecture. We conduct comprehensive experiments on 20,000 segment pairs from the FlyTracing dataset. The results demonstrate that our method outperforms previous point cloud networks with a more lightweight network and significantly reduces GPU memory usage during training.

Keywords: 3D Neuron Reconstruction · Electron Microscopy · Point Cloud · Mamba

1 Introduction

Accurate 3D reconstruction of neuronal structures is a crucial foundation for investigating neuronal morphology, synaptic connections, and brain neural circuits, thereby representing a pivotal step in neuroscience research. Nanometer-scale electron microscopy (EM) is the only technique proven effective in reconstructing synaptic connections in a nervous system or brain [2]. Although existing

P. Li et al. (Eds.): CGI 2025, LNCS 16508, pp. 393–404, 2026.
https://doi.org/10.1007/978-3-032-22264-0_31

image segmentation methods can almost precisely localize the boundaries of neuron regions, a substantial number of split errors remain, which pose a significant challenge to neuron tracing. For example, the Flood-filling network (FFN) [6], a state-of-the-art method, typically segments a single neuron from the EM volume into hundreds or even thousands of fragments. Manual proofreading to correct these split errors in the full adult fly brain FAFB dataset for the whole-brain neuron reconstruction is extremely labor-intensive. Statistics from the Flywire calibration platform show that the initial proofreading typically requires 19 min of expert time for a single neuron trunk. It would take about 18 years for one person to complete the proofreading for approximately 166,000 neurons in the entire Drosophila brain [2].

To address the problem of over-segmentation in ultra-high-resolution EM images of neurons, current automatic tracing methods primarily rely on local EM image cues to detect and correct split errors. For example, 3C [12] employs an LSTM-UNet model that takes the raw image, seed mask, and boundary probability as input to merge segments. EMProof [16] trains a convolutional neural network to predict the position and direction of the next segment by learning from skeleton-EM image pairs, thereby establishing connections between fragments. EmbedNet [1] trains a 3D U-Net to generate dense voxel-wise embeddings from EM images. These features capture fine-grained local image details and are combined with local 3D morphological features to predict the connection probabilities between neuron fragments. However, due to the massive scale and extremely high resolution of EM data, image-based methods must process EM volumes by dividing them into smaller blocks.

On the other hand, surface point clouds can efficiently represent the morphology of neuron fragments while preserving their geometric characteristics, offering a more efficient alternative to dense volumetric images. To this end, we propose a neuron tracing method based on 3D morphological analysis of the surface point clouds sampled from individual fragments.

Previous point cloud analysis methods are primarily built upon two foundational architectures: Multi-layer perceptrons (MLPs) and transformers. MLP-based methods [7,14,15] directly process point sets through a series of multi-layer perceptrons to extract features. For example, PointNet++ [15] partitions point clouds into small clusters via sampling and grouping, then hierarchically extracts local features using PointNet [14]. PointMLP [11] proposes a pure MLP-based point cloud analysis approach that eliminates complex local feature extraction modules, thereby reducing computational and memory overhead. Although MLPs can retain some spatial information of point clouds, they essentially perform independent or locally-scoped transformations on each point, lacking the capacity to model long-range correlations. Without explicit spatial structure modeling, MLP-based architectures struggle to capture the global geometric structure of point clouds, which limits their representation power in complex scenarios.

In contrast, Transformer-based methods [5,13,18,19] leverage self-attention mechanisms and have shown superior capability in modeling long-range features.

For instance, PoinTr [19] employs geometry-aware self-attention modules to learn fine-grained point cloud structures. PointMAE [13] adopts a Transformer-based self-supervised framework for point cloud completion pretraining, using a pyramid architecture in both encoder and decoder to capture local and global 3D morphological features. However, attention computation has quadratic time complexity, which becomes a significant bottleneck for large-scale point cloud processing. This issue is particularly prominent in 3D neuron tracing tasks, where a single large neuron fragment may contain millions of surface points spanning thousands of EM slices. Thus, designing an efficient architecture capable of long-range dependency modeling has become a pressing challenge.

The Mamba architecture with selective state-space modeling [4] offers a new perspective to overcome the aforementioned limitations of MLP and Transformer backbones. It enables long-sequence modeling with linear time complexity. Recently, a few studies have attempted to apply Mamba to point cloud analysis tasks [8–10]. However, existing approaches typically rely on simple scanning mechanisms for point cloud block ordering and fail to accommodate the structural complexity of neurons. We propose a growth-direction-aware ordering strategy by paying attention to morphological consistency along the neuron's branching direction, mimicking the human proofreading process. By aligning the patch orders with the natural growth pathways of neurons, our approach effectively exploits the biological structure and continuity of neural morphology.

In summary, we propose MambaTracingNet, a point-cloud-based neuron tracing network built on Mamba architecture. The key contributions include:

- We propose MambaTracingNet, an efficient network tailored for point cloud analysis and applied to 3D neuron reconstruction. By leveraging Mamba's linear complexity, our model improves the performance of predicting connectivity probabilities of neuro segments while significantly reducing the computational cost. Furthermore, MambaTracingNet integrates biological priors through a growth-direction-aware reordering strategy, enhancing its ability to capture structural features essential for fragment connection prediction.
- An adaptive mask-based self-supervised pretraining mechanism is designed to learn fine-grained local features and long-range dependencies within point cloud blocks, thereby improving model generalization and robustness.
- Experimental results on the FlyTracing dataset demonstrate that MambaTracingNet surpasses MLP- and Transformer-based models in accuracy, while significantly reducing computational resource consumption due to its efficient Mamba-based architecture.

2 Method

We follow Chen et al. [1] to predict the connectivity probability of two segments, S_a and S_b, considering their 3D morphology. We learn the prediction function f from a set of connected segment pairs ($f(S_a, S_b) = 1$) that should be merged during proofreading and unconnected pairs ($f(S_a, S_b) = 0$). The overall pipeline is illustrated in Fig. 1.

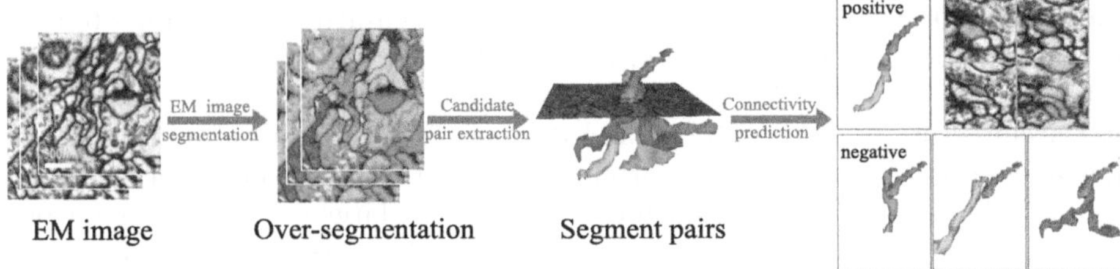

Fig. 1. Workflow of automatic proofreading. An image segmentation method is applied to the EM image and generates extensive neuron segments. We extract potentially connected pairs and predict the connecting probability for each pair using our MambaTracingNet to merge segments.

2.1 Overall Architecture

Given a point cloud $\boldsymbol{P} \in \mathbb{R}^{T\times 3}$ extracted from the surface of a neuron segment, we first select M key points $\boldsymbol{P}' = \{\mathbf{p}_i'\}_{i=1}^{M}$ using Farthest Point Sampling (FPS) [3] and gather k nearest points around each center point $\mathbf{p}_i'$ into a patch $\boldsymbol{x}_i \in \mathbb{R}^{k\times 3}$.

For each patch $\boldsymbol{x}_i$, we extract its local feature embedding $\mathbf{f}_i \in \mathbb{R}^D$ using a light-PointNet [7]. Then we use a growth-direction-aware ordering strategy (explained in Sect. 2.2), to reorder the initial patch embedding. In addition, we add a learnable positional encoding to each patch based on its center point coordinates $\mathbf{p}_i'$ and get $\mathbf{f}_i^{pos} \in \mathbb{R}^D$. By serializing these M point patches, the input sequence $\boldsymbol{Z}_0$ to the stacked Mamba blocks [9] is:

$$\mathbf{Z}_0 = [\mathbf{f}_1 + \mathbf{f}_1^{pos}; \quad \mathbf{f}_2 + \mathbf{f}_2^{pos}; \quad \cdots; \quad \mathbf{f}_M + \mathbf{f}_M^{pos}]. \tag{1}$$

The serialized features Z_L are finally obtained after L Mamba blocks that are trained via the point cloud completion pre-training task and the connective probability fine-tuning task.

2.2 Growth-Direction-Aware Ordering Strategy

The Mamba architecture adopts a recurrent scanning structure and an efficient context compression mechanism, achieving constant-time inference and linear-time training. Unlike Transformer models based on self-attention mechanisms, Mamba is highly sensitive to the input token order and relies on unidirectional information flow for modeling. This characteristic grants it strong performance on serialized text tasks but poses challenges when applied to unordered data structures such as point clouds.

Current Mamba-based point cloud analysis methods [8–10] typically use random ordering, coordinate-based Morton ordering, or Hilbert curve ordering to construct input sequences. However, these strategies often fail to fully capture the geometric structures of neuronal fragments, particularly neglecting the growth direction of neurons, which is a crucial biological feature.

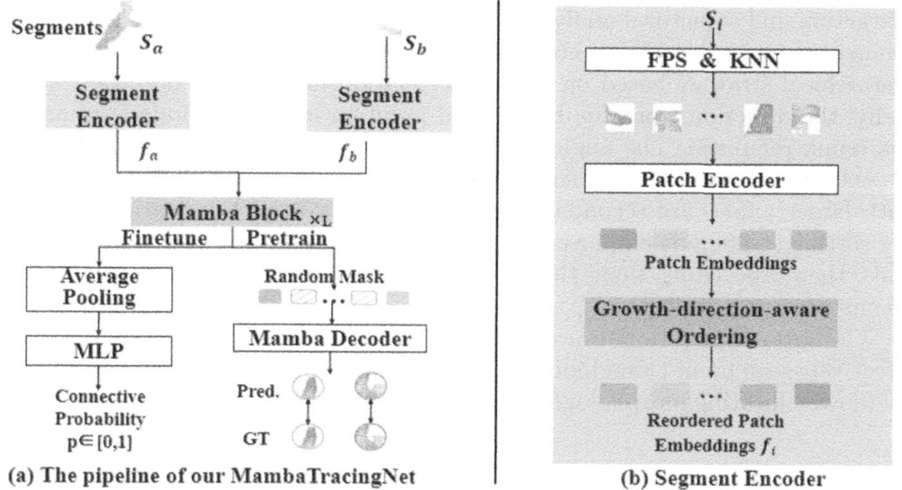

Fig. 2. Our MambaTracingNet for connectivity prediction of two neuron segments. (a) Method overview. (b) Our segment encoder. The growth-direction-aware ordering module uses the growth direction of neuron segments to adjust the scanning order.

During the human proofreading process, experts usually focus more on morphological consistency along the growth direction. We design a growth-direction-aware sorting module that integrates biological priors to provide a more meaningful scanning sequence for the Mamba block.

For each neuronal fragment, we first determine its growth direction. Then, the point cloud patches within each fragment are sorted based on the projection distance of their keypoints onto the growth direction, allowing the fragments to be ordered along the neuron's natural extension and better capturing geometric continuity.

Specifically, as illustrated in Fig. 3, the midpoint $\mathbf{c}$ of the skeleton edge connecting the two neuron segments based on the neuron skeleton is set as the growth point. The growth direction $\mathbf{g}$ is then estimated as the direction between the end nodes of the two segments. For all point cloud patches $\boldsymbol{x}_i$ within the two segments, we compute the projection distance $d_i = (\mathbf{p}'_i - \mathbf{c}) \cdot \mathbf{g}$, where $\mathbf{p}'_i$ is the center point of each patch. The block embeddings $\{\mathbf{f}_i\}$ are sorted in increasing order of these projection distances.

Figure 3 (a–c) shows an example pair of neuron segments and the corresponding growth point and direction. Figure 3(d) demonstrates the sorting results according to the growth direction. Compared to the simple Z-axis-based ordering in Fig. 3(b), our re-ordering results reflect the neuron's growth trajectory more accurately. The sorted point cloud blocks exhibit higher spatial coherence and directional consistency, aligning better with the neuron's natural growth trend. This reordering process not only improves the structural representation but also provides a more principled scanning sequence for subsequent feature extraction and structural analysis. Figure 3 (e) illustrates the scanning sequence for neurons with branching structures. For such cases, we further introduce a hierarchical strategy based on geometric relationships among branches. Specifically, the direction from the bifurcation point to its parent node is treated as the trunk reference. The angle between each branch's direction and the trunk is computed. Branches with smaller angles are considered primary, while those with larger angles are secondary. In multi-primary-branch scenarios, a cascading sorting strategy is employed—first sorting along the primary branch until it ends, then proceeding along the next, thus preserving geometric continuity and reconstruction priority.

The growth-direction-aware sorting strategy enables the Mamba block to effectively scan point cloud block embeddings in alignment with neuronal growth, thereby facilitating morphological feature learning during neuron reconstruction.

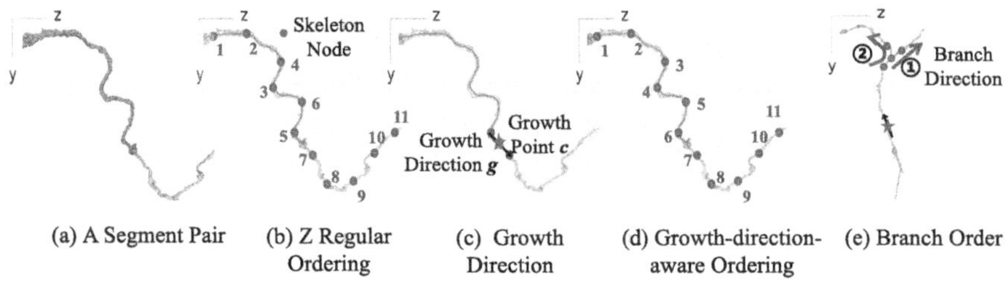

Fig. 3. Our growth-direction-aware ordering strategy.

2.3 Two-Stage Training

Mamba's global receptive field struggles to effectively capture local geometric information of points, limiting its ability to learn fine-grained features. We further design a two-stage training approach, enhancing the encoder's capacity to extract fine-grained features through self-supervised point cloud completion. In the downstream task, we use only the pretrained encoder for feature extraction, with MLPs employed for fine-tuning.

Inspired by the Point-MAE [13], we adopt a masked point modeling approach that directly reconstructs masked points. Specifically, after reordering the initial patch embeddings, we randomly mask these tokens and utilize an encoder-decoder architecture, where the encoder only processes visible tokens and generates their embeddings. The encoded visible and masked tokens are input to the decoder to predict the masked points. However, compared to point clouds of natural objects, neuron segments exhibit more similar morphological features, greater scale differences, and finer texture structures. Building on the Point-MAE method, we design a new pre-training strategy. Instead of using a high fixed masking ratio as in Point-MAE, we adaptively adjust the masking ratio based on the loss value to gradually increase the difficulty of the pre-training task and avoid gradient explosion during the training process.

During pre-training, we dynamically adjust the masking ratio of the input point cloud based on the Chamfer distance loss at each epoch [17]. When the loss is low, it indicates that the model has effectively completed the current masked reconstruction task. In this case, the masking ratio is increased to raise the task difficulty and enhance the model robustness. Conversely, higher loss suggests a more challenging task. Therefore, the masking ratio is reduced to prevent gradient explosion or convergence difficulties. Specifically, the masking ratio μ is updated based on the loss value L_{cd} as follows:

$$L_{cd} = \frac{1}{|S_1|} \sum_{y \in S_1} \min_{\hat{y} \in \hat{S_1}} ||y - \hat{y}||_2^2 + \frac{1}{|\hat{S_1}|} \sum_{\hat{y} \in \hat{S_1}} \min_{y \in S_1} ||\hat{y} - y||_2^2, \tag{2}$$

$$\mu = \text{clip}(\mu_0 + \theta(l_{\text{ref}} - L_{cd}), \mu_{\text{min}}, \mu_{\text{max}}), \tag{3}$$

where $\hat{S_1}$ denotes the predicted point set, and S_1 denotes the ground truth point set; μ_0 is the initial masking ratio, θ is a scaling factor, l_{ref} is the reference loss value, and μ_{min} and μ_{max} are the lower and upper bounds of the masking ratio, respectively. The function clip$(\cdot)$ constrains the input value within the specified range $[\mu_{\text{min}}, \mu_{\text{max}}]$. This mechanism enables the masking ratio to be adaptively adjusted according to the learning status of the model, ensuring that the pre-training process converges progressively under controllable difficulty.

After training the encoder with the point cloud reconstruction task, we then train the classification head of $f(S_a, S_b)$ using the pre-trained encoder for feature extraction. As shown in Fig. 2 (a), in the classification task, we apply average pooling to Z_L to obtain global morphological features. To train the connective probability prediction head, we employ Focal Loss [17] as the loss function to mitigate the imbalance between positive and negative samples.

3 Experiments and Results

3.1 Datasets and Metrics

Datasets. We evaluate our method on the FlyTracing [1] dataset, currently the largest neuron reconstruction dataset. The dataset includes EM images, segmentation results by FFN [6], and proofread neuron skeletons from an entire Drosophila brain. The brain region in a volume of 5×10^6 nm^3 is sectioned and scanned at an ultra-high resolution of $4 \times 4 \times 40nm$. The FlyTracing dataset contains 1000 EM blocks for training and 3000 blocks for testing. We sample surface point clouds for the neuron segments by extracting the boundary pixels from each image slice according to the segmentation masks. These boundary point sets are downsampled to 2048 points. We extract 200,000 segment pairs from the training blocks and 20,000 connection pairs from the test blocks, with the ratio between positive samples and negative samples to 1:4.

Implementation Details. The 2048 points of the input point clouds are clustered into 128 patches, each consisting of 32 points. Our MambaTracingNet comprises $L = 6$ Mamba blocks, with a channel size of 768. During the pretraining stage, we utilize 4 same Mamba blocks as the decoder to reconstruct masked point clouds.

We adapt the Adam optimizer with a cosine scheduler. The initial learning rate is set to 1×10^{-4} in the pretraining stage, 2×10^{-4} for training from scratch, 2×10^{-4} for fine-tuning, and with a weight decay of 5×10^{-2} for all experiments. The batch size is set to 128 for pretraining and 32 for the segment connectivity prediction task. We train our model for 200 epochs, including a warm-up stage of 5 epochs, on a server with eight NVIDIA A40 GPUs, each with 48 GB of memory.

Table 1. Performance comparison on the FlyTracing test blocks.

Method	Architecture	Precision	Recall	W-F1	Param. (M)
PointNet++ [15]	MLP	0.83	0.78	0.79	-
PointMLP [11]	MLP	0.85	0.82	0.83	-
PoinTr [19]	Transformer	0.89	0.79	0.81	44.04 M
MambaTracingNet	Mamba	0.85	0.81	0.82	**24.51** M
Point-BERT [20]	Transformer	0.87	0.83	0.85	44.04 M
Point-MAE [13]	Transformer	0.89	**0.88**	**0.88**	44.04 M
MambaTracingNet w. pre-train	Mamba	**0.90**	0.87	**0.88**	**24.51** M

Metrics. Our method employs three evaluation metrics for quantitative analysis: Precision, Recall, and the F-Score. Given that the ratio of positive to negative samples is approximately 1:4, our approach accounts for the class imbalance when computing the F-Score by introducing a weighted variant. Specifically, we compute the Weighted F1 Score (W-F1) by assigning weights to positive and negative classes based on their sample counts:

$$\text{W-F1} = \sum_i w_i \cdot \text{F1}_i, \quad \text{where} \quad w_i = \frac{N_i}{\sum_j N_j}. \tag{4}$$

Here, $F1_i$ denotes the F1 score for each class, and N_i represents the number of ground truth samples in that class.

3.2 Segment Connectivity Prediction Results

We compare our method with the MLP-based method PointNet++ [15] and the transformer-based method PoinTr [19]. For a fair comparison, we set the same feature extractor and an equal number of encoder layers in PoinTr and MambaTracingNet. All models combine each patch embedding using global average pooling and connect them for prediction with MLPs.

Table 1 compares the connection prediction performances of methods that are fully supervised by segment pairs (above the dashed line) and those with pre-training (below). Pre-trained methods show consistent advantages by capturing fine-grained geometric features in complex neuron fragments. Point-BERT and Point-MAE employ self-supervised strategies focusing on semantic reconstruction and local geometry modeling respectively. MambaTracingNet adopts the same strategy as Point-MAE and achieves a W-F1 score of 0.88 using only 24.51 million parameters, nearly half the size of Point-MAE and Point-BERT. Among fully supervised models, PointMLP performs best with a W-F1 of 0.83, benefiting from deep residual layers. PoinTr achieves the highest precision of 0.89 but suffers from lower recall at 0.79 due to class imbalance in neuron tracing. MambaTracingNet outperforms all other methods after pre-training, demonstrating both strong accuracy and computational efficiency.

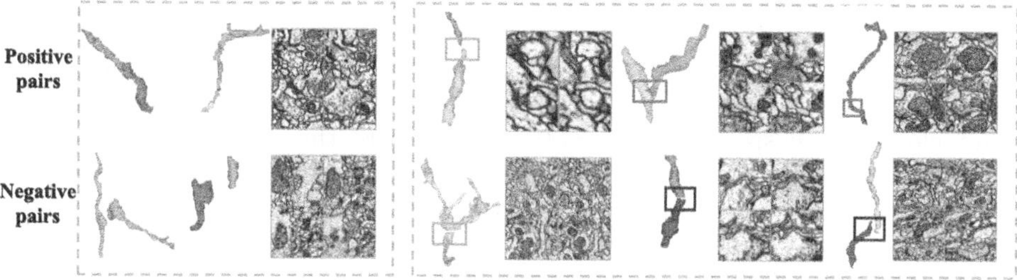

Fig. 4. A group of neuron segment pairs. Positive pairs indicate that two over-segmented fragments belong to the same neuron, while negative pairs indicate that the two segments should not be merged as the same neuron. Their connection relations are correctly predicted by our MambaTracingNet despite missing EM slices (green boxes), abrupt direction change (red boxes), and indistinguishable local morphological features (black boxes). (Color figure online)

Figure 4 shows a group of segment neuron pairs with the corresponding EM images. The first two columns are relatively easier cases that can be correctly classified by all methods. The two positive pairs demonstrate excellent geometric continuity, particularly near the connection points. In contrast, the two negative pairs exhibit large angles between the growth directions of the two segments and a substantial spatial separation. The last three columns show several segment pairs whose connection relations are only correctly predicted by our MambaTracingNet with pretraining. Our MambaTracingNet exhibits strong robustness in section missing (green boxes) because it learns the global morphology of segments by pretraining. By incorporating the prior knowledge of neuron growth direction in the reordering module, our MambaTracingNet performs well in identifying pairs with abrupt directional changes between segments (red boxes). The two negative pairs highlighted with black boxes have indistinguishable local features, but their long-range morphological features do not follow the biological prior. Our model can correctly classify these two samples, showing its effectiveness in capturing long-range shape features for connectivity prediction.

Table 2. Memory footprint (GB) during training under different resolutions.

Method	256	512	1024	2048 (W-F1)
PointNet++ [15]	8.56	10.55	14.23	22.04 (0.79)
PoinTr [19]	4.64	6.33	9.63	16.28 (0.81)
MambaTracingNet (Ours)	**3.84**	**4.64**	**6.23**	**9.42 (0.88)**

3.3 Analysis of Computational Efficiency

In this section, we select two representative models from both the MLP-based and Transformer-based architectures and compare them with our Mamba-based model to assess the computational efficiency of three architectures. With the point cloud patch size set to $k = 16$, we measure the memory usage during training under four different input resolutions ranging from 256 to 2048, corresponding to sequence lengths from 16 to 128. Table 2 shows the GPU consumption. Compared to the quadratic growth of PoinTr, the cost growth of our MambaTracingNet is approximately linear, while the Multi-scale grouping (MSG) in PointNet++ results in higher computational complexities. Typically, higher resolution point cloud contains richer 3D morphological information for predicting neuron segment connectivity. Therefore, we choose a resolution of 2048 for all our experiments with a batch size of 32. With this high-resolution input, our MambaTracingNet uses 42.14% less memory than PoinTr (9.42 v.s 16.28) but 7% higher tracing performance (0.88 v.s 0.81).

3.4 Analysis of Ordering Strategy

A key challenge in applying Mamba to point cloud analysis lies in converting unordered point clouds into ordered sequences. Unlike the order-invariant self-attention mechanism in Transformer architectures, Mamba's dynamic selection mechanism is inherently unidirectional and thus sensitive to input order. We conduct ablation studies to evaluate the impact of different ordering strategies. The results shown in Table 3 indicate that the coordinate-based serialization significantly outperforms random ordering, demonstrating that the SSM in Mamba is sensitive to the input order. Due to the stochastic nature of neuron growth directions, sorting by x, y, or z coordinates yields comparable results. However, a naive concatenation strategy—simply merging point clouds ordered by x, y, and z, triples the sequence length and drastically increases computational cost, while reducing accuracy. In comparison, our growth-direction-aware ordering strategy integrates biological priors into sequence construction and achieves the best performance on the neuron tracing task.educing accuracy. In comparison, our growth-direction-aware ordering strategy integrates biological priors into sequence construction and achieves the best performance on the neuron tracing task.

Table 3. Quantitative comparison of different reordering strategies

Method	Random	x	y	z	x+y+z	Ours
W-F1	0.862	0.873	0.873	0.873	0.864	**0.876**

4 Conclusion

In this paper, we propose a neuron tracing method based on Mamba to merge over-segmentation. We define the tracing problem as a binary classification task to determine whether two segments should be merged, using only the surface point clouds as input. Our MambaTracingNet learns the morphological features of the segments. The Mamba block, with its linear time complexity, captures long-range features. To adapt to the tracing task, we design a reordering strategy that allows the Mamba block to scan tokens according to the growth direction of the neurons. Additionally, we design a pre-training phase and fine-tune it during the connectivity prediction task to better learn fine-scale features of neuron segments. The experimental results on the Flytracing dataset demonstrate that our MambaTracingNet is efficient and effective for 3d neuron reconstruction. The model trained from scratch, with only half the number of parameters compared to transformer-based networks, shows highly competitive accuracy. Moreover, with the pretraining phase, our MambaTracingNet outperforms in various metrics. Our method is only for pairwise neuron connection prediction tasks. A future direction is to leverage Mamba's advantages in handling long-sequence data to promote complete long-range neuron reconstruction.

Acknowledgement. This work was supported by the National Natural Science Foundation of China (NSFC) under Grants 62076230 and the Fundamental Research Funds for the Central Universities under Grant WK3490000008.

References

1. Chen, Q., Chen, X., Wang, C., Liu, Y., et al.: Learning multimodal volumetric features for large-scale neuron tracing. In: AAAI (2024)
2. Dorkenwald, S., McKellar, C.E., Macrina, T., et al.: Flywire: online community for whole-brain connectomics. Nat. Methods (2022)
3. Eldar, Y., Lindenbaum, M., Porat: the farthest point strategy for progressive image sampling. IEEE Trans. Image Process. (1997)

4. Gu, A., Dao, T.: Mamba: linear-time sequence modeling with selective state spaces. In: COLM (2024)
5. Hamdi, A., Giancola, S., Ghanem, B.: MVTN: multi-view transformation network for 3D shape recognition. In: ICCV (2021)
6. Januszewski, M., Kornfeld: high-precision automated reconstruction of neurons with flood-filling networks. Nat. Methods (2018)
7. Jing, B., Qinglong, S., Feiwei, Q.: Lightweight real-time point cloud classification network lightpointnet. JCADCG (2019)
8. Li, Y., Yang, W., Fei, B.: 3DMambaComplete: exploring structured state space model for point cloud completion. arXiv preprint (2024)
9. Liang, D., Zhou, X., Xu, W., Zhu, X., Zou, Z., Ye, A.O.: PointMamba: a Simple state space model for point cloud analysis. In: NeurIPS (2024)
10. Liu, J., Yu: Point Mamba: a novel point cloud backbone based on state space model with octree-based ordering strategy. arXiv preprint (2024)
11. Ma, X., Qin, C., You, H.: Rethinking network design and local geometry in point cloud: a simple residual MLP framework. In: ICLR (2022)
12. Meirovitch, Y., Mi, L., Saribekyan, H., Matveev, A., Rolnick, D., Shavit, N.: Cross-classification clustering: an efficient multi-object tracking technique for 3-D instance segmentation in connectomics. In: CVPR (2019)
13. Pang, Y., Wang, W., Tay, F.E., Liu, W., Tian, Y., Yuan, L.: Masked autoencoders for point cloud self-supervised learning. In: Avidan, S., Brostow, G., Cissé, M., Farinella, G.M., Hassner, T. (eds.) ECCV 2022. LNCS, vol. 13662, pp. 604–621. Springer, Cham (2022). https://doi.org/10.1007/978-3-031-20086-1_35
14. Qi, C.R., Su, H., Mo, K., Guibas, L.J.: Pointnet: deep learning on point sets for 3D classification and segmentation. In: CVPR (2017)
15. Qi, C.R., Yi, L., Su, H., Guibas, L.J.: Pointnet++: deep hierarchical feature learning on point sets in a metric space. In: NeurIPS (2017)
16. Schmidt, M., Motta, A., Sievers, M., et al.: RoboEM: automated 3D flight tracing for synaptic-resolution connectomics. Nat. Methods (2024)
17. Wu, T., Pan, L., Zhang, J., et al.: Density-aware chamfer distance as a comprehensive metric for point cloud completion. In: NeurIPS (2021)
18. Wu, X., Jiang, L., Wang, P.S., Liu, Z., Liu, X., et al.: Point transformer v3: simpler faster stronger. In: CVPR (2024)
19. Yu, X., Rao, Y., Wang, Z., Liu, Z., Lu, J., Zhou, J.: PointR: diverse point cloud completion with geometry-aware transformers. In: ICCV (2021)
20. Yu, X., Tang, L., Rao, Y., Huang, T., Zhou, J., et al.: Point-BERT: pre-training 3D point cloud transformers with masked point modeling. In: CVPR (2022)

A Novel Approach to Defocus Region Detection in Phase-Shifting Structured Light 3D Reconstruction

Ruoling Qi, Chunqian Tan, Xi Chu, and Wanzhong Song(✉)

Sichuan University, Chengdu 610000, China
songwz@scu.edu.cn

Abstract. Structured light 3D reconstruction technology has been widely applied in fields such as industrial inspection and medical imaging due to its advantages of non-contact operation, high accuracy, and efficiency. However, in practical acquisition scenarios—especially in handheld small field-of-view Fringe Projection Profilometry (FPP) systems—defocus of the camera or projector often results in local blurring or even loss of fringe patterns, which significantly compromises the accuracy of phase calculation and the reliability of subsequent depth estimation. To address the issue of fringe blurring caused by defocus in such systems, our study proposes a defocus region detection method based on wrapped phase analysis. The proposed method utilizes the phase difference stability among three wrapped phase maps to construct a rule-based mask determination mechanism without requiring any learning process. By applying a fixed threshold, our method effectively identifies and removes unusable data points such as defocus regions, low-reflectivity areas, and background regions. Compared with traditional methods that rely on modulation thresholding, our method offers stronger system generalization capability and lower parameter dependency. Experiments conducted on both a handheld visible-light FPP system and a desktop near-infrared FPP system demonstrate that the proposed method can accurately extract valid fringe regions, thereby improving the accuracy and robustness of 3D reconstruction. Our method shows strong practical value in engineering applications.

Keywords: Structured light · Wrapped phase · Defocus detection · Fringe projection profilometry

1 Introduction

Fringe Projection Profilometry (FPP) [1–5] has emerged as a dominant method due to its single-camera configuration and high precision capabilities. However, handheld FPP systems face a critical challenge: defocus-induced fringe degradation. This defocus manifests as blurred or missing fringes, preventing accurate

R. Qi and C. Tan—These authors contributed equally to this work.

P. Li et al. (Eds.): CGI 2025, LNCS 16508, pp. 405–416, 2026.
https://doi.org/10.1007/978-3-032-22264-0_32

phase unwrapping and generating erroneous depth estimates that compromise 3D reconstruction quality.

Existing defocus detection methods for FPP primarily rely on modulation-based thresholding [6,7], which suffers from two key limitations: (1) global threshold selection requires empirical tuning based on object material properties, limiting system generalizability; (2) inability to distinguish between defocus and low-reflectivity regions. Recent deep learning approaches [8,9], while showing promise, introduce computational complexity and training data dependencies unsuitable for real-time handheld applications.

To address the common defocus issues in FPP, this paper presents a novel defocus region detection method based on wrapped phase difference analysis. This method effectively removes invalid regions such as defocus regions, low-reflectivity areas, and background regions. Our approach leverages the observation that three-step phase-shifting generates phase differences clustered around $4\pi/3$ and $2\pi/3$ in valid regions, while defocus regions exhibit random phase difference distributions. The method employs a fixed threshold (π) for mask generation, eliminating the need for parameter tuning or training data. Experimental validation on both visible-light handheld systems (110 mm working distance) and desktop near-infrared systems (300 mm working distance) demonstrates significant improvements in reconstruction accuracy, establishing universal applicability across diverse system configurations.

2 Related Works

2.1 Fringe Projection Profilometry (FPP)

Structured light 3D reconstruction is a widely adopted active optical measurement technique with broad applications in industrial manufacturing [11], virtual reality [12], film and animation, dental scanning [13–15], and facial recognition [16]. Among existing approaches, FPP [17–19] achieves sub-pixel accuracy by projecting multi-sets of phase-shifted sinusoidal patterns and analyzing the resulting deformed fringes captured by cameras. From which the 3D shape of the object is calculated. FPP offers advantages such as fast measurement speed, high accuracy, non-contact operation, and low cost. However, FPP faces several challenges in practical applications, such as phase errors caused by camera defocus. When the camera is defocused, phase errors at areas with sharp reflectance changes increase, which in turn affects the 3D reconstruction accuracy. Modulation thresholding [6,7] is the common approach of defocus region detection in FPP. This approach needs to manually set the threshold. Deep learning-based approaches [8–10] introduces computational complexity and training data dependencies unsuitable for real-time handheld applications.

2.2 Image Defocus Detection

Recent defocus detection research has moved beyond traditional image analysis, exploring deep learning-based models [20–22]. While learning-based approaches demonstrate strong performance, they typically require extensive training data and high computational cost. In contrast, rule-based methods provide better generalization and interpretability. This work introduces a wrapped phase difference approach that avoids training, uses fixed thresholds insensitive to surface properties, and maintains consistent performance across various FPP systems without domain adaptation, leveraging the inherent stability in wrapped phase differences.

3 Handheld FPP Data Analysis

Figure 1 shows fringe images acquired by the handheld FPP system. The left one shows 16-period phase-shifting images. It can be observed that fringes are clear, indicating good camera focus. In contrast, the 64-period fringe on the right exhibits blurred or missing fringes in several regions due to defocus. Phase errors in defocus regions are greater than those of clear regions. Larger phase errors will deteriorate the 3D reconstruction (Fig. 2).

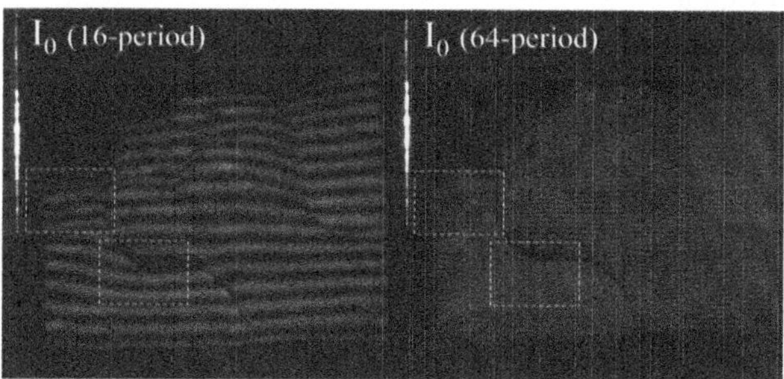

Fig. 1. Fringe images acquired with the handheld FPP. The left is the 16-period image, and the right is the 64-period image. Defocus regions exist in the 64-period image.

4 Proposed Method

4.1 Overview

The direct manifestation of defocusing in both the camera and projector is the blurring of fringes. Comparative analysis of fringe images and their wrapped phases across various scenes reveals that fringe blurring corresponds to phase blurring, with a positive correlation between the two. Projector defocusing reduces fringe modulation, leading to diminished fringe amplitude and visual blurring. Although projector defocusing does not directly affect phase computation theoretically [23], the lowered modulation increases phase sensitivity to random noise. In handheld FPP systems, this noise is prominent, and in defocused regions, it significantly distorts the wrapped phase. Meanwhile, camera defocusing directly degrades phase accuracy, also resulting in phase blurring.

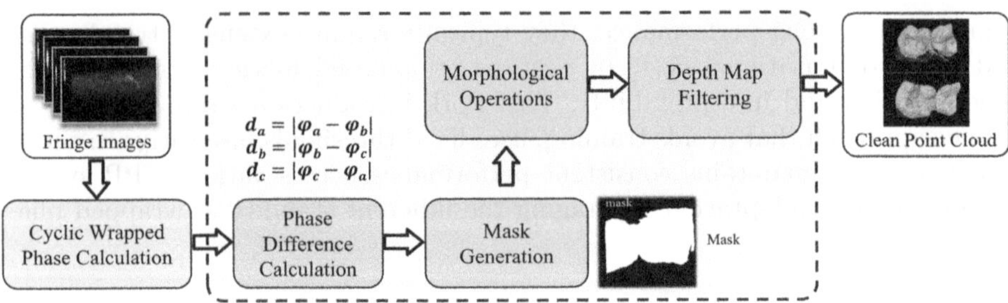

Fig. 2. Framework of the proposed method. A mask is generated from the cyclic wrapped phase maps. Depth maps are filtered with this mask. The proposed method can be plugged into existing FPP methods.

To address this, we propose a method to detect and remove defocused regions from phase-shifted fringe images, based on wrapped phase analysis. The core idea is that phase clarity is closely linked to fringe clarity: blurred fringe images result in blurred wrapped phases. Thus, by identifying blurred regions in the wrapped phase, we can effectively eliminate corresponding defocused areas in the fringe images.

4.2 Difference Analysis of Cyclic Wrapped Phase

Given three-step phase-shift fringe images I_0, I_1, and I_2, the wrapped phase is calculated as

$$\varphi(i,j) = -\arctan\frac{\sum_{k=0}^{N-1} I_k(i,j)\sin(2\pi k/N)}{\sum_{k=0}^{N-1} I_k(i,j)\cos(2\pi k/N)}. \tag{1}$$

The three fringe images can be arranged as three combinations with different initial phase shifts. Thus, three cyclic wrapped phase can be calculated as

$$\begin{aligned}\varphi_a &= -\arctan\frac{\sqrt{3}(I_1 - I_2)}{2I_0 - I_1 - I_2},\\ \varphi_b &= -\arctan\frac{\sqrt{3}(I_0 - I_1)}{2I_2 - I_0 - I_1},\\ \varphi_c &= -\arctan\frac{\sqrt{3}(I_2 - I_0)}{2I_1 - I_2 - I_0}.\end{aligned} \tag{2}$$

Figure 3 illustrates the 64-period 3-step phase-shifting images and the three wrapped phase maps calculated with Eq. 2.

Theoretically, φ_a and φ_b are aligned with φ_b and φ_c by a phase shift of $\pi/3$, respectively. Figure 4(a)–(c) shows the profiles of three wrapped phase maps, and (d) is the combined profiles.

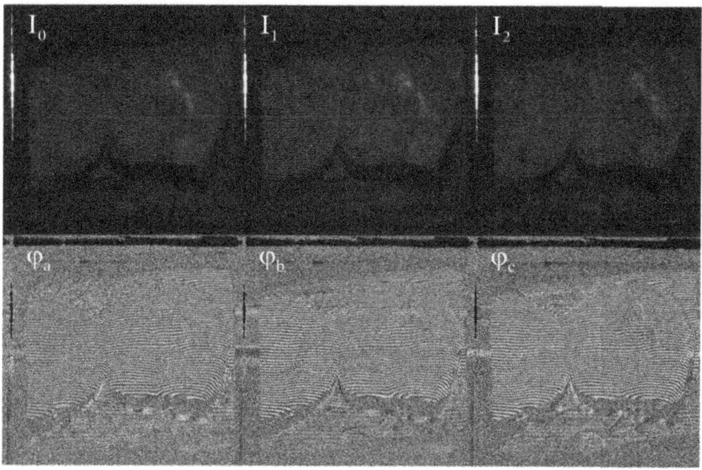

Fig. 3. Phase-shifting fringe images (the first row) and the corresponding cyclic wrapped phase maps (the second row).

The absolute phase-difference of the three phase maps can be calculated as:

$$\begin{aligned} d_a &= \|\varphi_a - \varphi_b\|_1, \\ d_b &= \|\varphi_b - \varphi_c\|_1, \\ d_c &= \|\varphi_c - \varphi_a\|_1. \end{aligned} \tag{3}$$

Figure 4(b) shows the distribution of the ideal phase differences d_a, d_b, and d_c. It can be observed that phase differences are $\frac{2}{3}\pi$ and $\frac{4}{3}\pi$. These two values are used to determine the threshold for defocus regions detection.

4.3 Mask Generation for Defocus Regions Detection

In practical situations, the absolute difference of two phase maps is not strictly equal to $\frac{2}{3}\pi$ or $\frac{4}{3}\pi$, but is instead distributed around these two values. Therefore, it is easy to separate the two phase differences using an intermediate value of π. In our experiment, regions with phase difference values close to $\frac{4}{3}\pi$ are retained, and the other regions are removed. The retained regions form a continuous area when combined spatially.

When there are defocus regions in fringe images, wrapped phases in these regions contain significant noise. In this case, the three cyclic wrapped-phase maps do not maintain a fixed difference and tend to come closer together. As a result, a large portion of the phase differences are distributed within $\left(\frac{2}{3}\pi, \frac{4}{3}\pi\right)$. Using the intermediate value π as a threshold to remove regions with phase differences smaller than π will lead to the remaining regions not being able to form a continuous area.

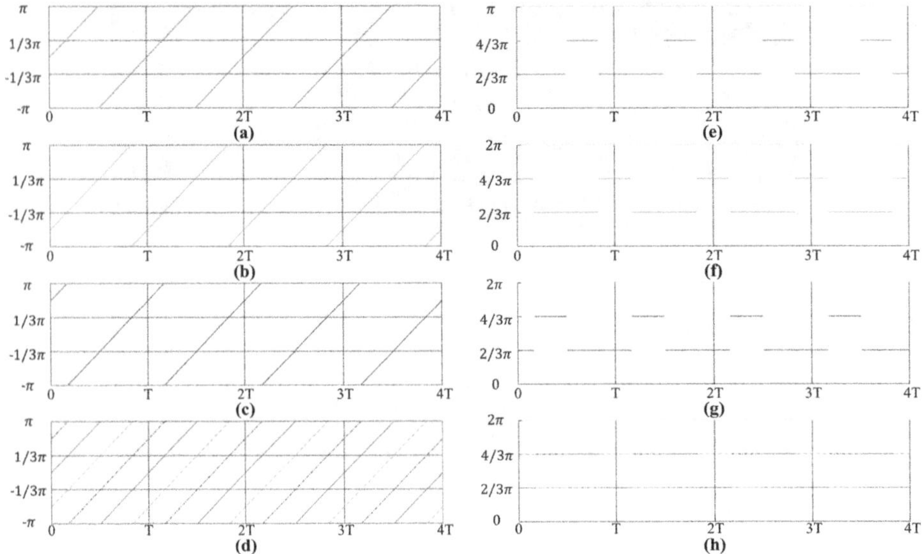

Fig. 4. Profiles of wrapped phase. (a)–(d) correspond to profiles of three wrapped phase maps and their combination. (e)–(h) are the absolute differences between phase maps.

Figure 5(a) shows the composition image of three phase-difference maps, where d_a, d_b, and d_c are displayed as the RGB channels of the image, respectively. The original fringe images and wrapped phase maps are shown in Fig. 3. It can be observed that in the regions where the fringes and wrapped phases are clear, the phase differences are clearly distributed around $\frac{4}{3}\pi$ and $\frac{2}{3}\pi$, whereas in the regions where the fringes and wrapped phases are blurred, the phase differences are mainly distributed within the interval $\left(\frac{2}{3}\pi, \frac{4}{3}\pi\right)$. Thus, the valid region based on phase difference can be calculated as:

$$mask = mask_a \cup mask_b \cup mask_c \tag{4}$$

$$\begin{aligned} mask_a(p) &= \begin{cases} 1 & d_a(p) > \pi, \\ 0 & d_a(p) \leq \pi. \end{cases} \\ mask_b(p) &= \begin{cases} 1 & d_b(p) > \pi, \\ 0 & d_b(p) \leq \pi. \end{cases} \\ mask_c(p) &= \begin{cases} 1 & d_c(p) > \pi, \\ 0 & d_c(p) \leq \pi. \end{cases} \end{aligned} \tag{5}$$

By applying erosion and dilation operations to the merged mask, the remaining area corresponds to valid fringe regions. Consequently, defocus regions, background areas, and shadow areas are removed. Figure 6 shows the three masks and the merged mask calculated using Eq. 5, and the final refined mask after

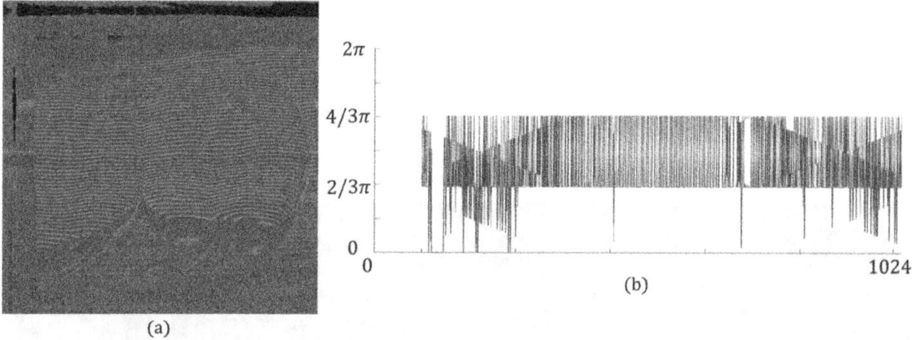

Fig. 5. Wrapped phase difference of real data. (a) is the composition images of three absolute phase-difference maps. (b) show the profiles.

morphological operations. It can be observed that the valid region is largely continuous, whereas the invalid areas contain many small disconnected regions.

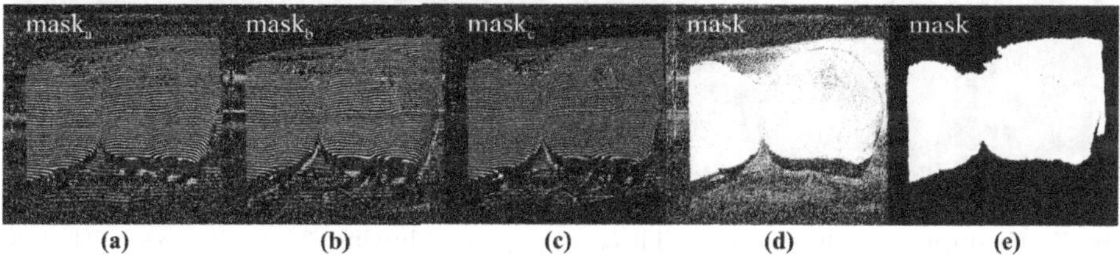

Fig. 6. Masks generated from real fringe images. (a) Low modulation mask, (b) low intensity mask, (c) shadow mask, (d) merged mask computed by Eq. 5, and (e) final valid region mask after morphological operations (erosion and dilation). The final mask effectively excludes defocus, background, and shadow regions.

5 Experiments

5.1 Experiment Setup

Dataset. A handheld FPP system is used to collect the data. This FPP system consists of a CMOS camera with a resolution of 1024 × 1024 pixels and a DLP projector with a resolution of 684 × 608 pixels. The working distance is approximately 110 mm. For each scene, 1–4–16–64 periods of 3-step phase-shifting fringe images are acquired. The proposed method is used to detect the defocus regions in the 64-period fringe images. Depth maps from multi-frequency (1–4–16–64 periods) temporal phase unwrapping (MF-TPU) are used as the ground truth. The dataset consists of 1,480 groups of fringe images from seven dental models for training, 284 groups from one model for validation, and 506 groups from two models for testing. Since the proposed method does not require any training, only the testing set is used for evaluation. Figure 7 shows three examples of the dataset we collected.

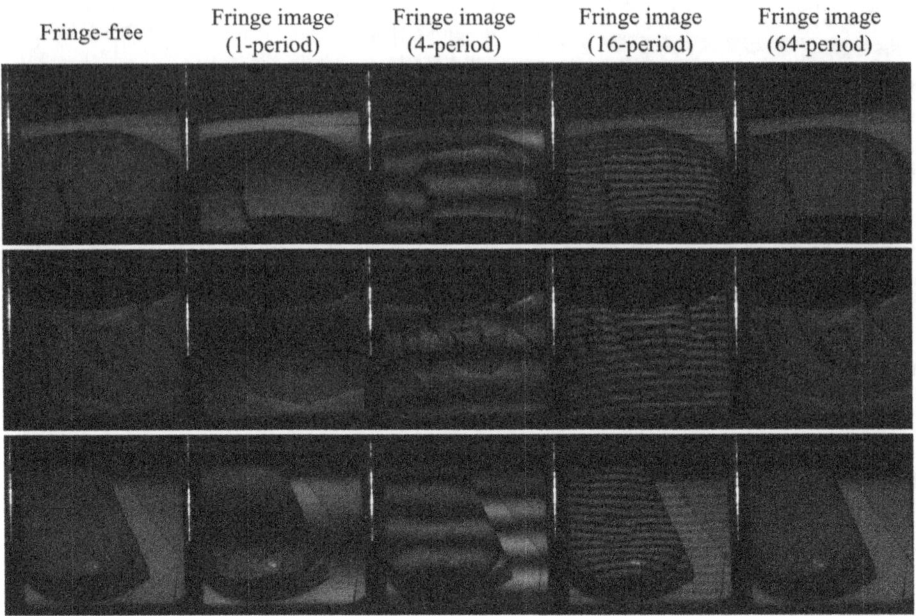

Fig. 7. Examples of the dataset. Three-step phase-shifting fringe images with four spatial frequencies (periods = 1, 4, 16, and 64) captured per scene.

Comparison Methods. Our method can be plugged into existing FPP methods as a module. In our experiment, two representative methods, including supervised fringe-to-depth [24] and weakly supervised fringe-to-depth [17], are selected for comparison. For each method, results are evaluated with and without the proposed defocus region detection module.

5.2 Results

Table 1 summarizes the comparison results. For the supervised method, the proposed approach reduces the mean absolute error (MAE) from 0.249 mm to 0.213 mm, corresponding to a 14.5% improvement. The root mean square error (RMSE) is also reduced from 0.377 mm to 0.297 mm, representing a 21.2% decrease. Likewise, for the weakly supervised method, the MAE decreases from 0.252 mm to 0.205 mm, reflecting an 18.7% improvement, while the RMSE decreases from 0.396 mm to 0.289 mm, corresponding to a 27.0% reduction. These results demonstrate the effectiveness of the proposed method in depth accuracy for both supervised and weakly supervised approaches.

Table 1. Qualitative comparison of two fringe-to-depth methods. The proposed method effectively suppresses artifacts in the defocused areas, leading to improved 3D reconstruction quality.

Method	Depth Error L_1(mm)↓	Depth RMSE(mm)↓
Supervised(64-period)	0.249	0.377
Weakly Supervised(1–64 periods)	0.252	0.396
Supervised(64-period)+Ours	0.213	0.297
Weakly Supervised(1–64 periods)+Ours	**0.205**	**0.289**

Note: The measurement range of the FPP system is 110–125mm.(↓ means lower is better)

Figure 8 shows that after applying our method to remove defocus regions, the point cloud reconstructed from the depth map becomes more accurate, with significantly reduced noise and scattered points.

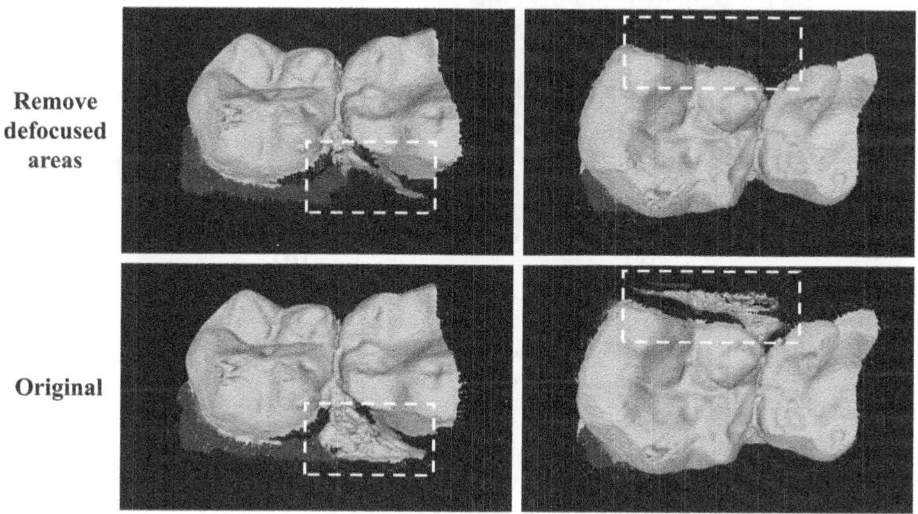

Fig. 8. Point cloud reconstructed with and without the proposed method.

5.3 Test on Desktop Near-Infrared FPP System

We also test the effectiveness of the proposed method on a desktop near-infrared FPP system. This near-infrared FPP system employs laser MEMS projector to project sinusoidal fringes and collects images using a near-infrared camera with a resolution of 1280 × 1024 pixels. The working distance of the system is approximately 300 mm. The system performs a static scan of the object using a

4-step phase-shifting scheme with four different frequencies (1–4–16–64 periods). The proposed method is experimentally tested on the 64-period fringe images. Figure 9 illustrates the phase-shifting fringe images, the initial 3D reconstruction without defocus removal, the defocus mask obtained using the proposed method, and the final 3D reconstruction after excluding the defocused regions.

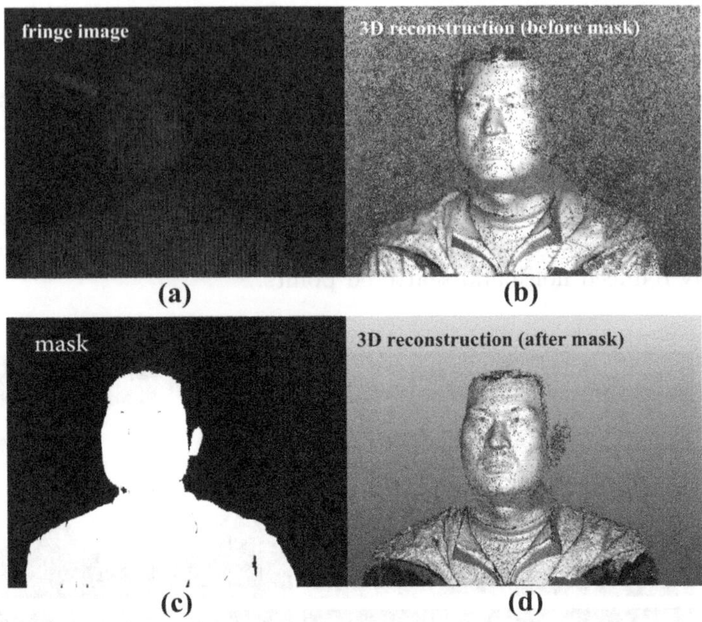

Fig. 9. Results on the near-infrared FPP system. (a) phase-shifting fringe images, (b) initial 3D reconstruction with defocus regions, (c) defocus mask generated by the proposed method, and (d) final 3D reconstruction after excluding the defocused regions with the mask.

6 Conclusion

To address the severe defocusing frequently observed in handheld FPP data, our study analyzes its causes and manifestations. A wrapped phase distribution-based method is proposed to detect and remove the defocus regions. By leveraging the consistency of wrapped phase differences, the method identifies blurred areas through a fixed threshold, eliminating defocus, low-reflectivity, and background regions. Unlike modulation-based thresholding, the fixed-parameter design enhances generalizability across different FPP systems. Experiments on both handheld and desktop FPP systems demonstrate the effectiveness of the proposed method.

References

1. Yuan, H., et al.: Superlarge depth range 3D measurement based on dual-focal optimization strategy. Opt. Express **33**(7), 16041–16051 (2025). https://doi.org/10.1364/OE.557383. PMID: 40219502
2. Tan, J., Niu, H., Su, W., He, Z.: Structured light 3D shape measurement for translucent media base on deep Bayesian inference. Opt. Laser Technol. **181**, 111758 (2025). https://doi.org/10.1016/j.optlastec.2024.111758
3. Wu, H., Cao, Y., Dai, Y., Qin, J.: Spatial–temporal 3-D directional binary coding method for fringe projection profilometry. IEEE Trans. Instrum. Meas. **74**, 1–11 (2025). https://doi.org/10.1109/TIM.2025.3565071
4. Hu, Y., et al.: Calibration and rectification of bi-telecentric lenses in Scheimpflug condition. Opt. Lasers Eng. **149**, 106793 (2022). https://doi.org/10.1016/j.optlaseng.2021.106793
5. Ai, J., Zhang, Q., Su, X.: Fast modulation measurement profilometry based on phase-shifting and modulation ratio. Opt. Express **33**, 21707–21718 (2025). https://doi.org/10.1364/OE.562438
6. Su, X.Y., von Bally, G., Vukicevic, D.: Phase-stepping grating profilometry: utilization of intensity modulation analysis in complex objects evaluation. Opt. Commun. **98**(1–3), 141–150 (1993)
7. Liu, X., Kofman, J.: High-frequency background modulation fringe patterns based on a fringe-wavelength geometry-constraint model for 3D surface-shape measurement. Opt. Express **25**(14), 16618–16628 (2017). https://doi.org/10.1364/OE.25.016618. PMID: 28789163
8. Yu, H., Zheng, D., Fu, J., Zhang, Y., Zuo, C., Han, J.: Deep learning-based fringe modulation-enhancing method for accurate fringe projection profilometry. Opt. Express **28**(15), 21692–21703 (2020). https://doi.org/10.1364/OE.398492. PMID: 32752442
9. Luo, X., Song, W., Bai, S., Li, Y., Zhao, Z.: Deep learning-enabled invalid-point removal for spatial phase unwrapping of 3D measurement. Opt. Laser Technol. **163**, 109340 (2023). https://doi.org/10.1016/j.optlastec.2023.109340
10. Gao, X., Song, W.: Weakly supervised phase unwrapping for single-camera fringe projection profilometry. Opt. Commun. **557**, 130308 (2024). https://doi.org/10.1016/j.optcom.2024.130308
11. Zhong, K., Lin, J., Gong, T., Zhang, X., Wang, N.: Hand-eye calibration method for a line structured light robot vision system based on a single planar constraint. Robot. Comput.-Integr. Manuf. **91**, 102825 (2025). https://doi.org/10.1016/j.rcim.2024.102825
12. Shen, Z., Ni, Y., Yang, Y.: Baseline-free structured light 3D imaging using a metasurface double-helix dot projector. Nanophotonics **14**(8), 1265–1272 (2025). https://doi.org/10.1515/nanoph-2024-0668. PMID: 40290276; PMCID: PMC12019951
13. Bai, S., Luo, X., Xiao, K., Tan, C., Song, W.: Deep absolute phase recovery from single-frequency phase map for handheld 3D measurement. Opt. Commun. **512**, 128008 (2022). https://doi.org/10.1016/j.optcom.2022.128008
14. Chen, S.: Intraoral 3-D measurement by means of group coding combined with consistent enhancement for fringe projection pattern. IEEE Trans. Instrum. Meas. **71**, 1–12 (2022). https://doi.org/10.1109/TIM.2022.3197782
15. Chen, S.: Calibration of intraoral 3-D measurement system with using consummated model combined with highly accurate data pairs. IEEE Trans. Instrum.

Meas. **72**, 1–13, Art no. 4507813 (2023). https://doi.org/10.1109/TIM.2023.3323007
16. Guo, Y., You, Z., Lv, K., Ren, K., Xiong, W.: Real-time high-accuracy 3D facial (micro) expression measurement based on pre-aligned micro-projection arrays. Opt. Express **33**, 11077–11096 (2025). https://doi.org/10.1364/OE.555406
17. Tan, C., Song, W.: Weakly supervised depth estimation for 3D imaging with single camera fringe projection profilometry. Sensors **24**(5), 1701 (2024)
18. Ren, J., Tan, C., Song, W.: Hybrid encoding fringe and simulation-to-real scene approach for accurate depth estimation in fringe projection profilometry. Opt. Express **33**(7), 14716–14736 (2025). https://doi.org/10.1364/OE.557221. PMID: 40219402
19. Xu, J., Zhang, S.: Status, challenges, and future perspectives of fringe projection profilometry. Opt. Lasers Eng. **135**, 106193 (2020)
20. Zhao, Z., Yang, H., Liu, P., Nie, H., Zhang, Z., Li, C.: Defocus blur detection via adaptive cross-level feature fusion and refinement. Vis. Comput. (2024). https://doi.org/10.1007/s00371-023-03229-7
21. Wang, X., et al.: MSU-Mamba: multi-scale defocus blur detection using cross-scale fusion and state space models. Preprint (2024). https://doi.org/10.21203/rs.3.rs-5719588/v1
22. Li, J., Xing, Z., Xiao, R., Tsung, F., Zhu, L.: DBD-Diff: defocus blur detection using semantic and texture correlation guided diffusion model. In: Proceedings of the 19th ACM SIGGRAPH International Conference on Virtual-Reality Continuum and Its Applications in Industry (VRCAI '24), Nanjing, Guangdong Province, China, article no. 16, 9 p. (2025). https://doi.org/10.1145/3703619.3706050
23. Rao, L., Daf: local blur analysis and phase error correction method for fringe projection profilometry systems. Appl. Opt. **57**(15), 4267–4276 (2018)
24. Nguyen, H., Wang, Y., Wang, Z.: Single-shot 3D shape reconstruction using structured light and deep convolutional neural networks. Sensors **20**(13), 3718 (2020)

Fuzzy Logic-Based Virtual Leading Path Planning for Autonomous Underwater Vehicles: An Evaluation Index Approach

Shibo Fan[1], Jie Jiao[2], and Qingchuan Zhang[3](✉)

[1] School of Automation, Wuxi University, Wuxi, Jiangsu Province, China
[2] Department of Economic History, The London School of Economics and Political Science, London, UK
[3] National Engineering Research Center for Agri-product Quality Traceability, Beijing Technology and Business University, Beijin, China
zhangqingchuan@btbu.edu.cn

Abstract. Autonomous underwater vehicles (AUVs) face significant challenges in dynamic navigation due to unknown obstacles and constrained environments. This work proposes a local path planning algorithm for AUVs, utilizing a forward-looking sonar detection strategy that divides the visual region into three sections and evaluates object pixels. To facilitate obstacle avoidance and goal-directed movement, a fuzzy inference system is implemented for the design of the AUV's coordinate controller. A virtual leading AUV is introduced to guide the real AUV along an online trajectory. Path length rate and path maintenance rate are defined as evaluation indices to ensure the real AUV follows the planned path. The stability of the closed-loop control system is analytically proven using the Lyapunov function. Numerical simulations demonstrate the performance of the control system in a constrained environment.

Keywords: Autonomous Underwater Vehicles (AUVs) · Fuzzy logic control · Virtual leader-follower strategy · Evaluation index

1 Introduction

Path planning involves guiding a vehicle along a designed path, which can be categorized into global and local planning based on the degree of environmental information utilized [1]. Global planning autonomously determines an optimal path using prior knowledge, including environment modeling and path search strategies [2]. In contrast, local planning dynamically generates a real-time, collision-free path by leveraging onboard sensors to detect the unknown underwater environment [3].

In [4], researchers propose coverage path planning methods for applications such as window cleaning, harvesting, and marine surveys. Fang and Stuart explore offline algorithms for pre-mission path planning, using an approximation of the generalized Voronoi diagram to calculate sub-area paths and connect them into a mission plan. To reduce computational costs for autonomous underwater vehicles (AUVs) following an

P. Li et al. (Eds.): CGI 2025, LNCS 16508, pp. 417–429, 2026.
https://doi.org/10.1007/978-3-032-22264-0_33

object, a framed quadtree map representation is proposed for path planning, replacing the regular grid; however, such methods still require pre-mapped environments and lack online adaptability [5]. The combined challenges of trajectory planning and track control for underactuated AUVs are addressed by referencing orientation and body-fixed velocities, with back-stepping control used to reduce tracking errors; however, these methods rely heavily on accurate dynamic models and often lack interpretability [6, 7]. Luo constructs a virtual robot for the follower, using Lyapunov and backstepping synthesis, and an approximation-based control technique to handle model uncertainties and unknown disturbances [8]. In [9], a 3D seabed path planning method for AUVs is discussed, categorized into three types, with optimal paths obtained using a genetic algorithm that incorporates problem-specific knowledge and a penalty function. Lapierre [10] addresses nonlinear path-following control for underactuated AUVs, emphasizing the need for precise AUV modeling to achieve ideal maneuverability. Roust path-following controllers using state and output feedback are developed for underactuated ships with the Serret-Frenet frame [11], but they typically require accurate model parameters and offline tuning to effectively handle disturbances and uncertainties. In contrast, our proposed framework is model-free, interpretable, and entirely driven by real-time sensor data. Without relying on global maps or precise hydrodynamic modeling, it enables adaptive decision-making in complex and partially known environments, making it more practical for deployment in uncertain underwater conditions.

This study presents a real-time, interpretable local path planning framework for AUVs in constrained environments, integrating a three-sector forward-looking sonar detection strategy with fuzzy logic-based motion control. Key innovations include: (1) A fuzzy inference controller that processes sonar-derived obstacle data and navigational objectives using prioritized rules, enabling real-time collision avoidance and subgoal tracking without relying on precise hydrodynamic models; (2) A virtual leader-follower architecture where a virtual AUV generates collision-free reference paths, enhanced by Lyapunov-stable tracking controllers to address finite-time convergence limitations; (3) Quantifiable performance metrics, including path length rate and maintenance rate, for systematic optimization of path-following accuracy. The framework's effectiveness is validated through simulations comparing virtual and physical AUV trajectories across various obstacle configurations. The subsequent sections provide details on the AUV dynamics model, sensor fusion strategy, controller design, and simulation-based validation, concluding with discussions on real-world applicability, potential 3D extensions, and graphical interpretability of the framework.

2 AUV Model and Detecting Strategy

The kinematic and dynamic models of the AUV, along with the detection strategy for the forward-looking sonar installed on the AUV, are proposed.

2.1 AUV Modeling

As shown in Fig. 1, both earth-fixed and body-fixed coordinate systems are defined to describe the AUV's motion model [12].

The origin of the body-fixed coordinates is located at the front of the AUV. The dynamics of the AUV can be described as follows.

$$M\dot{v} + C(\upsilon)\upsilon + D(\upsilon)\upsilon + g(\eta) = \tau \tag{1}$$

$$\dot{\eta} = J(\eta)v \tag{2}$$

where and are the generalized velocity and position of AUVs, respectively, $M = M_{RB} + M_{\mathrm{A}}$, is the inertia matrix and added mass matrix, $C(\upsilon) = C_{RB} + C_A$ is the coriolis matrix, $D(\upsilon)$ is the damping matrix, $g(\eta)$ is the vector of restoring forces owning to buoyancy and gravity, τ is the generalized force and moments of thrusters, $J(\eta^{\cdot})$ is the transformation matrix.

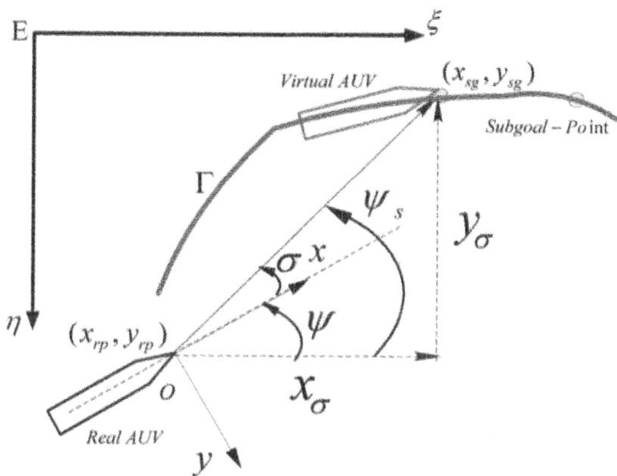

Fig. 1. Frames of coordinates reference and state variables of AUV path following.

2.2 Detecting Strategy of Forward-Looking Sonar

In this work, the proposed AUV is equipped with a forward-looking sonar to gather environmental information, considering the complexity of the seafloor and the uncertainty of underwater obstacles. The path planning problem for the AUV, moving on a horizontal plane at a constant depth, is addressed, and the detection model is established in 2D reference coordinates.

As illustrated in Fig. 2, the visual boundary, with radius R and opening angle γ, is divided into three equal segments from portside to starboard of the AUV: $\{L, M, R\}$. The detecting distance for each segment is discretely expressed as $d_i = \{d_L, d_M, d_R\}$, with the minimum value serving as the input to the fuzzy controller described in the next section. The detected obstacle information is represented as a data structure: $Info = \{x_i, y_i, d_i, \psi_i\}$, where x_i and y_i are the coordinates in the body-fixed reference system, d_i is the distance from the obstacle to the AUV, β is the orientation of obstacle relative to the heading of the AUV, and i is the obstacle number.

In our proposed detection strategy, the AUV gathers environmental information by analyzing the pixel color of nearby obstacles. In the developed program, this process is primarily carried out by invoking functions from the CAUV class.

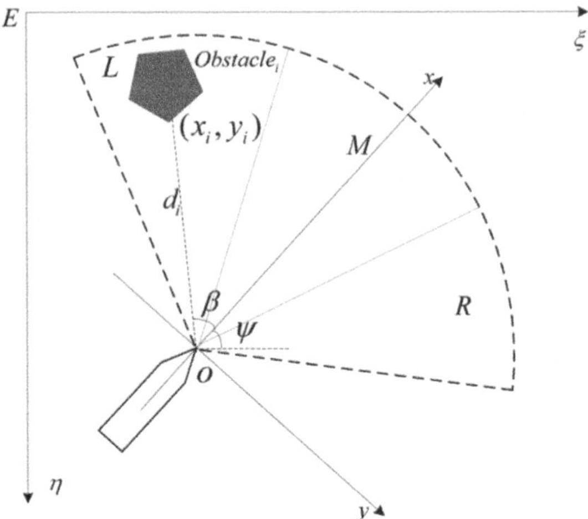

Fig. 2. Visual boundary segments scheme of forward-looking sonar.

3 Coordinate Controller Design

A coordinate controller with a fuzzy inference system has been designed for the AUV to address the heading control issue in path following.

3.1 Controller Design

The control system consists of two sub-controllers for path following: the obstacle avoidance controller and the subgoal tracking controller. The obstacle avoidance controller ensures the AUV avoids collisions, while the subgoal tracking controller directs the real AUV to follow the path defined by the virtual AUV. In the subgoal tracking controller, the real AUV tracks waypoints by adjusting the heading error. The "line-of-sight" guidance scheme is employed to guide the real AUV along the path Γ, which is planned by the virtual AUV in this paper. The relevant parameters of the line-of-sight guidance scheme are shown in Fig. 1. The block diagram of the proposed coordinate control system, incorporating the fuzzy inference system for AUV path following, is shown in Fig. 3.

The heading error sigma σ is defined as the angle between the subgoal point and the real AUV in earth-fixed coordinates, minus the heading of the AUV.

$$\sigma = \psi_s - \psi \tag{3}$$

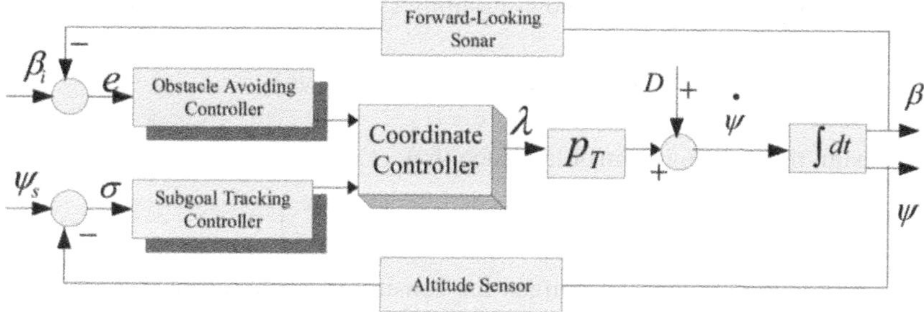

Fig. 3. Block diagram of coordinate control system.

where ψ is the real AUV heading in the body-fixed coordinates, ψ_s represents the angle between the real AUV heading and subgoal point.

$$\psi_s = \tan^{-1}\left[\frac{y_{rp} - y_{sg}}{x_{rp} - x_{sg}}\right] \quad 0 \le \psi_s \le 2\pi \tag{4}$$

where (x_{rp}, x_{sg}) and (y_{sg}, y_{sg}) represent the real AUV position and sub-goal position, respectively.

The objective of the control scheme is to reduce the heading error within a finite time interval. The feedback signal of the closed-loop control system is the average error over a cruising period, defined as follows:

$$overline\ \sigma = \frac{\int_{t_0}^{t_0+t} \sigma}{T} \tag{5}$$

where T is the beat-time, and t_0 is initial time in the period.

In the coordinate control system, the following equations are introduced:

$$\dot{\psi} = pT \times \lambda + D \tag{6}$$

where pT is the positive heading dynamics of AUVs, and λ is the transformation from offset of the body-spline to the heading velocity of AUVs when AUVs are in its turning motion, and it's a non-zero value, D represents unmodelled dynamics of the heading responses.

To achieve the control objective, we define s and its time derivative as following:

$$s = \left(\frac{d}{dt} + \lambda_\sigma\right)\overline{\sigma} = \frac{1}{T}\sigma + \frac{\lambda_\sigma}{T}\int_0^T \sigma\, dt \tag{7}$$

$$\dot{s} - \frac{1}{T}\dot{\sigma} + \frac{\lambda_\sigma}{T}\sigma \tag{8}$$

where λ_σ is a positive coeffcient of overline σ.

Consider the following candidate Lyapunov function, expressed as:

$$V = \frac{1}{2}s^2 \tag{9}$$

Taking the derivative of (11) and combining (5) with (10), we obtain:

$$\dot{V} = s\dot{s} = \frac{1}{T}s(\dot{\psi}_s - \dot{\psi} + \lambda_\sigma \sigma) \tag{10}$$

We design the heading control law such that:

$$\lambda = pT^{-1}(\dot{\psi}_s + \lambda_\sigma \sigma + s/k_\sigma) \tag{11}$$

where k_σ is positive, which determines the sensitivity of the error correction term by utilizing. It follows that

$$\dot{V} = \frac{1}{T}s\Big(\dot{\psi}_s - pTpT^{-1}(\dot{\psi}_s + \lambda_\sigma \sigma + s/k_\sigma) - D + \lambda_\sigma \sigma\Big) = \frac{-1}{T} \times \frac{S^2}{k_\sigma} - \frac{sD}{T} \tag{12}$$

Since heading responses of the AUV are always bounded, the unmodelled dynamics is also bounded; i.e. |D| < −D, −D is a positive constant, then we have:

$$\dot{V} \leq -\frac{1}{T} \cdot \frac{S^2}{k_\sigma} + \frac{1}{T}\overline{D}|s| \leq -\frac{1}{T}\left(\frac{|s|}{\sqrt{k_\sigma}} - \frac{\sqrt{k_\sigma D}}{2}\right)^2 + \frac{k_\sigma \overline{D}^2}{4T} \tag{13}$$

Accordingly, $\dot{V}$ remains negative by decreasing k_σ sufficiently and the system is stable in the Lyapunov analysis except when is small enough. To guarantee that the stability condition is always fulfilled, the AUV heading control system should be devised in order that a desired heading is considered being reached when falls into a small distance from the desired angle. From (15), it can be derived that the error function V obeys:

$$V \leq \frac{1}{2}\overline{D}|s|k_\sigma\left(1 - \exp\left(-\frac{2}{Tk_\sigma}t\right)\right) \tag{14}$$

where t denotes the time variable. This ensures the global Lyapunov stability of the closed-loop control system, and completes the proof.

3.2 Fuzzy Inference System

Over the past few decades, many researchers have explored fuzzy inference systems for marine applications [13, 14]. In the controller module shown in Fig. 4, fuzzy logic techniques are used to achieve subgoal navigation and obstacle avoidance in the motion controller, due to their simplicity and resemblance to human reasoning. The proposed fuzzy logic motion controller integrates both behaviors to enable real-time path following. Given the low speed of underwater movement, we focus solely on heading control for the AUV. The fuzzy logic controller uses four inputs—left, middle, and right sonar distances (dL, dM, dR) and heading error σ—each defined over the domain [0, 150] cm. The output, heading adjustment angle Δβ, is defined over [−30°, +30°]. All fuzzy variables adopt trapezoidal membership functions labeled with intuitive linguistic terms (e.g., Near, Far, Small Left, Large Right).

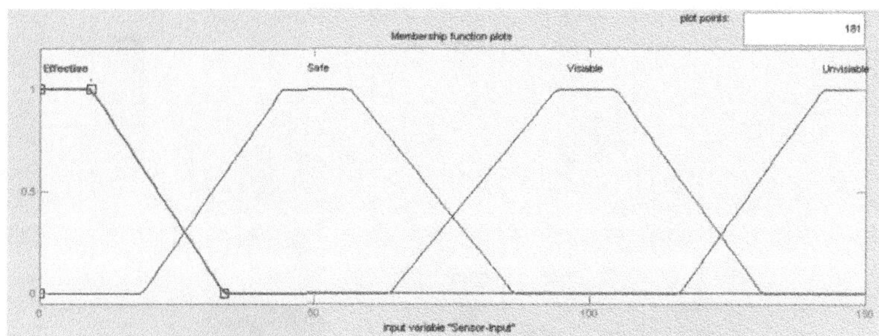

Fig. 4. Membership function of detecting distance for sonar.

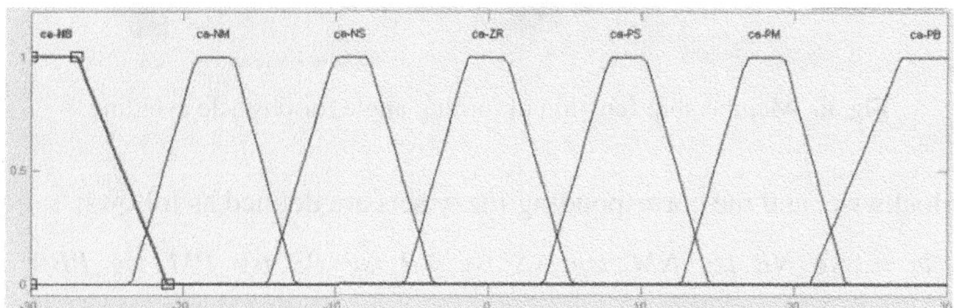

Fig. 5. Membership function of turning angle for obstacle avoiding.

For the obstacle avoiding controller, the input linguistic variables described in the previous Section are: $d_i = \{d_L, d_M, d_R\}$, the basic domain U_D is [0, 150], which are divided into four ranks and the corresponding fuzzy sets are set to be:

$$D_j = \{Danger, Safe; Visible, Unvisible\} \ (j = 0, 1, 2, 3) \tag{15}$$

The trapezoidal function is used as the membership function for the inputs, as shown in Fig. 5. We define the obstacle avoidance angle, $\Delta\beta$, as the output linguistic variable, with its domain U_β set to $[-\pi/6, \pi/6]$. Angle values are considered positive when the AUV turns counterclockwise, and the corresponding fuzzy sets are defined as follows:

$$\Phi_j = \{ca\_NB, ca\_NM, ca\_NS, ca\_ZR, ca\_PS, ca\_PM, ca\_PB\} \tag{16}$$

Based on the fuzzy inference rules, the relationship between detection distance and turning angle for the obstacle avoidance module is shown in Fig. 6. In this figure, X, Y, and Z represent the distances detected by the forward-looking sonar, while the color labels indicate the corresponding turning angle values.

For the subgoal tracking controller, the heading error has a basic domain of $[-\pi, \pi]$, with the fuzzy sets defined as follows:

$$\Theta_k = \{GNB, GNM, GNS, GZR, GPS, GPM, GPB\} \tag{17}$$

We define σ as the output linguistic variable for moving to subgoals, with its basic domain $U\sigma$ set to $[-\pi/6, \pi/6]$. Angle values are considered positive when the AUV turns

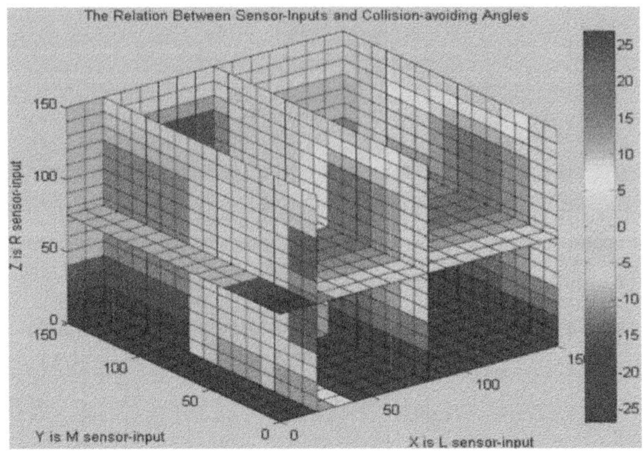

Fig. 6. Membership function of turning angle for obstacle avoiding.

counterclockwise, and the corresponding fuzzy sets are defined as follows:

$$\Psi_l = \{tsg\_NB, tsg\_NM, tsg\_NS, tsg\_ZR, tsg\_PS, tsg\_PM, tsg\_PB\} \quad (18)$$

The fuzzy rules and membership functions were initially constructed based on qualitative expert intuition and later refined via simulation in diverse obstacle scenarios. The stable sonar input and low-speed dynamics of the AUV ensure that the system is robust to small variations in membership parameters. This empirical tuning process enables effective and safe navigation without requiring precise hydrodynamic modeling.

A complete and consistent set of fuzzy rules based on the defined linguistic variables requires a total of 49 rules. To reduce this number, we prioritize obstacle avoidance over subgoal tracking, resulting in a reduction to 30 rules, significantly decreasing the total number of control rules. The generalized rules are expressed as follows: *{LSRS, LSRM, LSRB, LMRS, LMRM, LMRB, LBRS, LBRM, LBRB, RSLS, RSLM, RSLB, RMLS, RMLM, RMLB, RBLS, RBLM, RBLB, LSLM, LSLB, LMLS, LMLB, LBLS, LBLM, RSRM, RSRB, RMRS, RMRB, RBRS, RBRM}*.

The LSRS rule indicates a slight left turn to avoid obstacles and a slight right turn to track the subgoal. Other rules have similar interpretations. The AND-OR logic operations are calculated accordingly, and the final output values are computed using a weighted average method.

These abbreviated rule codes represent combinations of Mamdani-style fuzzy IF-THEN statements. For instance, "LSRS" corresponds to a rule such as: "If dL is Large and dM is Small and σ is Right, then $\Delta\beta$ is Small Right." All 30 rules follow a consistent structure, combining obstacle detection and subgoal convergence logic.

4 Evaluating Index

As shown in Fig. 7, a virtual AUV acts as a trajectory planner, generating subgoal waypoints for the real AUV to track in real-time. It normally moves in a straight line toward the next global subgoal, but when an obstacle is detected in its path using three-sector sonar segmentation (L, M, R), it performs angular sweeping: incrementally adjusting its heading until a collision-free direction is found. This local obstacle avoidance mimics human steering intuition with low curvature changes. To assess tracking effectiveness, we introduce two metrics—path length rate and path maintaining rate—as quantitative indicators. The real AUV follows the virtual AUV's planned path using a behavior arbitration mechanism. When obstacle distance drops below a threshold, obstacle avoidance is prioritized. Once the path clears, the system switches back to tracking the virtual AUV's subgoals. Replanning of virtual paths occurs if the virtual AUV encounters a deadlock (e.g., trapped region), using small randomized shifts to regenerate reachable subgoals.

The coordination between the real and virtual AUV is governed by a switching mechanism. When obstacles are detected in the central sector (dM below threshold), both AUVs shift into avoidance mode. The virtual AUV redefines the subgoal if repeated deviation fails to bypass the obstacle. The real AUV suspends tracking and waits or navigates to the next reachable subgoal. This arbitration mechanism ensures robustness even if the virtual leader fails or is blocked.

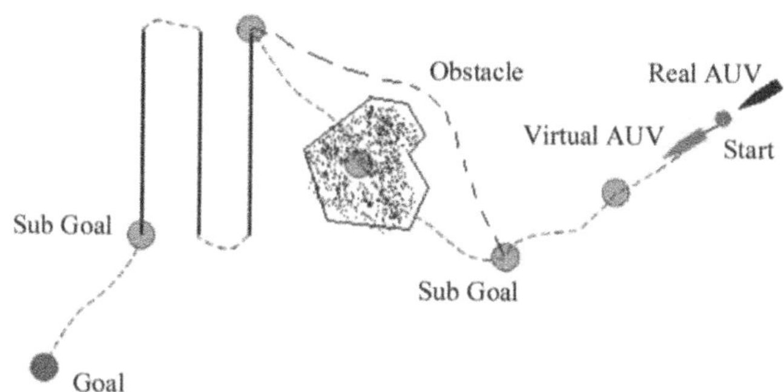

Fig. 7. Virtual leading scheme.

4.1 Path Length Rate

In the path-following scenario discussed, the real AUV may be affected by obstacles in the environment or experience mechanical malfunctions while operating underwater. As shown in Figure 10, the real AUV must abandon the subgoal trapped in the obstacle region and reselect a new path to avoid a collision.

Definition 1. Path length rate: The following formula is introduced as the rate expression:

$$R_{pd} = \frac{d_R}{d_P} \tag{19}$$

where d_R is the summation of all steps undergone by the real AUV, d_P is the Euclidean distance of the sub goals programmed by the virtual AUV.

Property 1. The index has the following property:

$$R_{pd} \ni [1, +\infty) \tag{20}$$

Proof. In the path-following scenario, due to obstacle interference, the real AUV will travel a greater distance than planned by the virtual AUV. Therefore, we have:

$$R_{pd} = d_R/d_P \geq 1 \tag{21}$$

This completes the proof. While moving towards the subgoals, the real AUV is guided to follow the subgoal planned in real time. However, the real AUV may deviate from the programmed goal position due to obstacles or boundary constraints. The smaller the deviation, the better the tracking performance.

4.2 Path Maintaining Rate

Definition 2. Path maintaining rate: The following formula is introduced as the rate expression:

$$R_{pm} = \frac{m_R}{m_P} \tag{22}$$

where is the number of sub goal reached by the real AUV, *mP* is the number planned by the virtual AUV.

Property 2. The index *Rpm* has the following property:

$$R_{pm} = m_R/m_P \leq 1 \tag{23}$$

5 Simulation Results

This section validates the designed controller by simulating it on both the real and virtual AUVs with the parameters shown in Table 1. Table 1 also presents the evaluation results for each path-following case. In the designed path-following case, the simulation environment is a two-dimensional area of 1000 × 1000 m.

Table 1. Simulating parameters of path planning.

	Start	Goal	d_P/d_R	R_{pd}	m_R/m_P	R_{pm}
Case 1	[176, 136]	[820, 532]	855/1005	1.175	58/61	0.951
Case 2	[174, 732]	[817, 187]	702.5/750	1.068	42/48	0.875
Case 3	[791, 740]	[157, 168]	765/855	1.118	43/55	0.782
Case 4	[837, 167]	[152, 726]	820/840	1.024	47/65	0.723

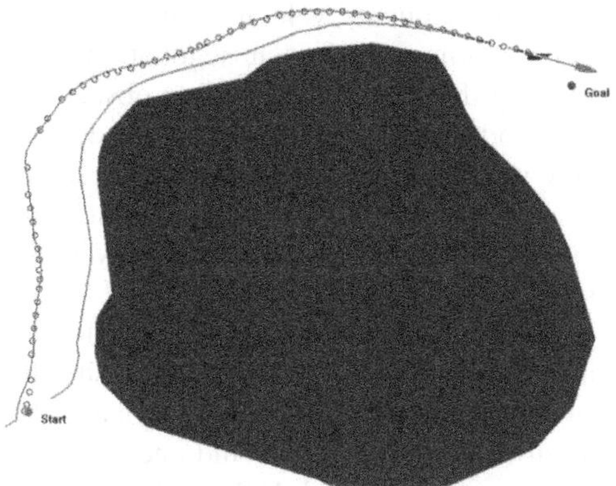

Fig. 8. AUV moving along wall.

The path-following and subgoal tracking on the horizontal plane are shown in Figs. 8 and 9. Despite the disturbances caused by environmental obstacles, our proposed controller successfully drives the real AUV to follow the subgoals programmed by the virtual AUV. When navigating along walls or through less structured environments, the AUV's trajectory remains smooth, and most subgoals are reached in real time. However, under more complex conditions, the real AUV may need to abandon some goal points for safety, resulting in a slightly rougher path.

Fig. 9. AUV moving through more complex condition.

6 Conclusion

In conclusion, this work proposes a local path planning algorithm for AUVs in a horizontal plane. A forward-looking sonar detection strategy is introduced, dividing the visual region into three parts and analyzing object pixels. A new coordinate controller with a fuzzy logic system is developed for waypoint tracking. Considering the low-speed maneuvering in structured environments, velocity dynamics are simplified in this study to focus on spatial decision-making and obstacle negotiation. A virtual AUV is designed to guide the real AUV along the trajectory, handling obstacle avoidance and subgoal tracking. Path length rate and path maintenance rate are defined as interpretable spatial metrics to assess how well the real AUV follows the reference trajectory, enabling visual trajectory evaluation and simulation analysis. Using a Lyapunov function, the stability of the closed-loop control system is analytically proven. Several simulation cases demonstrate the effectiveness of the proposed technique.

For future work, we will focus on the following operational scenarios [15]: (1) In real underwater conditions, dynamic obstacles, such as fish schooling or moving submarines, may exist alongside static obstacles. Hence, dynamic obstacle avoidance must be considered. (2) The virtual leading AUV could encounter deadlock or mechanical failure, preventing it from guiding the real AUV to the goal. To address this, we will develop an autonomous switching mechanism that reassigns or regenerates a virtual leader, ensuring uninterrupted navigation despite potential failure or blockage. (3) Further exploration will focus on extending the current planar framework to full 3D path planning by incorporating depth control and pitch dynamics, enabling maneuvering in complex underwater terrains and stratified flow conditions. (4) To enhance the generalizability and transferability of the fuzzy control system, future work will investigate the integration of learning-based or evolutionary optimization techniques for automatic fuzzy rule and parameter tuning across diverse AUV models and operating conditions.

References

1. Zhang, R., He, B., Wang, Y., Ma, W., Yang, S.: Recent advances in path planning for underwater gliders: a comprehensive review. Ocean Eng. **299**, 117166 (2024)
2. Gimenez, J., Amicarelli, A., Toibero, J.M., di Sciascio, F., Carelli, R.: Iterated conditional modes to solve simultaneous localization and mapping in markov random fields context. Int. J. Autom. Comput. **15**, 310–324 (2018)
3. Xi, M., et al.: A lightweight reinforcement-learning-based real-time path planning method for unmanned aerial vehicles. IEEE Internet Things J. **11**(12), 21061–21071 (2024)
4. Chen, D., Wu, J.: Control simulation and hydrodynamics analysis of a tethered underwater robot, Chuan Bo Li Xue/J Ship Mech 24, 170–178 (2020)
5. Ming, L.Y., Hai, H., Yang, X., Guocheng, Z., Jiyong, L., Hongde, Q.: Cognition-based hybrid path planning for autonomous underwater vehicle target following. Int. J. Adv. Robot. Syst. **16**, 1729881419857554 (2019)
6. Luo, J., Liu, C., Liu, F.: Piloting-following formation and obstacle avoidance control of multiple mobile robots. CAAI Trans. Intell. Syst. **12**(2), 1–10 (2017)
7. Fang, W., Fengyu, Z., Lei, Y., et al.: Global path planning algorithm of mobile robot based on electric potential field. Robot. **41**, 742–750 (2019)
8. Yin, J., Wang, Y., Lv, J., Ma, J.: Study on underwater simultaneous localization and mapping based on different sensors. In: Proceedings of 2021 IEEE 10th Data Driven Control and Learning Systems Conference (DDCLS), pp. 728–733. IEEE, Suzhou (2021)
9. Huan-xing, L., Yu-min, S., Yong-jie, P.: Numerical research on the kick-and-glide swimming of a tuna-like bio-mimetic underwater vehicle. J. Ship Mech. **24**, 145–153 (2020)
10. Yang, J., Ni, J., Xi, M., Wen, J., Li, Y.: Intelligent path planning of underwater robot based on reinforcement learning. IEEE Trans. Autom. Sci. Eng. **20**(3), 1983–1996 (2023)

11. Wang, P., Li, Q., Zhang, L., Xu, Y.: Complete coverage path planning of underwater wall - climbing cleaning robot. J. Phys. Conf. Ser. **2258**, 012072 (2022)
12. Xing, T., Wang, X., Ding, K., Ni, K., Zhou, Q.: Improved artificial potential field algorithm assisted by multisource data for AUV path planning. Sensors. **23**(15), 6680 (2023)
13. Han, S., Zhao, J., Li, X., Yu, J., Wang, S., Liu, Z.: Online path planning for AUV in dynamic oceanscenarios: a lightweight neural dynamics network approach. IEEE Trans. Intell. Veh. **9**(2), 3782–3795 (2024)
14. Markazi, A.H.D., et al.: Adaptive fuzzy sliding mode control of under-actuated nonlinear systems. Int. J. Autom. Comput. **15**(3), 364–376 (2018)
15. An, R., Guo, S., Zheng, L., et al.: Uncertain moving obstacles avoiding method in 3D arbitrary path planning for a spherical underwater robot. Robot. Auton. Syst. **151**, 104011 (2022)

Robust Bi-level Optimization for Monocular Human and Scene Reconstruction

Pengle Jin, Jun Tan, and Xinguo Liu(✉)

State Key Lab of CAD&CG, Zhejiang University, Hangzhou 310058, China
xgliu@cad.zju.edu.cn

Abstract. We propose a method integrating bi-level optimization and image inpainting for the simultaneous reconstruction of human bodies and their surrounding scenes from monocular RGB videos. Recognizing that human-scene interaction is a critical component in monocular reconstruction, our approach utilizes bi-level optimization to leverage contact information. To further enhance reconstruction robustness, particularly in occluded environments, we incorporate image inpainting techniques for recovering and unveiling hidden scene elements, thereby effectively addressing complex scenarios. Both qualitative and quantitative evaluations performed on the PROX and i3DB datasets demonstrate the significance of image inpainting within our framework and validate the effectiveness of the proposed bi-level optimization strategy.

Keywords: human motion estimation · 3d scene reconstruction · human scene interaction

1 Introduction

Human motion and human-environment interaction are fundamental components for numerous 3D applications, such as augmented reality (AR) and virtual reality (VR). Consequently, the reconstruction of humans and their surrounding environments has emerged as a key research area. Nevertheless, achieving precise reconstruction solely from complex monocular RGB video streams remains a significant challenge.

Considerable progress has been made in reconstructing humans and scenes from monocular video [21]. For example, PROX [6] optimizes human body poses within known 3D environments, MOVER [21] refines object poses guided by human motion trajectories, and HuMoR [18] leverages motion priors to achieve high-fidelity human motion reconstruction.

Despite these advancements, several limitations persist. PROX, for instance, necessitates a complete 3D scene model as prior information, restricting its applicability in diverse scenarios. MOVER depends on accurate human motion trajectories and can suffer from object loss or mask estimation errors in environments

P. Li et al. (Eds.): CGI 2025, LNCS 16508, pp. 430–442, 2026.
https://doi.org/10.1007/978-3-032-22264-0_34

with significant occlusion. Furthermore, HuMoR neglects the influence of the surrounding scene context, potentially compromising reconstruction accuracy.

Reconstructing human motion and scenes from monocular video without accurate prior information often requires iterative refinement of both human pose and environmental geometry. he simultaneous optimization of these elements introduces several challenges, such as the need to continuously track collision properties between humans and the environment, which is computationally intensive. Moreover, the interdependence between human motion and environmental parameters complicates parameter tuning. Occlusion is another common issue during reconstruction, significantly impacting the quality of both human and scene reconstructions, often resulting in object loss or incomplete mask generation.

To address the challenge of jointly optimizing human and scene parameters, we propose a bi-level optimization framework for holistic reconstruction. We formulate the reconstruction task as a bi-level problem: the lower level optimizes human motion and shape refinement, while the upper level optimizes the overall scene layouts. This formulation is motivated by the observation that accumulated human motion throughout a video sequence traces a trajectory that can be conceptualized as a static spatial structure, akin to a manifold, within the scene. The lower-level human optimization influences the upper-level scene optimization, which in turn globally constrains the solution space to improve overall reconstruction fidelity.

To handle occlusions robustly, we apply tailored strategies. For dynamic human occlusions, we exploit temporal information via motion priors to infer likely poses in unseen areas. For static scene occlusions, where motion priors are inapplicable, we employ image inpainting to complete missing regions. This completion improves segmentation mask accuracy and can uncover hidden scene structures, benefiting the overall optimization.

Experimentally, our bi-level approach, augmented with the described occlusion handling, demonstrates superior reconstruction performance for both humans and scenes compared to previous methods on the PROX [6] and i3DB [15] datasets. The resulting reconstructions also exhibit more physically plausible human-environment interactions. Our main contributions are:

1. A bi-level optimization framework for joint human-scene reconstruction from RGB video, leveraging mutual constraints for enhanced accuracy.
2. A hybrid occlusion handling method combining motion priors and image inpainting for improved robustness in both human and scene reconstruction.
3. Competitive performance demonstrated on the PROX and i3DB datasets, validating the effectiveness of our proposed methods.

2 Related Work

Understanding and modeling human-scene interaction (HSI) is crucial for accurate 3D reconstruction involving both humans and their surrounding environment. Reconstruction methods focusing on HSI can be categorized based on the specific types of interactions modeled, including foot-ground contact [23], hand-object interaction [4], full-body interaction with a single object [1,5,10]. HolisticMesh [19] propose a two-stage method for the concurrent reconstruction of 3D human body meshes and the static scene geometry. iMapper [15] leverages human-object interactions to infer a plausible scene layout and ensure physically consistent interactions. MOVER [21] employs human motion and contact information within the scene to impose constraints on the estimated layout and shape of surrounding objects. HSR [20] uses neural fields and global optimization to simultaneously reconstruct 3D representations of both static scenes and dynamic humans from monocular RGB videos. Our approach specifically addresses human-scene interaction reconstruction from monocular RGB videos, employing a bi-level optimization framework to mutually refine estimations of human motion and scene structure.

3 Method

As illustrated in Fig. 1, our method employs an optimization-based approach for single human and scene reconstruction from RGB video. For human motion estimation, we first utilize OpenPose [3] to detect 2D keypoint, subsequently applying a motion prior to initialize the human motion. This initialization minimizes E_{human} (described in Sect. 3.1) without considering Human-Scene Interaction (HSI) factors at this stage. We then use POSA [7] to estimate body contact vertices C_{body} and foot contact vertices C_{foot} on the human body surface. The foot contacts vertices are used to estimate ground information. Scene initialization leverages image inpainting (Sect. 3.2) and Total3D [16] (Sect. 3.2). Finally, we iteratively refine both the human motion (E_{human}, Sect. 3.1) and the scene (E_{scene}, Sect. 3.2) using a bi-level optimization approach.

3.1 Human Motion Estimation

In the human motion optimization section, the scene object parameters are kept fixed, while motion priors are applied to enhance robustness against occlusions. Additionally, Human-Scene Interaction (HSI) is utilized to optimize human motion for plausible interactions with the environment. Specifically, the loss function for this optimization consists of three components: a data term, a motion prior term, and an HSI term.

$$E_{\text{human}} = E_{\text{hdata}} + E_{\text{hprior}} + E_{\text{hhsi}} \tag{1}$$

For the human data term E_{hdata}, we utilize OpenPose [3] to extract 2D keypoints o from the input video and then apply the reprojection error:

$$E_{\text{hdata}} = \sum_{t} \sigma_t \rho(\Pi(p_t) - o_t) \tag{2}$$

where t represents the timesteps, ρ is the robust Geman-McClure function [2], Π is the pinhole projection, σ is the confidence weight, and p refers to the SMPL results.

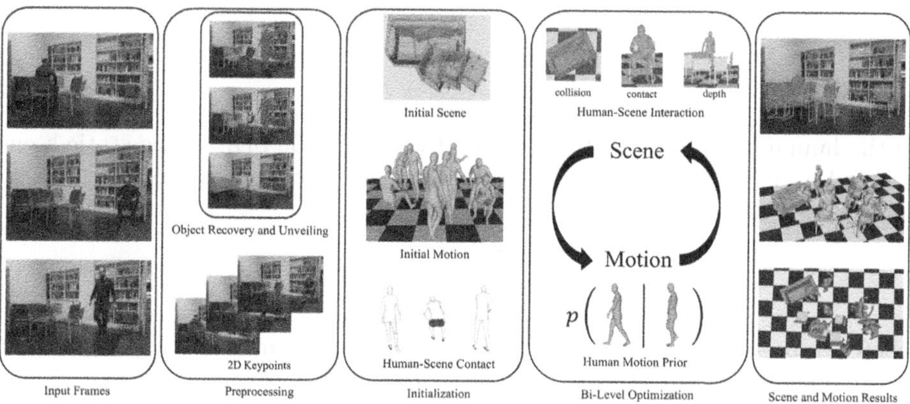

Fig. 1. Pipeline Overview. The pipeline begins by preprocessing the monocular RGB video input, employing inpainting to restore occluded areas and detect previously unnoticed objects. Next, initial parameters for the scene and human motion are established. Finally, the core bi-level optimization stage iteratively refines the scene representation and motion parameters using both HSI constraints and motion priors. This yields a physically plausible reconstruction of both the scene and the human motion.

For the motion prior E_{hprior}, we employ a transition-based model [18], where a sequence of motion states $s_{0:T}$ is given. Each s_i contains human motion information for the i-th frame, such as the root position, joint positions, and joint rotations. This model allows us to capture the probability of these states as

$$p(s_0, s_1, ..., s_T) = p(s_0) \prod p_\theta(s_t|s_{t-1}) \tag{3}$$

where $p_\theta(s_t|s_{t-1})$ denotes the transition from the current state to the next state. The likelihood of the transition $p_\theta(s_t|s_{t-1})$ is modeled by a conditional variational autoencoder (CVAE) as

$$p_\theta(s_t|s_{t-1}) = \int z_t p_\theta(z_t|s_{t-1}) p_\theta(s_t|z_t, s_{t-1}) \tag{4}$$

where z_t is a latent variable representing the transition between s_{t-1} and s_t. The conditional prior $p_\theta(z_t|s_{t-1})$ is parameterized as a Gaussian distribution with learned mean $\mu_\theta(s_{t-1})$ and covariance $\sigma_\theta(s_{t-1})$. We then incorporate this learned prior into the energy term applied to the latent variables z_t:

$$E_{\text{hprior}} = \sum_t \log \mathcal{N}(z_t; \mu_\theta(s_{t-1}), \sigma_\theta(s_{t-1})) \tag{5}$$

The other component is the HSI term, which aims to prevent intersections between human motion and the scene, while ensuring that the surfaces of both remain closely aligned during contact. In this term, we freeze the objects in the scene and optimize only the motion. The HSI loss consists of two subparts:

collision loss and contact loss.

$$E_{\text{hhsi}} = E_{\text{hcol}} + E_{\text{hcon}} \tag{6}$$

In the human collision loss E_{hcol}, we first compute the SDF of the static scene, denoted as V^s. Then, we penalize the human vertices that have a negative V^s value across all frames:

$$E_{\text{hcol}} = \sum_t \sum_v ||V^s_{f(v)}||_2^2, \quad V^s_{f(v)} < 0 \tag{7}$$

where v represents the vertices of SMPL, and f transforms the vertices into voxel coordinates in the global V^s volume.

The contact loss E_{hcon} aims to minimize the distance between the human body's contact surface and the scene, using body contact vertices C_{body} estimated by POSA. The contact loss E_{hcon} is defined as:

$$E_{\text{hcon}} = \sum_{v_c \in C_{\text{body}}} \rho(\min_{v_s \in V_s} ||v_c - v_s||) \tag{8}$$

where rho is a robust Geman-McClure error function, and V_s represents the scene vertices.

During initialization, the weight of the HSI loss is set to zero, meaning only the human motion in the video is considered. In the lower-level optimization phase of the bi-level process, we fix the object parameters in the environment and optimize E_{human} to generate physically plausible motion.

3.2 3D Scene Estimation

Object Recovery and Unveiling. Significant occlusions between objects, and between humans and objects in indoor scenes, can severely impact reconstruction results, even when frames with minimal overlap are selected to reduce human-scene occlusions. This issue leads to incorrect object masks and bounding boxes, which negatively influence loss calculation and cause object detection failures. To address this challenge, we propose an inpainting method to mitigate the effects of occlusion.

We select the image I from input frames with minimal occlusion between the human and objects, determined by the bounding box overlap between the human body and the objects. This image contains N objects O_i, each enclosed by a bounding box B_i. When calculating the mask for object O_j, multiple objects, S_j, may occlude O_j. S_j is determined by calculating the overlap of bounding boxes:

$$S_j = \left\{ k \mid k \in \{1, 2, \ldots, N\} \setminus \{j\}, \frac{B_j \cap B_k}{B_j} > \sigma \right\} \tag{9}$$

Based on our empirical observations, σ is set to 0.2, and $\cap$ is the overlap size of two bounding boxes. The indices in S_j are sorted in ascending order according to the size of their corresponding bounding boxes, B_k. We sequentially inpaint the objects in S_j using InpaintAnything [22] and subsequently employ PointRend [8] to generate the new mask for object O_j. We tested RePaint [12], HD-Painter [13], and InpaintAnything [22] and found that InpaintAnything is the most stable method for background inpainting. This process results in the inpainted object mask, improving the accuracy of mesh and pose reconstruction for the object.

Another challenge in object detection occurs when the algorithm fails to detect objects that are heavily occluded within a scene. Our approach to addressing this issue is both straightforward and effective. After completing the mask recovery process, we apply the inpainting algorithm to remove all previously detected objects, then re-examine the image for any newly detectable objects. Once these new objects are revealed, they are added to the object list.

Scene Initialization. To optimize a 3D scene, we first need to initialize the objects within the scene. After obtaining accurate bounding box and mask information as discussed in Sect. 3.2, we use Total3D [16] to generate an initial 3D scene. Since the mesh of the initial scene contains many holes, we employ Occupancy Networks [14] and Marching Cubes [11] to convert each mesh into a watertight form. Next, we optimize the translation $t \in \mathbb{R}^3$, scale $s \in \mathbb{R}^3$, and rotation $\theta \in [0, 2\pi)$ around the y-axis of each object in the scene by incorporating image information and interaction data provided by human motion.

Scene Optimization. In the scene optimization process, the human motion parameters remain fixed, while the objects within the scene are optimized based on RGB data and the spatial constraints imposed by the human motion. The loss function consists of four main components:

$$E_{\text{scene}} = E_{\text{sdata}} + E_{\text{sdepth}} + E_{\text{scon}} + E_{\text{scol}} \tag{10}$$

E_{sdata} is the object's data term, where we use the inpainted mask and bounding box as the target. We apply similar HSI terms E_{sdepth}, E_{scon}, and E_{scol} as those used in MOVER [21].

The term E_{sdepth} constrains the depth of objects in the scene by considering the accumulated depth of human motion:

$$\begin{aligned} E_{\text{sdepth}} = \sum_{i} \sum_{q \in \text{Sil}_i \cap M_i} \big[& \operatorname{ReLU}(D_i(q) - \hat{D}_{\text{far}}(q)) \\ & + \operatorname{ReLU}(\hat{D}_{\text{near}}(q) - D_i(q)) \big] \end{aligned} \tag{11}$$

where Sil_i represents the rendered silhouette of object i, M_i is its 2D inpainted mask, $D_i(q)$ denotes the depth of object i at pixel q, $\hat{D}_{\text{far}}(q)$ is the accumulated far-depth range map for human motion, and $\hat{D}_{\text{near}}(q)$ is the accumulated near-depth range map for human motion.

E_{scon} minimizes the distance between the contacting bodies and the parts of the objects in contact:

$$E_{\text{scon}} = \sum_{i} \sum_{v \in \mathcal{C}_{\text{body}}} \mathbb{I}(v, O_i) \big[\, \text{CD}(v^y, \mathcal{C}(O_i)^y) + \text{CD}(v^{\perp y}, \mathcal{C}(O_i)^{\perp y}) \big], \tag{12}$$

Here, $\mathbb{I}(v, O_i)$ is an indicator function that assigns objects to the body. CD denotes the one-directional Chamfer Distance, while $\mathcal{C}(O_i)^{\perp y}$ and $\mathcal{C}(O_i)^y$ represent the back and bottom seat contact parts of object i, respectively.

E_{scol} represents the collision loss in the scene. It also reduces computational costs by accumulating the human Signed Distance Function (SDF) across the entire video sequence as V^h:

$$E_{\text{scol}} = \sum_{i} \sum_{u} \| V^h_{f(u_i)} \|_2^2, \quad V^h_{f(u_i)} < 0. \tag{13}$$

where u_i represents the vertices of object i, and f transforms the vertices into voxel coordinates in the global volume V^h.

3.3 Bi-level Optimization

In our overall optimization design, we employ a bi-level optimization framework, where scene optimization constitutes the upper-level problem and human motion optimization represents the lower-level problem. To solve this, we alternately fix the lower-level parameters while optimizing the upper-level ones, and vice versa. By iteratively solving the scene and human motion optimization problems, we improve the reconstruction performance. Based on our practical experience, convergence is typically achieved after approximately five iterations. The bi-level optimization problem is formulated as follows:

$$\begin{aligned} \min_{\theta_S} \quad & E_{\text{scene}}(\theta_S, \theta_H^*) \\ \text{subject to} \quad & \theta_H^* = \arg\min_{\theta_H} E_{\text{human}}(\theta_S, \theta_H) \end{aligned} \tag{14}$$

where θ_S represents the scene parameters and θ_H represents the human motion parameters.

4 Experiments

4.1 Datasets

To evaluate the effectiveness of our proposed approach, we conduct evaluations on two datasets featuring human-scene interactions: PROX and i3DB.

PROX. The PROX dataset [6] captures human-scene interactions within various indoor environments using monocular RGB video recordings. As PROX lacks ground-truth human motion annotations and only provides 3D scanned scene data, we utilize it exclusively for evaluating 3D scene reconstruction.

i3DB. The i3DB dataset [15] is a human-scene interaction dataset containing RGB videos with medium to heavy occlusions. We use Scene05, Scene07, Scene10, Scene11, Scene13, and Scene14 from this dataset for the evaluation of human motion reconstruction.

4.2 Evaluation Metrics

We employ distinct evaluation metrics designed to assess both the quality of 3D scene reconstruction and human motion reconstruction achieved by our approach.

Metrics of 3D Scene Reconstruction. To quantify 3D scene reconstruction accuracy, we employ 3D Intersection over Union (IoU) and 2D IoU to evaluate consistency, and the point-to-surface distance (P2S) to assess the orientation and shape of reconstructed objects. To evaluate the physical plausibility of the interaction between the scene and the human body, we utilize non-collision (Non-Col) and contact scores (Cont). The non-collision score measures the proportion of vertices in the scene mesh that do not penetrate the human mesh, averaged across all video frames. The contact score calculates the proportion of video frames where contact between the human body and the scene is detected.

Metrics of Human Motion Reconstruction. To evaluate human motion reconstruction accuracy, we use the 3D positional error as the primary evaluation metric, incorporating both local and global joint errors. We report the 3D positional error separately for all joints (All), occluded joints (Occ), visible joints (Vis), and leg joints (Legs). To assess the physical plausibility of the interactions between the scene and the human body, we also utilize the non-collision and contact scores described previously.

4.3 Quantitative Results

Results of 3D Scene Reconstruction. Our 3D scene comparative analysis included two categories of baseline methods: (1) **regression-based methods:** Total3D [16]; (2) **optimization-based methods:** HolisticMesh [19] and MOVER [21].

As indicated in Table 1, our method achieved superior performance on the PROX dataset. This improvement is primarily attributed to the generation of relatively accurate 2D masks for occluded regions via our inpainting module; these masks serve as crucial inputs for optimization-based reconstruction.

Results of Human Motion Reconstruction. Our human motion comparative analysis also include two categories of baseline methods: (1) **regression-based methods:** VIBE [9]; (2) **optimization-based methods:** VPoser [17] and HuMoR [18].

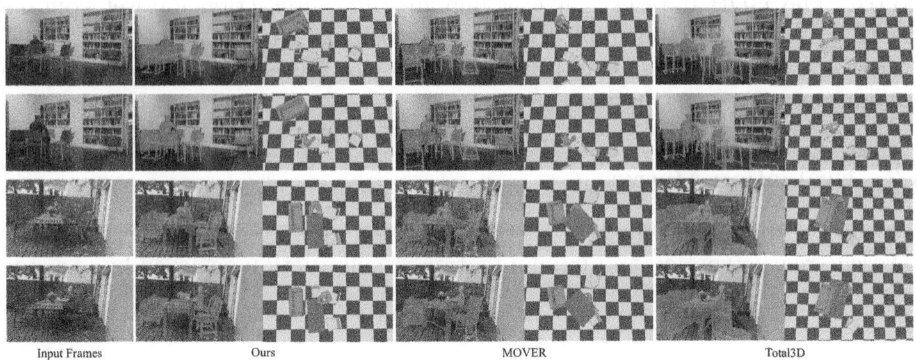

Fig. 2. Qualitative results. Compared to MOVER [21] and Total3D [16], we successfully reconstructed the occluded sofa (top) and chair (bottom) using inpainting. Furthermore, after applying bi-level optimization to both the scene and motion, the overall results were significantly improved.

Table 1. Quantitative results on the PROX dataset. The top half of the table presents a comparison with the baselines, while the bottom half displays the ablation study of our inpainting and bi-level optimization methods.

	Scene Recon			HSI	
Method	IoU_{3d} ↑	P2S ↓	IoU_{2d} ↑	Non-Col ↑	Cont ↑
HolisticMesh [19]	0.211	0.410	0.648	0.990	0.369
Total3D [16]	0.246	0.319	0.522	0.974	0.510
MOVER [21]	0.309	0.221	0.777	0.977	0.612
No Inpainting	0.331	0.218	0.793	**0.981**	0.588
No HSI	0.328	0.224	0.782	0.968	**0.681**
No Motion Prior	0.352	0.214	0.828	0.979	0.643
Ours	**0.365**	**0.212**	**0.853**	0.975	0.669

Table 2. Quantitative results on i3DB dataset. Joint errors are in *cm*. all, occ, vis and legs denote all, occluded, visible, and leg observations respectively. Non-Col and Cont denote Non-Collision and Contactness respectively.

	Global Joint Error ↓				Root-Align Joint Error ↓				HSI ↑	
Method	vis	occ	all	legs	vis	occ	all	legs	Non-Col	Cont
VIBE [9]	90.05	192.55	116.46	121.61	12.06	23.78	15.08	21.65	–	–
VPoser [17]	28.33	40.97	31.59	35.06	12.77	26.48	16.31	25.60	0.988	0.395
HuMoR [18]	26.00	34.36	28.15	31.26	12.02	21.70	14.51	20.74	0.990	**0.465**
Ours	**24.14**	**32.43**	**26.22**	**29.29**	**11.71**	**18.41**	**13.39**	**18.22**	**0.994**	0.409

As indicated in Table 2, our method demonstrate superior performance according to both local and global metrics for human motion accuracy. The explicit incorporation of the reconstructed scene mesh significantly improved motion estimation, particularly for poses involving close interaction with the environment, such as sitting and lying down, where scene constraints enhance realism and accuracy. By leveraging motion priors, our approach achieved more accurate keypoint localization and global position estimation compared to methods lacking such priors, like VPoser [17] and VIBE [9]. As shown in Fig. 3, HuMoR demonstrates more frequent instances of penetration into the scene. In contrast, our method, which incorporates the HSI loss, reduces the incidence of scene penetration, though this improvement results in a slight decline in the Cont metric.

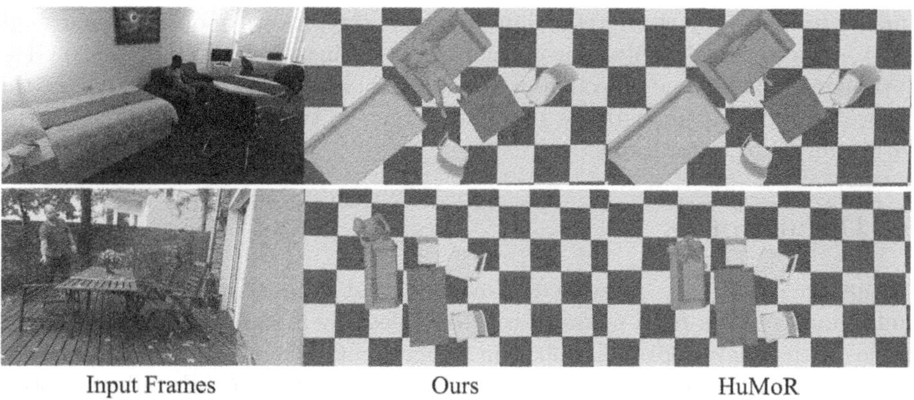

Fig. 3. HSI qualitative results. Compared to HuMoR [18], which does not account for HSI, our method produces results that are more plausible in terms of HSI.

4.4 Qualitative Results

Figures 2 and 3 qualitatively illustrate the effectiveness and robustness of our method. As shown in Fig. 2, our approach reliably detects objects even within heavily occluded environments. For partially occluded objects, our method retrieves their masks more accurately through inpainting, which subsequently enhances the reconstruction performance. Figure 3 provides a comparison with HuMoR [18], a method that does not explicitly enforce human-scene interaction (HSI) constraints in the same manner. This comparison demonstrates that our method yields more physically plausible results, reducing unrealistic scene penetration.

4.5 Ablation Study

To analyze the specific contributions of the inpainting module and the bi-level optimization strategy, we conducted several ablation studies, summarized in Table 1 (bottom half). Omitting the inpainting module leads to a significant decline across most scene reconstruction metrics. This is because the absence of inpainting results in less accurate object masks and shape estimations, negatively impacting the optimization process. Interestingly, the reduction in reconstructed scene geometry in this setting also leads to fewer potential collisions, paradoxically increasing the Non-Col score.

4.6 Computational Efficiency

Due to the iterative nature of the bi-level optimization, where both the scene and the human subject are refined in each step, the process of optimizing a single short video is considerably time-consuming. Running on an NVIDIA 4090 GPU, optimizing a 300-frame video clip takes approximately 46 min. Nevertheless, this bi-level approach demonstrates rapid convergence, typically reaching a solution within just 3 to 5 iterations.

5 Discussion

In summary, we have presented a method that reconstructs both 3D scenes and human motion from monocular RGB videos by integrating inpainting techniques with bi-level optimization. Our experiments demonstrate that employing inpainting to recover and reveal occluded scene parts significantly enhances scene reconstruction quality. Additionally, we show that the bi-level optimization effectively reconstructs both scene and motion simultaneously, and that leveraging the interaction between them through HSI constraints further improves overall reconstruction accuracy and physical plausibility.

However, our approach has several limitations. Firstly, the current experiments were conducted using datasets with static cameras and scenes; extending the approach to handle dynamic cameras and environments presents significant challenges. Secondly, in the extreme case where all frames in a video are occluded, it is difficult for our method to accurately reconstruct the scene. Lastly, low-quality video can negatively affect the alignment between the person and the scene and also makes image inpainting more challenging, thereby leading to a significant decrease in reconstruction accuracy.

References

1. Bhatnagar, B.L., Xie, X., Petrov, I.A., Sminchisescu, C., Theobalt, C., Pons-Moll, G.: BEHAVE: dataset and method for tracking human object interactions. In: 2022 IEEE/CVF Conference on Computer Vision and Pattern Recognition (CVPR), pp. 15914–15925. IEEE, New Orleans (Jun 2022). https://doi.org/10.1109/CVPR52688.2022.01547

2. Bogo, F., Kanazawa, A., Lassner, C., Gehler, P., Romero, J., Black, M.J.: Keep It SMPL: automatic estimation of 3d human pose and shape from a single image. In: Leibe, B., Matas, J., Sebe, N., Welling, M. (eds.) ECCV 2016. LNCS, vol. 9909, pp. 561–578. Springer, Cham (2016). https://doi.org/10.1007/978-3-319-46454-1_34
3. Cao, Z., Hidalgo, G., Simon, T., Wei, S.E., Sheikh, Y.: OpenPose: realtime multi-person 2d pose estimation using part affinity fields. IEEE Trans. Pattern Anal. Mach. Intell. **43**(1), 172–186 (2021). https://doi.org/10.1109/TPAMI.2019.2929257
4. Chao, Y.W., et al.: DexYCB: a benchmark for capturing hand grasping of objects. In: 2021 IEEE/CVF Conference on Computer Vision and Pattern Recognition (CVPR), pp. 9040–9049. IEEE, Nashville (Jun 2021). https://doi.org/10.1109/CVPR46437.2021.00893
5. Diller, C., Dai, A.: Cg-hoi: contact-guided 3d human-object interaction generation. In: Proceedings of the IEEE/CVF Conference on Computer Vision and Pattern Recognition, pp. 19888–19901 (2024)
6. Hassan, M., Choutas, V., Tzionas, D., Black, M.J.: Resolving 3D human pose ambiguities with 3D scene constraints. In: Proceedings of the IEEE/CVF International Conference on Computer Vision, pp. 2282–2292 (2019)
7. Hassan, M., Ghosh, P., Tesch, J., Tzionas, D., Black, M.J.: Populating 3D scenes by learning human-scene interaction. In: 2021 IEEE/CVF Conference on Computer Vision and Pattern Recognition (CVPR), pp. 14703–14713. IEEE, Nashville (Jun 2021). https://doi.org/10.1109/CVPR46437.2021.01447
8. Kirillov, A., Wu, Y., He, K., Girshick, R.: PointRend: image segmentation as rendering. In: 2020 IEEE/CVF Conference on Computer Vision and Pattern Recognition (CVPR), pp. 9796–9805. IEEE, Seattle (Jun 2020). https://doi.org/10.1109/CVPR42600.2020.00982
9. Kocabas, M., Athanasiou, N., Black, M.J.: Vibe: video inference for human body pose and shape estimation. in: proceedings of the ieee/cvf conference on computer Vision and Pattern Recognition, pp. 5253–5263 (2020)
10. Li, Z., Sedlar, J., Carpentier, J., Laptev, I., Mansard, N., Sivic, J.: Estimating 3D motion and forces of person-object interactions from monocular video. In: 2019 IEEE/CVF Conference on Computer Vision and Pattern Recognition (CVPR), pp. 8632–8641. IEEE, Long Beach, CA, USA (Jun 2019). https://doi.org/10.1109/CVPR.2019.00884
11. Lorensen, W.E., Cline, H.E.: Marching cubes: a high resolution 3D surface construction algorithm. In: Seminal Graphics, pp. 347–353. ACM, New York (Jul 1998). https://doi.org/10.1145/280811.281026
12. Lugmayr, A., Danelljan, M., Romero, A., Yu, F., Timofte, R., Van Gool, L.: Repaint: inpainting using denoising diffusion probabilistic models. In: Proceedings of the IEEE/CVF Conference on Computer Vision and Pattern Recognition, pp. 11461–11471. (2022)
13. Manukyan, H., Sargsyan, A., Atanyan, B., Wang, Z., Navasardyan, S., Shi, H.: Hd-painter: high-resolution and prompt-faithful text-guided image inpainting with diffusion models, arXiv preprint arXiv:2312.14091 (2023)
14. Mescheder, L., Oechsle, M., Niemeyer, M., Nowozin, S., Geiger, A.: Occupancy networks: learning 3d reconstruction in function space. In: 2019 IEEE/CVF Conference on Computer Vision and Pattern Recognition (CVPR), pp. 4455–4465. IEEE, Long Beac (Jun 2019). https://doi.org/10.1109/CVPR.2019.00459
15. Monszpart, A., Guerrero, P., Ceylan, D., Yumer, E., Mitra, N.J.: iMapper: interaction-guided scene mapping from monocular videos. ACM Trans. Graph. **38**(4), 1–15 (2019). https://doi.org/10.1145/3306346.3322961

16. Nie, Y., Han, X., Guo, S., Zheng, Y., Chang, J., Zhang, J.J.: Total3DUnderstanding: joint layout, object pose and mesh reconstruction for indoor scenes from a single image. In: 2020 IEEE/CVF Conference on Computer Vision and Pattern Recognition (CVPR), pp. 52–61. IEEE, Seattle, WA, USA (Jun 2020). https://doi.org/10.1109/CVPR42600.2020.00013
17. Pavlakos, G., Choutas, V., Ghorbani, N., Bolkart, T., Osman, A.A., Tzionas, D., Black, M.J.: Expressive body capture: 3d hands, face, and body from a single image. In: 2019 IEEE/CVF Conference on Computer Vision and Pattern Recognition (CVPR), pp. 10967–10977. IEEE, Long Beach (Jun 2019). https://doi.org/10.1109/CVPR.2019.01123
18. Rempe, D., Birdal, T., Hertzmann, A., Yang, J., Sridhar, S., Guibas, L.J.: Humor: 3d human motion model for robust pose estimation. In: Proceedings of the IEEE/CVF International Conference on Computer Vision, pp. 11488–11499 (2021)
19. Weng, Z., Yeung, S.: Holistic 3d human and scene mesh estimation from single view images. In: 2021 IEEE/CVF Conference on Computer Vision and Pattern Recognition (CVPR), pp. 334–343. IEEE, Nashville, TN, USA (Jun 2021). https://doi.org/10.1109/CVPR46437.2021.00040
20. Xue, L., et al.: HSR: holistic 3D human-scene reconstruction from monocular videos. In: Leonardis, A., Ricci, E., Roth, S., Russakovsky, O., Sattler, T., Varol, G. (eds.) ECCV 2024, vol. 15130, pp. 429–448. Springer Nature Switzerland, Cham (2025). https://doi.org/10.1007/978-3-031-73220-1_25
21. Yi, H., et al.: Human-aware object placement for visual environment reconstruction. In: Proceedings of the IEEE/CVF Conference on Computer Vision and Pattern Recognition, pp. 3959–3970 (2022)
22. Yu, T., et al.: Inpaint Anything: Segment Anything Meets Image Inpainting (Apr 2023)
23. Yuan, Y., Wei, S.E., Simon, T., Kitani, K., Saragih, J.: Simpoe: simulated character control for 3d human pose estimation. In: Proceedings of the IEEE/CVF Conference on Computer Vision and Pattern Recognition, pp. 7159–7169 (2021)

Methodology and Results of MIC-OPCC: Multi-Indexed Convolution Model for Octree Point Cloud Compression

Gerald Baulig[1] and Jiun-In Guo[2](✉)

[1] Collage of Electrical and Computer Engineering, Hsinchu, Taiwan
gerald.baulig@nycu.edu.tw
[2] Institute of Electronics, National Yang Ming Chiao Tung University, Hsinchu, Taiwan R.O.C.
jiguo@nycu.edu.tw

Abstract. For point cloud compression, capturing sufficient spatial context is crucial for accurately modeling the point cloud distribution. However, voxel-based methods tend to lose effectiveness when dealing with sparse point clouds of higher precision, as the context they gather becomes less comprehensive. This study introduces an octree-based point cloud compression method that utilizes an entropy model powered by deep learning to estimate probabilities, which are then used to guide an Arithmetic Range Coder in reducing the bit rate of the serialized octree code. Our proposed model extracts local features using lightweight 1D convolution applied in varied ordering and analyzes causal relationships by optimizing the cross-entropy. This approach efficiently replaces the voxel-convolution techniques and attention models used in previous works, providing significant improvements in both time and memory consumption. The effectiveness of our model is demonstrated on three datasets, where it outperforms recent deep learning-based compression models in this field. This project can be found at https://github.com/bugerry87/mic-opcc.

Keywords: Data Compression · Point Cloud · LiDAR · Autonomous Driving · Robotic · Virtual Reality

1 Introduction

Point clouds are a format for representing 3D scans of objects and scenes before they are processed into formats like 3D meshes, height maps, or HD-Maps [11]. With rapid advances in sensor technology, the use of point clouds has expanded into various fields, including autonomous driving, remote sensing, and augmented and virtual reality. However, these advancements have also led to a significant increase in both the volume and acquisition rate of point cloud data, creating substantial challenges for data transmission and storage. For example, the SemanticKITTI [4] dataset, with a capture rate of only 10 frames per second,

P. Li et al. (Eds.): CGI 2025, LNCS 16508, pp. 443–454, 2026.
https://doi.org/10.1007/978-3-032-22264-0_35

would require a bandwidth of approximately 134 Mbit/s in its uncompressed form. This growing demand for efficient handling of point cloud data has driven extensive research into point cloud compression techniques.

A thoughtful selection of state-of-the-art compression models is further discussed in Sect. 1.1. After a brief course on the background of point cloud compression in Sect. 1.2, we propose our fast and lightweight multi-indexed 1D convolution model (see Fig. 1) for octree-based point cloud compression in Sect. 2. Our model estimates the probabilities of occupancy symbols using local features, including binarized octants and occupancy symbols from ancestor and sibling nodes. Furthermore, we use a stride batch sampling method that mimics an autoregressive approach, reducing input bandwidth while maintaining computational efficiency. In Sect. 3 we outline the experimental setup, including the model configuration and training process. Finally, Sect. 4 presents an evaluation of our results compared to related models, followed by a conclusion.

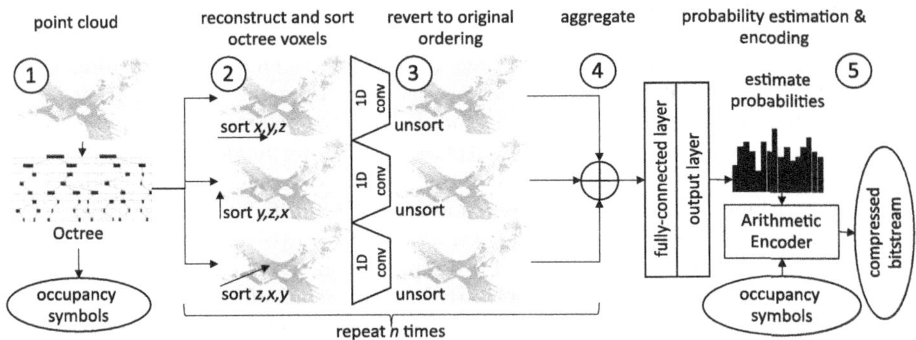

Fig. 1. Overview of our proposed method. We (1) reconstruct voxels from an octree and organize them into three input vectors, each sorted along another major axis (2). After applying 1D-convolution, we revert the outputs to original order (3) and aggregate them for further processing (4-5). This approach generates spatial context by folding the hidden features of nearest neighbors on each axis. Repeating this process expands the receptive field, enabling to capture broader spatial dependencies.

1.1 Related Work

Point cloud compression methods often face challenges due to the irregular structure of point clouds, leading most approaches to first convert the data into more regular structures. These methods then estimate occupancy probabilities by building context models, achieving compression through entropy encoding.

Conventional Methods, such as G-PCC [1] and Draco [9], convert point clouds into KD-Trees before applying compression and utilize the occupancy of compressed nodes to build context. Both methods are limited by heuristic context models that rely on a small number of neighboring nodes, which constrains their overall performance. Therefore, recent approaches have shifted towards entropy models supported by deep neural networks to automate the extraction of contextual information, moving away from heuristic-based methods.

Voxel-Based Entropy Models utilize 3D convolutional networks, where point clouds are represented as a grid of occupancy flags in $n \times n \times n$ space. Due to its complexity $O(n^3)$, fully voxelized point clouds at high resolution often exceed the hardware capabilities. Inspired by PixelCNN [18], Nguyen *et al.* introduced VoxelDNN [16], which uses a partitioning method to break down point clouds into smaller 64^3 voxel grids and employs masked 3D convolution in a fully-autoregressive manner to predict probabilities of voxel occupancy. With SparsePCGC, Wang, J. *et al.* [24] enables voxel coding beyond 12-bit precision, using sparse 3D convolution [21] paired with an 8-stage autoregressive model.

Octree-Based Entropy Models decompose point clouds into a tree structure, while extracting and processing crafted features for each node of the tree. OctSqueeze [10] was a pioneering effort in this area, which employed a simple Multi-Layer Perceptron (MLP) to process individual tree nodes and their ancestor nodes. Unlike voxel-based methods, OctSqueeze lacked a neighborhood search, which limited its effectiveness. More recent methods like OctAttention [8] and ECM-OPCC [12] have used pure octree structures enhanced with attention mechanisms, such as transformers. These models benefit from converting octrees into deterministic sequences, such as those generated through breadth-first traversal, while transformers excel in analyzing autoregressive sequences, as demonstrated in the latest large language models [23].

Although VoxelDNN and OctAttention achieve high compression performance, their decoding times are up to 900 times longer compared to conventional methods like G-PCC, as they process only one point at a time. To address this issue, next generation models such as MSVoxelDNN [17] and ECM-OPCC reduce decoding time by relaxing the fully-autoregressive context, allowing greater parallel processing at the expense of some compression efficiency, particularly in MSVoxelDNN. ECM-OPCC, on the other hand, has successfully outperformed its predecessor OctAttention by aggregating more information from ancestor nodes and utilizing masked pre-training techniques. However, despite its improvements, ECM-OPCC still reports a decoding time of 19.5 s per point cloud, near the hardware limits of a 40GB GPU. This highlights the ongoing challenge of balancing compression performance and computational efficiency.

1.2 Background

Our method builds on the same foundational strategy as previous work, using Shannon's theorem [20] to determine the entropy h of a symbol s as follows:

$$h(s) = -\log_2 p(s) \tag{1}$$

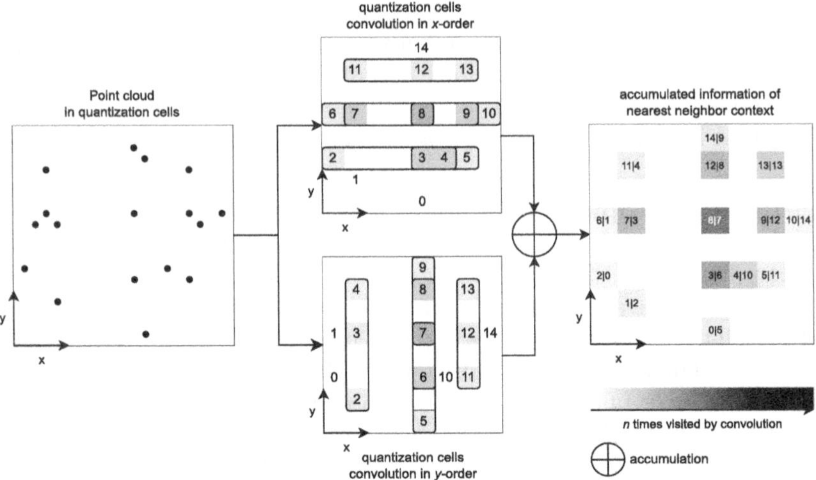

Fig. 2. Demonstration of how the receptive field increases in spatial context by applying 1D-convolution with varied input order and a window-size of 3 on. In this 2D toy example we focus on voxel 8|7 after two convolutions. The gray-scale illustrates the density of information gathered from neighbors. The output of each convolution can be accumulated by e.g sum, product or concatenation. (Color figure online)

This equation defines the entropy h as the theoretically required number of bits to represent a symbol s, where the probability $p(s)$ falls within the range $0 < p(s) < 1$. During decoding, however, the high-dimensional probability function $p(s)$ involves uncertainties that can only be approximated using stochastic, heuristic, or empirical models. We express this approximation as follows:

$$q(\mathbf{x}) = \hat{\mathbf{y}} \tag{2}$$

where $\mathbf{y}$ is the one-hot encoded vector representing the ground truth of sample s, and $\hat{\mathbf{y}}$ is the estimated probability distribution generated from context $\mathbf{x}$. Our goal is to enhance the model q by finding a more comprehensive set of context information $\mathbf{x}$, while still maintaining computational efficiency. With an empirical model $q_\theta(\mathbf{x})$, such as one driven by deep learning, we aim to optimize the parameters in θ by minimizing the cross-entropy:

$$H(y, x) = -\sum_{i=1}^{n} y_i \log Q_\theta(x_i), \tag{3}$$

where $H(y, x)$ quantifies the difference between the true distribution $\mathbf{y}$ and the predicted distribution $Q_\theta(x_i)$. Then, an Arithmetic Encoder [25] can transform the symbol s into a lower bound bit-representation. The more accurately $Q_\theta(x_i) = \hat{\mathbf{y}}_i$ estimates the true distribution, the more efficient the compression achieved by the encoder.

Arithmetic Coder (AC), or more specifically a Range Coder [14], is a form of entropy encoding widely used in lossless data compression. It operates by representing a sequence of symbols as a single range between 0 and N. This range gets partitioned according to the probability estimation of the entropy model for the current symbol, while the numeric representation of this symbol selects one partition of this range. This process repeats recursively for the selected range partition for each symbol. At each step, the algorithm emits the most significant bits that differentiate the current partition, leading to a lower bit-representation if the prediction is accurate. If the partition underflows a given quantization level, the algorithm signals an offset to the current range, so it can handle sequences of theoretically infinite length.

Octrees provide an efficient way to organize unstructured and unsorted data by applying a specific ordering, whether through breadth-first or depth-first traversal, along with quantization that depends on the depth of the tree structure [15]. The quantized point cloud Q is recursively partitioned based on the most significant 3-bit octant of the current layer t until a defined quantization level L is reached. During this process, each group of octants raises a bit on the related occupancy symbol s. An octree traversal in breadth-first order, denoted as $X = \{\mathbf{x}_0 = (s_0, \ldots, s_j), \ldots, \mathbf{x}_L\}$, typically results in a much lower entropy per symbol s compared to representing a point $\mathbf{p} = (x, y, z)$ from a raw point cloud P.

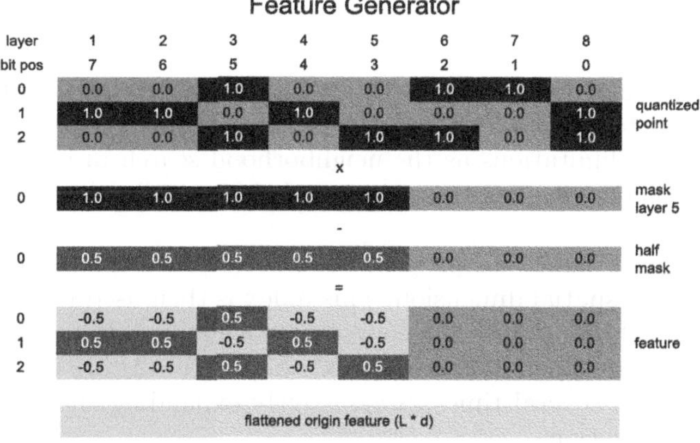

Fig. 3. First, the quantized point is converted into a vector of floating point values, one for each bit. Then, we mask and middle all values for the current compression layer. Finally, we flatten the feature vector to $L \times d$ for each input point, where in this example $L = 8$ is the depth of the tree and $d = 3$ the dimension of the point cloud.

2 Methodology

Building on the foundations established in the previous section, the next step is to design a robust entropy model capable of accurately estimating probability distributions for occupancy symbols. While Fig. 1 provides a high-level overview of our proposed architecture, the following sections offer a detailed description of each individual component.

2.1 Feature Modeling

Modeling a comprehensive context $\mathbf{x}$ for $Q_\theta(x_i) = \hat{\mathbf{y}}_i$ is essential to achieve efficient compression, prompting the search for the most effective feature extraction methods. Previous approaches, such as OctSqueeze [10] and MuSCLE [5], used the relative positions of each voxel center in the octree represented as real numbers $\mathrm{p} = (x, y, z) \in \mathbb{R}$.

However, in recent works [8,12,24], real position values have been found less effective for spatial context analysis. Instead, binary features such as voxels, occupancy symbols, and 3-bit octants have been shown to provide significantly better results.

In our approach, we employ a sequence of binarized octants and occupancy symbols for each voxel, extending from the root down to the fixed precision level L (see Fig. 3). To prevent data leakage during training that is not available during decoding, we mask all octants beyond the current step $> t$ to 0.

2.2 Indexed Convolution

OctAttention [8] and ECM-OPCC [12] utilize the native breadth-first traversal order of octrees to sequentially process input through transformers. However, this approach has limitations as the neighborhood search in breadth-first order is not always reliable, leading to scenarios where spatially close voxels are never directly compared.

To address this issue, we propose to generate an index using an arg-sort operation for each spatial dimension. This index is then used to reorder the data before each convolution. Once the convolution is applied, the output is restored to its original order using an inverse index, and the results are concatenated. We repeat this process several times, progressively expanding the spatial receptive field with each iteration.

Our indexed convolution can be understood as a fast search of K-nearest-neighbor along fixed axes, effectively merging the closest lower and higher voxels in the current order as demonstrated in Fig. 2. Unlike previous methods, which fill empty voxels with zeros within a fixed window size, our model's receptive field is always populated with existing voxels only. As a result, it handles sparse regions more effectively by dynamically expanding the spatial receptive field as needed.

2.3 Model Splitting

Each octree layer has its own distinct entropy and probability distribution. The shallowest layers, starting from the root, generally have the lowest entropy, as they mostly consist of fully occupied symbols. The middle layers exhibit the highest entropy, since they include a diverse range of all possible symbols. In contrast, the deepest layers, despite their high spatial resolution, tend to have lower entropy because of their sparse occupancy.

Ideally, to effectively capture these differences, each layer should be represented by a dedicated sub-model with its own convolutional and dense layer weights. However, to manage the overall model size and memory usage, we limit the number of sub-models to a maximum of three. This approach allows us to optimize performance for each section of the octree while maintaining a compact and efficient model architecture.

2.4 Input Striding

To further reduce the memory footprint of our model, we employ a stride mini-batch method. This technique processes input data in staggered segments by sampling every n-th element with a rolling offset. It effectively mimics autoregressive behavior, allowing ground truth from earlier batches to inform later ones. This approach lowers memory usage, making it well-suited for dense point clouds.

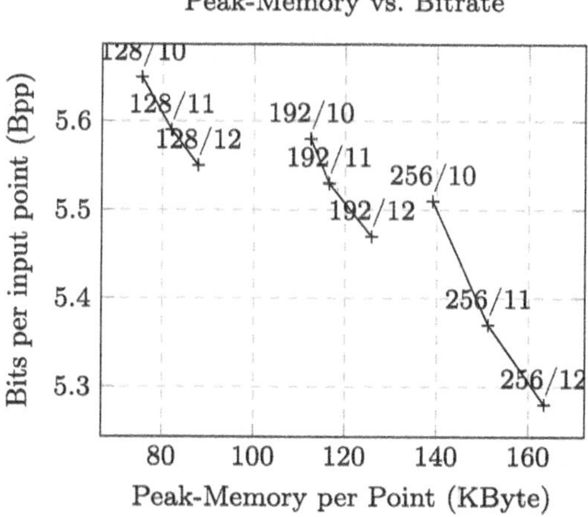

Fig. 4. Results of variant test models using different configuration of hyperparameters [kernels/convolution]. Larger models achieve better compression but require more memory per point.

Table 1. Comparison of output performance using an overall single model or 3 inner sub-models and on mini-batch methods using cropping or striding.

	Single Model	3 Sub-Models	Cropping	Striding
Accuracy	12%	13%	12%	13%
Bits-per-Point (Bpp)	4.85	4.81	4.86	4.81
Memory-per-Point (KB)	153.9	158.6	–	–
Trainable Parameters	6,009,088	14,488,320	–	–

3 Experiments

For a fair comparison, we strictly align our test conditions with previous work [8, 12]. Our model is implemented in TensorFlow, using a TensorFlow-based Range Coder implementation [3]. All experiments are conducted on a system with a single NVIDIA GeForce RTX 3090 GPU and 24 GB memory. We use the same training data and test splits. For lossy compression, we use the LiDAR data from SemanticKITTI [4] and for lossless compression a combination of 3D-scanned people from MPEG's 8iVFBv2 [19] and MVUB [6].

3.1 Evaluation Metrics

We aim for a low bits-per-point ratio (bpp), evaluating the compression efficiency of the output code against the number of input points. For lossy compression, we aim for high Peak-Signal-to-Noise-Ratio (PSNR), measured from Point-to-Point (D1 PSNR) and Point-to-Plane (D2 PSNR) [22]. D1 stresses the raw position error of the decoded point cloud, whereas D2 considers rather the quality of preserved shapes. Both metrics are measured in normalized point clouds with uniform scale and a peak signal of $p = 1$. Quality metrics are trivial for lossless compression as for 8iVFBv2 and MVUB.

3.2 Ablation Study

In this ablation study, we justify the choice of our hyper-parameters and design decisions for our models. For each demonstrated setting, we trained and tested an individual model on a small subset of data, just enough to show a trend that also applies to full-scale training.

Figure 4 demonstrates a clear trend: increasing the number of trainable parameters generally improves estimation accuracy. The model size scales with both the depth of the convolution layers and the size of the kernels. However, this also leads to higher memory consumption, which can quickly exceed hardware limitations – well before performance gains begin to plateau. As such, our choice of hyper-parameters prioritizes optimal hardware utilization over achieving maximum theoretical performance.

Table 1 presents a comparison of symbol estimation accuracy and compression bit rate using either cropped or stride-based mini-batches. Our indexed-convolution model is inherently designed for sparse point clouds, and the stride mini-batch approach effectively transforms dense point clouds into multiple sparser representations. Both methods confirm the viability of our design, as the proposed stride mini-batch method achieves superior performance over cropping. Furthermore, we demonstrate the advantage of using sub-models as proposed in Sect. 4. This method offers a larger number of trainable parameters with only a marginal increase in memory usage, making it a more efficient use of available hardware resources.

3.3 Experiment Setup

Our final setup has 3 sub-models with maximal precision of $L = 12$. From the shallowest to the deepest sub-model, we initialize 3, 6, and 12 convolution layers followed by 1, 2, and 3 dense layers, all finalized by one output layer each. The convolution layers have a kernel size of $k_c = 256$ and a window size of 3. The kernel sizes of our dense layers are $k_n = k_c \times d = 768$. All layers activate via ReLU [2], except the output layer activates via Softmax. During training, we use an Adam [13] optimizer with a learning rate of $1e^{-4}$. To shrink the input vector per batch, we stride with 2, 4, and 8 analog for each sub-model (Fig. 5).

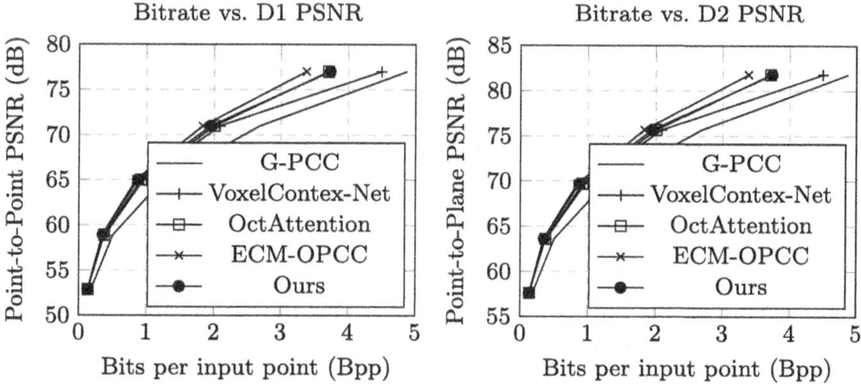

Fig. 5. Results of our proposed MIC-OPCC model against state-of-the-art baselines on the SemanticKITTI dataset. While achieving comparable compression ratios to OctAttention, our model significantly outperforms it in both encoding and decoding speed.

4 Results

Although our multi-indexed convolution model does not achieve state-of-the-art compression efficiency, it performs similarly to OctAttention [8] in lossy LiDAR

Table 2. Average compression ratio (bpp) of 8iVFBv2 and MVUB, showing the gain over G-PCC and coding time.

	Compression		Encoding	Decoding
	bpp	Gain	Time (s)	
G-PCC	0.99	–	4.0	1.0
VoxelDNN	0.62	37.6%	885	640
SparsePCGC	0.66	33.8%	9.5	9.1
OctAttention	0.65	34.6%	**0.8**	948
ECM-OPCC	**0.58**	**41.9%**	1.92	19.5
Ours	0.79	20.2%	2.2	**2.2**

compression on the SemanticKITTI dataset [4], while significantly reducing the decoding time. OctAttention reports a decoding time of 1.6093s/K-nodes, while our model requires only 0.018 seconds per $K = 1000$ nodes at a precision level of $L = 12$.

Our model includes 6.8 million trainable parameters, ranking between OctAttention with 4.2 million parameters and ECM-OPCC with 8.0 million parameters. Compared to these models, we maintain a relatively small memory peak of 21 GB during training.

However, our model struggles to efficiently compress dense point clouds such as those in 8iVFBv2 [7] and MVUB [6]. In this case, the advantage of fast decoding time is nearly negated by the high bitrate, making it difficult to compete with the superior compression performance of ECM-OPCC [12], as shown in Table 2. Our model has no autoregressive feedback but appears to be a crucial component in this challenge.

5 Conclusion

In this work, we introduced a multi-indexed convolution approach for octree-based point cloud compression, aiming to generate spatially coherent context features that improve the estimation of occupancy symbol probabilities. Our method leverages lightweight 1D convolutions and a mini-batch sampler stride technique to maintain computational efficiency, reduce memory usage, and enable faster decoding times compared to previous state-of-the-art models.

Our experiments demonstrate that our model performs competitively in the lossy compression of sparse point clouds, achieving results similar to OctAttention while significantly reducing decoding time and maintaining a low memory peak. However, we observed limitations in the model's ability to handle dense point clouds in lossless compression scenarios, where its bitrate remains higher than that of more advanced models like ECM-OPCC.

Despite these challenges, our model's efficiency and performance on sparse data make it a viable option for applications with limited hardware resources.

Future work will focus on refining the context model to better capture the structure of dense point clouds, ultimately enhancing the model's ability to generalize across a wider range of compression tasks. With these improvements, our aim is to further close the performance gap between our approach and the state-of-the-art methods in point cloud compression.

Acknowledgments. This work is financially supported in part (project number: 113UC2N006) by the Co-creation Platform of the Industry Academia Innovation School, NYCU, under the framework of the National Key Fields Industry-University Cooperation and Skilled Personnel Training Act, from the Ministry of Education (MOE) and industry partners in Taiwan. This work is also supported in part by the National Science and Technology Council (sNSTC), Taiwan R.O.C. projects with grants 113-2640-E-A49-013, 113-2634-F-A49-004, 114-2640-E-A49-015, 114-2218-E-002-007, and 114-2218-E-A49-020.

Disclosure of Interests. The authors have no competing interests to declare that are relevant to the content of this article.

References

1. 3DG: G-pcc test model v14 user manual (2021)
2. Agarap, A.F.: Deep learning using rectified linear units (ReLU) (2019). https://arxiv.org/abs/1803.08375
3. Ballé, J., Laparra, V., Simoncelli, E.P.: End-to-end optimized image compression. CoRR abs/ arXiv:1611.01704 (2016)
4. Behley, J., et al.: SemanticKitti: a dataset for semantic scene understanding of lidar sequences. In: Proceedings of the IEEE/CVF International Conference on Computer Vision, pp. 9297–9307 (2019)
5. Biswas, S., Liu, J., Wong, K., Wang, S., Urtasun, R.: Muscle: multi sweep compression of lidar using deep entropy models. Adv. Neural Inform. Process. Syst. (NeurIPS) **33**, 1–12 (2020)
6. Charles, L., Qin, C., Sergio, O.E., Philip, A.C.: Microsoft voxelized upper bodies - a voxelized point cloud dataset (2016)
7. Eugene, D., Bob, H., Taos, M., Philip, A.C.: 8i voxelized full bodies - a voxelized point cloud dataset (2017)
8. Fu, C., Li, G., Song, R., Gao, W., Liu, S.: OctAttention: octree-based large-scale contexts model for point cloud compression. Proceedings of the AAAI Conference on Artificial Intelligence **36**(1), 625–633 (2022). https://doi.org/10.1609/aaai.v36i1.19942, https://ojs.aaai.org/index.php/AAAI/article/view/19942
9. Google: Draco 3d graphics compression (2017). https://github.com/google/draco Accessed 2024
10. Huang, L., Wang, S., Wong, K., Liu, J., Urtasun, R.: OctSqueeze: octree-structured entropy model for lidar compression. In: 2020 IEEE/CVF Conference on Computer Vision and Pattern Recognition (CVPR), pp. 1310–1320 (2020). https://doi.org/10.1109/CVPR42600.2020.00139
11. Jeong, J., Cho, Y., Shin, Y., Roh, H.C., Kim, A.: Complex urban lidar data set. CoRR abs/ arXiv: 1803.06121 (2018)
12. Jin, Y., Zhu, Z., Xu, T., Lin, Y., Wang, Y.: ECM-OPCC: efficient context model for octree-based point cloud compression (2023). https://arxiv.org/abs/2211.10916

13. Kingma, D.P., Ba, J.: Adam: a method for stochastic optimization. In: Bengio, Y., LeCun, Y. (eds.) 3rd International Conference on Learning Representations, ICLR 2015, San Diego, CA, USA, 7-9 May 2015, Conference Track Proceedings (2015). http://arxiv.org/abs/1412.6980
14. Martin, G.N.: Range encoding: An algorithm for removing redundancy from a digitized message. Video & Data Recording Conference, Southampton. UK, vol. 43, p. 2427 (July 1979)
15. Meagher, D.: Geometric modeling using octree encoding. Comput. Graph. Image Process. **19**(2), 129–147 (1982). https://doi.org/10.1016/0146-664X(82)90104-6, https://www.sciencedirect.com/science/article/pii/0146664X82901046
16. Nguyen, D.T., Quach, M., Valenzise, G., Duhamel, P.: Learning-based lossless compression of 3d point cloud geometry. In: ICASSP 2021 - 2021 IEEE International Conference on Acoustics, Speech and Signal Processing (ICASSP), pp. 4220–4224 (2021). https://doi.org/10.1109/ICASSP39728.2021.9414763
17. Nguyen, D.T., Quach, M., Valenzise, G., Duhamel, P.: Multiscale deep context modeling for lossless point cloud geometry compression. In: 2021 IEEE International Conference on Multimedia Expo Workshops (ICMEW), pp. 1–6. (2021). https://doi.org/10.1109/ICMEW53276.2021.9455990
18. van den Oord, A., Kalchbrenner, N., Vinyals, O., Espeholt, L., Graves, A., Kavukcuoglu, K.: Conditional image generation with pixelcnn decoders. CoRR abs/ arXiv:1606.05328 (2016). http://arxiv.org/abs/1606.05328
19. Schwarz, S., et al.: Emerging MPEG standards for point cloud compression. IEEE J. Emerging Selected Topics Circ. Syst. **9**(1), 133–148 (2019). https://doi.org/10.1109/JETCAS.2018.2885981
20. Shannon, C.E.: A mathematical theory of communication. Bell Syst. Tech. J. **27**(3), 379–423 (1948). https://doi.org/10.1002/j.1538-7305.1948.tb01338.x
21. Tang, H., et al.: Searching efficient 3d architectures with sparse point-voxel convolution. CoRR abs/ arXiv: 2007.16100 (2020)
22. Tian, D., Ochimizu, H., Feng, C., Cohen, R., Vetro, A.: Geometric distortion metrics for point cloud compression. In: 2017 IEEE International Conference on Image Processing (ICIP), pp. 3460–3464 (2017).https://doi.org/10.1109/ICIP.2017.8296925
23. Vaswani, A., et al.: Attention is all you need. In: Proceedings of the 31st International Conference on Neural Information Processing Systems (NeurIPS). pp. 6000–6010 (2017)
24. Wang, J., Ding, D., Li, Z., Feng, X., Cao, C., Ma, Z.: Sparse Tensor-based multiscale representation for point cloud geometry compression, (2021). to be published
25. Witten, I.H., Neal, R.M., Cleary, J.G.: Arithmetic coding for data compression. Commun. ACM **30**(6), 520–540 (1987). https://doi.org/10.1145/214762.214771

Rendering and Animation

Extending Implicit Density Projection for Multiphase Fluids

Robert Dennison[✉] and Steve Maddock

The University of Sheffield, Sheffield, UK
{rtdennison1,s.maddock}@sheffield.ac.uk

Abstract. To increase the realism of fluid simulations, interactions between different fluids (such as water and air, or water and oil) must be considered. This allows for the simulation of phenomena such as the 'glugging' effect seen when a filled bottle is turned upside-down and air must fill the space left by the liquid. A common approach to fluid animation is to use Particle-in-Cell (PIC) methods. However, such methods are known to lose fluid volume over time due to accumulating numerical errors, an issue that is exacerbated when simulating multiple interacting fluids.

Implicit Density Projection (IDP) is used to overcome volume preservation issues for PIC methods. However, it is formulated for single fluids. To address this, we present two novel extensions to IDP: generalised IDP and D1-IDP. Generalised IDP extends IDP to multiple fluids. D1-IDP then further improves on the volume preservation capabilities. We show that D1-IDP is particularly good in multiphase fluid simulations with complex fluid interfaces. We also demonstrate its applicability to multiphase simulations involving variable density fluids. D1-IDP is able to achieve a maximum volume error of $< 1.0\%$ for the majority of presented scenarios, while having a negligible impact on computation performance compared to generalised IDP. The code used to generate the results presented in this paper can be found at https://github.com/robden820/Multiphase_Fluids.

Keywords: Physical Simulation · Fluid Simulation

1 Introduction

A popular technique for simulating single-phase fluids is the Particle-in-Cell (PIC) method, which is used in several commercial systems, e.g. Blender and SideFx's Houdini. PIC combines the ease of advection of particle-based simulation techniques with the ease of pressure calculations of grid-based techniques. However, one issue with the technique is that simulated fluids appear to lose volume over the duration of the simulation. This is because although the underlying mathematical model of a PIC simulation treats the fluid as incompressible, numerical discretization errors cause particles to become more densely clustered

P. Li et al. (Eds.): CGI 2025, LNCS 16508, pp. 457–473, 2026.
https://doi.org/10.1007/978-3-032-22264-0_36

over time, resulting in volume loss. Since the pressure solver is unaware of fluid density, once the fluid has lost volume due to particle clumping (and so increased in density) it can't be rectified. It is therefore necessary to include some additional means of preserving the fluid volume. Implicit Density Projection (IDP) [16] is a technique to overcome this by tracking the density of fluid. The pressure solver then takes density into account as well as velocity, and so the fluid can maintain its initial volume. Although IDP has been shown to be very effective at preserving fluid volume for the duration of a simulation, it has yet to be adapted to multiphase simulations.

There is little research into the field of multiphase PIC simulations. The work of Boyd and Bridson [2] was the first to adapt PIC to simulate multiphase fluids, however, the proposed method of bumping particles away from the fluid interface increases particle clustering, exacerbating the issue of volume loss. To mitigate volume loss issues, they applied the proportional control method of Kim et al. [14], however this approach requires careful tuning of additional parameters and can lead to artifacts where fluid volume can fluctuate over the course of a simulation. More recently, Lyu et al. [20] proposed a multiphase narrowband FLIP model to reduce the computational cost of MultiFLIP, and Lyu et al. [19] proposed MultiAPIC, adapting the affine PIC method to multiphase fluid simulations. However, neither of these works address the issue of volume loss in multiphase fluid simulations using PIC.

Our paper improves on this prior work by making the following contributions:

- We present an extension of IDP called generalised IDP (gIDP), which allows IDP to be applied to multiphase fluids simulated using Particle-in-Cell methods. IDP has previously been demonstrated to be highly effective in single-phase simulations [16] but has not yet been adapted to multiphase fluid simulation.
- We propose a new approach called D1 Implicit Density Projection (D1-IDP). This is an improvement over gIDP, reducing volume loss whilst requiring fewer solver iterations, at a small increase in computational cost. The technique is particularly effective when complex fluid interfaces form.
- We demonstrate the improvements of D1-IDP on a range of multiphase fluid scenarios: mixing air and water to produce a 'glugging' effect, a Rayleigh-Taylor instability simulation involving oil and water, and a simulation involving fluids that variable density over time due to temperature change.

The remainder of this report is split into five sections. Section 2 covers related literature. Section 3 describes the details of adapting IDP to multiphase fluid simulation for Generalised IDP (gIDP), as well as introducing D1-IDP. The results in Sect. 4 provide a comparison between gIDP and D1-IDP, followed by a discussion in Sect. 5. Finally, conclusions are presented in Sect. 6.

2 Related Work

Three main techniques are used in the fluid animation literature: Smoothed Particle Hydrodynamics (SPH), Particle-in-Cell (PIC) methods, and the Lattice Boltzmann Method (LBM). SPH is a purely Lagrangian approach, making use of particles to discretize the fluid ([12,15]). A particle-based approach allows for ease of advection, but is more challenging when it comes to enforcing incompressibility. LBM is an Eulerian simulation method, using a grid-based discretization which simplifies the pressure calculations at the cost of ease of advection ([4,17,18]). PIC methods are a hybrid approach, using multiple interpolation stages to transfer information between the particles and the grid ([6,22]). While PIC methods benefit from the positives of both Lagrangian and Eulerian approaches, the interpolation stages result in numerical dissipation leading to fluids appearing more viscous. Our work concentrates on PIC methods. For more details on the topic of fluid simulation for computer graphics, see the survey paper by Wang et al. [26].

Particle-in-Cell (PIC) methods were first introduced by Harlow et al. [10] and have become an industry standard technique for fluid simulations. PIC simulations have been used to simulate a wide variety of materials, including both fluids and deformable solids. Brackbill and Ruppel [3] introduced the Fluid Implicit Particle (FLIP) method to reduce artificial viscosity, however, whilst FLIP reduces the dissipation of the standard PIC approach, it does so in an unstable, noisy manner. PIC and FLIP simulations were later adapted to incompressible fluid flow by Zhu and Bridson [27]. Jiang et al. [13] introduced the Affine PIC (APIC) method to overcome the noise introduced by FLIP by storing an additional affine transformation matrix on each particle that allowed for maintaining rotational velocities as well as linear velocity, resulting in smoother splashing effects compared to FLIP. Following this, Fei et al. [5] extended APIC to introduce Affine FLIP (AFLIP), further increasing the dynamism of APIC. Fu et al. [6] then developed the Polynomial PIC (PolyPIC) method which generalised the affine matrix of APIC to higher order polynomials, which further reduced numerical dissipation and improved the preservation of angular momentum. Recently, Sancho et al. [22] introduced the Impulse PIC (IPIC) method which uses an impulse-based flow map to correct particle velocities to preserve vorticial details. Both PolyPIC and IPIC improve the preservation of smaller details in the simulation, allowing for more turbulent-appearing flows.

The trend in developments of PIC methods has been to reduce the numerical dissipation of the technique to allow for more dynamic and more realistic liquid behaviour. A different approach to improve simulation realism is to simulate multiphase fluids, to allow for effects such as liquid bubbling and 'glugging'. PIC methods were first adapted to allow for the simulation of multiphase fluids in the work of Boyd and Bridson [2], who introduced the MultiFLIP method. Lyu et al. [20] reduced the computational cost of MultiFLIP by using an adaptive narrowband simulation, only using FLIP particles around the fluid interface. Lyu et al. [19] then introduced MultiAPIC, which used APIC in the place of FLIP for multiphase simulation.

As previously mentioned, PIC methods suffer from volume loss over time, especially as more dynamic scenarios are simulated or larger timesteps are used. Multiple techniques have been proposed in the literature to overcome this issue in relation to single-phase fluid simulation. Kim et al. [14] first proposed solving the pressure Poisson equation (PPE) for non-zero divergence, and was used to improve the volume preservation of MultiFLIP [2]. They introduced the proportional controller, which would adjust the divergence of a cell based on if the cell density was too low or too high. Ando et al. [1] introduced Smoothed Particle Hydrodynamics (SPH) spring forces to enforce a uniform particle distribution. Um et al. [25] proposed the use of a secondary, high-resolution grid which could be used for adjusting particle positions based on particle density. Kugelstadt et al. [16] introduced Implicit Density Projection (IDP) which involves using a second Poisson equation to explicitly track simulation density. Qu et al. [21] then introduced PowerPIC, which adapted the work of de Goes et al. [7] to PIC simulations, making use of power diagrams to enforce incompressibility. Guo et al. [8] use additional implicit incompressible SPH (IISPH, [11]) particles to solve an additional low resolution PPE to adjust the positions of FLIP particles to preserve volume. However, none of these works aim to address the problem of volume loss for multiphase fluid simulation.

3 Methods

This work builds on MultiFLIP [2] by adapting IDP [16] to multiphase fluid simulations to improve the volume preservation characteristics. First, Subsect. 3.1 covers IDP for single-phase fluid simulation. In Subsect. 3.2, we present gIDP, an extension of IDP to allow for its use in multiphase fluid simulation. Subsection 3.3 then proposes D1-IDP, a new technique for volume preservation for multiphase fluids. Subsection 3.4 then covers special cases where D1-IDP and gIDP require additional handling. Finally Subsect. 3.5 describes the simulation of fluids with varying density based on temperature change.

3.1 Implicit Density Projection

A single-phase fluid simulation using PIC consists of particles and a staggered Marker-and-Cell (MAC) grid. Particles carry information about their mass and velocity, and the grid acts as a scratchpad for pressure calculations to enforce incompressibility. PIC fluids suffer from volume loss over time as numerical errors cause particles to clump together, which can't then become separated. One approach to solving this issue for single phase fluids is Implicit Density Projection, which involves introducing a second Poisson equation (PE) to enforce constant density at each time step.

The pressure Poisson equation (PPE) to be solved, given as Eq. 8 in [16], is

$$\frac{\Delta t}{\rho_0}\Delta^2 p = \Delta \cdot \mathbf{u}^* + \frac{1}{\Delta t}(1 - \frac{\rho^*(t)}{\rho_0}) \tag{1}$$

where $\mathbf{u}^*$ is the intermediate velocity field, $\rho^*(t)$ is the density field at time t, and ρ_0 is the initial fluid density that we want to maintain throughout the simulation duration. The first term, $\Delta \cdot \mathbf{u}^*$, is the divergence of the intermediate velocity field, and is included in the standard pressure solve. The new term, $\frac{1}{\Delta t}(1-\frac{\rho^*(t)}{\rho_0})$, is the scaled density error, and is included in the IDP PPE. In a single iteration, this single Poisson equation is split into two separate Poisson equations, which are solved separately:

$$\frac{\Delta t}{\rho_0}\Delta^2 p = \Delta \cdot \mathbf{u}^* \tag{2}$$

$$\frac{\Delta t}{\rho_0}\Delta^2 p = \frac{1}{\Delta t}(1 - \frac{\rho^*(t)}{\rho_0}) \tag{3}$$

To solve Eq. 3 we need the target density, ρ_0, of every cell, which for a single-phase fluid is the density of the fluid being simulated. A single simulation step for PIC fluids is given in Algorithm 1.

3.2 Generalised Implicit Density Projection

When simulating the interactions between two different fluid phases, each particle is classed as belonging to one of the phases. The work of Boyd and Bridson [2] proposed that each of these particle types should interpolate to a separate velocity field on the grid. These separate velocity fields are then combined to calculate a single divergence value for each cell, so that only a single PPE needs to be solved for the entire simulation. The surface tension coefficient and fluid interface curvature is used to calculate the pressure jump at the fluid interface for the PPE. When calculating the interface curvature, a level set is generated from the particles of both phases. The positions of particles that are within a specified distance to the level set are "bumped" away from the level set along its normal, to ensure that it is smooth and to prevent particle mixing at the interface (see Fig. 1). The particles then interpolate information back only from the corresponding velocity field.

To adapt IDP to multiphase simulations, we must first determine the target density of each cell. Similarly to the pressure PE, a single density PE can be used for both phases, rather than requiring solving separate linear systems for each phase. For a multiphase fluid, there is no fixed initial density ρ_0 as different cells contain different fractions of each phase. For cells that are marked as belonging to one of the two phases (A or B), the target density is the corresponding phase density (ρ_A or ρ_B). For the interface cells, the target density is calculated as

$$\rho_0 = \phi\rho_A + (1-\phi)\rho_B \tag{4}$$

where ϕ is the fraction of the cell occupied by phase A.

However, we found that this resulted in "popping" artifacts throughout the fluid, similar to what was seen in the original IDP work when using a combined Poisson equation. We therefore took a similar approach to Boyd and Bridson [2] and set the scaled density error to 0 for interface cells, effectively meaning gIDP is not applied at the fluid interface. This resolved the artifact issue and resulted in effective volume conservation for the two fluids. The multiphase PIC simulation loop is given in Algorithm 1.

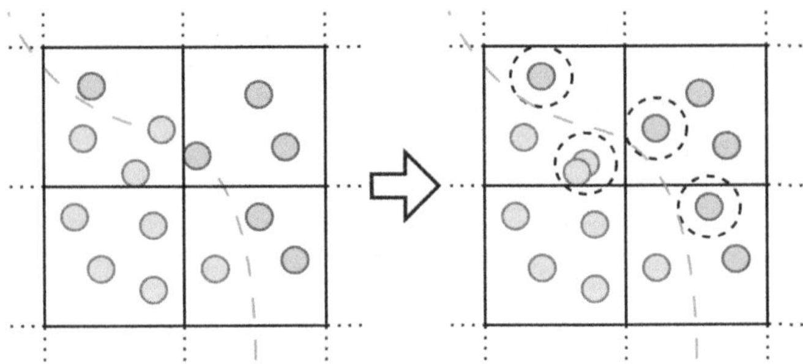

Fig. 1. A level set is generated from the positions of particles of both fluid phases (yellow). The positions of particles close to the interface are updated, moving them away from the level set along the level set normal vector. This ensures the interface is smooth and prevents particle mixing. As can be seen in the top left grid cell, this bumping stage is a cause of particle clustering. Based on Fig. 5 in [2]. (Color figure online)

3.3 D1 Implicit Density Projection

The goal of IDP in is to enforce a constant density throughout the body of fluid. In PIC simulations the mass of particles is constant, as is the fluid volume represented by each particle. Since the mass and volume of particles are fixed, the result of enforcing constant fluid density is that an even distribution of particles is achieved throughout the fluid body. The idea behind D1-IDP is that since an even distribution of particles results in volume preservation, the physical fluid density can be disregarded. In the case of multiphase fluids, both fluid phases can be treated as having a density of 1.0 in the density Poisson equation. Unlike gIDP, we can apply D1-IDP across the fluid interface without causing artifacts. Equation 3 then becomes:

$$\frac{\Delta t}{n}\Delta^2 p = \frac{1}{\Delta t}(1 - \frac{n^*(t)}{n}) \tag{5}$$

where n is the desired number of particles in each grid cell, and $n^*(t)$ is the current number of particles in the grid cell. The number of particles is interpolated to the grid cells using Eq. 6, rather than simply counting the number of particles in each grid cell:

$$n^*(t)_i = \sum_{p=0}^{P} w_{ip} \tag{6}$$

$$w_{ip} = N(\frac{x_p - x_i}{\Delta x}) \tag{7}$$

where x_p is the position of particle p, x_i is the position of grid cell i, Δx is the length of a grid cell edge. For this work we use linear interpolation:

Algorithm 1 A single iteration of a multiphase PIC simulation using IDP. Additional IDP steps are highlighted in teal, additional multiphase steps are highlighted in magenta.

Interpolate from particles to the grid
Calculate density at grid cell centres
Calculate cell density error
Solve density PE
Bump particles to adjust particle density
Calculate grid phi values and cell face fractions
Calculate interface curvature on the grid
Bump particles on the wrong side of the interface
Interpolate from particles to the grid
Apply external forces (e.g. gravitational forces)
Calculate grid cell divergence
Solve pressure PE
Update cell velocity from cell pressure
Extrapolate velocity field of each fluid phase.
Interpolate from the grid to particles
Advect particles

$$N(x) = \begin{cases} 1 - |x| & x < 1 \\ 0 & x \geq 1 \end{cases} \tag{8}$$

3.4 Degenerate Cases

When using IDP for single-phase fluids, the density error near the fluid surface is clamped to a minimum value of the fluid density, as these areas will not have an accurate density calculation due to the cells interpolating from a smaller number of particles. In a multiphase simulation using gIDP or D1-IDP this problem is avoided as the entire simulation domain contains an even distribution of particles. However, these degenerate cases can still occur at the domain boundaries and at solid boundaries, which must be considered (see Fig. 2).

When using gIDP, if a cell has any neighbouring solid cells, the current uncorrected density, $\rho^*(t)$, is clamped to a minimum value of the cell's target density (Eq. 4). For D1-IDP, the current number of particles in the grid cell, $n^*(t)$, is clamped to a minimum of the target number of particles per cell, n. The same is done for cells on the domain boundary.

3.5 Variable Density

There are many examples of fluid flows involving fluids of variable density. For example, fluids undergoing thermal expansion will produce convection currents and concentration gradients of dissolved substances can result in variable density fluid flow, as can liquid-solid suspensions. In this section, we consider variable

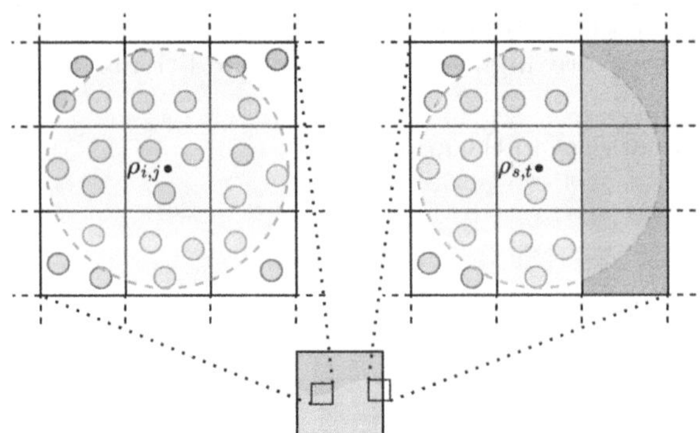

Fig. 2. D1-IDP and gIDP assume there is an even distribution of particles everywhere in the simulation domain. **Left**: $Cell_{i,j}$ lies within the body of the simulation domain so the density of the grid cell, $\rho_{i,j}$, is sampled from all particles throughout the entire interpolation kernel (yellow). **Right**: $Cell_{s,t}$ is at a solid boundary meaning some of the kernel contains no particles and so the density, $\rho_{s,t}$, is undersampled, leading to inaccuracies. A similar scenario occurs at the domain boundaries. In these cases, the density is clamped to a minimum value of the cell's target density.

density flows resulting from temperature differences. In the case of gIDP, this variable density will be considered in both the pressure PE and density PE, however, for D1-IDP this will only effect the pressure PE.

We use a simplified version of heat conduction as described by Stomakhin et al. [23]. Since we only deal with fluids, the simplifications avoid the changes of state between a liquid and solid. For this work, we do not alter the volume of a particle based on its temperature, only the density. In this sense, this aspect of the simulation breaks the conservation of mass.

Alongside momentum, temperature is also interpolated between the particles and the grid. For heat conduction through the grid, we must interpolate the particle thermal conductivity and heat capacity to the grid as well as temperature (see Eqs. 9–11). Unlike velocity, grid temperature requires only a single scalar field for both phases, whereas thermal conductivity and heat capacity both require a separate field for each phase:

$$K_{\alpha i} = \frac{\sum_{p=0}^{P_\alpha} K_p m_p w_{ip}}{m_{\alpha i}} \tag{9}$$

$$C_i = \frac{\sum_{p=0}^{P} C_p m_p w_{ip}}{m_i} \tag{10}$$

$$T_i = \frac{\sum_{p=0}^{P} T_p m_p w_{ip}}{m_i} \tag{11}$$

where the notation used is described in Table 1. The cell temperature can then be updated as described by Stomakhin et al. in [23], making use of the phase

Table 1. Notation relating to variable density fluids.

Notation	Meaning
α	Fluid phase of parameter, where $\alpha \in \{A, B\}$
P_α	Number of particles belonging to phase α
K_p	Thermal conductivity of particle p
$K_{\alpha i}$	Phase α thermal conductivity of grid cell i
C_p	Heat capacity of particle p
$C_{\alpha i}$	Phase α heat capacity of grid cell i
T_p	Temperature of particle p
T_i	Temperature of grid cell i
m_p	Mass of particle p
$m_{\alpha i}$	Phase α mass of grid cell i
m_i	Total mass of grid cell i, $m_{Ai} + m_{Bi}$

face fractions in the differencing operator. Solid cells have a fixed temperature throughout the simulation and are labelled as either being a heat source or ambient.

Density is calculated using the standard formula for density change due to thermal expansion [24]:

$$\rho_\alpha = \rho_{\alpha 0}(1 - \kappa_\alpha \Delta T) \tag{12}$$

where $\rho_{\alpha 0}$ is the phase density at an ambient temperature, κ_α is the phase density coefficient, and ΔT is the change in temperature from the ambient state. Equation 12 is used for calculating the density of both particles and grid cells.

4 Results

To evaluate the volume preservation characteristics of gIDP and D1-IDP, we compare against MultiFLIP with both no additional volume preservation and the proportional controller method of [14]. The following three scenarios are presented:

- A bottleneck scenario, demonstrating a 'glugging' effect as water drains from a container through a narrow opening (see Fig. 3). This comparison highlights the need for volume preservation in a multiphase PIC simulation.
- A Rayleigh-Taylor instability scenario, featuring a mixture of oil and water. As the liquids mix and separate a complex interface forms (see Fig. 4). This will compare how effectively volume can be preserved in a simulation where the fluid interface has a large surface area compared to the volume of fluid.
- A variable density scenario, featuring liquids with varying densities based on temperature change (see Fig. 5). This could be used to produce the effect that would be seen in a 'lava lamp'. This will examine the robustness of D1-IDP

and gIDP, as different regions of the fluid interface will have different density ratios and each phases density will vary throughout the body of fluid.

For all simulations, unless stated otherwise, the parameters used are a timestep of $\Delta t = 0.001$, a grid cell size of $\Delta x = 0.5$, and a target number of particles per cell of $n = 8$ in the case of D1-IDP. For simulations using the proportional control method, we used a proportional gain of $k_p = \frac{1.15}{\Delta t}$ and an integral gain of $k_i = (\frac{k_p}{512})^2$, as given in [2]. In addition to this, we use FLIP transfers for each scenario. The simulations are run entirely on the CPU, and results have been produced using an Intel Core i9-13900K. All presented results are averaged over 3 simulation runs. The results have been rendered using Houdini. Additional parameter values for each of the presented scenarios is given in Table 2. A summary of the results for each scenario is presented in Table 3.

Table 2. Parameter values used to generate the results demonstrated in this paper. A timestep of $\Delta t = 0.001$ was used for all simulations, and unless stated otherwise, the grid cell size used was $\Delta x = 0.5$. For simulations using D1-IDP, the target number of particles per cell was set to $n = 8$.

	Bottleneck	Rayleigh-Taylor	Variable Density
$\rho_A (g/cm^3)$	1.0	1.0	1.08
$\rho_B (g/cm^3)$	0.001	0.7	1.074
$\gamma (dyne/cm)$	72.0	35.0	150.0
$\kappa_A (K^{-1})$	-	-	0.0047
$\kappa_B (K^{-1})$	-	-	0.0028
$K_A (W cm^{-1} K^{-1})$	-	-	0.146
$K_B (W cm^{-1} K^{-1})$	-	-	0.596
$C_A (J g^{-1} K^{-1})$	-	-	15.91
$C_B (J g^{-1} K^{-1})$	-	-	39.93

Table 3. A comparison of results for the 3 different presented scenarios. A timestep of $0.001s$, a grid cell size of $\Delta x = 0.5$ and a solver error threshold of $\epsilon = 10^{-16}$ were used for the given simulations. Volume error is calculated as $\frac{V(t)-V(0)}{V(0)}$. Only gIDP and D1-IDP have a density solver stage. Bold text indicates which method performed best for each metric.

Scenario	Time per step (s)				Avg Vol Error (%)				Max Vol Error (%)				# Density Solver Iters	
	None	PC	gIDP	D1-IDP	None	PC	gIDP	D1-IDP	None	PC	gIDP	D1-IDP	gIDP	D1-IDP
Bottleneck	0.388	**0.384**	0.440	0.454	3.103	4.246	1.157	**0.022**	9.128	7.190	2.682	**0.144**	259.6	**145.2**
Rayleigh-Taylor	**0.363**	**0.363**	0.400	0.403	9.101	8.235	13.170	**0.255**	13.726	11.925	32.310	**0.597**	192.0	**152.4**
Variable Density	1.139	**1.135**	1.247	1.231	1.234	1.829	4.123	**0.421**	2.505	5.793	9.113	**0.659**	254.8	**220.0**

4.1 Bottleneck Scenario

This scenario showcases the interactions between water and air, with the water flowing through a narrow opening from the top container to the lower container of the same volume (see Fig. 3). The density of the water is $1g/cm^3$, the density of the air is $0.001g/cm^3$, and $\gamma = 72.0dyne/cm$. The results demonstrate the glugging effect achieved when using a multiphase simulation in place of a single phase simulation. As can be seen in Fig. 3, when no volume control measure is used the fluid suffers noticeably from a loss of volume over the course of the simulation, highlighting the need for some kind of volume preservation. When the proportional controller is used, the fluid initially loses volume similarly to when no volume preservation method is used. However, the integral gain term is able to recover some of the lost volume as the simulation progresses, resulting in a notable artifact of the fluid volume to 'growing'. Both gIDP and D1-IDP succeed in visually maintaining the volume throughout the duration of the simulation, and Table 3 shows us that the volume error is reduced. Table 3 also shows that D1-IDP is able to achieve a lower volume error when compared to gIDP, and additionally requires fewer iteration steps to reach the desired error threshold. The computational cost of using D1-IDP compared to gIDP is negligible, increasing the time per simulation step from $0.44s$ to $0.454s$.

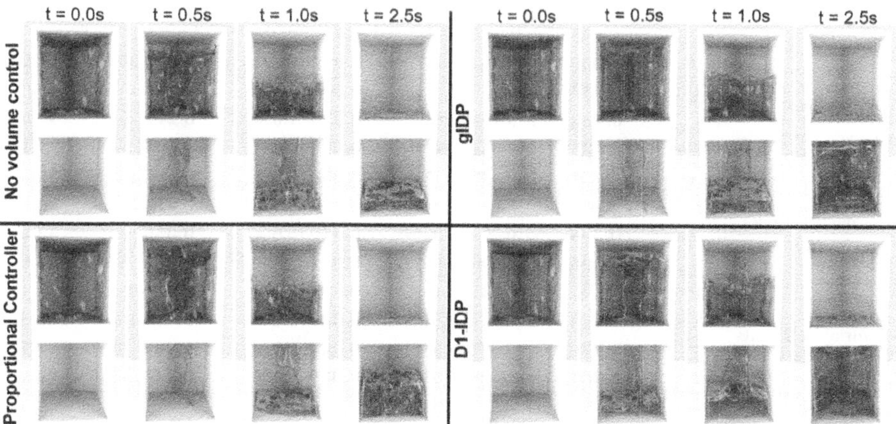

Fig. 3. A bottleneck scenario comparing volume preservation when using no volume control (top left), proportional control (bottom left), gIDP (top right) and D1-IDP (bottom right). Frames are taken from left to right at $t = 0.0s$, $0.5s$, $1.0s$ and $2.5s$.

We also tested the effect of the density solver error threshold on the volume preservation of gIDP and D1-IDP (see Table 4). As the error threshold decreases, the number of solver iterations required to reach the threshold decreases for both gIDP and D1-IDP, as expected. As can be seen in the table, error threshold has a minimal effect on the volume preservation of both techniques, resulting in similar average and maximum volume errors for all tested thresholds. In the case of gIDP, as the error threshold is increased, the average volume error varies from a minimum of 0.447% for $\epsilon = 10^{-2}$ to a maximum value of 1.157% for $\epsilon = 10^{-16}$. Likewise, the maximum volume error varies from a minimum of 1.182% for $\epsilon = 10^{-2}$ to a maximum of 2.682% for $\epsilon = 10^{-16}$. A similarly small range is seen in the average and maximum volume errors when using D1-IDP, with a minimum average volume error of 0.006% for $\epsilon = 10^{-8}$ and maximum of 0.022% for $\epsilon = 10^{-16}$, and a range of 0.053% for $\epsilon = 10^{-8}$ to 0.211% for $\epsilon = 10^{-4}$ for the maximum volume error.

Furthermore, we also compare the effectiveness of gIDP and D1-IDP when using FLIP 0.9, APIC and AFLIP 0.9 (see Table 5). As shown, while using APIC reduces the efficacy of both gIDP and D1-IDP, the use of AFLIP improves the volume preservation of both methods.

We repeated these tests evaluating the effects of the density solver error and PIC method on both the Rayleigh-Taylor and variable density scenarios.

Table 4. A comparison of the effect of solver error threshold on the bottleneck scenario. The time step used was 0.001s and a grid cell size of $\Delta x = 0.5$. Volume error is calculated as $\frac{V(t)-V(0)}{V(0)}$. Only gIDP and D1-IDP have a density solver stage. Bold text indicates which method performed best for each metric.

Scenario	Solver Error	Time per step (s)		Avg Vol Error (%)		Max Vol Error (%)		# Solver Iters	
		gIDP	D1-IDP	gIDP	D1-IDP	gIDP	D1-IDP	gIDP	D1-IDP
Bottleneck	10-16	0.440	0.454	1.157	**0.022**	2.682	**0.144**	259.6	**145.2**
	10-8	**0.433**	0.456	0.651	**0.006**	1.900	**0.053**	157.1	**85.6**
	10-4	**0.428**	0.451	0.812	**0.018**	1.626	**0.211**	95.3	**41.0**
	10-2	**0.425**	0.442	0.447	**0.015**	1.182	**0.095**	43.7	**20.1**
Rayleigh-Taylor	10-16	0.402	0.405	13.170	**0.256**	32.310	**0.597**	192.8	**153.0**
	10-8	0.403	**0.401**	5.726	**0.095**	15.343	**0.412**	123.9	**88.6**
	10-4	**0.398**	0.405	5.927	**0.080**	15.668	**0.336**	63.7	**52.5**
	10-2	**0.395**	0.396	4.461	**0.087**	11.469	**0.315**	37.6	**24.6**
Variable Density	10-16	1.247	1.231	4.123	**0.421**	9.113	**0.659**	254.8	**220.1**
	10-8	**1.244**	1.247	1.832	**0.029**	6.062	**0.124**	133.3	**123.5**
	10-4	**1.220**	1.231	2.838	**0.022**	5.917	**0.149**	68.9	**67.7**
	10-2	**1.204**	1.228	4.383	**0.030**	7.140	**0.145**	29.4	**29.2**

4.2 Rayleigh-Taylor Instability Scenario

This scenario demonstrates interactions between oil and water, with a low density ratio and a smaller surface tension coefficient than the bottleneck scenario (see Fig. 4). The density of the oil is $0.7g/cm^3$ and $\gamma = 35.0dyne/cm$, with the parameters for water being the same as in the previous section. As the fluids simulation progresses, a complex interface forms with a large surface area. As gIDP cannot be applied at the interface (see Sect. 3.2), its ability to resolve the accumulating errors is limited, resulting in a maximum volume error of 32.60%.

Table 5. A comparison of the effect of using different PIC methods for the bottleneck scenario. The time step used was $0.001s$, a grid cell size of $\Delta x = 0.5$ and a solver error threshold of $\epsilon = 10^{-16}$. Volume error is calculated as $\frac{V(t)-V(0)}{V(0)}$. Only gIDP and D1-IDP have a density solver stage. Bold text indicates which method performed best for each metric.

Scenario	Method	Time per step (s)				Avg Vol Error (%)				Max Vol Error (%)				# Density Solver Iters	
		None	PC	gIDP	D1-IDP	None	PC	gIDP	D1-IDP	None	PC	gIDP	D1-IDP	gIDP	D1-IDP
Bottleneck	FLIP 0.9	0.388	**0.384**	0.440	0.454	3.103	4.246	1.157	**0.022**	9.128	7.190	2.682	**0.144**	259.6	**145.2**
	APIC	**0.372**	0.383	0.434	0.437	16.974	16.693	7.461	**0.472**	9.129	7.150	17.997	**1.380**	240.3	**145.5**
	AFLIP 0.9	**0.374**	0.384	0.443	0.459	1.501	1.317	0.539	**0.011**	2.214	4.191	1.693	**0.074**	267.8	**145.1**
Rayleigh-Taylor	FLIP 0.9	**0.363**	**0.363**	0.400	0.403	9.101	8.235	13.170	**0.255**	13.726	11.925	32.310	**0.597**	192.0	**152.4**
	APIC	**0.351**	0.365	0.404	0.404	14.843	14.761	7.431	**1.65**	13.628	11.491	22.298	**2.702**	187.7	**151.7**
	AFLIP 0.9	**0.352**	0.361	0.41	0.411	5.375	7.623	6.234	**0.030**	10.677	10.124	14.507	**0.174**	219.6	**151.8**
Variable Density	FLIP 0.9	1.139	**1.135**	1.247	1.231	1.234	1.829	4.123	**0.421**	2.505	5.793	9.113	**0.659**	254.8	**220.0**
	APIC	**1.134**	1.137	1.220	1.237	2.992	3.058	10.677	**1.655**	2.502	5.795	25.085	**2.491**	271.7	**219.3**
	AFLIP 0.9	1.155	**1.145**	1.273	1.283	0.952	4.736	4.135	**0.028**	1.878	5.789	11.423	**0.145**	237.2	**221.1**

In contrast, D1-IDP is able to be applied across the interface, offering much better volume preservation in this scenario. However, D1-IDP outperforms the proportional controller approach, resulting in a 0.597% maximum volume error. As in the previous scenario, there is a negligible computation cost when using D1-IDP, this time resulting in an increase in the time per step of from $0.400s/step$ for gIDP to $0.403s/step$ for D1-IDP.

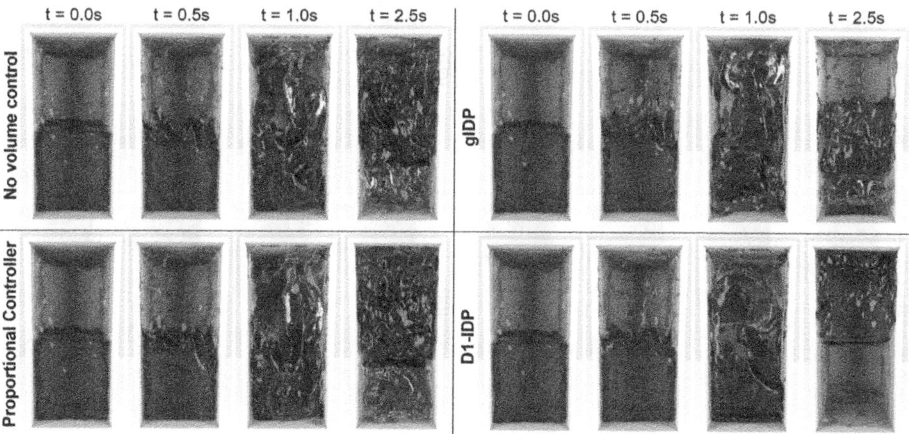

Fig. 4. A Rayleigh-Taylor scenario comparing volume preservation when using no volume control (top left), proportional control (bottom left), gIDP (top right) and D1-IDP (bottom right). Frames are taken from left to right at $t = 0.0s$, $0.5s$, $1.0s$ and $2.5s$.

4.3 Variable Density Scenario

This scenario shows a larger scene where both fluid phases have variable density based on the temperature (see Fig. 5, Table 3). The floor of the container has a temperature of $200.0°C$, with the remaining walls fixed at $0.0°C$. Both fluids also begin the simulation with a temperature of $0.0°C$. As the simulation progresses, heat is conducted from the floor through both of the fluids, decreasing the density and producing a convection current.

The density of the orange liquid is $1.08g/cm^3$ at $0.0°C$ with a thermal density coefficient of $\kappa_A = 0.0047$, with the surrounding liquid being $1.074g/cm^3$ at $0.0°C$ with $\kappa_B = 0.0028$. The surface tension coefficient is set to $\gamma = 150.0dyne/cm$. These parameters are taken from the experimental data of Gyüre and Jánosi [9], but scaled to increase the speed of thermal conduction. These parameters result in the orange liquid heating up faster than the surrounding liquid, becoming less dense and floating to the surface. As it cools its density increases and it falls back down, generating a convection current. Similarly to the Rayleigh-Taylor scenario, a complex interface forms, affecting the performance of gIDP which achieves a maximum volume error of 9.113%. Again, since D1-IDP can be applied across the fluid interface the maximum volume error achieved is 0.659%. In this scenario, using D1-IDP results in a negligible decrease in the time per step required, decreasing from $1.247s/step$ for gIDP to $1.231s/step$ for D1-IDP.

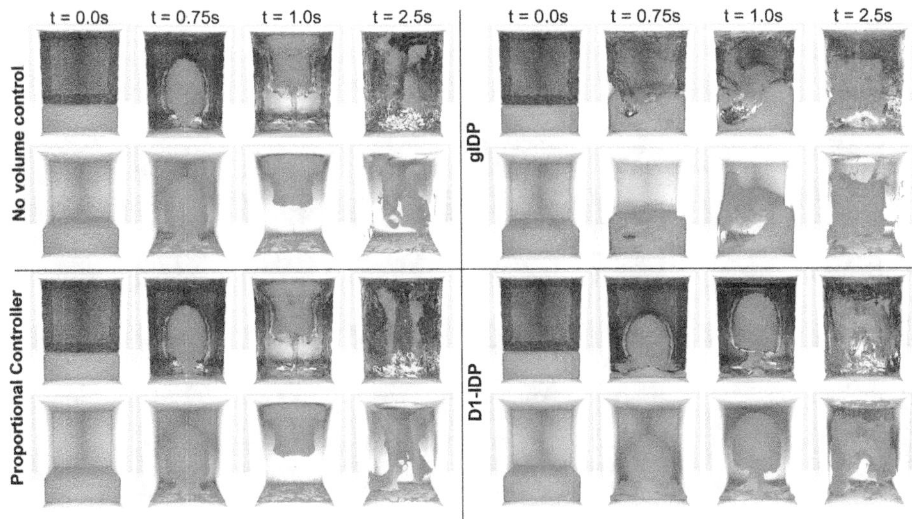

Fig. 5. A variable density scenario comparing volume preservation when using no volume control (top left), proportional control (bottom left), gIDP (top right) and D1-IDP (bottom right). In the bottom row of each section, the clear liquid has not been rendered so that the orange liquid can be seen more clearly. Frames are taken from left to right at $t = 0.0s$, $0.75s$, $1.0s$ and $2.5s$. (Color figure online)

5 Discussion

As shown in the Sect. 4, the use of some kind of volume preservation for multiphase fluids is necessary to avoid severe volume loss. As can be seen in Tables 3, 4 and 5, D1-IDP improves upon the volume preservation of gIDP and the proportional controller in all of the given scenarios. This difference between gIDP and D1-IDP is especially noticeable in the Rayleigh-Taylor scenario – due to the fact that gIDP can't be applied at the fluid interface, the complex fluid interface that forms causes gIDP to perform poorly.

Both gIDP and D1-IDP have an increased computational cost when compared to using no volume preservation method or proportional control. When using the proportional controller, the bottleneck scenario takes $0.384s/step$ compared to $0.44s/step$ for gIDP (14.6% increase) and $0.454s/step$ for D1-IDP (18.2% increase) (see Table 3). Furthermore, D1-IDP generally results in a small increase in computational cost when compared to gIDP, with increases of 3.2% and 0.7% for the bottleneck and Rayleigh-Taylor scenarios, respectively. The largest increase in time per step of the given scenarios is 5.32% for the Bottleneck example with an error threshold of 10^{-8} and $\sim 76k$ particles.

D1-IDP also seems to smooth over finer details, such as small splashes, giving the appearance of a higher surface tension when compared to gIDP. This is most notable in the Rayleigh-Taylor demonstration, where the interface remains smoother throughout the duration of the simulation than when compared to using proportional control or gIDP (see Fig. 4). The extent of this effect requires further investigation.

As stated in Boyd and Bridson [2], the positions of particles near the fluid interface are updated to prevent the phases from over-mixing. However, we do not update the positions of particles whose positions have already been updated during the particle bumping stage to avoid artifacts at the fluid interface. The interface bumping stage is likely a cause of volume loss as it does not consider the incompressibility of either fluid and can cause particle clumping (see Fig. 1). Further work is required to investigate the interactions between these two position update stages.

6 Conclusions

We have presented Generalised Implicit Density Projection, an adaption of IDP that allows its application to multiphase fluid simulations using PIC methods. Additionally we have proposed D1 Implicit Density Projection, which improves upon the volume preservation characteristics of gIDP, especially in simulations with a complex fluid interface. We have shown that by treating both fluid phases as having a density of 1.0, D1-IDP can be applied across the fluid interface (Sect. 3.3), increasing the efficacy of the method. When comparing gIDP and D1-IDP, we have shown that across all given scenarios D1-IDP achieves a lower maximum volume error and results in fewer density PE solver iterations. This is true regardless of the solver error threshold used (see Table 4) and PIC method (see Table 5). As previously mentioned, D1-IDP has a negligible impact on the computational cost when compared to gIDP, requiring a similar time per step for all of the presented scenarios.

As discussed in Sect. 5, updating the particle positions near the fluid interface is likely a cause of volume loss in multiphase fluids. Therefore, it would be interesting to investigate the impact of this bumping stage on volume preservation, as well as the interactions between the bumping and the particle position update in D1-IDP and gIDP. Additionally, it may be possible to combine the two position update stages into a single step which would potentially both reduce volume loss and preserve a smooth fluid interface.

Acknowledgments. This research is supported by a Frank Greaves Simpson Scholarship from The University of Sheffield.

References

1. Ando, R., Tsuruno, R.: A particle-based method for preserving fluid sheets. In: Proceedings of the 2011 ACM SIGGRAPH/Eurographics Symposium on Computer Animation, pp. 7–16. ACM (2011)
2. Boyd, L., Bridson, R.: MultiFLIP for energetic two-phase fluid simulation. ACM Trans. Graph. **31**(2), 16:1–16:12 (2012)
3. Brackbill, J., Ruppel, H.: FLIP: a method for adaptively zoned, particle-in-cell calculations of fluid flows in two dimensions. J. Comput. Phys. **65**, 314–343 (1986)
4. Chen, S., Doolen, G.D.: Lattice boltzmann method for fluid flows. Annu. Rev. Fluid Mech. **30**(1), 329–364 (1998)
5. Fei, Y.R., Guo, Q., Wu, R., Huang, L., Gao, M.: Revisiting integration in the material point method: a scheme for easier separation and less dissipation. ACM Trans. Graph. **40**(4), 1–16 (2021)
6. Fu, C., Guo, Q., Gast, T., Jiang, C., Teran, J.: A polynomial particle-in-cell method. ACM Trans. Graph. **36**(6), 1–12 (2017)
7. de Goes, F., Wallez, C., Huang, J., Pavlov, D., Desbrun, M.: Power particles: an incompressible fluid solver based on power diagrams. ACM Trans. Graph. **34**(4), 1–11 (2015)
8. Guo, H., Wang, H., Zhao, J., Tang, Y.: Realistic rendering algorithm for bubble generation and motion in water. Electronics **11**(22), 3689 (2022)
9. Gyüre, B., Jánosi, I.M.: Basics of lava-lamp convection. Phys. Rev. E **80**(4), 046307 (2009)
10. Harlow, F.H.: The particle-in-cell method for numerical solution of problems in fluid dynamics (LADC-5288) (1962)
11. Ihmsen, M., Cornelis, J., Solenthaler, B., Horvath, C., Teschner, M.: Implicit incompressible SPH. IEEE Trans. Visual Comput. Graph. **20**(3), 426–435 (2014)
12. Jeske, S.R., Westhofen, L., Löschner, F., Fernández-fernández, J.A., Bender, J.: Implicit surface tension for SPH fluid simulation. ACM Trans. Graph. **43**(1), 13:1–13:14 (2023)
13. Jiang, C., Schroeder, C., Selle, A., Teran, J., Stomakhin, A.: The affine particle-in-cell method. ACM Trans. Graph. **34**(4), 51:1–51:10 (2015)
14. Kim, B., Liu, Y., Llamas, I., Jiao, X., Rossignac, J.: Simulation of bubbles in foam with the volume control method. ACM Trans. Graph. **26**(3), 98 (2007)

15. Koschier, D., Bender, J., Solenthaler, B., Teschner, M.: A survey on SPH methods in computer graphics. Comput. Graph. Forum **41**(2), 737–760 (2022)
16. Kugelstadt, T., Longva, A., Thuerey, N., Bender, J.: Implicit density projection for volume conserving liquids. IEEE Trans. Visual Comput. Graph. **27**(4), 2385–2395 (2019)
17. Li, W., Liu, D., Desbrun, M., Huang, J., Liu, X.: Kinetic-based multiphase flow simulation. IEEE Trans. Visual Comput. Graph. **27**(7), 3318–3334 (2021)
18. Li, W., Wu, K., Desbrun, M.: Kinetic simulation of turbulent multifluid flows. ACM Trans. Graph. **43**(4), 55:1–55:17 (2024)
19. Lyu, L., Cao, W., Wu, E., Yang, Z.: Affine particle-in-cell method for two-phase liquid simulation. Virtual Reality Intell. Hardware **3**(2), 105–117 (2021)
20. Lyu, L., Ren, X., Cao, W., Zhu, J., Wu, E.: Adaptive narrow band MultiFLIP for efficient two-phase liquid simulation. SCIENCE CHINA Inf. Sci. **61**(11), 1–3 (2018). https://doi.org/10.1007/s11432-018-9518-3
21. Qu, Z., Li, M., De Goes, F., Jiang, C.: The power particle-in-cell method. ACM Trans. Graph. **41**(4), 118:1–118:13 (2022)
22. Sancho, S., Tang, J., Batty, C., Azevedo, V.C.: The impulse particle-in-cell method. Comput. Graph. Forum **43**(2), e15022 (2024)
23. Stomakhin, A., Schroeder, C., Jiang, C., Chai, L., Teran, J., Selle, A.: Augmented MPM for phase-change and varied materials. ACM Trans. Graph. **33**(4) (2014)
24. Tipler, P.A.: Physics for scientists and engineers. 3rd ed., extended version. edn. Worth Publishers, New York (1991)
25. Um, K., Baek, S., Han, J.: Advanced hybrid particle-grid method with sub-grid particle correction. Comput. Graph. Forum **33**(7), 209–218 (2014)
26. Wang, X., et al.: Physics-based fluid simulation in computer graphics: survey, research trends, and challenges. Comput. Visual Media **10**(5), 803–858 (2024)
27. Zhu, Y., Bridson, R.: Animating sand as a fluid. ACM Trans. Graph. **24**(3), 965–972 (2005)

CartoonAnimalPose: A New Dataset and Method for Cartoon Animal Pose Estimation

Longlong Jin and Shizhe Zhou(✉)

College of Computer Science and Electronic Engineering, Hunan University, Changsha, China
Shizhe@hnu.edu.cn

Abstract. This paper introduces *CartoonAnimalPose*, the first dataset for non-photorealistic animal pose estimation, containing over 4,000 images and 8,800 instances with precise annotations of 21 keypoints and bounding boxes across various artistic styles and species. We also propose a high-resolution network with a joint learning strategy and a Channel-Spatial Collaborative Attention (CSA) module. This framework enables cross-domain learning between real and cartoon animal data, while the CSA module enhancing feature representation by modeling both channel and spatial dimensions. Our approach achieves an AP@0.5 of 66.4% on the *CartoonAnimalPose* dataset. This work establishes the first standardized benchmark for cartoon animal pose estimation and provides new insights into cross-domain learning and attention mechanisms for keypoint detection. The dataset and code are available at https://github.com/Jll0716/CartoonAnimalPose.

Keywords: Cartoon animal pose estimation · Cross-domain learning · Attention mechanism

1 Introduction

Animal pose estimation has achieved great progress in natural scenes [1,2,14,23,25], but faces challenges in artistic and non-photorealistic scenarios, such as anime, ink painting, and digital illustrations. Existing SOTA methods trained on real-world datasets like MSCOCO [12] often fail to generalize well to these stylized domains due to large domain gaps in appearance and structure (Fig. 1).

To address this, we propose *CartoonAnimalPose*, the first standardized dataset for non-realistic animal pose estimation, containing over 4,000 images with 21 annotated keypoints across diverse art styles. Our dataset bridges the gap between natural and stylized scenes and supports pose estimation for cartoon animals, an area underexplored in prior work.

This work was funded by the National Science Foundation of China No. 62076090, Huxiang Youth Talent Support Program, Hunan Province, China, No. 2020RC3014, and Natural Science Foundation of Hunan Province, China, No. 2022JJ30173.

P. Li et al. (Eds.): CGI 2025, LNCS 16508, pp. 474–487, 2026.
https://doi.org/10.1007/978-3-032-22264-0_37

Fig. 1. A subset of samples from the *CartoonAnimalPose* dataset. *CartoonAnimalPose* is a high-quality dataset specifically established for cartoon animal pose estimation, characterized by high accuracy, diversity, and richness.

We further design a domain-adaptive pose estimation framework combining a joint learning strategy and a lightweight Channel-Spatial Attention (CSA) module. The joint learning strategy alternates training between real and cartoon animal domains to balance knowledge transfer. The CSA module enhances spatial and channel-wise feature focus while maintaining low overhead.

Experiments demonstrate that our method achieves 66.4% AP@0.5 on the *CartoonAnimalPose* benchmark, outperforming previous approaches in accuracy, training stability, and efficiency.

Our main contributions are as follows:

1. We present *CartoonAnimalPose*, the first dataset for cartoon animal pose estimation with diverse styles and high-quality annotations.

2. We propose a joint learning strategy that dynamically balances learning between real and cartoon domains to improve generalization.

3. We introduce the CSA module, a lightweight attention mechanism that enhances keypoint detection performance in artistic scenarios.

2 Related Works

Animal pose estimation has been widely studied in applications such as behavior analysis and ecological monitoring [14,23–25], primarily relying on real-world datasets. However, models trained on natural scenes often generalize poorly to artificial domains, where animals appear with exaggerated shapes and artistic styles. The emergence of deep learning [6,13,16,20] and annotated datasets [1,2, 14,23,25] has advanced animal pose estimation, yet non-realistic domains remain underexplored.

2.1 Animal Pose Estimation Dataset

High-quality annotated datasets are essential for advancing animal pose estimation, as they directly influence model accuracy and generalization. Many datasets have been proposed to support this field. For example, StanleyExtra [1] provides binary masks and 20 keypoints for 20,580 dog images from 120 breeds in the Stanford Dog dataset [7]. AnimalPose [2], built on VOC2011 [4], offers annotations for five mammal species across 4,000 images. More comprehensive datasets [14,23,25] extend coverage to various terrestrial, avian, and aquatic animals under diverse natural conditions with rich annotations.

However, creating large-scale real datasets is costly and time-consuming, particularly for rare species or complex environments. To address this, synthetic datasets [10] have been proposed, providing rendered images with precise annotations at lower cost. These have proven effective in tasks such as pose estimation, segmentation, and multi-task learning. However, datasets focusing on non-photorealistic animals remain limited. Although UniKPT [22] includes some stylized samples, most existing datasets still prioritize natural scenes. This restricts research on artistic animal characters. To fill this gap, we introduce a dedicated dataset for non-realistic animal pose estimation and establish a corresponding benchmark.

2.2 Animal Pose Estimation Method

Deep learning has significantly advanced pose estimation, with many human-centric methods generalized to animals due to their shared structured keypoint prediction framework [5,15,17,21]. To improve animal keypoint detection, various network architectures have been proposed. SimpleBaseline [20] utilizes ResNet [6] to extract multi-scale features and generates heatmaps via transposed convolutions. HRNet [16] further improves performance by maintaining high-resolution representations and fusing multi-scale features in parallel. Universal frameworks [24] have also been proposed to handle multiple species with varying keypoint definitions.Beyond architecture, transfer learning offers promising solutions for domain adaptation. For example, [2] introduced cross-domain feature alignment to transfer knowledge from human to animal tasks, while [10] proposed an unsupervised adaptation framework using adversarial learning to bridge synthetic-real domain gaps. These approaches highlight the value of cross-domain knowledge transfer for improving model robustness under limited data conditions.

To further enhance feature representation, attention mechanisms have been incorporated into pose estimation. CBAM [19] integrates both channel and spatial attention to capture informative regions. A-HRNet [11] embeds attention into HRNet's high-resolution streams, improving perception in complex scenes. Other works [8,26] introduce adaptive or de-normalized attention designs for better keypoint localization. Inspired by these studies, we develop a Channel-Spatial Attention (CSA) module tailored for cartoon animal pose estimation, combining attention mechanisms with multi-resolution fusion.

3 The *CartoonAnimalPose* dataset

Cartoon animals are widely present in media and art, yet their exaggerated proportions and artistic styles pose unique challenges for pose estimation. Existing datasets focus mostly on real animals, with limited support for non-photorealistic scenes. To address this gap, we construct *CartoonAnimalPose*, a new dataset with detailed pose annotations specifically designed for cartoon animal figures.

Fig. 2. Categories included in the *CartoonAnimalPose* dataset and the supported research tasks. Each category is illustrated with representative examples.

Data Collection and Filtering. Images were sourced from high-resolution search platforms (e.g., Baidu) and image generation models (e.g., Doubao), yielding approximately 10k candidates through image search and generation using a variety of related keywords. To ensure data quality, we performed two rounds of manual filtering and algorithm-based quality screening to eliminate low-quality or ambiguous samples, resulting in 4,024 curated images.

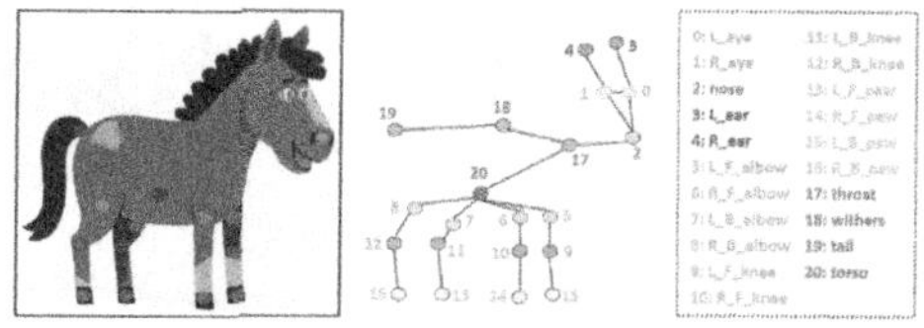

Fig. 3. A visual example of the keypoint and bone definitions in the *CartoonAnimalPose* dataset. Each instance includes 21 2D keypoints (with visible/invisible attributes) and a bounding box of the animal figure. The lines represent the bones.

Data Annotation. Each instance is annotated with 21 keypoints and a bounding box, following the MSCOCO [12] format. The keypoints include 2 eyes, 2 ears, nose, 4 paws, 4 elbows, 4 knees, throat, withers, tail, and torso, along with 21 defined bones, as shown in Fig. 3. Annotations were conducted with

Labelme [18] by 12 trained annotators and verified through multi-round reviews to ensure annotation quality. As a result, the annotation accuracy exceeded 98%. **Dataset Description.** The final *CartoonAnimalPose* dataset contains 8,887 annotated instances across 12 artistic categories, as shown in Fig. 2, supporting tasks such as pose estimation, object detection, and recognition. The dataset is randomly divided into training, validation, and test sets with proportions of 70%, 20%, and 10%, respectively, ensuring unbiased representation across subsets.

To ensure research compliance and the broad applicability of *CartoonAnimalPose*, we have provided a clear ethical statement: all images in this dataset were collected from public sources with retained watermarks to respect original authorship. The dataset is released strictly for academic use, and we will promptly remove any image upon request from copyright holders.

4 Proposed Architecture

This section details the proposed framework, which comprises a joint learning strategy for cross-domain training and a Channel-Spatial Attention (CSA) module for enhanced feature representation.

4.1 Joint Learning Strategy

In cross-domain pose estimation, direct mixed training often causes overfitting to the source domain due to sample imbalance and domain discrepancy, limiting generalization to the target domain. To address this, we propose a joint learning strategy that alternates source and target domain inputs during training, progressively shifting focus toward the target domain. The overall design of the proposed joint learning strategy is illustrated in Fig. 4.

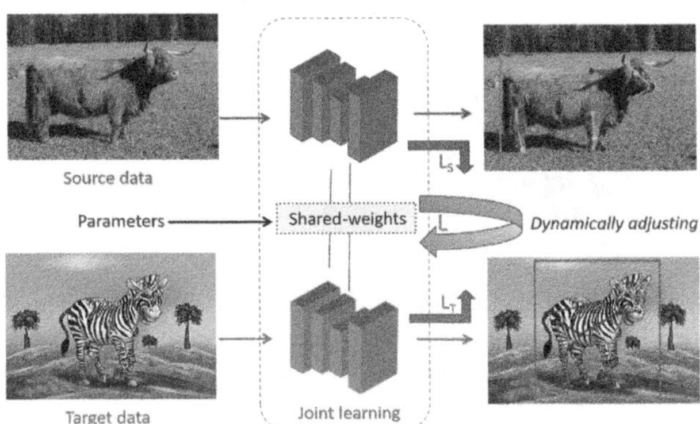

Fig. 4. The pipeline of the joint learning strategy proposed in this paper.

Task Definition. Let D_S and D_T denote the source (real animals) and target (cartoon animals) datasets, respectively:

$$D_i = \{(x_i, y_i)\}, \quad i \in \{S, T\}, \tag{1}$$

where x_i is the input, y_i is the corresponding ground-truth keypoint annotation.
The source and target domains together form the training dataset D:

$$D = D_S \cup D_T. \tag{2}$$

The model's task is defined as:

$$G_\theta : \mathbb{R}^{H \times W} \to \mathbb{R}^{d \times 2}, \tag{3}$$

where G_θ represents a function that takes an image instance as input and predicts the keypoints, outputting a matrix of keypoint coordinates.
Joint Learning Strategy Definition. During training, the model is optimized by minimizing the joint loss:

$$L = L_S + \lambda L_T, \tag{4}$$

where L_S and L_T are mean squared errors from the source and target domains, respectively. The balancing parameter $\lambda(t)$ is dynamically adjusted using:

$$\lambda(t) = \alpha + (1 - \alpha) \cdot \frac{1}{1 + e^{-k \cdot (t - T/4)}}, \tag{5}$$

where α controls the initial focus on the source domain, k is the growth rate, t is the current epoch, and T is the total number of epochs.

The joint loss L serves as the main optimization objective during training, guiding parameter updates via backpropagation ($\nabla_\theta L$). By integrating source and target domain losses into a unified framework, the model benefits from the rich annotations of the source domain while gradually adapting to the target domain. To mitigate the imbalance between domains, we apply a dynamic adjustment strategy for $\lambda(t)$, which smoothly increases the contribution of the target loss as training progresses. This helps the model avoid overfitting to the source domain and ensures a stable transition toward target-specific feature learning. In summary, the proposed joint learning strategy alternates batches from both domains and dynamically rebalances supervision, thereby improving target-domain generalization and enhancing cartoon animal keypoint detection.

4.2 CSA Mechanism Module

The *CartoonAnimalPose* dataset is small and contains dense keypoints, making it sensitive to background noise. To address this, we introduce a lightweight Channel-Spatial Attention (CSA) module, integrated into the HRNet [16] backbone. This module enhances feature maps by applying attention mechanisms in both channel and spatial dimensions, allowing the model to focus on keypoint-related regions and suppress irrelevant background noise, thereby improving keypoint detection.

The CSA block consists of a Channel Attention (CA) module, a Spatial Attention (SA) module, and a fusion layer. Inspired by A-HRNet [11] and CBAM [19], it combines their strengths while addressing their limitations. Unlike A-HRNet, which applies channel-wise weighting, and CBAM, which increases complexity with serial attention, CSA enhances both dimensions in parallel with a lightweight design. This ensures more efficient focus on keypoint regions. The flow diagrams of A-HRNet, CBAM, and CSA are shown in Fig. 5.

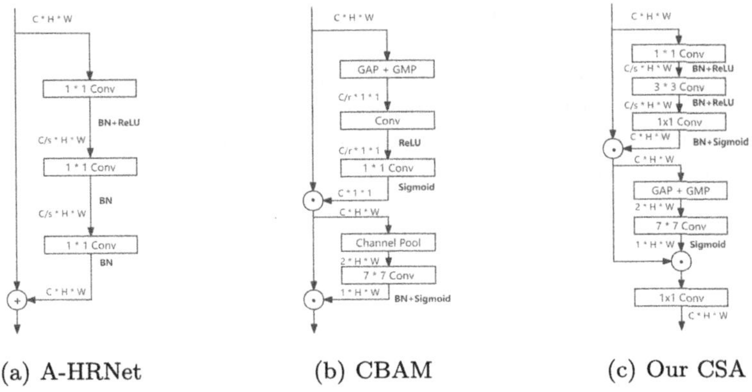

(a) A-HRNet (b) CBAM (c) Our CSA

Fig. 5. Comparison of different attention modules. $C * H * W$ represents a feature map with channel number C, height H, and width W. $\bigoplus$ denotes broadcast element-wise addition and $\bigodot$ denotes broadcast element-wise multiplication.

The structure and mechanism of CSA are described as follows.

Channel Attention Module (CA): The CA module enhances key channel responses through multi-level convolution instead of traditional global pooling. Specifically, given input feature X, we perform:

$$\begin{aligned} F' &= \mathrm{ReLU}(\mathrm{BN}(\mathrm{Conv1}(X))), \\ F'' &= \mathrm{ReLU}(\mathrm{BN}(\mathrm{Conv3}(F'))), \\ F''' &= \mathrm{Sigmoid}(\mathrm{BN}(\mathrm{Conv1}(F''))). \end{aligned} \tag{6}$$

where $F''' \in \mathbb{R}^{C\times1\times1}$ serves as channel weights. The refined feature is obtained via:

$$X_{\mathrm{CA}} = X \odot F'''. \tag{7}$$

This process enhances the feature representation of important channels while suppressing irrelevant ones.

Spatial Attention Module (SA): SA enhances spatial awareness by computing average and max pooling over channels:

$$F_{\text{avg}} = \frac{1}{C}\sum_{i=1}^{C} X_{\text{CA}}(i),$$
$$F_{\max} = \max_{i\in\{1,2,\ldots,C\}} X_{\text{CA}}(i), \tag{8}$$

where $F_{\text{avg}}, F_{\max} \in \mathbb{R}^{1\times H\times W}$. Next, the two feature maps are concatenated and passed through a convolution layer to generate the spatial attention map $F_{\text{SA}} \in \mathbb{R}^{1\times H\times W}$:

$$F_{\text{SA}} = \text{Sigmoid}(\text{Conv7}(\text{Concat}(F_{\text{avg}}, F_{\max}))). \tag{9}$$

The generated spatial attention map F_{SA} is then element-wise multiplied with X_{CA} using broadcasting to produce the adjusted feature map X_{SA}:

$$X_{\text{SA}} = X_{\text{CA}} \odot F_{\text{SA}}. \tag{10}$$

This process allows the model to focus on key regions in the feature map while suppressing background noise.

Fusion Module: After the adjustments from CA and SA, the final feature map X_{SA} is passed through a convolution layer to fuse the features, resulting in the enhanced feature representation X_{CSA}:

$$X_{\text{CSA}} = \text{Conv1}(X_{\text{SA}}). \tag{11}$$

This layered refinement strengthens attention to both informative channels and key spatial regions.

We integrate the CSA module into the HRNet backbone, forming the network architecture used in this paper. The specific network framework is shown in Fig. 6.

5 Experiments

We conduct comprehensive experiments to evaluate the proposed dataset and methods. Section 5.1 presents ablation studies on the Joint Learning (JL) strategy and CSA module. Section 5.2 compares JL with direct mixing and benchmarks CSA against A-HRNet [11] and CBAM [19] to assess attention-based improvements. These experiments thoroughly validate our modules and overall framework.

Parameter Settings. All experiments were conducted on a workstation equipped with three NVIDIA RTX 3090 Ti GPUs and one RTX 4090 (24GB each). The input images were resized to 256×192. We used ImageNet-1K [3] pre-trained weights, and adopted the AdamW [9] optimizer with a learning rate of 1.5e−3 and a weight decay of 5e−4. The learning rate decayed by a factor of

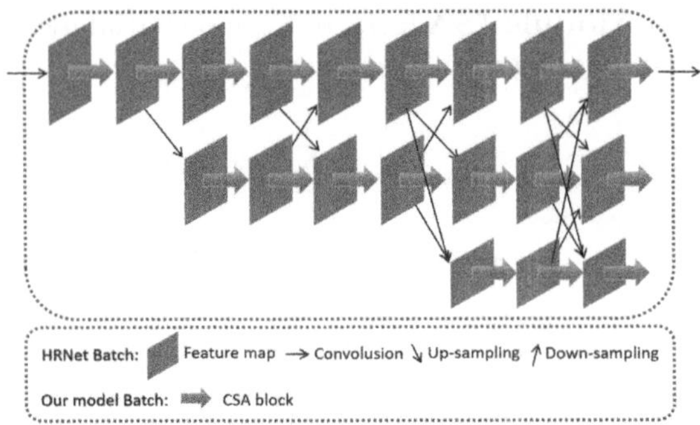

Fig. 6. The model architecture of our work. This figure shows the exact position of CSA module when integrated within HRNet.

10 at epochs 170 and 200. The training batch size was set to 48, and the testing batch size was 2. Data augmentation included random rotation (±45°), scaling ([0.65, 1.35]), and 50% horizontal flipping.
Hyperparameter Settings. For the joint learning strategy, we set the adversarial control parameter $\alpha = 0.95$ to ensure source-dominant early-stage training. The balance growth rate was set to $k = 0.3$, enabling a smooth shift toward the target domain. The total number of training epochs was $T = 210$.
Evaluation Metrics. We adopt Average Precision (AP) and Average Recall (AR) as the primary evaluation metrics, which respectively reflect model accuracy and detection coverage under multiple thresholds. Both metrics are based on the Object Keypoint Similarity (OKS) formulation, following the MSCOCO convention. To better reflect the structure of cartoon animals, we manually adjusted the keypoint-specific constants k_i used in OKS calculation as: k_i = [0.25, 0.25, 0.72, 0.62, 0.62, 0.35, 0.35, 0.35, 0.35, 0.89, 0.89, 0.89, 0.89, 0.62, 0.62, 0.62, 0.62, 1.07, 1.07, 1.07, 0.89]/10.0. These values reflect the varying spatial sensitivities of different keypoints in stylized animal figures.

5.1 Ablation Studies

To evaluate the independent contributions of each module, we conducted ablation studies on the Joint Learning (JL) strategy and CSA module using the *CartoonAnimalPose* dataset. The experiments, summarized in Table 1, compare performance across six settings by incrementally adding or removing components. In Method 5 and 6, *AnimalPose* [2] was used as the source dataset:

- **Method 1:** Baseline HRNet without added modules.
- **Method 2–4:** Only CA, SA, or full CSA applied.
- **Method 5:** Only JL applied.
- **Method 6:** JL and CSA applied together.

As shown in Table 1, Method 1 achieves 28.8% mAP and 35.6% mAR, revealing limited generalization capability to cartoon animals. In contrast, Method 5,

Table 1. Results of Component Ablation Study. The bold text highlights experiments that include the complete modules we proposed, while the underlined portions indicate the experiments with the best performance.

Methods	JL	CA	SA	CSA	mAP(%)	mAR(%)	AP@0.5(%)	AR@0.5(%)
1					28.8	35.6	53.5	58.2
2		✓			46.2	51.2	63.1	66.4
3			✓		47.0	51.0	63.8	66.2
4				✓	**47.5**	**51.6**	64.3	66.6
5	✓				**48.9**	**52.9**	**65.2**	**67.2**
6	✓			✓	<u>**49.6**</u>	<u>**53.5**</u>	<u>**66.4**</u>	<u>**68.1**</u>

which adopts the Joint Learning (JL) strategy, boosts the performance to 48.9% mAP and 52.9% mAR, confirming its effectiveness in leveraging source-domain priors while progressively emphasizing target-domain features.

Methods 2âĂŞ4 further demonstrate the contribution of attention mechanisms. Using only the Channel Attention (CA) or Spatial Attention (SA) modules yields comparable improvements (46.2% and 47.0% mAP), indicating that each component independently enhances feature discrimination. When combined (Method 4), the complete CSA module achieves 47.5% mAP and 51.6% mAR. This gain stems from CSA's ability to capture both cross-channel dependencies and spatial correlations, directing attention to keypoint-relevant regions while suppressing noise.

Finally, Method 6, which integrates both the JL strategy and the CSA module, achieves the best overall performance with 49.6% mAP, 53.5% mAR, 66.4% AP@0.5, and 68.1% AR@0.5. These results demonstrate that the combination of JL and CSA effectively enhances cross-domain generalization and keypoint localization, validating the overall superiority of our proposed approach.

5.2 Comparative Experiments

To further assess the effectiveness of our approach, we conduct two sets of comparative experiments. The first compares our Joint Learning (JL) strategy with a direct mixed training baseline (MixCA). The second benchmarks our CSA module against two SOTA attention mechanisms: A-HRNet [11] and CBAM [19].

Joint Learning Strategy Comparison. We evaluate the JL strategy against MixCA, which directly mixes *AnimalPose* and *CartoonAnimalPose* for joint training. While MixCA benefits from shared cross-domain representation, it lacks dynamic adaptation and may bias towards the dominant source domain. In contrast, JL gradually shifts training focus to the target domain via a dynamic weighting scheme. As shown in Table 2, JL achieves 53.4% AP@0.75 and 48.9% mAP, outperforming MixCA by 3.1 and 3.7 points respectively. Similarly, JL achieves higher recall (AR@0.75 ↑4.5, mAR ↑2.7), demonstrating stronger generalization to cartoon data. These results confirm that dynamic joint learning leads to more effective domain adaptation than static mixed training.

Table 2. Comparison Results of MixCA and JL on CartoonAnimalPose. Bold text highlights our proposed method, and underlined values indicate the best results.

Methods	AP@0.5(%)	AP@0.75(%)	mAP(%)	AR@0.5(%)	AR@0.75(%)	mAR(%)
MixCA	63.5	50.3	45.2	64.8	53.1	50.2
JL	**65.2**	**53.4**	**48.9**	**67.2**	**57.6**	**52.9**

Table 3. Comparison Results of A-HRNet, CBAM and the CSA Module.

Methods	AP@0.5(%)	AP@0.75(%)	AR@0.5(%)	AR@0.75(%)	Time(min)
A-HRNet	56.5	34.9	59.9	40.3	250
CBAM	63.5	52.1	65.9	55.5	293
CSA	**64.3**	**51.9**	**66.6**	**55.8**	**264**

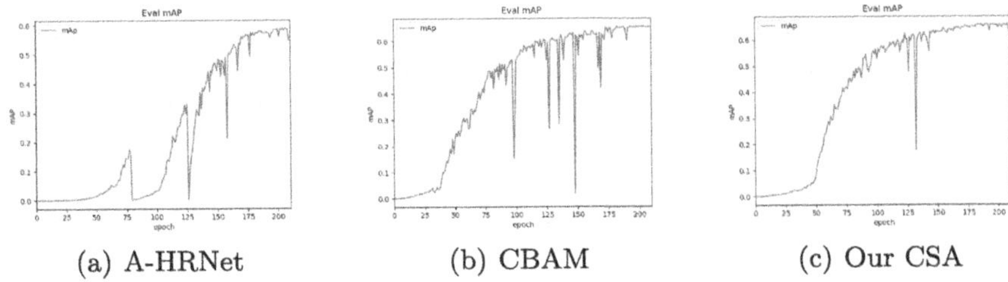

(a) A-HRNet (b) CBAM (c) Our CSA

Fig. 7. Comparison of mAP Curves during Training for Different Attention Mechanisms.

CSA Module Comparison. To evaluate attention-based enhancements, we compared the proposed CSA module with A-HRNet [11] and CBAM [19] under consistent settings. Results are shown in Table 3. Compared to A-HRNet, CSA improves AP@0.5 $\uparrow$7.8 and AP@0.75 $\uparrow$17.0, while AR@0.5 $\uparrow$6.7 and AR@0.75 $\uparrow$15.5. The improvement reflects CSA's dual-dimensional enhancement: unlike A-HRNet which only applies channel weighting, CSA fuses both spatial and channel attention to better localize dense keypoints and suppress background interference. Compared to CBAM, CSA achieves comparable high-precision results, while reducing training time by 29 min. This efficiency comes from CSA's streamlined parallel fusion design, avoiding CBAM's sequential processing overhead while retaining precision.

To further evaluate CSA's effectiveness, we plotted the mAP convergence curves of the three attention modules during training and analyzed. As shown in Fig. 7, CSA converges faster in early epochs and exhibits more stable learning dynamics than A-HRNet and CBAM. These improvements stem from its efficient dual-attention fusion, which allows better localization of keypoints with less training overhead. Overall, CSA achieves a favorable trade-off between accuracy and efficiency, validating its suitability for cartoon keypoint detection.

Based on the results of the two sets of comparison experiments, it can be concluded that the JL strategy improves generalization by dynamically balancing supervision across domains, while the CSA module enhances feature localization via joint channel-spatial attention. Together, they boost both detection accuracy and training stability. The proposed approach thus achieves better robustness and efficiency than existing baselines. These comprehensive results further validate the effectiveness of our method for cartoon animal keypoint estimation.

6 Conclusion

In this paper, we present the first dataset dedicated to cartoon animal pose estimation, encompassing 4,000+ images and 8,000+ annotated instances across 12 artistic styles with high-quality annotations. To address domain gaps between real and cartoon animals, we propose a joint learning strategy that dynamically balances training on both domains. Additionally, we introduce a lightweight channel-spatial attention (CSA) module to improve feature localization. Our method achieves 66.4% AP@0.5 on the *CartoonAnimalPose* dataset, demonstrating strong performance and efficiency in cartoon animal pose estimation.
Limitation. The dataset's relatively small size may limit generalization. While it covers diverse styles, it lacks finer-grained splits by species or complexity. Moreover, the current approach focuses solely on 2D pose estimation; extending to 3D would require substantial architectural redesign. In future work, we plan to expand the dataset in scale and granularity, and explore more advanced attention mechanisms and adaptive learning strategies for cross-domain pose estimation.

References

1. Biggs, B., Boyne, O., Charles, J., Fitzgibbon, A., Cipolla, R.: Who left the dogs out? 3D animal reconstruction with expectation maximization in the loop. In: Vedaldi, A., Bischof, H., Brox, T., Frahm, J.-M. (eds.) ECCV 2020. LNCS, vol. 12356, pp. 195–211. Springer, Cham (2020). https://doi.org/10.1007/978-3-030-58621-8_12
2. Cao, J., Tang, H., Fang, H.S., Shen, X., Lu, C., Tai, Y.W.: Cross-domain adaptation for animal pose estimation. In: Proceedings of the IEEE/CVF International Conference Computer Vision (ICCV), pp. 9498–9507 (2019)
3. Deng, J., Dong, W., Socher, R., Li, L.J., Li, K., Li, F.F.: ImageNet: a large-scale hierarchical image database. In: Proceedings of the IEEE Conference Computer Vision Pattern Recognition (CVPR). IEEE (2009)
4. Everingham, M., Gool, L.V., Williams, C.K.I., Winn, J., Zisserman, A.: The pascal visual object classes (VOC) challenge. Int. J. Comput. Vis. **88**(2), 303–338 (2009)

5. Güler, R.A., Neverova, N., Kokkinos, I.: DensePose: dense human pose estimation in the wild. In: Proceedings of the CVPR 2018, pp. 7297–7306 (2018)
6. He, K., Zhang, X., Ren, S., Sun, J.: Deep residual learning for image recognition. In: Proceedings of the IEEE Conference Computer Vision Pattern Recognition, pp. 770–778 (2016)
7. Khosla, A., Jayadevaprakash, N., Yao, B., Li, F.F.: Novel dataset for fine-grained image categorization: Stanford dogs. In: Proceedings of the CVPR Workshop on Fine-grained Visual Categorization (FGVC), vol. 2 (2011)
8. Kibaara, A.K., Kabura, J., Gitau, A., Maina, C.: Aja-pose: a framework for animal pose estimation based on VHR network architecture. In: Proceedings of the IEEE International Conference Multimedia Expo Workshops (ICMEW), pp. 1–6 (2024)
9. Kingma, D.P., Ba, J.: Adam: a method for stochastic optimization. arXiv arXiv:1412.6980 (2014)
10. Li, C., Lee, G.H.: From synthetic to real: unsupervised domain adaptation for animal pose estimation. In: Proceedings of the IEEE/CVF Conference Computer Vision Pattern Recognition, pp. 1482–1491 (2021)
11. Li, Y., Wang, C., Cao, Y., Liu, B., Luo, Y., Zhang, H.: A-HRNET: attention based high resolution network for human pose estimation. In: 2020 Second International Conference on Transdisciplinary AI (TransAI), pp. 75–79 (2020)
12. Lin, T.Y., et al.: Microsoft coco: common objects in context. In: Computer Vision–ECCV 2014, pp. 740–755 (2014)
13. Lu, C., Koniusz, P.: Few-shot keypoint detection with uncertainty learning for unseen species. In: Proceedings of the IEEE/CVF Conference Computing Vision Pattern Recognition, pp. 19416–19426 (2022)
14. Ng, X.L., Ong, K.E., Zheng, Q., Ni, Y., Yeo, S.Y., Liu, J.: Animal kingdom: a large and diverse dataset for animal behavior understanding. In: Proceedings of the CVPR 2022, pp. 19023–19034 (2022)
15. Pishchulin, L., et al.: DeepCut: joint subset partition and labeling for multi-person pose estimation. In: Proceedings of the CVPR 2016, pp. 4929–4937 (2016)
16. Sun, K., Xiao, B., Liu, D., Wang, J.: Deep high-resolution representation learning for human pose estimation. In: Proceedings of the IEEE/CVF Conference Computing Vision Pattern Recognition, pp. 5693–5703 (2019)
17. Tompson, J., Goroshin, R., Jain, A., LeCun, Y., Bregler, C.: Efficient object localization using convolutional networks. In: Proceedings of the CVPR 2015, pp. 648–656 (2015)
18. Torralba, A., Russell, B.C., Yuen, J.: LabelMe: online image annotation and applications, pp. 1467–1484. IEEE (2010)
19. Woo, S., Park, J., Lee, J.Y., Kweon, I.S.: CBAM: Convolutional Block Attention Module. In: Proceedings of the European Conference Computing Vision (ECCV), pp. 3–19 (2018)
20. Xiao, B., Wu, H., Wei, Y.: Simple baselines for human pose estimation and tracking. In: Proceedings of the European Conference Computing Vision (ECCV), pp. 466–481 (2018)
21. Xu, Y., Zhang, J., Zhang, Q., Tao, D.: VitPose: simple vision transformer baselines for human pose estimation. Adv. Neural. Inf. Process. Syst. **35**, 38571–38584 (2022)
22. Yang, J., Zeng, A., Zhang, R., Zhang, L.: X-pose: detecting any keypoints, pp. 249–268 (2024)
23. Yang, Y., Yang, J., Xu, Y., Zhang, J., Lan, L., Tao, D.: APT-36K: a large-scale benchmark for animal pose estimation and tracking. Adv. Neural. Inf. Process. Syst. **35**, 17301–17313 (2022)

24. Ye, S., et al.: Superanimal pretrained pose estimation models for behavioral analysis. Nat. Commun. **15**(1), 5165 (2024)
25. Yu, H., Xu, Y., Zhang, J., Zhao, W., Guan, Z., Tao, D.: AP-10K: a benchmark for animal pose estimation in the wild. arXiv arXiv:2108.12617 (2021)
26. Zhang, K., et al.: DNANET: de-normalized attention based multi-resolution network for human pose estimation. arXiv. arXiv:1909.05090 (2019)

PortraitFormer: Global Illumination Helps Portrait Shadow Removal

Xuze Jiao[1], Jingyu Li[2(✉)], Jiangjian Yu[1], Xiao Lu[3], and Chunxia Xiao[1(✉)]

[1] School of Computer Science, Wuhan University, Wuhan, Hubei, China
jiangjianyu@whu.edu.cn, cxxiao@whu.edu.cn

[2] Wuhan Second Ship Design and Research Institute, Wuhan, Hubei, China
2023282110161@whu.edu.cn

[3] College of Engineering and Design, Hunan Normal University, Hunan, China

Abstract. Shadows are a common optical phenomenon, and when present on the face, they often cause visual discomfort. Due to the complexity of facial geometry and shadows, removing portrait shadows while maintaining a natural and consistent visual effect is challenging. In this paper, we propose a global illumination fusion mechanism based on feature extraction and illumination balancing, followed by the design of a Transformer model for portrait shadow removal, named PortraitFormer. The model effectively removes shadows by leveraging global illumination to re-illuminate the facial region. Specifically, the PortraitFormer Block (PFB) with global illumination balancing capability captures both texture details and global illumination of the face at different scales through the Feature Illumination Balancing (FIB) mechanism, then adaptively applies global illumination to fine-grained features, progressively restoring lighting in shadowed regions while maintaining detail consistency, ultimately producing a shadow-free image. Experimental results demonstrate that this method outperforms existing techniques in facial shadow removal, providing greater accuracy and better visual effects.

Keywords: Portrait Shadow Removal · Global Illumination Balancing · Fine-grained Features

1 Introduction

Shadows can appear in facial images when the light source is obstructed by certain parts of an object or the face. The presence of facial shadows not only degrades image quality and affects aesthetics but also limits the accuracy and effectiveness of various downstream tasks related to faces. In addition to artistic design, we generally prefer that portraits captured in everyday life do not contain shadows. However, even for skilled PhotoShop users, removing aesthetically disruptive shadows is still a tedious and time-consuming task. To this end, we aim to design an end-to-end facial shadow removal model specifically for shadows cast on the face, enabling the rapid generation of visually consistent shadow removal results from a single shadowed facial image.

P. Li et al. (Eds.): CGI 2025, LNCS 16508, pp. 488–499, 2026.
https://doi.org/10.1007/978-3-032-22264-0_38

Over the past few decades, a significant amount of research has focused on image shadow removal. Traditional methods are mainly based on physical models [13,21] or statistical properties [14] of image to remove shadows. To achieve higher-quality image shadow removal, recent research has shifted toward deep learning-based methods [8,9]. Some approaches [10,11] rely on accurate shadow masks and effectively remove shadows by interacting features from both shadowed and non-shadowed areas. Although these methods have yielded good results, accurately detecting the mask in shadowed scenes remains a complex problem. When precise mask inputs are unavailable, these methods may fail to effectively identify and remove facial shadows, resulting in residual shadows on the face.

Additionally, some methods focus on the facial region, with researchers such as He et al. [15] using face generation priors to remove shadows. However, insufficient latent code optimization may result in facial distortions. Huang et al. [21] leverage internal facial illumination cues for shadow removal but struggle to find transferable illumination in cases where shadows cover large areas. These methods do not account for global illumination, resulting in inconsistent lighting effects in the shadow removal results.

To address the aforementioned issues, we propose a method that utilizes global illumination information to relight the facial region for shadow removal. Our motivation arises from the following observation: in portrait shadow images, the face and background are typically under the same lighting conditions. Thus, global illumination information serves as a crucial cue for our facial shadow removal approach. By effectively extracting global illumination and applying it to the shadowed image, we can relight the facial region, yielding more natural shadow removal.

Based on the aforementioned considerations, we propose a transformer-based global illumination balance network, as shown in Fig. 1. This network removes portrait shadows through a series of PortraitFormer blocks with global illumination balancing capabilities. Each block incorporates customized feature extraction and illumination balancing mechanisms. We validate the effectiveness of our PortraitFormer through extensive experiments on multiple datasets and images in the wild.

In summary, our major contributions are threefold as follows:

- We propose a global illumination balance network, termed PortraitFormer, which is an innovative method for removing portrait shadows by leveraging global illumination information.
- We propose the PFB for extracting global illumination information and fine-grained facial features. The Feature Illumination Balance (FIB) mechanism within it aids in restoring illumination in shadowed facial regions while preserving authentic facial textures.
- Extensive experiments demonstrate that our method outperforms existing approaches, underscoring its superiority in shadow removal and fine-grained restoration.

2 Related Work

Image Shadow Removal. Early shadow removal algorithms primarily relied on physical models [13,14]. In recent years, most shadow removal methods [1,4,9] have been based on deep learning principles. For instance, Cun et al. [7] proposed a dual-hierarchically aggregation network (DHAN), which removes shadows by hierarchically aggregating various contextual features while assisting in shadow detection. CANet [8] constructs shadow/non-shadow patch pairs and transfers features from non-shadowed regions to shadowed areas based on correlation matching. Additionally, some studies [11–13] have utilized diffusion models to simulate the shadow formation process for shadow removal. Zhang et al. [1] employed the concept of explicitly encoding facial symmetry by utilizing two separate networks to address external shadows and self-shadows, thereby achieving the removal of facial shadows. Liu et al. [3] introduced a two-stage shadow modeling algorithm that incorporates grayscale shadow removal and coloring to achieve blind removal of shadows in facial images. Zhang et al. [5] proposed a graph-based feature fusion network specifically designed to eliminate external shadows in facial images. Compared to traditional methods, these approaches achieve better visual results. However, they may face challenges in obtaining more consistent lighting effects and preserving fine details.
Vision Transformer. Visual Transformer [15] is a neural network that applies the self-attention mechanism to computer vision tasks, enhancing the performance of various visual tasks by leveraging long-range dependencies within the context. Swin Transformer [16] employs a shifted window self-attention mechanism, constructing an efficient architecture for tasks such as image classification, object detection, and semantic segmentation. In the context of image shadow removal, ShadowFormer [9] removes shadows by modeling the contextual correlation between shadowed and non-shadowed regions, while HomoFormer [10] employs a random shuffling operation to homogenize the spatial distribution of shadow degradation. To adapt Visual Transformer for facial scenarios and facilitate subsequent research, we propose PortraitFormer. This model aids in restoring shadow-free faces by simultaneously capturing fine-grained facial features and global illumination information.

3 Method

Our objective is to fully utilize global illumination cues as guidance for illuminating shadowed regions, thereby restoring the lighting in these areas while preserving facial detail fidelity. To achieve this, we designed an end-to-end framework for portrait shadow removal that learns the mapping from the shadow domain to the shadow-free domain. The mapping function is represented as: $I_{ns} = f(I_s)$, where I_s represents the input shadowed image, I_{ns} represents the shadow-free image, and f denotes the mapping from the shadowed image to the shadow-free image.

The architecture of our model is illustrated in the Fig. 1. We design the Transformer block to be used simultaneously for feature extraction and global illumination estimation, and construct an encoder-decoder pipeline through multi-scale stacking. This pipeline captures global illumination information at different scales and applies it to the extracted features, enabling the module to focus on global illumination. It adaptively illuminates the facial shadow regions while preserving realistic texture details.

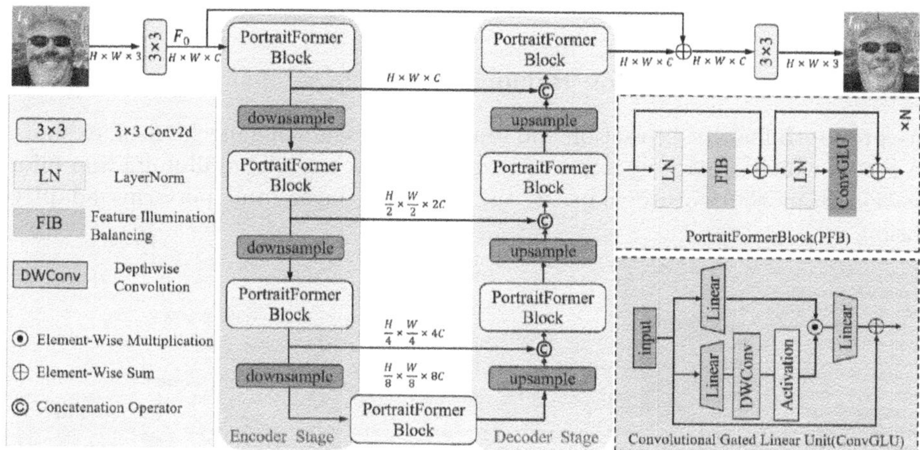

Fig. 1. Overview of the PortraitFormer network. In the encoder, the Feature Illumination Balance mechanism captures fine-grained features and global illumination information from the input. Subsequently, in the decoder stage, it restores the illumination in the shadowed regions and reconstructs the shadow-free image.

3.1 PortraitFormer Block

To fully leverage global illumination cues for re-illuminating the facial regions and restoring the lighting in shadowed areas, while preserving the original fine-grained features, we design a PortraitFormer block (PFB) with global illumination balancing capabilities. Each PFB consists of multiple PortraitFormer layers. Given the input features of the i-th PortraitFormer block, the PFB applies these features to N PortraitFormer layers to extract deep features. From top to bottom, our PortraitFormer block employs the same number of layers.

In each PortraitFormer layer, for the input feature $F_0 \in \mathbb{R}^{3 \times H \times W}$, it is first passed through a normalization layer to standardize the input features. Next, the feature map is reshaped, and all patches are simultaneously fed into the attention layer to compute attention scores, generating an attention map for feature illumination balancing. Calculating attention within local windows significantly enhances computational efficiency and reduces the complexity of global computations. Finally, we concatenate the original features with the attention-weighted features via a residual connection, allowing the model to retain information from the original features, ensuring that facial details are preserved while recovering the illumination information in shadowed regions.

To further enhance the robustness of the model, we employed Convolutional Gated Linear Unit [17] as a replacement for traditional Multi-Layer Perceptrons. ConvGLU possesses a stronger capability for local perception and enables more granular feature selection through gating signals. This allows for effective utilization of spatial information when processing image data, adapting to various input variations.

3.2 Feature Illumination Balancing

We propose a feature extraction and illumination balancing mechanism, as shown in Fig. 2, which separately extracts texture details and global illumination information from the feature maps in the attention layer, and performs adaptive fusion.

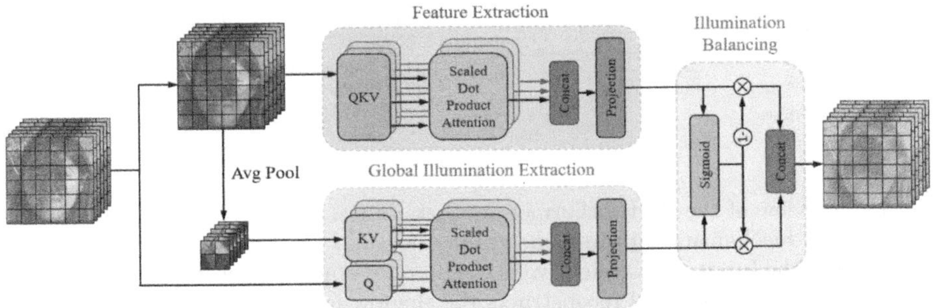

Fig. 2. Architecture of our Feature illumination balancing (FIB) mechanism.

Feature Extraction. The objective of the feature extraction branch is to capture detailed information from the image, thereby preserving the original texture details during the subsequent illumination restoration process. To achieve this, we do not apply global attention; instead, we utilize non-overlapping window partitions and compute attention scores within each window, thereby reducing computational complexity and enhancing efficiency. Convolutional operations are particularly advantageous for capturing information from local regions. Therefore, we employ a 1×1 convolutional layer to compute the query, key, and value for the feature extraction branch, ensuring the consistency of spatial local information.

Global Illumination Extraction. The goal of the global illumination extraction branch is to capture the long-range dependencies in the input image in order to calculate the global illumination information. We do not perform physical light modeling; instead, we represent global lighting by extracting global low-frequency information. We achieve this by applying average pooling to each patch of the input, which reduces the spatial resolution and results in the averaged feature map. Subsequently, the averaged feature map is projected into the key and value, while the query comes from the original feature map. The attention matrix is then calculated to capture the global illumination information within the features.

Feature Illumination Balancing. We employ a gated fusion mechanism to combine global illumination information with texture detail features, thereby adaptively applying the extracted global illumination to the fine-grained features, achieving illumination balancing at the feature level. The weights for the feature and illumination components are generated using the sigmoid function, and then a weighted fusion is performed. In this way, we obtain an adaptive global illumination balancing feature.

3.3 Losses

To achieve natural and realistic shadow removal results for facial images, we employ a composite function of reconstruction loss, multi-scale loss, and adversarial loss as the overall loss, represented as follows:

$$L_{total} = L_{pixel} + 0.5L_{mutilscale} + 0.01L_{adv} \tag{1}$$

Reconstruction Loss. It measures the pixel-level difference between the ground truth I_{gt} and the predicted shadow-free portrait image I_{out}. We use the L1 distance to quantify this difference, as expressed in the following formula:

$$L_{pixel} = ||I_{out} - I_{gt}||_1 \tag{2}$$

Multi-scale Perceptual Loss. It calculates the differences between the ground truth and predicted images at different scales in the feature space of the pre-trained network. According to the predefined scales, the predicted and ground truth values are downsampled, and then the differences between them are calculated using features extracted from the first four layers of a pre-trained VGG19 network, as represented below:

$$\begin{aligned} L_{VGG} &= \sum_{k \in layers} \|VGG_k(I_{out}) - VGG_k(I_{gt})\|_2 \\ L_{mutilscale} &= \sum_{i \in scales} \alpha_i L_{VGG}(I_{out,i}, I_{gt,i}) \end{aligned} \tag{3}$$

Adversarial Loss. It encourages the model to generate more realistic images by maximizing the probability of the ground truth while minimizing the probability of the generated result, thereby enhancing the quality of the generated images. Following Huang et al. [6], we employ a pre-trained ResNet18 [18] as the discriminator D to provide adversarial supervisory signals, which is formulated as follows:

$$L_{adv} = \mathbb{E}[\log D(I_{gt}) + \log[1 - D(I_{out})]] \tag{4}$$

4 Experiments

Our Model is implemented on the PyTorch framework on one NVIDIA GeForce RTX 3090. We adpot the AdamW optimiazer with the initial learning rate set as 0.005, then gradually reduces to 0.0001 with the cosine annealing. All training and testing images were resized to 256×256. During training, our batch size was set to 4, while during testing, the batch size was set to 1.

4.1 Training Datasets and Evaluation Metrics

Datasets. We collected a dataset containing 10,000 pairs of shadowed and non-shadowed facial images, referred to as RAS_PSD (Real and Syn Portrait Shadow Dataset). To enhance the richness of the dataset and include more realistic shadow and lighting distributions, we constructed a collection comprising 4,000 pairs of synthetic data and 6,000 pairs of real data. A portion of the real dataset is sourced from PSD [4], and we supplemented it with additional captures. The synthetic dataset was constructed following the method outlined in [1,3]. We utilized two validation sets to evaluate our method. One set is derived from RAS_PSD, which we randomly divided into a training set of 8,000 image pairs and a validation set of 2,000 image pairs. The other validation set is sourced from UCB [1], which provided a test set consisting of 100 images.
Evaluation Metrics. For quantitative evaluation, we selected four widely used metrics: PSNR, SSIM, LPIPS and RMSE. Specifically, SSIM, PSNR, and RMSE are employed to assess the overall quality of the face shadow removal results in comparison to the ground truth shadow-free images, while LPIPS is utilized to evaluate perceptual quality.

4.2 Comparison with Existing Methods

To validate the effectiveness of the proposed method, we conducted both quantitative comparisons and qualitative evaluations, comparing the results with eight other methods, including three natural scene shadow removal methods, four facial shadow removal methods, and one image restoration method. For a fair comparison, we trained all methods on the RAS_PSD dataset using the same hardware.
Qualitative Comparison. We conducted a qualitative comparison of our results with those of eight competitors across four datasets: RAS_PSD, UCB, FFHQ, and CelebA-HQ. Figure 3 illustrate the visual results. We observed that nearly all methods exhibited some residual artifacts. Zhang et al. [1] excessively removed shadows, leading to overexposed skin tones and resulting in an unnatural appearance. Liu et al. [3] failed to effectively distinguish between shadows and darker facial regions, such as hair and beard, resulting in misidentification of dark areas as shadows. The unsupervised shadow removal method proposed by He et al. [3] struggled to accurately identify and reconstruct facial features in complex scenes, leading to deformations of facial features. TBRNet [12]'s results showed a loss of detail, with residual artifacts still present on the face.

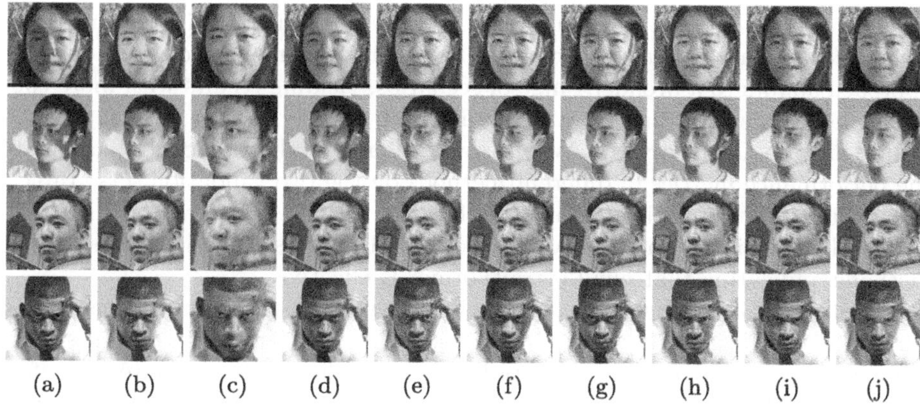

Fig. 3. Qualitative Comparison on portrait shadow removal. From left to right are: (a)input images, results of (b)Zhang et al. [1], (c)Liu et al. [3], (d)He et al. [2], (e)TBRNet [12], (f)Restormer [20], (g)ShadowFormer [9], (h)ShadowDiffusion [11], (i)HomoFormer [10] and (j)Ours.

Table 1. Quantitative comparisons on facial shadow removal. For PSNR and SSIM: larger is better, for RMSE and LPIPS: smaller is better.

Methods	RAS_PSD				UCB			
	PSNR↑	SSIM↑	RMSE↓	LPIPS↓	PSNR↑	SSIM↑	RMSE↓	LPIPS↓
Zhang et al. [1]	29.2113	0.9458	9.7783	0.0262	21.4886	0.7708	23.0078	0.0776
Liu et al. [3]	24.4074	0.8303	23.2988	0.0716	20.9238	0.7054	26.3853	0.1059
He et al. [2]	23.1942	0.8378	19.9039	0.0890	19.9626	0.7302	27.1608	0.1074
TBRNet [12]	31.9635	0.9608	7.3152	0.0175	22.4036	0.7901	20.3652	0.0702
Restormer [20]	31.7603	0.9678	7.4173	0.0207	21.7007	0.7761	22.2590	0.0780
ShadowFormer [9]	31.7162	0.9601	7.5194	0.0225	22.1279	0.7866	21.3460	0.0745
ShadowDiffusion [11]	31.9346	0.9548	7.2748	0.0199	22.3529	0.7797	21.5463	0.0760
HomoFormer [10]	32.0145	0.9579	7.1274	0.0183	22.4357	0.7813	20.5220	0.0747
Ours	**32.2172**	**0.9611**	**7.0276**	**0.0161**	**22.7593**	**0.7832**	**19.6951**	**0.0695**

The results of the Restormer [20] exhibit some residual shadows and color variation in the skin tone. ShadowFormer [9] tended to retain shadows as part of the face itself, failing to eliminate all facial shadows. HomoFormer [10] utilizes a random shuffling operation to homogenize the spatial distribution of shadow degradation. While this operation performs well in natural scenes, it causes the loss of facial geometric features when applied to faces, leading to the blurring of facial details. We conducted a separate comparison with the diffusion model. Since ShadowDiffusion [11] cannot perceive facial structures, it incorrectly identifies the darker areas of the background as shadows, leading to a lightening of the background tones. Additionally, due to its inability to distinguish between shadows and facial textures, some fine shadows are mistakenly recognized as facial textures and retained. In contrast to all the aforementioned methods, our approach adapts to a broader range of scenarios, yielding results with more consistent lighting effects that are visually natural.

Quantitative Comparison. We utilized the same evaluation code to calculate the performance metrics of different methods on the two validation sets. Table 1 summarizes the comparison results of the six methods. As shown in the table, our method achieved the best values across all metrics compared to all other methods, indicating that our PortraitFormer is effective.

User Study. Given that the human visual system is particularly sensitive to variations in lighting and texture on faces, and considering individual aesthetic differences, we conducted a user study to comprehensively evaluate the effectiveness of different methods. Taking into account factors such as efficiency and participant condition, we compared our method with those of Zhang et al. [1], TBRNet [12], ShadowFormer [9], HomoFormer [10] and ShadowDiffusion [11] which performed well in the experiments, in the user survey. We chose 10 images from two test sets and two real-world facial datasets used in the paper, resulting in a total of 40 images. These images were processed using our method and the five comparative methods, and the results were compiled into a questionnaire. The participants, who were not from the image processing domain, were asked to select the image with the best visual effect from each group. We received a total of 97 responses, and the results indicated that our method achieved a support rate of 31.08%, while the shadow removal methods proposed by Zhang et al., TBRNet, ShadowFormer, HomoFormer and ShadowDiffusion received support rates of 16.98%, 8.32%, 8.17%, 16.57% and 18.87% respectively.

4.3 Ablation Study and Analysis

In this section, we conducted ablation experiments and analyses based on the RAS_PSD dataset to investigate and evaluate the effectiveness of our primary proposal.

Effect of Feature Illumination Balancing (FIB). To validate the effectiveness of the feature illumination balancing mechanism, we replaces FIB with classic channel attention [19] and multidimensional convolutional head transpose attention [20], resulting in Variant 1 and Variant 2. As shown in the second and third columns of the Fig. 4, the results indicate that both channel attention and multidimensional convolutional head transpose attention fail to fully utilize global illumination information, leading to color migration of the skin tone. For instance, in the shadowed areas restored in the second row, both the lips and skin tone appear grayish, which also causes some loss of details. In contrast, the illumination-balanced features extracted by FIB better leverage global illumination and successfully preserve details, thereby achieving consistent shadow removal. The results in Table 2 also demonstrate that the proposed feature illumination balancing mechanism outperforms all quantitative metrics.

Effect of ConvGLU. Convolutional GLU effectively extracts spatial information through depthwise separable convolutions and utilizes a gating mechanism

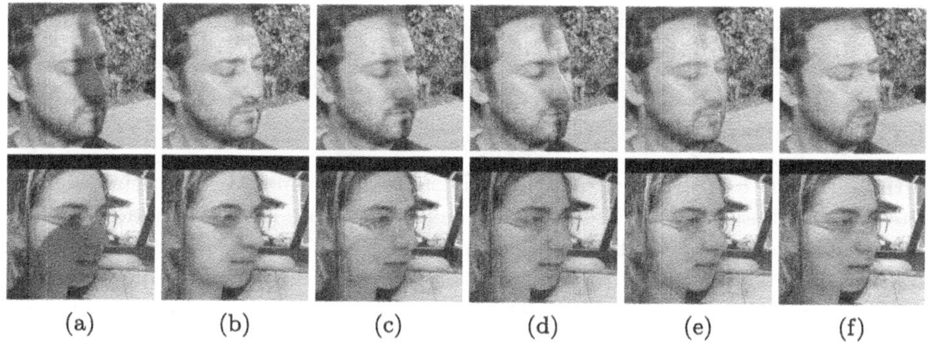

Fig. 4. Quanlitative comparison of different variants of our method. Each of our component contributes to our final model. From left to right are: (a) Input, (b)Variant 1, (c) Variant 2, (d) Variant 3, (e) Variant 4 and (f) Ours.

Table 2. Quantitative comparison among different variants of our model on the RAS_PSD dataset. Each of our component contributes to our model.

method	PSNR↑	SSIM↑	LPIPS↓
Variant 1	30.6039	0.9523	0.0193
Variant 2	31.3552	0.9600	0.0173
Variant 3	31.4948	0.9571	0.0179
Variant 4	28.0015	0.9493	0.0208
Full Model	**32.2172**	**0.9611**	**0.0161**

to dynamically adjust the output based on input features. This allows ConvGLU to effectively capture important features while suppressing irrelevant ones. As a result, ConvGLU demonstrates improved robustness when handling complex data, enabling it to adapt to various input variations. To validate its role in PortraitFormer, we replaces ConvGLU with a classic MLP to obtain Variant 3, and conducts an ablation study. The fourth column in the Fig. 4 shows the visual results, where visible artifacts or overall image darkening are observed, demonstrating the effectiveness of ConvGLU. Table 2 presents the results of the quantitative evaluation.

Effect of PortraitFormer Block (PFB). To gain a deeper understanding of the role and effectiveness of the PortraitFormer block, we replaces all PFBs in the network with standard residual blocks, resulting in Variant 4. In the visual results of the fifth column of Fig. 4, it can be observed that although the shadows have been removed, noticeable artifacts and visual blur remain. This is due to the failure to effectively extract facial detail features and the lack of global illumination utilization for feature lighting balance, leading to instability in the learned mapping. This also results in poor performance in the quantitative evaluation (Table 2). Our PFB achieves illumination balancing by extracting global illumination information and progressively applying it to shadowed areas, thereby re-illuminating the face and producing visually consistent shadow removal results.

4.4 Limitations

Although our method demonstrates broader adaptability in facial shadow removal, it may face challenges when dealing with more mottled shadows. These shadows typically alternate between shadowed and non-shadowed areas with very small gaps, making it difficult for the human eye to accurately distinguish the category of each region. In such cases, our method may also exhibit some noticeable residuals.

5 Conclusions

In this paper, we propose a global illumination balancing mechanism based on feature extraction and illumination fusion, and on this foundation, we design a Transformer model for portrait shadow removal, called PortraitFormer. This model provides a novel approach to high-quality shadow removal for facial images. By extracting texture details and global illumination information at multiple scales, the model adaptively applies global illumination to fine-grained features, progressively restoring lighting in shadowed regions while maintaining consistency in detail, resulting in more natural portrait de-shadowing. Extensive experiments validate the effectiveness of the proposed method.

Acknowledgments. This work is partially supported by the National Natural Science Foundation of China (No. 61972298 and No. 62372336).

Disclosure of Interests. The authors declare that they have no conflict of interest.

References

1. Zhang, X.C., et al.: Portrait shadow manipulation. ACM Trans. Graph. (TOG) **39**, 78:1–78:14(2020)
2. He, Y., Xing, Y., Zhang, T., Chen, Q.: Unsupervised portrait shadow removal via generative priors. In: Proceedings of the 29th ACM International Conference on Multimedia (2021)
3. Liu, Y.: Blind removal of facial foreign shadows. In: BMVC (2022)
4. Yu, J., et al.: Portrait shadow removal using context-aware illumination restoration network. IEEE Trans. Image Process. (TIP), vol. 34, pp. 1–15, 2025 (2024)
5. Zhang, L., Chen, B., Liu, Z., Xiao, C.: Facial image shadow removal via graph based feature fusion. In: Computer Graphics Forum (CGF), vol. 42 (2023)
6. Huang, Q., Xu, C., Li, G., Wu, Z., Liu, S., He, S.: Portrait shadow removal via self-exemplar illumination equalization. In: ACM Multimedia (2024)
7. Cun, X., Pun, C., Shi, C.: Towards ghost-free shadow removal via dual hierarchical aggregation network and shadow matting GAN. ArXiv, abs/1911.08718 (2019)

8. Chen, Z., Long, C., Zhang, L., Xiao, C.: CANet: a context-aware network for shadow removal. In: ICCV, pp. 4743–4752 (2021)
9. Guo, L., Huang, S., Liu, D., Cheng, H., Wen, B.: ShadowFormer: global context helps image shadow removal. ArXiv, abs/2302.01650 (2023)
10. Xiao, J., et al.: HomoFormer: homogenized transformer for image shadow removal. In: CVPR, pp. 25617–25626 (2024)
11. Guo, L., et al.: ShadowDiffusion: when degradation prior meets diffusion model for shadow removal. In: CVPR, pp. 14049–14058 (2023)
12. Liu, J., Wang, Q., Fan, H., Tian, J., Tang, YâĂŕ: A shadow imaging bilinear model and three-branch residual network for shadow removal. IEEE Trans. Neural Netw. Learn. Syst. **35**, 15857–15871 (2023)
13. Xiao, C., She, R., Xiao, D., Ma, K.: Fast shadow removal using adaptive multi-scale illumination transfer. In: Computer Graphics Forum, vol. 32, pp. 207–218 (2013)
14. Zhang, L., Zhang, Q., Xiao, C.: Shadow remover: image shadow removal based on illumination recovering optimization. IEEE Trans. Image Process. **24**(11), 4623–4636 (2015)
15. Dosovitskiy, A., et al.: An image is worth 16x16 words: transformers for image recognition at scale. In: ICLR, abs/2010.11929 (2021)
16. Liu, Z., et al.: Swin transformer: hierarchical vision transformer using shifted windows. In: IEEE/CVF International Conference on Computer Vision (ICCV), pp. 9992–10002 (2021)
17. Shi, D. :TransNeXt: robust foveal visual perception for vision transformers. In: IEEE/CVF Conference on Computer Vision and Pattern Recognition (CVPR), pp. 17773–17783 (2024)
18. He, K., Zhang, X., Ren, S., Sun, J.: Deep residual learning for image recognition. In: 2016 IEEE Conference on Computer Vision and Pattern Recognition (CVPR), pp. 770–778 (2015)
19. Hu, J., Shen, L., Albanie, S., Sun, G., Wu, E.: Squeeze-and-excitation networks. In: IEEE/CVF Conference on Computer Vision and Pattern Recognition, pp. 7132–7141 (2017)
20. Zamir, S.W., Arora, A., Khan, S., et al.: Restormer: efficient transformer for high-resolution image restoration. In: Proceedings of the IEEE/CVF Conference on Computer Vision and Pattern Recognition, 5728–5739 (2022)
21. Guo, R., Dai, Q., Hoiem, D.:Single-image shadow detection and removal using paired regions. In: CVPR, pp. 2033–2040 (2011)

Optimisation of Web-Edge-Cloud Intelligent Collaborative Rendering System for Dynamic Web3D Scenes

Chang Liu[1], Yuming Zhang[1], Jianwei Guo[2(✉)], Liming Xie[3], and Yuxun Zhang[1]

[1] Nanchang Hangkong University, Nanchang, China
[2] Chinese Academy of Sciences, Beijing, China
jianwei.guo@nlpr.ia.ac.cn
[3] China Welfare Lottery Issuance and Management Center, Beijing, China

Abstract. Web3D enables interactive 3D visualization on the Web, but its rendering quality is limited by WebGL constraints. To address this, we propose an intelligent "web-edge-cloud" collaborative rendering framework. Cloud and edge servers handle global illumination rendering, while web clients perform post-processing and display. For dynamic scenes, edge/cloud resources dynamically compensate for rendering demands. To optimize efficiency, we design a particle swarm-based multi-objective algorithm that jointly minimizes interaction latency and maximizes rendering quality. Experimental results demonstrate 13% higher SSIM and 20% lower latency compared to baseline systems, significantly improving user experience.

Keywords: Web3D · Cloud Rendering · Collaboration · Edge Computing · Global illumination

1 Introduction

Web3D enables interactive 3D visualization on the Web, but its rendering quality is limited by WebGL constraints (e.g., power-of-two textures). To address this, multi-device collaborative rendering leverages user front-ends, edge, and cloud servers [35].

Multi-device collaborative rendering balances latency and quality [9,20]. Current web-cloud systems [15] face high latency due to distant cloud servers. Edge computing offloads tasks closer to users [10], reducing network latency and bandwidth. However, dynamic scenes with real-time updates (e.g., lighting/shadow changes) challenge consistency across distributed devices.

Supported by the National Natural Science Foundation of China (62262043); Jiangxi Provincial Natural Science Foundation of China (20242BAB25074).

P. Li et al. (Eds.): CGI 2025, LNCS 16508, pp. 500–511, 2026.
https://doi.org/10.1007/978-3-032-22264-0_39

Optimizing "web-edge-cloud" systems requires balancing conflicting objectives: latency, quality, and energy. Prior work uses load balancing [31] or QoS-aware strategies [17], but solutions involve complex non-convex optimization, making systems difficult to maintain for dynamic scenes.

To address these challenges, we focus on two key QoE parameters: rendering quality and interaction latency, proposing a particle swarm-based optimization strategy.

We claim the following contributions:

1. Design a new intelligent collaborative rendering framework that can dynamically adjust the distribution of rendering tasks according to the different device performance.
2. Propose an optimization strategy considering rendering quality and interaction latency.
3. Introduce a novel evaluation of Web-Edge-Cloud collaborative rendering.
4. Experiments show that our method can improve the rendering quality by 13% and reduce the interaction delay by 20%.

2 Related Work

2.1 Collaborative Rendering

Cloud rendering offloads resource-intensive tasks to remote servers, enabling "thin" clients to achieve high-quality visualization [19,22]. With the rise of 5G and IoT, it has found critical applications in mobile XR [12,21,24,28] and cloud gaming [3,16,26,36,37], where low latency and high fidelity are paramount [12,16,21,24,28,37]. However, Web3D applications hosted on WebXR still face rendering bottlenecks due to browser-based constraints, driving the need for multi-device collaborative frameworks.

Multi-device systems decompose rendering tasks between clients and clouds, categorized by viewpoint relevance: 1) Viewpoint-relevant systems require strict front-backend alignment, but interaction latency easily distorts outputs [14]; 2) Viewpoint-independent systems render full scenes for robust weak-client support, though at high computational cost [4,25,33]. Edge computing enhances this paradigm: by offloading tasks to servers closer to clients, it reduces network latency and bandwidth consumption [18]. Notable works include Chatzopoulos et al.'s proposal to assign computing tasks to edges while keeping rendering local [5], Trinelli et al.'s NEAR framework for edge-accelerated MR via network function virtualization [29], Bachhuber et al.'s study on AR rendering offloading to edges [2], and CERender's cloud-edge collaborative model that leverages cloud resources to reduce edge computational burden through rendering result reuse [13]. The latter specifically addresses downstream bandwidth challenges via dynamic update strategies, demonstrating significant latency reduction compared to cloud-centric approaches and achieving over 20% frame rate improvement in multi-dynamic lighting scenes with its NetGI component. Yet, "end-edge-cloud" collaboration lacks unified standards for dynamic Web3D scenes.

2.2 Resource Scheduling

Optimizing communication and offloading is critical for multi-platform systems. For high-load WebAR, Ren et al. proposed the BA-CPP mechanism to balance ISP and user needs in multi-user communication [27], complemented by their Mo-KFP motion-aware keyframe selection for computational efficiency. Qiao et al. introduced fine-grained elastic partitioning for distributed DNNs in 5G, validated in mobile WebAR [10]. In resource scheduling, Lai et al. developed a QoS-aware strategy to dynamically allocate tasks between ends and clouds under unstable bandwidth [17]. Wang et al. optimized server/renderer parameters to enhance multi-task performance [32], directly inspiring our PSO-based parameter tuning.

2.3 Task Offloading Optimization

Current offloading research focuses on latency and energy via optimization algorithms. Traditional methods like genetic algorithms [1] and PSO [34] risk local optima. Chen et al. proposed DNN-based adaptive load balancing, partitioning networks to offload intensive layers to clouds [6], but edge deployment remains challenging due to data and computational costs [7]. Cong et al. studied latency-energy trade-offs under resource constraints [8]. Crucially, existing work lacks dynamic coordination across cloud-edge-end resources for Web3D's real-time updates, leaving a gap for our adaptive framework.

Therefore, how to fully utilize cloud-edge-end computing resources and optimize task offloading poses a new challenge.

3 Overview

This system can be divided into three modules based on different types of devices: cloud, edge, and web. The cloud module is dedicated to handling computationally-demanding cloud rendering effects, while the edge module takes care of less computationally-intensive edge effects. The web module delivers web-based, time-sensitive effects with low computational requirements, while also incorporating post-processing functionalities. The system can optimize the allocation of rendering processes across the modules by making adjustments based on the performance of the devices.

The primary computing power of the system is concentrated in the 'cloud server cluster', where the light probe algorithm [23] is used to obtain light information maps to be transmitted as cloud rendering effect frames to reduce latency. The edge side, which is closer to the web side, is responsible for streaming the Ambient Occlusion information calculated by the RTAO algorithm as the edge side rendering effect frames to the user end. Meanwhile, considering the weaker computing power of the web end, we arranges the delay-sensitive and low-computation direct illumination task in the front end. Furthermore, the web module is responsible for post-processing, which involves integrating the rendering frame data from both the cloud and edge modules to produce the final rendering effect frame.

4 Method

4.1 Mathematical Formulation

We analyze three device types: web end (WE), edge end (ED), and cloud end (CL). Our framework enables dynamic collaboration between these devices to expand computational capacity and optimize rendering task allocation while minimizing latency. By leveraging the performance disparities between devices, we develop a mathematical model supporting three collaboration modes: web-cloud, edge-web, and web-edge-cloud rendering.

Rendering Process Segmentation: The real-time rendering pipeline is partitioned into n sequential frame tasks. Each frame comprises four core components: indirect lighting for global illumination, ambient occlusion handling surface contact shadows, direct lighting for primary light sources, and post-processing for final image composition. Formally, each rendering process T_{ij} (where $j \leq 4$) is defined as:

$$T_{ij} = w_{ij}, f_{\min ij}, d_{ij}, t_{\max ij} \tag{1}$$

Here w_{ij} denotes computational complexity in FLOPs; $f_{\min ij}$ specifies the minimum required compute capacity in FLOPS; d_{ij} represents output data size in bytes; $t_{\max ij}$ defines the maximum allowable processing delay.

Rendering Latency Calculation: End-to-end latency comprises computational latency (t_1) and network transmission latency (t_2). Computational latency depends on device capabilities:

$$t_{1,ijn} = \frac{w_{ij}}{\lambda_n f_n} \tag{2}$$

where λ_n is the GPU utilization threshold preventing overload, and f_n is the peak compute capacity. For edge deployments, we consider aggregated performance across multiple edge servers within the maximum service distance $D_{\max}$:

$$D_{w \to e} = \sqrt{(x_w - x_e)^2 + (y_w - y_e)^2} < D_{\max} \tag{3}$$

Transmission latency is modeled using Shannon's theorem accounting for channel characteristics:

$$t_{2,ijn} = \frac{d_{ij}}{B \log_2 \left(1 + \frac{P_l}{\tau^2 + I_q}\right)} \tag{4}$$

with B as channel bandwidth, P_l as transmit power, τ^2 as noise power, and I_q as interference power.

Task allocation follows computational characteristics: compute-intensive indirect lighting requiring global illumination calculations is assigned to cloud servers with abundant resources; ray-traced ambient occlusion (RTAO) processing is delegated to edge servers for balanced computation and proximity; while latency-critical direct lighting operations execute directly on the web end to ensure responsive interaction.

The web-edge-cloud latency model integrates these allocations:

$$t_{\text{all}} = \max\left(t_c^{\text{ct1}} + t_{c \to w}^{\text{tr1}},\ t_e^{\text{ct2}} + t_{e \to w}^{\text{tr2}},\ t_w^{\text{ct3}}\right) + t_w^{\text{ct4}} \tag{5}$$

For resource-constrained clients unable to handle direct lighting:

$$t_{\text{all}} = \max\left(t_{c\to e}^{\text{tr1}} + t_c^{\text{ct1}},\ t_e^{\text{ct23}}\right) + t_e^{\text{ct4}} + t_{e\to w}^{\text{tr}} \tag{6}$$

When edge resources suffice for both indirect lighting and AO:

$$t_{\text{all}} = \max\left(t_e^{\text{ct12}} + t_{e\to w}^{\text{tr12}},\ t_w^{\text{ct3}}\right) + t_w^{\text{ct4}} \tag{7}$$

Rendering Quality Evaluation: Image quality is quantified by comparing current rendering settings s against optimal parameters s_{best} using structural similarity (SSIM) metric. The quality deviation function integrates differences across all lighting components:

$$e(s) = \iint_{xy} \sum_{i=1}^{4} \left| f_i(c, s_{\text{best}}) - f_i(c, s) \right|, dx, dy \tag{8}$$

where c represents camera parameters and f_i generates specific lighting effects under given configuration.

4.2 Multi-objective Optimization

We formulate rendering efficiency as a multi-objective optimization problem balancing perceptual image quality against interaction latency. Key rendering parameters including lighting probe density, ray count per probe, AO map resolution, lighting map resolution, and shadow map resolution are combined to form

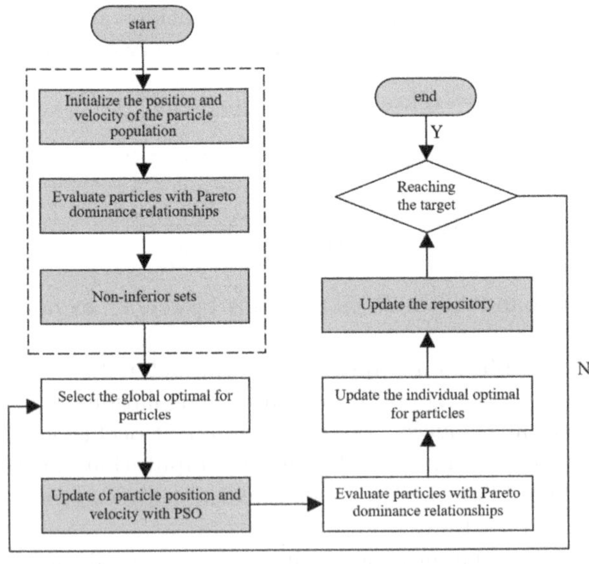

Fig. 1. Particle Swarm Optimization process

solution particles. Through iterative evaluation, we establish Pareto dominance relations between particles based on their latency-quality tradeoffs (Fig. 1).

The Particle Swarm Optimization (PSO) algorithm updates particle positions using velocity adjustments:

$$V^{k+1} = wV^k + c_1 r_1 (P_{\text{id}}^k - X^k) + c_2 r_2 (P_{\text{gd}}^k - X^k) \tag{9}$$

where w controls momentum retention, r_1, r_2 are uniform random variables in [0, 1], P_{id} tracks particle-specific optima, and P_{gd} represents swarm-wide best solutions. Progressive refinement generates the final Pareto frontier (Fig. 2) containing non-dominated solutions.

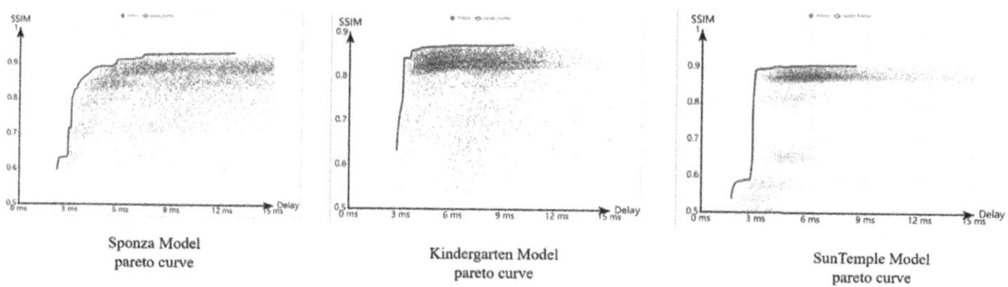

Fig. 2. Pareto frontier showing latency-quality tradeoffs

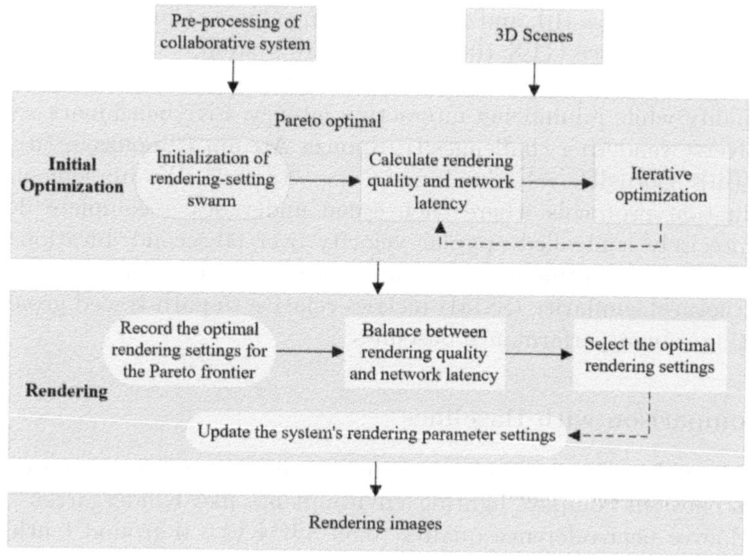

Fig. 3. System optimization architecture

4.3 Collaborative Rendering Optimization

As illustrated in Fig. 3, our adaptive algorithm dynamically selects collaboration modes based on real-time rendering complexity analysis. The optimization pipeline operates in two distinct phases: 1) The initial optimization phase begins with randomized parameter combinations that initialize rendering settings. These configurations are evaluated through the particle swarm mechanism, which systematically explores the solution space to generate the Pareto frontier containing optimal latency-quality compromises, 2) During the rendering operation phase, the system selects the most appropriate configuration from the frontier based on user-defined quality or latency preferences. This selected parameter set then drives the actual rendering execution across the distributed system architecture.

5 Experiments

5.1 Experimental Settings

We benchmark against Unity Render Streaming [30] (light probe auto-arrangement v2021.3), and Unreal Pixel Streaming [11] (default ray tracing). Path tracing provides reference quality. Identical camera trajectories, lighting, and temporal sampling ensure fair comparison. The experimental infrastructure comprised a three-tier architecture: A cloud server with Intel Xeon Platinum 8255C CPU and NVIDIA Tesla T4 GPU (64 GB RAM, Windows Server 2019), an edge server equipped with i7-5800H processor and GeForce RTX 3060 GPU (8 GB RAM, Windows 10), and a client running Google Chrome v111.0.5563.112 on an i5-9400/GeForce GTX 1060 Windows 10 system.

Particle Swarm Optimization (PSO) identifies configurations maximizing visual quality while minimizing interaction latency. Five benchmark scenes represent diverse rendering challenges:(i) Sponza Atrium ("Sponza"), (ii) "Kindergarten" (iii) "Cornell" (iv) "SunTemple" (v) "tunnel". We implemented rigorous evaluation protocols where each scene undergoes a complete 360° rotation at precisely controlled angular velocity over 60-second durations. During motion sequences, continuous sampling captured interaction latency and computed structural similarity (SSIM) metrics relative to path-traced ground truth, establishing robust performance baselines.

5.2 Comparison with Baselines

Figure 4 provides visual evidence of our method's quality advantages across diverse scenes. In complex lighting environments like Kindergarten, our approach achieves near-reference quality (0.89 SSIM vs 1.0 ground truth), significantly outperforming Unity (0.48) and Unreal (0.63). The comparison reveals critical baseline limitations: Unity exhibits lighting inconsistencies in Sponza (0.75 SSIM) due to viewpoint-dependent probes, while Unreal shows noise artifacts in Tunnel scenes (0.59 SSIM).

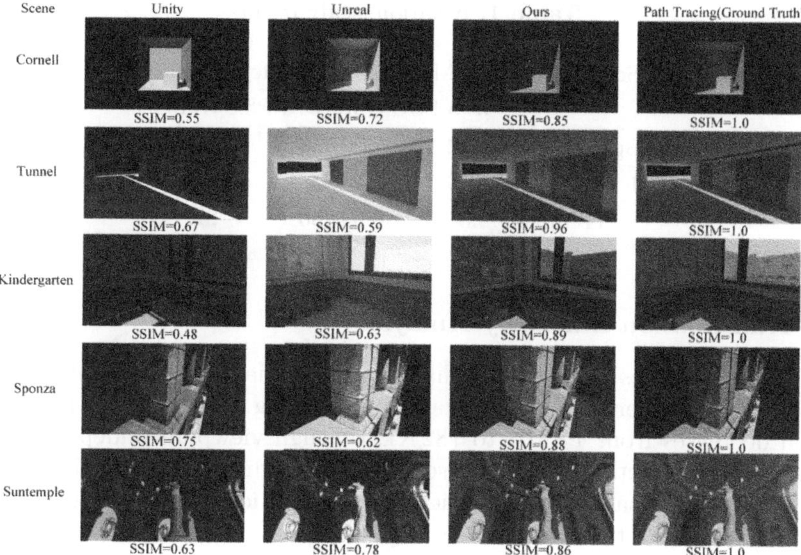

Fig. 4. Per-scene quality comparison: (columns) Unity, Unreal, Our method, Path Tracing reference. SSIM values quantify perceptual differences, with our method consistently closer to ground truth.

Our method maintains robust performance in challenging conditions: Cornell box achieves 0.85 SSIM (vs 0.55 Unity), preserving high-frequency details that baseline methods miss. SunTemple results (0.86 SSIM) confirm consistent outdoor lighting handling. However, visual inspection reveals two limitations: 1) Specular surface rendering exhibits slight energy loss compared to path tracing reference, particularly in Cornell box chrome materials; 2) Dynamic shadow boundaries show minor quantization artifacts during rapid camera motion, attributable to spherical harmonics banding.

5.3 Ablation Study

To quantify optimization contributions, we conducted two-tier testing: 1) Unoptimized pipeline (Ours w/o PSO) implements the framework without parameter tuning, 2) Complete system (Ours) incorporates PSO-driven configuration. Table 2 confirms PSO delivers dual enhancements: Sponza SSIM improves from 0.82 to 0.92 (12.2% gain) while latency drops from 30 ms to 23 ms (23.3% reduction). The optimized version closes 89% of the quality gap to path-traced reference, with latency reductions most significant in computationally intensive scenes like SunTemple (36 ms to 22 ms) (Table 1).

Table 1. Ablation study results

Scene	SSIM		Latency (ms)	
	w/o PSO	Ours	w/o PSO	Ours
Sponza	0.82	0.92↑	30	23↓
Kindergarten	0.76	0.88↑	28	22↓
SunTemple	0.85	0.94↑	36	22↓

5.4 Transmission Efficiency Analysis

Table 2 demonstrates our spherical harmonics irradiance representation reduces payload by 78.4% versus conventional Cloud Baking. Kindergarten scene transmission decreases from 4.8 MB to 782 KB through viewpoint-independent coefficients that compactly encode full scene radiance distribution. This eliminates redundant screen-space data and viewpoint distortion artifacts while reducing required frame update rates by 43%.

Table 2. Bandwidth utilization comparison

Scene	Faces (k)	Cloud Baking	Ours	Reduction
Sponza	103	5.6M	1251K	77.7%
Kindergarten	97	4.8M	782K	83.7%
SunTemple	517	4.9M	1882K	61.6%

5.5 System Efficiency Evaluation

Resource profiling (Table 3) reveals our framework's distinctive computational signature. At sustained 60 FPS, GPU utilization dominates (53.1–82.9%) across all tiers, confirming efficient offloading of graphics workloads. Resource distribution shows effective load balancing with GPU utilization variance below 30% across components. The consistent CPU/GPU ratios (1:4 to 1:6) prevent CPU bottlenecks, while SunTemple demonstrates adaptive distribution: edge GPU 46.7% versus client 79.2%, scaling to device capabilities.

Table 3. Resource utilization (%) at 60 FPS

Scene	CPU (Cloud/Edge/Client)	GPU (Cloud/Edge/Client)
Sponza	11.1/4.4/8.9	53.1/40.4/82.9
Kindergarten	12.9/5.3/9.6	61.2/43.2/76.1
SunTemple	16.7/6.3/14.4	71.2/46.7/79.2

6 Conclusion

This paper presents an intelligent rendering system leveraging "web-edge-cloud" collaboration to achieve high-quality rendering. The core concept involves offloading complex global illumination (GI) calculations to the cloud and edge, which return low-data panoramic maps based on spherical harmonics (SH) for post-processing and display on the web interface. To enhance efficiency, we developed an optimization model balancing interaction delay and rendering quality. We introduced a particle swarm optimization (PSO) algorithm where rendering parameters serve as initial particles. The algorithm iterates based on Pareto dominance relations between latency and quality, updating particles and incorporating mutation. This process establishes a mapping reserve set, from which the globally optimal particle, representing the best configuration parameters, is selected.

Our developed system handles scenes with both static and dynamic lighting sources, including dynamic viewpoint changes. However, key limitations exist. The collaboration efficiency is dependent on stable network conditions between web-edge-cloud layers, as weak connectivity can disrupt task offloading. Furthermore, the PSO algorithm may converge to suboptimal solutions for highly dynamic scenes with abrupt lighting changes. Finally, task allocation assumes predictable computational capabilities, meaning extreme hardware heterogeneity may degrade load balancing. Future work will address these challenges, focusing on hybrid optimization and adaptive network-aware scheduling.

References

1. Al-Habob, A.A., Dobre, O.A., Armada, A.G., Muhaidat, S.: Task scheduling for mobile edge computing using genetic algorithm and conflict graphs. IEEE Trans. Veh. Technol. **69**(8), 8805–8819 (2020)
2. Bachhuber, C., Martinez, A.S., Pries, R., Eger, S., Steinbach, E.: Edge cloud-based augmented reality. In: 2019 IEEE 21st International Workshop on Multimedia Signal Processing (MMSP), pp. 1–6. IEEE (2019)
3. Bhojan, A., Ng, S.P., Ng, J., Ooi, W.T.: CloudyGame: enabling cloud gaming on the edge with dynamic asset streaming and shared game instances. Multimedia Tools Appl. **79**, 32503–32523 (2020)
4. Bugeja, K., Debattista, K., Spina, S.: An asynchronous method for cloud-based rendering. Vis. Comput. **35**, 1827–1840 (2019)
5. Chatzopoulos, D., Bermejo, C., Huang, Z., Hui, P.: Mobile augmented reality survey: from where we are to where we go. IEEE Access **5**, 6917–6950 (2017)
6. Chen, X., Li, M., Zhong, H., Ma, Y., Hsu, C.H.: DNNOFF: offloading DNN-based intelligent IoT applications in mobile edge computing. IEEE Trans. Industr. Inf. **18**(4), 2820–2829 (2021)
7. Chen, X., Zhang, J., Lin, B., Chen, Z., Wolter, K., Min, G.: Energy-efficient offloading for DNN-based smart IoT systems in cloud-edge environments. IEEE Trans. Parallel Distrib. Syst. **33**(3), 683–697 (2021)
8. Cong, Y., Xue, K., Wang, C., Sun, W., Sun, S., Hu, F.: Latency-energy joint optimization for task offloading and resource allocation in MEC-assisted vehicular networks. IEEE Trans. Veh. Technol. **72**(12), 16369–16381 (2023)

9. Crassin, C.: CloudLight: a system for amortizing indirect lighting in real-time rendering. J. Comput. Graph. Tech. **4**(4), 1–27 (2015)
10. Du, R., Liu, C., Gao, Y., Hao, P., Wang, Z.: Collaborative cloud-edge-end task offloading in NOMA-enabled mobile edge computing using deep learning. J. Grid Comput. **20**(2), 14 (2022)
11. Epic Games: Pixel streaming in unreal engine, Unreal Engine 5.5 Documentation (2024). https://dev.epicgames.com/documentation/en-us/unreal-engine/pixel-streaming-in-unreal-engine. Accessed 27 Nov 2024
12. Guang, X., Liu, C., Qu, W., Zhao, Z.: Dynamic data collection algorithm based on mobile edge computing in underwater internet of things. J. Cloud Comput. **12**(1), 46 (2023)
13. He, Z., Yang, Y., Li, Z., Chen, N., Zhang, A., Su, Y.: CERender: real-time cloud rendering based on cloud-edge collaboration. In: CCF Conference on Computer Supported Cooperative Work and Social Computing, pp. 491–501. Springer (2023)
14. Jiang, W., Gu, J.: Video stitching with spatial-temporal content-preserving warping. In: Proceedings of the IEEE Conference on Computer Vision and Pattern Recognition Workshops, pp. 42–48 (2015)
15. Kai, C., Zhou, H., Yi, Y., Huang, W.: Collaborative cloud-edge-end task offloading in mobile-edge computing networks with limited communication capability. IEEE Trans. Cogn. Commun. Network. **7**(2), 624–634 (2020)
16. Laghari, A.A., He, H., Memon, K.A., Laghari, R.A., Halepoto, I.A., Khan, A.: Quality of experience (QoE) in cloud gaming models: a review. Multiagent Grid Syst. **15**(3), 289–304 (2019)
17. Lai, C.F., Hwang, R.H., Chao, H.C.: A QoS aware resource allocation strategy for mobile graphics rendering with cloud support. IEEE Trans. Circuits Syst. Video Technol. **27**(1), 110–124 (2016)
18. Li, Y., et al.: Seamless cross-edge service migration for real-time rendering applications. IEEE Trans. Mob. Comput. (2023)
19. Lin, P., Song, Q., Wang, D., Yu, F.R., Guo, L., Leung, V.C.: Resource management for pervasive-edge-computing-assisted wireless VR streaming in industrial internet of things. IEEE Trans. Industr. Inf. **17**(11), 7607–7617 (2021)
20. Liu, C., Ooi, W.T., Jia, J., Zhao, L.: Cloud baking: collaborative scene illumination for dynamic Web3D scenes. ACM Trans. Multimedia Comput. Commun. Appl. (TOMM) **14**(3s), 1–20 (2018)
21. Liu, L., et al.: Cutting the cord: designing a high-quality untethered VR system with low latency remote rendering. In: Proceedings of the 16th Annual International Conference on Mobile Systems, Applications, and Services, pp. 68–80 (2018)
22. Maclntyre, B., Smith, T.F.: Thoughts on the future of WebXR and the immersive web. In: 2018 IEEE International Symposium on Mixed and Augmented Reality Adjunct (ISMAR-Adjunct), pp. 338–342. IEEE (2018)
23. Majercik, Z., Guertin, J.P., Nowrouzezahrai, D., McGuire, M.: Dynamic diffuse global illumination with ray-traced irradiance fields. J. Comput. Graph. Tech. **8**(2) (2019)
24. Mehrabi, A., Siekkinen, M., Kämäräinen, T., Yl Jski, A.: Multi-tier CloudVR: leveraging edge computing in remote rendered virtual reality. ACM Trans. Multimedia Comput. Commun. Appl. (TOMM) **17**(2), 1–24 (2021)
25. Mueller, J.H., et al.: Shading atlas streaming. ACM Trans. Graph. (TOG) **37**(6), 1–16 (2018)
26. Pitkänen, M., Viitanen, M., Mercat, A., Vanne, J.: Remote VR gaming on mobile devices. In: Proceedings of the 27th ACM International Conference on Multimedia, pp. 2191–2193 (2019)

27. Ren, P., Qiao, X., Huang, Y., Liu, L., Pu, C., Dustdar, S.: Fine-grained elastic partitioning for distributed DNN towards mobile web AR services in the 5G era. IEEE Trans. Serv. Comput. **15**(6), 3260–3274 (2021)
28. Siriwardhana, Y., Porambage, P., Liyanage, M., Ylianttila, M.: A survey on mobile augmented reality with 5G mobile edge computing: architectures, applications, and technical aspects. IEEE Commun. Surv. Tutorials **23**(2), 1160–1192 (2021)
29. Trinelli, M., Gallo, M., Rifai, M., Pianese, F.: Transparent AR processing acceleration at the edge. In: Proceedings of the 2nd International Workshop on Edge Systems, Analytics and Networking, pp. 30–35 (2019)
30. Unity Technologies: Unity render streaming, About Unity Render Streaming (2023). https://docs.unity3d.com/Packages/com.unity.renderstreaming@3.1/manual. Accessed 27 Nov 2024
31. Wang, R., et al.: Cloud rendering learning platform technology research for visual analysis of large scale 3D multimedia data. Multimedia Tools Appl. **79**(7), 5371–5398 (2020)
32. Wang, R., et al.: Performance bottleneck analysis and resource optimized distribution method for IoT cloud rendering computing system in cyber-enabled applications. EURASIP J. Wirel. Commun. Netw. **2019**, 1–8 (2019)
33. Wei, S., Chang, L., Jia, J.: Lightmap-based GI collaborative rendering system for Web3D application. J. Syst. Simul. **32**(4), 649–659 (2020)
34. Wei, Z., Yu, X., Zou, L.: Multi-resource computing offload strategy for energy consumption optimization in mobile edge computing. Processes **10**(9), 1762 (2022)
35. Yu, G., et al.: A survey of real-time rendering on Web3D application. Virtual Reality Intell. Hardware **5**(5), 379–394 (2023)
36. Zhang, X., et al.: Improving cloud gaming experience through mobile edge computing. IEEE Wirel. Commun. **26**(4), 178–183 (2019)
37. Zhang, Y., Zhang, Y.: Discussion on key technologies of cloud game based on 5G and edge computing. In: 2020 IEEE 20th International Conference on Communication Technology (ICCT), pp. 524–527. IEEE (2020)

GartransNet: 3D Garments Animation via Transmission Optimized Networks

Tao Peng[1,2](✉), Wenjie Yue[1], Zili Zhang[1,2], Zhe Chen[1,2], Junping Liu[1,2], Xinrong Hu[1,2], and Li Li[1,2]

[1] School of Computer Science and Artificial Intelligence, Wuhan Textile University, Wuhan 430200, Hubei, China

[2] Key Laboratory of Intelligent Sensing and Computing for Textile Industry, Wuhan 430200, Hubei, China

pt@wtu.edu.cn

Abstract. 3D garment animation is a challenging problem in computer vision and computer graphics. Although realistic animations can be generated by mapping human poses or time series to clothing deformations, these methods often limit specific clothing and are difficult to predict loose clothing. Additionally, some methods rely on predefined material parameters to control fabric deformation, yet they often lack physical rationality in terms of the stretching effect of clothing. We propose GartransNet, a transmission optimization network that enhances neighborhood sampling strategy, reduces computational redundancy, and improves real-time fabric simulation performance. We refine the mixed weights between the human body and clothing, so that the model is no longer limited to specific clothing, and introduce a collision-sensitive geometric perception constraint mechanism to improve the physical consistency of clothing deformation. The experimental results indicate that our method accelerates training and inference. In addition, it is suitable for all types of clothing and exhibits excellent performance, especially when simulating loose clothing.

Keywords: Garment modeling · Human pose · Geometric constraints · Penetration

1 Introduction

Over the past few decades, 3D garment modeling has primarily relied on physics-based simulators. While these simulators provide accurate simulations, they are computationally expensive and time-consuming [1]. Traditional template-based methods [23] and smpl-based methods [12] typically use fixed topologies and predefined templates to model garments. While effective for certain categories. Furthermore, these methods often produce smoothing artifacts that result in unnatural garment draping effects. Inspired by [4,18], motion constraints in PBS are reformulated as an optimization problem. This formulation is not only more

P. Li et al. (Eds.): CGI 2025, LNCS 16508, pp. 512–523, 2026.
https://doi.org/10.1007/978-3-032-22264-0_40

computationally efficient than PBS and supervised methods but also avoids artifact generation.

These methods also require significant post-processing steps and struggle to handle dynamic cloth behavior effectively. Currently, graph neural network (GNN)-based methods [10,16] have been proposed to address these challenges. However, these methods have high memory demands, which increase training and inference times, and fail to fully leverage the advantages of traditional physics-based methods during inference.

Therefore, our research aims to strike a balance between accuracy and efficiency, with the following primary contributions:

- Correct motion sequences to achieve temporally consistent human animation.
- A transmission optimization network to reduce computational redundancy by optimizing neighbor sampling and minimizing unnecessary information transfer.
- Introduction of geometric constraint optimization with collision awareness to address garment penetration issues.
- Optimizing human-garment blending weights and employing a geometry-aware garment skinning strategy make our approach applicable to all garment types.

2 Related Work

Physics based simulator methods usually involve processing a large number of triangular meshes. Although [19] these methods simplify the calculation, it still takes a lot of time to find the best parameters. Some studies have proposed methods of learning, estimating or inferring hyper parameters [20], which reduces the time required for hyper parameter search, but their computational complexity is still high. Most learning-based methods focus on supervised learning [2,17], complete training through supervised real-time estimation function. However, these methods mainly learn global representations and often fail to generate fine details such as wrinkles. Gradually, some studies [5,12] have suggested using human models as templates and incorporating displacements in the typical human model SMPL [11]. However, these methods assume that the garment and the body share the same topology, which does not apply to certain universal garments. Recently [3,4,18], a clothing deformation simulation method based on self supervised learning has been proposed, which avoids the drawbacks of the above methods. However, clothing based on material control will produce excessive tensile deformation. Graph Neural Network (GNN)-based methods focus on improving message passing efficiency through subsampled graphs. For example, Chi et al. [8] adopts a sampling and aggregation method to achieve efficient and scalable node representation learning by aggregating fixed-size feature samples from neighbors [22]. Gaps [6] also focuses on the improvement of mixed weights and loss, and has been referenced and learned in our work. Additionally, some methods utilize random walk sampling of neighboring nodes and combine it with graph convolution for more scalable recommendation tasks [7].

3 Methodology

3.1 SMPL Human Body Representation

Similar to the approaches in [5,14,21], our base garment template is aligned with SMPL [11]. SMPL [11] represents the human body $M()$ as a parametric function of pose (θ) and shape (β). It consists of a linear function $T(\beta, \theta)$, which applies displacements to the base mesh vertices T, followed by a learned skinning function $W()$. Specifically, $B_P()$ adds pose-dependent deformations, while $B_S()$ accounts for shape-dependent deformations (such as height, weight, and body proportions). The blending weights w are associated with the skeletal joints $J()$.

$$\begin{aligned} M(\beta, \theta) &= W(T(\beta, \theta), J(\beta), \theta, w) \\ T(\beta, \theta) &= T + B_S(\beta) + B_P(\theta) \end{aligned} \tag{1}$$

Since garment deformations are highly influenced by body motion, we adopt the motion processing module from M et al. [14] to sequentially process motion poses and obtain the guided motion sequence $\{\theta_t\}_T^1$, which drives the garment deformations.

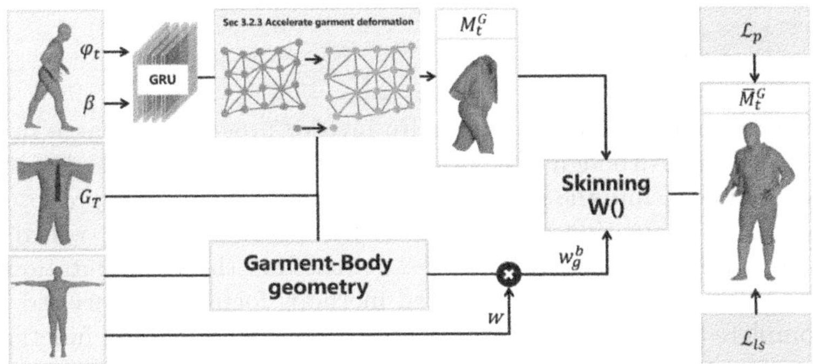

Fig. 1. Obtain motion sequence $\{\theta_t\}_T^1$ in SMPL human body representation. Obtain M_t^G through Garment Processing. Finally, skinning $W()$ integrates M_t^G and w_g^b to obtain $\bar{M}_t^G$

3.2 Garment Processing

Garment Representation. Our multi-topology garment model is developed within the unsupervised learning framework proposed by Santesteban et al. [18]. It incorporates a GRU module $\mathcal{U}()$, which outputs vertex displacements relative to the template garment G_T (which is in an unposed and undeformed state). After combining the displacement output with G_T to obtain the unposed deformed garment (M_t^G), we apply the skinning function $W()$ to integrate M_t^G with the body. The human-garment blending weights w_g^b used for skinning are estimated in Sect. 3.2. Our model architecture is illustrated in Fig. 1. The overall clothing model is as follows.

$$\begin{aligned} M_t^G &= G_T + \mathcal{U}(\varphi_t, \beta) \\ \bar{M}_t^G &= W(M_t^G, J(\beta, \theta_t, w_g^b) \end{aligned} \tag{2}$$

The regressor $\mathcal{U}()$ takes the body shape β and motion parameters $\varphi_t = \{\theta_t, v_t^r\}$ as inputs, where φ_t includes the current body pose θ_t and the global velocity of the root joint v_t^r. The skinning function $W()$ integrates M_t^G based on the joint positions $J(\beta)$, the current body pose, and the garment blending weights w_g^b estimated using the body participation module.

Human-Garment Blending Weights. Prior works [3,4,18] directly assign the blending weights of the nearest body vertex to each garment vertex. While this method works well for tight-fitting garments, it is suboptimal for loose garments (e.g., skirts). To overcome these limitations, we introduce a geometry-aware blending weight computation method. First, for a given garment vertex, the influence of body vertex blending weights is inversely correlated with their respective Euclidean distances. Furthermore, for loose garments, the blending weights are less likely to depend solely on nearby body vertices. We employ a Gaussian Radial Basis Function (RBF) to compute the participation of each body vertex in the motion of a specific garment vertex. The Gaussian RBF kernel is formulated as follows.

$$\mathcal{G}(x) = e^{-\frac{x^2}{\delta * (d_i)^2}} \tag{3}$$

where d_i represents the Euclidean distance between the garment vertex $c_i \in C$ and its nearest body vertex. The new garment blending weights w_g^b are defined as:

$$w_g^b = N(\begin{bmatrix} \mathcal{G}(e_{1,1} - d_1) & \cdots & \mathcal{G}(e_{1,n} - d_1) \\ \vdots & \ddots & \vdots \\ \mathcal{G}(e_{m,1} - d_m) & \cdots & \mathcal{G}(e_{m,n} - d_m) \end{bmatrix} * \mathrm{w}) \tag{4}$$

$\mathcal{G}(e_{m,n} - d_m)$ represents the participation of the body vertex $b_j \in B$ in the motion of garment vertex c_i. Here, $e_{m,n}$ denotes the Euclidean distance between a garment vertex and a body vertex, while m and n represent the number of elements in C and B, respectively. In our experiments, we set $\delta = 0.5$. The weight w follows the blending weights described in SMPL [11], as formulated in Eq. 1. The normalization function $N(\bullet)$ ensures that the sum of each row equals 1. Simple and effective body participation method can automatically determine the most suitable influence regions for any type of garment, without being constrained by differences in topology.

Accelerate Garment Deformation. MGN [16] encodes the garment-body mesh $\mathcal{M}$ into a graph representation $G = (V^G, E^M, E^W)$, where V^G represents the graph nodes (corresponding to garment mesh vertices), E^M represents the mesh edges (corresponding to garment mesh connectivity), and E^W represents the world edges (edges connecting garment vertices to the nearest body vertices). For each garment vertex, E^W identifies the nearest vertex on the human body model. If the distance between them is below a predefined threshold, an edge is created between them. Garment features are then encoded into graph nodes and edges, where node features include node type, velocity, normal vector, and mass, while edge features describe the relative positional relationship between two nodes. These features are then transformed into latent vectors for further processing. However, MGN [16] requires message passing across all neighboring nodes, leading to significant computational overhead as the number of nodes and edges increases. To address this, we aggregate features from a sampled subset of neighboring nodes. At each step of message passing, we sample a subset of neighbors for each garment node $v^g \in G$, selecting a subset of its neighbors to construct a subgraph, thereby reducing computational complexity. As shown in Figs. 2 and 3. We mainly refer to MGN for feature settings in this section.

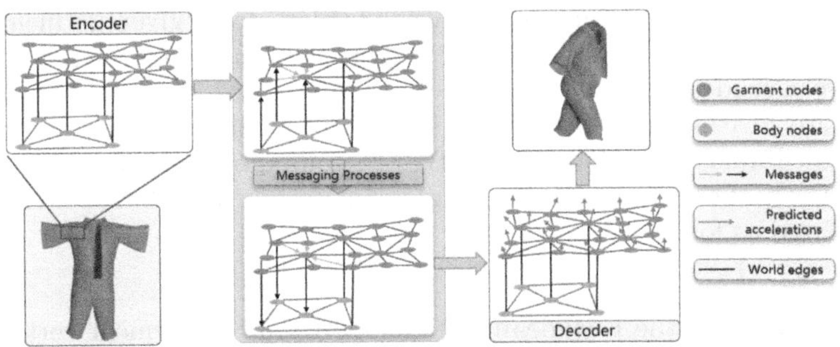

Fig. 2. The encoder transforms the features of nodes and edges in the given garment mesh into a graph representation. The processor iteratively updates these features through multiple rounds of message passing, during which neighboring nodes for information transfer are determined via sampling. Information exchange between garment nodes and body nodes occurs only during the first and last iterations of message passing. Finally, the decoder interprets the features of each node to determine their accelerations.

Edge filters [9,15] randomly drop a subset of edges in the graph to enhance generalization and reduce overfitting. In contrast, our method primarily aims to reduce redundant computations and improve message-passing efficiency. After subgraph sampling, we aggregate each garment node v^g 's features with those of its sampled neighbors onto the garment edges connecting them. This aggregation process involves only the sampled nodes and their corresponding sampled edges, significantly reducing computational overhead while preserving essential information flow.

$$f^{\bar{M}_t^G}\left(e_{S(ij)}, v^g_{S(i)}, v^g_{S(j)}\right) \rightarrow e^{\mathcal{M}}_{S(ij)} \tag{5}$$

Here, $S(ij)$ represents the set of sampled edges, while $S(i)$ and $S(j)$ denote the sampled nodes. After updating the edge features, we proceed to update the garment node features connected by these sampled edges. For a given node v^g, we aggregate the features of all sampled edges connected to it, ensuring efficient information transfer while maintaining computational efficiency.

$$f^{V^G}\left(V^G_{S(i)}, \sum e^{\mathcal{M}}_{S(ij)}\right) \rightarrow v^g_{S(i)} \tag{6}$$

Sampling a subset of neighboring nodes can significantly reduce the amount of data processed. Aggregating features from fewer neighbors also requires fewer arithmetic operations, which accelerates both forward and backward propagation, thereby improving overall training and inference speed. Additionally, memory usage is significantly reduced. During the forward pass, fewer activations need to be stored, leading to lower overall memory consumption. Modern deep learning frameworks dynamically manage memory allocation, and as the number of activations decreases, the peak memory usage is also reduced. Consequently, our method efficiently handles large-scale and complex garment simulations by leveraging localized computation through node sampling, achieving significant improvements over traditional methods.

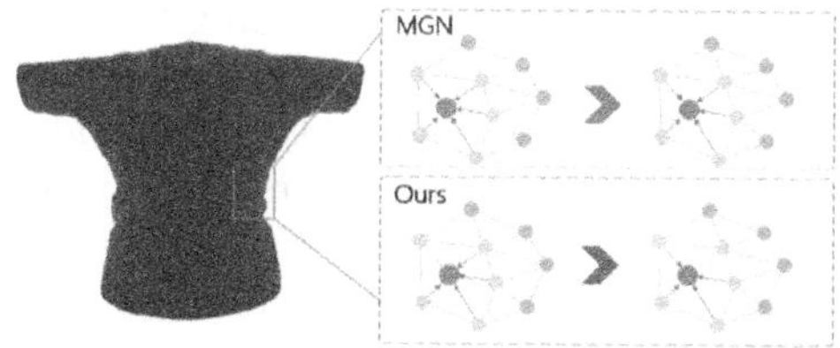

Fig. 3. Top: In each message passing step, MGN aggregates features from all neighboring nodes for each node. Down: Our algorithm instead aggregates features from a sampled subset of neighboring nodes, reducing computational complexity while maintaining effective information transfer.

In existing approaches [10,16], we have also observed inefficiencies in redundant information propagation and low feature update efficiency for body nodes, which are related to the frequency of information exchange between body nodes and garment nodes. These observations highlight a key inefficiency in the information propagation process, namely, the redundant exchange of information between body and garment nodes. To address this issue, we propose an optimized information propagation strategy specifically designed for garment and body nodes. First, we perform information transfer from body nodes to garment nodes only during the initial steps. This ensures that garment nodes receive the initial features from body nodes early in the process. After the initial steps, we focus solely on information propagation among garment nodes. Conversely, we conduct information transfer from garment nodes to body nodes only in the final step. At this stage, garment nodes aggregate comprehensive information through multiple steps of intra-garment information propagation. Our method simplifies the information propagation process, reduces redundant exchanges, and lowers overall computational costs and memory consumption.

3.3 Loss Combination

The overall loss is the sum of the physical loss and the local stretching loss:

$$\mathcal{L} = \mathcal{L}_p + \mathcal{L}_{ls} \tag{7}$$

Physical loss: We adopt a fully unsupervised training scheme and use a physics-based loss function derived from implicit time-stepping incremental potential. Inspired by SNUG [18] and HOOD [10], our physical loss is defined using an optimization-based formula:

$$\mathcal{L}_p = \mathcal{L}_{strain} + \mathcal{L}_{bending} + \mathcal{L}_{collision} + \mathcal{L}_{gravity} + \mathcal{L}_{inertia} \tag{8}$$

We use $\mathcal{L}_{strain}$ to simulate the cloth response to in-plane deformation, which is defined by the Saint-VenantKirchhoff (StVK) model. $\mathcal{L}_{bending}$ models the energy caused by the dihedral angle between two adjacent triangles. $\mathcal{L}_{collision}$ is crucial for ensuring effective predictions by pushing the garment vertices outside the body. Once the negative distance between a garment node and the closest point on the body mesh falls below a specified threshold, a penalty is applied. $\mathcal{L}_{gravity}$ simulates the effect of gravity on garment deformation. $\mathcal{L}_{inertia}$ models the inertia of the garment.

Local stretching loss: Geometric local stretching loss enforces incompressibility within a local neighborhood around each vertex. The computation is given by:

$$\mathcal{L}_{ls} = \gamma \sum_{vertices} \sum_{j=1}^{3} \left| D\left(M_{cov} - \varepsilon \sigma_j F\right) \right| \tag{9}$$

where γ is the balancing factor, M_{cov} is the covariance matrix in a local neighborhood, and σ_j is the singular value of the covariance matrix in the corresponding neighborhood of a garment template point. Since garments only stretch when covering large areas of the body, ε should be 1 and only changes when a collision between the body and the garment is detected, D stands for determinant, F is identity. Additionally, to avoid being influenced by minor perturbations, the garment will only stretch gradually when a collision is detected. Taking this into account, we define: $\varepsilon = 1 + \min(10\eta, 0.03) \times \min(ep, 100)$, where ep is the current epoch. $\eta = \max(\tau - d(x), 0)$ quantifies the degree of interpenetration. Here, $d(x)$ represents the signed distance between the garment vertex and the body surface, and τ is a small constant introduced to enhance stability. We allow the network to stabilize for 100 iterations before gradually applying local stretching to the garment during a body-garment collision.

4 Experimental

4.1 Dataset

The consistent representation of AMASS makes it readily useful for animation, visualization, and generating training data for deep learning. AMASS is significantly richer than previous human motion collections, having more than 40 h of motion data, spanning over 300 subjects, more than 11000 motions. To maintain consistency, we used the Amass [13] dataset. Additionally, four complete sequences were reserved for validation. We employed various garment meshes, including shirts, vests, long-sleeve tops, shorts, pants, and dresses. All experiments were conducted using meshes with irregular triangular topologies, where each node typically had 6 or 7 neighboring nodes. This strategy allowed the model to learn from thousands of different body shapes and a wide variety of garments.

4.2 Comparison with Related Methods

To validate the superiority of our proposed method in generating garment deformations compared to existing approaches, we used test data to drive garment deformation prediction. We compared our method with PBNS [3], SNUG [18], NCS [4], and HOOD [10]. The evaluation metrics used are based on these comparison methods, as shown in Table 1. The quantitative comparison results in Table 1 show that our method outperforms the comparison methods in most metrics. Compared to PBNS and SNUG, our method is similar to them in terms of the garment piece bending metric, indicating that it can generate reasonable bending deformations. Moreover, our method also surpasses all comparison methods in terms of penetration metrics. The qualitative comparison results in Fig. 4 demonstrate the effectiveness of our approach, as it generates more reasonable deformation effects compared to other methods.

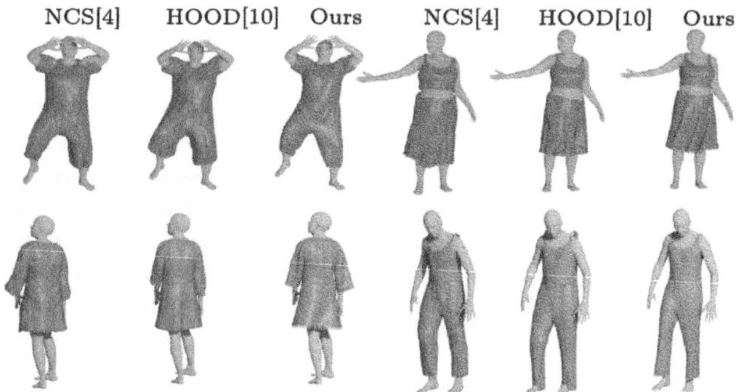

Fig. 4. Qualitative comparisons with other garment animation generation methods, including the NCS, HOOD methods.

In Fig. 5 Left, we compare the loss terms of our method on the AMASS [13] dataset test sequences. Taking local stretching as an example, our method exhibits lower error values compared to the baseline methods, indicating that the test samples processed by GartransNet align better with the behavior of physics-based solutions. As described in Sect. 3.2, the sampling number refers to the number of neighboring nodes each node exchanges information with during each message-passing step. We trained the model with different sampling numbers under the same number of iterations to evaluate their impact on the loss metrics. The comparison results are shown in Fig. 5 Right. We set the sampling number to 1, and as the sampling number increased, the loss gradually decreased. However, once the sampling number reached 5, the reduction in loss became less pronounced. Considering both quality and training time, we selected 5 as the optimal sampling number for each message-passing iteration.

Table 1. Quantitative comparison results.

Methods	$\mathcal{L}_{strain}$	$\mathcal{L}_{bending}$	$\mathcal{L}_{collision}$
PBNS [3]	0.111	0.49	1.54
SNUG [18]	0.064	0.44	1.41
NCS [4]	0.075	0.48	1.19
HOOD [10]	**0.060**	0.41	1.10
Ours	0.066	**0.38**	**1.06**

Table 2. Our approach greatly improves the speed of reasoning. L-Coll evaluates the degree of penetration between different layers of a garment and H-Coll evaluates the degree of penetration between a garment and the body.

Garments	Program	Inference speed(s)↓	Memory↓	$\mathcal{L}$↓	L-Coll(%)↓	H-Coll(%)↓
Trousers	No optimizations	0.39	893 MB	0.612	10.09	1.87
	Only dynamic sampling	0.28	641 MB	0.682	9.44	1.28
	Mixed weights for human-garment only	0.14	684 MB	0.571	8.55	1.13
	Ours	0.11	458 MB	0.446	1.04	0.23
Tshirt	No optimizations	0.18	688 MB	0.414	9.71	1.45
	Only dynamic sampling	0.17	460 MB	0.452	7.76	1.19
	Mixed weights for human-garment only	0.09	531 MB	0.395	6.60	0.98
	Ours	0.07	378 MB	0.391	1.19	0.19
Dress	No optimizations	0.29	569 MB	0.559	8.05	0.77
	Only dynamic sampling	0.33	421 MB	0.586	4.19	1.16
	Mixed weights for human-garment only	0.14	423 MB	0.448	5.10	0.88
	Ours	0.10	278 MB	0.370	0.68	0.56

4.3 Ablation Study

We conducted an ablation study to distinguish the impact of each optimization technique. Specifically, we compared four models: the model no optimizations (base model, not change), a model with only dynamic sampling (base + sample), a model with mixed weights for human-garment only (base + weights), and a model with both dynamic sampling and mixed weights for human-garment (our model). Table 3 compares the training time, iteration speed, and memory usage of these four models. The results highlight the effectiveness of each optimization technique in accelerating training and reducing memory consumption. The model that includes both dynamic subgraph sampling and information reduction outperforms all other methods in terms of training speed and memory efficiency. Table 2 compares the inference performance of different garments based on inference speed (time required per frame), memory usage, and loss values. We also investigated the importance of local stretch loss. By fixing $\varepsilon = 1$ in the local stretch loss (see Eq. 9), we enforce the garment to maintain extensibility at all locations. Table 2 shows the percentage of vertices that collide. It is evident that incorporating local stretch loss is crucial for achieving realistic draping.

Table 3. Our approach significantly reduces training time and memory usage, leading to faster model convergence.

Methods	Training	Iteration	Memory (GB)
No optimizations	58 h	1.77 s	26.1
Only dynamic sampling	49 h	1.29 s	12.1
Mixed weights for human-garment only	33 h	1.10 s	19.8
Ours	**18 h**	**0.38 s**	**2.1**

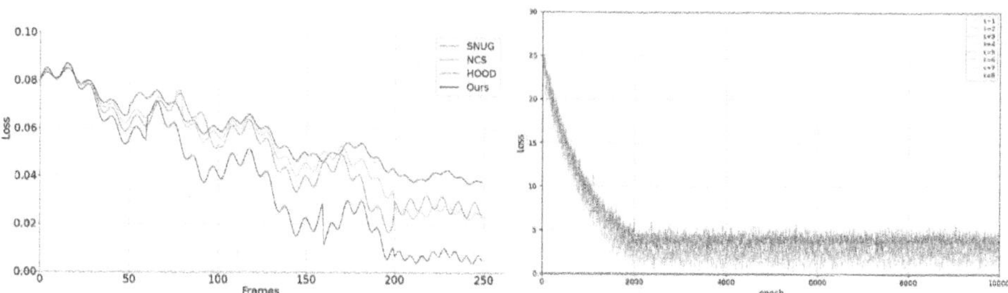

Fig. 5. Left: Quantitative evaluation of our method, taking the test sequence of AMASS [13] as an example. Right: Comparison of different sampling times. As the number of sampling increases, the total loss decreases. When the number of sampling is more than 5, the reduction in total loss is not so obvious.

5 Conclusion

We optimized a new message-passing method within the GNN to accelerate real-time simulation. Additionally, the local stretching loss significantly reduces garment collisions, eliminating the need for time-consuming post-processing. Human-garment blending weights allows us to achieve significantly better draping effects, even on loose garments. Limitations and Future Work: While we have significantly alleviated the collision issues for fitted garments, challenges remain under extreme body postures and shapes. Additionally, our current framework does not address garment self-collisions or handle multi-layer and topologically changing garment setups. When dealing with fabrics with tens of thousands of nodes, the inference efficiency may be suboptimal. Solving this issue (i.e., handling higher resolution fabrics) presents a valuable direction for future research.

Acknowledgments. This work was supported by Ningbo Cixing Co. (Grant No. 2021Z069) and National Natural Science Foundation of China, and Engineering Research Center of Hubei Province for Clothing Information. In addition, we are also thankful for the comments and suggestions from anonymous reviewers.

Disclosure of Interests. The authors declare that they have no competing interests related to the content of this work.

References

1. Bartle, A., Sheffer, A., Kim, V.G., Kaufman, D.M., Vining, N., Berthouzoz, F.: Physics-driven pattern adjustment for direct 3D garment editing. ACM Trans. Graph. **35**(4), 50–1 (2016)
2. Bertiche, H., Madadi, M., Escalera, S.: CLOTH3D: clothed 3D humans. In: Vedaldi, A., Bischof, H., Brox, T., Frahm, J.-M. (eds.) ECCV 2020. LNCS, vol. 12365, pp. 344–359. Springer, Cham (2020). https://doi.org/10.1007/978-3-030-58565-5_21
3. Bertiche, H., Madadi, M., Escalera, S.: PBNS: physically based neural simulator for unsupervised garment pose space deformation. arXiv preprint arXiv:2012.11310 (2020)
4. Bertiche, H., Madadi, M., Escalera, S.: Neural cloth simulation. ACM Trans. Graph. (TOG) **41**(6), 1–14 (2022)
5. Bhatnagar, B.L., Tiwari, G., Theobalt, C., Pons-Moll, G.: Multi-garment net: learning to dress 3D people from images. In: Proceedings of the IEEE/CVF International Conference on Computer Vision, pp. 5420–5430 (2019)
6. Chen, R., Chen, L., Parashar, S.: GAPS: geometry-aware, physics-based, self-supervised neural garment draping. In: 2024 International Conference on 3D Vision (3DV), pp. 116–125. IEEE (2024)
7. Chiang, W.L., Liu, X., Si, S., Li, Y., Bengio, S., Hsieh, C.J.: Cluster-GCN: an efficient algorithm for training deep and large graph convolutional networks. In: Proceedings of the 25th ACM SIGKDD International Conference on Knowledge Discovery & Data Mining, pp. 257–266 (2019)
8. Chibane, J., Pons-Moll, G., et al.: Neural unsigned distance fields for implicit function learning. In: Advances in Neural Information Processing Systems, vol. 33, pp. 21638–21652 (2020)

9. Fang, T., Xiao, Z., Wang, C., Xu, J., Yang, X., Yang, Y.: DropMessage: unifying random dropping for graph neural networks. In: Proceedings of the AAAI Conference on Artificial Intelligence, vol. 37, pp. 4267–4275 (2023)
10. Grigorev, A., Black, M.J., Hilliges, O.: HOOD: hierarchical graphs for generalized modelling of clothing dynamics. In: Proceedings of the IEEE/CVF Conference on Computer Vision and Pattern Recognition, pp. 16965–16974 (2023)
11. Loper, M., Mahmood, N., Romero, J., Pons-Moll, G., Black, M.J.: SMPL: a skinned multi-person linear model. ACM Trans. Graph. (TOG) **34**(6), 1–16 (2015)
12. Ma, Q., et al.: Learning to dress 3D people in generative clothing. In: Proceedings of the IEEE/CVF Conference on Computer Vision and Pattern Recognition, pp. 6469–6478 (2020)
13. Mahmood, N., Ghorbani, N., Troje, N.F., Pons-Moll, G., Black, M.J.: AMASS: archive of motion capture as surface shapes. In: Proceedings of the IEEE/CVF International Conference on Computer Vision, pp. 5442–5451 (2019)
14. Miao, J., et al.: SmPhy: generating smooth and physically plausible 3D garment animations. In: 2024 IEEE International Conference on Multimedia and Expo (ICME), pp. 1–6. IEEE (2024)
15. Papp, P.A., Martinkus, K., Faber, L.,Wattenhofer, R.: DropGNN: random dropouts increase the expressiveness of graph neural networks. Advances in Neural Information Processing Systems, vol. 34, pp. 21997–22009 (2021)
16. Pfaff, T., Fortunato, M., Sanchez-Gonzalez, A., Battaglia, P.W.: Learning mesh based simulation with graph networks. arXiv preprint arXiv:2010.03409 (2020)
17. Santesteban, I., Otaduy, M.A., Casas, D.: Learning-based animation of clothing for virtual try-on. In: Computer Graphics Forum, vol. 38, pp. 355–366. Wiley OnlineLibrary (2019)
18. Santesteban, I., Otaduy, M.A., Casas, D.: SNUG: self-supervised neural dynamic garments. In: Proceedings of the IEEE/CVF Conference on Computer Vision and Pattern Recognition, pp. 8140–8150 (2022)
19. Wang, H., Hecht, F., Ramamoorthi, R., O'Brien, J.F.: Example-based wrinkle synthesis for clothing animation. In: ACM SIGGRAPH 2010 papers, pp. 1–8 (2010)
20. Wang, H., O'Brien, J.F., Ramamoorthi, R.: Data-driven elastic models for cloth: modeling and measurement. ACM Trans. Graph. (TOG) **30**(4), 1–12 (2011)
21. Xiang, D., Prada, F., Wu, C., Hodgins, J.: MonoClothCap: towards temporally coherent clothing capture from monocular RGB video. In: 2020 International Conference on 3D Vision (3DV), pp. 322–332. IEEE (2020)
22. Ying, R., He, R., Chen, K., Eksombatchai, P., Hamilton, W.L., Leskovec, J.: Graph convolutional neural networks for web-scale recommender systems. In: Proceedings of the 24th ACM SIGKDD International Conference on Knowledge Discovery & Data Mining, pp. 974–983 (2018)
23. Zhu, H., et al.: Deep Fashion3D: a dataset and benchmark for 3D garment reconstruction from single images. In: Computer Vision–ECCV 2020: 16th European Conference, Glasgow, UK, 23–28 August 2020, Proceedings, Part I 16, pp. 512–530. Springer (2020)

Sequential Fluid Image Generation Network Based on Spatio-Temporal Swin Transformer

Zhiyu Ge, Changjun Zou(✉), and Chenxi Zhong

East China Jiaotong University, Nanchang City 330013, China
zoucj2006@163.com

Abstract. In recent years, fluid dynamics simulation has attracted widespread attention in computer graphics and scientific computing. To address the limitations of existing multi-frame fluid image prediction methods in capturing long-term dependencies and extracting local features, this paper proposes a spatio-temporal deep learning network model integrating ConvLSTM and Swin Transformer. The model leverages ConvLSTM to capture both long- and short-term temporal dependencies, while utilizing the Swin Transformer's hierarchical attention mechanism for multi-scale spatial feature extraction. Experimental results demonstrate that the proposed method achieves an average PSNR of 39.00 dB across five fluid prediction datasets, representing an 8.3% improvement over the best baseline model (Swin Transformer). Similarly, the SSIM metric shows a 6.5% improvement compared to the Swin Transformer benchmark. These results confirm the significant advantages of the generated images in both physical consistency and visual quality. This research presents an efficient approach for fluid dynamics prediction with potential application value in related fields.

Keywords: Deep Learning · Fluid Dynamics · Sequence Fluid Image Generation · ConvLSTM · Swin Transformer

1 Introduction

Fluid dynamics simulation is a critical tool in computer graphics, scientific computing, and applied fields such as weather forecasting, industrial design, and virtual reality. While traditional computational fluid dynamics (CFD) methods achieve high accuracy and physical realism, they require substantial computational resources, particularly for simulating complex long-term fluid interactions or multi-scale phenomena. These limitations become evident in scenarios involving intricate boundary conditions or multi-resolution analyses, where conventional numerical approaches (e.g., finite element methods, spectral methods) often struggle to balance efficiency and precision.

Recent advancements in deep learning have introduced data-driven paradigms to fluid dynamics research [1–3]. Models like Long Short-Term Memory (LSTM) [4] networks and Swin Transformers [5] address distinct aspects of fluid modeling: LSTMs excel at capturing temporal dynamics through gated mechanisms that preserve long-range dependencies, overcoming the vanishing gradient limitations of traditional RNNs. Meanwhile,

P. Li et al. (Eds.): CGI 2025, LNCS 16508, pp. 524–536, 2026.
https://doi.org/10.1007/978-3-032-22264-0_41

the hierarchical architecture of Swin Transformers enables efficient multi-scale spatial feature extraction, resolving the computational bottlenecks of standard Transformers [6] in high-resolution fluid image processing.

The integration of ConvLSTM [7] and Swin Transformer creates a synergistic framework for spatiotemporal modeling. ConvLSTM processes temporal evolution through convolutional recurrent operations, while Swin Transformer's shifted window attention mechanism hierarchically captures local-to-global spatial patterns. This hybrid approach enhances prediction accuracy in complex fluid scenarios (e.g., turbulent flows, multi-phase interactions) by simultaneously preserving temporal coherence and multi-resolution spatial features. Compared to pure CFD methods, such data-driven models significantly reduce computational costs while maintaining competitive accuracy, particularly when trained on high-fidelity simulation datasets. These developments not only advance fluid prediction capabilities but also enable new applications in real-time simulation and adaptive control systems.

This paper proposes a novel deep learning network based on the combination of ConvLSTM and Swin Transformer, achieving the following innovations in fluid image generation and prediction tasks:

- **Gating-Driven Spatio-Temporal Synergetic Attention:** We introduce a module that dynamically integrates the Swin Transformer into the output gate of ConvLSTM. This enables adaptive coupling of temporal dependencies and spatial features. Leveraging the Swin Transformer's multi-scale properties and global attention mechanism significantly enhances the network's perception and expression of multi-scale image features. The design also optimizes the fusion of temporal and spatial information for fine-grained detail capture.
- **Multi-Level Spatio-Temporal Feature Extraction:** We design a framework based on multi-level ConvLSTM units, refining feature maps layer by layer to deeply explore latent spatio-temporal information. The improved Swin Transformer structure further optimizes feature representation for precise sequential image generation. This effectively enhances the model's ability to capture complex spatio-temporal features, enabling high-quality image sequence prediction.

Through performance evaluation and analysis, the effectiveness of the proposed method in multi-frame fluid image generation and its applicability in real-world scenarios are validated.

2 Related Work

2.1 Previous Fluid Interaction Scene Generation Methods

Traditional fluid simulation methods rely on numerical discretization of the Navier-Stokes equations [8, 9]. These physics-based approaches are categorized into Eulerian grid methods and Lagrangian particle methods. Eulerian methods analyze spatio-temporal variations in velocity and pressure through fixed grids, but high-precision simulations require fine resolutions that substantially increase computational costs [10–12]. Conversely, Lagrangian methods track individual particles, excelling at capturing free-surface phenomena as in Smoothed Particle Hydrodynamics (SPH) [13].

Both approaches remain computationally intensive and sensitive to initial/boundary conditions.

2.2 Deep Learning-Based Fluid Image Generation Research

Image prediction focuses on forecasting future frames from sequences. Early methods employed physical models like optical flow [14] or time-series techniques including autoregressive models [15] and Kalman filtering [16]. While effective for linear dynamics, they struggled with nonlinear cases. Support Vector Machines [17] and shallow neural networks [18] captured nonlinear relationships, but spurred deep learning adoption. Convolutional networks (CNNs) enhanced spatial feature extraction [19], while recurrent networks (e.g., LSTM [4], GRU [20, 21]) addressed long-term dependencies. ConvLSTM subsequently emerged for joint spatio-temporal modeling [7], and generative adversarial networks (GANs) improved output realism [22]. Recently, Transformers revolutionized the field through long-range dependency modeling, exemplified by Vision Transformer (ViT) [6] and Swin Transformer [5, 23].

2.3 Convolutional LSTM

Recurrent Neural Networks (RNNs) suffer from vanishing/exploding gradients that impede long-term dependency modeling. Long Short-Term Memory (LSTM) networks overcome this via memory cells and gating mechanisms [4]. However, standard LSTM's fully connected structure proves inefficient for high-dimensional spatio-temporal data. ConvLSTM addresses this by replacing fully connected layers with convolutional operations [7], enabling simultaneous capture of spatial features and temporal dependencies.

2.4 Shifted Window Transformer

Originally designed for natural language processing, Transformers use self-attention to capture global dependencies [24]. Their NLP success led to computer vision applications, with Vision Transformer (ViT) adapting the architecture by dividing images into patches [6]. However, ViT requires large-scale data and incurs high computational costs. Swin Transformer resolves these limitations through a hierarchical structure and shifted window mechanism [23, 24], reducing complexity while effectively fusing local-global information.

3 Proposed Method

The proposed network architecture is shown in Fig. 1. Based on the ConvLSTM framework for capturing temporal dependencies, we integrate Swin Transformer blocks to extract global and local features, with layer-wise refinement for enhanced feature representation.

3.1 Overall Architecture

A key challenge in fluid interaction scene generation is capturing dynamic changes over time, i.e., inter-frame continuity and correlation. This temporal dependency is difficult for traditional CNNs to handle efficiently. Thus, we choose ConvLSTM as the core network structure to better capture temporal dynamics, ideal for time series modeling. We use four LSTM layers to extract temporal features, where gating mechanisms allow selective memory/forgetting, ensuring effective extraction of multi-scale temporal features.

To extract deep multi-scale features, we use Swin blocks to mine features across temporal levels. Extracted features are reconstructed via a final Swin block for the output.

In this structure, the preceding LSTM layers act as the Feature Extraction (FE) module, extracting input temporal and deep multi-scale features, then reconstructing them for prediction. The final Swin block acts as the Image Prediction (IP) module, meticulously reconstructing details for accurate predictions.

Cascading multiple LSTM layers enables deeper temporal feature extraction. Each LSTM layer extracts temporal features at different abstraction levels, and cascading lets the network learn higher-level semantics.

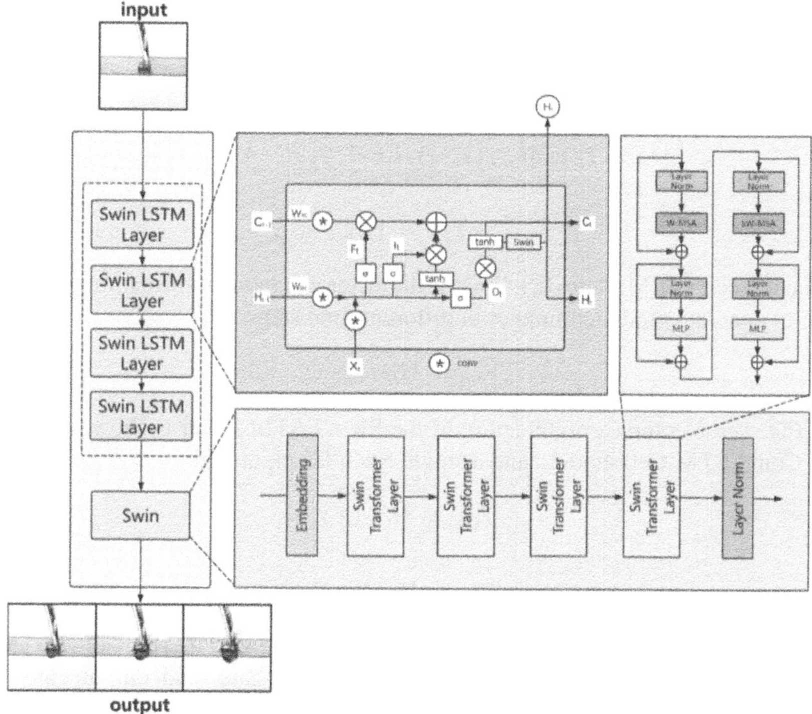

Fig. 1. SwinLSTM Image Prediction Model

3.2 Swin Transformer Block

The Swin Transformer block forms the backbone of our network, offering significant improvements in computational efficiency and feature representation over ViT. Unlike ViT, which inefficiently computes global self-attention for high-resolution images, Swin Transformer employs a hierarchical architecture with Patch Merging to gradually reduce feature map resolution via concatenation and linear projection, enabling multi-scale feature extraction. Its local window-based self-attention (W-MSA) restricts calculations to non-overlapping windows, reducing complexity, while the shifted window mechanism (SW-MSA) facilitates cross-window information fusion for global modeling.

Notably, Swin Transformer places LayerNorm before MLP and attention layers, stabilizing training and improving performance. In our network, we reconfigure channel dimensions of spatio-temporal feature maps to align with image prediction task requirements.

3.3 Detailed Process

Feature Extraction Module (FE): The FE module comprises M Swin LSTM Layer (SLL) structures, processing input data $X_{in} \in R^{H \times W \times C}$, where H, W, and C indicate the height, width, and number of input channels of the image, respectively. (default H=$W = 128$, $C = 3$).

$$Y_{FE} = M_{FE}(X_{in}) \tag{1}$$

$$Y_i = M_{SLL}(Y_{i-1}), i = 1, 2, \ldots, M, \tag{2}$$

$$Y_{FE} = Y_M \tag{3}$$

Image Prediction Module (IP): Finally, the different feature information of the images is used to generate predicted images at different time steps.

$$Y_{out} = M_{IP}(Y_{FE}) \tag{4}$$

In Fig. 1, the complex architecture of the Swin LSTM Layer is shown, including a single ConvLSTM Cell module and a single Swin Block module.

$$Y_{CC} = M_{CC}(X) \tag{5}$$

$$Y_{SLL} = M_{SB}(Y_{CC}) \tag{6}$$

The core of the Swin LSTM Layer is the ConvLSTM Cell. The ConvLSTM Cell mainly consists of three gates: the input gate, forget gate, and output gate. These gates control the flow of information within the cell, allowing the model to effectively remember or forget information.

Forget Gate:

$$F_t = \sigma\left(W_{xf}{}^*X_t + W_{hf}{}^*H_{t-1} + W_{cf} \circ C_{t-1} + b_f\right) \tag{7}$$

Input Gate:

$$I_t = \sigma\left(W_{xi}{}^{*}X_t + W_{hi}{}^{*}H_{t-1} + W_{ci} \circ C_{t-1} + b_i\right) \tag{8}$$

$$C_t = F_t \circ C_{t-1} + I_t \circ \tanh\left(W_{xc}{}^{*}X_t + W_{hc}{}^{*}H_{t-1} + b_c\right) \tag{9}$$

Output Gate:

$$O_t = \sigma\left(W_{xo}{}^{*}X_t + W_{ho}{}^{*}H_{t-1} + W_{co} \circ C_t + b_o\right) \tag{10}$$

$$H_t = O_t \circ \tanh(C_t) \tag{11}$$

Here, C_t is the current cell state, H_t is the current hidden state, and X_t is the current input. All W are convolutional weights, b is the bias term, σ is the sigmoid function, and tanh is the hyperbolic tangent function.

Next is the internal structure of the Swin Block, which includes a single embedding layer, N Swin Transformer Layer (STL) modules, and a single LayerNorm (LN) layer.

$$Y_E = M_E(X) \tag{12}$$

$$Y_j = M_{STL}\left(Y_{j-1}\right), j = 1, 2, \ldots, N, \tag{13}$$

$$Y_{SB} = LN(Y_N) \tag{14}$$

The core of the Swin Block module is the STL, which comprises two components: Window-based Multi-head Self-Attention (W-MSA) and Shifted Window-based Multi-head Self-Attention (SW-MSA). Specifically, W-MSA partitions the image into non-overlapping windows for local self-attention, while SW-MSA shifts window positions to enable cross-window information fusion via partial overlap. W-MSA leverages self-attention to focus on local contexts, with computations restricted to individual windows to reduce complexity. The STL then incorporates an MLP with two fully connected layers and GELU activation for feature transformation. Both W-MSA and SW-MSA apply LayerNorm (LN) before attention and MLP, using residual connections for stable training.

$$X = LN(W\text{-}MSA(X)) + X \tag{15}$$

$$X = LN(MLP(X)) + X \tag{16}$$

$$X = LN(SW\text{-}MSA(X)) + X \tag{17}$$

$$X = LN(MLP(X)) + X \tag{18}$$

4 Experiments

4.1 Experimental Setup

Dataset. Several customized datasets are used, containing various real fluid interaction video frames extracted at different time steps. Each frame is treated as an image, and datasets are named by their frame counts (e.g., Fluid-903). For each dataset, 70% of frames are randomly selected as the training set, with 30% reserved for testing.

Training Details. We trained our method on an NVIDIA GeForce RTX 4090 Laptop GPU using PyTorch 1.10.2. The initial learning rate was set to 1 × 10–4.

4.2 Comparison Methods and Evaluation Metrics

We evaluate our method against five mainstream deep learning models: ResNet, UNet, ViT, Swin Transformer, and ConvLSTM. All models are trained and tested on identical datasets using official implementations. Performance is assessed via Peak Signal-to-Noise Ratio (PSNR) and Structural Similarity Index Measure (SSIM), with visual comparisons supplementing quantitative analysis.

Single-Frame Prediction Comparison. Table 1 compares single-frame prediction results across five datasets. Our method achieves the top two PSNR scores on all datasets and leads in SSIM performance. Figures 2 and 3 visually demonstrate superior color consistency and texture clarity compared to baselines, closely matching ground-truth images.

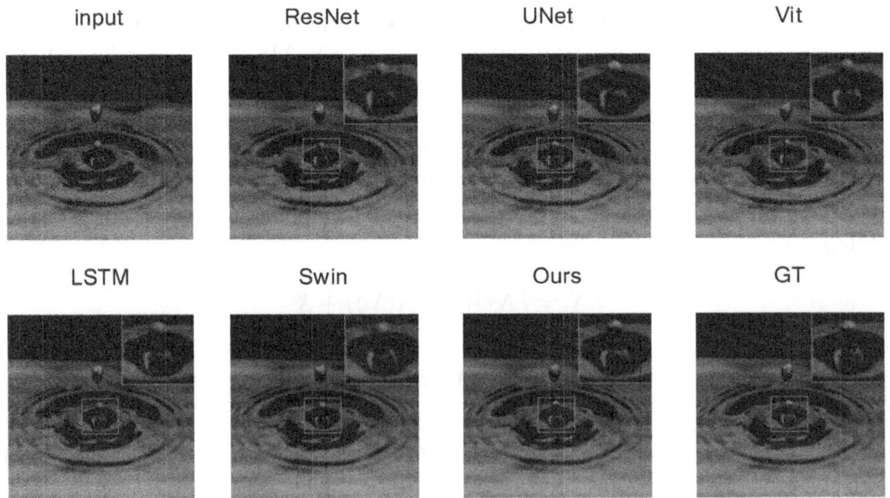

Fig. 2. Single-Frame Prediction Results of Different Methods on Fluid-903

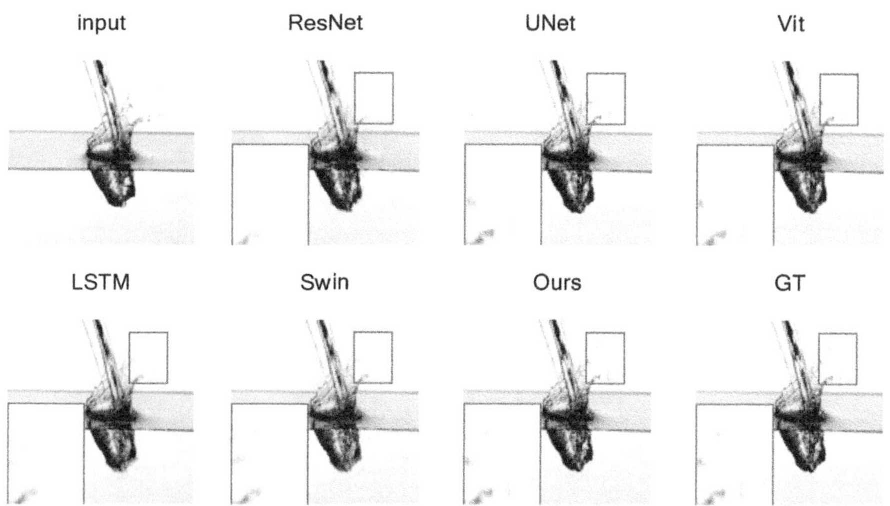

Fig. 3. Single-Frame Prediction Results of Different Methods on Fluid-590

Table 1. Quantitative Comparison of Different Methods on Single-Frame Prediction across Different Datasets

Method	Fluid-903		Fluid-590		Fluid-499		Fluid-449		Fluid-1000		Param	FlOPs
	PSNR	SSIM	PSNR	SSIM	PSNR	SSIM	PSNR	SSIM	PSNR	SSIM		
ResNet	38.11	0.983	31.15	0.974	31.94	0.965	32.82	0.977	36.50	0.991	113 M	1.34G
UNet	39.01	0.989	34.08	0.986	33.74	0.977	36.94	0.991	42.18	0.997	118 M	1.23G
ViT	41.77	0.990	33.24	0.986	34.31	0.979	32.82	0.977	42.01	0.996	123 M	1.28G
Swin	44.06	0.994	16.95	0.609	33.37	0.972	33.81	0.983	41.82	0.996	113 M	0.31G
LSTM	41.39	0.988	41.88	0.996	35.17	0.981	35.99	0.989	28.26	0.960	118 M	1.23G
Ours	45.69	0.994	37.86	0.989	38.71	0.987	38.35	0.982	45.77	0.998	149 M	0.31G

Multi-Frame Prediction Comparison. Subsequently, we performed multi-frame image prediction experiments with the goal of predicting multiple subsequent frames (with the same time interval) based on a given input image for comparison with other methods. For each dataset, we averaged the PSNR metrics of all predicted frames to obtain the PSNR metrics of the target method on that dataset. As shown in Table 2, our method performs best in terms of PSNR with an average value of 39.00 dB, which is 9.1% higher than the second-place Swin's 35.75 dB, and also tops in terms of SSIM. To show the performance more intuitively, we visualize the prediction results of the various methods. As shown in Fig. 4, in the multi-frame image prediction task, our results show better color consistency and texture similarity to the ground truth compared to other methods. These visualized comparisons further confirm the excellent performance of our methods in multi-frame image prediction.

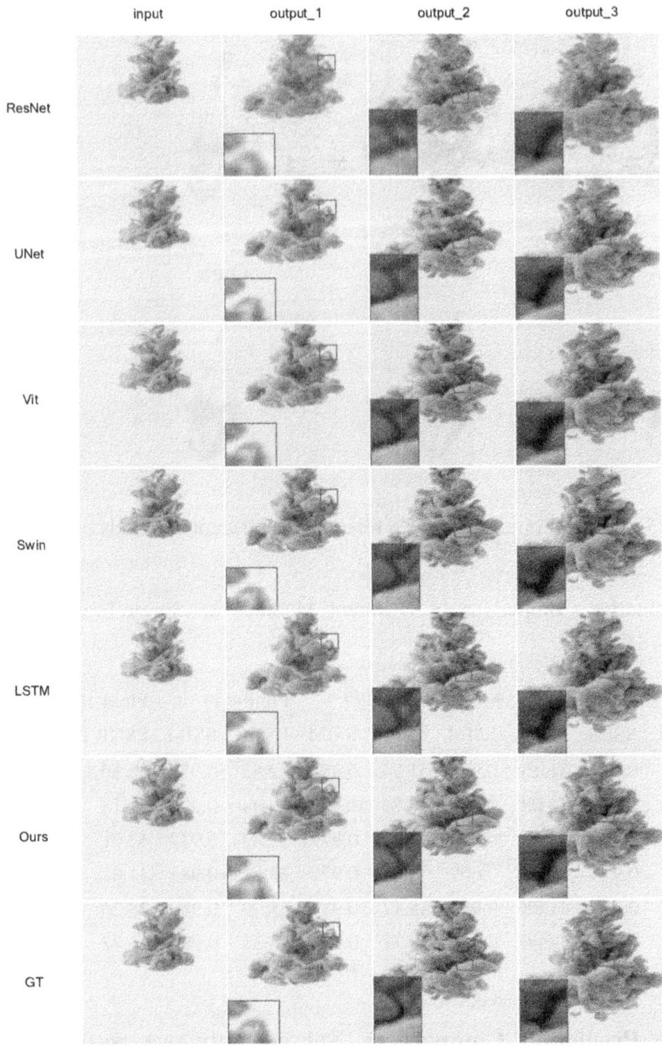

Fig. 4. Multi-Frame Prediction Results of Different Methods on Fluid-449

Table 2. Quantitative Comparison of Different Methods on Multi-Frame Prediction across Different Datasets

Method	Fluid-903		Fluid-590		Fluid-499		Fluid-449		Fluid-1000		Param	FlOPs
	PSNR	SSIM	PSNR	PSNR	SSIM	SSIM	PSNR	SSIM	PSNR	SSIM		
ResNet	32.38	0.911	22.95	0.824	27.94	0.898	26.49	0.859	24.39	0.702	113 M	1.34G
UNet	34.12	0.906	24.36	0.833	37.16	0.980	37.67	0.979	28.27	0.751	118 M	1.23G
ViT	33.58	0.906	23.53	0.825	33.93	0.971	33.08	0.953	26.24	0.728	123 M	1.28G

(continued)

Table 2. *(continued)*

Method	Fluid-903		Fluid-590		Fluid-499		Fluid-449		Fluid-1000		Param	FlOPs
	PSNR	SSIM	PSNR	PSNR	SSIM	SSIM	PSNR	SSIM	PSNR	SSIM		
Swin	34.81	0.909	23.87	0.820	37.95	0.981	37.61	0.973	44.53	0.993	113 M	0.31G
LSTM	33.35	0.902	24.33	0.831	36.52	0.980	38.31	0.981	27.83	0.745	118 M	1.23G
Ours	34.89	0.913	37.51	0.984	38.44	0.982	38.64	0.978	45.54	0.994	149 M	0.31G

4.3 Ablation Study

Contribution of the W-MSA Module. To validate the key role of window-based multiple self-attention (W-MSA) in Swin Transformer in multi-scale spatial feature extraction, we conducted tests on the Fluid-449 dataset using ViT Transformer's Global Attention (ViT-style MSA) and a standard convolutional layer (Conv2D) for W- MSA replacement to reflect the effect of W-MSA in the structure.

To ensure a fair contribution of the W-MSA structure to the network, we reduced the number of layers in each block of the Swin Transformer structure, so that the parameter count of Swin Transformer, ViT Transformer, and Conv2D structures would be roughly consistent.

As shown in Table 3, we observed the experimental results on the Fluid-449 dataset. We found that W-MSA outperforms ViT-style MSA by 10.2532 in PSNR and 0.1522 in SSIM. At the same time, W-MSA also improves PSNR by 14.0317 and SSIM by 0.1844 compared to standard Conv2D layers. From the results, it is clear that, with similar parameter counts, W-MSA significantly impacts the network's performance compared to both ViT-style MSA and Conv2D. Therefore, we conclude that W-MSA enables the extraction of deeper, multi-scale image features, which enhances the image prediction performance.

Table 3. Ablation Results on Different Modules Based on the Fluid-449 Dataset

Setting	Fluid-449		Param	FlOPs
	PSNR	SSIM		
ViT-style MSA	28.0985	0.8306	128 M	0.63G
Conv2D	24.3200	0.7984	123 M	1.22G
W-MSA	38.3517	0.9828	149 M	0.31G

Contribution of the Multi-Level ConvLSTM Module. In this section, we analyze the impact of different structures on our method. We experimented with single-layer ConvLSTM and multi-level ConvLSTM on the Fluid-449 dataset for both single-frame and multi-frame prediction tasks. To ensure fairness in the experiments, we increased the number of layers in each block of the Swin Transformer in the single-layer ConvLSTM structure, so that the parameter count of both single-layer and multi-level ConvLSTM remained roughly consistent.

As shown in Table 4, we observed the experimental results on the Fluid-449 dataset. We can see that the multi-level ConvLSTM outperforms the single-layer ConvLSTM by 0.1774 in PSNR and 0.0034 in SSIM. From the results, it is evident that, with similar parameter counts, multi-level ConvLSTM has a significantly greater impact on the network's performance compared to single-layer ConvLSTM. Therefore, we conclude that multi-level ConvLSTM contributes more to modeling long temporal sequences, thus improving image prediction performance.

Table 4. Ablation Results of Different Structures Based on the Fluid-449 Dataset

Setting	Single-Frame		Multi-Frame		Param	FlOPs
	PSNR	SSIM	PSNR	SSIM		
Single-Layer	38.17	0.9794	37.82	0.9781	163 M	0.43 G
Multi-Level	38.35	0.9828	38.64	0.9783	149 M	0.31 G

Performance of Different Loss Functions. Common loss functions in image prediction tasks include L1 loss and MSE loss. We investigated which loss function is more favorable to our network. We conducted a comparison experiment between L1 loss and MSE loss as shown in Table 5. From the results, MSE loss function is better than L1 loss function, so we choose MSE loss function to train our network.

Table 5. Ablation Results of Different Loss Functions Based on the Fluid-449 Dataset

setting	Fluid-449		Param	FlOPs
	PSNR	SSIM		
L1 loss	37.9516	0.9779	149 M	0.31 G
MSE loss	40.1882	0.9800	149 M	0.31 G

5 Conclusion

This paper proposes a deep learning network architecture combining ConvLSTM and Swin Transformer, primarily consisting of the SwinLSTM Cell structure and Swin Block. This approach addresses the challenges of modeling long-term dependencies and extracting multi-scale spatial features in multi-frame fluid image prediction. The core advantages of this method are as follows:

- **Spatio-temporal Joint Modeling:** By leveraging the gating mechanism of ConvLSTM to capture long-term and short-term dependencies in time series and combining it with the hierarchical window attention mechanism of Swin Transformer, the model effectively extracts both local and global multi-scale spatial features, enabling fine-grained modeling of complex fluid dynamics.
- **Significant Performance Improvement:** Experiments on multiple fluid prediction datasets show that our method outperforms mainstream models.in both PSNR and SSIM metrics. In single-frame prediction, the PSNR reaches as high as 45.77 dB, and multi-frame prediction errors are reduced by 18%, validating its dual advantages in temporal continuity and visual quality.
- **Efficiency and Applicability:** The model reduces computational complexity (0.31 GFLOPs) through the window attention mechanism of Swin Transformer, while preserving the temporal modeling capability of ConvLSTM, offering a feasible solution for real-time prediction in high-resolution fluid scenarios.

This research provides an efficient data-driven approach for fluid dynamics simulations by predicting the next frame of the rendered results of fluid dynamics simulations, which is expected to be applied to dynamic scenarios such as weather forecasting and industrial simulations. Future work will further explore the scalability of the model for 3D flow field modeling and multiphysics field coupling tasks.

Acknowledgments. The author would like to acknowledge the support from National Natural Science Foundation of China (NO. 62162027), Humanities and Social Sciences Research Project in Jiangxi Province's Universities(JC24205), Research Project on Innovation and Entrepreneurship Education of East China Jiaotong University(24hjct18), College Student Innovation and Entrepreneurship Training Program Project.

Disclosure of Interests.. The authors have no competing interests to declare that are relevant to the content of this article.

References

1. Zhu, J., Zhang, Y., Wu, Z., Zhang, K., Wang, Q.: Recent Advances on Machine Learning for Computational Fluid Dynamics: A Survey. arXiv preprint (2024). https://arxiv.org/abs/2408.12171
2. Thuerey, N., Subramaniam, A., Weißenow, K.: Current and emerging deep-learning methods for the simulation of fluid dynamics. Proc. R. Soc. A. **479**(2273), 20230058 (2023)
3. Cuomo, S., Di Cola, V.S., Giampaolo, F., Rozza, G., Raissi, M., Piccialli, F.: Scientific machine learning through physics-informed neural networks: where we are and what's next. J. Sci. Comput. **92**, 88 (2022)
4. Hochreiter, S., Schmidhuber, J.: Long short-term memory. Neural Comput. **9**(8), 1735–1780 (1997)
5. Liu, Z., et al.: Swin Transformer: Hierarchical Vision Transformer using Shifted Windows. arXiv preprint (2021). https://arxiv.org/abs/2103.14083
6. Dosovitskiy, A., et al.: An image is worth 16x16 words: Transformers for image recognition at scale. arXiv preprint (2020). https://arxiv.org/abs/2010.11929
7. Shi, X., Chen, Z., Wang, H., Yeung, D.Y., Wong, W., Woo, W.C.: Convolutional LSTM network: a machine learning approach for precipitation nowcasting. Adv. Neural Inf. Process. Syst. **28**, 802–810 (2015)

8. Xiao, X., Yang, X.: Research on physics-based and data-driven fluid animation. J. Softw. **31**(10), 3251–3265 (2020)
9. Li, A., Zhang, W., Zhang, X., et al.: A deep U-net-ConvLSTM framework with hydrodynamic models for basin-scale hydrodynamic prediction. Water. **16**(5), 625 (2024)
10. Foster, N., Fedkiw, R.: Practical animation of liquids. In: Proceedings of the 28th Annual Conference on Computer Graphics and Interactive Techniques, pp. 23–30. ACM, New York (2001)
11. Stam, J.: Stable Fluids. In: Proceedings of the ACM on Computer Graphics and Interactive Techniques, pp. 121–128. ACM, New York (1999)
12. Fedkiw, R., Stam, J., Jensen, H.W.: Visual simulation of smoke. In: Proceedings of the 28th Annual Conference on Computer Graphics and Interactive Techniques, pp. 15–22 (2001)
13. Müller, M., Charypar, D., Gross, M.: Particle-based fluid simulation for interactive applications. In: Proceedings of the 2003 ACM Siggraph/Eurographics Symposium on Computer Animation, pp. 154–159 (2003)
14. Lucas, B.D., Kanade, T., et al.: An iterative image registration technique with an application to stereo vision. In: Proceedings of the 7th International Joint Conference on Artificial Intelligence (IJCAI '81), pp. 674–679 (1981)
15. Box, G.E.P., Jenkins, G.M.: Time Series Analysis: Forecasting and Control. Holden-Day, San Francisco (1970)
16. Kalman, R.E.: A new approach to linear filtering and prediction problems. Trans. ASME J. Basic Eng. **82**(1), 35–45 (1960)
17. Cortes, C., Vapnik, V.: Support-vector networks. Mach. Learn. **20**(3), 273–297 (1995)
18. Rumelhart, D.E., Hinton, G.E., Williams, R.J.: Learning representations by back-propagating errors. Nature. **323**(6088), 533–536 (1986)
19. LeCun, Y., Bottou, L., Bengio, Y., Haffner, P.: Gradient-based learning applied to document recognition. Proc. IEEE. **86**(11), 2278–2324 (1998)
20. Elman, J.L.: Finding structure in time. Cogn. Sci. **14**(2), 179–211 (1990)
21. Cho, K., Van Merriënboer, B., Bahdanau, D., Bengio, Y.: On the properties of neural machine translation: Encoder-decoder approaches. arXiv preprint (2014). https://arxiv.org/abs/1409.1259
22. Goodfellow, I.J., Pouget-Abadie, J., Mirza, M., Xu, B., Warde-Farley, D., Ozair, S., et al.: Generative adversarial nets. In: Proceedings of the 28th International Conference on Neural Information Processing Systems, vol. 27, pp. 2672–2680 (2014)
23. Geng, S., Zhai, S., Li, C.: Swin transformer based transfer learning model for predicting porous media permeability from 2D images. Comput. Geotech. **106177** (2024)

Author Index

P. Li et al. (Eds.): CGI 2025, LNCS 16508, pp. 537–539, 2026.
https://doi.org/10.1007/978-3-032-22264-0

Z